WILEY

IAS 98

Interpretation and Application of

INTERNATIONAL ACCOUNTING STANDARDS 1998

WILEY

IAS 98

Interpretation and Application of

INTERNATIONAL ACCOUNTING STANDARDS 1998

Barry J. Epstein

Abbas Ali Mirza

Forewords by Sir Bryan Carsberg and Juan R. Herrera

JOHN WILEY & SONS, INC.

New York • Chichester • Weinheim • Brisbane • Singapore • Toronto

Permissions

Portions of this book have their origins in copyrighted materials from the International Accounting Standards Committee. These are noted by reference to the specific pronouncements, except for certain of the definitions introduced in bold type, which appear in a separate section at the beginning of each chapter. Complete copies of the international standards are available from the IASC. Copyright © International Accounting Standards Committee, 167 Fleet Street, London EC4A 2ES, England.

ISBN 0-471-16296-5

Printed in the United States of America
10 9 8 7 6 5 4 3 2 1

Contents

Foreword 1998

The first edition of this book, *IAS 97*, first came to our attention during the Global Accounting Standards Forum '97 held in Dubai in May, 1997. It has been a very long time since we read with so much enjoyment a book about accounting theory. When you notice you are re-reading paragraph after paragraph simply because you are captivated by the style and by the clarity of explanations, you cannot but realize that what you hold in your hands is an outstanding publication.

We find the most salient feature of this book to be the ease with which the reader understands what is presented. Here are International Accounting Standards laid bare for all to grasp. But the book contains a lot more than just standards. There are very logical explanations of the how and why the standards require given treatments, as well as comprehensive and up-to-date examples that help the reader see the standards actually applied and bring home the fine points they are intended to convey. The book also has an added bonus: comparisons of the requirements of certain international accounting standards with those of national standards of countries such as the US and the UK. All things considered, it is the most complete publication I have seen about International Accounting Standards. It is the perfect companion to the IAS themselves. And I dare add, if you only have the IAS, you are missing half the message.

The second edition, *IAS 98*, expands and updates the first edition to include IAS and exposure drafts issued in the last year. This presents the reader, between the covers of a single book, all there is to know about IAS to date. The inclusion of exposure drafts presents the opportunity of peeking into the future, and seeing not only what new standards are being considered, but what amendments to existing standards are in the pipeline. It is the most up-to-date information available, included in the proper context and within the corresponding subject matter.

IAS 98 and *IAS 97* are excellent text books as well as reference books. They are of use to professionals and students alike, to accountants in public practice and in business and industry, to business owners, regulators and standard setters. We must also recognize the tangible support they represent of the goals and objectives of the International Federation of Accountants (IFAC) and the International Accounting Standards Committee (IASC).

With these books, Barry Epstein and Abbas Ali Mirza have made a contribution of enormous usefulness. There can be no widespread use of International Accounting Standards if people do not understand them. We are certain that these books will increase the number of businessmen and accountants who will, at last, understand and begin to apply IAS. They will be a great boost to the efforts of our profession to give the corporate world the much needed harmonization of standards it requires to function in a globalized economy. These books will also help national standard setters clearly perceive the differences between national and international standards, if any, thus speeding the process of breaching the gaps which may separate them. They are, therefore, highly useful. Considering the expected endorsement of IAS by IOSCO in the near future, they are also most timely.

Congratulations are in order to the authors. They now have an important commitment with the business world and the accounting profession as a whole. By including in the titles of the books the years in which they have been published, the authors have created the expectation that they will update them every year. We sincerely hope and pray that they will be able to do so.

Juan R. Herrera, President
International Federation of
Accountants (IFAC)
Santo Domingo

September, 1997

Foreword to the 1997 Edition

The International Accounting Standards Committee (IASC) has been working for 23 years to develop a set of accounting standards which can be used to bring about uniformity in financial reporting around the world. Uniform accounting will reduce the costs of preparing financial statements for multinational companies and, perhaps more importantly, facilitate the jobs of investment analysts, investors, and other users in assessing business results.

This has always been recognized as a good idea, but it has been surprisingly long in yielding fruit. Only in the last few years have the benefits of global uniformity become sufficiently important to override domestic concerns. The last year or two has seen remarkable changes in the world for cross-border exchange listings but there are three very important exceptions: the stock exchanges of Canada, Japan, and the United States. An agreement made with IOSCO, the international organization of the securities regulators, in July 1995 will lead to completion of the core set of International Accounting Standards which we plan by 1998. IOSCO has said that this will clear the way for their endorsement of International Accounting Standards, after which we hope that the standards will be accepted universally for the purposes of cross-border listings. The SEC in the United States has said that it supports our objectives and will work with IOSCO to help achieve this goal.

Similar good progress has been seen in Europe. The European Commission now regards International Accounting Standards as the way to harmonize accounting in the European Union. France is moving ahead in a dramatic way by introducing a new law which will provide for the recognition of International Accounting Standards for domestic use in France as well as overseas by French companies. IASC must play its part by completing good quality standards on a timely basis.

As a standard-setting body makes progress towards widespread acceptance and use of its standards in practice, so interest increases in understanding those standards, acquiring expertise in using them, and conducting research into their merits and effects. Textbooks are needed, conferences must be held, and university teachers must undertake research projects. All of these beneficial developments are well underway for International Accounting Standards. This book by Barry Jay Epstein and Abbas Ali Mirza is one of the pioneers in the textbook field. I wish it success. The need for it is great.

Sir Bryan Carsberg
Secretary General
International Accounting Standards
Committee (IASC)

September 18, 1996

Acknowledgements

The authors are indebted to the many individuals who have inspired us to undertake this project and who have assisted us in bringing it to completion. This project had its inception in a series of conferences held in the Middle East in 1994 and 1995, which were cosponsored by a major public accounting firm, Talal Abu-Ghazaleh & Co. (TAGCO), with substantial support from the International Accounting Standards Committee. The authors express their gratitude particularly to Mr. Talal Abu-Ghazaleh and to Sir Bryan Carsberg, currently the secretary general of the IASC, for their ongoing support. We also appreciate the assistance of Qusay Abu-Ghazaleh and Hazem Farah, both of TAGCO, and of IASC board member Rolf Rundfelt of KPMG in Stockholm, Sweden. Mr. Abbas Ali Mirza expresses thanks to Graham Martins (PKF, United Arab Emirates), his father Ali Mirza, and his brother Dr. Hume Mirza for editorial assistance; to Bahadur Chacha for inspiration and moral support, and to his mother. Dr. Barry Epstein acknowledges the substantial copy editing contributions by his daughter, Brett Jocelyn Epstein, whose career intentions also include professional writing. Of course, the authors are very grateful to the production staff at John Wiley's DeKalb, Illinois, facility for their careful and timely efforts, and to the John Wiley editors in New York.

Acknowledgements

About the Authors

Barry J. Epstein, PhD, CPA, is a partner in the Chicago office of the major international accounting firm BDO Seidman, LLP, where he specializes in litigation consulting and also is involved widely in technical accounting and auditing issues affecting the firm and its clients. In the litigation practice he is active principally in accountants' malpractice defense work and other matters, such as contractual disputes, which revolve around the interpretation of the professional accounting and auditing literature. Prior to joining BDO Seidman in 1997, he was partner in charge of quality control for several large regional CPA firms for over 15 years, was a technical manager in the national office of another large firm for over 8 years, taught at the college level for 5 years, and served a stint as a financial executive with a Fortune 250 company. He has authored or coauthored six books (one of which, *Wiley GAAP '98*, has been a standard reference work on US accounting principles for the past 15 years), many professional articles, and a regular business column for a major newspaper. Dr. Epstein has served on numerous technical committees at the state and national levels and was a member of the AICPA's Board of Examiners for 5 years. He has lectured widely in the US, Canada, and the Middle East, and has been regularly involved in training professionals both for his firms, and through continuing education programs in the community. Dr. Epstein holds the PhD in management information systems and finance from the University of Pittsburgh, the MBA from the University of Chicago, and the BSC in accountancy and finance from DePaul University.

Abbas Ali Mirza, ACA, Grad. CWA, CPA, has had a distinguished career in the fields of auditing, finance and taxation, and has worked for major accounting firms around the globe including the United States of America and the Middle East. His diversified auditing experience encompasses many industries. In his Middle Eastern accounting and audit experience he has pioneered the practical application of "International Accounting Standards." Currently, he is Director for Professional Development at Talal Abu-Ghazaleh & Co., a major Middle Eastern CPA firm, and is responsible for quality assurance and technical support on complex accounting and auditing issues to the firm's 34 offices throughout the Arab World. He is a frequent principal speaker and a workshop leader at global conferences on International Accounting Standards and US GAAP. He is widely published in international accounting journals and coauthors a business column in a leading English newspaper of the Middle East, the "KHALEEJ TIMES," which addresses current issues in international accounting, auditing, and finance.

WILEY

IAS 98

Interpretation and Application of
INTERNATIONAL ACCOUNTING STANDARDS
1998

1 INTRODUCTION TO INTERNATIONAL ACCOUNTING STANDARDS

NEED FOR ACCOUNTING STANDARDS

Development of accounting and financial reporting. Accounting was created as a tool to aid in measuring economic activity. Renaissance era monk Fra Luca Pacioli is normally credited with the invention of double entry bookkeeping, designed for trading accounts in Italian city-states of the fourteenth and fifteenth centuries. From these origins, double entry bookkeeping can be traced to Germany and France, and then to Britain, where it proliferated due to the dominant world position held by the British Empire during the seventeenth and eighteenth centuries. British investments into the insurance and railroad industries of North America and Commonwealth countries brought about the accounting influence evident even today. Similarly, during this same era, Dutch accounting followed the discoveries and settlements made in Indonesia and South Africa. Other patterns of influence can be traced from their European origins throughout the world, as from Spain to Latin American nations. Later, with its economic ascendancy, the United States became the prime developer of accounting theory and exported its financial reporting model around the globe.

The evolution of accounting in various countries has inevitably led to different practices and regulations. As the economic systems and trading conditions vary from one country to another, so do the accounting models and methods. Factors influencing these variations include the degree of centralization in the economy, ranging from state control to unfettered free enterprise; the nature of economic activity, from simple agrarian societies to the most sophisticated and complex business enterprises; the stage of economic development, from emerging economies to fully matured postindustrial ones; the pattern and rate of economic growth, ranging from stagnation to the explosive growth of certain Asian economies; and the stability of the local currency, which connotes the inflationary experience of the local economy.

In addition to the economic system differences, disparate legal systems have had a profound effect on the approach to accounting and financial reporting. These are addressed in the following section.

Accounting and reporting models. Whatever the economic and legal system, in virtually every country in the free world there is some degree of regulation of the accounting profession by either government regulatory bodies or professional societies, or by both. The overall result is a complex agglomeration of laws, rules, and standards. In understanding the evolution of accounting principles, and the present and projected future state of those systems of reporting requirements, it is useful to review the factors that have led to the different approaches to accounting and reporting theory and regulations.

It is not the objective of this book to present a detailed comparison of accounting practices among the nations of the world. Rather, the focus will be on the rapidly evolving area of international accounting standards, which have the potential to eclipse the national standards of most of the world's developed and developing countries, eventually even those of the United States and the United Kingdom. (However, it must be appreciated that the international standards issued to date have been heavily based on US and UK standards.) The following abbreviated discussion, then, is intended merely to set the stage for the body of this book, which is a detailed consideration of the international standards.

Among the more developed countries of the world, there are two distinct types of regulatory environments, which in turn have fostered two different paths of evolution of accounting theory and practice. While there is a vast range of differences even within these groupings, it seems that a key distinction has been between those countries that have had a **common law** custom versus those that have followed a **code law** tradition. Those nations that have codified many rules of behavior have tended to formally prescribe accounting and financial reporting matters as well, and most often the role of financial reporting has been made subservient to the taxing system of the country. The Napoleonic Code is the universally referenced model of code law, and indeed most of the nations that were dominated by France during the reign of Napoleon subscribe to this approach.

The polar opposite to the code law approach and the analogous process of setting financial reporting standards by governmental actions is the common law tradition exemplified by England and those nations, including the United States, which were influenced by Great Britain. Whereas code law countries tend to prescribe what must be done, common law nations tend to be permissive until rulings are made regarding actions that cannot be taken, such as those proscribing fraudulent financial reporting. Common law countries tend not to define financial reporting requirements in their national laws, and the rules that have developed are largely those of the private sector, having over time been established by practitioners working through their professional societies, as well as by the labors of academicians. In common law countries, the goals of financial reporting are often at variance with those of national tax policy.

In addition to the code law versus common law dichotomy, there are other factors that have played roles in the manner in which the accounting professions and accounting and financial reporting rules have developed in various nations. Among these are the tradition of free enterprise versus centrally planned economies, the respective nations' experiences with price instability, and the extent to which the respective economies have developed and have fostered the growth of large-scale, complex business organizations.

A nation's tradition of free enterprise has historically been important to the development of accounting rules and of the profession of accounting. Nations that had thriving trading cultures hundreds of years ago, such as England and the Netherlands, not surprisingly had early needs for meaningful financial reporting. It is arguable whether the trading culture encouraged the development of accounting or whether the evolution of financial reporting encouraged the growth of business enterprises (both are probably true to a great extent), but clearly the profession flourished first in these environments. At the opposite extreme, nations that at one time had a Communist economic system had far less reason to focus on the development of financial reporting models, since production quotas, not enterprise economic performance, were of greater concern to central planners.

Experience with changing prices has also significantly influenced the development of accounting and financial reporting. The virtues of historical cost-based financial reporting (objectivity, reliability) have been most impressive in the context of price stability, but when prices are rapidly changing, these traits become less important than the characteristics exhibited by inflation-adjusted reporting (greater decision relevance, understandability, comparability). Nations that have had long histories of price instability (notably, Latin American countries) have been more supportive of departures from historical cost financial reporting, although none of the assorted approaches to financial reporting adjusted on the basis of general price level and specific price (current replacement cost) have been entirely satisfactory, and many even believe that the very fact that reported financial results are often adjusted contributes to these nations' inability to achieve a stable price regime. It is interesting to note that even those nations which traditionally have experienced relative price stability (e.g., the United States and the United Kingdom), have witnessed sporadic episodes of double-digit inflation (such as occurred during the 1920s and 1970s) accompanied by calls for and experiments with inflation-adjusted financial reporting, but as soon as price stability was reestablished, this interest waned dramatically.

Finally, those nations that have witnessed the growth of large and complex business organizations, particularly when accompanied by absentee ownership, have also seen the rise of the accounting profession and the development of more comprehensive theories of financial reporting. Large multinational companies tend to be headquartered in nations that have skilled labor forces, including professional accountants, and are subject to accounting rules established in those jurisdictions. Besides the United States and the United Kingdom, the countries of western Europe and Japan have the highest concentration of these characteristics.

Taking the foregoing factors together, one can conclude that there is a basic dichotomy between historically code law nations having governmentally sanctioned accounting and reporting rules heavily oriented toward tax compliance, and common law nations having accounting rules developed essentially in the private sector and not contrived to serve the government's fiscal objectives. This is further modified by other factors that, to greater or lesser degrees, encourage the development of comprehensive models of financial reporting that may or may not address the lack of price stability in the economy. This leads to a classification scheme that places the United States and the United Kingdom in one category; the nations of western, continental Europe (possibly including Japan) in another; the formerly communist nations of eastern Europe, including the former USSR, in yet another; and developing (third world) nations in a final category.

Setting accounting standards. The standard-setting process has proceeded by varying routes in the major nations of the developed world. To illustrate this thesis briefly, consider the United States, the United Kingdom, Germany, France, Japan, and several Latin American nations. The United States and the United Kingdom have been influenced by the same traditions of common law, capitalism, highly educated and professional work forces, large and sophisticated companies that raise equity capital in the public markets, and a belief in the responsibility of managements to report on their stewardship to the owners of the respective businesses. The early development of accounting theory, and the first flowering of the public accounting profession, took place in the United Kingdom, with most of the earliest US firms being offshoots of British ones.

The principle of full disclosure is very important in both the United States and the United Kingdom. Financial statements are expected to be transparent, so that the users, generally assumed to be investors and creditors, are able to understand fully the nature of the reporting enterprise's operations and finances. Rules are largely established by the profession itself (even when, as in the United States, the government has some statutory authority to establish accounting principles), and tax reporting is a distinct and separate matter, which does not drive financial reporting.

Accounting principles in the United Kingdom are established largely in the private sector, with enabling provisions being contained in the Companies Acts of 1985 and 1989. The present standard-setting structure actually dates only from 1990, replacing an earlier structure that was in place for 20 years. While there is due process, there is less openness to the opinions of interested parties outside the accountancy profession, and there is no British equivalent to the American Securities and Exchange Commission having a statutory oversight role.

One distinction between UK and US accounting is that there are many legal and institutional regulations that apply only to public companies (in the United States, the only accounting rules that are limited to public companies under current generally accepted accounting principles (GAAP) are those related to segment reporting and earnings per share). This is said to be a reflection of the historical development of accounting as a mechanism to protect shareholders, which still drives much of the standard-setting process in the United Kingdom.

Apart from the foregoing distinctions and the fact that the Companies Acts dictate the formats in which financial statements may be presented, the British accounting model is very similar to that of the United States. This is not unexpected, given that both derived from almost identical traditions.

Standard setting in the United States is also in the private sector, although the public markets regulator, the Securities and Exchange Commission (the SEC) has statutory authority to establish GAAP for public companies, which it has virtually never exercised, although supplementary disclosures have been required and other interpretive guidance has been issued from time to time. For the past 20 years the Financial Accounting Standards Board (the FASB) has been the primary US accounting standard setter, with a lesser role still being played by the American Institute of Certified Public Accountants (the AICPA). The FASB was created as a full-time body to remedy the perceived inadequacies of its predecessor, the part-time Accounting Principles Board (the APB), which also suffered a diminished credibility by being a creature of the AICPA, which is the body representing the auditing profession. Since the advent of the FASB, the responsibility for setting accounting standards has been divorced from the process of making auditing rules.

US GAAP contains by far the largest number of specific rules, currently comprising 31 APB opinions, 131 FASB statements, and scores of interpretations and technical bulletins, statements of position, and accounting guides issued by the AICPA, and other relevant professional literature. The international standard setter (the IASC) has stated that it has no intention of trying to duplicate this body of guidance, and indeed, subscribes to a philosophy of providing general guidance rather than detailed "cookbook recipes" addressing every nuance of business practice. There are many who believe that the troubles experienced by accountants in recent years, particularly the explosion of litigation against them, can be traced to the attempt (doomed to fail, some would argue) to establish specific guidance for a vast array of transactions and events. The IASC has determined not to follow that course of action.

General purpose financial reporting in the United States, as in the United Kingdom, is intended to serve the needs of investors, lenders, and other interested parties, that can also include regulatory authorities. However, there is no pretense that GAAP will measure taxable income, and indeed the reason for deferred income tax accounting is that tax reporting will almost always differ from financial reporting prepared in conformity with GAAP.

As compared with the United States and the United Kingdom, countries in Europe, plus Japan, have capitalist economic systems that rely far less on public equity markets and much more on bank financing. The relationships between the borrowers and lenders are much closer than those that generally exist between companies and their equity investors, as there are typically far fewer lenders than stockholders, and each lender has a much greater stake in the outcome of events than do passive investors. Thus, there is greater ability to obtain information informally: that is, key lenders can demand information from their borrowers at will, and are not limited by what disclosures are mandated by accounting standards, or by the frequency with which financial reporting is made to shareholders. The implication is that accounting rules are of less importance in these environments.

Both France and Germany have code law traditions and in both nations the private sector accounting profession has limited influence on the development of accounting and financial reporting requirements. Financial reporting is dictated by law, which makes some distinctions between large or publicly held companies and small or privately held ones. The French system is very similar to the German, in fact, having been substantially influenced by the German during the World War II occupation. Furthermore, most of the basic underlying concepts, such as accrual basis accounting and the going concern assumption, are identical with those recognized by US and UK GAAP.

As an illustration of the sharp differences between UK and US accounting on the one hand, and French and German reporting on the other, consider the topic of interperiod tax allocation. Although the concepts of deferred income taxes are recognized in both France and Germany, there are few instances in which material amounts of deferred taxes appear on balance sheets, since most tax deductions are conditioned on the item being expensed currently for financial reporting purposes. To the limited extent that deferred taxes are provided, the deferred method is more commonly employed in France, while the liability approach is required in Germany.

As another example, consider the provision of **reserves**. In both of these nations, regulations exist to require that a defined percentage of earnings (currently 5%) be appropriated to a legal reserve account, until that account (shown in stockholders' equity) equals a defined amount (10% of share capital in France, 10% of the par value of share capital in Germany, in general). While these are allocations from earnings, and not charges against profits, per se, they do communicate that some fraction of earnings is, in a sense, not available currently to shareholders. Furthermore, especially in Germany, where accrual (by charges against earnings) of contingencies is governed by the concept of prudence, it is well known that earnings tend to be very conservatively stated even before the reserve appropriation is made. Thus, while it may be said that general contingency reserves, long prohibited in the US and many other nations, are also not permitted in France and Germany, nonetheless the overall effect of the conservative, prudent accounting which is subscribed to in both nations, plus the impact of providing so-called legal reserves, does tend to imply a greater tolerance for some degree of income smoothing. The goal of creditor protection, while possibly a worthy one, particularly given the historical dependence on debt financing in both France and Germany, leads to an understatement, in many cases, of net equity available to shareholders.

Japanese financial reporting rules were originally modeled after German accounting, as a result of the close association between those two nations in the first half of this century, although more recently they have been influenced by US standards. The overriding concern is with creditor protection, since most financing is provided by large commercial banks, not by individual shareholders. Japanese society is structured to be focused far more on the collective good, and this value system has also affected financial accounting. For example, accounting procedures to achieve income smoothing are tolerated if they can be shown to contribute to the success of the business enterprise over the long term, as that would tend to benefit society at large.

Despite the postwar influence of the United States, which dictated the structure of its public accounting profession, Japanese accounting and financial reporting continues to follow the European model closely. Thus statutory reserves are provided, thereby reducing reported profits from what would be acknowledged under US or UK GAAP. Prudence (i.e., conservatism) is the most significant concept underlying Japanese accounting principles. There is a high degree of correlation between tax reporting and financial accounting, and thus deferred tax accounting is not typically an issue.

Although the nations of Central and South America which were colonized and culturally influenced by Spain or Portugal employ financial reporting very similar to those of European nations, a major distinction is that the historical cost model is held in less reverence. This is the obvious result of many decades' experience with high levels of price inflation in most Latin American nations. Argentina, Bolivia, Brazil, and Chile require that financial statements be restated comprehensively to compensate for changes in the general price level. Certain Latin American nations require periodic revaluations of plant assets, which other countries permit on an elective basis.

Frequent currency devaluations, coupled with wage and other contractual agreements that call for automatic adjustments for the impact of changes in the general level of prices, have perhaps desensitized the public to the ravages of inflation and thus contributed to the rampant inflation experienced by many of these nations throughout the post-World War II era. Ill-advised government fiscal and monetary policies have contributed to the pervasiveness of this problem. The intractability of inflation has even led to acceptance of revaluations of plant assets as a basis for computing tax depreciation in a few Latin American nations, including Bolivia and Brazil. In general, tax policies are given the greatest consideration in the setting of financial reporting requirements, and the needs of government economic planners are viewed as more important than those of either stockholders or creditors.

Need for International Accounting Standards

While differing national traditions and experiences led to the development of alternative financial reporting models, the pressures for intensified development in the global environment have been evident as the needs of the ever-changing economy demand international harmonization. Major changes in business practices following World War II have led to demands for the internationalization of accounting and auditing practices. These changes are found principally in the evolution of multinational enterprises and, more recently, international capital markets. From these flow numerous professional practice issues.

Multinational companies (MNC) have grown dramatically and over the past 25 years have assumed a dominant role in many market segments, affecting almost every country, every government, and every person. From an accounting perspective, the complexity of conducting international business operations across national borders, each with a different set of business regulations and often different accounting methods, presents a daunting challenge for accountants and the professional bodies that establish accounting and auditing rules. Some of the significant complexities confronting international accountants are caused by the nature of the huge multinational enterprises themselves. The diversity of applicable accounting, auditing, and tax rules may affect the enterprise's ability to prepare reliable financial information necessary for a careful analysis of investment opportunities. As the number of countries of activity increases, so does the complexity.

There are some national differences in accounting and reporting approaches that should be addressed. A prime example is the complaint of many US companies about the competitive disadvantage that results from the US rules regarding accounting for goodwill. Entities complying with accounting standards of most European countries, including the United Kingdom, do not need to amortize goodwill, because it can be charged directly against shareholders' equity at the date of the business acquisition. Other international accounting and reporting matters, such as inflation accounting adjustments, deferred tax accounting, and translation of foreign subsidiaries' financial statements, also create disadvantages for some companies, and the persistence of these differences puts pressure on standard setters to work harder to achieve a "level playing field."

The globalization of capital markets has also contributed to the need to address harmonization of financial reporting requirements. Capital needs were once supplied almost exclusively from domestic sources, especially in the pre-World War II era. However, since that time, and especially as a result of major international economic assistance programs after the war, there has been a significant growth and development of international capital markets. There are now highly developed Eurodollar, Eurocurrency, and Asia-dollar capital markets in the developed world economies, especially those in the United States, the United Kingdom, Japan, and parts of Europe. That the financial marketplace is now global is abundantly evident from the October 1987 stock market crash, in which all major markets plunged by similar magnitudes.

This vast global capital market needs, but does not yet have, a common accounting "language" for the communication of financial information. Recognition of this need is another significant influence and a major force in the development of, and progress toward, internationalized accounting and auditing standards. Without this "common language" there is some doubt that given diverse national standards, a truly efficient international market will develop, and this may impair the ability of capital-seeking corporations to compete effectively for the capital otherwise available in the world markets.

National securities regulators, as well as the International Organization of Securities Commissioners (IOSCO), an organization of securities regulators from more than 80 countries promoting international coordination, have recently given increased support to the need for improved international accounting standards, and therefore to the IASC's harmonization proposal. As discussed elsewhere in this chapter, the IASC-IOSCO agreement promises greatly increased support for harmonization once the IASC completes its core set of standards, now promised by mid-1998. Given the obvious need for global harmonization of financial reporting practices, if not outright uniformity of generally accepted accounting principles, the importance of the IASC's efforts can readily be appreciated.

The International Accounting Standards Committee

The International Accounting Standards Committee was founded in 1973 by representatives of professional bodies in Australia, Canada, France, Germany, Japan, Mexico, the Netherlands, the United Kingdom and Ireland, and the United States, and presently includes representatives from 85 countries. Since 1983, the IASC's members have included all the professional accountancy bodies that are members of the International Federation of Accountants (IFAC) which, as of January 1997, comprised 119 member bodies (plus six associate members) from 88 countries.

Since its formation, the IASC has engaged in a standard-setting program that has now gained worldwide recognition. IASC has issued 33 international accounting standards (IAS), of which 31 remain in force (two early standards having been superseded by later pronouncements). A number of these standards are now in their second iteration, as a major project undertaken to revise the standards, principally to eliminate some previously acceptable alternative treatments and to update certain of the standards (most notably, to substitute cash flow reporting for funds flow statements), was largely completed in 1994. Also issued to date have been a conceptual release on the *Framework for the Preparation and Presentation of Financial Statements* and a number of exposure drafts (at least one exposure draft preceded each standard), about seven of which are currently outstanding.

Objectives and approach to standard setting. The objectives of IASC, as set forth in its constitution, are twofold. The first is to formulate and publish in the public interest accounting standards to be observed in the presentation of financial statements and to promote their worldwide acceptance and observance. The second is to work generally for the improvement and harmonization of regulations, accounting standards, and procedures relating to the presentation of financial statements.

Recognizing that differing accounting principles on a given subject exist in different countries, and that there are many accounting subjects which have not even been addressed in some jurisdictions, the IASC decided on a multipronged approach designed to serve the largest possible audience. The IASC has employed a range of strategies, including

1. Urging member bodies to invite IASC to participate whenever two or more countries that do not share common legislation are proposing to hold discussions on accounting standards;
2. Encouraging countries that have not previously established national accounting standards to adopt International Accounting Standards (IAS) as the country's own standards;
3. Inviting other countries, which may have some national standards but none on particular topics, to adapt IAS as a basis for a national standard on a particular subject, guaranteeing a certain level of quality and compatibility for the particular standard, and reducing both the time and the development costs required to produce a national standard;
4. Suggesting that where national standards already exist, countries compare them with IAS and seek to eliminate any material differences; and
5. Endeavoring to demonstrate for those countries where the framework of accounting practice is contained in law the benefits of harmonization with IAS.

To accommodate such diverse approaches, the IASC has strived to deal mostly with broad principles and to avoid excessive details. The result is that the IAS seem avant-garde in some countries (primarily those without their own extensive national standards) but elementary in others (particularly the United States and the United Kingdom, which have fully developed systems of generally accepted accounting principles). The goal is, however, to filter out unsound practices over a period of time, recognizing the evolutionary nature of the task and the challenges that are to be faced in the process. Recently, there has been a trend toward including more detailed guidance in the IAS, largely in response to IOSCO demands (which in turn are heavily influenced by the US standard setter, the FASB, and the US securities regulator, the SEC) for a comprehensive "core set of standards" with consistent interpretation and application. While the attempt to accommodate IOSCO's wishes has forced the IASC to deviate somewhat from its historical practice and stated philosophy, achieving IOSCO endorsement of the IAS is of such importance that this has been done with few recriminations or regrets.

Stages of Development in the International Accounting Standard-Setting Process

Reviewing the history of the IASC, it is possible to identify three stages through which it has passed in its development as a standard-setting body. These are, respectively, the early years of attempting to demonstrate attention to all the major accounting issues; the middle period of consolidation, when allowable alternative treatments were reduced as part of the effort to improve comparability; and the current era, when the core set of standards necessary to obtain the support of the international capital markets is being completed.

The stages through which the international standard-setting process has progressed are indicated by the history of the standards that have been issued to date. The first phase represented an attempt to establish a common body of standards on major topics, such as accounting for inventory, for leases, and for plant assets. Essentially (although the IASC might not care to admit to this) the strategy was to endorse virtually all the mainstream methods used in any of the major nations of the world. This "lowest common denominator" approach resulted in the promulgation of a number of standards that permitted the application of diverse accounting principles to similar fact situations, without necessarily setting forth any clear conceptual basis for allowing these alternative treatments. However, despite the limited achievement this represented, it did serve to establish the IASC's legitimacy as a transnational standard-setting body, albeit one without any enforcement mechanism.

The second phase in the IASC's evolution was marked by the Comparability/Improvements Project which began with the release of Exposure Draft 32, *Comparability of Financial Statements*, in 1989, and concluded with the promulgation of 10 revised standards that took effect in 1995. The objective of this project was to narrow the range of the acceptable accounting treatments that could be brought to bear upon given fact situations. The project was a qualified success, as indeed the number of acceptable alternatives was reduced, although perhaps too many alternatives still remained available even when the project had been completed.

This experience reveals the very difficult task faced by the IASC, as a body whose only tool has been moral suasion. For example, in taking up the question of inventory accounting, which had been dealt with by IAS 2, which had granted financial statement preparers free choice among the FIFO, weighted-average, LIFO, and base stock costing methods, the committee determined that the LIFO and base stock methods should be prohibited. However, in a number of countries, LIFO is both a popular method and one that depends on conformity between financial reporting and tax reporting (i.e., tax advantages are available only if published financial statements conform to the method used in the tax returns). As a result, the IASC found it necessary to accept the continued existence of LIFO, which was demoted to **allowed alternative** status, with FIFO and weighted-average costing becoming the **benchmarks**. (As a practical matter, there is no distinction between benchmark and alternative treatments, since reporting enterprises are not penalized for availing themselves of the alternatives. A proposal made by the IASC at the time the 10 revised standards were being developed--to require presentation of a reconciliation of net income to amounts that would have been produced by application of the benchmark standard--was dropped.)

Notwithstanding the fact that the range of alternatives was not narrowed as much as might have been hoped, the Comparability/Improvements Project had its achievements. These accomplishments are summarized as follows:

IAS 2 Inventories

The base stock method was dropped and the LIFO method was relegated to allowed alternative status.

IAS 8 Net Profit or Loss for the Period, Fundamental Errors and Changes in Accounting Policies

The original standard addressed the reporting of unusual items, prior period items, and changes in accounting policies and accounting estimates. In the revised standard, benchmark and allowed alternative treatments are prescribed for correction of what are called "fundamental" errors, with the benchmark involving adjustment of retained earnings and restatement of comparative prior periods, and the alternative being inclusion of the effect of the correction in current period income. The new standard also requires that extraordinary items be set forth separately on the face of the income statement, and the expanded disclosure of certain unusual items that are included in ordinary income (e.g., write-downs of inventories to net realizable values) and of discontinued operations. The effect of this revised standard was to bring the international accounting standard into closer conformity with the US standard and to improve financial statement disclosures.

IAS 9 Research and Development Costs

The original standard required expensing research costs but permitted either capitalization or expensing of defined development costs. The revised standard continues to require expensing of all research costs but sets standards for capitalization of certain development costs. If the standards are met in a given fact situation, the costs must be capitalized and amortized; if not, they must be expensed at once. Thus, this revision did fully achieve the goal of eliminating alternative treatments.

IAS 11 Construction Contracts

The initial standard permitted a free choice between percentage-of-completion and completed-contract accounting, while the revised standard requires percentage-of-completion. Once again, the goal of narrowing alternatives was fully achieved.

IAS 16 Property, Plant, and Equipment

The original standard permitted either historical cost or revalued amounts as the basis for reporting plant assets; these remain in the revised standard, but historical cost is now designated as the benchmark treatment, with revalued amounts being relegated to the allowed alternative category. A number of other changes were also made, including incorporating the formerly separate guidance of IAS 4, *Depreciation Accounting,* and requiring that any revaluations be to fair value and that these be updated regularly (at least every 3 years). Although this revised standard offers guidance superior to its predecessor, it nonetheless still permits diverse accounting methods.

IAS 18 Revenue Recognition

Whereas the original standard permitted either percentage-of-completion or completed-contract accounting for recognition of revenue related to the rendering of services, in the revision only the percentage-of-completion method is allowed, if specified conditions are met.

IAS 19 Retirement Benefit Costs

Accounting for retirement benefits by employers was, and remains, a very complicated topic. In the first version of the standard, the guidance was very general, essentially only demanding that costs be rationally allocated to the periods of benefit. The revised standard, on the other hand, is far more detailed but nonetheless still permits a range of methods, most notably defining the accrued benefit valuation method as the benchmark and the projected benefit method as the allowed alternative (contrasted to the US standard, SFAS 87, which mandates exclusive use of the projected benefit method alone). The revised standard also requires that actuarial valuations regarding projected salaries, past service costs, experience adjustments, and the effects of changes in actuarial assumptions be allocated to income on a systematic basis. Yet another revision to this standard is promised as part of the core set of standards project, discussed later in the chapter.

IAS 21 Effects of Changes in Foreign Exchange Rates

The revisions to this standard were rather modest in scope; certain choices relative to the deferral and amortization of exchange differences on long-term monetary items, on translation of income statements of foreign entities at the closing rate, and on translation of financial statements of foreign entities that report in the currency of a hyperinflationary economy without prior restatement, all were narrowed. Additional disclosures were also mandated by the revised standard. The revised standard largely duplicates the corresponding US standard, SFAS 52.

IAS 22 Accounting for Business Combinations

The revision more clearly defined which combinations (known as **acquisitions**) are to be accounted for using the purchase method and which (**unitings of interests**) must be accounted for as poolings. The criteria for unitings are quite restrictive but are simpler than those in the parallel US standard, APB 16 (the latter defines 12 criteria that must all be met, while the former sets forth only 3). Furthermore, the revised IAS 22 prohibits the immediate write-off of goodwill against stockholders' equity that was allowed previously. On the other hand, the revised standard sets forth benchmark and allowed alternatives with regard to the measurement of minority interest and for the accounting for negative goodwill. Thus, alternative accounting for essentially identical events has not been eliminated completely.

IAS 23 Borrowing Costs

The maiden standard permitted either capitalization or expensing of borrowing costs incurred in connection with construction of assets, while the revision slightly alters this by defining expensing as the benchmark treatment and capitalization as the allowed alternative. This change is only a modest achievement, given that enterprises are under no real burden to conform to the benchmark treatment.

The IASC entered its third distinct phase of existence some 18 months ago when it embarked on its mission to complete what has been defined as the "core set of standards." In a historic agreement with IOSCO, the IASC undertook to complete revisions of the set of standards which were deemed essential to IOSCO's willingness to consider endorsing the IAS for purposes of cross border securities registrations by mid-1999 (later further accelerated to early 1998, and now seen as likely by mid-1998). Since this endorsement, which actually has limited value, given that each member regulatory agency retains the power to individually decide whether to permit use of IAS by entities seeking to register securities on each sovereign nation's securities exchange, is absolutely key to the ultimate legitimization of the international accounting standards, it was both prudent and necessary that the IASC agree to this time schedule.

As the deadline looms ever closer, several things have become more or less apparent. First, the IASC has in fact accomplished a great deal, notwithstanding its limited resources (e.g., its funding is less than 10% of that for the US standard setting body) and the logistical nightmare of conducting meetings around the globe. Second, the IASC may miss its self-imposed deadline of March 1998, but probably not by much; June 1998 seems like a feasible date for completion, with the possible exception of the financial instruments recognition and measurement project.

Third, as it becomes clearer that IASC may, indeed, accomplish its herculean task, some nominal supporters, particularly in the US standard-setting and regulatory community, have been very prominent in equivocating support for the process, criticizing, for example, the speed with which certain topics are being addressed (notable particularly in contrast with FASB's elaborate and time consuming due process procedures, which have caused some major projects such as financial instruments, consolidations, and stock based compensation to take as long as 10 years to be completed). The implication of such overt or implied criticism is that high quality standards cannot, ipso facto, result from such an expedited process. This, however, ignores the fact that IASC is able to benefit from all the research which has already been conducted and deliberations which have already taken place by those other standard setters. Finally, it appears that some of the other major standard setters have begun to fear the possible emerging primacy of international accounting standards, and have begun to place their own survival into the political equation, with the result that support for the international harmonization program is wavering somewhat.

In light of the IASC's achievements to date, and the political issues which remain to be successfully traversed if the IOSCO endorsement is to be made as promised, the next 12 months will be very critical. Completion of the core set of standards is virtually assured even if delayed by 3 months or so. The next step will be for IOSCO to review the standards to determine if they do in fact represent a cohesive, comprehensive set of high quality standards. If IOSCO does vote to endorse these for cross-border securities registrations, there will be tremendous momentum which should lead to acceptance by major national securities regulators, including the SEC. This would mark a major milestone in the true global harmonization of financial reporting.

There is the possibility of complications arising from this program, however. Since entities registering their securities in other countries will be able to submit financial statements prepared in conformity with IAS, some pressure will probably also develop to conform national standards with IAS. Otherwise, domestic registrants will be (from one perspective, at least) at a disadvantage in terms of types of disclosures and similar factors. This would be particularly true in countries such as the United States, where national accounting standards are more demanding than IAS in terms of financial statement disclosure. Although it is clearly too early to anticipate the outcome, it is very likely that the completion of the core set project, and the honoring of IOSCO's promised quid pro quo, will prove to be a watershed event in the history of IASC.

The actual agreement between IASC and IOSCO involved the formal acceptance of a work plan that sets forth a number of projects to be completed on a targeted schedule (originally mid-1999, but later revised so that the entire project could be completed by early 1998). The standards to be addressed included accounting for income taxes (which has since been achieved by revised IAS 12, issued in late 1996); financial instruments (which was bifurcated into a project on presentation and disclosure, completed with the issuance of IAS 32 in 1995, and one on recognition and measurement, on which an exposure draft is due by the end of 1997); earnings per share reporting (completed with the issuance of IAS 33 in mid-1997); segment reporting (revised IAS 14 was approved in early 1997 and issued in mid-1997); financial statement presentation (revised IAS 1, superseding IAS 1, 5, and 13, was issued in mid-1997); accounting for intangibles, research and development and goodwill (exposure draft E60 was published in mid-1997); retirement benefit costs (E54 issued late 1996); interim financial reporting (E57 published mid-1997); reporting of discontinuing operations (E58 released mid-1997); provisions and contingencies (E59 published mid-1997); and impairment of assets (E55 issued in mid-1997). The expectation is that, once these individual efforts are completed, IOSCO will endorse them collectively for use in cross-border securities registrations, having earlier rejected a perhaps more logical approach, namely endorsing the standard-setting process itself, rather than the particular standards.

Other breakthroughs for IASC. In late 1995, the announcement by the European Commission's (EC) Single Market Commissioner that the European Union had abandoned its long-cherished goal of developing unique European standards of accounting gave a clear boost to the IASC's efforts. By effectively deferring to international accounting standards (IAS), the EC has removed the specter of yet another layer of national and supranational accounting standards and contributed to a quantum leap toward true internationalization of financial reporting and harmonization of accounting principles.

In fact, the EC's gesture of support has apparently had an impact, as the pace of adoptions of IAS has accelerated over the past 18 months worldwide. A growing list of important nations have either adopted IAS outright or have crafted national standards around a core of IAS principles; in some cases nominally national standards are no more than thinly veiled international standards, without any substantive departures save the titles. Among the more important recent converts to or protagonists of IAS are Germany, China, France, Australia, and Japan. Other adopters include Hong Kong, Malta, Korea, Barbados, Zimbabwe, Lebanon, Turkey, Trinidad and Tobago, Uganda, and Mongolia.

A new pan-European securities market (known as EASDAQ) now permits the use of international accounting standards by its registrants. Furthermore, the Federation of Euro-Asian Stock Exchanges (FEAS), with 20 member exchanges in 18 nations in Europe (outside the EU and EFTA), Central and South Asia and the Middle East has recommended that its members should require the use of international accounting standards. Recently, a joint declaration was issued by the Arab Society of Certified Accountants and IASC, calling for all Arab nations to adopt IAS no later than 1998.

To summarize, the international accounting standard-setting process has evolved through three stages and is now poised on the brink of achieving widespread legitimacy, which may result, over time, in the IASC's becoming the premier accounting standard setter. If both parties to the IASC-IOSCO agreement abide by their respective commitments, by the end of the decade (and century) the globalization of accounting standards may well be in sight.

Recent developments. In September 1996, the IASC approved the creation of the Standing Interpretations Committee (SIC). Apart from the obvious wisdom of taking this step, it was also done to accommodate the wishes of IOSCO and in particular the US regulatory community, which was concerned that absent a mechanism to ensure that IAS were uniformly interpreted and applied, there was no assurance that current diversity of practice would really be narrowed as intended. This group held its organizational meeting in April 1997 and, as of mid-1997, the SIC had issued three draft interpretations. These are discussed in this book in the sections to which they pertain.

In operation, the SIC receives recommendations from its constituencies concerning topics which are thought to contain ambiguities, and also may by other means identify issues which may need to be addressed. Typically these will be either narrow interpretation matters or applications to particular industries or types of operations. The SIC has indicated that it will deal with those suggested matters which involve interpretations of existing IAS (i.e., its role is not to break new ground), which has practical and widespread relevance, which relates to a specific fact pattern, and on which there is substantial divergence of practice. The IASC has published a suggested structure for the submission of suggested topics to the SIC.

If the 12-member committee is able to reach a consensus, a draft interpretation is first published and, after comments are received and considered, a final interpretation is adopted. In other cases, the SIC may urge the IASC itself to take up a project, if a need for new accounting standards is indicated which is beyond the scope of the SIC's efforts.

The IASC has also recently constituted a Strategy Working Party. The role of this group is to consider the need for restructuring the IASC itself, as it has grown so large and unwieldy that progress on substantive issues may be hampered. One suggestion is for a "bicameral" organization, with a smaller board to do the actual standard writing, subject to ratification or oversight by a larger board (which would be essentially the same as the current IASC). One concern, however, is that a smaller executive group might be comprised of representatives of the world's current major standard-setting organizations, and if so that the IAS-development process would be reduced to a matter of political "horse trading" among those dominant groups. A somewhat contrary suggestion is that the executive board be comprised primarily of representatives of nations already complying with IAS; this would, for the time being at least, largely exclude the world's major standard-setting bodies.

Another issue being tackled by the IASC pertains to the providing of expanded implementation guidance. Currently, the IAS are very concise, conceptual documents, with little in the way of practical guidelines or examples (hence the need for this book). Many users of the international standards have requested that the IAS be made more like the US or UK standards, which typically contain substantially more detailed guidance. To date, the IASC has been sensitive to the fact that developing nations and smaller enterprises constitute a large fraction of its current constituency, and from a cost/benefit perspective it is not clear that imposing thousands of pages of detailed rules on such entities would be justified. On the other hand, however, gaining support from the major standard-setting bodies and regulatory agencies for the hoped-for IOSCO endorsement of the core set of standards may necessitate some gesture toward providing this type of expanded implementation assistance.

The foregoing are only some of the more important activities and developments currently occupying the IASC and impacting the course of future developments. These serve to underline the great significance of the year 1998 in determining the ultimate success of global harmonization of accounting standards.

Benefits From Global Harmonization of Accounting Principles

From the standpoint of the users of financial statements (e.g., bankers and investors), it is rather difficult to make relative evaluations of companies that use diverse accounting standards. This tends to restrict the market for the shares of these companies and therefore greatly affects their rankings and attributed value. Today, for most businesses, the biggest opportunities lie in international markets: They have economic activities that extend far beyond domestic markets, they seek investment capital in foreign countries, and they conduct their operations through facilities in foreign lands. It is also fairly evident that in the share market arena, global fighters are emerging as winners since investors seem to be ignoring domestic competitors and clearly casting their ballot in favor of international champions. Thus, harmonization of accounting standards worldwide will greatly help the users of accounting and financial information in making informed economic decisions about these companies.

From the standpoint of preparers of financial statements, the burden of financial reporting would be greatly lessened with increased harmonization, which would simplify the process of preparing individual as well as group financial statements. It is a well-known fact that multinational groups that have nondomestic subsidiaries have huge added costs of preparation of financial statements. To elaborate the point, consider an example of a company which has a subsidiary that is operating out of Saudi Arabia, with its parent company based in the United Kingdom, and whose shares are listed on the New York Stock Exchange. This company will have to prepare three sets of financial statements.

1. Financial statements to comply with the Saudi standards, to meet the requirements of the Saudi Arabian company
2. Financial statements to comply with the consolidation requirements in the United Kingdom

3. Financial statements to meet the registration and filing requirements in the United States

This means that enormous additional financial costs have to be incurred not only in the preparation of such financial statements but also in getting them audited. Imagine if this company were a multinational corporation (MNC) operating out of, say, 50 countries, most of which had local licensing regulations that required financial reporting to be tailored according to their national standards. The company's accounting travails would then be extremely unpleasant, to say the least. Thus it is obvious that enormous benefits will emanate from harmonization of accounting standards worldwide.

Impediments to Harmonization

Based on an authoritative study on the subject of harmonization of international accounting standards, a paper was prepared by the International Federation of Accountants and distributed by the International Capital Markets Group. According to this study, the major barrier to harmonization seems to be the "manifestation of national sovereignty." A second very important factor is the "varying attitudes of standard setters around the world to the purpose of the financial statements." When the purpose is perceived as **creditor protection**, the tendency is to understate profits (and thereby require retention of profits) compared with countries where **shareholder protection** is the dominant feature. Further, countries where creditor protection is a high priority also tend to be more tax driven in their financial reporting, which means that in such countries recognition of expenses is influenced by the provisions of the tax code more than the principles of commercial accounting.

Reporting Anomalies Resulting From Diversity in Accounting Standards Worldwide

Significant diversity in accounting standards of different countries not only poses the problem of additional cost to be incurred for financial reporting but could cause other difficulties for multinational companies. For instance, it is quite possible for a transaction to give rise to a profit under the accounting standards of one country, whereas it would require a deferral under the standards of another country. When a multinational company has to report under the standards of both countries, one is amazed to see some extremely odd financial results which could sometimes also be embarrassing. The case of lopsided financial reporting that instantly comes to mind is that of German industrial giant Daimler-Benz AG, which sought listing of its shares in the United States in 1993 and ended up reporting a massive loss of $1 billion under US GAAP, when in fact it had reported a profit of $370 million under its own national (German) GAAP.

Major Differences in National Accounting Standards

The following analysis is by no means an authoritative study of differences in accounting standards worldwide but is being attempted with the limited purpose of highlighting some of the well-known major differences in accounting standards. Four countries have been chosen for this comparison: the United Kingdom, the United States, France, and Japan.

1. **Measurement subsequent to initial recognition of fixed assets (historical cost vs. revaluations).** Revaluation is more of a choice than a requirement or stipulation. Even those standards that permit revaluations offer it as an alternative to the historical cost. It is prohibited in countries such as the United States and Japan, and if used would be considered a departure from GAAP. In the United Kingdom and France revaluation of assets is permitted, but not all assets are allowed to be carried at revalued amounts. In the United Kingdom the items that are permitted to be revalued are property, plant, equipment, and investments. In France, revaluations are rare, except when prescribed by law.
2. **Timing of recognition vs. deferrals**. Recognition of profits and losses causes major differences in financial reporting. Sometimes the method used in recognizing profits or losses could cause differences, and sometimes the number of years over which amortization is spread could cause disparities in the reporting of financial results. Two examples illustrating the foregoing causes of differences follow.

   a. **Accounting for goodwill.** There is great disparity among standards with regard to the accounting treatment of goodwill. Some countries have traditionally given a free choice of either writing it off to reserves on acquisition or capitalizing and recognizing it on the balance sheet. The other controversy is with regard to the number of years over which goodwill is to be amortized. The following summarizes these differences:

      (1) *United States and France.* Both treat goodwill as an asset and amortize it over its useful life. (Under US GAAP the amortization period is 40 years, while in France no set limit is prescribed but shorter periods are used.)

      (2) *United Kingdom.* Traditionally, alternatives are allowed: Goodwill could either be written off on acquisition by a charge to reserves (**not** to the income statement) **or** capitalized and amortized over its useful life. However, recent amendments have modified this approach.

      (3) *Japan.* Goodwill is capitalized and written off over 5 years, but this can be extended if a longer life can be justified.

b. **Accounting for long-term contracts**. Long-term contracts could be accounted under either the percentage-of-completion method or the completed contract method. Profit recognition under the methods is vastly different. While the completed contract method postpones the recognition of profits until the contact is completed, the percentage-of-completion method recognizes profits during the life of the contract. Following are the methods prescribed under the various standards:

(1) *United States, France, and Japan.* Both methods are permitted.
(2) *United Kingdom.* Only the percentage-of-completion method is permitted.

3. **Recognition of substance over form in accounting for leases: capital vs. operating**

a. *United Kingdom and United States.* Certain categories of leases (called **finance leases** in the United Kingdom and **capital leases** in the United States) have to be capitalized (capital value of asset leased is recorded as an asset and future lease payments recorded as liability).
b. *France.* Capitalizing is prohibited, except for consolidated accounts, for which it is optional.
c. *Japan.* Although this treatment is not specifically prohibited, there are no accounting rules on this subject.

4. **Financial statement disclosures**

a. **Related party transactions**

(1) *United States and France.* There are significant disclosure requirements on related party transactions.
(2) *United Kingdom.* Traditionally, only details of certain transactions with directors (and other specified personnel) were required to be disclosed. However, with the recent promulgation of a new standard (FRS 8), the related party disclosure requirements have been broadened.
(3) *Japan.* All material transactions with related parties must be disclosed under a footnote captioned "Conditions of Business Group."

b. **Segmental information**

(1) *United States.* Applicable only to publicly held (listed) companies.
(2) *France and United Kingdom.* Applicable in case of all companies.
(3) *Japan.* Applicable in case of listed companies and should be reported by the parent company for the group; to be disclosed in a footnote captioned "Conditions of Business Group."

Relevance of IAS to the Developing Countries of the World

Many developing nations do not have their own national accounting standards. The generally accepted accounting principles (GAAP) that they follow are either the UK, US, or international standards. In certain countries, governments and central banks have made the IAS mandatory. Rather than reinventing the wheel, the adoption of IAS, which are high-quality standards, developed after a truly international "due process," seems to be a step in the right direction, as it will help the process of uniformity in international financial reporting.

APPENDIX

INTERNATIONAL ACCOUNTING STANDARDS EFFECTIVE 1998

IAS 1 Presentation of Financial Statements (revised July 1997; effective for periods beginning on or after July 1, 1998)

Note that former IAS 1 remains effective until IAS 1 (revised) is implemented.

IAS 2 Inventories

IAS 4 Depreciation Accounting

IAS 5 Information to be Disclosed in Financial Statements (to be superseded by IAS 1 [revised] effective for periods beginning on or after July 1, 1998)

IAS 7 Cash Flow Statements

IAS 8 Net Profit or Loss for the Period, Fundamental Errors and Changes in Accounting Policies

IAS 9 Research and Development Costs

IAS 10 Contingencies and Events Occurring After the Balance Sheet Date

IAS 11 Construction Contracts

IAS 12 Accounting for Taxes on Income (revised September 1996; effective for periods beginning on or after January 1, 1998)

IAS 13 Presentation of Current Assets and Current Liabilities (to be replaced by IAS 1[revised] effective for periods beginning on or after July 1, 1998)

IAS 14 Reporting Financial Information by Segment

IAS 15 Information Reflecting the Effects of Changing Prices

IAS 16 Property, Plant, and Equipment

IAS 17 Accounting for Leases

IAS 18 Revenue

IAS 19 Retirement Benefit Costs

IAS 20 Accounting for Government Grants and Disclosure of Government Assistance

IAS 21 The Effects of Changes in Foreign Exchange Rates

IAS 22 Business Combinations

IAS 23 Borrowing Costs

IAS 24 Related Party Disclosures

IAS 25 Accounting for Investments

IAS 26 Accounting and Reporting by Retirement Benefit Plans

IAS 27 Consolidated Financial Statements and Accounting for Investments in Subsidiaries

IAS 28 Accounting for Investments in Associates

IAS 29 Financial Reporting in Hyperinflationary Economies

IAS 30 Disclosures in the Financial Statements of Banks and Similar Financial Institutions

IAS 31 Financial Reporting of Interests in Joint Ventures

IAS 32 Financial Instruments: Disclosures and Presentation

IAS 33 Earnings Per Share (issued February 1997; effective for periods beginning on or after January 1, 1998)

2 BALANCE SHEET

PERSPECTIVE AND ISSUES

The objective of presenting financial statements in a manner consistent with that outlined by the IASC in its *Framework for the Preparation and Presentation of Financial Statements* is to provide information regarding an enterprise's financial position, performance, and changes in financial position to a broad spectrum of users, to enable them to make rational and informed economic decisions. According to the IASC's *Framework*, the financial statements are meant to report on the "results of stewardship of the management, or the accountability of management for the resources entrusted to it."

These provisions of the *Framework* are consistent with the long debated, recently issued IAS 1 (revised), *Presentation of Financial Statements.* The revised standard, while eloquently referring to financial statements as "a structured financial representation of the financial position of and the transactions undertaken by an enterprise," elaborates further upon their purpose or objective. According to this standard, the objective of the "general purpose financial statements" is to provide information about an enterprise's "financial position," its "performance," and its "cash flows," which information is then utilized by a wide spectrum of end-users in making economic decisions. This information is presented through a complete set of financial statements which, according to IAS 1 (revised 1997), para 7, comprises the following components:

1. The balance sheet
2. An income statement
3. Another statement showing either
    a. All changes in equity, or
    b. Changes in equity other than those arising from capital transactions with owners and distributions to owners
4. A cash flow statement
5. Accounting policies and other explanatory notes

The fact that revised IAS 1 provides a somewhat ambiguous definition of the financial statement which will summarize some or all changes in equity during the reporting period is particularly interesting. It will be remembered that this statement's immediate predecessor, Exposure Draft E53, required that an enterprise present a basic financial statement to be captioned as the "statement of nonowner movement in equity." In the interim, while comments on E53 were being received and considered, the US accounting standard setter imposed a somewhat similar requirement, for the presentation of a new "statement of comprehensive income," on US companies complying with GAAP (while this statement can be combined with the income statement or incorporated into a statement of changes in stockholders' equity, the same essential requirements have to be fulfilled in any event). Furthermore, the UK GAAP requirements had earlier been revised to mandate the presentation of a somewhat similar financial statement, the "statement of total recognized gains and losses." Thus, the easing of the requirements which were signaled by E53 is somewhat puzzling, although it appears at this early date that the practical differences between what was to have been imposed and what has now been codified might be minor.

A balance sheet, which is a major component of the financial statements, is a statement of financial position that presents assets, liabilities, and shareholders' equity (net worth) at a given point in time. The balance sheet reflects the financial status of an enterprise in conformity with the accounting principles on which the financial statements have been prepared; for instance, the international accounting standards. Alone among the traditional financial statements, it reports the aggregate effect of transactions at a point in time, whereas the other components of the financial statements, that is, the income statement, the newly prescribed statement showing **either** "all changes in equity" or "changes in equity other than those arising from capital transactions with owners and distributions to owners," and the statement of cash flows, summarize the totality of transactions over a period of time.

Whereas the early history of financial reporting was one of almost universal emphasis on the balance sheet (in fact, there was a time when only the balance sheet was presented for review by those outside an organization), for an extended period beginning in the 1960s, users of financial statements placed greater emphasis on the income statement than on the balance sheet. During this period, enterprise desirability was measured largely by earnings growth, as investors became more interested in short-run maximization of earnings per share. However, the cycles of worldwide inflation and recession that began during the 1970s, replete with "credit crunches" that precipitated the demise of many once-high-flying entities, brought about a renewed emphasis on the balance sheet. By the mid- to late 1980s a more balanced view became dominant, with both balance sheet and income statement (the cash flow statement did not achieve prominence until the very late 1980s and early 1990s) receiving close scrutiny.

This shift of emphasis back toward the balance sheet has signaled a departure from the traditional transaction-based concept of income toward a capital maintenance concept. This has historically been more favored by economists than by accountants, consistent with the former group's concern with real, not merely nominal, wealth creation. Under the capital maintenance approach to income measurement, the amount of beginning net assets (ideally measured by real economic value, not by accounting book values) would be compared to the amount of ending net assets, and the difference would be adjusted for dividends and capital transactions. Only to the extent that an entity maintained its net assets (after adjusting for capital transactions) would income be deemed to have been earned. By using a capital maintenance concept, it is argued, investors can better predict the overall profit potential of the firm. Notwithstanding the recognition of this, however, financial reporting almost universally continues to be grounded in historical costs, except in those economies where experience with hyperinflation has made such financial reporting obviously meaningless.

Financial statements should provide information that helps users make rational investment, credit, or economic decisions. The balance sheet must be studied to assess a firm's liquidity, its financial flexibility, and its ability to generate profits, pay its debts as they become due, and pay dividends. **Liquidity** refers to an entity's present cash and near-cash position as well as to the timing of its future cash flows which are anticipated to occur in the normal course of business. Liquidity thus refers to the enterprise's ability to meet its obligations as they fall due.

The concept of financial flexibility is broader than the concept of liquidity. **Financial flexibility** is the ability to take effective actions to alter the amounts and timings of cash flows so that it can respond to unexpected needs and opportunities. Financial flexibility includes the ability to raise new capital or tap into unused lines of credit.

Another important objective of financial reporting is to provide information that is useful in assessing the amounts, timing, and uncertainty of future cash flows. There have been two pertinent suggestions to make the balance sheet more useful in assessing a firm's liquidity. The first is to make alterations to the balance sheet's format. The second is to provide expanded information about liquidity in the notes to the balance sheet.

For most businesses, balance sheets are more meaningful if they are classified into categories. Assets are classified as **current assets** if they are used in the enterprise's operating activities and are reasonably expected to be converted into cash, sold, or consumed either within 12 months of the reporting date or in the normal course of one operating cycle, whichever is longer. Assets are also classified as current assets when they are held primarily for trading or short-term investment purposes and are expected to be realized within 12 months of the reporting date. Liabilities are classified as **current liabilities** if they are expected to be liquidated through the use of current assets or the creation of other current liabilities. The excess of current assets over current liabilities is known universally as **net working capital**.

For some other businesses, however, the concept of **working capital** has little or no relevance and the balance sheet is accordingly not classified. Such businesses include banks, similar financial institutions and insurance enterprises. Personal financial statements are unclassified for the same reason (refer to Chapter 21 for details).

Ultimately, each reporting entity must decide whether a classified balance sheet would be meaningful to users. IAS 1 (revised 1997) makes it incumbent upon each enterprise to make a determination, based on the nature of its operations, whether or not to present current and noncurrent assets and current and noncurrent liabilities as separate classifications on the face of the balance sheet. Even the predecessor to this standard, IAS 13, left it up to the reporting entity to resolve this matter; thus this position is not a new one in the context of the international accounting standards.

Additionally, the revised standard IAS 1 makes it incumbent upon enterprises, whether they choose to present a classified balance sheet or not, to disclose, for each asset and liability item, the amounts expected to be recovered or settled after more than 12 months. In imposing this new requirement, the revised standard on the presentation of financial statements recognizes that information about the maturities dates of financial assets and financial liabilities is now required by IAS 32, *Financial Instruments: Disclosure and Presentation.* IAS 1 (revised) thus builds upon this foundation, and emphasizes that additional information concerning the expected dates of recovery and settlement of nonmonetary assets and liabilities, like inventories or provisions, is also useful (whether or not an enterprise presents a classified balance sheet).

Sources of IAS

IAS 1 (revised 1997), 5 (repealed by IAS 1), 7, 10, 13 (repealed by IAS 1), 24, 30, 32

IASC's Framework for the Preparation and Presentation of Financial Statements

Exposure Draft on Presentation of Financial Statements, E53
(predecessor to the revised IAS 1)

Exposure Draft on Intangible Assets, E50

DEFINITIONS OF TERMS

The IASC's *Framework* defines elements of the financial statements of business enterprises and several related concepts. Elements are the basic categories that appear on financial statements. To be included in financial statements, an item must meet the definitional requirements, recognition requirements, and measurement requirements. Although there may be other elements of financial statements, the

IASC's *Framework* defines only those elements that relate to the status and performance of a business and which are therefore relevant to decisions that would require the commitment of resources to the business. Three of the 10 elements (assets, liabilities, and equity) are related to the status of an entity at a particular point in time. The other elements, such as comprehensive income and expenses, are related to the performance of an entity over a period of time. The two categories of elements articulate. That is, a change in one category will affect the other.

Elements of balance sheets.

> ***Assets****--Probable future economic benefits obtained or controlled by a particular entity as a result of past transactions or events.*

The following three characteristics must be present for an item to qualify as an asset:

1. The asset must provide probable future economic benefit which enables it to provide future net cash inflows.
2. The entity is able to receive the benefit and restrict other entities' access to that benefit.
3. The event that provides the entity with the right to the benefit has occurred.

Assets remain an economic resource of an enterprise as long as they continue to meet the three requirements identified above. Transactions and operations act to change an entity's assets.

A valuation account is neither an asset nor a liability. Rather, it alters the carrying value of an asset and is not independent of that related asset.

Assets have features that help identify them in that they are exchangeable, legally enforceable, and have future economic benefit (service potential). It is that potential that eventually brings in cash to the entity and that underlies the concept of an asset.

> ***Liabilities****--Probable future sacrifices of economic benefits arising from present obligations of a particular entity to transfer assets or provide services to other entities in the future as a result of past transactions or events.*

The following three characteristics must be present for an item to qualify as a liability:

1. A liability requires that the entity settle a present obligation by the probable future transfer of an asset on demand when a specified event occurs or at a particular date.
2. The obligation cannot be avoided.
3. The event that obligates the entity has occurred.

Liabilities usually result from transactions that enable entities to obtain resources. Other liabilities may arise from nonreciprocal transfers, such as the declaration of dividends to the owners of the entity or the pledge of assets to charitable organizations.

An entity may involuntarily incur a liability. A liability may be imposed on the entity by government or by the court system in the form of taxes, fines, or levies. A liability may arise from price changes or interest rate changes. Liabilities may be legally enforceable or they may be equitable obligations that arise from social, ethical, or moral requirements. Liabilities continue in existence until the entity is no longer responsible for discharging them. A valuation account is not an independent item. It alters the carrying value of a liability and is directly related to that liability.

Most liabilities stem from financial instruments, contracts, and laws, which are legal concepts invented by a sophisticated economy. Enterprises incur liabilities primarily as part of their ongoing economic activities, in exchange for economic resources and services required to operate the business. The end result of a liability is that it takes the use of an asset or the creation of another liability to liquidate it. Liabilities are imposed by agreement, by law, by court, by equitable or constructive obligation, and by business ethics and custom.

The diagram that follows, which is taken from a document that formed part of the conceptual framework project by the US standard-setting body, the Financial Accounting Standards Board, identifies the three classes of events that affect an entity.

> ***Equity***--*The residual interest in the assets that remains after deducting its liabilities. In a business enterprise, the equity is the ownership interest.*

Equity arises from the ownership relation and is the basis for distributions of earnings to the owners. Distributions of enterprise assets to owners are voluntary. Equity is increased by owners' investments and comprehensive income and is reduced by distributions to owners. In practice, the distinction between equity and liabilities may be difficult to ascertain. Securities such as convertible debt and certain types of preferred stock may have characteristics of both equity (residual ownership interest) and liabilities (nondiscretionary future sacrifices).

The other elements that change assets, liabilities, and equities are identified and defined in Chapter 3.

CONCEPTS, RULES, AND EXAMPLES

General Concepts

Under international accounting standards, assets and liabilities are recorded in financial statements under the historical cost principle, although in selected cases subsequent changes in values can be recognized. Historical exchange prices are used because they are objective and capable of being verified independently. When a balance sheet is presented, most assets are reported at cost. One very important

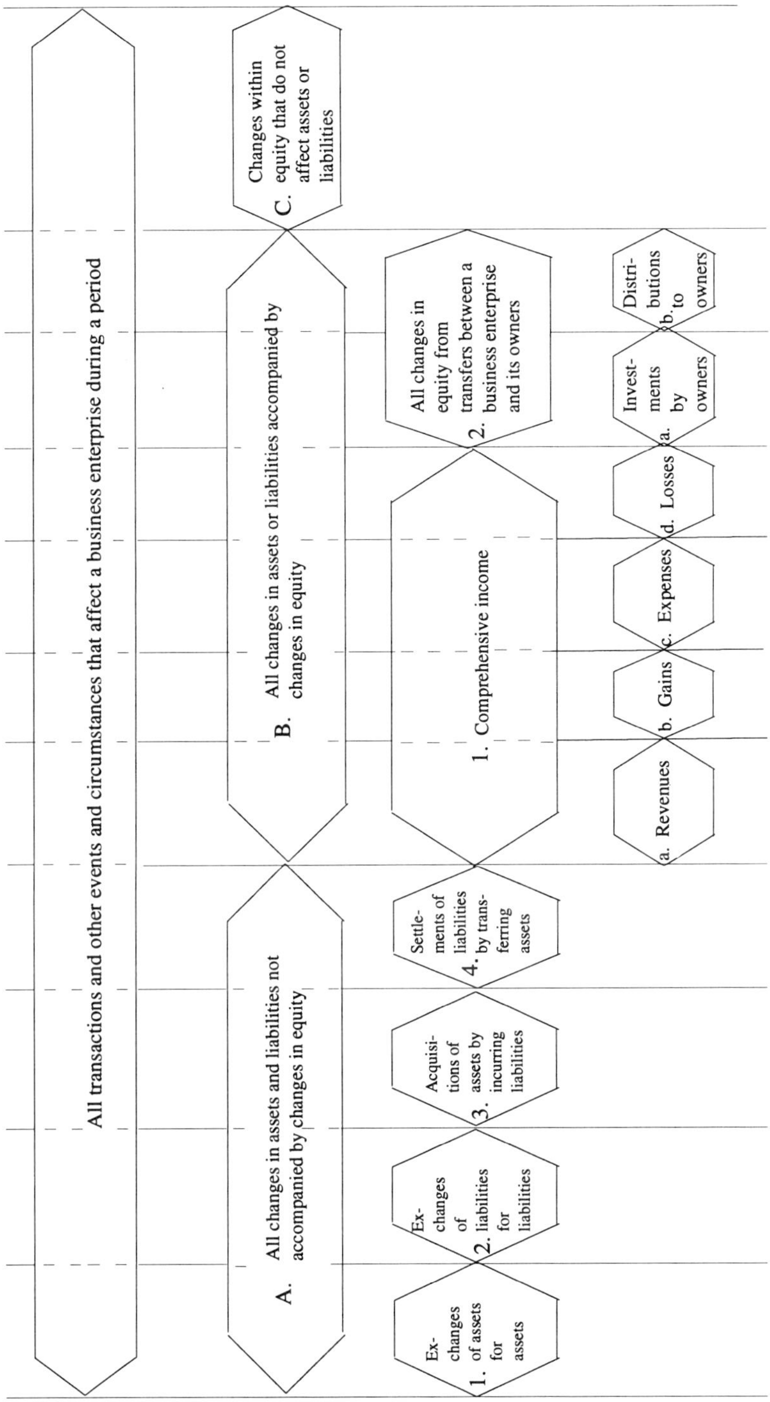
All transactions and other events and circumstances that affect a business enterprise during a period
A. All changes in assets and liabilities not accompanied by changes in equity
B. All changes in assets or liabilities accompanied by changes in equity
C. Changes within equity that do not affect assets or liabilities
1. Ex-changes of assets for assets
2. Ex-changes of liabilities for liabilities
3. Acquisi-tions of assets by incurring liabilities
4. Settle-ments of liabilities by trans-ferring assets
1. Comprehensive income
2. All changes in equity from transfers between a business enterprise and its owners
a. Revenues
b. Gains
c. Expenses
d. Losses
a. Invest-ments by owners
b. Distri-butions to owners

limitation is that historical cost does not always (or even typically) reflect current value, and thus the balance sheet will not generally be indicative of the economic value of an enterprise.

Generally accepted accounting principles allow or require certain exceptions to the historical cost principle. For example, inventories and marketable equity securities may be reported at lower of cost or market, and certain long-term investments may be reported under the equity method, but neither of these exceptions is intended to result in a balance sheet that reflects current economic value. Depreciation, depletion, and amortization of long-term assets are acceptable practices, but appreciation of assets is not generally recorded. Appreciation of assets is usually recorded only when realized through an arm's-length transaction (sale), although international accounting standards do provide the option of revaluation for plant assets and for certain other investment assets, as described in more detail in Chapters 8 and 9.

Many accountants, of course, believe that the balance sheet would be more useful if all assets were restated in terms of current values, and a number of strategies to accomplish this have been proposed or tried over the years. In general, these current values could be market related (i.e., based on changes in specific prices) or could simply be historical costs adjusted for the changing value of the dollar (i.e., based on changes in the general price level). For a range of reasons, none of these approaches have been widely accepted in practice, and thus the historical cost approach continues as the most widely employed measurement model for financial reporting. However, under current generally accepted accounting principles, although assets are usually stated at historical cost, if market information indicates a permanent and material decline in value, recognition of the economic loss is immediate.

Another limitation of historical cost-based balance sheets is a consequence of the fact that estimates are used to determine the carrying, or book, values of many of the assets. Estimates are used in determining the collectibility of receivables, salability of inventory, and useful life of long-term assets, among other things. Estimates are necessary in order to divide and separate economic events occurring between two distinct accounting periods. However, such estimates require informed judgments for which there is perhaps not enough guidance in accounting literature.

An additional failing of the balance sheet is that it ignores items that are of financial value to the firm but the worth of which cannot be determined objectively. For example, internally generated goodwill, human resources, and secret processes are of financial value, but since these values are not measurable under current accounting principles and practices, they are not recorded on the balance sheet. Only assets obtained in a market transaction are incorporated into the financial statements of an entity. As the service economy becomes ever more dominant, the importance of assets that are not reflected in the traditional balance sheet (particularly those relating to human capital) will become a more critical issue which the accounting professions will eventually have to address.

A final constraint on the usefulness of the balance sheet is that it largely ignores the time value of its elements. Although certain receivables and payables may be discounted, most items are stated at face value regardless of the timing of the cash flows that they will generate. This tends to exacerbate the divergence between net worth as reported in balance sheets and the value of the enterprise in real economic terms.

The net result of the foregoing is that the balance sheet contains a mixture of historical costs and current values that may restrict its utility to users. It is true that, in the case of some assets and liabilities, cost is a reasonably close approximation of current value. Monetary assets such as cash, short-term investments, and receivables closely approximate current value. Current liabilities are payable within a short period, and the amounts reported thus also closely approximate current values. If these values were discounted, any discrepancy would be immaterial because of the short time period before payment. Current liabilities are not classified strictly on the basis of maturity value but on the concept that a current liability is one that requires either a current asset or another current liability to liquidate, and should be shown on the balance sheet at face value. Productive assets such as property, plant, and equipment, and intangibles are reported at cost less any reduction due to depreciation, depletion, or amortization. Long-term liabilities are recorded as the discounted value of future payments to be made under contract, since, on the date of issuance, the discount rate equals the market rate. However, as time passes and the market rate fluctuates, the recorded cost will not necessarily approximate the current value.

The rights of the common shareholders of a firm and the rights of other capital-supplying parties (bondholders and other lenders, and preferred stockholders) of a firm are many and varied. Both sources of capital are concerned with two basic rights: the right to share in the cash or property disbursements (interest and dividends) and the right to share in the assets in the event of liquidation. The disclosure of these rights is an important objective in the presentation of financial statements.

Form of Balance Sheet

The titles commonly given to the primary financial statement that presents an entity's financial position are balance sheet, statement of financial position, or statement of financial condition. Use of any of these terms implies that the statement was prepared in conformity with generally accepted accounting principles. If some other comprehensive basis of accounting, such as income tax or cash, is adhered to instead, the title of the financial statement should be adjusted to reflect this departure. Thus, a title such as "Statements of Assets and Liabilities" would be necessary to differentiate the financial statement being presented from a balance sheet.

The three elements that are displayed in the heading of a balance sheet are

1. The entity whose financial position is being presented
2. The title of the statement
3. The date of the statement

The entity's name should appear exactly as written in the legal document that created it (e.g., the certificate of incorporation, partnership agreement, etc.). The title should also clearly reflect the legal status of the enterprise as a corporation, partnership, sole proprietorship, or division of some other entity. Where the entity's name does not disclose its legal status, supplemental information should be added to the title to clarify that status. A few examples are

ABC Company
(A partnership)

ABC Company
(A limited partnership)

ABC Company
(A sole proprietorship)

ABC Company
(A division of DEF, Inc.)

The title of the financial statement should generally be "Balance Sheet" unless another name is indicative of the terminology used in the industry. For example, in the securities industry, the title "Statement of Financial Condition" is more widely used.

Finally, the last day of the month should be used as the statement date unless the entity uses a fiscal reporting period always ending on a particular day of the week, such as a Friday or Sunday (e.g., the last Friday in December, or the Sunday falling closest to December 31). In these cases, the balance sheet can appropriately be dated accordingly (i.e., December 26, October 1, etc.). In all cases, the implication is that the balance sheet captures the pertinent amounts as of the close of business on the date noted.

Balance sheets should generally be uniform in appearance from one period to the next, as indeed should all of the entity's financial statements. The form, terminology, captions, and pattern of combining insignificant items should be consistent. The goal is to enhance usefulness by maintaining a consistent manner of presentation unless there are good reasons to change these and the changes are duly reported.

Classification of Assets

Assets, liabilities, and stockholders' equity are separated in the balance sheet so that important relationships can be shown and so that attention can be focused on significant subtotals.

Current assets. According to IAS 1 (revised 1997), an asset should be classified as a current asset when it

1. Is expected to be realized in, or is held for sale or consumption in, the normal course of the enterprise's operating cycle; or
2. Is held primarily for trading purposes or for the short term, and is expected to be realized within 12 months of the balance sheet date; or
3. Is cash or a cash equivalent asset which is not restricted in its use.

All other assets should be classified as noncurrent assets, if a classified balance sheet is to be presented in the financial statements.

Thus, current assets include cash, cash equivalents and other assets which can be expected to be realized in cash or sold or consumed during one normal operating cycle of the business. The operating cycle of an enterprise is the time between the acquisition of materials entering into a process and its realization in cash or an instrument that is readily convertible into cash. The default assumption is that the operating cycle is a period of 12 months, and thus the current assets are expected to be realized within the period of 12 months. IAS 1 (revised 1997) makes an exception in the case of "inventories" and "trade receivables" and specifically states that even if these assets are not expected to be realized within 12 months from the balance sheet date they should still be classified as "current assets" in a classified balance sheet. However, "marketable securities" could only be classified as current assets if they are expected to be realized within 12 months of the balance sheet date, even though most would deem marketable securities to be more liquid than inventories and possibly even than receivables. The following items would be classified as current assets:

1. **Cash** and cash equivalents include cash on hand, consisting of coins, currency, and undeposited checks; money orders and drafts; and deposits in banks. Anything accepted by a bank for deposit would be considered as cash. Cash must be available for a demand withdrawal: Assets such as certificates of deposit would not be considered cash because of the time restrictions on withdrawal. Also, to be classified as a current asset, cash must be available for current use. According to IAS 1 (revised 1997), cash that is restricted in use and whose restrictions will not expire within the operating cycle, or cash restricted for a noncurrent use, would not be included in current assets. According to IAS 7 (revised 1992), cash equivalents include short-term, highly liquid investments that (1) are readily convertible to known amounts of cash, and (2) are so near their maturity (original maturi-

ties of 3 months or less) that they present negligible risk of changes in value because of changes in interest rates. Treasury bills, commercial paper, and money market funds are all examples of cash equivalents.

2. **Short-term investments** are readily marketable securities which are normally acquired through the use of temporarily idle cash. The basis of reporting of these items need not be reported on the face of the balance sheet provided that the different reporting classifications are reconciled in the notes. The balance sheet presentation would be as follows:

Marketable securities	$xxx

3. **Receivables** include accounts and notes receivable, receivables from affiliate companies, and officer and employee receivables. The term **accounts receivable** represents amounts due from customers arising from transactions in the ordinary course of business. Allowances due to lack of collectibility and any amounts discounted or pledged should be stated clearly. The allowances may be based on a relationship to sales or based on direct analysis of the receivables. If material, the receivables should be analyzed into their component parts. The receivables section may be presented as follows:

Receivables:			
Accounts	$xxx		
Notes	xxx	$xxxx	
Less allowance for doubtful accounts		(xxx)	$xxxx
Associated companies			xxx
Officers and employees			xxx
Total			$xxxx

4. **Inventories** are assets held, either for sale in the ordinary course of business or in the process of production for such sale, or in the form of materials or supplies to be consumed in the production process or in the rendering of services (IAS 2). The basis of valuation and the method of pricing should be disclosed.

Inventories--at the lower of cost (FIFO) or net realizable value	$xxx

In the case of a manufacturing concern, raw materials, work in process, and finished goods should be disclosed separately on the balance sheet or in the footnotes.

Inventories:		
Finished goods	$xxx	
Work in process	xxx	
Raw materials	xxx	$xxx

5. **Prepaid expenses** are assets created by the prepayment of cash or incurrence of a liability. They expire and become expenses with the passage of time, use, or events (e.g., prepaid rent, prepaid insurance, and deferred taxes).

Noncurrent assets. IAS 1 (revised 1997) uses the term "noncurrent" to include tangible, intangible, operating, and financial assets of a long-term nature. It does not prohibit the use of alternative descriptions, as long as the meaning is clear. Noncurrent assets include long-term investments, property and equipment, intangible assets and miscellaneous other assets, as described in the following paragraphs.

Long-term investments. Investments that are intended to be held for an extended period of time (longer than one operating cycle) would be classified as long-term investments. The following are the three major types of long-term investments:

1. **Debt and equity securities** are stocks, bonds, and long-term notes. The basis of reporting of these items is not reported on the face of the balance sheet but should be reported in the notes.

Long-term investments:			
Investments in A company stock	$xxx		
Notes receivable	xxx		
Less discount on notes receivable	(xxx)	xxx	
Investment in B company bonds		xxx	$xxx

2. **Tangible assets** not currently used in operations, such as surplus machinery being held on a standby basis.
3. **Investments held in special funds** (e.g., sinking funds, pension funds, amounts held for plant expansion, and cash surrender values of life insurance policies).

Property, plant, and equipment. Tangible assets that are held by an enterprise for use in the production or supply of goods or services, or for rental to others, or for administrative purposes and which are expected to be used during more than one period. Included are such items as land, buildings, machinery and equipment, furniture and fixtures, motor vehicles and equipment. These should be disclosed, with the related accumulated depreciation, as follows:

Machinery and equipment	$xxx	
Less accumulated depreciation	(xxx)	$xxx
or		
Machinery and equipment (net of $xxx accumulated depreciation)		$xxx

Accumulated depreciation should be shown by major classes of depreciable assets. In addition to showing this amount on the balance sheet, the notes to the financial statements should contain balances of major classes of depreciable assets, by nature or function, at the balance sheet date, along with a general description of the method or methods used in computing depreciation with respect to major classes of depreciable assets (IAS 16).

Intangible assets. Noncurrent, nonmaterialistic assets of a business, the possession of which provides anticipative benefits to the owner. Included in this category are such items as goodwill, trademarks, patents, copyrights, and organizational costs. These are defined by IASC's *Exposure Draft on Intangible Assets*, E50, as "identifiable, nonmonetary assets without physical substance that:

1. Are controlled by an enterprise for use in the production or supply of goods or services, for rental to others, or for administrative purposes and
2. Are expected to be used during more than one period."

Generally, the amortization of an intangible asset is credited directly to the asset account, although it is acceptable to use an accumulated amortization account. The tradition of reporting tangible assets on a gross basis, with accumulated depreciation shown separately, developed from the goal of providing the reader with enough information to make a rough calculation of the age of plant assets used by the enterprise, partly to enable an assessment of the amount and timing of capital needed for the replacement of those assets. Intangible assets are not as regularly subject to replacement, however, and are often written down in carrying value for reasons other than the simple passage of time, and therefore amortization is typically, but not necessarily, credited directly to the asset account.

Other assets. An all-inclusive heading for accounts that do not fit neatly into any of the other asset categories (e.g., long-term prepaid expenses, deferred taxes, deferred bond issue costs, noncurrent receivables, and restricted cash).

Classification of Liabilities

The liabilities are normally displayed on the balance sheet in the order of payment.

Current liabilities. According to IAS 1 (revised 1997), a liability should be classified as a current liability when it

1. Is expected to be settled in the normal course of the enterprise's operating cycle; or
2. Is due to be settled within 12 months of the balance sheet date.

All other liabilities should be classified as noncurrent liabilities.

In other words, current liabilities are obligations the liquidation of which is reasonably expected to require the use of existing resources properly classifiable as current assets, or the creation of other current obligations. Obligations which are due on demand or which are callable at any time by the lender are classified as current regardless of the present intent of the entity or of the lender concerning early demand for repayment.

1. Obligations arising from the acquisition of goods and services entering the operating cycle (e.g., accounts payable, short-term notes payable, wages payable, taxes payable, and other miscellaneous payables).
2. Collections of money in advance for the future delivery of goods or performance of services, such as rent received in advance and unearned subscription revenues.
3. Other obligations maturing within the current operating cycle to be met through the use of current assets, such as the current maturity of bonds and long-term notes.

Per IAS 1 (revised 1997), certain liabilities, such as trade payables and accruals for operating costs, which form part of the working capital used in the normal operating cycle of the business, are to be classified as "current liabilities" even if they are due to be settled after more than 12 months from the balance sheet date.

Other current liabilities which are not settled as part of the operating cycle, but which are due for settlement within 12 months of the balance sheet date, such as dividends payable and the current portion of long-term debt, should also be classified as "current liabilities." However, interest-bearing liabilities that provide the financing for working capital on a long-term basis, and which are not scheduled for settlement within 12 months, should not be classified as "current liabilities."

IAS 1 (revised 1997) provides another exception to the general rule that a liability due to be repaid within 12 months of the balance sheet date should be classified as a "current liability." If the original term was for a period longer than 12 months, and the enterprise intended to refinance the obligation on a long-term basis prior to the balance sheet date, and that intention is supported by an agreement to refinance, or to reschedule payments, which agreement is completed before the financial statements are approved, then the debt is to be reclassified as noncurrent as of the balance sheet date.

In two cases, obligations to be paid within one period should not be classified as current liabilities. Debt expected to be refinanced through another long-term issue, and debt that will be retired through the use of noncurrent assets, such as from the amount accumulated in a bond sinking fund, are treated as noncurrent liabilities because the liquidation does not require the use of current assets or the creation of other current liabilities.

The distinction between current and noncurrent liquid assets generally rests upon both the ability of the entity and the intent of the entity to liquidate or not to liquidate within the traditional 1-year concept. Intent is not of similar significance with regard to the classification of liabilities, however, because the creditor has the legal right to demand satisfaction of a currently due obligation, and even an expression of intent not to exercise that right does not diminish the entity's burden should there be a change in that intention. Thus, whereas an entity can control its use of current assets, it cannot be the master of its own fate with regard to current liabilities, and accordingly, accounting for current liabilities (with the two exceptions noted above) is based on legal terms, not expressions of intent.

Noncurrent liabilities. Obligations that are not expected to be liquidated within the current operating cycle, including

1. Obligations arising through the acquisition of assets, such as the issuance of bonds, long-term notes, and lease obligations;
2. Obligations arising out of the normal course of operations, such as pension obligations; and
3. Contingent obligations involving uncertainty as to possible losses. These are resolved by the occurrence or nonoccurrence of one or more future events that confirm the amount payable, the payee, and/or the date payable, such as product warranties (see the contingency section).

For all long-term liabilities, the maturity date, nature of obligation, rate of interest, and description of any security pledged to support the agreement should be clearly shown. Also, in the case of bonds and long-term notes, any premium or discount should be reported separately as an addition to or subtraction from the par (or face) value of the bond or note. Long-term obligations which contain certain covenants that must be adhered to are classified as current liabilities if any of those covenants have been violated and the lender has the right to demand payment. Unless the lender expressly waives that right or the conditions causing the default are corrected, the obligation is current.

Other liabilities. Items that do not meet the definition of a liability, such as deferred income taxes or deferred investment tax credits, where measured by the deferred method. Often these items will be included in current or noncurrent liabilities even though technically, they are not similar.

Offsetting assets and liabilities. In general, assets and liabilities should not be offset against each other. The reduction of accounts receivable by the allowance for doubtful accounts, or of property, plant, and equipment by the accumulated depreciation, are acts that reduce these assets by the appropriate valuation accounts. These are not equivalent to offsetting assets and liabilities, however.

The right of setoff must exist for the offsetting in the financial statements to be a proper presentation. This right of setoff exists only when all the following conditions are met:

1. Each of the two parties owes the other determinable amounts (although they may be in different currencies and bear different rates of interest).
2. The entity has the right to set off against the amount owed by the other party.
3. The entity intends to offset.
4. The right of setoff is legally enforceable.

In particular cases, laws of certain countries, including some bankruptcy laws, may impose restrictions or prohibitions against the right of setoff. Furthermore, when maturities differ, only the party with the nearest maturity can offset because the party with the longer maturity must settle in the manner determined by the earlier maturity party.

In the context of the presentation of current assets and current liabilities in financial statements, IAS 1 (revised 1997) clearly states that unless a legal right of setoff exists and offsetting represents the expectation as to the realization of the asset or settlement of the liability, amounts should not be offset against each other.

IAS 30 establishes disclosure requirements for banks and similar financial institutions. It prohibits offsetting of assets or liabilities on similar grounds. The offsetting of cash or other assets against a tax liability or other amounts due to governmental bodies is also not acceptable except under limited circumstances. The only exception is when it is clear that the purchase of securities is in substance an advance payment of taxes payable in the near future and that the securities are acceptable for the payment of taxes. This occurs primarily as an accommodation to governmental bodies.

For forwards, interest rate swaps, currency swaps, options, and other conditional or exchange contracts, the conditions for the right of offset must exist or the fair value of contracts in a loss position cannot be offset against the fair value of contracts in a gain position. Neither can accrued receivable amounts be offset against accrued payable amounts. If, however, there is a master netting arrangement, fair value amounts recognized for forwards, interest or currency swaps, options, or other such contracts may be offset without respect to the conditions specified previously.

Classification of Stockholders' Equity

Stockholders' equity represents the interest of the stockholders in the assets of a corporation. It shows the cumulative net results of past transactions and other events.

Share capital. This consists of the par or stated value of preferred and common shares. The number of shares authorized, the number issued, and the number outstanding should be clearly shown. For preferred share capital, the preference features must also be stated as follows:

6% cumulative preference shares, $100 par value, callable at $115, 10,000 shares authorized and outstanding	$xxx
Equity shares, $10 par value per share, 2,000,000 shares authorized, 1,500,000 shares issued and outstanding	$xxx

Preference share capital that is redeemable at the option of the holder is not considered to be part of equity but is usually shown in a separate caption between liabilities and equity. However, IAS 32 makes it clear that substance prevails over form in the case of compound financial instruments, including equity instruments such as mandatorily redeemable preference shares, which accordingly should be shown in the liability section of the balance sheet.

Additional paid-in capital. There are two major categories of additional paid-in capital.

1. Paid-in capital in excess of par or stated value, which is the difference between the actual issue price and par or stated value. Amounts in excess should be disclosed separately for equity shares and each issue of preferred shares as follows:

Additional paid-in capital--6% preference shares	$xxx
Additional paid-in capital--equity shares	$xxx

2. Paid-in capital from other transactions, which includes treasury stock, retirement of stock, stock dividends recorded at market, proceeds from the lapse of stock purchase warrants, proceeds from the conversion of convertible bonds in excess of the par value of the stock, and any other additional capital arising from the company's own stock transactions.

Donated capital. Donations of a noncash variety from either stockholders or outside parties, such as land, securities, buildings, and equipment. The most typical scenario giving rise to donated capital is when a governmental agency makes a contribution to induce a business to locate in the community, in the belief that the resulting job creation will boost the local economy.

Retained earnings. Accumulated earnings that have not been distributed to the shareholders.

1. **Appropriated**--A certain amount of retained earnings that are not to be distributed to stockholders as dividends.
2. **Unappropriated**--Earnings available to be distributed as dividends.

A balance sheet disclosure should reveal the pertinent provisions, source of restriction, amount subject to restriction, and restrictions on other items, such as working capital and additional borrowings. If a company appropriated retained earnings to satisfy bond indebtedness, the presentation would be as follows:

Retained earnings		
Appropriated for bond indebtedness	$xxx	
Free and unappropriated	xxx	$xxx

Many corporations do not record the restrictions in appropriated and unappropriated accounts but merely explain the restrictions in the footnotes, because financial statement users often believe the appropriation is held as cash.

Also included in the equity section of the balance sheet is treasury stock representing issued shares reacquired by the issuer. These are generally stated at their cost of acquisition and as a reduction of shareholders' equity.

Finally, net unrealized losses on noncurrent portfolios of marketable equity securities, the excess of minimum pension liability over unrecognized prior service cost, and unrealized gains (losses) on foreign currency translations will also be shown as adjustments of equity.

Classification of Partners' Capital

In partnership entities, the balance sheet is the same as for all other entities, except for the net worth section. In a partnership, this section is usually referred to as partners' capital. In partnership accounting, the net worth section of the balance sheet includes the equity interests of the partners. Although each individual partner's capital need not be displayed, the totals for each class of partner, general or limited, should be shown.

Loans to or from partners should be displayed as assets and liabilities of the partnership and not as reductions or additions to partners' capital, although a separate line item on the balance sheet may be combined with net worth in a separately defined subtotal on the balance sheet. Payments to partners of interest on loans are properly classified as expenses on the income statement. Payments of interest on capital or salaries to partners are considered an allocation of profits and are usually not expensed on the income statement. However, in an attempt to emulate corporate financial reporting, some partnerships, with adequate disclosure, do display part or all of such payments as expenses.

Relationship of the Balance Sheet to the Income Statement

The balance sheet and income statement are interrelated through the changes that take place in each as a result of business transactions. Choosing a method of valuing inventory determines the method of calculating cost of goods sold. This articulation enables the users of financial information to use the statements as predictive indicators of future cash flows.

In assessing information about overall firm performance, users are interested in bringing together information in the income statement and the balance sheet. The balance sheet can also be used as a guide to give an indication of a firm's continuing ability to earn income and pay dividends. By combining the two statements, investors can develop some important financial ratios. For example, users may wish to express income as a rate of return on net operating assets.

Supplemental Disclosures

In addition to the measurement accounting principles that guide the values placed on the elements included in the balance sheet, there are disclosure accounting principles which are necessary to make the financial statements not misleading because of their omission. The following are five techniques of disclosure:

1. Parenthetical explanations
2. Footnotes
3. Supporting schedules
4. Cross-references
5. Valuation accounts

Parenthetical explanations. Supplemental information is disclosed by means of parenthetical explanations following the appropriate balance sheet items. For example

Equity share capital ($10 par value, 200,000 shares authorized, 150,000 issued)	$1,500,000

Parenthetical explanations have an advantage over both footnotes and supporting schedules. Parenthetical explanations place the disclosure in the body of the statement. The supplemental information tends to be overlooked when it is placed in a footnote.

Footnotes. If the additional information cannot be disclosed in a relatively short and concise parenthetical explanation, a footnote should be used. For example

Inventories (see note 1)	$2,550,000

The notes to the financial statements would then contain the following:

Note 1: Inventories are stated at the lower of cost or market. Cost is determined by the first-in, first-out method, and market is determined on the basis of estimated net realizable value. As of the balance sheet date, the market value of the inventory is $2,720,000.

Supporting schedules. To present adequate detail regarding certain balance sheet items, a supporting schedule may be used. Current receivables may be a single line item on the balance sheet, as follows:

Current receivables (see Schedule 2)	$2,500,000

A separate schedule for current receivables would then be presented as follows:

Schedule 2
Current Receivables

Customers' accounts and notes	$2,000,000
Associated companies	300,000
Nonconsolidated affiliates	322,000
Other	18,000
	2,640,000
Less allowance for doubtful accounts	(140,000)
	$2,500,000

Cross-references. Cross-referencing is used when there is a direct relationship between two accounts on the balance sheet. For example, among the current assets, the following might be shown if $1,500,000 of accounts receivable were required to be pledged as collateral for a $1,200,000 bank loan:

Accounts receivable pledged to bank	$1,500,000

Included in the current liabilities would be the following:

Bank loan payable--secured by accounts receivable	$1,200,000

Valuation accounts. Valuation accounts are used to reduce or increase the carrying amount of some assets and liabilities in financial statements. Accumulated depreciation reduces the book value for property, plant, and equipment, and a bond premium (discount) increases (decreases) the face value of a bond payable as shown in the following illustrations:

Equipment	$18,000,000	
Less accumulated depreciation	(1,625,000)	$16,375,000
Bonds payable	$20,000,000	
Less discount on bonds payable	(1,300,000)	$18,700,000
Bonds payable	$20,000,000	
Add premium on bonds payable	1,300,000	$21,300,000

Accounting policies. There are many different methods of valuing assets and assigning costs. IAS 1 (revised 1997) requires financial statements to include clear and concise disclosure of all significant accounting policies that have been used in the preparation of those financial statements. Financial statement users must be aware of the accounting policies used by enterprises so that sound economic decisions can be made. The disclosures should identify and describe the accounting principles followed by the entity and methods of applying those principles that materially affect the determination of financial position, changes in cash flows, or results of operations. The accounting policies should encompass those accounting principles and methods that involve the following:

1. Selection from acceptable alternatives
2. Principles and methods peculiar to the industry
3. Unique applications of IAS

Fairness exception under IAS 1 (revised). In what has become a somewhat controversial move, the IASC inserted what may be called a "fairness exception" in IAS 1 (revised), which was not included in the precedent exposure draft E53. This acknowledges that, while the use of IAS will result **in virtually all circumstances** in financial statements which achieve a fair presentation, in some instances this may not be the case. In such eventualities, IAS 1 (revised) permits departure from the standards to achieve the greater good of fair presentation, provided, however, that the enterprise discloses the following:

1. That management has concluded that the financial statements fairly present the entity's financial position, financial performance and cash flows;
2. That the entity has complied in all material respects with applicable IAS except that it departed from a standard to achieve a fair presentation; and
3. The standard from which the entity has departed; the nature of the departure, including the accounting treatment which the standard would have required; the reason why that treatment would have been misleading in the circumstances; the alternative treatment which was in fact applied; and the financial impact of the departure on profit or loss, assets, liabilities, equity, and cash flows for each period presented.

It might be noted that in the US, there is no similar exception under the accounting standards, but under US auditing standards there is a provision which provides that an "unqualified opinion" may be rendered even when there has been a GAAP departure, if the auditor concludes that it provides a fairer presentation than would have resulted had GAAP been strictly adhered to. Under IAS, this logic is built into the accounting standards themselves, and thus is not dependent upon the level of service, if any, being rendered by an independent accountant, but rather makes it a management responsibility, including the need to disclose the logic and the financial statement impact.

IAS 1 (revised 1997) requires that disclosure of these policies be an integral part of the financial statements. It recommends that these policies be disclosed in one location rather than being scattered throughout the footnotes. Though it makes it mandatory on enterprises to disclose all significant accounting policies, IAS 1 also recognizes that disclosure cannot rectify an incorrect or inappropriate treatment. Three considerations that govern the selection and application of the appropriate accounting policies are

1. Prudence
2. Substance over form
3. Materiality

The IASC not only encourages enterprises to present financial statements in conformity with the standards but also requires enterprises to disclose whether they have complied with or departed from the requirements of the standards (IAS 1 [revised 1997]; and the IASC's *Framework*).

Related parties disclosures. According to IAS 24, *Related Party Disclosures*, financial statements should include disclosure of material related party transactions which are defined by the standard as "transfer of resources or obligations between related parties, regardless of whether a price is charged."

A **related party** is essentially any party that controls or can significantly influence the financial or operating decisions of the company to the extent that the company may be prevented from fully pursuing its own interests. Such groups would include associates, investees accounted for by the equity method, trusts for the benefit of employees, principal owners, key management personnel, and immediate family members of owners or management.

Disclosures should take place even if there is no accounting recognition made for such transactions (e.g., a service is performed without payment). Disclosures should generally not imply that such related party transactions were on terms essentially equivalent to arm's-length dealings. Additionally, when one or more companies are under common control such that the financial statements might vary from those that would have been obtained if the companies were autonomous, the nature of the control relationship should be disclosed even if there are no transactions between the companies.

The disclosures generally should include

1. Nature of relationship
2. Description of transactions and effects of such transactions on the financial statements for each period for which an income statement is presented
3. Dollar amount of transactions for each period for which an income statement is presented and effects of any change in establishing the terms of such transactions different from that used in prior periods
4. Amounts due to and from such related parties as of the date of each balance sheet presented together with the terms and manner of settlement

Reporting comparative amounts for the preceding period. IAS 1 (revised 1997) requires that financial statements should show corresponding figures for the preceding period. To increase the usefulness of financial statements, many companies include in their annual reports 5- or 10-year summaries of condensed financial information. These comparative statements allow investment analysts and other interested readers to perform comparative analysis of pertinent information. The presentation of comparative financial statements in annual reports enhances the usefulness of such reports and brings out more clearly the nature and trends of current changes affecting the enterprise. Such presentation emphasizes the fact that the statements for a series of periods are far more significant than those for a single period and that the accounts for one period are but an installment of what is essentially a continuous history.

When comparative financial statements are presented (as they normally will be), the related footnote disclosures must also be presented on a comparative basis, except for items of disclosure that would be not meaningful, or might even be confusing, if set forth in such a manner. Although there is no official guidance on this issue, certain details, such as schedules of debt maturities as of the year earlier balance sheet date, would be of little interest to users of the current statements and would be largely redundant with information provided for the more recent year end. Accordingly, such details are often omitted from comparative financial statements. Another example of superfluous comparative data is the amount of undrawn borrowing capacity at the earlier year end. Most other disclosures, however, continue to be meaningful and should be presented for all years for which basic financial statements are displayed.

Subsequent events. The balance sheet is dated as of the last day of the fiscal period, but a period of time may elapse before the financial statements are actually prepared and issued. During this period, significant events or transactions may have occurred that materially affect the company's financial position. These events and transactions are usually referred to as **subsequent events**. IAS 10 refers to them as "events occurring after the balance sheet date." If not disclosed, significant events occurring between the balance sheet date and issue date could make the financial statements misleading.

There are two types of subsequent events described by IAS 10. The first type consists of events that provide additional evidence with respect to conditions that existed at the date of the balance sheet and affect the estimates inherent in the process of preparing financial statements. The second type consists of events that provide evidence with respect to conditions that did not exist at the date of the balance sheet being reported on but arose subsequent to that date. The first type results in adjustments of the financial statements. The second type does not require adjustment of the financial statements but may require disclosure to keep the financial statements from being misleading. Disclosure can be made in the form of footnotes, supporting schedules, and pro forma statements.

Examples of subsequent events

1. A loss on an uncollectible trade account receivable as a result of a customer's deteriorating financial condition leading to bankruptcy subsequent to the balance sheet date would be indicative of conditions existing at the balance sheet date, thereby calling for adjustment of the financial statements before their issuance. On the other hand, a loss on an uncollectible trade account receivable resulting from a customer's major casualty, such as a fire or flood subsequent to the balance sheet date, would not be indicative of conditions existing at the balance sheet date and adjustment of the financial statements would not be appropriate. However, if the amount is material, disclosure would be required.
2. A loss arising from the recognition after the balance sheet date that an asset such as plant and equipment had suffered a material decline in value arising out of reduced marketability for the product or service it can produce. Such a reduction would be considered an economic event in process at the balance sheet date and would require adjustment and recognition of the loss.
3. The second type of events, those not existing at the balance sheet date, require disclosure but not adjustment, and include

   a. Sale of a bond or share capital issue.
   b. Purchase of a business.
   c. Settlement of litigation when the event giving rise to the claim took place subsequent to the balance sheet date. The settlement is an economic event that would be accounted for in the period of occurrence.

d. Loss of plant or inventories as a result of fire or flood.
e. Losses on receivables resulting from conditions (such as a customer's major casualty) arising subsequent to the balance sheet date.
f. Gains or losses on certain marketable securities.

Contingencies. A contingency is defined in IAS 10 as a condition or situation the ultimate outcome of which, gain or loss, will be confirmed only on the occurrence or nonoccurrence of one or more uncertain future events. Resolution of the uncertainty may confirm the acquisition of an asset, the reduction of a liability, the loss or impairment of an asset, or the incurrence of a liability.

An estimated loss from a loss contingency is accrued by a charge to income and the recording of a liability if both of the following conditions are met:

1. Information available prior to issuance of the financial statements indicates that it is **probable** that an asset had been impaired or a liability had been incurred at the date of the financial statements.
2. The amount of loss can be **reasonably estimated**.

The likelihood of a loss on a contingency may be broken down into the following three classifications:

1. **Probable**--The future event or events are likely to occur.
2. **Reasonably possible**--The chance of the future event or events occurring is more than remote but less than likely.
3. **Remote**--The chance of the future event or events occurring is slight.

If the loss contingency is probable but only a range of estimated values can be ascertained, the minimum point of the range should be accrued and the maximum point should be disclosed.

If the loss contingency is at least reasonably possible, a liability should not be recorded, but disclosure is required. If feasible, that disclosure should include an estimate of the loss or range of loss. If a reasonable estimate of the loss cannot be made, that fact should be disclosed.

Certain contingencies are remote, but their disclosure is expected in financial statements because a guarantee has been given. No disclosure is required for unasserted claims or assessments when no act by the potential claimant has transpired. In addition, general or unspecific business risks are neither accrued nor disclosed.

Examples of loss contingencies

1. Collectibility of receivables
2. Obligations related to product warranties and product defects
3. Risk of loss or damage of enterprise property by fire, explosion, or other hazards
4. Threat of expropriation of assets
5. Pending or threatened litigation

6. Actual or possible claims and assessments
7. Risk of loss from catastrophes assumed by property and casualty insurance companies including reinsurance companies
8. Guarantees of indebtedness of other entities
9. Obligations of commercial banks under standby letters of credit
10. Agreements to repurchase receivables (or to repurchase the related property) that have been sold

Accrual and disclosure of loss contingencies should be based on an evaluation of the facts in each particular case. Accrual is not a substitute for disclosure, and disclosure is not a substitute for accrual.

An estimated gain from a gain contingency usually is not reflected in the accounts since to do so might be to recognize revenue prior to its realization. Adequate disclosure of the gain contingency shall be made, but care must be taken to avoid misleading implications as to the likelihood of realization.

Contracts and negotiations. All significant contractual agreements and negotiations should be disclosed in the footnotes to the financial statements. For example, lease contract provisions, pension obligations, requirements contracts, bond indenture covenants, and stock option plans should be clearly disclosed in the footnotes.

Other disclosures required by IAS 1 (revised). IAS 1 (revised) has added several new, required disclosure items. If not otherwise disclosed within the financial statements, these items should be reported in the footnotes.

1. The domicile and legal form of the entity, its country of incorporation, and the address of the registered office (or principal place of business, if different);
2. A description of the nature of the enterprise's operations and its principal activities;
3. The name of the parent entity and the ultimate parent of the group; and
4. The number of employees either at the end of the period or an average during the period being reported upon.

These disclosures (which may have been modeled on those already imposed under UK GAAP) are particularly of interest given the multinational character of many enterprises reporting in conformity with IAS.

Balance Sheet Format

The format of a balance sheet is not presently specified by International Accounting Standards but has become established as a matter of tradition and, in some circumstances, as a result of specific industry practices. IAS 5 categorically states that "this Standard does not propose a particular format for the presentation of financial statements." However, the appendix to IAS 1 (revised 1997) gives an example of a balance sheet format but also clarifies that it be considered as an example of the way in which the requirements of the proposed standard might be put into practice.

In general, the two types of formats are the report form and the account form. In the **report form** the balance sheet continues line by line from top to bottom as follows:

Assets	$xxx
Liabilities	$xxx
Stockholders' equity	xxx
Total liabilities and stockholders' equity	$xxx

In the **account form** the balance sheet appears in a balancing concept with assets on the left and liabilities and equity amounts on the right as follows:

Assets	$ xxx	Liabilities	$ xxx
		Stockholders' equity	xxx
Total assets	$ xxx	Total liabilities and stockholders' equity	$ xxx

Example of balance sheet classification and presentation

The system of balance sheet classification and presentations is illustrated by the following comprehensive balance sheet:

ABC Corporation
Balance Sheet
December 31, 1996

Assets		
Current assets:		
Cash and bank deposits		
Restricted to current bond maturity	$xxx	
Unrestricted	xxx	$xxx
Short-term investments		
Marketable equity securities		xxx
Marketable debt securities		xxx
Refundable income taxes		xxx
Receivables from associates		xxx
Accounts receivable	xxx	
Less allowance for doubtful accounts	(xxx)	xxx
Notes receivable due in 1997	xxx	
Less notes receivable discounted	(xxx)	xxx
Dishonored notes receivable		xxx
Installment notes due in 1997		xxx
Interest receivable		xxx
Creditors' accounts with debit balances		xxx
Advances to employees		xxx

Inventories (carried at lower of cost or market by FIFO):			
Finished goods	xxx		
Work in process	xxx		
Raw materials	xxx	xxx	
Prepaid expenses:			
Prepaid rent	xxx		
Prepaid insurance	xxx	xxx	
Total current assets			$xxx
Long-term investments:			
Investments in equity securities		xxx	
Investments in bonds		xxx	
Investments in equity securities (at cost, plus equity in undistributed net earnings since acquisition)		xxx	
Investments in unused land and facilities		xxx	
Cash surrender value of officers' life insurance policies		xxx	
Sinking fund for bond retirement		xxx	
Plant expansion fund		xxx	
Total long-term investments			$xxx
Property, plant, and equipment:			
Land		$xxx	
Buildings		xxx	
Machinery and equipment		xxx	
Furniture and fixtures		xxx	
Leasehold improvements		xxx	
Less accumulated depreciation and amortization		(xxx)	
Total property, plant, and equipment			xxx
Intangible assets net of amortization:			
Excess of cost over net assets of acquired businesses (goodwill)		$xxx	
Patents		xxx	
Trademarks		xxx	
Organization costs		xxx	
Total intangible assets, net			xxx
Other assets:			
Installment notes due after 1997		$xxx	
Unamortized bond issue costs		xxx	
Total other noncurrent assets			xxx
Total assets			$xxx

Liabilities and Stockholders' Equity			
Current liabilities:			
Commercial paper and other short-term notes	$xxx		
Accounts payable	xxx		
Salaries, wages, and commissions	xxx		
Taxes withheld from employees	xxx		
Income taxes payable	xxx		
Dividends payable	xxx		
Rent revenue collected in advance	xxx		
Other advances from customers	xxx		
Current portion of long-term debt	xxx		
Current obligations under capital leases	xxx		
Deferred tax liability	xxx		
Short-term portion of accrued warranty	xxx		
Other accrued liabilities	xxx		
Total current liabilities			$xxx
Noncurrent liabilities:			
Notes payable due after 1997	$xxx		
Plus unamortized note premium	xxx	$xxx	
Long-term bonds:			
10% debentures due 2012	xxx		
9-1/2% collateralized obligations maturing serially to 1998	xxx		
8% convertible subordinated debentures due 2012	xxx		
Less unamortized discounts net of premiums	(xxx)	xxx	
Accrued pension cost		xxx	
Obligations under capital leases		xxx	
Deferred tax liability		xxx	
Long-term portion of accrued warranty		xxx	
Total noncurrent liabilities			xxx
Total liabilities			$xxx
Share capital:			
$12.50 convertible preference shares stock, $100 stated value, 200,000 shares authorized, 175,000 outstanding	$xxx		
12% cumulative preferrence shares, $100 stated value, callable at $115, 100,000 shares authorized and outstanding	xxx		
Equity shares, $10 stated value, 500,000 shares authorized, 450,000 issued, 15,000 held in treasury	xxx		
Equity shares subscribed 10,000 shares	xxx		
Less: Subscriptions receivable	(xxx)	$xxx	

Additional paid-in capital:			
From 12% cumulative preferrence	xxx		
From equity shares	xxx		
From treasury stock transactions	xxx		
From stock dividends	xxx		
From expiration of stock options	xxx		
Warrants outstanding	xxx	xxx	
Retained earnings:			
Appropriated for bond indebtedness	xxx		
Free and unappropriated	xxx	xxx	
		xxx	
Less: Treasury stock at cost	(xxx)		
Net unrealized loss on available-for-sale securities	(xxx)		
Unrealized loss from foreign currency translation	(xxx)		
Excess of minimum pension liability over unrecognized prior service cost	(xxx)	(xxx)	
Total stockholders' equity			$xxx
Total liabilities and stockholders' equity			$xxx

The format of the balance sheet as illustrated by the appendix to IAS 1 (revised 1997) is the following:

XYZ Limited
Consolidated Balance Sheet
as at 31 December 19X2
(in thousands of currency units)

	19X2	*19X2*	*19X1*	*19X1*
Assets				
Noncurrent assets	x		x	
Property, plant and equipment	x		x	
Goodwill	x		x	
Investments in associates	x		x	
Other financial assets	x	xx	x	xx
Current assets				
Inventories	x		x	
Trade and other receivables	x		x	
Prepayments	x		x	
Cash and cash equivalents	x	xx	x	xx
Total assets		xx		xx
Equity and Liabilities				
Capital and reserves				
Issued capital (Note__)	x		x	
Reserves (Note__)	x		x	
Accumulated profit (losses)	x	xx	x	xx
Minority interest		xx		xx
Noncurrent liabilities				
Interest-bearing borrowings	x		x	
Deferred taxes	x		x	
Retirement benefit obligations	x	xx	x	xx
Current liabilities				
Trade and other payables	x		x	
Short-term borrowings	x		x	
Current portion of interest-bearing borrowings	x		x	
Warranty provisions	x	xx	x	xx
Total equity and liabilities		xx		xx

3 INCOME STATEMENT, STATEMENT OF CHANGES IN EQUITY, AND STATEMENT OF RECOGNIZED GAINS AND LOSSES

PERSPECTIVE AND ISSUES

In discussing the concept of performance, the IASC's *Framework for the Preparation and Presentation of Financial Statements* states that profit is frequently used as a measure of performance. Historically, under all sets of extant accounting standards, the income statement has provided this vital piece of information about what is sometimes referred to as the "bottom line" for the enterprise, the ultimate measure of entity economic performance. However, under both IAS and various national GAAP standards, over the years a number of sources of changes in owner net worth, excluding investments by or distributions to the owners themselves, have become excluded from this "bottom line" measure, for various reasons. For example, revaluations of plant assets, which are sanctioned by IAS 16, are not considered to be culminations of the normal earnings process (inasmuch as commercial enterprises are not typically organized to speculate on the changing values of their productive assets), and thus such items have been relegated to equity accounts such as revaluation surplus. As a consequence, the income statement cannot and does not purport to reveal the totality of economic changes in the enterprise for the period.

To deal with the fact that the income statement has diverged increasingly from being a complete picture of the economic changes affecting the reporting entity over the course of the period, accounting standard setters in the US and the UK, as well as the IASC, have of late been deliberating the need either for an expanded income statement (one which would include the various changes which have, under the respective sets of standards, been consigned to assorted "contra equity" or "additional equity" accounts) or for a new financial statement which would summarize these changes in some other fashion. E53 did propose to require such a new statement, the statement of nonowner movements in equity, which would have included all these various nonincome statement changes in net worth, excluding owner transactions, plus net income. The US standard setter, the FASB, in fact has recently mandated just such a statement, the statement of comprehensive income.

A good deal of opposition was voiced to the IASC's proposal in E53, however, and the final standard, recently issued as IAS 1 (revised), has retreated somewhat from the earlier recommendation. However, to comply with IAS 1 (revised 1997) it will in fact be necessary to add one of two possible new financial statements, with expanded footnote disclosures needed under certain conditions. These are explored later in this chapter. The IASC has also established a new project, on reporting financial performance, which will reexamine this issue, possibly leading eventually to further changes to the form and content of the financial statement or statements which are intended to convey the substance of an entity's financial performance for a period. Thus, the present status, following the issuance of IAS 1 (revised), should be viewed as an interim solution.

The traditional income statement is known by many titles. The international accounting standards, such as IAS 1 (revised 1997), *Presentation of Financial Statements,* and IAS 8, *Net Profit or Loss for the Period, Fundamental Errors and Changes in Accounting Polices,* refer to this statement as the income statement, but internationally it has a number of other common appellations. For instance, in the United Kingdom and certain developing countries it is also referred to as the profit and loss account; and in the United States other names, such as the statement of income, statement of earnings, or statement of operations, are sometimes used. By whatever name, this statement is a major component of an entity's periodic financial reporting and captures most of the changes in the entity's economic position over the course of the reporting period, which is most often 1 year.

Since the late 1960s or early 1970s, the income statement has been widely perceived by investors, creditors, management, and other interested parties as the single most important of an enterprise's basic financial statements. Investors consider the past income of a business as the most useful predictor of future earnings and performance, which in turn is widely deemed to be the best indicator of future dividends and market stock price performance. In fact, the reason that many other changes in net worth, such as that resulting from changes in fair values of plant assets or investments, are excluded from the income statement is that these are **not** considered to be useful as predictors of future economic performance.

Creditors look principally to the income statement for insight into the borrower's ability to generate the future cash flows needed to repay the obligations (while the cash flow statement would appear more logically to be the source for these insights, that statement is a relatively late development and not universally understood yet; thus, traditionally, financial statement users have been more comfortable drawing these inferences from the income statement). Management, then, must be concerned with the income statement by virtue of the importance placed on it by investors and creditors. Additionally, management uses the income statement as a gauge of its effectiveness and efficiency in combining the factors of production into the goods and/or services that it creates and sells.

The information provided by the income statement, relating to individual items of income and expense and to different combinations of these items (such as the amounts reported as gross margin or profit before interest and taxes), facilitate the process of financial analysis, especially that relating to the entity's profitability. Further, the manner of presentation of certain items of income and expense on the face of the income statement can provide relevant information for proper economic decision making.

For one example of this last matter, it is normal practice to distinguish between those items of income and expense that arise from ordinary activities and those that do not. IAS 8 requires that income and expenses (and profit or loss) from ordinary activities be disclosed separately on the face of the income statement, distinguishing them from any extraordinary items, which must be identified clearly and disclosed separately. The standard also requires that individual items of income and expense within profit or loss from ordinary activities, if due to materiality considerations or because of their nature or incidence, need disclosure to assist the user of the financial statements in understanding the performance of the enterprise, these must be given separate disclosure. The paramount concern is that financial statement users be able to assess the ability of the enterprise to replicate the item and thus to generate earnings and ultimately cash and cash equivalents in the future.

Much of current accounting theory is concerned with the measurement of income. Even with the renewed interest in the balance sheet, the income statement remains of great importance to the majority of financial statement users. This chapter focuses on key income measurement issues and on matters of income statement presentation and disclosure. It also explains and illustrates the presentation of the new component of financial statements prescribed by IAS 1 (revised 1997), **statement of changes in equity** (or, alternatively, the **statement of recognized gains and losses** together with the required footnote disclosure).

IAS 1 (revised 1997) has added, in a somewhat controversial move, what may be deemed a "fairness exception" to compliance with IAS. If management concludes that application of a particular provision of a standard would cause the financial statements to be misleading, it may choose to depart from that provision in order to achieve a fair presentation. In such circumstances, however, the fact of the departure, the nature of it, the treatment which IAS would have required, and why it was deemed to be misleading, must all be included in the notes to the financial statements.

Sources of IAS

IAS 1 (revised 1997), 8, 14 (revised 1997), 16, 18, 21, 25, 30
IASC's Framework for the Preparation and Presentation of Financial Statements
ED 58, *Discontinuing Operations*

DEFINITIONS OF TERMS

Elements of Financial Statements

Comprehensive income. The change in equity of an entity during a period from transactions and other events and circumstances from nonowner sources. It includes all changes in equity during a period, except those resulting from investments by owners and distributions to owners.

Expenses. Decreases in economic benefits during the accounting period in the form of outflows or depletions of assets or incurrences of liabilities that result in decreases in equity, other than those relating to distributions to equity participants. The term **expenses** is broad enough to include **losses** as well as normal categories of expenses; thus, the international standard differs from its US counterpart, which deems losses to be a separate and distinct element to be accounted for, denoting decreases in equity from peripheral or incidental transactions.

Income. Increases in economic benefits during the accounting period in the form of inflows or enhancements of assets that result in increases in equity, other than those relating to contributions from equity participants. The IASC's *Framework* clarifies that this definition of income encompasses both revenue and gains. Again, the corresponding US accounting standard holds that revenues and gains constitute two separate elements of financial reporting, with gains denoting increases in equity from peripheral or incidental transactions.

Statement of changes in equity. As prescribed by IAS 1 (revised 1997), *Presentation of Financial Statements*, an enterprise should present, as a separate component of financial statements, along with the traditional financial statements, a statement showing

1. The net profit or loss for the period;
2. Items of income (including gain) and expense (including loss) which are recognized in equity, as required by this standard, and the total of these items;
3. The cumulative effect of changes in accounting policy and the correction of fundamental errors (when the benchmark treatment, retrospective application and adjustment of beginning retained earnings, respectively, is elected under IAS 8);
4. Capital transactions and distributions with/to owners of the enterprise;
5. The balance of accumulated profit or loss at the beginning of the period and at the balance sheet date, and the movements for the period; and

6. A reconciliation between the carrying amounts of each class of equity capital, share premium and each reserve at the beginning and the end of the period, separately disclosing each movement.

Statement of recognized gains and losses. As an alternative to a statement of changes in equity (above), as prescribed by the IAS 1 (revised 1997), *Presentation of Financial Statements,* an enterprise may present, along with the traditional financial statements, a statement of recognized gains and losses. This statement highlights items of income and expense that are not recognized in the income statement and it reports all changes in equity, including net income, other than those resulting from investments by and distributions to owners (items 1-3 shown under the foregoing, should be presented in this statement). When an enterprise chooses to present the statement of recognized gains and losses, it should, additionally, present in footnotes to the financial statements, items 4 to 6 shown under the discussion of the statement of changes in equity, above.

Other Terminology

Discontinued operations. These result from the sale or abandonment of an operation that represents a separate, major line of business of an enterprise and of which the assets, net profits or loss, and activities can be distinguished physically, operationally, and for financial reporting purposes.

Extraordinary item. Events and transactions that are clearly distinct from the ordinary activities of the enterprise and are distinguished by the infrequency of their occurrence.

Major line of business. In the context of discontinued operations, IAS 8 defines a major line of business as a separate line of business of an enterprise that is "distinguishable from other business activities," such as a segment, as determined in accordance with IAS 14.

Ordinary activities. Activities that are undertaken by the enterprise as part of its normal business and include related activities that are incidental to or are pursued in furtherance of regular business.

Realization. The process of converting noncash resources and rights into money or, more precisely, the sale of an asset for cash or claims to cash.

Recognition. The process of formally recording or incorporating in the financial statements of an entity items that meet the definition of an element and satisfy the criteria for recognition.

Segment of a business. A distinguishable component of an enterprise which is engaged in providing products or services which are subject to risks and returns different from other "business segments" or "geographical segments." A segment may be in the form of a subsidiary, a division, a department, a joint venture or other nonsubsidiary investee. Its assets, results of operations, and activities can be clearly distinguished (physically and operationally, and for financial reporting purposes) from the other assets, results of operations, and activities of the entity. Business segments are distinguishable components of an enterprise engaged in providing different products or services, or a different group of related products or services, primarily to customers outside an enterprise. Geographical segments are distinguishable components of an enterprise engaged in operations in different countries or group of countries within particular geographical areas as may be determined to be appropriate in an enterprise's particular circumstances.

CONCEPTS, RULES, AND EXAMPLES

Concepts of Income

Economists have generally adopted a wealth maintenance concept of income. Under this concept, income is the maximum amount that can be consumed during a period and still leave the enterprise with the same amount of wealth at the end of the period as existed at the beginning. Wealth is determined with reference to the current market values of the net productive assets at the beginning and end of the period. Therefore, the economists' definition of income would fully incorporate market value changes (both increases and decreases in wealth) in the determination of periodic income.

Accountants, on the other hand, have generally defined income by reference to specific events that give rise to recognizable elements of revenue and expense during a reporting period. The events that produce reportable items of revenue and expense comprise a subset of economic events that determine economic income. Many changes in the market values of wealth components are deliberately excluded from the measurement of accounting income but are included in the measurement of economic income.

The discrepancy between the accounting and economic measures of income are the result of a preference on the part of accountants and financial statement users for information that is reliable. Since many fluctuations in the market values of assets are matters of conjecture, accountants have retained the historical cost model, which generally precludes the recognition of market value changes until realized by a transaction. Similarly, both accountants and economists understand that the earnings process occurs throughout the various stages of production, sales, and final delivery of the product. However, the difficulty in measuring the precise rate at which this earnings process is taking place has led accountants to conclude that income should normally be recognized only when it is fully realized. Realization generally implies that the enterprise producing the item has completed all of its obligations relating to the product and that collection of the resulting receivable is assured beyond reasonable doubt. For very sound reasons, accountants have developed a reliable system of income recognition that is based on generally accepted accounting principles applied consistently from period to period. The interplay between recognition and realization generally means that values on the balance sheet are recognized only when realized through an income statement transaction.

A separate but equally important reason for the disparity between the accounting and economic measures of income relates to the need for periodic reporting. The economic measure of income would be relatively simple to apply on a life cycle basis. Economic income would be measured by the difference between its wealth at the termination point and its wealth at the origination date, plus withdrawals or other distributions and minus additional investments over the course of its life. However, applying the same measurement strategy to discrete fiscal periods, as accountants apply, is much more difficult. The continual earnings process, in which the earnings of a business occur throughout the various stages of production and delivery of a product, is conceptually straightforward. Allocating those earnings to individual years, quarters, or months is substantially more difficult, requiring both estimates and judgment. Consequently, accountants have concluded that there must be unambiguous guidelines for revenue recognition. These have required recognition only at the completion of the earnings cycle.

The appropriate measurement of income is partially dependent on the vantage point of the party doing the measuring. From the perspective of outside investors taken as a whole, income might be defined as earnings before any payments to those investors, including bondholders and preferred stockholders, as well as common shareholders. On the other hand, from the viewpoint of the common shareholders, income might better be defined as earnings after payments to other investors, including creditors and preferred shareholders. Currently, net income is defined as earnings available for the preferred and common stockholders. However, in various statistics and special reports, a variety of these concepts are employed.

Recognition and Measurement

Recognition involves the depiction of an item in words and by a monetary amount, and the inclusion of that amount in the balance sheet or the income statement. For recognition of an item on financial statements, it should meet the definition of an element as prescribed by the IASC's *Framework* and satisfy the criteria for recognition as set out in that document. The criteria are needed to assist accountants in determining which economic events are in the domain of items included in the measurement of income. The IASC's *Framework* has identified the following recognition criteria, which have not been altered by the issuance of IAS 1 (revised):

1. **Item must meet the definition of an element.** To be recognized, an item must meet one of the definitions of an element of the financial statements. For instance, a resource must meet the definition of an asset, an obligation must meet the definition of a liability, and so on. It is interesting to note that sometimes the interrelationship between the elements requires that an

item that meets the definition and recognition criteria for a particular element, for instance, an asset, automatically requires the recognition of another element, for example, income or a liability.

2. **Assessment of degree of uncertainty regarding future economic benefits.** This refers to the degree of uncertainty that the future economic benefits associated with an item will flow to or from the enterprise. The assessment of this uncertainty is made on the basis of evidence available at the time of preparation of the financial statements. This concept can be illustrated through the following example: At year end while valuing inventory, if it is uncertain whether or not the full cost of the inventory could be recovered in the future, say, when part of the inventory is damaged, recognition is given to this uncertainty and the inventory is written down to its net realizable value.
3. **Item's cost or value can be measured with reliability.** An item must possess a relevant attribute, such as cost or value, which can be quantified in monetary units with sufficient reliability. Measurability must be considered in terms of both relevance and reliability, the two primary qualitative characteristics of accounting information.
4. **Relevance.** An item is relevant if the information about it has the capacity to make a difference in investors', creditors', or other users' decisions. The relevance of information is affected by its nature and materiality.
5. **Reliability.** An item is reliable if the information about it is representationally faithful, free of material errors, and is neutral or free from bias. Further, to possess the quality of reliability, two more features should be present.

   a. The transactions and other events the information purports to represent should be accounted for and presented in accordance with their *substance* and economic reality and *not merely their legal form.*
   b. The preparers of financial statements, while dealing with and recognizing uncertainties, should exercise judgment or a degree of caution: in other words, *prudence.*

To be given accounting recognition, an asset, liability, or item of income or expense would have to meet the above-mentioned five criteria.

Income. According to the IASC's *Framework*

> ***Income*** *is increases in economic benefits during the accounting period in the form of inflows or enhancements of assets or decreases of liabilities that result in increases in equity, other than those relating to contributions from equity participants. The definition of income encompasses both revenue and gains, and revenue arises in the course of ordinary activities of an enterprise and is referred to by different names, such as sales, fees, interest, dividends, royalties, and rent.*

IAS 18 is the standard that deals with the accounting for revenue. It sets forth the following characteristics of the term **revenue**:

1. Inflows of economic benefits arise in the course of ordinary activities of an enterprise.
2. Inflows are to be reported gross.
3. Inflows result in increases in equity, other than increases relating to contributions from equity participants.

The measurement concept requires that revenue be measured at the fair value of the consideration received or receivable. **Fair value** is defined as

> *the amount for which an asset could be exchanged, or a liability settled, between knowledgeable, willing parties in an arm's length transaction.*

The realization concept stipulates that revenue is recognized only when the following occur:

1. The earnings process is complete or virtually complete.
2. Revenue is evidenced by the existence of an exchange transaction that has taken place.

The existence of an exchange transaction is critical to the accounting recognition of revenue. Generally, it means that a sale to an outside party has occurred, resulting in the receipt of cash or the obligation by the purchaser to make future payment for the item received. However, an exchange transaction is viewed in a broader sense than the legal concept of a sale. Whenever an exchange of rights and privileges takes place, an exchange transaction is deemed to have occurred. For example, interest revenue and interest expense are earned or incurred ratably over a period without a discrete transaction taking place. Accruals are recorded periodically to reflect the interest realized by the passage of time. Similarly, the percentage-of-completion method recognizes revenue based on the measure of progress on a long-term construction project. The earnings process is considered to occur simultaneously with the measure of progress (e.g., the incurrence of costs).

The conditions for the timing of revenue recognition would also be varied if the production of certain commodities takes place in environments in which the ultimate realization of revenue is so assured that it can be recognized upon the completion of the production process. At the opposite extreme is the situation in which the exchange transaction has taken place but significant uncertainty exists as to the ultimate collectibility of the amount. For example, in certain sales of real estate, where the down payment percentage is extremely small and the security for the buyer's notes is minimal, revenue is often not recognized until collections are actually received.

Expenses. According to the IASC's *Framework*

> ***Expenses** are decreases in economic benefits during an accounting period in the form of outflows or depletions of assets or incurrences of liabilities that result in decreases in equity, other than those relating to distributions to equity participants. Thus the characteristics of expenses include the following:*
>
> 1. *Sacrifices involved in carrying out the earnings process*
> 2. *Actual or expected cash outflows resulting from ordinary activities*
> 3. *Outflows reported gross*

Expenses are expired costs, or items that were assets but are no longer assets because they have no future value. The matching principle requires that all expenses incurred in the generating of revenue be recognized in the same accounting period as the revenues are recognized. The matching principle is broken down into three pervasive measurement principles: associating cause and effect, systematic and rational allocation, and immediate recognition.

Costs such as materials and direct labor consumed in the manufacturing process are relatively easy to identify with the related revenue elements. These cost elements are included in inventory and expensed as cost of sales when the product is sold and revenue from the sale is recognized. This is associating cause and effect.

Some costs are more closely associated with specific accounting periods. In the absence of a cause and effect relationship, the asset's cost should be allocated to benefiting accounting periods in a systematic and rational manner. This form of expense recognition involves assumptions about the expected length of benefit and the relationship between benefit and cost of each period. Depreciation of fixed assets, amortization of intangibles, and allocation of rent and insurance are examples of costs that would be recognized by the use of a systematic and rational method.

All other costs are normally expensed in the period in which they are incurred. This would include those costs for which no clear-cut future benefits can be identified, costs that were recorded as assets in prior periods but for which no remaining future benefits can be identified, and those other elements of administrative or general expense for which no rational allocation scheme can be devised. The general approach is first to attempt to match costs with the related revenues. Next, a method of systematic and rational allocation should be attempted. If neither of these measurement principles is beneficial, the cost should be immediately expensed.

As stated in the IASC's *Framework*, the term **expenses** is broad enough to include losses as well. Expenses that arise in the course of the ordinary activities of an enterprise include such items as cost of sales, wages, and depreciation. They usually take the form of an outflow of cash or depletion of other assets.

Losses also represent decreases in economic benefits and are similar in nature to expenses. However, there is a subtle difference between the two concepts: losses may or may not arise in the course of ordinary activities, whereas expenses arise from ordinary activities. Thus, a loss from an extraordinary item such as a natural disaster would also qualify as a loss according to this definition. It is to be noted that even unrealized losses are covered here. For example, losses arising from the effects of increases or decreases in the exchange rates for a foreign currency in respect of the borrowings of an enterprise in that currency, which are unrealized losses, are also contemplated by this definition.

It is interesting to note that in the United States, the FASB's conceptual framework project defined expenses as "outflows or other using up of assets or incurrences of liabilities (or a combination of the two) resulting from delivery of goods, rendering of services, or other activities constituting the enterprise's major or central operations." This definition, although crisp and concise, is quite comprehensive; it seems to cover all conceivable ways of incurring expenses. For instance, the expression "a combination of the two" probably was intended to be a catch-all clause but for some reason has not been included in the definition given in IASC's *Framework.*

Gains and losses. According to the IASC's *Framework*

> *Gains (losses) represent items that meet the definition of income (expenses) and may or may not arise in the course of ordinary activities of an enterprise. Gains (losses) represent increases (decreases) in economic benefits and as such are no different in nature from revenue (expenses). Hence they are not regarded as separate elements in IASC's* ***Framework****. Characteristics of gains and losses include the following:*
>
> 1. *Result from peripheral transactions and circumstances that may be beyond entity's control*
> 2. *May be classified according to sources or as operating and nonoperating*

The recognition of gains and losses should follow the principles stated below.

1. Gains often result from transactions and other events that involve no earnings process; therefore, in terms of recognition, it is more significant that the gain be realized than earned.
2. Losses are recognized when it becomes evident that future economic benefits of a previously recognized asset have been reduced or eliminated, or that a liability has been incurred without associated economic benefits. The main difference between expenses and losses is that expenses result from continuing operations, whereas losses result from peripheral transactions that may be beyond the entity's control.

Statement of changes in equity and statement of recognized gains and losses. IAS 1 (revised 1997) prescribes a new component of financial statements (to be presented along with the traditional financial statements). While the IASC had earlier been intending to mandate a new prescribed financial statement, the statement of nonowner movements in equity, opposition to its proposal in E53 has resulted in a somewhat modified final standard. Although different in some particulars and offering more options in terms of format, this will nonetheless reveal to financial statement users the full scope of changes in economic position, whether due to traditional items of income and expense, or to such other phenomena as revaluations of plan assets and investments, or the translations of foreign subsidiaries' and affiliates' balance sheets.

IAS 1 (revised) offers preparers two principal mechanisms for reporting the changes in enterprise equity for a period. The first of these would have the reporting entity present a new financial statement, to be captioned the **statement of changes in equity**. This statement should present

1. An enterprise's total recognized gains or losses for the period, including those that are recognized directly in equity (giving details of each item of income, expense, gain or loss which are required by other IAS to be shown directly in equity, along with the total of these items, plus net profit or loss for the period and cumulative effect of changes in accounting policy and of correction of fundamental errors if accounted for by the benchmark treatments prescribed by IAS 8); and, in addition,
2. Also present, other changes in the equity accounts, along with a reconciliations of beginning and ending balances in each of the components of equity (giving details by each class of equity capital) and balances of accumulated profit or loss (giving details of the movements for the period).

An example of the statement of changes in equity is presented in the following section of this chapter.

Under the second of the two permitted approaches, the enterprise would present a **statement of recognized gains and losses** for the period, which would only include the **net** effect of income, expense, gain or loss reported in the income statement for the period. That is, net income or loss, including if applicable the cumulative effect of changes in accounting policy and of the correction of any fundamental errors accounted for by the benchmark treatments prescribed by IAS 8, would be added to the other items of income, expense, gain or loss which are carried directly to equity, with the total of these being presented as the final amount in the statement of recognized gains and losses.

If the second approach is utilized, the changes in other capital accounts resulting from transactions with owners, as well as the changes in retained earnings (referred to in IAS 1 as accumulated profit or loss), must be presented elsewhere in the notes to the financial statements. An example of this second approach is also shown in the following section of this chapter.

IAS 1 (revised 1997) explains that it is important to take into consideration all income, expenses, gains, and losses (including those not recognized in the income statement) in assessing the overall financial performance of an enterprise. Thus, the revised standard on presentation of financial statements has prescribed this new component of financial statements, to capture those items of gains or losses that are not included in the determination of net income or loss for the period. This standard further justifies the need for the presentation of this new component of financial statements, by setting forth the following reasoning for its prescription:

1. Since IAS 8 requires that all items of income and expense in a period be included in the determination of net profit or loss for the period, unless an international accounting standard requires or permits otherwise; and also
2. Since other standards, such as IAS 16, IAS 25, and IAS 21, require that specified gains and losses, such as revaluation surpluses or deficits and foreign currency translation differences, be recognized directly as changes in equity along with capital transactions with and distributions to the enterprise's owners; thus,
3. In order to capture all gains or losses that have a bearing on the enterprise's financial position, it is important that a separate component of financial statements be presented along with the traditional components of financial statement.

While the new standard refers to this as "a separate component of the financial statements," what, in fact, is required is a new financial statement, per se, which (depending in which alternative version is adopted) may also require additional footnote materials. This "separate component" will have to be presented as an integral part of all complete sets of financial statements, and accordingly, once IAS 1 (revised) becomes operative, any set of financial statements would be considered incomplete without this new statement.

It is to be noted that the IASC's action is in line with the current thinking in the UK and US. In the US, recently promulgated SFAS 129 prescribes a similar statement to be presented as a separate component of the financial statements, based on the FASB's concept of "comprehensive income." In the UK, which was the first to take this step, the treatment is very similar to that embraced by IAS 1 (revised), and the new component of financial statement prescribed under FRS 3 of the UK GAAP is captioned the "statement of total recognized gains and losses," which is similar to that suggested by IAS 1 when the second suggested approach is utilized.

Examples of the new statements alternatively required by IAS 1 (revised 1997).

Example 1: If the statement of changes in equity is to be employed

XYZ Malta Inc.
Statement of Changes in Equity
For the Year Ended December 31, 19X8

(in thousands of US dollars)

	Share capital	*Share premium*	*Revaluation reserve*	*Currency translation*	*Accumulated profits*	*Total*
Balance at Dec. 31, 19X6	1,000	100	200	200	100	1,600
Changes in accounting policy	--	--	--	--	50	50
Opening balances, as restated	1,000	100	200	200	150	1,650
Currency translation difference	--	--	--	(50)	--	(50)
Surplus from revaluation of buildings	--	--	100	--	--	100
Net gains and losses not recognized in income statement	--	--	100	(50)	--	50
Net profit for the period	--	--	--	--	100	100
Issuance of share capital	100	10	--	--	--	110
Balance at Dec. 31, 19X7	1,100	110	300	150	250	1,910
Currency translation difference	--	--	--	150	--	150
Deficit on revaluation of investments	--	--	--	--	(50)	(50)
Net gains and losses not recognized in income statement	--	--	--	150	(50)	100
Net profit for the period	--	--	--	--	200	200
Dividends	--	--	--	--	(50)	(50)
Balance at Dec. 31, 19X8	1,100	110	300	300	350	2,160

Example 2: If the statement of recognized gains and losses is to be presented (see note below)

ABC Barbados Co. Ltd.
Statement of Recognized Gains and Losses
For the Year Ended December 31, 19X8

(in thousands of US dollars)

	19X8	*19X7*
Surplus on revaluation of buildings	500	--
Surplus (deficit) on revaluation of investments	1,000	(1,000)
Exchange differences on translation of the financial statements of a foreign subsidiary	2,000	(2,000)
Net gains (losses) not recognized in the income statement	3,500	(3,000)
Net profit for the year	5,000	2,800
Total recognized gains and losses	8,500	(200)
Effect of changes in accounting policy	--	500

NOTE: If this approach is used, then a reconciliation of the opening and closing balances of share capital, reserves, and retained earnings (accumulated profits) as illustrated in the first example, above, should be presented in the footnotes to the financial statements.

Impact of Legal Form on Financial Reporting

Revenues and expenses of a corporation are easily identified and separated from the revenues and expenses of the shareholders. In both the sole proprietorship and partnership form of entity, the identification process can be more difficult. Items such as interest or salaries paid to partners or owners may be thought of as distributions of profits rather than expenses. However, many entities adopt the philosophy that income reporting should be the same regardless of legal form (economic substance takes precedence over legal form). Under the corporate form of business, interest on stockholder loans and salaries paid to stockholders are clearly classified as expenses and not as distributions. Accordingly, under this theory, these items may be treated as expenses for both partnerships and sole proprietorships. However, full disclosure and consistency of financial reporting treatment would be required. Circumstances may involve treating certain payments, such as guaranteed salaries, as expenses while classifying other "salaries" as profit distributions.

Income Statement Classification and Presentation

Statement title. Income statements measure economic performance for a period of time and, except for this variation, follow the same basic rule for headings and titles as do balance sheets. For instance, the legal name of the entity must be used to identify the financial statements and the title "Income Statement" used to distinguish the statement from other information presented in the annual report. This is important also so that users can identify the information that is presented in accordance with international accounting standards from other information which may not be the subject of accounting requirements.

If another comprehensive basis of accounting is used, as is explicitly contemplated under US GAAP, such as the "cash basis" or "income tax basis," the title of the financial statement should be modified accordingly. "Statement of Revenue and Expenses--Income Tax Basis" or "Statement of Revenue and Expense--Modified Cash Basis" are examples of such titles. However, it should be noted that international accounting standards neither refer to nor contain guidance relating to these so-called other comprehensive bases of accounting. One could interpret this omission to mean that current international accounting standards (i.e., the IASC's *Framework*, IAS 1 (revised 1997), *Presentation of Financial Statements)* recognize only the accrual basis of accounting.

Reporting Period. The period covered by the income statement must clearly be identified, such as "year ending (ended) December 31, 1997." Such dating informs the user of the financial statements not only about the length of the period covered by the income statement, but also the starting and ending dates. Dating such as "the period ending March 31, 1997" or "through March 31, 1997" would represent a violation of accounting principles because of the lack of precise definition in these titles. Income statements are normally presented annually (i.e., for a period of 12 months or a year). However, in exceptional circumstances, income statements could be presented for periods in excess of 1 year or for shorter periods as well, say for 5 months or a quarter of a year. IAS 1 (revised 1997) requires that when financial statements are presented for periods other than a year, the following additional disclosures should be made:

1. The reason for presenting the income statement (and other financial statements, such as the cash flow statement, statement of changes in equity and notes) for a period other than 1 year; and,
2. The fact that the comparatives information presented (in the income statement, changes in equity, cash flow statement and notes) is not truly comparable.

Entities whose operations form a natural cycle may have a reporting period end on a specific day (e.g., the last Friday of the month). Certain enterprises (typically retail enterprises) prepare income statements for a fiscal period of 52 or 53 weeks instead of a year (thus, to always end on a day, such as Sunday, on which no business is transacted, so that inventory may be taken). These entities should clearly state that the income statement has been presented, for instance, "for the 52-week period ended March 28, 1997." The new standard on presentation of financial statements specifically addresses enterprises that prefer to report consistently for a 52- or 53-week period, and states categorically that it does not preclude this practice since it is unlikely that the financial statements thus presented would be materially different from those that are presented for 1 full year.

In order that the presentation and classification of items in the income statement be consistent from period to period, items of income and expenses should be uniform both with respect to appearance and categories from one time period through the next. That is, if a decision is made to change classification schemes, the comparative prior-period financials should be restated to conform and thus to maintain comparability between the two periods being presented together. Disclosure must, of course, be made of this reclassification, since the earlier period financial statements being presented currently will differ in appearance from those nominally same statements presented in the earlier year.

Aggregating items. Aggregation of items should not serve to conceal significant information, such as netting revenues against expenses or combining elements of interest to readers, such as bad debts and depreciation. The categories "other" or "miscellaneous expense" should contain, at maximum, an immaterial total amount of aggregated insignificant elements. Once this total approaches, say, 10% of total expenses (or any other materiality threshold), some other aggregations with explanatory titles should be selected.

Information is **material** if its omission or misstatement or nondisclosure could influence the economic decisions of users taken on the basis of the financial statements. Materiality depends on the size of the item judged in the particular circumstances of its omission (IASC's *Framework*, para 30). But it is often forgotten that materiality is also linked with understandability and the level of precision in which the financial statements are to be presented. For instance, the financial statements are often rendered more understandable by rounding information to the nearest thousand currency units (i.e., US dollars). This obviates the necessity of loading the financial statements with unnecessary detail. However, it should be borne in mind that the use of the level of precision that makes presentation possible in the nearest thousands of currency units is acceptable only as long as the threshold of materiality is not surpassed.

Offsetting items of revenue and expense. Materiality also plays a role in the matter of allowing or disallowing offsetting of the items of income and expense. The new standard IAS 1 (revised 1997) addresses this issue and prescribes rules in this area. According to this standard, items of income and expense should be offset when, and only when

1. An international accounting standard requires or permits it. For example, IAS 30 permits banks and similar financial institutions to offset income and expense items relating to hedging; or
2. Gains, losses, and related expenses arising from the same or similar transactions and events are not material. Such amounts should be aggregated in such cases.

The standard also states that immaterial amounts should be aggregated with amounts of similar nature or function and need not be presented separately. However, when such gains or losses are individually material then they should not be offset, but instead should be presented on a gross basis. For example, gain on the sale of a building is $5 million and loss on the sale of land during the same accounting period is $10 million. If both of these amounts are individually material, they should not be offset but be shown on a gross basis.

Usually, losses and gains on disposal of noncurrent assets are seen reported on a net basis, which may be due to the fact that they are not material individually (compared to other items on the income statement). However, if they were material individually, as in the example above, it goes without saying that they would need to be disclosed separately according to the requirements of IAS 1 (revised 1997). It is the authors' opinion that even under the existing international accounting standards, they would not be required to be offset and shown on a net basis. For instance, IAS 16 stipulates that "gains or losses arising from the retirement or disposals of an item of property, plant, and equipment...should be recognized as income or expense in the income statement." Read in the light of the guidelines contained in the IASC's *Framework*, which categorically states that "when gains (losses) are recognized in the income statement, they are usually displayed separately because knowledge of them is useful for the purpose of making economic decisions," it would be unreasonable to interpret that IAS 16 does not require disclosure of gains or losses arising from the retirement or disposal of property, plant, and equipment.

Further, based on the discussion above, it seems unreasonable to read between the lines of IAS 16 in an attempt to reach a conclusion, as some have done, that it does **not** require the disclosure of gains or losses arising from the retirement or disposal of property, plant, and equipment, and therefore that such gains or losses may be included as an undisclosed net amount within broad expense categories such as "general and administrative expenses." In the authors' opinion, although gains or losses arising from retirement or disposal of property, plant, and equipment are not mentioned in the disclosure section of IAS 16, they are specifically dealt with in an earlier paragraph of that IAS. Thus, reading all the provisions of IAS 16, together with the IASC's *Framework* (as explained earlier), it would not be unreasonable to interpret that such gains or losses should be disclosed separately in the income statement, if material.

IAS 1 (revised 1997) further clarifies that when items of income or expense are offset, the enterprise should nevertheless consider, based on materiality, the need to disclose the gross amounts in the notes to the financial statements. This new standard gives the following examples of transactions that are incidental to the main revenue generating activities of an enterprise and whose results when presented by offsetting or reporting on a net basis, such as netting any gains with related expenses, reflect the substance of the transaction:

1. Gains or losses on the disposal of noncurrent assets, including investments and operating assets, are reported by deducting from the proceeds on disposal the carrying amounts of the asset and related selling expenses.
2. Extraordinary items are presented net of related taxation and minority interest.
3. Expenditure that is reimbursed under a contractual arrangement with a third party may be netted against the related reimbursement.

For example, an enterprise based on a time-share arrangement processes computerized accounting data electronically for its own accounting department as well as for certain other companies in the area and incurs a total expenditure of $5 million for an accounting period. The expenditure it incurs on this data-processing activity should be presented after netting the related reimbursable expenditure, which amounts to $3 million. Thus, the income statement presentation would display the net figure (expense) of $2 million (instead of a gross basis presentation of a $5 million expense and a $3 million income). This financial statement presentation reflects the substance of the transaction. (It should be noted, however, that a disclosure of the gross amounts, if they are material, may need to be made in the notes to the financial statements; this is also a requirement of IAS 1 [revised 1997] and was explained earlier in this chapter.)

Major components of the income statement. IAS 1 (revised) stipulates that, at the minimum, the income statement must include line items which present the following items (if they are pertinent to the entity's operations for the period in question):

1. Revenue
2. Results of operating activities
3. Finance costs
4. Share of profits and losses of associates and joint ventures accounted for by the equity method
5. Tax expense
6. Profit or loss from ordinary activities
7. Extraordinary items
8. Minority interest
9. Net profit for the period

The foregoing items represent the barest minimum: Other line items can be included as deemed useful or necessary to fairly communicate the results of the enterprise's operations. It should be carefully noted that this requirement must be satisfied by presentation on the face of the income statement; it cannot be dealt with by incorporating the items into the notes to the financial statements.

While the objectives of the line items are uniform across all reporting entities, the manner of presentation may differ. Specifically, IAS 1 (revised) offers preparers two different manners of classifying operating and other expenses: the so-called natural scheme, or the functional one. While entities are encouraged to apply one or the other of these on the face of the income statement, it would be permissible to relegate this information to the notes.

The natural expense classification scheme identifies costs and expenses in terms of their character, such as salaries and wages, raw materials consumed, and depreciation of plant assets. On the other hand, the functional classification scheme (also referred to as the "cost of sales" method) reports on the purpose of the expenditure, such as for manufacturing, distribution, and administration. Note that the minimum line item disclosures mandated by the standard must be met in any case; thus, finance costs must be so identified regardless of which classification scheme is employed.

Certain projects presently being pursued by the IASC will inevitably affect how income statement presentation will be accomplished. For example, the project on discontinuing operations (exposure draft E58 was recently published for comments) will determine how the results of those operations which management has determined are to be discontinued will be presented in the income statement (and the balance sheet and statement of cash flows as well). The new standard on discontinuing operations, incidentally, will address presentation and disclosure matters only; measurement will be guided by other IAS, such as the proposed new standard on impairment. Readers should therefore be alert to the possibility that later standards will impact on the requirements set forth in IAS 1 (revised 1997).

IAS 1 (revised) furthermore stipulates that if a reporting entity adopts the functional classification scheme, it must also provide information on the nature of its expenses, including depreciation and amortization and staff costs (salaries and wages). The standard does not provide detailed guidance on this requirement, however. Presumably the traditional disclosures (e.g., depreciation expense as defined in IAS 16, etc.) would be sufficient to satisfy this rule.

As a practical matter, most traditionally structured income statements employ a combination of functional and natural classifications, or are effectively supplemented by disclosures made in other financial statements or in the footnotes. For example, even when depreciation is not set forth as a line item on the income statement, it will appear on the cash flow statement (if the popular indirect method is employed). As noted, finance costs must be separately stated on the income statement, whichever classification scheme is primarily used.

Finally, IAS 1 (revised) requires that dividends, on a per share basis, be disclosed either on the face of the income statement or in the notes thereto. Dividends include both those paid and those declared but unpaid at year end.

While IAS does not require the inclusion of subsidiary schedules to support major captions in the income statement, it is commonly found that, for example, detailed schedules of costs of goods manufactured and/or sold are included in full sets of financial statements. These will be illustrated in the following section to provide a more expansive discussion of the meaning of certain major sections of the income statement.

Income from ordinary activities. This section of the income statement will serve to summarize the revenues and expenses of the company's central operations.

1. Sales or other operating revenues are charges to customers for the goods and/or services provided to them during the period. This section of the income statement should include information about discounts, allowances, and returns, to determine net sales or net revenues.
2. Cost of goods sold is the cost of the inventory items sold during the period. In the case of a merchandising firm, net purchases (purchases less discounts, returns, and allowances plus freight-in) are added to beginning inventory to obtain the cost of goods available for sale. From the cost of goods available for sale amount, the ending inventory is deducted to compute cost of goods sold.

Example of schedule of cost of goods sold

ABC Merchandising Company
Schedule of Cost of Goods Sold
For the Year Ended December 31, 19X6

Beginning inventory			$xxx
Add: Purchases		$xxx	
Freight-in		xxx	
Cost of purchases		xxx	
Less: Purchase discounts	$xx		
Purchase R&A	xx	(xxx)	
Net purchases			xxx
Cost of goods available for sale			xxx
Less: Ending inventory			(xxx)
Cost of goods sold			$xxx

A manufacturing enterprise computes the cost of goods sold in a slightly different way. Cost of goods manufactured would be added to the beginning inventory to arrive at cost of goods available for sale. The ending inventory is then deducted from the cost of goods available for sale to determine the cost of goods sold. Cost of goods manufactured is computed by adding to raw (direct) materials on hand at the beginning of the period the raw materials purchases during the period and all other costs of production, such as labor and direct overhead, thereby yielding the cost of goods placed in production during the period. When adjusted for changes in work in process during the period and for raw materials on hand at the end of the period, this results in the calculation of goods produced.

Example of schedules of cost of goods manufactured and sold

XYZ Manufacturing Company
Schedule of Cost of Goods Manufactured
For the Year Ended December 31, 19X6

Direct materials inventory 1/1/X6	$xxx	
Purchases of materials (including freight-in and deducting purchase discounts)	xxx	
Total direct materials available	$xxx	
Direct materials inventory 12/31/X6	(xxx)	
Direct materials used		$xxx
Direct labor		xxx
Factory overhead:		
Depreciation of factory equipment	$xxx	
Utilities	xxx	
Indirect factory labor	xxx	
Indirect materials	xxx	
Other overhead items	xxx	xxx
Manufacturing cost incurred in 19X6		$xxx
Add: Work in process 1/1/X6		xxx
Less: Work in process 12/31/X6		(xxx)
Cost of goods manufactured		$xxx

XYZ Manufacturing Company
Schedule of Cost of Goods Sold
For the Year Ended December 31, 19X6

Finished goods inventory 1/1/X6	$xxx
Add: Cost of goods manufactured	xxx
Cost of goods available for sale	$xxx
Less: Finished goods inventory 12/31/X6	(xxx)
Cost of goods sold	$xxx

3. Operating expenses are primary recurring costs associated with central operations, other than cost of goods sold, that are incurred to generate sales. Operating expenses are normally classified into the following two categories:

   a. Selling expenses
   b. General and administrative expenses

   Selling expenses are those expenses related directly to the company's efforts to generate sales (e.g., sales salaries, commissions, advertising, delivery expenses, depreciation of store furniture and equipment, and store supplies). General and administrative expenses are expenses related to the general administration of the company's operations (e.g., officers and office salaries, office supplies, depreciation of office furniture and fixtures, telephone, postage, accounting and legal services, and business licenses and fees).

4. Gains and losses stem from the peripheral transactions of the entity. These items are shown with the normal recurring revenues and expenses. If they are *material,* they should be disclosed separately and shown above income (loss) from continuing operations before income taxes. Examples are write-downs of inventories and receivables, effects of a strike, and gains and losses from exchange or translation of foreign currencies.
5. Other revenues and expenses are revenues and expenses not related to the central operations of the company (e.g., gains and losses on the disposal of equipment, interest revenues and expenses, and dividend revenues).
6. Separate disclosure items are items that are within the profit or loss from the ordinary activities but are such size, nature, or incidence that their disclosure becomes important in order to explain the performance of the enterprise for the period. They should be reported as a separate component of income from continuing operations. Examples of items that require such disclosure are as follows:

   a. Write-down of inventories to net realizable value, or of property, plant, and equipment to recoverable amounts, and subsequent reversals of such write-downs
   b. Costs of restructuring the activities of an enterprise and any subsequent reversals of such provisions
   c. Gains or losses resulting from disposals of items of property, plant, and equipment
   d. Gains or losses from disposals of long-term investments
   e. Results of discontinued operations
   f. Costs of litigation settlements
   g. Other reversals of provisions

7. Discontinued operations must be reported in those circumstances when an enterprise sells or abandons a separate major line of business, such as a **segment** (as that term is defined by revised IAS 14). IAS 8 prescribes the following disclosures for each discontinued operation:

   a. The nature of the discontinued operation
   b. The business and geographical segment in which it is reported in accordance with revised IAS 14
   c. The effective date of discontinuance for accounting purposes
   d. The manner of discontinuance (whether by sale or abandonment)
   e. The gain or loss on discontinuance and the accounting policy used to measure that gain or loss

f. The revenue and the net profit or loss from the ordinary activities of the operation for the period, together with the corresponding amount for each prior period presented

The standard further requires that when it is known at the date on which the financial statements are authorized for issue that an operation was discontinued subsequent to the balance sheet date or will be discontinued, the above-noted disclosures, to the extent they can be reliably estimated, should be presented.

Generally, the results of discontinued operations are included in the profit or loss from ordinary activities. However, if the discontinuance results from events or transactions that are clearly different from the enterprise's ordinary activities and are not expected to recur, the income or expenses that arise from such discontinuance should be reported as extraordinary items. For example, if the discontinuance of a major line of business was caused by an earthquake or a natural disaster, losses sustained as a result of that event will be treated as an extraordinary item and not as part of ordinary activities.

8. Income tax expense related to ordinary activities is that portion of the total income tax expense applicable to continuing operations.
9. Extraordinary items are income or expenses that arise from events or transactions that are clearly distinct from ordinary activities of an enterprise.

Only on rare occasions does an event or a transaction give rise to an extraordinary item. The nature of the event in relation to the business ordinarily carried out by the enterprise determines whether or not an event is clearly distinct from the ordinary activities of the enterprise and hence should be classified as an extraordinary event. Thus an event may be extraordinary for one enterprise but may not be extraordinary for another enterprise. For instance, losses sustained from a hurricane would be an extraordinary event for most enterprises but claims resulting from such a natural disaster by an insurance company do not qualify for such treatment (since such claims are part of the ordinary activities of an insurance company's business).

Examples of events or transactions that generally qualify as extraordinary items, as included in IAS 8, are the following:

a. Losses resulting from the expropriation of assets
b. Losses sustained from natural disasters such as an earthquake

The nature and the amount of each extraordinary item should be disclosed separately. Disclosures may be made either on the face of the income statement or in footnotes to the financial statements.

Example of presentation of extraordinary item

XYX Malta, Ltd.
Income Statement
For the Year Ended December 31, 1996

	1996	*1995*
Sales	$1,000,000	$ 800,000
Cost of sales	(700,000)	(600,000)
Gross profit	300,000	200,000
Distribution costs	(50,000)	(40,000)
Administrative expenses	(30,000)	(40,000)
Net financing costs	(20,000)	(20,000)
Loss from sale of scooter division (Note 1)	(50,000)	--
Profit from ordinary activities, before taxes	150,000	100,000
Income tax expense	(60,000)	(40,000)
Extraordinary item		
Loss on expropriation of Suzukiyo moped Manufacturing operations in India (Net of income taxes of $30,000)(Note 2)	--	(30,000)
Net profit for the year	$ 90,000	$ 30,000

Note 1: On September 1, 1996, the company sold its scooter division. The results of this operation had previously been reported in the scooter industry segment and the domestic geographic segment. The loss on the sale was computed based on the sale proceeds and the net carrying amounts of assets and liabilities of the operation at the date of the sale. The revenues recognized relating to this operation from January 1, 1996 until the date of sale, September 1, 1996, were $100,000 (the comparable 1995 amount was $150,000), and the profits before income taxes were $30,000 ($40,000 in 1995).

Note 2: On July 1, 1995, the company's Suzukiyo moped manufacturing operations were expropriated in India, without compensation, by government decree. The results of this operation had previously been reported in the moped industry segment and the Far East geographic segment. The extraordinary loss from this operation was computed using the carrying amounts of assets and liabilities at the date of expropriation. The revenues recognized relating to this operation from January 1, 1995 to July 1, 1995 were $50,000, and the profits before tax were $22,000.

APPENDIX A

PRESENTATION OF DISCONTINUED OPERATIONS

Currently extant international accounting standards mandate that certain expanded disclosures be made for the effects of discontinued operations, as discussed in this chapter. Under IAS 8 discontinued operations are (with very rare exceptions) to be included in profit or loss from ordinary activities. This contrasts markedly with the approach under the corresponding US GAAP, as set forth in APB Opinion 30. Under the guidance of that standard, the income statement is classified into two major segments (where conditions warrant), comprising continuing operations and discontinued operations, respectively. Due to lack of detailed guidance regarding the reporting of discontinued operations in IAS 8, the authors had previously suggested that financial statement preparers could benefit from the guidance offered by US GAAP, with appropriate tailoring, when attempting to construct financial statement presentation and related disclosures concerning discontinued operations. This is no longer the case, however, since the IASC has in 1997 clearly indicated the road it intends to follow for what it is now calling "discontinuing operations."

Recently, the IASC has published an exposure draft, E58, of a new standard on reporting discontinuing operations. A final standard is expected by early to mid-1998. Given that this is an important topic, on which guidance under international accounting standards was previously quite sparse, the essential components of this proposal will be set forth here. The reader is cautioned, however, that the final standard may differ from what is discussed here. This risk is particularly heightened in the case of this project, since the exposure draft differs markedly from the IASC's earlier draft statement of principles (DSOP) on this very same topic. Thus, further changes cannot be ruled out.

If the IASC issues a final standard consistent with the exposure draft, it will provide that a discontinuing operation is a component of a business which, pursuant to a single plan, is either to be disposed of substantially in its entirety or to be terminated through abandonment or piecemeal sale of assets and settlement of liabilities. In order to qualify as a discontinuing operation, it would need to comprise either a separate major line of business, geographical area of operations, or class of customer, and furthermore be organized such that it could be distinguished both operationally and for financial reporting purposes.

In other words, while a discontinuing operation would **not** have to meet the test of being a segment as that term is defined in IAS 14 (revised), it clearly would have to be a substantial operation and be readily identifiable both in terms of its actual physical operations (e.g., by having separate factory facilities, etc.) as well as from a financial reporting perspective (e.g., by having divisional financial statements prepared for management use, etc.). Also, to qualify as a discontinuing operation, the act of discontinuing the operation would have to involve a significant management event, such as the sale or abandonment of the entire operation or an organized, even if piecemeal, effort to sell off the assets and settle the obligations of the operation.

The exposure draft notes that major product lines and portions of segments (as that term is defined in IAS 14) would often qualify as discontinuing operations, provided that certain conditions were met. If operating assets and liabilities, and income, could be attributed to the component, and at least a majority of its operating expenses could be attributed to it, then it would likely be valid under the new standard to define this operation (if it were being sold or abandoned) as a discontinuing operation. It should be noted that under the proposed standard the term "discontinuing" is used instead of "discontinued," largely to acknowledge that the disclosures are being made while the act of discontinuation is in process. However, the meaning is intended to be essential that which was earlier ascribed to the previously employed terminology.

The applicable and long-standing US standard, APB Opinion 30, had stipulated two significant dates which drove the financial statement disclosures: the so-called "measurement date," and the actual disposal date. The former was the date a decision was made by management to discontinue the operation, and once made segregation of operating results on the income statement is necessary, not merely for the current reporting period containing the measurement date, but also retrospectively for any comparative periods presented. Furthermore, accrual of estimated losses, if any, to be incurred from remaining operations of the discontinued operation, including that on ultimate disposal, is required as of the measurement date. IAS 8 did not define either of these terms, and did not require either segregation of operating results in the income statement, nor accrual of estimated future losses.

The proposed new standard, however, defines two key dates: the "initial disclosure date" and the "segregation date." These are quite distinct from the dates defined in the corresponding US standard, but will also have major bearings on how the discontinuing operation is to be reported on. Inasmuch as the implications of the two dates defined by E58 are quite different from those set forth in APB Opinion 30, further reference to the US standard, which was helpful in implementing IAS 8 in the absence of detailed guidance under that international accounting standard, would no longer be useful. For that reason, further consideration of the US reporting requirements is not provided.

Under E58's provisions, an initial disclosure event is that which first causes the enterprise to disclose, in the notes to the financial statements, **not** on the face of the income statement or any other financial statement, initial information about a planned discontinuance. There are two incidences which must **both** have occurred before the initial disclosure even can be said to have happened:

1. The enterprise's governing board (board of directors, etc.) must have actually approved a detailed formal plan for the discontinuance; and
2. The enterprise has publicly announced that plan.

Under the provisions of E58, after the initial disclosure event has occurred, the entity would need to make certain disclosures in its financial statements, until such time as the second key event, called the segregation event, has occurred. Until that time, the entity would have to disclose the following:

1. A description of the discontinuing operation;
2. The business or geographical segment (as defined by IAS 14) in which it is reported;
3. The date on which the plan for discontinuance was publicly announced;
4. The date by which discontinuance is expected to be completed;
5. The carrying amounts, as of the balance sheet date, of the assets and liabilities to be disposed of; these would be the book values, not adjusted to expected realizable amounts (see further discussion below);
6. The amount of pretax profit or loss from the ordinary activities of the discontinuing operation during the current reporting period;
7. The amount of net cash flow from operating activities of the discontinuing operation during the current reporting period; and
8. If the assets are being sold and the liabilities are being settled piecemeal, the amount of the net selling price (net of expected disposal costs) received or expected from the sale of only those assets as to which the entity has entered into binding sales agreements, as well as the expected timing of the related cash flows and the carrying amounts of the assets.

The reason that the carrying amounts and reportable amounts of discontinuing operations would be equal to the existing book values is that E58 does not address measurement matters as such; rather, it presumes that other IAS deal with these concerns, and that the carrying values of assets (whether to be disposed of or not) have already been adjusted for any impairment (which is the subject of another exposure draft, E55, which is discussed in Chapter 8). Thus, if the carrying amounts of assets needed to be adjusted upon being declared to be part of a discontinuing operation, this would imply that international accounting standards (including the projected impairment standard) had not been complied with. If all existing impairments had been properly recognized, then logically the mere act of declaring an operational segment a discontinuing operation would not have any impact on carrying value.

E58 states that if the initial disclosure event occurs after the balance sheet date, but before the financial statements have been issued, the disclosures enumerated above would need to be made.

It is worth emphasizing that the occurrence of the initial disclosure event only triggers disclosures in the notes to the financial statements. It will **not** result in segregation on the face of the income statement, as the initial "measurement date" event does under US GAAP. The IAS will differ significantly from both earlier guidance under IAS 8 and from the far more detailed guidance under the US standard often looked to for guidance, APB Opinion 30. The IASC has concluded that until there has been a public announcement there remains a real possibility that the plan will be aborted, and furthermore, that premature financial statement disclosure could imperil consummation of the underlying negotiations.

The second of the two key events discussed in E58 is referred to as the segregation event, and it is defined as an action by management which demonstrably commits the enterprise to the discontinuance. This is presumed to have occurred for pending sales of an operation when there exists a binding sales agreement. For other forms of discontinuance's this is presumed to have occurred when the reporting entity has no realistic possibility of withdrawing from its detailed and announced plan for the discontinuance.

The segregation event triggers, as the name suggests, segregation of the discontinuing operation's assets and liabilities, revenues and expenses, and cash flows within the enterprise's financial statements. If comparative financial statements are prepared, the earlier period must be restated to conform the manner of presentation. (This is similar to the financial reporting dictated by US GAAP when the first event, the "measurement date," has occurred.) Again, however, it is assumed that no adjustments to carrying value would be necessary if, in fact, all other applicable international accounting standards, particularly the expected standard on impairments, had been adhered to. The segregation event may occur simultaneously with the initial disclosure event, it may occur later in the same reporting period, or it may occur much later in time. If the segregation event occurs after the balance sheet date but before financial statements are published, the requirements should be applied to those statements also. The following rules will apply:

1. Total assets and liabilities pertaining to the discontinuing operation should be distinguished from those applicable to continuing operations. This can be accomplished either by segregating the assets and liabilities on the face of the balance sheet itself, or by means of disclosure in the notes to the financial statements.
2. By means of disclosures on the face of the income statement or via the footnotes to the financials, the following information will need to be disclosed: the income attributable to the discontinuing operation, either in the aggregate or by categories of income; expenses attributable to the discontinuing operation, either in the aggregate or by categories of expense; income tax expense attributable to the profit or loss from the ordinary activities of the discontinuing operation consistent with IAS 12 (revised); and after-tax profit or loss from the ordinary activities of the discontinuing operation.
3. The after-tax profit or loss from the ordinary activities of the discontinuing operation will have to be included in results from operating activities, as defined in IAS 1.

4. If any gain or loss is recognized upon the disposition of assets or settlement of liabilities attributable to the discontinuing operation, the face of the income statement or the notes thereto will need to disclose the amount of after-tax gain or loss and the income tax expense related thereto.
5. It will be prohibited to report income or expense related to discontinuing operations as part of extraordinary items. The IAS 8 definition of extraordinary activities is quite restrictive (versus, say, that which is set forth under US GAAP), and discontinuing operations, being a major portion of the business which management has adopted a plan to dispense with, cannot meet that definition.
6. Cash flows relating to discontinuing operations should be clearly distinguished from those relating to continuing operations; this can be accomplished by segregating those cash flows in the cash flow statement, or by presenting appropriate disclosures in the footnotes.
7. Other disclosures to be made after the segregation event has occurred largely parallel the information already required after the initial disclosure date. Furthermore, the date of the segregation event must be stated, as must the net selling price (i.e., net of disposal costs) received or expected from sales or binding sales agreements, the expected timing of related cash flows, and carrying amounts of related assets.
8. For any period after the one in which the segregation event occurred, significant activities or events relating to the discontinuing operation must be disclosed, including changes in estimates regarding the amounts or timing of cash flows relating to the assets to be disposed of or the liabilities to be settled.
9. If the reporting entity has more than one discontinuing operation, disclosures for each should be presented separately.

The IASC's intention (as of fall, 1997) is to enact this new standard in early to mid-1998, for initial application to financial statements covering periods beginning after 1998. Earlier application would, however, be encouraged.

APPENDIX B

PRESENTATION OF EXTRAORDINARY ITEMS

The guidance offered by IAS 8 concerning extraordinary items is limited. The definition of extraordinary items in that standard was presented in the body of this chapter, and at present the IASC has no plan to either expand the definition or to provide more detailed financial statement presentation and disclosure recommendations or examples. Accordingly, this appendix will briefly summarize the materials contained in the corresponding US standard, APB Opinion 30, which does offer somewhat more generous insight into this topic. Readers are cautioned that this is only offered to provide context for developing presentation and disclosure in compliance with IAS 8, and must be appropriately modified based on the facts and circumstances of each situation.

Extraordinary items. Under the provisions of APB 30, both of the following criteria must be met to classify an event or transaction as an extraordinary item:

1. **Unusual nature.** The underlying event or transaction should possess a high degree of abnormality and be of a type clearly unrelated to, or only incidentally related to, the ordinary and typical activities of the entity, taking into account the environment in which the entity operates. Special characteristics of the entity include the following:

    a. Type and scope of operations
    b. Lines of business
    c. Operating policies

2. **Infrequency of occurrence.** The underlying event or transaction should be of a type that would not reasonably be expected to recur in the foreseeable future, taking into account the environment in which the entity operates. In addition, other US accounting pronouncements have specifically required the following items to be disclosed as extraordinary, even though they do not meet the criteria stated above (these are noted merely to provide further guidance in attempting to operationalize the requirements under international accounting standards, which of course do not identify these items):

    a. Material gains and losses from the extinguishment of debt, other than gains and losses from extinguishments of debt made to satisfy sinking-fund requirements that an enterprise must meet within 1 year of the date of extinguishment
    b. Profit or loss resulting from the disposal of a significant part of the assets or a separable segment of previously separate companies, provided that the profit or loss is material and the disposal is within 2 years after a pooling of interest
    c. Write-off of operating rights of motor carriers

d. The investor's share of an investee's extraordinary item when the investor uses the equity method of accounting for the investee
e. Gains of a debtor related to a troubled debt restructuring

Among other guidance under US GAAP is an interpretation that neither the cost incurred by a company to defend itself from a takeover attempt nor the cost incurred as part of a "standstill" agreement meet the criteria for extraordinary classifications as discussed in APB 30.

Extraordinary items should be segregated from the results of ordinary operations and be shown net of taxes in a separate section of the income statement, following "discontinued operations" and preceding "cumulative effect of a change in accounting principle," if any. Under international standards, however, discontinued operations are included in ordinary activities; although these can and probably should be broken out as a discrete subsection. The following illustrations are based on US GAAP and should be considered a starting point for developing useful presentations under IAS.

Example of the income statement presentation for extraordinary items

An extraordinary item would be presented as follows:

Income before extraordinary items	$xxx
Extraordinary items (less applicable income taxes of $__) (Note __)	xxx
Net income	$xxx

APPENDIX C

FINANCIAL REPORTING FOR DEVELOPMENT STAGE ENTERPRISES

A recurring concern among newly established enterprises is that, given what is often a multiyear process of achieving a normal level of operations and absorbing the typically heavy startup costs needed to achieve this, the income statements prepared and presented under generally accepted accounting principles may be insufficient to provide the user with meaningful insights into the operations and potential of the entity. In years gone by, a commonly employed solution was to defer many costs that normally are deemed to be period costs, and then to amortize these over what was often an arbitrary period, say, 5 years. The logic was that these costs were incurred to benefit operations after the entity began to operate in a normal fashion, and to expense these upon incurrence would result, most commonly, in reportable losses which would imply that future successful operations would not be achieved.

The obvious flaw in the deferral of startup costs, from a financial reporting perspective, is that these deferred costs would necessarily be presented as assets on the enterprise's balance sheet, when in fact these sunk costs would have no demonstrable value for the future, particularly if the entity's strategies proved unsuccessful. Thus, there is an inherent conflict among some of accounting's most fundamental concepts: the going concern assumption, realization, and conservatism. Ultimately, the US standards setters had to rule that costs must be accounted for by development stage enterprises no differently than by operating enterprises: If the cost represents an asset, it is accounted for as such, but if a sunk cost does not meet the definition of an asset, it must be expensed when incurred.

In recognition of the not unreasonable argument that strict application of the foregoing rule would result in income statements for development stage enterprises which might not be as meaningful as would be hoped, the US standard provides that **cumulative** statements of income be presented for development stage enterprises, so that users can better understand the full scope of the activities undertaken to achieve normal operations. Although there is currently no corresponding standard under IAS, there is also no prohibition that such statements (at least on a supplementary basis) could not be presented.

Development stage enterprises defined. Under the applicable US GAAP standard, SFAS 7, a development stage enterprise is defined as one that is devoting substantially all of its efforts to establishing a new business, and **either** of the following conditions exists:

1. Planned principal operations have not begun.
2. Planned principal operations have begun but there has been no significant revenue.

SFAS 7 indicates that these enterprises should prepare their financial statements in accordance with the same GAAP applicable to established operating entities.

SFAS 7 indicated that specialized accounting practices are unacceptable and that development stage enterprises were to follow the same generally accepted accounting principles as those that applied to an established operating entity. SFAS 7 also provided that a development stage enterprise should disclose certain additional information that would alert readers to the fact that the company is in the development stage. Disclosure requirements include

1. All disclosures applicable to operating entities
2. Identification of the statements as those of a development stage enterprise
3 Disclosure of the nature of development stage activities
4. A balance sheet that includes the cumulative net losses since inception in the equity section
5. An income statement showing current-period revenue and expense as well as the cumulative amount from the inception of the entity
6. A statement of cash flows showing cash flows for the period as well as those from inception
7. A statement of stockholders' equity showing the following from the enterprise's inception:

    a. For each issuance, the date and number of equity securities issued for cash or other consideration
    b. For each issuance, the dollar amounts per share assigned to the consideration received for equity securities
    c. For each issuance involving noncash consideration, the nature of the consideration and the basis used in assigning the valuation

8. For the first period in which an enterprise is no longer a development stage enterprise, it shall be disclosed that in prior periods the entity was a development stage enterprise. If comparative statements are presented, the foregoing disclosure presentations (2 through 7) need not be shown.

4 CASH FLOW STATEMENTS

PERSPECTIVE AND ISSUES

The IASC issued revised IAS 7, *Cash Flow Statements*, in 1992, superseding the original standard, also denoted as IAS 7, which had been issued in 1977 and which required enterprises to prepare the statement of changes in financial position (commonly referred to as the **funds flow statement**) as an integral part of the financial reporting process. This revised standard, which established the currently applicable rules for cash flow reporting, became operative for financial statements of periods beginning on or after January 1, 1994.

The primary purpose of the statement of cash flows is to provide information about the cash receipts and cash payments of an entity during a period. A secondary purpose is to provide insight into the investing and financing activities of the entity. More specifically, the statement of cash flows should help investors and creditors assess

1. The ability to generate future positive cash flows
2. The ability to meet obligations and pay dividends
3. Reasons for differences between income and cash receipts and payments
4. Both cash and noncash aspects of entities' investing and financing transactions

The adoption of a requirement for cash flow reporting by the IASC completes what has been virtually a universal movement away from the formerly popular funds flow mode of reporting to cash reporting. In the United States, the move was completed with the issuance of SFAS 95 (which became effective in 1988). A similar change in the United Kingdom occurred with the issuance of FRS 1 in 1991. (However, the UK rules were substantially revised in October 1996, so that financial reporting of cash flow information in the UK now differs significantly from practice under both US and International standards, as noted in greater detail below.) The purpose of this shift was to provide external users of financial statements with a better tool to project future cash flows, which is now deemed to be the ultimate concern of investors and creditors. While the formerly popular concept of funds did permit this assessment to be made, albeit with difficulty on the part of the users of the statements, cash flow reporting is now seen as being a central objective of the financial reporting process. The requirements of IAS 7 are generally similar to the requirements of both SFAS 95 and the **original** UK FRS 1, as it stood before its overhaul in 1996, although IAS 7 does contain a few peculiarities, which are highlighted in the following discussion.

Sources of IAS
IAS 7

DEFINITIONS OF TERMS

Cash. Cash on hand and demand deposits with banks or other financial institutions.

Cash equivalents. Short-term highly liquid investments that are (1) readily convertible to known amounts of cash, and (2) so near their maturity (original maturity of 3 months or less) that they present negligible risk of changes in value because of changes in interest rates. Treasury bills, commercial paper, and money market funds are all examples of cash equivalents.

Direct method. A method that derives the net cash provided by or used in operating activities from major components of operating cash receipts and payments.

Financing activities. The transactions that cause changes in the size and composition of an enterprise's capital and borrowings.

Indirect (reconciliation) method. A method that derives the net cash provided by or used in operating activities by adjusting net income (loss) for the effects of transactions of a noncash nature, any deferrals or accruals of past or future operating cash receipts or payments, and items of income or expense associated with investing or financing activities.

Investing activities. The acquisition and disposal of long-term assets and other investments not included in cash equivalents.

Operating activities. The transactions not classified as financing or investing activities, generally involving producing and delivering goods or providing services.

CONCEPTS, RULES, AND EXAMPLES

Benefits of Cash Flow Statements

The concepts underlying the balance sheet and the income statement have long been established in financial reporting; they are, respectively, the stock measure or a snapshot at a point in time of an entity's resources and obligations, and a summary of the entity's economic performance over a period of time. The third major financial statement, the cash flow statement, is a more recent innovation but has evolved substantially since introduced. What has ultimately developed into the cash flow statement began life as a flow statement which reconciled changes in enterprise resources over a period of time but in a fundamentally different manner than did the income statement.

Most of the basic progress on this financial statement occurred in the United States, where during the 1950s and early 1960s a variety of formats and concepts were experimented with. By the mid-1960s the most common approach in the United States was that of reporting the sources and applications (or uses) of funds, although such reporting did not become mandatory until 1971, and even then, **funds** could be defined by the reporting entity in at least four different ways, including as cash and as net working capital (current assets minus current liabilities).

One reason why the financial statement preparer community did not more quickly embrace a cash flow concept is that the accounting profession had long had a significant aversion to the cash basis measurement of enterprise operating performance. This was largely the result of its commitment to accrual basis accounting, which recognizes revenues when earned and expenses when incurred, and which views cash flow reporting as a back door approach to cash basis accounting. By focusing instead on **funds**, which most typically was defined as net working capital, items such as receivables and payables were included, thereby preserving the essential accrual basis characteristic of the flow measurement. On the other hand, this failed to give statement users meaningful insight into the entities' sources and uses of cash per se.

By the 1970s there was widespread recognition of the myriad problems associated with funds flow reporting, including the required use of the **all financial resources** approach, under which all major, noncash (and nonfund) transactions, such as exchanges of stock or debt for plant assets, were included in the funds flow statement. This ultimately led to a renewed call for cash flow reporting. Most significantly, the FASB's conceptual framework project of the late 1970s to mid-1980s identified usefulness in predicting future cash flows as a central purpose of the financial reporting process. This presaged the nearly universal move away from funds flows to cash flows as a third standard measurement to be incorporated in financial reports.

Cash flow statements thus became required in the late 1980s in the United States, with the United Kingdom following along soon thereafter, with an approach that largely mirrored the US standard; albeit with a somewhat refined classification scheme, which solves some of the problems inherent in the US model (as described in greater detail below) and which, in the 1996 revision of FRS 1, has embraced an even more extensive classification scheme, as described below. The international accounting standard, which was adopted a year after that of the United Kingdom (both of these were revisions to earlier requirements that had mandated the use of funds flow statements), embraces the somewhat simpler US approach but offers greater flexibility, thus effectively incorporating the UK view without adding to the structural complexity of the cash flow statement itself.

Today, the clear consensus of national and international accounting standard setters is that the statement of cash flows is a necessary component of complete financial reporting. The perceived benefits of presenting the statement of cash flows in conjunction with the statement of financial position (balance sheet) and the statement of income (or operations) have been highlighted by IAS 7 to be as follows:

1. It provides an insight into the financial structure of the enterprise (including its liquidity and solvency) and its ability to affect the amounts and timing of cash flows in order to adapt to changing circumstances and opportunities.

The statement of cash flows discloses important information about the cash flows from operating, investing, and financing activities, information that is not available or as clearly discernible in either the balance sheet or the income statement. The additional disclosures which are either recommended by IAS 7 (such as those relating to undrawn borrowing facilities or cash flows that represent increases in operating capacity) or required to be disclosed by the standard (such as that about cash held by the enterprise but not available for use) provide a wealth of information for the informed user of financial statements. Taken together, the statement of cash flows coupled with these required or recommended disclosures provide the user with vastly more insight into the entity's performance and position, and its probable future results, than would the balance sheet and income statement alone.

2. It provides additional information to the users of financial statements for evaluating changes in assets, liabilities, and equity of an enterprise.

When comparative balance sheets are presented, users are given information about the enterprise's assets and liabilities at the end of each of the years. Were the statement of cash flows not presented as an integral part of the financial statements, it would be necessary for users of comparative financial statements either to wonder how and why certain amounts reported on the balance sheet changed from one period to another, or to compute (at least for the latest year presented) approximations of these items for themselves. At best, however, such a do-it-yourself approach would derive the net changes (the increase or decrease) in the individual assets and liabilities and attribute these to normally related income statement accounts. (For example, the net change in accounts receivable from the beginning to the end of the year would be used to convert reported sales to cash basis sales or cash collected from customers.) More complex combinations of events (such as the acquisition of another entity, along with its accounts receivables, which would be an increase in that asset which was not related to sales to customers by the reporting entity during the period) would not immediately be comprehensible and might lead to incorrect interpretations of the data unless an actual cash flow statement were presented.

3. It enhances the comparability of reporting of operating performance by different enterprises because it eliminates the effects of using different accounting treatments for the same transactions and events.

There was considerable debate even as early as the 1960s and 1970s over accounting standardization, which led to the emergence of cash flow accounting. The principal argument in support of cash flow accounting by its earliest proponents was that it avoids the arbitrary allocations inherent in accrual accounting. For example, cash flows provided by or used in operating activities are derived, under the indirect method, by adjusting net income (or loss) for items such as depreciation and amortization, which might have been computed by different entities using different accounting methods. Thus, accounting standardization will be achieved by converting the accrual basis net income to cash basis income, and the resultant figures will become comparable across enterprises.

4. It serves as an indicator of the amount, timing, and certainty of future cash flows. Furthermore, if an enterprise has a system in place to project its future cash flows, the statement of cash flows could be used as a touchstone to evaluate the accuracy of past projections of those future cash flows. This benefit is elucidated by the standard as follows:

    a. The statement of cash flows is useful in comparing past assessments of future cash flows against current year's cash flow information, and
    b. It is of value in appraising the relationship between profitability and net cash flows, and in assessing the impact of changing prices.

Exclusion of Noncash Transactions

The statement of cash flows includes only inflows and outflows of cash and cash equivalents. On the other hand, it excludes all transactions that do not directly affect cash receipts and payments. However, IAS 7 does require that the effects of transactions not resulting in receipts or payments of cash be disclosed elsewhere in the financial statements. The reason for not including noncash transactions in the statement of cash flows and placing them elsewhere in the financial statements (e.g., the footnotes) is that it preserves the statement's primary focus on cash flows from operating, investing, and financing activities.

Components of Cash and Cash Equivalents

The statement of cash flows, under the various national and international standards, may or may not include transactions in cash equivalents as well as cash. Under US standards, for example, preparers may choose to define cash as "cash and cash equivalents," as long as the same definition is used in the balance sheet as in the cash flow statement (i.e., the cash flow statement must tie to a single caption on the balance sheet). With the recent dramatic revision to the UK standard on cash flow reporting, on the other hand, the **revised** UK FRS 1 now defines cash flows to include movements only in "cash." IAS 7, on the other hand, rather clearly required that the changes in both cash and cash equivalents be explained by the cash flow statement. Thus, the three major standards (US, UK, and International) have taken three different roads (optionally including cash equivalents; mandatorily excluding cash equivalents; and including cash equivalents) to the presentation of the statement of cash flows.

Cash and cash equivalents include unrestricted cash (meaning cash actually on hand, or bank balances whose immediate use is determined by the management), other demand deposits, and short-term investments whose maturities at the date of acquisition by the enterprise were 3 months or less. **Equity investments** do not qualify as cash equivalents unless they fit the definition above of short-term maturities of 3 months or less. **Redeemable preference shares**, if acquired within 3 months of their predetermined redemption date, would meet the criteria above since they are, in substance, cash equivalents. These are very infrequently encountered circumstances, however.

Bank borrowings are normally considered as financing activities. However, in some countries, bank overdrafts play an integral part in the enterprise's cash management, and as such, overdrafts are to be included as a component of cash equivalents if the following conditions are met:

1. The bank overdraft is repayable on demand, and
2. The bank balance often fluctuates from positive to negative (overdraft).

Postdated checks (cheques), commonly referred to as **PDC**, are used a great deal in business transactions in certain countries. In such situations, vendors usually insist upon PDC to back up the credit extended by them in the normal course of business. Banks will then offer to discount these postdated checks (on a recourse basis, normally) if the discounting party's credit is strong, and thus vendors may end up collecting their receivables before the due date. Under such circumstances, where vendors use PDC as an integral component of their cash management strategy, it could very well be argued that PDC should be considered cash equivalents. However, if it is not certain at the balance sheet date whether or not the PDC are to be discounted, a case could be made to at least consider those PDC that mature within 3 months after the balance sheet date as cash equivalents (while those having original maturities longer than 3 months would be precluded from being so treated). The customer who issued those PDC, however, has no control over them once they are issued and would not be able to use them as an integral part of its cash management; thus, in the debtors' financial statements PDC are simply accounts payable and are not cash transactions until the dates of the PDC occur.

Statutory deposits by banks (i.e., those held with the central bank for regulatory compliance purposes) are often included in the same balance sheet caption as cash. There is difference of opinion and even some controversy in certain countries, which is fairly evident from scrutiny of published financial statements of banks, as to whether these deposits should be considered a cash equivalent or an operating asset. If the latter, changes in amount would be presented in the operating activities section of the cash flow statement, and the item could not then be combined with cash in the balance sheet. Since the appendix to IAS 7, which illustrates the application of the standard to cash flow statements of financial institutions, does not include statutory deposits with the central bank as a cash equivalent, the authors have concluded that there is little logic to support the alternative presentation of this item as a cash equivalent. Given the fact that deposits with central banks are more or less permanent (and in fact would be more likely to increase over time than to be diminished, given a going concern assumption about the reporting financial institution) the presumption must be that these are not cash equivalents in normal practice.

Classifications in the Statement of Cash Flows

The statement of cash flows prepared in accordance with international accounting standards (and also in accordance with US GAAP) requires classification into these three categories:

1. **Investing activities** include the acquisition and disposition of property, plant and equipment and other long-term assets and debt and equity instruments of other enterprises that are not considered cash equivalents or held for dealing or trading purposes. Investing activities include cash advances and collections on loans made to other parties (other than advances and loans of a financial institution).
2. **Financing activities** include obtaining resources from and returning resources to the owners. Also included is obtaining resources through borrowings (short-term or long-term) and repayments of the amounts borrowed.
3. **Operating activities** include all transactions that are not investing and financing activities. In general, cash flows that relate to, or are the corollary of, items reported in the income statement are operating cash flows. Operating activities are principal revenue-producing activities of an enterprise and include delivering or producing goods for sale and providing services.

While both US and international accounting standards define these three components of cash flows, the international standards offer somewhat more flexibility in how certain types of cash flows are categorized. For example, under US GAAP, interest paid must be included in operating activities, but under the provisions of IAS 7 this may consistently be included in either operating or financing activities. (These and other discrepancies among the standards will be discussed further throughout this chapter.) This is a reflection of the fact that although interest expense is operating in the sense of being an item that is reported in the income statement, it also clearly relates to the entity's financing activities.

The **original** UK standard on cash flow reporting, FRS 1, tried to solve this dilemma by defining **five**, not merely three, categories for the cash flow statement. In addition to the three standard classifications discussed above, it added two others: "returns on investments and servicing of finance," and "taxation." The first of these added categories was used to report all dividends and interest paid or received, leaving the traditional financing section to report only principal transactions, and averting the issue of whether dividends and interest are operating, investing, or financing in nature. The segregation of taxation into a category of its own avoids a very similar debate, since taxation can be the result of normal operating activities as well as of investing or financing events.

The recently **revised** UK standard on cash flow reporting, which is also denoted as FRS 1, now requires classification into the following **eight** categories:

1. Operating activities
2. Returns on investments and servicing of finance
3. Taxation
4. Capital expenditure and financial investment
5. Acquisitions and disposals
6. Equity dividends paid
7. Management of liquid resources
8. Financing

As a result of this new classification scheme, financial statements prepared in conformity with UK GAAP will differ rather notably from those prepared under either UK GAAP or IAS. With the growing world-wide interest in the standardization of financial reporting in general, and in the international accounting standards in particular, it remains to be seen how well this unorthodox approach will be accepted. In any event, it is deemed to be extremely unlikely that the IAS will be modified to acknowledge the UK approach.

The following are examples of the statement of cash flows classification under the provisions of IAS 7:

	Operating	Investing	Financing
Cash inflows	• Receipts from sale of goods or services • Sale of loans, debt, or equity instruments carried in trading portfolio • Returns on loans (interest) • Returns on equity securities (dividends)	• Principal collections from loans and sales of other entities' debt instruments • Sale of equity instruments of other enterprises and from returns of investment in those instruments • Sale of plant and equipment	• Proceeds from issuing share capital • Proceeds from issuing debt (short-term or long-term) • Not-for-profits' donor restricted cash that is limited to long-term purposes
Cash outflows	• Payments to suppliers for goods and other services • Payments to or on behalf of employees • Payments of taxes • Payments of interest • Purchase of loans, debt, or equity instruments carried in trading portfolio	• Loans made and acquisition of other entities' debt instruments • Purchase of equity instruments* of other enterprises • Purchase of plant and equipment	• Payment of dividends • Repurchase of company's shares • Repayment of debt principal, including capital lease obligations

**Unless held for trading purposes or considered to be cash equivalents.*

Noncash investing and financing activities should, according to IAS 7, be disclosed in the footnotes to financial statements ("elsewhere" is how the standard actually identifies this), but apparently are not intended to be included in the cash flow statement itself. This contrasts somewhat with the US standard, SFAS 95, which encourages inclusion of this supplemental information on the face of the statement of cash flows, although it can, under that standard, be relegated to a footnote as well. (The UK standard on cash flow reporting, FRS 1, revised in 1996, also requires that major noncash transactions be disclosed in a note to the cash flow statement.) Examples of significant noncash financing and investing activities might include

1. Acquiring an asset through a finance lease
2. Conversion of debt to equity
3. Exchange of noncash assets or liabilities for other noncash assets or liabilities
4. Issuance of stock to acquire assets

Basic example of a classified statement of cash flows

Liquid Corporation
Statement of Cash Flows
For the Year Ended December 31, 19XX

Net cash flows from operating activities		$ xxx
Cash flows from investing activities:		
Purchase of property, plant, and equipment	$(xxx)	
Sale of equipment	xx	
Collection of notes receivable	xx	
Net cash **used** in investing activities		(xx)
Cash flows from financing activities:		
Proceeds from issuance of share capital	xxx	
Repayment of long-term debt	(xx)	
Reduction of notes payable	(xx)	
Net cash **provided** by financing activities		xx
Effect of exchange rate changes on cash		xx
Net increase in cash and cash equivalents		$ xxx
Cash and cash equivalents at beginning of year		xxx
Cash and cash equivalents at end of year		$xxxx

Footnote Disclosure of Noncash Investing and Financing Activities

Note 4: Supplemental Cash Flow Statement Information

Significant noncash investing and financing transactions:

Conversion of bonds into common stock	$ xxx
Property acquired under finance leases	xxx
	$ xxx

Reporting Cash Flows From Operating Activities

Direct vs. indirect method. The operating activities section of the statement of cash flows can be presented under the direct or the indirect method. However, the IASC has expressed a preference for the direct method of presenting net cash from operating activities. In this regard the IASC was probably following in the well-worn path of the FASB in the United States, which similarly urged that the direct method of reporting be adhered to. Under UK GAAP, however, though the UK Accounting Standards Board considered the advantages of the "direct method" in developing FRS 1, it was noted that it did not believe that in all cases the benefits to users outweighed the costs to the reporting entity of providing that mode of reporting. The UK Board remains of this view, and the revised FRS 1 continues to encourage the "direct method" only where the potential benefits to users outweigh the costs of providing it. For their part, preparers of financial statements in the other parts of the world, like those in the US, have chosen overwhelmingly to ignore the recommendation of the IASC, preferring by a very large margin to use the "indirect method" in lieu of the recommended "direct method."

The **direct method** shows the items that affected cash flow and the magnitude of those cash flows. Cash received from, and cash paid to, specific sources (such as customers and suppliers) are presented, as opposed to the indirect method's converting accrual basis net income (loss) to cash flow information by means of a series of add-backs and deductions. Entities using the direct method are required by IAS 7 to report the following major classes of gross cash receipts and gross cash payments:

1. Cash collected from customers
2. Interest and dividends received*
3. Cash paid to employees and other suppliers
4. Interest paid**
5. Income taxes paid
6. Other operating cash receipts and payments

Given the availability of alternative modes of presentation of interest and dividends received, and of interest paid, it is particularly critical that the policy adopted be followed consistently. Since the face of the statement of cash flows will in almost all cases make it clear what approach has been elected, it is not usually necessary to spell this out in the accounting policy note to the financial statements, although this certainly can be done if it would be useful to do so.

An important advantage of the direct method is that it permits the user to better comprehend the relationships between the company's net income (loss) and its cash flows. For example, payments of expenses are shown as cash disbursements and are deducted from cash receipts. In this way the user is able to recognize the cash receipts and cash payments for the period. Formulas for conversion of various income statement amounts for the direct method presentation from the accrual basis to the cash basis are summarized below.

---

* *Alternatively, interest and dividends received may be classified as investing cash flows rather than as operating cash flows because they are returns on investments. In this important regard, the IAS differs from the corresponding US rule, which does not permit this elective treatment, making the operating cash flow presentation mandatory.*

** *Alternatively, also, IAS 7 permits interest paid to be classified as a financing cash flow, because this is the cost of obtaining financing. As with the foregoing, the availability of alternative treatments differs from the US approach, which makes the operating cash flow presentation the only choice.*

Accrual basis	*Additions*	*Deductions*	*Cash basis*
Net sales	+ Beginning AR	– Ending AR AR written off	= Cash received from customers
Cost of goods sold	+ Ending inventory Beginning AP	– Depreciation and amortization* Beginning inventory Ending AP	= Cash paid to suppliers
Operating expenses	+ Ending prepaid expenses Beginning accrued expenses	– Depreciation and amortization Beginning prepaid expenses Ending accrued expenses payable Bad debts expense	= Cash paid for operating expenses

**Applies to a manufacturing entity only*

From the foregoing it can be appreciated that the amounts to be included in the operating section of the statement of cash flows, when the direct approach is utilized, are derived amounts that must be computed (although the computations are not onerous); they are not, generally, amounts that exist as account balances simply to be looked up and then placed in the statement. The extra effort needed to prepare the direct method operating cash flow data may be a contributing cause of why this method has been distinctly unpopular with preparers. (There is an extra reason why the direct method is unpopular with entities that report in conformity with US GAAP: SFAS 95 requires that when the direct method is used, a supplementary schedule be prepared reconciling net income to net cash flows from operating activities, which effectively means that **both** the direct and indirect methods must be employed. This rule does not apply under international accounting standards, however.)

The **indirect method** (sometimes referred to as the reconciliation method) is the most widely used means of presentation of cash from operating activities, primarily because it is easier to prepare. It focuses on the differences between net operating results and cash flows. The indirect format begins with net income (or loss), which can be obtained directly from the income statement. Revenue and expense items not affecting cash are added or deducted to arrive at net cash provided by operating activities. For example, depreciation and amortization would be added back because these expenses reduce net income without affecting cash.

The statement of cash flows prepared using the indirect method emphasizes changes in the components of most current asset and current liability accounts. Changes in inventory, accounts receivable, and other current accounts are used to determine the cash flow from operating activities. Although most of these adjustments are obvious (most preparers simply relate each current asset or current liability on the balance sheet to a single caption in the income statement), some changes require more careful analysis. For example, it is important to compute cash collected from sales by relating sales revenue to both the change in accounts receivable and the change in the related bad debt allowance account.

As another example of possible complexity in computing the cash from operating activities, the change in short-term borrowings resulting from the purchase of equipment would not be included, since it is not related to operating activities. Instead, these short-term borrowings would be classified as a financing activity. Other adjustments under the indirect method include changes in the account balances of deferred income taxes, minority interest, unrealized foreign currency gains or losses and the income (loss) from investments under the equity method.

IAS 7 offers yet another alternative way of presenting the cash flows from operating activities. This could be referred to as the **modified indirect method**. Under this variant of the indirect method, the starting point is not net income but rather revenues and expenses as reported in the income statement. In essence, this approach is virtually the same as the regular indirect method, with two more details: revenues and expenses for the period. There is no equivalent rule under US GAAP.

The following summary, actually simply an expanded balance sheet equation, may facilitate understanding of the adjustments to net income necessary for converting accrual-basis net income to cash-basis net income when using the indirect method.

	*Current assets**	–	*Fixed assets*	=	*Current liabilities*	+	*Long-term liabilities*	+	*Income*	*Accrual income adjustment to convert to cash flow*
1.	Increase			=					Increase	Decrease
2.	Decrease			=					Decrease	Increase
3.				=	Increase				Decrease	Increase
4.				=	Decrease				Increase	Decrease

**Other than cash and cash equivalents*

For example, using row 1 in the above chart, a credit sale would increase accounts receivable and accrual-basis income but would not affect cash. Therefore, its effect must be removed from the accrual income to convert to cash income. The last column indicates that the increase in a current asset balance must be deducted from income to obtain cash flow.

Similarly, an increase in a current liability, row 3, must be added to income to obtain cash flows (e.g., accrued wages are on the income statement as an expense, but they do not require cash; the increase in wages payable must be added back to remove this noncash flow expense from accrual-basis income).

Under the US GAAP, when the indirect method is employed, the amount of interest and income taxes paid must be included in the related disclosures (supplemental schedule). However, under international accounting standards, as illustrated by the appendix to IAS 7, instead of disclosing them in the supplemental schedules, they are shown as part of the operating activities under both the direct and indirect methods. (Examples presented later in the chapter illustrate this.)

The major drawback to the indirect method involves the user's difficulty in comprehending the information presented. This method does not show from where the cash was received or to where the cash was paid. Only adjustments to accrual basis net income are shown. In some cases the adjustments can be confusing. For instance, the sale of equipment resulting in an accrual basis loss would require that the loss be added to net income to arrive at net cash from operating activities. (The loss was deducted in the computation of net income, but because the sale will be shown as an investing activity, the loss must be added back to net income.)

Although the indirect method is more commonly used in practice, the IASC and the FASB both encourage enterprises to use the direct method. As pointed out by IAS 7, a distinct advantage of the direct method is that it provides information that may be useful in estimating or projecting future cash flows, a benefit that is clearly not achieved when the indirect method is utilized instead. Both the direct and indirect methods are presented below.

Direct method

Cash flows from operating activities:		
Cash received from sale of goods	$xxx	
Cash dividends received*	xxx	
Cash provided by operating activities		$xxx
Cash paid to suppliers	(xxx)	
Cash paid for operating expenses	(xxx)	
Cash paid for income taxes**	(xxx)	
Cash disbursed for operating activities		($xxx)
Net cash flows from operating activities		$xxx

* *Alternatively, could be classified as investing cash flow.*

** *Taxes paid are usually classified as operating activities. However, when it is practical to identify the tax cash flow with an individual transaction that gives rise to cash flows that are classified as investing or financing activities, then the tax cash flow is classified as an investing or financing activity as appropriate.*

Indirect method

Cash flows from operating activities:	
Net income before income taxes	$ xx
Adjustments for:	
Depreciation	xx
Unrealized loss on foreign exchange	xx
Interest expense	xx
Operating profit before working capital changes***	
Increase in accounts receivable	(xx)
Decrease in inventories	xx

Increase in accounts payable	xx
Cash generated from operations	
Interest paid	(xx)
Income taxes paid (see note**above)	(xx)
Net cash flows from operating activities	$xxx

*** *The appendix to IAS 7 uses the term "working capital changes," but the authors believe that "changes in operating assets and liabilities" is preferable since the emphasis has clearly shifted from working capital changes, and the related concept of fund flows, to cash flows by the supplanting of the erstwhile IAS 7, which dealt with the now obsolete "statement of changes in financial position."*

Other Requirements

Gross vs. net basis. The emphasis in the statement of cash flows is on gross cash receipts and cash payments. For instance, reporting the net change in bonds payable would obscure the financing activities of the entity by not disclosing separately cash inflows from issuing bonds and cash outflows from retiring bonds.

IAS 7 (paragraph 22) specifies two exceptions where netting of cash flows is allowed. Items with quick turnovers, large amounts, and short maturities may be presented as net cash flows. Cash receipts and payments on behalf of customers when the cash flows reflect the activities of the customers rather than those of the enterprise may also be reported on a net rather than a gross basis.

Foreign currency cash flows. Foreign operations must prepare a separate statement of cash flows and translate the statement to the reporting currency using the exchange rate in effect at the time of the cash flow (a weighted-average exchange rate may be used if the result is substantially the same). This translated statement is then used in the preparation of the consolidated statement of cash flows. Noncash exchange gains and losses recognized on the income statement should be reported as a separate item when reconciling net income and operating activities. For a more detailed discussion about the exchange rate effects on the statement of cash flows, see Chapter 20.

Cash flow per share. There is presently no requirement either under the international accounting standards or under US GAAP to disclose such information in the financial statements of an enterprise, unlike the requirement to report earnings per share (EPS). In fact, cash flow per share is a somewhat disreputable concept, since it was sometimes touted, in an earlier era, as being indicative of an entity's "real" performance, when of course it is not a meaningful alternative to earnings per share; because, for example, enterprises that are self-liquidating by selling productive assets can generate very positive total cash flows, and hence cash flows per share, while decimating the potential for future earnings. Since, unlike a comprehensive cash flow statement, cash flow per share cannot reveal the components of cash flow (operating, investing, and financing), its usage could be misleading.

Exemption From Presentation of a Statement of Cash Flows Under US GAAP and IAS

Under US GAAP, as set forth in FASB 102, a statement of cash flows is not required for a defined benefit pension plan that presents financial information consistent with the guidelines of FASB 35. Other employee benefit plans are exempted provided that the financial information presented is similar to the requirements of FASB 35. Investment enterprises or a common trust fund held for the collective investment and reinvestment of moneys are not required to provide a statement of cash flows if the following conditions are met:

1. Substantially all of the entity's investments are highly liquid
2. Entity's investments are carried at market value
3. Entity had little or no debt, based on average debt outstanding during the period in relation to average total assets
4. Entity provides a statement of changes in net assets

However, with the issuance of FASB 117, the requirements for presentation of statements of cash flows have been made almost universal except in the case of investment companies and employee benefit plans, which are still exempted. IAS 7, on the other hand, categorically states that all enterprises regardless of the nature of their activities should present a statement of cash flows as an integral part of their financial reports. No exceptions have been identified to this requirement.

Net Reporting by Financial Institutions

IAS 7 permits financial institutions to report cash flows arising from certain activities on a net basis. These activities, and the related conditions under which net reporting would be acceptable, are as follows:

1. Cash receipts and payments on behalf of customers, when the cash flows reflect the activities of the customers rather than those of the bank. For example, the acceptance and repayment of demand deposits
2. Cash flows relating to deposits with fixed maturity dates
3. Placements and withdrawals of deposits from other financial institutions
4. Cash advances and loans to banks customers and repayments thereon

US GAAP has similar requirements. According to FASB 104, banks, savings institutions, and credit unions are allowed to report net cash receipts and payments for the following:

1. Deposits placed with other financial institutions
2. Withdrawals of deposits
3. Time deposits accepted
4. Repayments of deposits
5. Loans made to customers

6. Principal collections of loans

Reporting Futures, Forward Contracts, Options, and Swaps

IAS 7 stipulates that cash payments for and cash receipts from futures contracts, forward contracts, option contracts, and swap contracts are normally classified as investing activities, except

1. When such contracts are held for dealing or trading purposes and thus represent operating activities
2. When the payments or receipts are considered by the enterprise as financing activities and are reported accordingly

Further, when a contract is accounted for as a hedge of an identifiable position, the cash flows of the contract are classified in the same manner as the cash flows of the position being hedged. In this matter, US GAAP establishes similar requirements (by SFAS 104).

Reporting Extraordinary Items in the Cash Flow Statement

The cash flows associated with extraordinary items should be disclosed separately as arising from operating, investing, or financing activities in the statement of cash flows, as appropriate. By way of contrast, US GAAP permits, but does not require, separate disclosure of cash flows related to extraordinary items. If an entity reporting under US GAAP chooses to make this disclosure, however, it is expected to do so consistently in all periods.

Reconciliation of Cash and Cash Equivalents

An enterprise should disclose the components of cash and cash equivalents and should present a reconciliation of the difference, if any, between the amounts reported in the statement of cash flows and equivalent items reported in the balance sheet. By contrast, under the US GAAP the definition must tie to a specific caption on the balance sheet. For example, if short-term investments are shown as a separate caption in the balance sheet, the definition of cash for the purposes of the statement of cash flows must include "cash" alone (and not also include short-term investments). On the other hand, if "cash and cash equivalents" is the adopted definition in the statement of cash flows, a single caption in the balance sheet must include both "cash" and "short-term investments."

Acquisitions and Disposals of Subsidiaries and Other Business Units

IAS 7 requires that the aggregate cash flows from acquisitions and from disposals of subsidiaries or other business units should be presented separately as part of the investing activities section of the statement of cash flows. The following disclosures have also been prescribed by IAS 7 in respect to both acquisitions and disposals:

1. The total consideration included
2. The portion thereof discharged by cash and cash equivalents
3. The amount of cash and cash equivalents in the subsidiary or business unit acquired or disposed
4. The amount of assets and liabilities (other than cash and cash equivalents) acquired or disposed, summarized by major category

Other Disclosures Required or Recommended by IAS 7

Certain additional information may be relevant to the users of financial statements in gaining an insight into the liquidity or solvency of an enterprise. With this objective in mind, IAS 7 sets forth other disclosures that are required or in some cases, recommended.

1. **Required disclosure**--Amount of significant cash and cash equivalent balances held by an enterprise that are not available for use by the group should be disclosed along with a commentary by management.
2. **Recommended disclosures**--The disclosures that are encouraged are the following:

    a. Amount of undrawn borrowing facilities, indicating restrictions on their use, if any
    b. In case of investments in joint ventures, which are accounted for using proportionate consolidation, the aggregate amount of cash flows from operating, investing and financing activities that are attributable to the investment in the joint venture
    c. Aggregate amount of cash flows that are attributable to the increase in operating capacity separately from those cash flows that are required to maintain operating capacity
    d. Amount of cash flows segregated by reported industry and geographical segments

The disclosures above recommended by the IAS 7, although difficult to present, are unique since such disclosures are not required even under the US GAAP. They are useful in enabling the users of financial statements to understand the enterprise's financial position better.

Basic example of the preparation of the cash flow statement under IAS 7 using a worksheet approach

Using the following financial information for ABC (Middle East) Ltd., preparation and presentation of the cash flow statement according to the requirements of IAS 7 are illustrated. (Note that all figures in this example are in thousands of US dollars.)

ABC (Middle East) Ltd.
Balance Sheets
As at December 31,1997 and 1996

Assets	*1997*	*1996*
Cash and cash equivalents	$ 3,000	$ 1,000
Debtors	5,000	2,500
Inventories	2,000	1,500
Preoperative expenses	1,000	1,500
Due from associates	19,000	19,000
Property, plant, and equipment cost	12,000	22,500
Accumulated depreciation	(5,000)	(6,000)
Property, plant, and equipment, net	7,000	16,500
Total assets	$37,000	$42,000
Liabilities		
Accounts payable	$ 5,000	$12,500
Income taxes payable	2,000	1,000
Deferred taxes payable	3,000	2,000
Total liabilities	10,000	15,500
Shareholders' equity		
Share capital	6,500	6,500
Retained earnings	20,500	20,000
Total shareholders' equity	27,000	26,500
Total liabilities and shareholders' equity	$37,000	$42,000

ABC (Middle East) Ltd.
Statement of Income
For the Year Ended December 31, 1997

Sales	$ 30,000
Cost of sales	(10,000)
Gross operating income	20,000
Administrative and selling expenses	(2,000)
Interest expenses	(2,000)
Depreciation of property, plant and equipment	(2,000)
Amortization of preoperative expenses	(500)
Investment income	2,000
Net income before taxation and extraordinary item	15,500
Extraordinary item--proceeds from settlement with government for expropriation of business	1,000
Net income after extraordinary item	16,500
Taxes on income	(4,000)
Net income	$ 12,500

The following additional information is relevant to the preparation of the statement of cash flows:

1. Equipment with a net book value of $7,500 and original cost of $10,500 was sold for $7,500.
2. All sales made by the company are credit sales.
3. The company received cash dividends (from investments) amounting to $2,000, recorded as income in the income statement for the year ended December 31,1997.
4. The company received $1,000 in settlement from government for the expropriation of business, which is accounted for as an extraordinary item.
5. The company declared and paid dividends of $12,000 to its shareholders.
6. Interest expense for the year 1997 was $2,000, which was fully paid during the year. All administration and selling expenses incurred were paid during the year.
7. Income tax expense for the year 1997 was provided at $4,000, out of which the company paid $2,000 during 1997 as an estimate.

A worksheet can be prepared to ease the development of the cash flow statement, as follows:

Cash Flow Worksheet

	1997	1996	Change	Operating	Investing	Financing	Cash and equivalents
Cash and equivalents	3,000	1,000	2,000				2,000
Debtors	5,000	2,500	2,500	(2,500)			
Inventories	2,000	1,500	500	(500)			
Preoperative expenses	1,000	1,500	(500)	500			
Due from associates	19,000	19,000	0				
Property, plant, and equipment	7,000	16,500	(9,500)	2,000	7,500		
Accounts payable	5,000	12,500	7,500	(7,500)			
Income taxes payable	2,000	1,000	1,000	1,000			
Deferred taxes payable	3,000	2,000	1,000	1,000			
Share capital	6,500	6,500	0				
Retained earnings	20,500	20,000	500	10,500	2,000	(12,000)	--
				4,500	9,500	(12,000)	2,000

ABC (Middle East) Ltd.
Statement of Cash Flows
For the Year Ended December 31, 1997
(Direct method)

Cash flows from operating activities		
Cash receipts from customers	$ 27,500	
Cash paid to suppliers and employees	(20,000)	
Cash generated from operations	7,500	
Interest paid	(2,000)	
Income taxes paid	(2,000)	
Cash flow before extraordinary item	3,500	
Proceeds from settlement with government for appropriation of business*	1,000	
Net cash from operating activities		$ 4,500

Cash flows from investing activities		
Proceeds from the sale of equipment	7,500	
Dividends received	2,000	
Net cash flow from investing activities		9,500
Cash flows from financing activities		
Dividends paid	(12,000)	
Net increase in cash and cash equivalents		(12,000)
Net increase in cash and cash equivalents		2,000
Cash and cash equivalents, beginning of year		1,000
Cash and cash equivalents, end of year		$ 3,000

**Cash flows associated with extraordinary items should be classified as arising from operating, investing, or financing activities as appropriate and disclosed separately. Thus, part of the proceeds (i.e., those pertaining to property, plant and equipment) could be presented as cash flows from investing activities, if information needed to do so is available.*

Details of the computations of amounts shown in the statement of cash flows are as follows:

Cash received from customers during the year		
Credit sales	30,000	
Plus: Accounts receivable, beginning of year	2,500	
Less: Accounts receivable, end of year	(5,000)	
Cash received from customers during the year		$27,500
Cash paid to suppliers and employees		
Cost of sales	10,000	
Less: Inventory, beginning of year	(1,500)	
Plus: Inventory, end of year	2,000	
Plus: Accounts payable, beginning of year	12,500	
Less: Accounts payable, end of year	(5,000)	
Plus: Administrative and selling expenses paid	2,000	
Cash paid to suppliers and employees during the year		$20,000
Interest paid equals interest expense charged to the income statement (per additional information)		$ 2,000

Income taxes paid during the year

Tax expense during the year (comprising current and deferred portions)	4,000	
Plus: Beginning income taxes payable	1,000	
Plus: Beginning deferred taxes payable	2,000	
Less: Ending income taxes payable	(2,000)	
Less: Ending deferred taxes payable	(3,000)	
Cash paid toward income taxes		$ 2,000
Proceeds from settlement with government--expropriation of business (per additional information)		$ 1,000
Proceeds from sale of equipment (per additional information)		$ 7,500
Dividends received during 1997 (per additional information)		$ 2,000
Dividends paid during 1997 (per additional information)		$12,000

ABC (Middle East) Ltd.
Statement of Cash Flows
For the Year Ended December 31, 1997
(Indirect method)*

Cash flows from operating activities		
Net income before taxation and extraordinary item	$ 15,500	
Adjustments for:		
Depreciation of property, plant and equipment	2,000	
Amortization of preoperative expenses	500	
Investment income	(2,000)	
Interest expense	2,000	
Operating income before working capital changes*	18,000	
Increase in accounts receivable	(2,500)	
Increase in inventories	(500)	
Decrease in accounts payable	(7,500)	
Cash generated from operations	7,500	
Interest paid	(2,000)	
Income taxes paid	(2,000)	
Cash flow before extraordinary item	3,500	
Proceeds from government settlement--expropriation of business**	1,000	
Net cash from operating activities		4,500
Cash flows from investing activities		
Proceeds from sale of equipment	7,500	
Dividends received	2,000	
Net cash from investing activities		9,500

Cash flows from financing activities		
Dividends paid	(12,000)	
Net cash used in financing activities		(12,000)
Net increase in cash and cash equivalents		2,000
Cash and cash equivalents, beginning of year		1,000
Cash and cash equivalents, end of year		$ 3,000

* *The format of the statement of cash flows presented under the indirect method is in accordance with the presentation in the appendix of IAS 7; thus the wording "working capital changes" has been used instead of "changes in operating assets and liabilities," as recommended by the authors. For a detailed discussion on this subject, refer to the earlier section of this chapter.*

** *Cash flows associated with extraordinary items should be classified as arising from operating, investing, or financing activities as appropriate and disclosed separately. Thus, part of the proceeds (i.e., those pertaining to property, plant and equipment) could be presented as cash flows from investing activities, if information needed to do so is available.*

A Comprehensive Example of the Preparation of the Cash Flow Statement Using the T-Account Approach

Under a cash and cash equivalents basis, the changes in the cash account and any cash equivalent account is the bottom line figure of the statement of cash flows. Using the 1996 and 1997 balance sheets shown below, an increase of $17,000 can be computed. This is the difference between the totals for cash and treasury bills between 1996 and 1997 ($33,000 – $16,000).

When preparing the statement of cash flows using the direct method, gross cash inflows from revenues and gross cash outflows to suppliers and for expenses are presented in the operating activities section.

In preparing the reconciliation of net income to net cash flow from operating activities (indirect method), changes in all accounts other than cash and cash equivalents that are related to operations are additions to or deductions from net income to arrive at net cash provided by operating activities.

A T-account analysis may be helpful when preparing the statement of cash flows. A T-account is set up for each account, and beginning (1996) and ending (1997) balances are taken from the appropriate balance sheet. Additionally, a T-account for cash and cash equivalents from operating activities and a master or summary T-account of cash and cash equivalents should be used.

Example of preparing a statement of cash flows

The financial statements will be used to prepare the statement of cash flows.

Johnson Company
Balance Sheets
December 31, 1997 and 1996

	1997	1996
Assets		
Current assets		
Cash	$ 29,000	$ 10,000
Treasury bills	4,000	6,000
Accounts receivable--net	9,000	11,000
Inventory	14,000	9,000
Prepaid expenses	10,000	13,000
Total current assets	$ 66,000	$ 49,000
Noncurrent assets		
Investment in XYZ (35%)	16,000	14,000
Patent	5,000	6,000
Leased asset	5,000	-0-
Property, plant, and equipment	39,000	37,000
Less accumulated depreciation	(7,000)	(3,000)
Total assets	$124,000	$103,000
Liabilities		
Current liabilities		
Accounts payable	$ 2,000	$ 12,000
Notes payable--current	9,000	--
Interest payable	3,000	2,000
Dividends payable	5,000	2,000
Income taxes payable	2,000	1,000
Lease obligation	700	-0-
Total current liabilities	21,700	17,000
Noncurrent liabilities		
Deferred tax liability	9,000	6,000
Bonds payable	10,000	25,000
Lease obligation	4,300	-0-
Total liabilities	$ 45,000	$ 48,000
Stockholders' equity		
Common stock, $10 par value	$ 33,000	$ 26,000
Additional paid-in capital	16,000	3,000
Retained earnings	30,000	26,000
Total stockholders' equity	$ 79,000	$ 55,000
Total liabilities and stockholders' equity	$124,000	$103,000

Johnson Company
Statement of Earnings
For the Year Ended December 31, 1997

Sales	$100,000
Other income	8,000
	$108,000
Cost of goods sold, excluding depreciation	60,000
Selling, general, and administrative expenses	12,000
Depreciation	8,000
Amortization of patents	1,000
Interest expense	2,000
	$ 83,000
Income before taxes	$ 25,000
Income taxes (36%)	9,000
Net income	$ 16,000

Additional information (relating to 1997)

1. Equipment costing $6,000 with a book value of $2,000 was sold for $5,000.
2. The company received a $3,000 dividend from its investment in XYZ, accounted for under the equity method and recorded income from the investment of $5,000, which is included in other income.
3. The company issued 200 shares of common stock for $5,000.
4. The company signed a note payable for $9,000.
5. Equipment was purchased for $8,000.
6. The company converted $15,000 bonds payable into 500 shares of common stock. The book value method was used to record the transaction.
7. A dividend of $12,000 was declared.
8. Equipment was leased on December 31, 1997. The principal portion of the first payment due December 31, 1998 is $700.

Summary of Cash and Cash Equivalents

	Inflows	Outflows	
(d)	5,000		
		8,000	(g)
(h)	5,000	9,000	(i)
(n)	9,000		
(s)	15,000		
	34,000	17,000	
		17,000	Net increase in cash
	34,000	34,000	

Cash and Cash Equivalents--oper. act.

	Debit	Credit	
(a)	16,000		
(b)	8,000		
(c)	1,000	3,000	(d)
(e)	3,000	5,000	(f)
(f)	3,000		
(j)	2,000		
(l)	3,000		
		5,000	(k)
(o)	1,000	10,000	(m)
(p)	1,000		
	38,000	23,000	
		15,000	(s)
	38,000	38,000	

Accounts Receivable (net)

Debit	Credit
11,000	
	2,000 (j)
9,000	

Inventory

Debit	Credit
9,000	
(k) 5,000	
14,000	

Prepaid Expenses

Debit	Credit
13,000	
	3,000 (l)
10,000	

Investment in XYZ

Debit	Credit
14,000	
(f) 5,000	3,000 (f)
16,000	

Patent

Debit	Credit
6,000	
	1,000 (c)
5,000	

Leased Equipment

Debit	Credit
(r) 5,000	
5,000	

Prop., Plant, & Equip.

Debit	Credit
37,000	
	6,000 (d)
(g) 8,000	
39,000	

Accumulated Depr.

Debit	Credit
	3,000
	8,000 (b)
(d) 4,000	
	7,000

Accounts Payable

Debit	Credit
	12,000
(m) 10,000	
	2,000

Notes Payable

Debit	Credit
	9,000 (n)
	9,000

Interest Payable

Debit	Credit
	2,000
(o) 1,000	2,000 (o)
	3,000

Dividends Payable

Debit	Credit
	2,000
(i) 9,000	12,000 (i)
	5,000

Income Taxes Payable

Debit	Credit
	1,000
(p) 5,000	6,000 (p)
	2,000

Deferred Tax Liability

Debit	Credit
	6,000
	3,000 (e)
	9,000

Bonds Payable

Debit	Credit
	25,000
(q) 15,000	
	10,000

Lease Obligation

Debit	Credit
	5,000 (r)
	5,000

Common Stock

Debit	Credit
	26,000
	2,000 (h)
	5,000 (q)
	33,000

Addl. Paid-in Capital

Debit	Credit
	3,000
	3,000 (h)
	10,000 (q)
	16,000

Retained Earnings

Debit	Credit
	26,000
	16,000 (a)
(i) 12,000	
	30,000

Explanation of entries

a. Cash and Cash Equivalents--Operating activities is debited for $16,000, and credited to Retained Earnings. This represents the net income figure.

b. Depreciation is not a cash flow; however, depreciation expense was deducted to arrive at net income. Therefore, Accumulated Depreciation is credited and Cash and Cash Equivalents--Operating activities is debited.

c. Amortization of patents is another expense not requiring cash; therefore, Cash and Cash Equivalents--Operating activities is debited and Patent is credited.

d. The sale of equipment (additional information, item 1) resulted in a $3,000 gain. The gain is computed by comparing the book value of $2,000 with the sales price of $5,000. Cash proceeds of $5,000 are an inflow of cash. Since the gain was included in net income, it must be deducted from net income to determine cash provided by operating activities. This is necessary to avoid counting the $3,000 gain both in cash provided by operating activities and in investing activities. The following entry would have been made on the date of sale:

Cash	5,000	
Accumulated depreciation (6,000 – 2,000)	4,000	
Property, plant, and equipment		6,000
Gain on sale of equipment (5,000 – 2,000)		3,000

Adjust the T-accounts as follows: debit Summary of Cash and Cash Equivalents for $5,000, debit Accumulated Depreciation for $4,000, credit Property, Plant, and Equipment for $6,000, and credit Cash and Cash Equivalents--Operating activities for $3,000.

e. The $3,000 increase in Deferred Income Taxes must be added to income from operations. Although the $3,000 was deducted as part of income tax expense in determining net income, it did not require an outflow of cash. Therefore, debit Cash and Cash Equivalents--Operating activities and credit Deferred Taxes.

f. Item 2 under the additional information indicates that the investment in XYZ is accounted for under the equity method. The investment in XYZ had a net increase of $2,000 during the year after considering the receipt of a $3,000 dividend. Dividends received (an inflow of cash) would reduce the investment in XYZ, while the equity in the income of XYZ would increase the investment without affecting cash. In order for the T-account to balance, a debit of $5,000 must have been made, indicating earnings of that amount. The journal entries would have been

Cash (dividend received)	3,000	
Investment in XYZ		3,000
Investment in XYZ	5,000	
Equity in earnings of XYZ		5,000

The dividend received ($3,000) is an inflow of cash, while the equity earnings are not. Debit Investment in XYZ for $5,000, credit Cash and Cash Equivalents--Operating activities for $5,000, debit Cash and Cash Equivalents--Operating activities for $3,000, and credit Investment in XYZ for $3,000.

g. The Property, Plant, and Equipment account increased because of the purchase of $8,000 (additional information, item 5). The purchase of assets is an outflow of cash. Debit Property, Plant, and Equipment for $8,000 and credit Summary of Cash and Cash Equivalents.

h. The company sold 200 shares of common stock during the year (additional information, item 3). The entry for the sale of stock was

Cash	5,000	
Common stock (200 shares x $10)		2,000
Additional paid-in capital		3,000

This transaction resulted in an inflow of cash. Debit Summary of Cash and Cash Equivalents $5,000, credit Common Stock $2,000, and credit Additional Paid-in Capital $3,000.

i. Dividends of $12,000 were declared (additional information, item 7). Only $9,000 was actually paid in cash resulting in an ending balance of $9,000 in the Dividends Payable account. Therefore, the following entries were made during the year:

Retained Earnings	12,000	
Dividends Payable		12,000
Dividends Payable	9,000	
Cash		9,000

These transactions result in an outflow of cash. Debit Retained Earnings $12,000 and credit Dividends Payable $12,000. Additionally, debit Dividends Payable $9,000 and credit Summary of Cash and Cash Equivalents $9,000 to indicate the cash dividends paid during the year.

j. Accounts Receivable (net) decreased by $2,000. This is added as an adjustment to net income in the computation of cash provided by operating activities. The decrease of $2,000 means that an additional $2,000 cash was collected on account above and beyond the sales reported in the income statement. Debit Cash and Cash Equivalents--Operating activities and credit Accounts Receivable for $2,000.

k. Inventories increased by $5,000. This is subtracted as an adjustment to net income in the computation of cash provided by operating activities. Although $5,000 additional cash was spent to increase inventories, this expenditure is not reflected in accrual-basis cost of goods sold. Debit Inventory and credit Cash and Cash Equivalents--Operating activities for $5,000.

l. Prepaid Expenses decreased by $3,000. This is added back to net income in the computation of cash provided by operating activities. The decrease means that no cash was spent when incurring the related expense. The cash was spent when the prepaid assets were purchased, not when they were expended on the income statement. Debit Cash and Cash Equivalents--Operating activities and credit Prepaid Expenses for $3,000.

m. Accounts Payable decreased by $10,000. This is subtracted as an adjustment to net income. The decrease of $10,000 means that an additional $10,000 of purchases were paid for in cash; therefore, income was not affected but cash was decreased. Debit Accounts Payable and credit Cash and Cash Equivalents--Operating activities for $10,000.

n. Notes Payable increased by $9,000 (additional information, item 4). This is an inflow of cash and would be included in the financing activities. Debit Summary of Cash and Cash Equivalents and credit Notes Payable for $9,000.

o. Interest Payable increased by $1,000, but interest expense from the income statement was $2,000. Therefore, although $2,000 was expensed, only $1,000 cash was paid ($2,000 expense – $1,000 increase in interest payable). Debit Cash and Cash

Equivalents--Operating activities for $1,000, debit Interest Payable for $1,000, and credit Interest Payable for $2,000.

p. The following entry was made to record the incurrence of the tax liability:

Income tax expense	9,000	
Income taxes payable		6,000
Deferred tax liability		3,000

Therefore, $9,000 was deducted in arriving at net income. The $3,000 credit to Deferred Income Taxes was accounted for in entry (e) above. The $6,000 credit to Taxes Payable does not, however, indicate that $6,000 cash was paid for taxes. Since Taxes Payable increased $1,000, only $5,000 must have been paid and $1,000 remains unpaid. Debit Cash and Cash Equivalents--Operating activities for $1,000, debit Income Taxes Payable for $5,000, and credit Income Taxes Payable for $6,000.

q. Item 6 under the additional information indicates that $15,000 of bonds payable were converted to common stock. This is a **noncash** financing activity and should be reported in a separate schedule. The following entry was made to record the transaction:

Bonds payable	15,000	
Common stock (500 shares x $10 par)		5,000
Additional paid-in capital		10,000

Adjust the T-accounts with a debit to Bonds Payable, $15,000; a credit to Common Stock, $5,000; and a credit to Additional Paid-in Capital, $10,000.

r. Item 8 under the additional information indicates that leased equipment was acquired on the last day of 1997. This is also a noncash financing activity and should be reported in a separate schedule. The following entry was made to record the lease transaction:

Leased asset	5,000	
Lease obligation		5,000

s. The cash and cash equivalents from operations ($15,000) is transferred to the Summary of Cash and Cash Equivalents.

Since all of the changes in the noncash accounts have been accounted for and the balance in the Summary of Cash and Cash Equivalents account of $17,000 is the amount of the year-to-year increase in cash and cash equivalents, the formal statement may now be prepared. The following classified SCF is prepared under the direct method and includes the reconciliation of net income to net cash provided by operating activities. The T-account, Cash and Cash Equivalents--Operating activities, is used in the preparation of this reconciliation. The calculations for gross receipts and gross payments needed for the direct method are shown below.

Johnson Company
Statement of Cash Flows
For the Year Ended December 31, 1997

Cash flow from operating activities		
Cash received from customers	$102,000 (a)	
Dividends received	3,000	
Cash provided by operating activities		$105,000
Cash paid to suppliers	$ 75,000 (b)	
Cash paid for expenses	9,000 (c)	
Interest paid	1,000 (d)	
Taxes paid	5,000 (e)	
Cash paid for operating activities		(90,000)
Net cash flow provided by operating activities		$ 15,000
Cash flows from investing activities		
Sale of equipment	5,000	
Purchase of property, plant, and equipment	(8,000)	
Net cash used in investing activities		(3,000)
Cash flow from financing activities		
Sale of common stock	$ 5,000	
Increase in notes payable	9,000	
Dividends paid	(9,000)	
Net cash provided by financing activities		5,000
Net increase in cash and cash equivalents		$ 17,000
Cash and cash equivalents at beginning of year		16,000
Cash and cash equivalents at end of year		$ 33,000

Calculation of amounts for operating activities section of Johnson Co.'s statement of cash flows

(a) Net sales + Beginning AR – Ending AR = Cash received from customers

$100,000 + $11,000 – $9,000 = $102,000

(b) Cost of goods sold + Beginning AP – Ending AP + Ending inventory – Beginning inventory = Cash paid to suppliers

$60,000 + $12,000 – $2,000 + $14,000 – $9,000 = $75,000

(c) Operating expenses + Ending prepaid expenses – Beginning prepaid expenses – Depreciation expense (and other noncash operating expenses) = Cash paid for operating expenses

$12,000 + $10,000 – $13,000 = $9,000

(d) Interest expense + Beginning interest payable – Ending interest payable = Interest paid

$2,000 + $2,000 – $3,000 = $1,000

(e) Income taxes + Beginning income taxes payable – Ending income taxes payable + Beginning deferred income taxes – Ending deferred income taxes = Taxes paid

$9,000 + $1,000 – $2,000 + $6,000 – $9,000 = $5,000

Reconciliation of net income to net cash provided by operating activities

Net income	$16,000	
Add (deduct) items not using (providing) cash:		
Depreciation	8,000	
Amortization	1,000	
Gain on sale of equipment	(3,000)	
Increase in deferred taxes	3,000	
Equity in XYZ	(2,000)	
Decrease in accounts receivable	2,000	
Increase in inventory	(5,000)	
Decrease in prepaid expenses	3,000	
Decrease in accounts payable	(10,000)	
Increase in interest payable	1,000	
Increase in income taxes payable	1,000	
Net cash flow provided by operating activities		$15,000

(The reconciliation above is required by US GAAP when the direct method is used, but there is no equivalent requirement under the international accounting standards. The reconciliation above illustrates the presentation of the operating section of the cash flow statement when the indirect method is used. The remaining sections [i.e., the investing and financing sections] of the statement of cash flows are common to both methods, hence have not been presented above.)

Schedule of noncash transactions (to be reported in the footnotes)

Conversion of bonds into common stock	$15,000
Acquisition of leased equipment	$ 5,000

Disclosure of accounting policy

For purposes of the statement of cash flows, the company considers all highly liquid debt instruments purchased with original maturities of 3 months or less to be cash equivalents.

Statement of Cash Flows for Consolidated Entities

A consolidated statement of cash flows must be presented when a complete set of consolidated financial statements is issued. The consolidated statement of cash flows would be the last statement to be prepared, as the information to prepare it will come from the other consolidated statements (consolidated balance sheet, income statement, and statement of retained earnings). The preparation of these other consolidated statements is discussed in Chapter 10.

The preparation of a consolidated statement of cash flows involves the same analysis and procedures as the statement for an individual entity, with a few additional items. The direct or indirect method of presentation may be used. When the indirect method is used, the additional noncash transactions relating to the business combination, such as the differential amortization, must also be reversed. Furthermore, all transfers to affiliates must be eliminated, as they do not represent a cash inflow or outflow of the consolidated entity.

All unrealized intercompany profits should have been eliminated in preparation of the other statements; thus, no additional entry of this sort should be required. Any income allocated to noncontrolling parties would need to be added back, as it would have been eliminated in computing consolidated net income but does not represent a true cash outflow. Finally, any dividend payments should be recorded as cash outflows in the financing activities section.

In preparing the operating activities section of the statement by the indirect method following a purchase business combination, the changes in assets and liabilities related to operations since acquisition should be derived by comparing the consolidated balance sheet as of the date of acquisition with the year-end consolidated balance sheet. These changes will be combined with those for the acquiring company up to the date of acquisition as adjustments to net income. The effects due to the acquisition of these assets and liabilities are reported under investing activities. Under the pooling-of-interests method the combination is treated as having occurred at the beginning of the year. Thus, the changes in assets and liabilities related to operations should be those derived by comparing the beginning of the year balance sheet amounts on a consolidated basis with the end of the year consolidated balance sheet amounts.

5 CASH, RECEIVABLES, AND FINANCIAL INSTRUMENTS

PERSPECTIVE AND ISSUES

Accounting for cash and for receivables has been fairly well settled for many years, although as new and innovative financing arrangements evolve, such as receivables factoring with recourse, accounting practice must also evolve. To the extent that these developments raise issues of recognition, measurement, or derecognition, the yet unresolved parts of the International Accounting Standards Committee's financial instruments project present an impediment. While the exposure drafts that preceded the recently promulgated standard on financial instruments did address these matters, the final standard merely contains guidance on presentation and disclosure issues, leaving the more daunting questions yet to be resolved.

Despite its limitations, IAS 32 does deal with many important matters and in some specific areas is more definitive and conceptually consistent than its US counterpart, which preceded IAS 32 by several years and which, like IAS 32, was the result of a bifurcation that has left recognition, measurement, and derecognition concerns still to be addressed.

IAS 32, first effective in 1996, embraces the traditional, but not always implemented, financial reporting approach of substance over form, and accordingly will result in some financial instruments that had previously been categorized as equity being reclassified as liabilities. It also requires the disaggregation of compound financial instruments, with appropriate display of each constituent element. The standard greatly expands the disclosure requirements, which will attach to all financial instruments, including information about concentrations and types of risk and the fair values of all financial assets as well as liabilities.

More recently, the IASC has published a comprehensive discussion paper which addresses recognition, derecognition, and measurement issues applicable to all financial instruments (and to some nonfinancial commodities as well). It is expected that this will result in one or more proposals which essentially will endorse fair value accounting for financial assets and liabilities, eschew the special hedge accounting which has developed under existing standards and which is central to the debate over accounting for so-called derivatives, and adopt a "financial components" approach to replace the formerly espoused "risks and rewards" approach. In recognition of the substantial impact that this document is expected to have on evolving accounting standards, the major issues and recommendations set forth in this discussion paper are presented later in this chapter.

Sources of IAS
IAS 32
Discussion Paper, Accounting for Financial Assets and Financial Liabilities

DEFINITIONS OF TERMS

Accounting loss. Loss that may have to be recognized due to credit and market risk as a direct result of the rights and obligations of a financial instrument.

Accounts receivable. Amounts due from customers for goods or services provided in the normal course of business operations.

Aging the accounts. Procedure for the computation of the adjustment for uncollectible accounts receivable based on the length of time the end-of-period outstanding accounts have been unpaid.

Assignment. Formal procedure for collateralization of borrowings through the use of accounts receivable. It normally does not involve debtor notification.

Carrying amount (value). Amount at which marketable equity securities are being carried, net of allowances. This amount is fair value.

Cash. Coins and currency on hand and balances in checking accounts available for immediate withdrawal.

Cash equivalents. Short-term, highly liquid investments that are readily convertible to known amounts of cash. Examples include treasury bills, commercial paper, and money market funds.

Cost (of a security). Original purchase price plus all costs incidental to the acquisition (e.g., brokerage fees and taxes) unless a new cost basis is assigned as a result of a decline in market value which is other than temporary.

Credit risk. Possibility that a loss may occur from the failure of another party to perform according to the terms of a contract.

Current assets. Assets that are reasonably expected to be realized in cash or sold or consumed within a year or within the normal operating cycle of the entity.

Equity instrument. Any contract that evidences a residual interest in the assets of an enterprise after deducting all its liabilities.

Factoring. Outright sale of accounts receivable to a third-party financing entity. The sale may be with or without recourse.

Fair value. Amount for which an asset could be exchanged, or a liability settled, between knowledgeable, willing parties in an arm's-length transaction.

Financial asset. Any asset that is

1. Cash

2. A contractual right to receive cash or another financial asset from another enterprise
3. A contractual right to exchange financial instruments with another enterprise under conditions that are potentially favorable
4. An equity instrument of another enterprise

Financial instrument. Any contract that gives rise to both a financial asset of one enterprise and a financial liability or equity instrument of another enterprise.

Financial instrument with off-balance-sheet risk. Financial instrument that has a risk of accounting loss if the risk to the entity may exceed the amount recognized as an asset, if any, or if the ultimate obligation may exceed the amount that is recognized as a liability in the statement of financial position.

Financial liability. Any liability that is a contractual obligation (1) to deliver cash or another financial asset to another enterprise, or (2) the obligation to exchange financial instruments with another enterprise under conditions that are potentially unfavorable.

Market risk. Possibility that future changes in market prices may make a financial instrument less valuable.

Market value. Amount obtainable from a sale, or payable on acquisition, of a financial instrument in an active market.

Marketable equity securities. Instruments representing actual ownership interest, or the rights to buy or sell such interests, which are actively traded or listed on a national securities exchange.

Monetary financial assets and financial liabilities. Financial assets and financial liabilities to be received or paid in fixed or determinable amounts of money.

Net realizable value. Amount of cash anticipated to be produced in the normal course of business from an asset, net of any direct costs of the conversion into cash.

Operating cycle. Average time between the acquisition of materials or services and the final cash realization from the sale of products or services.

Other-than-temporary decline. Downward movement in the value of a marketable equity security for which there are known causes. The decline indicates the remote likelihood of a price recovery.

Percentage-of-sales method. Procedure for computing the adjustment for uncollectible accounts receivable based on the historical relationship between bad debts and gross credit sales.

Pledging. Process of using an asset as collateral for borrowings. It generally refers to borrowings secured by accounts receivable.

Realized gain (loss). Difference between the cost or adjusted cost of a marketable security and the net selling price realized by the seller which is to be included in the determination of net income in the period of the sale.

Recourse. Right of the transferee (factor) of accounts receivable to seek recovery for an uncollectible account from the transferor. It is often limited to specific conditions.

Risk of accounting loss. Includes (1) the possibility that a loss may occur from the failure of another party to perform according to the terms of a contract (credit risk), (2) the possibility that future changes in market prices may make a financial instrument less valuable (market risk), and (3) the risk of theft or physical loss.

Short-term investments. Securities or other assets acquired with excess cash, having ready marketability and intended by management to be liquidated, if necessary, within the current operating cycle.

Temporary decline. Downward fluctuation in the value of a marketable equity security that has no known cause which suggests that the decline is of a permanent nature.

CONCEPTS, RULES, AND EXAMPLES

Cash

The promulgated international accounting standards for cash are, at present, rather minimal. While the yet-to-be-developed standard on financial instruments recognition and measurement will doubtless address cash (which does meet the definition of a financial instrument according to IAS 32), at the present time the only real guidance is that offered in IAS 5, *Information to be Disclosed in Financial Statements*; IAS 7, *Cash Flow Statements*; and IAS 13, *Presentation of Current Assets and Current Liabilities*.

As defined in IAS 5, cash includes cash on hand as well as current and other accounts with banks. Cash that is not immediately available for use should, according to the standard, be given separate disclosure. This wording, unfortunately, leaves the issue of formal balance sheet presentation somewhat ambiguous: Would, for example, footnote discussion of pertinent restrictions be adequate if restricted cash were included with unrestricted cash in the financial statement itself? As a practical matter, common practice (as well as national standards in the United States and elsewhere) is to exclude such items from the caption "cash" as presented on the balance sheet, reserving that designation for funds that are immediately accessible.

IAS 13 stipulates that cash and bank balances available for current operations should be included in current assets, assuming that the entity is presenting a classified balance sheet, of course. If the cash is subject to restrictions, the cash may be included in current assets only if the restrictions are set to lapse within a 1-year period.

Given the limited guidance offered by the standard, it is the authors' belief that to be included as cash in the balance sheet, funds must be represented by actual coins and currency on hand or demand deposits available without restriction. It must furthermore be management's intention that the cash be available for current purposes. For example, cash in a demand deposit account, which is being held for the retirement of long-term debts not maturing currently, should be excluded from current assets and shown as a noncurrent investment. This would apply only if management's intention was clear; it would not otherwise be necessary to segregate from the general cash account the funds that presumably will be needed for a scheduled debt retirement, as those funds could presumably be obtained from alternative sources, including new borrowings.

With the increased availability to, and popularity with, corporate investors of such short-term, safe earning assets as NOW accounts and money market funds, it has become more common to see the caption "cash and cash equivalents" in the balance sheet. This term includes other forms of near-cash as well as demand deposits and liquid, short-term securities. To justify inclusion, cash equivalents must be available upon demand.

IAS 7 defines these as short-term, highly liquid investments readily convertible into a known amount of cash which are subject to an insignificant risk of changes in value. The reasonable, if arbitrary, limit of 3 months is placed on the maturity dates of any instruments acquired to be part of cash equivalents. (This is, not coincidentally, the same limit applied by the US standard on cash flow statements, SFAS 95, the promulgation of which preceded the revision of IAS 7 by some years.)

Compensating balances are cash balances which are not immediately accessible by the owner. Pursuant to borrowing arrangements with lenders, an entity will often be required to maintain a minimum amount of cash on deposit (compensating balance). The purpose of this balance is to increase the yield on the loan to the lender. Since most organizations will need to maintain a certain working balance in their cash accounts simply to handle routine transactions and to cushion against unforeseen fluctuations in the demand for cash, borrowers will often not find compensating balance arrangements objectionable and may well have sufficient liquidity to maintain these with little hardship being incurred. They may even be viewed as comprising "rotating" normal cash balances which are flowing into and out of the bank on a regular basis. Notwithstanding how these are viewed by the debtor, however, the fact is that compensating balances are not available for unrestricted use and penalties will result if they are used rather than being left intact, as called for. Therefore, the portion of an entity's cash account that is a compensating balance must be segregated and shown as a noncurrent asset if the related borrowings are noncurrent liabilities. If the borrowings are current liabilities, it is acceptable to show the compensating balance as a separately captioned current asset, but under no circumstances should these be included in the caption "cash."

In some jurisdictions, certain cash deposits, such as savings accounts or corporate time deposits, are held by banks subject to terms and conditions that give the banks the right, which is not always exercised, to delay honoring withdrawal requests for a stated period of time, such as 7 days or 30 days. The reason for such rules is to discourage panic withdrawals and to give the depository institution adequate time to liquidate investments in an orderly fashion. Cash in savings accounts subject to a statutory notification requirement and cash in certificates of deposit maturing during the current operating cycle or within 1 year may be included as current assets, but as with compensating balances, should be separately captioned in the balance sheet to avoid the misleading implication that these funds are available immediately upon demand. Typically, such items will be included in the short-term investments caption, but these could also be labeled as time deposits or restricted cash deposits.

Petty cash and other imprest cash accounts are usually presented in financial statements with other cash accounts. Due to materiality considerations, these need not be set forth in a separate caption, although that may be done if desired.

Receivables

Receivables include trade receivables, which are amounts due from customers for goods sold or services performed in the normal course of business, as well as such other categories of receivables as notes receivable, trade acceptances, third-party instruments, and amounts due from officers, stockholders, employees, or affiliated companies.

Notes receivable are formalized obligations evidenced by written promissory notes. The latter categories of receivables generally arise from cash advances but could develop from sales of merchandise or the provision of services. The basic nature of amounts due from trade customers is often different from that of balances receivable from related parties, such as employees or stockholders. Thus, the general practice is to insist that the various classes of receivables be identified separately either on the face of the balance sheet or in the notes. The tabulation of receivables in IAS 7 suggests that this is a requirement under international standards, except that notes are not distinguished from open (trade) accounts and presumably may be commingled in the balance sheet.

International accounting standards do not address explicitly the recognition or measurement of receivables as a discrete topic, although presumably the forthcoming financial instruments' recognition and measurement standard will do so. However, a number of international standards do allude to the accounting for receivables. For example, IAS 18, *Revenue Recognition*, addresses the timing of revenue recognition, and hence also the matter of when the existence of receivables may be acknowledged. None of these address the key measurement issues.

For several reasons, receivables should be presented at net realizable amounts (i.e., amounts realistically anticipated to be collectible). First, the matching concept suggests that all costs of generating revenue be accrued and reported in the same period as the related revenue. By accruing an estimate of the amount of receivables due at the balance sheet date that are not likely to be collected, the matching objective will be largely achieved relative to the associated income statement. Second, the general concept of conservatism, which underlies much of financial reporting, demands that assets which are presented as representing claims to cash not be reported at amounts in excess of that which will ultimately be collected.

If the gross amount of receivables includes unearned interest or finance charges, these should be deducted in arriving at the net amount to be presented in the balance sheet. Deductions should be taken for amounts estimated to be uncollectible and also for the estimated returns, allowances, and other discounts to be taken by customers prior to or at the time of payment. In practice, the deductions that would be made for estimated returns, allowances, and trade discounts are usually deemed to be immaterial, and such adjustments are rarely made. However, if it is known that sales are often recorded for merchandise that is shipped on approval and available data suggests that a sizable proportion of such sales are returned by the customers, these estimated future returns must be accrued. Similarly, material amounts of anticipated discounts and allowances should be recorded in the period of sale.

The foregoing comments apply where revenues are recorded at the gross amount of the sale and subsequent sales discounts are recorded as debits (contra revenues). An alternative manner of recording revenue, which does away with any need to estimate future discounts, is to record the initial sale at the net amount; that is, at the amount that will be remitted if customers take advantage of the available discount terms. If customers pay the gross amount later (they fail to take the discounts), this additional revenue is recorded as income when it is remitted. The net method of recording sales, however, is rarely encountered in practice.

Bad Debts Expense

Whereas accrual of anticipated sales returns, allowances, and discounts is usually not required because of materiality, the recording of anticipated uncollectible amounts is almost always necessary. The direct write-off method, in which a receivable is charged off only when it is clear that it cannot be collected, is unsatisfactory since it results in a significant mismatching of revenues and expenses. Proper matching can be achieved only if bad debts expense is recorded in the same fiscal period as the revenues to which they are related. Since this expense is not known with certainty, an estimate must be made.

There are two popular estimation techniques. The percentage-of-sales method is principally oriented toward achieving the best possible matching of revenues and expenses. Aging the accounts is more oriented toward the presentation of the correct net realizable value of the trade receivables in the balance sheet. Both methods are acceptable and widely employed.

Percentage-of-sales method of estimating bad debts. Historical data are analyzed to ascertain the relationship between credit sales and bad debts. The derived percentage is then applied to the current period's sales revenues to arrive at the appropriate debit to bad debts expense for the year. The offsetting credit is made to allowance for uncollectibles. When specific customer accounts are subsequently identified as uncollectible, they are written off against this allowance.

Example of percentage-of-sales method

Total credit sales for year:	$7,500,000
Bad debt ratio from prior years or other data source:	1.75% of sales
Computed year-end adjustment for bad debts expense:	$ 131,250 ($7,500,000 x .0175)

The entry required is

Bad debts expense	131,250	
Allowance for uncollectibles		131,250

Note that the foregoing entry assumes that no bad debts expense has yet been recognized with respect to the year's credit sales. If some such expense has already been recognized, as a consequence of interim accruals, for example, the final adjusting entry would be suitably reduced.

Aging method of estimating bad debts. An analysis is prepared of the customer receivables at the balance sheet date. These accounts are categorized by the number of days or months they have remained outstanding. Based on the entity's past experience or on other available statistics, historical bad debts percentages are applied to each of these aggregate amounts, with larger percentages being applicable to the older accounts. The end result of this process is a computed total dollar amount that is the proper balance in the allowance for uncollectibles at the balance sheet date. As a result of the difference between the previous years' adjustments to the allowance for uncollectibles and the actual write-offs made to the account, there will usually be a balance in this account. Thus, the adjustment needed will be an amount other than that computed by the aging.

Example of the aging method

	Age of accounts			
	Under 30 days	*30-90 days*	*Over 90 days*	*Total*
Gross receivables	$1,100,000	$425,000	$360,000	
Bad debt percentage	0.5%	2.5%	15%	
Provision required	$5,500	$10,625	$54,000	$70,125

The credit balance required in the allowance account is $70,125. Assuming that a debit balance of $58,250 already exists in the allowance account (from charge-offs during the year), the necessary entry is

Bad debts expense	128,375	
Allowance for uncollectibles		128,375

Both of the estimation techniques should produce approximately the same result. This will be true especially over the course of a number of years. Nonetheless, it must be recognized that these adjustments are based on estimates and will never be totally accurate. When facts subsequently become available to indicate that the amount provided as an allowance for uncollectible accounts was incorrect, an adjustment classified as a change in estimate is made. According to IAS 8, adjustments of this nature are never considered fundamental errors subject to subsequent correction or restatement. Only if an actual clerical or mechanical error occurred in the recording of allowance for uncollectibles would correction as a fundamental error be warranted.

Pledging, Assigning, and Factoring Receivables

An organization can alter the timing of cash flows resulting from sales to its customers by using its accounts receivable as collateral for borrowings or by selling the receivables outright. A wide variety of arrangements can be structured by the borrower and lender, but the most common are pledging, assignment, and factoring. Although this topic has not yet been addressed formally by international accounting standards (it will be during the second phase of the IASC's financial instruments project), general guidance will be presented here.

Pledging of receivables. Pledging is an agreement whereby accounts receivable are used as collateral for loans. Generally, the lender has limited rights to inspect the borrower's records to achieve assurance that the receivables do exist. The customers whose accounts have been pledged are not aware of this event, and their payments are still remitted to the original obligee. The pledged accounts merely serve as security to the lender, giving comfort that sufficient assets exist that will generate cash flows adequate in amount and timing to repay the debt. However, the debt is paid by the borrower whether or not the pledged receivables are collected and whether or not the pattern of such collections matches the payments due on the debt.

The only accounting issue relating to pledging is that of adequate disclosure. The accounts receivable, which remain assets of the borrowing entity, continue to be shown as current assets in its financial statements but must be identified as having been pledged. This identification can be accomplished either parenthetically or by footnote disclosures. Similarly, the related debt should be identified as having been secured by the receivables.

Example of proper disclosure for pledged receivables

Current assets:	
Accounts receivable, net of allowance for doubtful accounts of $600,000 ($3,500,000 of which has been pledged as collateral for bank loans)	8,450,000
Current liabilities:	
Bank loans payable (secured by pledged accounts receivable)	2,700,000

A more common practice is to include the disclosure in the notes to the financial statements.

Assignment of receivables. The assignment of accounts receivable is a more formalized transfer of the asset to the lending institution. The lender will make an investigation of the specific receivables that are being proposed for assignment and will approve those that are deemed to be worthy as collateral. Customers are not usually aware that their accounts have been assigned and they continue to forward their payments to the original obligee. In some cases, the assignment agreement requires that collection proceeds be delivered to the lender immediately. The borrower is, however, the primary obligor and is required to make timely payment on the debt whether or not the receivables are collected as anticipated. The borrowing is with recourse, and the general credit of the borrower is pledged to the payment of the debt.

Since the lender knows that not all the receivables will be collected on a timely basis by the borrower, only a fraction of the face value of the receivables will be advanced as a loan to the borrower. Typically, this amount ranges from 70 to 90%, depending on the credit history and collection experience of the borrower.

Assigned accounts receivable remain the assets of the borrower and continue to be presented in its financial statements, with appropriate disclosure of the assignment similar to that illustrated for pledging. Prepaid finance charges would be debited to a prepaid expense account and amortized to expense over the period to which the charges apply.

Factoring of receivables. This category of financing is the most significant in terms of accounting implications. Factoring traditionally has involved the outright sale of receivables to a financing institution known as a factor. These arrangements involved (1) notification to the customer to forward future payments to the factor, and (2) the transfer of receivables without recourse. The factor assumes the risk of an inability to collect. Thus, once a factoring arrangement was completed, the entity had no further involvement with the accounts except for a return of merchandise.

The classical variety of factoring provides two financial services to the business: (1) it permits the entity to obtain cash earlier, and (2) the risk of bad debts is transferred to the factor. The factor is compensated for each of the services. Interest is charged based on the anticipated length of time between the date the factoring is consummated and the expected collection date of the receivables sold, and a fee is charged based on the factor's anticipated bad debt losses.

Some companies continue to factor receivables as a means of transferring the risk of bad debts but leave the cash on deposit with the factor until the weighted-average due date of the receivables, thereby avoiding interest charges. This arrangement is still referred to as factoring, since the customer receivables have been sold. However, the borrowing entity does not receive cash but instead has created a new receivable, usually captioned "due from factor." In contrast to the original customer receivables, this receivable is essentially riskless and will be presented in the balance sheet without a deduction for estimated uncollectibles.

Another variation is known as factoring with recourse. Some entities had such a poor history of uncollectible accounts that factors were willing to purchase their accounts only if a substantial fee were collected to compensate for the risk. When the company believed that the receivables were of better quality, a way to avoid excessive factoring fees was to sell these receivables with recourse. This variation of factoring was really an assignment of receivables with notification to the customers. Factoring does transfer title. Where there is a no recourse provision, the removal of these receivables from the borrower's balance sheet is clearly warranted.

Merchandise returns will normally be the responsibility of the original vendor, who must then make the appropriate settlement with the factor. To protect against the possibility of merchandise returns that diminish the total of receivables to be collected, very often a factoring arrangement will not advance the full amount of the factored receivables (less any interest and factoring fee deductions). Rather, the factor will retain a certain fraction of the total proceeds relating to the portion of sales that are anticipated to be returned by customers. This sum is known as the factor's **holdback**. When merchandise is returned to the borrower, an entry is made offsetting the receivable from the factor. At the end of the return privilege period, any remaining holdback will become due and payable to the borrower.

Examples of journal entries to be made by the borrower in a factoring situation

1. Thirsty Corp. on July 1, 1996, enters into an agreement with Rich Company to sell a group of its receivables without recourse. A total face value of $200,000 accounts receivable (against which a 5% allowance had been recorded) are involved. The factor will charge 20% interest computed on the (weighted) average time to maturity of the receivables of 36 days plus a 3% fee. A 5% holdback will also be retained.
2. Thirsty's customers return for credit $4,800 of merchandise.
3. The customer return privilege period expires and the remaining holdback is paid to the transferor.

The entries required are as follows:

1.	Cash	180,055	
	Allowance for bad debts (200,000 x .05)	10,000	
	Interest expense (or prepaid) (200,000 x .20 x 36/365)	3,945	
	Factoring fee (200,000 x .03)	6,000	
	Factor's holdback receivable (200,000 x .05)	10,000	
	Bad debts expense		10,000
	Accounts receivable		200,000

(Alternatively, the interest and factor's fee can be combined into a $9,945 charge to loss on sale of receivables.)

	Debit	Credit
2. Sales returns and allowances	4,800	
Factor's holdback receivable		4,800
3. Cash	5,200	
Factor's holdback receivable		5,200

Transfers of Receivables With Recourse

In recent years, a newer variant on factoring has become popular. This is what has been called factoring with recourse. When receivables are transferred with recourse, the arrangement is somewhat of a compromise between true factoring and an assignment of receivables, and accounting practice has varied considerably because of the hybrid nature of these transactions. A strong argument can be made, in fact, that factoring with recourse is nothing more than the assignment of receivables and that the proper accounting (as discussed above) is to present this as a secured borrowing, not as a sale of the receivables. It is expected that the second phase of the IASC's financial instruments project will address this matter. [It should be noted that even in the United States, where GAAP was developed to account for such transfers as sales under some circumstances (SFAS 77), the likelihood is that further revisions to professional standards will be made to end these practices, especially when recourse provisions are material to the transactions.]

FINANCIAL INSTRUMENTS

Financial Instruments Project: US Experience

Largely because the financial community has shown great creativity in developing a range of new and complex financial instruments over the past 10 to 15 years, and partly also as a result of a number of notorious financial scandals, ranging from the savings and loan industry collapse in the United States in the 1980s to the many derivatives-related debacles, including Barings Bank, in the early- to mid-1990s, the subject of financial instruments accounting has received a significant amount of attention from governmental and private sector standards setters. In the United States, for one example, almost one-half of new professional accounting standards, including interpretations and issues papers, have over the past 10 years addressed the topic of financial instruments in some manner or form. To set the stage for the following consideration of IAS 32, the developments in the United States, which largely, but not entirely, paved the way for the similar international standard-setting exercise, will be reviewed briefly next.

The experience in the US paralleled that of the international standards setting effort with regard to the respective financial instruments projects. Thus, the complex and controversial issues surrounding the questions of recognition and measurement have been proven to be the more difficult to solve, leaving the more straightforward issues of presentation and disclosure to be addressed first. In the

US, SFAS 105 was the first in a series of statements addressing financial instruments disclosures, focusing on the extent, nature, and terms of financial instruments with off-balance-sheet credit or market risk. In addition, this statement addresses concentrations of credit risk for all (i.e., on- or off-balance-sheet) financial instruments.

The foregoing was quickly followed by another disclosure standard, SFAS 107, which requires entities to communicate information about the fair value of all (recognized and unrecognized) financial instruments that are practicable to estimate, including liabilities. Pertinent descriptive information as to the fair value of the instrument is to be disclosed if an estimate of fair value cannot be made without incurring excessive costs. The standard excludes certain types of financial instruments, such as pensions, postretirement benefits, deferred compensation, defeased debt, insurance contracts, lease contracts, warranty obligations, and others from these requirements, much as IAS 32 does (see the later discussion). As a result of the substantial opposition engendered by SFAS 107 due to the universality of its requirements, the FASB recently, in SFAS 126, amended that standard to exempt enterprises having under $100 million in assets and no activities involving derivatives. Notwithstanding this temporary setback, however, it is expected that the FASB will, like the IASC, continue to move toward pure fair-value accounting for financial assets and liabilities.

Yet another disclosure standard was promulgated while the Financial Accounting Standards Board struggled with basic recognition and measurement issues, which have yet to be dealt with successfully. SFAS 119, issued in late 1994, requires issuers and holders of derivative financial instruments (DFI) to disclose new information about those instruments. (It also amended the disclosure requirements of SFAS 105 and SFAS 107.) In effect, the board was first beginning to address the central concerns of the entire financial instruments project, since it was derivatives (such as options, futures, swaps and complex combinations of these instruments, which derive their values from the worth of underlying commodities or basic financial instruments) which had created the public perception that there was a crisis in financial reporting.

DFI can be either on-balance-sheet or off-balance-sheet, and include

1. Option contracts
2. Interest rate caps
3. Interest rate floors
4. Fixed-rate loan commitments
5. Note issuance facilities
6. Letters of credit
7. Forward contracts
8. Forward interest rate agreements
9. Interest rate collars
10. Futures

11. Swaps
12. Instruments with similar characteristics

It should be noted that DFI, as defined by SFAS 119, exclude all on-balance-sheet receivables and payables including

1. Mortgage-backed securities
2. Interest-only obligations
3. Principal-only obligations
4. Indexed debt
5. Other optional characteristics incorporated within those receivables and payables (such as convertible bond conversion or call terms)

Thus, the definition of DFI used by the standard is somewhat more restrictive than the term as understood by most businesspersons.

In addition, DFI exclude contracts that either

1. Require exchange for a nonfinancial commodity, or
2. Permit settlement by delivering a nonfinancial commodity.

Thus, most product (petroleum, grain, etc.) future contracts would be excluded, while swaps (if settled in cash) would be included.

The basic business purpose of DFI is to manage some kind of risk, such as stock price movements, interest rate variations, currency fluctuations and commodity price volatility. The parties involved tend to be brokerage firms, financial institutions, insurance companies, and large corporations, although any two or more entities of any size can hold or issue derivatives. The DFI are contracts that are supposed to protect or hedge one or more of the parties from adverse movement in the underlying base.

Unfortunately, these protections or hedges are rarely perfect and sometimes the hedge, once established, is removed in order to engage in speculative activity. In this case, the DFI themselves can become risky and, if leveraged, small adverse price or interest rate variations can produce significant losses. Thus, instead of providing protection, many DFI have actually generated losses. Instruments such as interest rate swaps (exchanging variable or floating rate debt for fixed rate debt) and interest rate caps (limiting exposure to rising interest rates) have also resulted in losses, along with DFI such as mortgage-backed bonds and more exotic instruments, including "kitchen sink" bonds, structured notes, inverse floaters, and interest-only bonds. Accounting concerns about these losses involve the off-balance-sheet nature of many DFI, the amount of capital that should be required for trading DFI, and the suitability of DFI for holders, given the potential risks that have resulted. Thus, users and issuers are now reassessing their policies regarding DFI and examining their internal controls to limit the risk.

The FASB, incidentally, has not yet specified a preferred method of accounting for DFI, although it has been studying these and closely related issues of accounting for hedging for many years and has several times come close to proposing new standards on these matters. Reportedly, it will conclude on these issues by year end 1997. At this time, however, the accounting for these complex instruments has not been standardized. In many cases the individual positions are accounted for separately at fair value with the gains or losses reported in operating income or in net interest income. In other cases, hedge accounting is used, with its associated deferral of gains or losses. In addition, many of these DFI do not have a readily determined fair value. Without specifying the accounting to be used, the FASB has established requirements for minimum disclosures, in an attempt to provide relevant information so that indications of the risks associated with DFI can be assessed.

Currently, options held and other DFI are not disclosed under SFAS 105 because they are not off-balance-sheet and/or because they do not have off-balance-sheet risk of accounting loss. For DFI not included under the scope of SFAS 105, SFAS 119 amends SFAS 105 to require disclosure by category of financial instrument of

1. Face, contract, or notational principal amount
2. Nature and terms including
    a. Credit risk
    b. Market risk
    c. Cash requirements
    d. Accounting policy
    e. Leverage features (or multipliers) and their general effects on each of the above

As used in SFAS 119, the category of financial instrument denotes the class, business activity, risk, or other division consistent with managing these instruments. Whenever class of DFI is not used as the category for the disclosure, the class of financial instruments included in the category must be described. All DFI are to be classified as (1) trading (including dealing and all activities measured at fair value and reported in a trading account), or (2) other than trading.

For traded DFI, the required disclosures also include

1. Net gains or losses (net trading revenue) reported in income by category of financial instrument and where the net gains or losses are reported.
2. Average fair value of DFI during the period, together with the related value at the end of the period, differentiating assets and liabilities. Disclosure of this information is also encouraged for other types of financial instruments or nonfinancial assets that are traded.

For other than traded DFI, required disclosures also include

1. A description, including the class of DFI used, of
   a. Objectives for holding
   b. Context required to understand the objective
   c. Strategy for achieving the objectives
2. A description of how each class of DFI is reported in the statements including
   a. Recognition and measurement policies for DFI held or issued
   b. Location of DFI in the balance sheet and where the related gains or losses are reported in income
3. If held or issued and accounted for as hedges of anticipated transactions
   a. Information about the transaction being hedged and about the time period until occurrence
   b. Description of the classes of DFI used to hedge
   c. Amounts of explicitly deferred (i.e., in separate accounts as required by SFAS 52 and SFAS 80) hedging gains or losses
   d. Events that result in recognition in earnings of deferred items in c. above

Interest rate, commodity price, foreign exchange, or other market risk information that is useful for comparing strategic results with objectives of derivatives and which is consistent with the entity's management of risk is encouraged, but not required, to be disclosed. Different organizations will report this information in different ways. The development and evolution of effective ways of reporting the data above is encouraged.

In addition, SFAS 119 amends SFAS 105 to replace the term **class of financial instrument** with the term **category of financial instrument**. It also requires that financial instruments with off-balance-sheet risk (held or issued) be classified as (1) trading (includes dealing and all activities measured at fair value and reported in a trading account) or (2) other than trading.

The amendment of SFAS 107 requires that fair value information be presented along with the related carrying value so that it is clear whether they represent assets or liabilities. If disclosed in more than one note, a summary table containing the data above is required in one of these notes, with a cross-reference to the location of the other SFAS 107 notes. In addition, the relationship between the carrying amounts and what is reported in the balance sheet must be disclosed. Traded (including dealing and other activities measured at fair value with gains or losses recognized in earnings) financial instruments are to be distinguished from those that are categorized as other than traded. In disclosing the fair value of a DFI, that fair value should not be aggregated, netted, or combined (even if considered related) with either the fair value of a nonderivative financial instrument or other DFI, except as permitted by another FASB document, *Interpretation 39*.

Although FASB *Interpretation 39* makes an exception in the case of multiple forward, swap, and similar contracts executed with the same party under master netting arrangements, offsetting of assets and liabilities is improper except where a right of setoff exists. A **right of setoff** is a debtor's legal right to discharge debt owed to another party by applying against the debt an amount the other party owes to the debtor. The conditions to be met are

1. Each of the two parties owes the other determinable amounts.
2. The reporting party has the right to setoff.
3. The reporting party intends to set off.
4. The right of setoff is enforceable at law.

Accounting for Financial Instruments Under IAS 32: International Experience

As the following discussion will make clear, the international standard on financial instruments' presentation and disclosure very closely approximates the earlier pronouncements on the same matters by the US standard-setting body, the FASB. In fact, the only new ground broken by the IASC has been to commit to a strict "substance over form" approach and to require separate presentation of disparate elements of compound financial instruments; both of which were discussed in detail by the FASB in the early 1990s but that have yet to be incorporated into standards due to the controversy they generated at the time. Neither US nor international standards setters have been able to deal definitively with the recognition and measurement issues, which are by far the more difficult and which have been set aside for further deliberation in both of these domains.

Financial instruments defined. Under the international accounting standards (IAS 32, adopting the definitions first advanced by E40 and carried forward by E48), financial assets and liabilities are defined as follows:

1. **Financial asset**: Any asset that is
   a. Cash
   b. A contractual right to receive cash or another financial asset from another enterprise
   c. A contractual right to exchange financial instruments with another enterprise under conditions that are potentially favorable
   d. An equity instrument of another enterprise
2. **Financial liability**: Any liability that is a contractual obligation
   a. To deliver cash or another financial asset to another enterprise; or
   b. To exchange financial instruments with another enterprise under conditions that are potentially unfavorable.

According to this definition, financial instruments encompass a broad domain within the balance sheet. They include both primary instruments, such as stocks and bonds, and derivative instruments, such as options, forwards, and swaps. Physical assets, such as inventories or plant assets, and such long-lived intangible assets as patents and goodwill, are excluded from the definition; although control of such assets may create opportunities to generate future cash inflows, it does not grant to the holder a present right to receive cash or other financial assets. Similarly, liabilities that are not contractual in nature, such as income taxes payable (which are statutory, but not contractual, obligations), are not financial instruments either.

Some contractual rights and obligations do not involve the transfer of financial assets. For example, a commitment to deliver commodities such as agricultural products or precious metals is not a financial instrument, although in practice these contracts are often used for hedging purposes by enterprises and are often settled in cash (technically, the contracts are closed out by entering into offsetting transactions before their mandatory settlement dates). The fact that the contracts call for delivery of physical product, unless canceled by a closing market transaction prior to the maturity date, prevents these from being included within the definition of financial instruments.

Presentation Issues Addressed by IAS 32

Distinguishing liabilities from equity. One of the more challenging issues that US standards setters tried, unsuccessfully, to grapple with was that of distinguishing liabilities from equity. Conceptually, of course, this issue should not have been difficult to resolve, since the time-honored accounting tradition of substance over form should have provided clear guidance on this matter. However, a variety of reasons, including the prospect that a strict substance over form doctrine might have triggered severe legal complications, prevented the board from resolving this. One example of an anticipated problem is the case of mandatorily redeemable preferred stock, which is generally considered part of an entity's equity base despite having important characteristics of debt. However, requiring quasi equity issuances such as these to be recategorized as debt might have caused many entities to be deemed in violation of existing debt covenants and other contractual commitments. As a consequence, the FASB has yet to complete this phase of its project, despite having produced a comprehensive discussion memorandum on this topic in 1991, which, if adopted as a standard, would have necessitated that all debt-like instruments be classified as debt, not equity. It should be noted, however, that the FASB has recently announced that it would be pursuing two narrowly defined aspects of the broader liabilities vs. equity project, one of which is the matter of how redeemable preferred stock is to be classified on the balance sheet. The likely outcome will be that redeemable preferred will be reported as either a liability or some form of "mezzanine" capital outside the equity section.

Where the FASB feared to tread, however, the IASC has boldly stepped forward. Under the provisions of IAS 32, the issuer of a financial instrument must classify it, or its component parts, if a compound instrument (discussed in the next section), in accordance with the substance of the respective contractual arrangement. Thus it is quite clear that under the international standard, when the instrument gives rise to an obligation on the part of the issuer to deliver cash or another financial asset or to exchange financial instruments on potentially unfavorable terms, it is to be classified as a liability, not as equity. Mandatorily redeemable preferred stock and preferred stock issued with put options (options that can be exercised by the holder, requiring the issuer to redeem the shares at stipulated prices) would, under this definition, be presented as liabilities.

Less clear is the required presentation in the case of common stock subject to a buyout agreement with the entity's shareholders. Closely held enterprises commonly enter into these **buy-sell agreements** with each shareholder, which require that upon the occurrence of defined events such as a shareholder's retirement or death, the entity will be required to redeem the former shareholder's holdings at a defined or determinable price, such as fair or book value. The practical effect of buy-sell agreements is that all but the final shareholder will eventually become creditors; the last to retire or die will be the residual owner of the business, as the entity will be unable to redeem that holder's shares unless a new investor enters the picture. All the other owners who retire or die (as all must eventually do) will ultimately have been creditors, not true owners. IAS 32 does not address this situation explicitly, although circumstances of this sort are clearly within the language of the standard, which notes that "if a financial instrument labeled as a share gives the holder an option to require redemption upon the occurrence of a future event that is highly likely to occur, classification as a financial liability on initial recognition reflects the substance of the instrument." Nonetheless, it is not anticipated that enterprises will in fact reclassify the majority of stockholders' equity as debt in cases such as that described above.

IAS 32 goes beyond the literal terms of an instrument in seeking to determine whether it might be a liability. It also looks to the implied establishment of an obligation to redeem, as when preferred stock is issued that has a contractually increasing dividend requirement coupled with a call provision (giving the issuer the right, but not the obligation, to redeem the shares). In such a case, the practical effect is that the issuer will be compelled, at some point, to call the shares for redemption, and thus the instrument is to be defined as a liability upon its original issuance.

Classification of compound instruments. IAS 32 also addresses the difficult question of how compound instruments are to be categorized. Again, while the FASB clearly anticipated this issue a number of years earlier, it has thus far failed to rule on the matter, leaving it for the IASC to break this ground. Consistent with the substance over form stance it took in the case of simple debt or equity instruments, the IASC has mandated that compound instruments be analyzed into their constituent elements and accounted for accordingly at inception.

Compound instruments may be comprised of one or more liabilities and/or equities, which need to be evaluated as separate instruments. Since IAS 32 does not address recognition or measurement matters, no single method of valuation is prescribed. However, the standard does suggest two possible approaches.

1. Assign to the least easily measured components the residual amounts, after assigning values to the more easily measured components of the compound instrument
2. Measure the values of each component directly, and then, if necessary, adjust each on a pro rata basis if the total amounts exceed the proceeds from the issuance of the compound instrument

Example of value allocation using the residual value approach

Assume these facts.

1. 5,000 convertible bonds are sold January 1, 1996, due December 31, 1999.
2. Issuance price is par ($1,000 per bond); total issuance proceeds are $5,000,000.
3. Interest is due in arrears, semiannually, at a nominal rate of 5%.
4. Each bond is convertible into 150 shares of common stock of the issuer.
5. At issuance date, similar, nonconvertible, debt must yield 8%.
6. At issuance date, common shares are trading at $5, and expected dividends over the next 4 years are $ .20 per share per year.
7. The relevant risk-free rate on 4-year obligations is 4%.
8. The historical variability of the stock price is indicated by a standard deviation of annual returns of 25%.

The residual value of the equity component of the compound instrument is computed as follows:

1. Use the reference discount rate, 8%, to compute the market value of straight debt carrying a 5% yield:

PV of $5,000,000 due in 4 years	$3,653,451
PV of semiannual payments of $125,000	
for 8 periods	841,593
Total	$4,495,044

2. Compute the amount allocable to the conversion feature

Total proceeds from issuance of compound instrument	$5,000,000
Value allocable to debt	4,495,044
Residual value allocable to equity component	$ 504,956

Alternative approach using options pricing model. This approach values the conversion feature directly, using the Black-Scholes option pricing model (or its equivalent).

1. Compute the standard deviation of proportionate changes in the fair value of the asset underlying the option multiplied by the square root of the time to expiration of the option

$$.25 \times \sqrt{4} = .25 \times 2 = \underline{\underline{.50}}$$

2. Compute the ratio of the fair value of the asset underlying the option to the present value of the option exercise price

   a. The expected dividend per share is \$ .20 per year, the present value of this stream over 4 years would be (at the risk-free rate) \$.726.
   b. The shares are trading at \$5.00.
   c. Therefore, the value of the underlying optioned asset is

   $$\$5.00 - .726 = \$4.274 \text{ per share.}$$

   d. The implicit exercise price is \$1,000 ÷ 150 shares = \$6.667 per share. This must be discounted at the risk-free rate, 5%, over 4 years, assuming that conversion takes place at the expiration of the conversion period

   $$\$6.667 \div 1.05^4 = 6.667 \div 1.2155 = \$5.485$$

   e. Therefore, the ratio of the underlying asset, \$4.274, to the exercise price, \$5.485, is .7792.

3. Reference must now be made to a call option valuation table to assign a fair value to these two computed amounts (the standard deviation of proportionate changes in the fair value of the asset underlying the option multiplied by the square root of the time to expiration of the option, .50, and the ratio of the fair value of the asset underlying the option to the present value of the option exercise price, .7792). For this example, assume that the table value is 13.44% (meaning that the fair value of the option is 13.44%) of the fair value of the underlying asset.
4. The dollar valuation of the conversion option, then, is given as

   $$.1344 \times \$4.274 \text{ per share} \times 150 \text{ shares/bond} \times 5{,}000 \text{ bonds} = \$\underline{\underline{430{,}819}}$$

5. Since the fair value of the straight debt (computed above, \$4,495,044) plus the fair value of the options (\$430,819) does not equal the proceeds, \$5,000,000, both amounts should be adjusted pro rata (resulting in recording the debt at \$4,562,697 and the options at \$437,303).

Reporting interest, dividends, losses and gains. IAS 32 establishes that income earned while holding, and gains or losses from disposing of, financial instruments should be reported in the income statement. Dividends paid on equity instruments issued should be charged directly to equity. The balance sheet classification of the instrument drives the income statement classification of the related interest or dividends. For example, if mandatorily redeemable preferred shares have been categorized as debt on the issuer's balance sheet, dividend payments on the those shares must be reported in the income statement in the same manner as interest expense. Gains or losses on redemptions or refinancings of financial instruments classed as liabilities would be reported similarly in the income statement, while gains or losses on equity are credited or charged to equity directly.

Offsetting financial assets and liabilities. IAS 32 adopts an approach which closely mimics that which had earlier been embraced by the FASB in its Interpretations 39 and 41. Specifically, offsetting will be permitted only when the enterprise both (1) has the legally enforceable right to set off the recognized amounts, and (2) intends to settle the asset and liability on a net basis, or to realize the asset and settle the liability simultaneously. Offsetting does not give rise to gain or loss recognition, which distinguishes it from the derecognition of an instrument, which is not addressed by IAS 32 (or by any other international standard, at this date).

Simultaneous settlement of a financial asset and a financial liability can be presumed only under defined circumstances. The most typical of such cases is when both instruments will be settled through a clearinghouse functioning for an organized exchange. Other situations may superficially appear to warrant the same accounting treatment but in fact do not give rise to legitimate offsetting. For example, if the entity will exchange checks with a single counterparty for the settlement of both instruments, it becomes exposed to credit risk for a time, however brief, when it has paid the other party for the amount of the obligation owed to it but has yet to receive the counterparty's funds to settle the amount it is owed by the counterparty. Offsetting would not be warranted in such a context.

The standard sets forth a number of other circumstances in which offsetting would not be justified. These include

1. When several different instruments are used to synthesize the features of another type of instrument (which typically would involve a number of different counterparties, thus violating a basic principle of offsetting).
2. When financial assets and financial liabilities arise from instruments having the same primary risk exposure (such as when both are forward contracts) but with different counterparties.
3. When financial assets are pledged as collateral for nonrecourse financial liabilities (as the intention is not typically to effect offsetting, but rather, to settle the obligation and gain release of the collateral).
4. When financial assets are set aside in a trust for the purpose of discharging a financial obligation but the assets have not been formally accepted by the creditor (as when a sinking fund is established, or when in-substance defeasance of debt is arranged).

5. When obligations incurred as a consequence of events giving rise to losses are expected to be recovered from a third party by virtue of an insurance claim (again, different counterparties means that the entity is exposed to credit risk, however slight).

Even the existence of a master netting agreement does not automatically justify the offsetting of financial assets and financial liabilities. Only if both the stipulated conditions (both the right to offset and the intention to do so) are met can this accounting treatment be employed.

Disclosure Issues Addressed by IAS 32

Primacy of risk considerations. The major objective of the disclosure requirements established by IAS 32 is to give financial statement users the ability to assess on- and off-balance-sheet risks, which prominently includes risks relating to future cash flows associated with the financial instruments. The standard presents the following typology of risk:

1. **Price risk**, which implies not merely the risk of loss but also the potential for gain, and which is in turn comprised of

    a. **Currency risk**--The risk that the value of an instrument will vary due to changes in currency exchange rates.
    b. **Interest-rate risk**--The risk that the value of the instrument will fluctuate due to changes in market interest rates.
    c. **Market risk**--A broader concept that subsumes interest rate risk, this is, the risk that prices will fluctuate due to factors specific to the financial instrument or due to factors that are generally affecting other securities trading in the same markets.

2. **Credit risk** is related to the failure of one party to perform as it is required to contractually.
3. **Liquidity risk** (also known as **funding risk**) is a function of the possible difficulty to be encountered in raising funds to meet commitments; it may result from an inability to sell a financial asset at its fair value.
4. **Cash flow risk** is the risk that the future cash flows associated with a monetary financial instrument will fluctuate in amount, as when a debt instrument carries a floating interest rate, potentially causing a change in cash flows while fair values will remain constant (absent a coincidentally occurring change in creditworthiness).

The standard does address the means by which interest rate and credit risk factors are to be addressed in the financial statements, while cash flow and liquidity risk are discussed in general terms only.

Interest-rate risk in greater detail. Interest-rate risk is the risk associated with holding fixed-rate instruments in a changing interest rate environment. As market rates rise, the price of fixed interest rate instruments will decline, and vice versa. This relationship holds in all cases, irrespective of other specific factors, such as changes in perceived creditworthiness of the borrower. However, with certain complex instruments such as mortgage-backed bonds (a popular form of derivative instrument), where the behavior of the underlying debtors can be expected to be altered by changes in the interest rate environment (i.e., as market interest rates decline, prepayments by mortgagors increase in frequency, raising the risks to the bondholders and accordingly tempering the otherwise expected upward movement of the bond prices), this inverse relationship will be less than symmetrical.

IAS 32 requires that for each class of financial asset and financial liability, both those that are recognized (i.e., on-balance-sheet) and those that are not recognized (off-balance-sheet), the reporting entity should disclose information which will illuminate its exposure to interest-rate risk. This includes disclosure of contractual repricing dates or maturity dates, whichever are earlier, and effective interest rates, if applicable.

These data provide the user of the financial statements with an ability to predict cash flows, since fixed-rate instruments will generate cash inflows (if assets) or outflows (if liabilities) at a given rate until the maturity date or the earlier repricing date, although other features, such as optional call dates or serial retirements, can complicate this further. The combination of information on contractual (or "coupon") rates, maturity dates, and changing market conditions (not provided by the financial statements, but presumably available to anyone familiar with the financial press) also provides insight into the price risk of the underlying debt instruments, while for debt having floating rates of interest, knowledge of market conditions provides insight into cash flow risk.

The standard also suggests, but does not require, that when **expected** repricings are to occur at dates that differ significantly from contractual dates, such information be provided as well. An example is when the enterprise is an investor in fixed-rate mortgage loans and when prepayments can be reliably estimated; as the funds thereby generated will need to be reinvested at then-current market rates, altering the patterns and amounts of future cash flows from what a simple reading of the balance sheet might otherwise suggest. Information based on management expectations should be clearly distinguished from that which is based on contractual provisions.

IAS 32 suggests that a meaningful way to present this information is to group financial assets and financial liabilities into categories as follows:

1. Those debt instruments that have fixed rates and thus expose the reporting entity to interest-rate (price) risk
2. Those debt instruments that have floating rates and thus expose the entity to cash-flow risk

3. Those instruments, typically equity, which are not interest-rate sensitive

Effective interest rates, as used in this standard, means the internal rate of return, which is the discount rate that equates the present value of all future cash flows associated with the instrument with its current market price. Put another way, this is the measure of the time value of money as it relates to the financial instrument in question. Effective interest rates cannot be determined for derivative financial instruments such as swaps, forwards and options, although these are often affected by changes in interest rates, and the effective rate disclosures prescribed by IAS 32 do not apply in such cases. In any event, the risk characteristics of such instruments must be discussed in the footnote disclosures.

The nature of the reporting enterprise's business and the extent to which it holds financial assets or is obligated by financial liabilities will affect the manner in which such disclosures are presented, and no single method of making such disclosures will be suitable for every entity. The standard suggests that in many cases a tabular disclosure of amounts of financial instruments exposed to interest-rate risk will be useful, with the instruments grouped according to repricing or maturity dates (e.g., within 1 year, from 1 to 5 years, and over 5 years from the balance sheet date). In other cases (for financial institutions, for example), finer distinctions of maturities might be warranted. Similar tabular presentations of data on floating-rate instruments [which create cash-flow risk rather than interest-rate (price) risk] should also be presented, when pertinent. When other risk factors are also present, such as credit risk (discussed in the following section), a series of tabular presentations, segregating instruments into risk classes and then categorizing each in terms of maturities, and so on may be necessary to convey the risk dimensions adequately to readers.

Sensitivity analysis has been alluded to in a number of accounting standards over the years. Since it has always been presented as an optional feature, it has rarely been employed in actual disclosures, despite having great potential for being useful to readers. In the context of financial instruments, sensitivity analysis would imply a discussion of the effect on portfolio value of a hypothetical change (say, a 1% change, plus or minus) in interest rates. There are at least two reasons why such information, unless accompanied by an adequate discussion of the particular characteristics of the financial instruments in question, might be misleading to financial statement readers.

First, because of the phenomenon known as **convexity**, the value change of each successive 1% interest change in rates is not a constant, but rather, a function of current market rates. For example, if the market rate at the balance sheet date is 8%, a move to 9% might cause a $20,000 decline in value in a given bond portfolio, but a further change in the market rate from 9% to 10% would **not** have a further $20,000 effect. Instead, the effect would be an amount greater or lesser depending on the coupon (contractual) rate of interest of the underlying financial instruments. A reader, however, would rarely appreciate this fact and would probably extrapolate the sensitivity data in a linear manner, which could be materially misleading in the absence of further narrative information.

Second, sensitivity data most often are presented in a manner that suggests that they apply symmetrically. Thus, in the foregoing example, the presumption is that a 1% market rate decline would boost the portfolio value by $20,000 and that a 1% rate increase would depress it by a similar amount. However, some instruments, most notably those with embedded options (mortgage-backed bonds, having prepayment options, are the most common example cited, although exotic derivatives can be far more difficult to analyze) will not exhibit symmetrical price behavior, and the asymmetries will become exaggerated as hypothetical market rates stray further from the current rates. As a practical matter, the only way to convey these subtleties in a meaningful fashion would be to incorporate extensive tables of information into the footnotes, which many users would find to be impossibly confusing.

For these and possibly other reasons (including independent accountants' natural reluctance to include information that might be misleading to readers, who might then attempt to hold the accountants responsible for any consequent losses), although recommended by IAS 32, it is not anticipated that sensitivity data will be provided widely in the near term. If provided, however, any assumptions and the methodologies employed should be explained adequately, along with any needed caveats concerning the validity of extrapolation over greater ranges of market rate changes and over time.

Credit risk in greater detail. IAS 32 also demands that for each class of financial asset, both recognized (i.e., on-balance-sheet) and unrecognized (off-balance-sheet), information be provided as to exposure to credit risk. Specifically, the maximum amount of credit risk exposure as of the balance sheet date, without considering possible recoveries from any collateral that may have been provided, should be stated and any significant concentrations of credit risk should be discussed. This set of disclosure requirements is very similar to that first mandated under US GAAP by SFAS 105 over 5 years ago.

Credit risk is defined as the maximum amount of accounting loss that might be incurred by the reporting enterprise should the counterparty fail to perform. In many cases, this is simply the carrying value of such instruments; for example, accounts receivable net of any allowance for uncollectibles already provided would be the measure of credit risk associated with trade receivables. In other cases, the maximum loss would be an amount less than that which is revealed on the balance sheet, as when a legal right of offset exists but the financial asset was not presented on a net basis on the balance sheet because one of the required conditions set forth in IAS 32 (intention to settle on a net basis) was not met. In yet other circumstances, the maximum accounting loss that could be incurred would be greater, as when the asset is unrecognized in the balance sheet although otherwise disclosed in the footnotes as, for example, when the entity has guaranteed collection of receivables that have been sold to another party (often called factoring with recourse, discussed earlier).

There are a large number of potential combinations of factors that could affect maximum credit risk exposure, and in other than the most basic circumstances it is likely that extended narratives will be needed to convey the risks fully in the most meaningful way to users of the financial statements. For example, when an entity has financial assets owed from and financial liabilities owed to the same counterparty, with the right of offset but without having an intent to settle on a net basis, the maximum amount subject to credit risk may be lower than the carrying value of the asset. However, if past behavior suggests that the enterprise would probably respond to the debtor's difficulties by extending the maturity of the financial asset beyond the maturity of the related liability, it will voluntarily expose itself to greater risk since it will presumably settle its obligation and thus forfeit the opportunity to offset these related instruments.

When the maximum credit risk associated with a particular financial asset or group of assets is the same as the amount presented on the face of the balance sheet, it is not necessary to reiterate this fact in the footnotes. The presumption is that there will be disclosures made for all material items for which this fact does not hold, however.

In addition to disclosure of maximum credit risk, IAS 32 requires disclosure of concentrations of credit risk when these are not otherwise apparent from the financial statements. Common examples of this involve trade accounts receivable that are due from debtors within one geographic region or operating within one industry segment, as when a large fraction of receivables are due from, say, housing construction contractors in the Netherlands, many of which might find themselves in financial difficulty if economic conditions deteriorated in that market. In addition to geographic locale and industry, other factors to consider would include the creditworthiness of the debtors (e.g., if the reporting entity targets a market such as college students not having steady employment, or third-world governments) and the nature of the activities undertaken by the counterparties. The disclosures should provide a clear indication of the characteristics shared by the debtors.

Examples of disclosures of credit risk

Note 5: Interest Rate Swap Agreements

The differential to be paid or received is accrued as interest rates change and is recognized over the life of the agreements.

Note 8: Foreign Exchange Contracts

The corporation enters into foreign exchange contracts as a hedge against foreign accounts payable. Market value gains and losses are recognized, and the resulting credit or debit offsets foreign exchange losses or gains on those payables.

Note 13: Financial Instruments With Off-Balance-Sheet Risk

In the normal course of business, the corporation enters into or is a party to various financial instruments and contractual obligations that, under certain conditions, could give rise to or involve elements of market or credit risk in excess of that shown in the statement of financial condition. These financial instruments and contractual obligations include interest rate swaps, forward foreign exchange contracts, financial guarantees, and commitments to extend credit. The corporation monitors and limits its exposure to market risk through management policies designed to identify and reduce excess risk. The corporation limits its credit risk through monitoring of client credit exposure, reviews, and conservative estimates of allowances for bad debt and through the prudent use of collateral for large amounts of credit. The corporation monitors collateral values on a daily basis and requires additional collateral when deemed necessary.

Note 6: Interest Rate Swaps and Forward Exchange Contracts

The corporation enters into a variety of interest rate swaps and forward foreign exchange contracts. The primary use of these financial instruments is to reduce interest rate fluctuations and to stabilize costs or to hedge foreign currency liabilities or assets. Interest rate swap transactions involve the exchange of floating-rate and fixed-rate interest payment of obligations without the exchange of underlying notional amounts. The company is exposed to credit risk in the unlikely event of nonperformance by the counterparty. The differential to be received or paid is accrued as interest rates change and is recognized over the life of the agreement. Forward foreign exchange contracts represent commitments to exchange currencies at a specified future date. Gains (losses) on these contracts serve primarily to stabilize costs. Foreign currency exposure for the corporation will result in the unlikely event that the other party fails to perform under the contract.

Note 3: Financial Guarantees

Financial guarantees are conditional commitments to guarantee performance to third parties. These guarantees are primarily issued to guarantee borrowing arrangements. The corporation's credit risk exposure on these guarantees is not material.

Note 8: Commitment to Extend Credit

Loan commitments are agreements to extend credit under agreed-upon terms. The corporation's commitment to extend credit assists customers to meet their liquidity needs. These commitments generally have fixed expiration or other termination clauses. The corporation anticipates that not all of these commitments will be utilized. The amount of unused commitment does not necessarily represent future funding requirements.

Note 9: Summary of Off-Balance-Sheet Financial Instruments

The off-balance-sheet financial instruments are summarized as follows (in thousands):

Financial instruments whose notional or contract amounts exceed the amount of credit risk:

	Contract or Notional amount
Interest rate swap agreements	$8,765.40
Forward foreign exchange contracts	7,654.30

Financial instruments whose contract amount represents credit risk:

	Contract or Notional amount
Financial guarantees	$6,543.20
Commitments to extend credit	5,432.10

Concentration of credit risk for certain entities. For certain corporations, industry or regional concentrations of credit risk may be disclosed adequately by a description of the business. Some examples are

1. Credit risk for these off-balance-sheet financial instruments is concentrated in North America and in the trucking industry.
2. All financial instruments entered into by the corporation relate to US Government, international, and domestic commercial airline customers.

Example of disclosure of concentration of credit risk

Note 5: Significant Group Concentrations of Credit Risk

The corporation grants credit to customers throughout the nation. As of December 31, 1996, the five states where the corporation had the greatest amount of credit risk were as follows:

California	$8,765.40
Florida	7,654.30
Texas	6,543.20
New York	5,432.10
Washington	4,321.00

Disclosure of fair values. IAS 32 further requires that for each class of financial asset and financial liability, the reporting enterprise should disclose information about fair value. This virtually mirrors the requirement imposed in the United States by SFAS 107 and discussed above. As was the case with that standard, an escape valve is provided in the case when it is not deemed practicable within the constraints of timeliness or cost to determine fair value with sufficient reliability. However, when an entity avails itself of this option, it must disclose that fact, coupled with a summary of pertinent characteristics of the instrument, such that readers can make their own assessments of fair value should they so choose.

Stockholders and others have every reason to expect that management understands the values of the assets it acquires for the business or of the obligations it incurs. Therefore, a confession in the financial statements to the effect that fair values could not be determined, if made more than infrequently, would appear either disingenuous or an admission of managerial malfeasance. For this reason, a good-faith attempt to determine the fair value data requested by IAS 32, coupled with disclosures that set forth whatever caveats are deemed necessary to make the information not misleading, is probably the best course to follow.

Beyond the basic concern of computing fair values, there is the further issue of what this information is intended to imply. This question arises most commonly in the context of financial obligations, which represent contractual commitments to repay fixed sums at fixed points in time, which are not subject to adjustment for market-driven changes in value per se. For example, assume that an entity owes a bank loan carrying fixed 9.5% interest, with the principal due as a $300,000 balloon payment 3 years hence. If current rates are, say, 7%, the fair value of this obligation is something greater than its face value (in fact, the computed present value of future cash flows, discounted at 7%, is $342,060, which will be the surrogate for fair value) yet the contractual obligation is unchanged at the original $300,000. What, then, is the purpose of communicating to financial statement users that the fair value is the higher, $342,060, amount?

The explanation of this disclosure is that the economic burden being borne by the entity is heavier than would have been the case had a floating market rate of interest been attached to the debt. The spread between the disclosed fair value, $342,060, and the face amount of the debt, $300,000, is the present value of the additional interest to be paid in the future under the fixed-rate agreement over the amount that would be payable at the current market rate. Thus, fair value disclosure does not measure future cash flows, per se, but rather is an indication of economic burden or benefit in the assumed absence of any restructuring or other alteration of the debt.

Fair value is the exchange price in a current transaction (other than in a forced or liquidation sale) between willing parties. If a quoted market price is available, it should be used, after adjustment for transaction costs that would normally be incurred in a real transaction of this type. If there is more than one market price, the one used should be the one from the most active market. The possible effects on market price from the sale of large holdings and/or from thinly traded issues should generally be disregarded for purposes of this determination, since it would tend to introduce too much subjectivity into this measurement process.

If quoted market prices are unavailable, management's best estimate of fair value can be used. A number of standardized techniques, which attempt to tie the prices of various financial instruments to those having readily determinable fair values, are widely employed for this purpose. Some bases from which an estimate may be made include

1. Matrix pricing models
2. Option pricing models

3. Financial instruments with similar characteristics adjusted for risks involved
4. Financial instruments with similar valuation techniques (i.e. present value) adjusted for risks involved

IAS 32 notes that in some instances when the instruments are not traded in active markets (or perhaps when bid-ask prices are widely dispersed, as with thinly traded securities), rather than presenting a single fair value estimate, which might convey a sense of precision that is not warranted under the circumstances, a range of fair values should be displayed. Actually, in a number of earlier proposals and discussions among academics, standards setters, users, and others, the idea of matrix reporting, showing alternative valuations relating to defined conditions, this approach has been proffered, but it has rarely been seen as an attractive option. The opposition generally derives from the fear that offering readers alternative valuations will serve to cause confusion. Furthermore, it could devalue the financial reporting process in some eyes, since it might be read as a confession of an inability to ascertain the correct answer. It is the authors' expectation that few preparers will avail themselves of this suggestion and more likely will present a single fair value amount to be associated with each class of financial asset and financial liability, with appropriate caveats expressed, as needed, in the accompanying narrative disclosures.

Example

Note X: Financial Instruments Disclosures of Fair Value

The estimates of fair value of financial instruments are summarized as follows (in thousands):

Carrying amounts approximate fair values:

	Carrying amount
Cash	$987.6
Cash equivalents	876.5
Trade receivables	765.4
Trade payables	654.3

Fair values approximate carrying values because of the short time until realization or liquidation.

Fair values exceed carrying amounts:

	Carrying amount	*Fair value*
Short-term securities	$876.5	$987.6
Long-term investments	765.4	876.5
Forward foreign exchange contracts	654.3	765.4

Estimated fair values are based on available quoted market prices, present value calculations, and option pricing models.

Carrying amounts exceed fair values:

	Carrying amount	Fair value
Long-term debt	($543.2)	($432.1)

Estimated fair values are based on quoted market prices, present value calculations, and the prices of the same or similar instruments after considering risk, current interest rates, and remaining maturities.

Unrecognized financial instruments:

	Carrying amount	Fair value
Interest rate swap agreements		
Net receivable	$7,012.3	$7,865.4
Net payable	(1,753.1)	(1,543.2)
Commitments to extend credit	(5,432.1)	(4,321.0)
Financial guarantees	(6,543.2)	(7,654.3)

Estimated fair values after considering risk, current interest rates and remaining maturities were based on the following:

1. **Interest rate swaps**--Amounts to be received or paid to terminate swap agreements at reporting date.
2. **Credit commitments**--Value of the same or similar instruments after considering credit ratings of counterparties.
3. **Financial guarantees**--Cost to settle or terminate obligations with counterparties at reporting date.

Fair value not estimated:

	Carrying amount	Fair value
Long-term investment	$1,234.5	--

Fair value could not be estimated without incurring excessive costs. Investment is carried at original cost and represents an 8% investment in the common stock of a privately held untraded company that supplies the corporation. Management considers the risk of loss to be negligible.

Financial assets carried at amounts in excess of fair value. In certain circumstances, an entity carries one or several financial assets at amounts that exceed fair value, notwithstanding the general rule under accounting theory that such declines should be formally recognized in most instances. Normally, failure to recognize such declines is justified only when the decline is deemed to be temporary in nature.

IAS 32 requires that when one or more financial assets are reported at amounts that exceed fair value, disclosure should be made of both carrying amount and fair value, either individually or grouped in an appropriate manner, and the reasons for not reducing the carrying value to fair value should be set forth, including the nature of the evidence that provides the basis for management's belief that the carrying

value will be recovered. The purpose is to alert the financial statement readers to the risk that carrying amounts might later be reduced if a change in circumstances causes management to reassess the likelihood of recovery.

For example, a fixed-rate loan held as an investment may be carried at amortized cost, which may exceed fair value due to a temporary increase in the market rates of interest. In the absence of any evidence of increased risk of default by the borrower, and assuming an intention to hold the loan to maturity, there would not be a need to write this investment down to fair value (see discussion of IAS 25 in Chapter 9). On the other hand, if the reporting entity intends to sell its investment prior to maturity, or if a value decline that is other than temporary is expected to occur as a corollary to the changes in market rates (e.g., the increased costs of its other borrowings place a strain on the borrower that is expected to affect credit risk as well), a write-down is necessitated under pertinent accounting standards.

Hedges of anticipated transactions. As noted earlier, the entire subject of hedging accounting is controversial, complex, and largely unresolved. Conceptually, the accounting for hedging positions should be coordinated with that for the underlying position being hedged; so that, for example, if gains or losses on the "cash" position are being deferred, so will be the (hopefully offsetting) losses or gains on the hedge position. A special difficulty arises in the case of anticipated transactions, however, because the reporting entity does not have a hedged position on its balance sheet. It is permitted, under current rules, to defer gain or loss recognition on hedging positions related to anticipated transactions under certain circumstances.

IAS 32 requires that if the entity hedges anticipated transactions (e.g., by entering into currency forward transactions to hedge movements in exchange rates that may occur while purchases or sales of goods that will be settled in foreign currencies are being processed), disclosure be made of the nature of the anticipated transactions, including the period of time that will elapse until actual occurrence; the nature of the hedging transactions and instruments used; and the amount of any deferred or unrecognized gain or loss and the expected timing of ultimate recognition as income or expense.

Other disclosure requirements under IAS 32. IAS 32 encourages financial statement preparers to make other disclosures as warranted to enhance the readers' understanding of the financial statements and hence, of the operations of the enterprise being reported on. It suggests that these further disclosures could include such matters as

1. The total amount of change in the fair value of financial assets and financial liabilities that has been recognized in income for the period
2. The total amount of deferred or unrecognized gain or loss on hedging instruments other than those relating to anticipated transactions (which is already a disclosure issue, as noted above)

3. The average aggregate carrying amount during the year being reported on of recognized financial assets and financial liabilities; the average aggregate principal, stated, notional, or similar amounts of unrecognized financial assets and financial liabilities; and the average aggregate fair value of all financial assets and financial liabilities, all of which information is particularly useful when the amounts on hand at the balance sheet dates are not representative of the levels of activity during the period

Discussion paper on recognition and measurement. As noted above, the IASC was unable to resolve all the issues set forth in E48 and chose (like other standard setters have as well) to bifurcate its efforts. Presentation and disclosure issues were addressed in IAS 32, while recognition and measurement issues, which are inherently more difficult to resolve, have received further study. That study has recently resulted in the publication of a discussion paper, *Accounting for Financial Assets and Financial Liabilities,* and is likely as well to result in one or more exposure drafts and new standards. Briefly, the IASC appears to be inclined toward mandating pure fair-value accounting for all financial assets and liabilities. Special hedge accounting rules, now used (albeit not in a uniform manner across, or even within, nations and industries) to better accomplish matching of gains and losses incurred on hedging instruments with those incurred on the items being hedged, would be largely ended. The underlying accounting would conform to the so-called "financial components approach," which would supersede the "risks and rewards" approach espoused by E48 and its predecessor, E40.

The move from the "risks and rewards" approach to the "financial components approach" would be more than merely a theoretical adjustment; it would have concrete implications for financial reporting. The IASC believes that, given that compound instruments have become common and given that transactions often result in the transfer of **some** but not all risks and rewards, the former strategy (which was never really demonstrated to be workable, in any event) has been obsoleted. The financial components approach will permit accounting for the salc of those "portions" of compound instruments (e.g., groups of receivables) which in fact are transferred, while maintaining financial statement reporting for other portions (e.g., limited guarantees against credit risk made by transferor to transferee) which are retained. This is important, given the growing prevalence of disaggregating risks, rights and obligations, where applying the "risks and rewards" test might not even find that a transaction had actually occurred. Under the financial components approach, it will be easier to account for those events which have in fact occurred, without being thwarted by those which have not.

It should be noted that the US standard setter has been moving slowly toward the financial components approach, most notably in the recent SFAS 125 (issued in 1996). On the other hand, the UK accounting standard-setting agency, the ASB, continues to support the risks and rewards approach, most recently in FRS 5 (issued in 1994). While the IASC's discussion paper observes that the differences between

these alternatives may be more apparent than real, at least as operationalized by the US and UK standards, clearly one of the challenges for the IASC will be to rally support for its chosen philosophy. This may, in fact, be the very issue which provides the IASC with the opportunity to establish its role as a leader in accounting standard-setting, since the financial instruments matter has been the bane of all standards setters for many years.

The need for one or more new standards on financial instruments recognition and measurement is underlined by the fundamental changes in the ways in which commerce is now being conducted, even by smaller and privately held enterprises, vs. how things were being done as little as a decade ago. As the discussion paper notes, formerly most entities directed attention to manufacturing or distribution, which is to say on the conversion of raw materials or completed goods into other products or services. In many developed nations, currently, manufacturing plays a declining role in the economies; and even manufacturing or distributing enterprises more commonly give more substantial attention to the financial management side of the business than was previously the norm. While receivables were essentially the only financial asset on the typical balance sheet a decade ago, now many enterprises actively engage in a variety of activities to manage their risks, some of which involve on- or off-balance-sheet financial assets and liabilities.

For example, many enterprises enter into financial futures transactions to control risks attendant to fixed-rate borrowings. Others hedge foreign currency exposures arising from international trade on either the supply (vendor) side or the sales (customer) side of the business. Still others engage in hedging of assets being held as temporary investments. The easy availability of hedging instruments on organized exchanges, as well as the huge market in privately negotiated hedges, such as interest rate swaps, encourages this sort of activity, which in the main does reduce enterprise risk if properly conducted.

Thus, financial instruments are used to address and mitigate one or more categories of risk--currency, credit, interest rate, market, or liquidity. All of these, individually or in combination, expose an entity to one or (less commonly) both of two exposures: fair value or cash flow. As a simple example, interest rate risk exposes an entity obligated under the terms of a fixed-rate debt to fair value exposure; the same risk exposes an entity having floating-rate debt to cash flow exposure.

Accounting theory and financial reporting rules have been woefully slow to deal with these new realities, partly as a consequence of accounting's historical development within the industrial model. For this reason, accounting has had as its primary focus the determination of periodic results through the matching of costs and revenues, and a commitment to historical costing procedures, even as many departures from that orthodoxy have been permitted over the years. Accounting will have to deal with other complex issues in the immediate future, such as that of intellectual capital and other intangibles, which have been given little or no attention in the past (a new exposure draft on intangibles is expected this year from the IASC).

As a consequence of many widely publicized scandals involving derivatives and other complicated instruments, however, most accounting standard setters have been struggling for years to comprehensively address this topic, which has been probably the top priority for most of them.

The IASC has seemingly concluded that uniform rules for dealing with financial instrument recognition and measurement questions should be applicable to all enterprises (presumably meaning there will be no special industry rules), and the rather broad definition of financial instruments set forth in IAS 32 will be continued. The only instruments excluded systematically will be interests in subsidiaries, associates, and joint ventures; employer's obligations under employee stock option and purchase plans; and equity instruments issued by the reporting entity. It proposes to further study such matters as pension liabilities and insurance obligations, which may be ultimately included in the definition of financial instruments.

Recognition of an instrument will be mandated when an entity becomes a party to the contractual provisions that comprise the financial asset or liability; derecognition will follow when (for assets) the benefits specified in the contract have been realized, expired or surrendered, or (for liabilities) the obligations have been fulfilled, discharged, canceled, or expired. Initial recognition will be at fair value of the consideration given or received. Subsequent recognition will also be at fair value.

The IASC's position at this time is that all gains or losses on financial instruments should be recognized in income immediately. The most important implication of this conclusion is that hedge accounting (the deferral of gains or losses for better "matching" in a later period's income statement) cannot be supported. This rather neatly puts an end to the tortuous logic which has sometimes been invented (typically building on the otherwise solid foundation of the venerable matching concept) to support nonrecognition of gains or losses, placing them instead either as "deferred charges or credits" on the balance sheet, or into various "contra or additional equity" accounts, or as adjustments of the carrying values of the hedged assets or liabilities themselves. If the IASC indeed follows up this paper with a set of proposals based on this logic, all instruments, whether unhedged, hedged, or being held to hedge other instruments, will be marked to fair value, with the net gains and losses being fully reported in current earnings.

The only note of ambiguity in the discussion document concerns how gains or losses on hedging instruments held in connection with anticipated transactions other than the acquisition of assets or incurrence of liabilities would be reported. At this time, the sentiment is to offer reporting entities a choice of reporting these in earnings **or** in other comprehensive income, which is an as yet not fully defined category of gains and losses which are excluded from the statement of income but before net results for the period are transferred to retained earnings. Examples of the type of transactions which would qualify for such optional reporting would be currency forward contracts entered into in respect of future raw materials purchases from foreign suppliers or sales to foreign customers denominated in foreign currencies. It should be noted that the issue of hedges of anticipated transactions has been the most difficult for all the accounting standards setters to deal with, so the IASC will not likely be alone in reaching this somewhat unsatisfying solution.

The IASC will also likely modify IAS 32 to eliminate certain present requirements for fair value disclosures (unnecessary if all such assets and liabilities are adjusted to fair value), to expand disclosures about hedges of anticipated transactions, to provide more detail about financial instruments-related gains and losses included in income, and to expand disclosure of financial risk management strategies.

Realistically, the IASC has indicated that any new standard will receive a lengthier-than-normal phase-in period, and that a transitional working group will be formed to assist with implementation issues. It is likely that the resulting rules will be applicable to certain nonfinancial instruments as well, particularly to those commodities, such as certain precious metals and some agricultural goods, which are often settled for cash prior to the contract termination date. They will not apply to physical assets held as investments, however.

Short-Term Investments

IAS 25 addresses the accounting for (passive) investments, both short-term and long-term, and is discussed in Chapter 9.

6 INVENTORY

PERSPECTIVE AND ISSUES

The accounting for inventories is a major consideration for many entities because of its significance on both the income statement (cost of goods sold) and the balance sheet. Inventories are defined by IAS 2 as items that are

> *...held for sale in the ordinary course of business; in the process of production for such sale; or in the form of materials or supplies to be consumed in the production process or in the rendering of services.*

The complexity of accounting for inventories arises from several factors.

1. The high volume of activity (or turnover) in the account
2. The various cost flow alternatives that are acceptable
3. The classification of inventories

There are two types of entities for which we must consider the accounting for inventories. The merchandising entity (generally, a retailer or wholesaler) has a single inventory account that is usually titled **merchandise inventory**. These are the goods on hand that are purchased for resale. The other type of entity is the manufacturer. The manufacturer generally has three types of inventory: (1) raw materials, (2) work in process, and (3) finished goods. **Raw materials inventory** represents the goods purchased that will act as inputs in the production process leading to the finished product. **Work in process** (WIP) consists of the goods entered into production but not yet completed. **Finished goods inventory** is the completed product that is on hand awaiting sale.

In the case of either type of entity we are concerned with satisfying the same basic questions.

1. At what point in time should the items be included in inventory (ownership)?
2. What costs incurred should be included in the valuation of inventories?
3. What cost flow assumption should be used?
4. At what value should inventories be reported (net realizable value)?

The promulgated GAAP that addresses these questions is IAS 2. This standard discusses the definition, valuation, and classification of inventory. The extant standard is a modest revision of an earlier standard, the principal difference being that the base stock method formerly permitted is now prohibited. International standards are somewhat less detailed than national standards issued by certain jurisdictions, and in this chapter the requirements of IAS 2 are supplemented with guidance from other sources, where pertinent.

Under the provisions of IAS 2 as revised, the first-in, first-out and weighted-average cost methods are defined as benchmark treatments, with the last-in, first-out method relegated to allowable alternative treatment. Since the international standards went to some length to avoid naming certain methods as being preferred or recommended (hence the term "benchmark," which was deemed to be more neutral), it is fair to consider all three methods as being acceptable under the IAS. A proposed interpretation by the newly constituted Standing Interpretations Committee (SIC) of the IASC will, if enacted, state that entities should use the same cost formula for all inventories having similar nature and use. It furthermore states that differences in geographic location would not, *ipso facto*, justify the use of different cost formulas. In reaching this conclusion, the SIC analogized from the guidance on consolidations provided in IAS 27, and that on plant assets in IAS 16.

Sources of IAS
IAS 2

DEFINITIONS OF TERMS

Absorption (full) costing. Inclusion of all manufacturing costs (fixed and variable) in the cost of finished goods inventory, in accordance with GAAP.

Base stock. Based on the theory that a minimal level of inventory is a permanent investment, this amount is carried on the books at its historical cost.

By-products. Goods that result as an ancillary product from the production of a primary good; often having minor value when compared to the value of the principal product(s).

Ceiling. In lower of cost or market computations, market is limited to net realizable value. Market (replacement cost) cannot be higher than the ceiling (net realizable value). Net realizable value is selling price less selling costs and costs to complete.

Consignments. Marketing method in which the consignor ships goods to the consignee, who acts as an agent for the consignor in selling the goods. The inventory remains the property of the consignor until sold by the consignee.

Direct (variable) costing. Inclusion of only variable manufacturing costs in the cost of ending finished goods inventory. This method is not acceptable for financial reporting purposes.

Dollar-value LIFO. Variation of conventional LIFO in which layers of inventory are priced in dollars adjusted by price indexes instead of layers of inventory priced at unit prices.

Double-extension. Method used to compute the conversion price index. The index indicates the relationship between the base year and current prices in terms of a percentage.

Finished goods. Completed but unsold products produced by a manufacturing firm.

First-in, first-out (FIFO). Cost flow assumption; the first goods purchased or produced are assumed to be the first goods sold.

Floor. In lower of cost or market computations, market is limited to net realizable value less a normal profit, called the floor. Market (replacement cost) cannot be below the floor.

Goods in transit. Goods being shipped from seller to buyer at year end.

Gross profit method. Method used to estimate the amount of ending inventory based on the cost of goods available for sale, sales, and the gross profit percentage.

Inventory. Assets held for sale in the normal course of business, or which are in the process of production for such sale, or are in the form of materials or supplies to be consumed in the production process or in the rendering of services.

Inventory layer. Under the LIFO method, an increase in inventory quantity during a period.

Joint products. Two or more products produced jointly, where neither is viewed as being more important; in some cases additional production steps are applied to one or more joint products after a split off point.

Last-in, first-out (LIFO). Cost flow assumption; the last goods purchased are assumed to be the first goods sold.

LIFO liquidation. Liquidation of the LIFO base or old inventory layers when inventory quantities decrease. This can distort income since old costs are matched against current revenues.

LIFO retail. Inventory costing method that combines the LIFO cost flow assumption and the retail inventory method.

Link-chain. Method of applying dollar-value LIFO by developing a single cumulative index. This method may be used instead of double-extension only when there are substantial changes in product lines over the years.

Lower of cost or market. Inventories must be valued at lower of cost or market (replacement cost). Market cannot exceed the ceiling (net realizable value) or be less than the floor (net realizable value less a normal markup).

Markdown. Decrease below original retail price. A markdown cancelation is an increase (not above original retail price) in retail price after a markdown.

Markup. Increase above original retail price. A markup cancelation is a decrease (not below original retail price) in retail price after a markup.

Moving average. Inventory costing method used in conjunction with a perpetual inventory system. A weighted-average cost per unit is recomputed after every purchase. Goods sold are costed at the most recent moving average cost.

Net realizable value. Estimated selling price in the ordinary course of business less the estimated costs of completion and the estimated costs necessary to make the sale.

Periodic. Inventory system where quantities are determined only periodically by physical count.

Perpetual. Inventory system where up-to-date records of inventory quantities are kept.

Product financing arrangements. Arrangements whereby an entity buys inventory for another firm that agrees to purchase the inventory over a certain period at specified prices which include handling and financing costs; alternatively, an entity can buy inventory from another firm with the understanding that the seller will repurchase the goods at the original price plus defined storage and financing costs.

Purchase commitments. Noncancelable commitment to purchase goods. Losses on such commitments are recognized in the accounts.

Raw materials. For a manufacturing firm, materials on hand awaiting entry into the production process.

Replacement cost. Cost to reproduce an inventory item by purchase or manufacture. In lower of cost or market computations, the term **market** means replacement cost, subject to the ceiling and floor limitations.

Retail method. Inventory costing method that uses a cost ratio to reduce ending inventory (valued at retail) to cost.

Specific identification. Inventory system where the seller identifies which specific items are sold and which remain in ending inventory.

Standard costs. Predetermined unit costs, which are acceptable for financial reporting purposes if adjusted periodically to reflect current conditions.

Weighted-average. Periodic inventory costing method where ending inventory and cost of goods sold are priced at the weighted-average cost of all items available for sale.

Work in process. For a manufacturing firm, the inventory of partially completed products.

CONCEPTS, RULES, AND EXAMPLES

Basic Concept of Inventory Costing

International accounting standards (IAS 2, revised effective 1995) establish cost, not to exceed net realizable value, as the basis for valuation of inventories. In contrast to the standard for plant assets, there is no option for revaluing inventories to current replacement cost or fair value, presumably due to the far shorter period of time over which such assets are held, thereby limiting the cumulative impact of inflation on reported amounts. Furthermore, the benchmark treatment prescribes the relatively more conservative FIFO or weighted-average cost methods as the means of measuring historical cost of inventories, although the allowed alternative method, LIFO, may result in a somewhat more meaningful measure of earnings in periods of rising prices. These methods are discussed fully later in this chapter.

Ownership of Goods

From the accounting perspective, concern with the ownership of inventories is to assist in the determination of the actual physical quantity of inventory on hand. In general, an enterprise should record purchases and sales of inventory when legal title passes. Although strict adherence to this rule may not be important in daily transactions, a proper inventory cutoff at the end of an accounting period is crucial. Thus, for accounting purposes, to obtain an accurate measurement of inventory quantity and corresponding monetary representation of inventory and cost of goods sold in the financial statements, it is necessary to determine when title has passed.

The most common error made in this regard is to assume that title is synonymous with possession of goods on hand. This may be incorrect in two ways: (1) the goods on hand may not be owned, and (2) goods that are not on hand may be owned. There are four matters that may create a question as to proper ownership: (1) goods in transit, (2) consignment sales, (3) product financing arrangements, and (4) sales made with the buyer holding the right of return.

At year end, any **goods in transit** from seller to buyer may properly be includable in one, and only one, of those parties' inventories, based on the conditions of the sale. Under traditional legal and accounting interpretation, such goods are included in the inventory of the firm financially responsible for transportation costs. This responsibility may be indicated by shipping terms such as FOB, which is used in overland shipping contracts, and by FAS, CIF, C&F, and ex-ship, which are used in maritime contracts.

The term **FOB** stands for "free on board." If goods are shipped FOB destination, transportation costs are paid by the seller and title does not pass until the carrier delivers the goods to the buyer; thus these goods are part of the seller's inventory while in transit. If goods are shipped FOB shipping point, transportation costs are paid by the buyer and title passes when the carrier takes possession; thus these goods are part of the buyer's inventory while in transit. The terms **FOB destination** and **FOB shipping point** often indicate a specific location at which title to the goods is transferred, such as FOB Milan. This means that the seller retains title and risk of loss until the goods are delivered to a common carrier in Milan who will act as an agent for the buyer.

A seller who ships **FAS** (free alongside) must bear all expense and risk involved in delivering the goods to the dock next to (alongside) the vessel on which they are to be shipped. The buyer bears the cost of loading and of shipment; thus title passes when the carrier takes possession of the goods.

In a **CIF** (cost, insurance, and freight) contract the buyer agrees to pay in a lump sum the cost of the goods, insurance costs, and freight charges. In a C&F contract, the buyer promises to pay a lump sum that includes the cost of the goods and all freight charges. In either case, the seller must deliver the goods to the carrier and pay the costs of loading; thus both title and risk of loss pass to the buyer upon delivery of the goods to the carrier.

A seller who delivers goods **ex-ship** bears all expense and risk until the goods are unloaded, at which time both title and risk of loss pass to the buyer.

The foregoing is meant only to define normal terms and usage; actual contractual arrangements between a given buyer and a given seller can vary widely. The accounting treatment should in all cases strive to mirror the substance of the legal terms established between the parties.

In **consignments**, the consignor (seller) ships goods to the consignee (buyer), who acts as the agent of the consignor in trying to sell the goods. In some consignments, the consignee receives a commission; in other arrangements, the consignee "purchases" the goods simultaneously with the sale of the goods to the customer. Goods out on consignment are included in the inventory of the consignor and excluded from the inventory of the consignee.

A **product financing arrangement** is a transaction in which an entity sells and agrees to repurchase inventory with the repurchase price equal to the original sales price plus the carrying and financing costs. The purpose of this transaction is to allow the seller (sponsor) to arrange financing of its original purchase of the inventory. The substance of the transaction is illustrated by the diagram below.

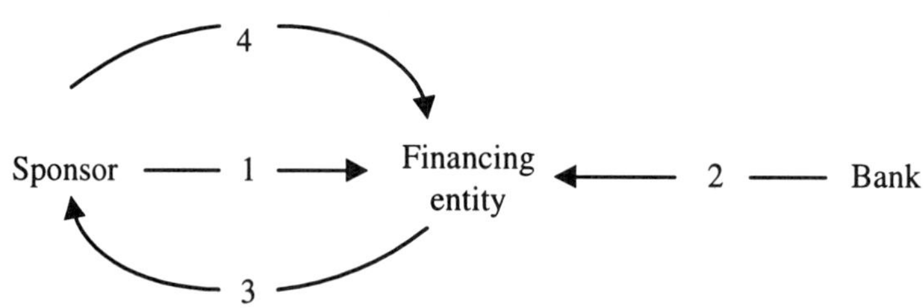

1. In the initial transaction the sponsor "sells" inventoriable items to the financing entity in return for the remittance of the sales price and at the same time agrees to repurchase the inventory at a specified price (usually the sales price plus carrying and financing costs) over a specified period of time.
2. The financing entity procures the funds remitted to the sponsor by borrowing from a bank (or other financial institution) using the newly purchased inventory as collateral.

3. The financing entity actually remits the funds to the sponsor and the sponsor presumably uses these funds to pay off the debt incurred as a result of the original purchase of the inventoriable debt.
4. The sponsor then repurchases the inventory for the specified price plus costs from the financing entity at a later time when the funds are available.

In a variant of this transaction, an entity can acquire goods from a manufacturer or dealer, with the contractual understanding that they will be resold to another entity at the same price, plus handling, storage, and financing costs.

The purpose of either variation of product financing arrangement is to enable the sponsor to acquire or control inventory without incurring additional reportable debt. Under international accounting standards, transactions of this type are not directly addressed, and thus it would appear that, if a "form over substance" approach is subscribed to, these transactions may successfully result in financing that is not reported in the balance sheet. It would therefore be instructive to look to the standard imposed in the United States by the FASB, which ruled that the substance of this type of transaction is that of a borrowing.

Under the pertinent US standard (SFAS 49, *Accounting for Product Financing Arrangements*), such transactions are, in substance, no different from those where a sponsor obtains third-party financing to purchase its inventory. As a result, the FASB ruled that when an entity sells inventory with a related arrangement to repurchase it, proper accounting is to record a liability when the funds are received for the initial transfer of the inventory in the amount of the selling price. The sponsor is then to accrue carrying and financing costs in accordance with its normal accounting policies. These accruals are eliminated and the liability satisfied when the sponsor repurchases the inventory. The inventory is not to be taken off the balance sheet of the sponsor and a sale is not to be recorded. Thus, although legal title has passed to the financing entity, for purposes of measuring and valuing inventory, the inventory is considered to be owned by the sponsor. Although the other variation on this financing arrangement, with a nominee entity acquiring the goods for the ultimate purchaser, is not addressed in SFAS 49, logic suggests that an analogous accounting treatment be prescribed.

A final issue that requires special consideration is the situation that exists when the buyer holds the right of return. Again, while international accounting standards do not address this topic directly, logical guidance is suggested by the US accounting standards. SFAS 48, *Revenue Recognition When Right of Return Exists*, addresses the propriety of recognizing revenue at the point of sale under these circumstances. Generally speaking, the sale is to be recorded if the future amount of the returns can reasonably be estimated. If the ability to make a reasonable estimate is precluded, the sale is not to be recorded until the returns are unlikely. In this situation, although legal title has passed to the buyer, the seller must continue to include the goods in its measurement and valuation of inventory. Absent a standard to the contrary under international GAAP, the "substance over form" dictum would seemingly support the guidelines suggested by SFAS 48.

Accounting for Inventories

Introduction. The major objectives of accounting for inventories is the matching of appropriate costs against revenues in order to arrive at the proper determination of periodic income, and accurate representation of inventories on hand as assets of the enterprise as of the balance sheet date. As it happens, these two goals are in conflict and, under any system of accounting in which the financial statements are fully articulated (i.e., where the balance sheet and income statement are linked together mechanically), it will be virtually impossible to achieve both fully.

The accounting for inventories is done under either a periodic or a perpetual system. In a **periodic inventory system**, the inventory quantity is determined periodically by a physical count. The quantity so determined is then priced in accordance with the cost method used. Cost of goods sold is computed by adding beginning inventory and net purchases (or cost of goods manufactured) and subtracting ending inventory.

Alternatively, a **perpetual inventory system** keeps a running total of the quantity (and possibly the cost) of inventory on hand by recording all sales and purchases as they occur. When inventory is purchased, the inventory account (rather than purchases) is debited. When inventory is sold, the cost of goods sold and reduction of inventory are recorded. Periodic physical counts are necessary only to verify the perpetual records and to satisfy the tax regulations (tax regulations require that a physical inventory be taken, at least annually).

Valuation of Inventories

According to IAS 2, the primary basis of accounting for inventories is cost. **Cost** is defined as the sum of all costs of purchase, costs of conversion, and other costs incurred in bringing the inventories to their present location and condition. This definition allows for significant interpretation of the costs to be included in inventory.

For raw materials and merchandise inventory that are purchased outright and not intended for further conversion, the identification of cost is relatively straightforward. The cost of these purchased inventories will include all expenditures incurred in bringing the goods to the point of sale and putting them in a salable condition. These costs include the purchase price, transportation costs, insurance, and handling costs. Trade discounts, rebates, and other such items are to be deducted in determining inventory costs; failure to do so would result in carrying inventory at amounts in excess of true historical costs.

The impact of interest costs as they relate to the valuation of inventoriable items (IAS 23) is discussed in Chapter 8. In general, even when the allowed alternative treatment prescribed by IAS 23 is employed, borrowing costs will not be capitalized in connection with inventory acquisitions, since the period required to ready the goods for sale will not be significant. However, where a lengthy production process is required to prepare the goods for sale, the provisions of IAS 23 would be applicable and a portion of borrowing costs would become part of the cost of inventory.

Conversion costs for manufactured goods should include all costs that are directly associated with the units produced, such as labor and overhead. The allocation of overhead costs, however, must be systematic and rational, and in the case of fixed overhead costs (i.e., those which do not vary directly with level of production) the allocation process should be based on normal production levels. In periods of unusually low levels of production, a portion of fixed overhead costs must accordingly be charged directly to operations, and not taken into inventory.

Costs other than material and conversion costs are inventoriable only to the extent they are necessary to bring the goods to their present condition and location. Examples might include certain design costs and other types of preproduction expenditures if intended to benefit specific classes of customers. On the other hand, all research costs and most development costs (per IAS 9, as discussed in Chapter 8) would typically **not** become part of inventory costs. Also generally excluded from inventory would be such costs as administrative and selling expenses, which must be treated as period costs; the cost of wasted materials, labor, or other production expenditures; and most storage costs. Included in overhead, and thus allocable to inventory, would be such categories as repairs, maintenance, utilities, rent, indirect labor, production supervisory wages, indirect materials and supplies, quality control and inspection, and the cost of small tools not capitalized.

Joint products and by-products. In some production processes, more than one product is produced simultaneously. Typically, if each product has significant value, they are referred to as **joint products**; if only one has substantial value, the others are known as **by-products**. Under IAS 2, when the costs of each jointly produced good cannot be clearly determined, a rational allocation among them is required. Generally, such allocation is made by reference to the relative values of the jointly produced goods, as measured by ultimate selling prices. Often, after a period of joint production the goods are split off, separately incurring additional costs before being completed and ready for sale. The allocation of joint costs should take into account the additional individual product costs yet to be incurred after the point at which joint production ceases.

By-products by definition are products that have limited value when measured with reference to the primary good being produced. IAS 2 suggests that by-products be valued at net realizable value, with the costs allocated to by-products thereby being deducted from the cost pool, being otherwise allocated to the sole or several principal products.

For example, products A and B have the same processes performed on them up to the split-off point. The total cost incurred to this point is $80,000. This cost can be assigned to products A and B using their relative sales value at the split-off point. If A could be sold for $60,000 and B for $40,000, the total sales value is $100,000. The cost would be assigned on the basis of each product's relative sales value. Thus, A would be assigned a cost of $48,000 (60,000/100,000 x 80,000) and B a cost of $32,000 (400,000/100,000 x 80,000).

If inventory is exchanged with another entity for similar goods, the earnings process is generally not culminated. Accordingly, the acquired items are recorded at the recorded, or book, value of the items given up.

In some jurisdictions, the categories of costs that are includable in inventory for tax purposes may differ from those that are permitted for financial reporting purposes under international accounting standards. To the extent that differential tax and financial reporting is possible (i.e., that there is no statutory requirement that the taxation rules constrain financial reporting) this situation will result in interperiod tax allocation. This is discussed more fully in Chapter 14.

Direct costing. The method of allocating fixed overhead to both ending inventory and cost of goods sold is commonly known as (full) absorption costing. IAS 2 requires that absorption costing be employed. However, often for managerial decision making purposes an alternative to absorption costing, variable or direct costing, is utilized. Direct costing requires classifying only direct materials, direct labor, and variable overhead related to production as inventory costs. All fixed costs are accounted for as period costs. The virtue of direct costing is that under this accounting strategy there will be a predictable, linear effect on marginal contribution from each unit of sales revenue, which can be useful in planning and controlling the business operation. However, such a costing method does not result in inventory which includes all costs of production, and therefore this is deemed not to be in accordance with GAAP under international standards. If an entity uses direct costing for internal budgeting or other purposes, adjustments must be made to develop alternative information for financial reporting purposes.

BENCHMARK METHODS OF INVENTORY COSTING

Specific Identification

The theoretical basis for valuing inventories and cost of goods sold requires assigning the production and/or acquisition costs to the specific goods to which they relate. For example, the cost of ending inventory for an entity in its first year, during which it produced 10 items (say, exclusive single family homes), might be the actual production cost of the first, sixth, and eighth unit produced if those are the actual units still on hand at the balance sheet date. This method of inventory valuation is usually referred to as **specific identification**.

Specific identification is generally not a practical technique, as the product will generally lose its separate identity as it passes through the production and sales process. Exceptions to this would arise in situations involving small inventory quantities with high unit value and low turnover rate. Under IAS 2, specific identification must be employed to cost inventories that are not ordinarily interchangeable, and goods and services produced and segregated for specific projects. For inventories meeting either of these criteria, the specific identification method is mandatory and the other benchmark methods cannot be used.

Because of the limited applicability of specific identification, it is more likely to be the case that certain assumptions regarding the cost flows associated with inventory will need to be made. One of accounting's peculiarities is that these cost flows may or may not reflect the physical flow of inventory. Over the years, much attention has been given to both the flow of physical goods and the assumed flow of costs associated with those goods. In most jurisdictions, it has long been recognized that the flow of costs need not mirror the actual flow of the goods with which those costs are associated. For example, a key provision in an early US accounting standard stated that

> *...cost for inventory purposes shall be determined under any one of several assumptions as to the flow of cost factors; the major objective in selecting a method should be to choose the one which, under the circumstances, most clearly reflects periodic income.*

Under international accounting standards, there are two benchmark cost flow assumptions, and one additional method, which is an allowed alternative treatment. The most common cost flow assumptions used are: (1) first-in, first-out (FIFO), (2) weighted-average, and (3) last-in, first-out (LIFO). Additionally, there are variations of each of these assumptions which have commonly been used in practice. In certain jurisdictions, other costing procedures, such as the base stock method, have also been permitted.

First-In, First-Out (FIFO)

The FIFO method of inventory valuation assumes that the first goods purchased are the first goods used or sold, regardless of the actual physical flow. This method is thought to parallel most closely the physical flow of the units for most industries having moderate to rapid turnover of goods. The strength of this cost flow assumption lies in the inventory amount reported on the balance sheet. Because the earliest goods purchased are the first ones removed from the inventory account, the remaining balance is composed of items acquired at more recent costs. This yields results similar to those obtained under current cost accounting on the balance sheet. However, the FIFO method does not necessarily reflect the most accurate income figure when viewed from the perspective of underlying economic performance, as older historical costs are being matched against current revenues. Depending on the rate of inventory turnover and the speed with which general and specific prices are changing, this mismatching could potentially have a material distorting effect on reported income. At the extreme, if reported earnings are fully distributed to owners as dividends, the enterprise could be left without sufficient resources to replenish its inventory stocks due to changing prices.

The following example illustrates the basic principles involved in the application of FIFO:

	Units available	*Units sold*	*Actual unit cost*	*Actual total cost*
Beginning inventory	100	--	$2.10	$210
Sale	--	75	--	--
Purchase	150	--	2.80	420
Sale	--	100	--	--
Purchase	50	--	3.00	150
Total	300	175		$780

Given these data, the cost of goods sold and the ending inventory balance are determined as follows:

	Units	*Unit cost*	*Total cost*
Cost of goods sold	100	$2.10	$210
	75	2.80	210
	175		$420
Ending inventory	50	3.00	$150
	75	2.80	210
	125		$360

Notice that the total of the units in cost of goods sold and ending inventory, as well as the sum of their total costs, is equal to the goods available for sale and their respective total costs.

The unique characteristic of the FIFO method is that it provides the same results under either the periodic or perpetual system. This will not be the case for any other costing method.

Weighted-Average

The other benchmark method of inventory valuation under IAS 2 involves averaging and is commonly referred to as the weighted-average method. The cost of goods available for sale (beginning inventory and net purchases) is divided by the units available for sale to obtain a weighted-average unit cost. Ending inventory and cost of goods sold are then priced at this average cost. For example, assume the following data:

	Units available	*Units sold*	*Actual unit cost*	*Actual total cost*
Beginning inventory	100	--	$2.10	$210
Sale	--	75	--	--
Purchase	150	--	2.80	420
Sale	--	100	--	--
Purchase	50	--	3.00	150
Total	300	175		$780

The weighted-average cost is $780/300, or $2.60. Ending inventory is 125 units at $2.60, or $325; cost of goods sold is 175 units at $2.60, or $455.

When the weighted-average assumption is applied to a perpetual inventory system, the average cost is recomputed after each purchase. This process is referred to as a moving average. Sales are costed at the most recent average. This combination is called the moving average method and is applied below to the same data used in the weighted-average example above.

	Units on hand	*Purchases in dollars*	*Sales in dollars*	*Total cost*	*Inventory unit cost*
Beginning inventory	100	$ --	$ --	$210.00	$2.10
Sale (75 units @ $2.10)	25	--	157.50	52.50	2.10
Purchase (150 units, $420)	175	420.00	--	472.50	2.70
Sale (100 units @ $2.70)	75	--	270.00	202.50	2.70
Purchase (50 units, $150)	125	150.00	--	352.50	2.82

Cost of goods sold is 75 units at $2.10 and 100 units at $2.70, or a total of $427.50.

Last-In, First-Out (LIFO)

The LIFO method of inventory valuation costs the ending inventory as if the last goods purchased were the first goods used or sold. This allows the matching of current costs with current revenue and as proponents of the method argue, provides the best measure of periodic income, which is a major objective for periodic financial reporting. However, unless costs remain relatively unchanged, the LIFO method will usually distort the ending inventory balance for balance sheet purposes because inventory usually consists of costs from earlier periods. Critics of the method also point out that LIFO does not usually follow the physical flow of merchandise or materials. However, this last argument should not affect the selection of a cost flow assumption, because the matching of physical flow is not considered to be an objective of accounting for inventories.

Despite the arguable logic of using a LIFO cost flow assumption during periods of changing prices, to achicvc a more meaningful measure of income, the method actually is not truly derived from a promulgated accounting principle. Rather, the basis for LIFO is found in various tax codes enacted in certain jurisdictions from time to time. Since rising general price levels have been almost the rule during the past half century, LIFO has been enacted as a form of tax relief by a number of important tax jurisdictions and was widely embraced for financial reporting purposes principally in those instances in which use for tax reporting purposes was linked to financial reporting. Other requirements of LIFO, largely dependent on local tax regulations, have included restrictions on abandoning the LIFO after first adopting it, and limitations on supplementary disclosures of income determined by alternative costing stategies. Given LIFO's genesis as an offspring of tax rules, the precise methods of applying LIFO that are permitted in different nations will vary widely; the following discussion sets forth many of the computational techniques that may validly be employed, but does not represent which, if any, may be permitted in any particular circumstance. (IAS 2 does not describe how LIFO is to be operationalized.)

The actual implementation of LIFO requires valuation of the quantity of ending inventory at prices in effect earlier. The quantity of ending inventory on hand in the year when the method is first applied is termed the **base layer**. This inventory is valued at actual (full absorption) cost, and unit cost is determined by dividing total cost by the quantity on hand. In subsequent periods, increases in the quantity of inventory on hand are referred to as **increments**, or **LIFO layers**. These increments are valued individually by applying one of several possible costs to the quantity of inventory representing a layer.

1. The actual cost of the goods most recently purchased or produced
2. The actual cost of the goods purchased or produced in order of acquisition
3. An average unit cost of all goods purchased or produced during the current year
4. A hybrid method that will more clearly reflect income

Thus, after using the LIFO method for 5 years, it is possible that an enterprise could have ending inventory consisting of the base layer and five additional layers (or increments) provided that the quantity of ending inventory increased every year.

Example of the single goods (unit) LIFO approach

Fenetre Co. is in its first year of operation and elects to use the periodic LIFO method of inventory valuation. The company sells only one product. Fenetre will apply the LIFO method using the order of current year acquisition cost. The following data are given for years 1 through 3:

	Units	Unit cost	Total cost
Year 1			
Purchase	200	$2.00	$400
Sale	100	--	--
Purchase	200	3.00	600
Sale	150	--	--
Year 2			
Purchase	300	$3.20	$960
Sale	200	--	--
Purchase	100	3.30	330
Year 3			
Purchase	100	$3.50	$350
Sale	200	--	--
Sale	100	--	--

In year 1 the following occurred:

1. The total goods available for sale were 400 units.

2. The total sales were 250 units.
3. Therefore, the ending inventory was 150 units.

The ending inventory is valued at the earliest current year acquisition cost of $2.00 per unit. Thus, ending inventory is valued at $300 (150 x $2.00).

Another way to look at this is to analyze both cost of goods sold and ending inventory.

	Units	*Unit cost*	*Total cost*
Cost of goods sold	200	$3.00	$600
	50	2.00	100
	250		$700
Ending inventory	150	$2.00	$300

Note that the base-year cost is $2.00 and that the base-year level is 150 units. Therefore, if ending inventory in the subsequent period exceeds 150 units, a new layer will be created.

Year 2	*Units*	*Unit cost*	*Total cost*
Cost of goods sold	100	$3.30	$330
	100	3.20	320
	200		$650
Ending inventory	150	$2.00	$300
	200	3.20	640
	350		$940

Now, if ending inventory exceeds 350 units in the next period, a new layer will be created.

Year 3	*Units*	*Unit cost*	*Total cost*
Cost of goods sold	100	$3.50	$350
	200	3.20	640
	300		$990
Ending inventory base year	150	$2.00	$300

Notice how the decrement of 200 units in year 3 eliminated the entire year 2 increment. Thus, any year 4 increase in the quantity of inventory would result in a new increment that would be valued at year 4 prices.

In situations where the ending inventory decreases from the level established at the close of the preceding year, the enterprise experiences a decrement or **LIFO liquidation**. Decrements will reduce or eliminate previously established LIFO layers. Once any part of a layer has been eliminated, it cannot be reinstated. For example, if in its first year after the election of LIFO an enterprise establishes a layer (increment) of 10 units, in the next year inventory decreases by 4 units, leaving the first layer at 6 units, the enterprise cannot reestablish the first layer (back up to 10 units) in the year that inventory next increases. Rather, it will be forced to create a new layer for the increase. The effect of LIFO liquidations in periods of rising prices is to release costs, which are significantly below the current cost being paid, into cost of goods sold from ending inventory. Thus, the resultant effect of a LIFO liquidation is to increase income, typically for both accounting and tax purposes (since most jurisdictions demand conformity between financial reporting and tax reporting). Because of this, LIFO is most commonly used by industries in which inventories are maintained or increased over time.

LIFO liquidations can take two forms, voluntary or involuntary. A **voluntary liquidation** exists when an enterprise decides, for one reason or another, to let inventory levels drop. Such a liquidation occurs because current prices may be too high, less inventory is needed for efficient production, or because of a transition in the product lines. **Involuntary LIFO liquidations** stem from reasons beyond the control of the enterprise, such as a strike, shortages, or shipping delay. Regardless of the reason, all liquidations result in a corresponding increase in income (assuming a trend of rising costs).

To compute the effect of the liquidation, the company must compute the difference between actual cost of sales and what cost of sales would have been had the inventory been reinstated. The Internal Revenue Service has ruled that this hypothetical reinstatement must be computed under the company's normal pricing procedures for valuing its LIFO increments. In the example above the effect of the year 3 LIFO liquidation would be computed as follows:

Inventory reinstatement:

200 units @ $3.50 – $3.20 = $60

Because the 200 units liquidated would have been stated at the year 3 price of $3.50 if there had been an increment, the difference between $3.50 and the actual amount charged to cost of sales for these units ($3.20) measures the effect of the liquidation.

An inordinate amount of recordkeeping is required in applying the unit LIFO method. Remember that the illustration above involved only one product. The recordkeeping burden becomes much greater as the number of products increases. For this reason a **pooling** approach is generally applied to LIFO inventories.

Pooling is the process of grouping items which are naturally related and then treating this group as a single unit in determining the LIFO cost. Because the quantity of ending inventory includes many more items, decreases in one item can be made up for by increases in others, whereas under the single goods unit approach a decrease in any one item results in a liquidation of LIFO layers.

The problem in applying the pooling method emanates from the tax regulations, not the practical side of application. In applying LIFO, the tax regulations state that each type of good in the opening inventory must be compared with a similar type in the closing inventory. These items must be similar as to character, quality, and price. This qualification has generally been interpreted to mean identical. The effect of this statement is to require a separate pool for each item under the unit LIFO method. The need for a simpler, more practical approach to using the LIFO concept and allowing for a greater use of the pooling concept was met by dollar-value LIFO.

Dollar-Value LIFO

Dollar-value LIFO may be employed in those jurisdictions where it is permitted by the tax or other regulatory authorities. The dollar-value LIFO method of inventory valuation determines the cost of inventories by expressing base-year costs in terms of total dollars rather than specific prices of specific units. As discussed later, the dollar-value method also gives rise to an expanded interpretation of the use of pools. Increments and liquidations are treated the same but are reflected only in terms of a net liquidation or increment for the entire pool.

Creating pools. Essentially three alternatives exist for determining pools under dollar-value LIFO: (1) the natural business unit, (2) multiple pools, and (3) pools for wholesalers, retailers, jobbers, and so on.

The natural business unit is defined by the existence of separate and distinct processing facilities and operations and the maintenance of separate income (loss) records. The concept of the natural business unit is generally dependent on the type of product, not the various stages of production for that project. Thus, the pool can (and will) contain raw materials, WIP, and finished goods. The three examples below, taken from treasury regulations, illustrate the application of the natural business unit concept.

Example 1

A corporation manufactures, in one division, automatic clothes washers and dryers of both commercial and domestic grade as well as electric ranges, mangles, and dishwashers. The corporation manufactures, in another division, radios and television sets. The manufacturing facilities and processes used in manufacturing radios and television sets are distinct from those used in manufacturing automatic clothes washers, for example. Under these circumstances, the enterprise would consist of two business units and two pools would be appropriate: one consisting of all of the LIFO inventories involved with the manufacture of clothes washers and dryers, electric ranges, mangles, and dishwashers, and the other consisting of all the LIFO inventories involved with the production of radios and television sets.

Example 2

An enterprise produces plastics in one of its plants. Substantial amounts of the production are sold as plastics. The remainder of the production is shipped to a second plant of the enterprise for the production of plastic toys which are sold to customers. The company operates its plastics plant and toy plant as separate divisions. Because of the different product lines and the separate divisions, the enterprise has two natural business units.

Example 3

A company is engaged in the manufacture of paper. At one stage of processing, uncoated paper is produced. Substantial amounts of uncoated paper are sold at this stage of processing. The remainder of the uncoated paper is transferred to the company's finishing mill, where coated paper is produced and sold. This company has only one natural business unit since coated and uncoated paper are within the same product line.

The multiple-pooling method is the grouping of substantially similar items. In determining substantially similar items, consideration should be given to the processing applied, the interchangeability, the similarity of use, and the customary practice of the industry. While the election of multiple pools will necessitate additional recordkeeping, it may result in a better estimation of periodic income. Depending on local tax regulations, diverse inventory types, such as inventory items of wholesalers, retailers, jobbers, and distributors, might be required to be placed into pools by major lines, types, or classes of goods.

All three methods of pooling allow for a change in the components of inventory. New items that properly fall within the pool may be added, and old items may disappear from the pool, but neither will necessarily effect a change in the total dollar value of the pool.

Computing dollar-value LIFO. The purpose of the dollar-value LIFO method of valuing inventory is to convert inventory that is priced at end-of-year prices to that same inventory priced at base-year (or applicable LIFO layer) prices. The dollar-value method achieves this result through the use of a conversion price index. The inventory at current year cost is divided by the appropriate index to arrive at the base-year cost. Thus, the main focus is on the determination of the conversion price index. There are three basic methods that can be used in computation of the LIFO value of a dollar-value pool: (1) double-extension, (2) link-chain, and (3) the index method. Each of these is discussed below with examples provided where appropriate.

Double-extension method. This was the method originally developed to compute the conversion price index. It involves extending the entire quantity of ending inventory for the current year at both base-year prices and end-of-year prices to arrive at a total dollar value for each, hence the title of double extension. The end-of-year dollar total is then divided by the base-year dollar total to arrive at the index, usually referred to as the **conversion price index**. This index indicates the relationship between the base-year and current prices in terms of a percentage. Each layer (or increment) is valued at its own percentage. Although a representative sample is allowed (meaning that not all of the items need be double extended; this is discussed in more detail under indexing), the recordkeeping under this method is very burdensome. The base-year price must be kept for each inventory item. Depending on the number of different items included in the inventory of the company, the necessary records may be too detailed to keep past the first year.

The following example illustrates the double-extension method of computing the LIFO value of inventory. The example presented is relatively simple and does not attempt to incorporate all of the complexities of inventory accounting.

Example of the double-extension LIFO method

Van de Voort, Inc. uses the dollar-value method of LIFO inventory valuation and computes its price index using the double-extension method. Van de Voort has a single pool that contains two inventory items, A and B. Year 1 is the company's initial year of operations. The following information is given for years 1 through 4:

Year	*Ending inventory current prices*	*Ending quantity (units) and current price* A		B	
1	$100,000	5,000	$6.00	7,000	$10.00
2	120,300	6,000	6.30	7,500	11.00
3	122,220	5,800	6.40	7,400	11.50
4	133,900	6,200	6.50	7,800	12.00

In year 1 there is no computation of an index; the index is 100%. The LIFO cost is the same as the actual current year cost. This is our base year.

In year 2 the first step is to double extend the quantity of ending inventory at base-year and current year costs. This is illustrated below.

Item	*Quantity*	*Base-year cost/unit*	*Extended*	*Current year cost/unit*	*Extended*
A	6,000	$ 6.00	$ 36,000	$ 6.30	$ 37,800
B	7,500	10.00	75,000	11.00	82,500
			$111,000		$120,300*

* *When using the double-extension method and extending* ***all*** *the inventory items to arrive at the index, this number must equal the ending inventory at current prices. If a sampling method is used (as discussed under indexing), this number* ***divided by*** *your ending inventory at current prices will give you the percentage sampled.*

Now we can compute the conversion price index which is

$$\frac{\text{Ending inventory at current year prices}}{\text{Ending inventory at base-year prices}}$$

In this case

$$\frac{120,300}{111,000} = 108.4\% \text{ (rounded)}$$

Next, the year 2 layer at the base-year cost is computed by taking the current year ending inventory at base-year prices (if only a sample of the inventory is extended, this number is arrived at by dividing the ending inventory at current year prices by the conversion price index) of $111,000 and subtracting the base-year cost of $100,000. In year 2 there is an increment (layer) of $11,000 at base-year costs.

The year 2 layer of $11,000 at base-year cost must be converted so that the layer is valued at the prices in effect when it came into existence (i.e., at year 2 prices). This is done by multiplying the increment at base-year cost ($11,000) by the conversion price index (1.08). The result is the year 2 layer at LIFO prices.

Base-year cost	$100,000
Year 2 layer ($11,000 x 1.084)	11,924
	$111,924

In year 3 the same basic procedure is followed.

Item	Quantity	Base-year cost/unit	Extended	Current year cost/unit	Extended
A	5,800	$ 6.00	$ 34,800	$ 6.40	$ 37,120
B	7,400	10.00	74,000	11.50	85,100
			$108,800		$122,220

There has been a decrease in the base-year cost of the ending inventory, which is referred to as a **decrement**. A decrement results in the decrease (or elimination) of layers provided previously. In this situation, computation of the index is not necessary, as there is no LIFO layer that requires valuation. If a sampling approach has been used, the index is needed to arrive at the ending inventory at base-year cost and thus to determine if there has been an increment or a decrement.

Now the ending inventory at base-year cost is $108,800. The base-year cost is still $100,000, so the total increment is $8,800. Since this is less than the $11,000 increment of year 2, no additional increment is established in year 3. The LIFO cost of the inventory is as shown below.

Base-year cost	$100,000
Year 2 layer ($8,800 x 1.084)	9,539
	$109,539

The fourth year then follows the same steps.

Item	Quantity	Base-year cost/unit	Extended	Current year cost/unit	Extended
A	6,200	$ 6.00	$ 37,200	$ 6.50	$ 40,300
B	7,800	10.00	78,000	12.00	93,600
			$115,200		$133,900

The conversion price index is 116.2% (133,900/115,200).

A current year increment exists because the ending inventory at base-year prices in year 4 of $115,200 exceeds the year 3 number of $108,800. The current year increment of $6,400 must be valued at year 4 prices. Thus the LIFO cost of the year 4 inventory is

Base-year layer	$100,000
Year 2 layer ($8,800 x 1.084)	9,539
Year 4 layer ($6,400 x 1.162)	7,437
	$116,976

It is important to point out that once a layer is reduced or eliminated, it is never replaced (as with the year 2 increment).

Link-chain method. As shown in this example, the computations for application of the double-extension method become arduous even if only a few items exist in the inventory. Also, consider the problems that arise when there is a constant change in the inventory mix or in situations in which the breadth of the inventory is large. The link-chain method of applying dollar-value LIFO was developed to combat these problems.

Another purpose served by the link-chain method is to eliminate the problem created by a significant turnover in the components of inventory. Under the double-extension or indexing method, it is presumed that any new products added to the inventory will be costed at base-year prices. If these are not available, the earliest cost available after the base year is used. If the item was not in existence in the base year, the reporting entity will attempt to reconstruct the base cost, using a reasonable method to determine what the cost would have been if the item had been in existence in the base year. Although this might not appear to be a problem upon first consideration, imagine identifying a cost from a base period 25 to 50 years past. Should that be impossible, a more recent cost would have to be identified to serve as the base-year cost value, which would eliminate some of the LIFO benefit.

Also imagine a situation faced by a high-tech industry where inventory is continually being replaced by newer, more advanced products. The effect of this rapid change under the double-extension method (because the new products did not exist in the base period) is to use current prices as base-year costs. Thus, when inventory has such a rapid turnover, the LIFO advantage is nonexistent, as current and base-year costs are sometimes synonymous. This is the major reason for the development of the link-chain method.

The link-chain method is the process of developing a single cumulative index that is applied to the ending inventory amount priced at the beginning-of-the-year costs. A separate cumulative index is used for each pool regardless of the variations in the components of these pools over the years. Technological change is allowed for by the method used to calculate each current year index. The index is derived by double extending a representative sample (between 50% and 75% of the dollar value of the pool is generally thought to be appropriate) at both beginning-of-year prices and end-of-year prices. This annual index is then applied (multiplied) to the previous period's cumulative index to arrive at the new current year cumulative index.

Example of the link-chain method

Notice that the end-of-year costs and inventory quantity used are the same as those used in the double-extension example. Assume the following inventory data for years 1 to 4. Year 1 is assumed to be the initial year of operation for the company. The LIFO method is elected on the first tax return. Assume that A and B constitute a single pool.

Product	Ending inventory quantity	Cost per unit Beg. of yr.	End of yr.	Extension Beginning	End
Year 1:					
A	5,000	N/A	$ 6.00	N/A	30,000
B	7,000	N/A	10.00	N/A	70,000
Year 2:					
A	6,000	$ 6.00	6.30	36,000	37,800
B	7,500	10.00	11.00	75,000	82,500
Year 3:					
A	5,800	6.30	6.40	36,540	37,120
B	7,400	11.00	11.50	81,400	85,100
Year 4:					
A	6,200	6.40	6.50	39,680	40,300
B	7,800	11.50	12.00	89,700	93,600

The initial year (base year) does not require the computation of an index under any LIFO method. The base-year index will always be 1.00.

Thus, the base-year inventory layer is $100,000 (the end-of-year inventory restated at base-year cost).

The second year requires the first index computation. Notice that in year 2 our extended totals are

	Beginning-of-year prices	End-of-year prices
A	$ 36,000	$ 37,800
B	75,000	82,500
	$111,000	$120,300

The year 2 index is 1.084 (120,300/111,000). This is the same as computed under the double-extension method because the beginning-of-the-year prices reflect the base-year price. This will not always be the case, as new items may sometimes be added to the pool, causing a change in the index.

Thus, the cumulative index is the 1.084 current year index multiplied by the preceding year index of 1.00 to arrive at a link-chain index of 1.084.

This index is then used to restate the inventory to base-year cost by dividing the inventory at end-of-year dollars by the cumulative index: $120,300/1.084 = $111,000. The determination of the LIFO increment or decrement is then basically the same as the double-extension method. In year 2 the increment (layer) at base-year cost is $11,000 ($111,000 – 100,000). This layer must be valued at the prices effective when the layer was created, or extended at the cumulative index for that year. This results in an ending inventory at LIFO cost of

	Base-year cost	Index	LIFO cost
Base year	$100,000	1.00	$100,000
Year 2 layer	11,000	1.084	11,924
	$111,000		$111,924

The index for year 3 is computed as follows:

	Beginning-of-year prices	End-of-year prices
A	$ 36,540	$ 37,120
B	81,400	85,100
	$117,940	$122,220

122,220/117,940 = 1.036

The next step is to determine the cumulative index, which is the product of the preceding year's cumulative index and the current year index, or 1.123 (1.084 x 1.036). The new cumulative index is used to restate the inventory at end-of-year dollars to base-year cost. This is accomplished by dividing the end-of-year inventory by the new cumulative index. Thus, current inventory at base-year cost is $108,833. In this instance we have experienced a decrement (a decrease from the prior year's $111,000). The determination of ending inventory is

	Base-year cost	Index	LIFO cost
Base year	$100,000	1.00	$100,000
Year 2 layer	8,833	1.084	9,575
Year 3 layer	--	1.123	--
	$108,833		$109,575

Finally, perform the same steps for the year 4 computation. The current year index is 1.035 (133,900/129,380). The new cumulative index is 1.162 (1.035 x 1.123). The base-year cost of the current inventory is $115,232 (133,900/1.162). Thus, LIFO inventory at the end of year 4 is

	Base-year cost	Index	LIFO cost
Base year	$100,000	1.00	$100,000
Year 2 layer	8,833	1.084	9,575
Year 3	--	1.123	--
Year 4 layer	6,399	1.162	7,435
	$115,232		$117,010

Notice how even though the numbers used were the same as those used in the double-extension example, the results were different (year 4 inventory under double extension was $116,976); however, not by a significant amount. It is much easier to keep track of beginning-of-the-year prices than it is to keep base-year prices, but perhaps more important, it is easier to establish beginning-of-the-year prices for **new items** than to establish their base-year price. The latter reason is why the link-chain method is so much more desirable than the double-extension method. However, before electing or applying this method, a company must be able to establish a sufficient need as defined in the treasury regulations.

Finally, it should be noted that the link-chain method was originally developed for those enterprises that wanted to use LIFO but because of substantial changes in product lines over time were unable to recreate or keep the historical records necessary to make accurate use of the double-extension method. It is important to note that the double-extension and link-chain methods are not intended to be selective alternatives for the same situation. The link-chain election requires that substantial change in product line be evident over the years, and it is not meant to be used solely because of its ease of application. The double-extension method, which is more accurate, should be demonstrated to be impractical before the link-chain method is invoked as an alternative.

Indexing. The last major alternative available for computing the dollar-value LIFO inventory is indexing. These indexing methods can basically be broken down into two types: (1) an internal index, and (2) an external index.

The **internal index** is merely a variation of the double-extension method. A representative sample (or some other statistical method) of the inventory will be double extended; the representative index computed from the sample is then used to restate the inventory to base-year cost and to value the new layer.

The **external index** method involves using indices published by governmental or private sources and applying the index chosen to the inventory figures. Because of this method's complexity and limited applicability, and due to the fact that local taxing authorities or other official agencies would have to endorse one or more indices for such use, this application is not discussed further.

The methods described for the application of LIFO, as noted above, have been based on tax rules rather than on financial accounting pronouncements. GAAP has tended to permit the use of LIFO, when it has, because it had earlier been endorsed by the taxing or other relevant authorities, not because of the theoretical validity of the technique, although it can be argued that LIFO does more accurately measure periodic income. In recognition of the lack of authoritative accounting guidelines in the implementation of LIFO in the United States, for example, the AICPA prepared an issues paper on this topic. This paper, *Identification and Discussion of Certain Financial Accounting and Reporting Issues Concerning LIFO Inventories*, described numerous accounting problems in the use of LIFO and includes advisory conclusions for these problems. Because of the possible applicability of the guidance in this paper to those entities that choose to use the available alternative method under IAS 2, selected sections of it are detailed in the appendix to this chapter.

Interim Treatment of LIFO

Interim financial reporting has not received formal attention from the international GAAP standard setters, although the topic is on the IASC draft work plan, with a projected date of mid-1997 for a discussion document. Under US GAAP, however, it is well established that interim periods are not equivalent to full fiscal periods, but rather, should be viewed as integral parts of the full period of which they will form a part. Thus, it is not expected that inventories will be taken at the end of each interim period, and estimation techniques such as the gross profit method can be used instead.

While for most issues of revenue or expense it is largely academic whether the interim period is treated as a stand-alone period or as a part of the fiscal year to which it belongs (as accrual accounting principles will dictate the same result in either case), entities using the LIFO inventory method will almost always be affected. The most commonly encountered issue is that of temporary liquidations of inventories; while these must be dealt with as permanent declines if occurring at year end, at interim dates these may be accounted for as temporary (assuming that this is supportable by the relevant facts and circumstances), with a "reserve" established for replenishment, thereby avoiding absorbing old, lower costs into cost of sales.

Although there are other measurement issues under GAAP that necessitate an annual perspective (such as the need to provide income taxes based on the entity's expected effective tax rate over the full year), inventory costing, particularly under LIFO, is probably the most notable interim reporting problem. The reason for permitting the use of a "reserve" is that LIFO was conceived of as an annual measurement strategy. US and other tax laws, where they permit LIFO inventory accounting, are strictly annual measures. Were companies permitted to treat LIFO measures as applicable to shorter reporting periods, depending on each company's possibly unique decisions regarding frequency of reporting, the results would not conform to the annual tax computations. This emphasizes the fact that LIFO has little conceptual validity and probably would not exist under GAAP were it not a popular tax strategy.

Comparison of Cost Assumptions

Of the three basic cost flow assumptions, LIFO and FIFO produce the most extreme results, with results using the weighted-average method generally falling somewhere in between. The selection of one of these methods involves a detailed analysis, including a determination of the organization's objectives and the current and future economic state.

As mentioned above, in periods of rising prices the LIFO method is generally thought best to fulfill the objective of providing the clearest measure of periodic income. It does not provide an accurate estimate of the inventory value in an inflationary environment; however, this can usually be overcome by the issuance of supplementary fair value data. In periods of rising prices a prudent business should use the LIFO method because it will result in a decrease in the current tax liability when compared to other alternatives, for those jurisdictions where the use of LIFO is acceptable. Yet in a deflationary period, the opposite is true.

FIFO is a balance sheet oriented costing method, as it gives the most accurate estimate of the current value of the inventory account during periods of changing prices. In periods of rising prices, the FIFO method will result in higher taxes than the other alternatives, while in a deflationary period FIFO provides for a reduced tax burden. However, a major advantage of the FIFO method is that it is not subject to all the regulations and requirements of the tax codes as LIFO typically is.

The average methods do not provide an estimate of current cost information on either the balance sheet or income statement. The average method will not serve to minimize the tax burden, nor will it result in the highest burden among the various alternatives.

Although price trends and underlying objectives are important in the selection of a cost flow assumption, other considerations, such as the risk of LIFO liquidations, cash flow, and capital maintenance, are also important but were not mentioned above.

Net Realizable Value

As stated in IAS 2

> *Net realizable value is the estimated selling price in the ordinary course of business less the estimated costs of completion and the estimated costs necessary to make the sale.*

The utility of an item of inventory is limited to the amount to be realized from its ultimate sale; where the item's recorded cost exceeds this amount, GAAP requires that a loss be recognized for the difference. The logic for this requirement is twofold: first, assets (in particular, current assets such as inventory) should not be reported at amounts that exceed net realizable value; and second, any decline in value in a period should be reported in that period's results of operations in order to achieve proper matching with current period's revenues. Were the inventory to be carried forward at an amount in excess of net realizable value, the loss would be recognized on the ultimate sale in a subsequent period. This would mean that a loss incurred in one period, when the value decline occurred, would have been deferred to a different period, which would clearly be inconsistent with several key accounting concepts, including conservatism.

IAS 2 states that estimates of net realizable value should be applied on an item-by-item basis in most instances, although it makes an exception for those situations where there are groups of related products or similar items that can be properly valued in the aggregate. As a general principle, item-by-item comparisons of cost to net realizable value are required, lest unrealized "gains" on some items (i.e., where the net realizable values exceed historical costs) offset the unrealized losses on other items, thereby reducing the net loss to be recognized. Since recognition of unrealized gains in earnings is generally proscribed under GAAP, evaluation of inventory declines on a grouped basis would be an indirect or "back door" mechanism to recognize gains that should not be given such recognition. Accordingly, the basic requirement is to apply the net realizable value tests on an individual item basis.

In many jurisdictions, the term **lower of cost or market** is used, as contrasted to IAS 2's **lower of cost or net realizable value**. As a practical matter, this difference in terminology will have little or no impact, since **market** is usually defined operationally as being replacement cost or net realizable value. However, one important distinction is that **market** is usually defined as a conditional term that contemplates a range of values, based not only on the costs to complete and sell an item, but also, in some circumstances, on the expected or normal profit to be earned on the sale. Since IAS 2 provides only general guidance concerning the determination of net realizable value, it will be useful to look to other existing standards for insight into how these measures are to be developed in a practical situation.

Measuring the decline to net realizable value. The IAS 2 definition of net realizable value makes explicit reference only to "costs of completion and costs incurred in order to make the sale." However, as illustrated below, if expected or normal profit margins on sales of inventory items are not taken into account, excessive profits or losses might be recognized in future periods, due to an incomplete application of the net realizable value concept.

The application of these principles is illustrated in the following example. In this example, replacement cost will be used as the primary operational definition of inventory value when that amount is lower than carrying value determined by historical cost. Replacement cost is a valid measure of the future utility of the inventory item since increases or decreases in the purchase price generally foreshadow related increases or decreases in the selling price. Assume the following information for products A, B, C, D, and E:

Item	*Cost*	*Replacement cost*	*Est. selling price*	*Cost to complete*	*Normal profit percentage*
A	$2.00	$1.80	$ 2.50	$0.50	24%
B	4.00	1.60	4.00	0.80	24%
C	6.00	6.60	10.00	1.00	18%
D	5.00	4.75	6.00	2.00	20%
E	1.00	1.05	1.20	0.25	12.5%

Consider item A: The net realizable value defined in accordance with IAS 2 is $2.50 – 0.50 = $2.00 (estimated selling price less costs to complete and sell). As it happens, this is exactly equal to historical cost, suggesting that there would be no adjustment required. However, if no adjustment is recorded, the profit realized upon the sale next period will be $2.50 – 2.00 – 0.50 = $0, which would be an unnaturally low net margin given the historical experience of a 24% margin. To preserve the normal margin, which would amount to $0.60 ($2.50 x 24%), the inventory would have to be written down to $1.40 ($2.50 – 0.50 – 0.60). However, the actual cost to replace the item in inventory is known to be $1.80, which suggests that the normal margin of 24% cannot be replicated under current conditions.

The foregoing explains why some standards setters and accounting theoreticians (but it should be stressed, not the IASC) have concluded that inventory should be reported at the lower of cost or market, where **market** is defined as replacement cost subject to ceiling and floor values; where **ceiling** is defined as net realizable value (NRV), and **floor** as the NRV minus the normal profit margin. Using this approach (which is the standard in the United States, Belgium, Canada, Germany,

Italy, the Netherlands, and Spain, among other jurisdictions), the amount of profit to be recognized in the period of later sale, absent other changes in the marketplace after the reporting date, will not be abnormally high or low.

To continue with this example, the data in the foregoing table are used to compute market values consistent with the definition set forth earlier. Note that the primary measure in all cases is replacement cost; if this falls between the ceiling and the floor, it becomes the measure of market, which is then compared to historical cost; the lower of cost or market is then used to actually value the inventory item. If the replacement cost exceeds the ceiling value (as for items D and E), the ceiling value becomes the market next to be compared to historical cost. On the other hand, if replacement cost is lower than the floor (as for items B and C), the floor is used as the market value to be compared next to the historical cost.

Determination of Net Realizable Value

Item	*Cost*	*Replacement cost*	*NRV (ceiling)*	*NRV less profit (floor)*	*Market*	*LCM*
A	$2.00	$1.80	$2.00	$1.40	$1.80	$1.80
B	4.00	1.60	3.20	2.24	2.24	2.24
C	6.00	6.60	9.00	7.20	7.20	6.00
D	5.00	4.75	4.00	2.80	4.00	4.00
E	1.00	1.05	0.95	0.80	0.95	0.95

Note that, under a strict reading of IAS 2, NRV would be compared directly to historical cost; the other values in the above table would not be given any consideration. However, it is the authors' opinion that there is sufficient flexibility in IAS 2 to permit some application of the principle of lower of cost or market as discussed above. If a strict application of the net realizable value rule were insisted upon, in contrast, item A would be valued at $2.00 instead of $1.80, resulting in a zero profit upon sale; and item B would be valued at $3.20 instead of $2.24, also resulting in a zero profit upon ultimate disposition. In general, the impact of using net realizable value, rather than market, would be to preclude preservation of some (if not a normal amount of) profit upon later sale of the item.

Recoveries of previously recognized losses. IAS 2 stipulates that a new assessment of net realizable value should be made in each subsequent period; when the reason for a previous write-down no longer exists (i.e., when net realizable value has improved), it should be reversed. Since the write-down was taken into income, the reversal should also be reflected in earnings.

Other Valuation Methods

There are instances in which an accountant must estimate the value of inventories. Whether for interim financial statements or as a check against perpetual records, the need for an inventory valuation without an actual physical count is required. Some of the methods used, which are discussed below, are the retail method, the LIFO retail method, and the gross profit method.

Retail method. IAS 2 notes that the retail method may be used by certain industry groups but does not provide details on how to employ this method, nor does it address the many variations of the technique. The conventional retail method is used by retailers as a method to estimate the cost of their ending inventory. The retailer can either take a physical inventory at retail prices or estimate ending retail inventory and then use the cost-to-retail ratio derived under this method to convert the ending inventory at retail to its estimated cost. This eliminates the process of going back to original invoices or other documents to determine the original cost for each inventoriable item. The retail method can be used under any of the three cost flow assumptions discussed earlier: FIFO, LIFO, or average cost. As with ordinary FIFO or average cost, the LCM rule can also be applied to the retail method when either one of these two cost assumptions is used.

The key to applying the retail method is determining the cost-to-retail ratio. The calculation of this number varies depending on the cost flow assumption selected. Essentially, the cost-to-retail ratio provides a relationship between the cost of goods available for sale and the retail price of these goods. This ratio is used to convert the ending retail inventory back to cost. Computation of the cost-to-retail ratio for each of the available methods is described below. The use of the LIFO cost flow assumption with this method is discussed in the next section and, therefore, is not addressed in this listing.

1. **FIFO cost**--The concept of FIFO indicates that the ending inventory is made up of the latest purchases; therefore, beginning inventory is excluded from computation of the cost-to-retail ratio, and the computation becomes net purchases divided by their retail value adjusted for both net markups and net markdowns.
2. **FIFO (using a lower of cost or market approach)**--The computation is basically the same as FIFO cost except that markdowns are excluded from the computation of the cost-to-retail ratio.
3. **Average cost**--Average cost assumes that ending inventory consists of all goods available for sale. Therefore, the cost-to-retail ratio is computed by dividing the cost of goods available for sale (Beginning inventory + Net purchases) by the retail value of these goods adjusted for both net markups and net markdowns.
4. **Average cost (using a lower of cost or market approach)**--This is computed in the same manner as average cost except that markdowns are excluded for the calculation of the cost-to-retail ratio.

A simple example illustrates the computation of the cost-to-retail ratio under both the FIFO cost and average cost methods in a situation where no markups or markdowns exist.

	FIFO cost			Average cost		
	Cost		Retail	Cost		Retail
Beginning inventory	$100,000		$ 200,000	$100,000		$ 200,000
Net purchases	500,000		800,000	500,000		800,000
Total goods available for sale	$600,000		1,000,000	$600,000		1,000,000
Sales at retail			(800,000)			(800,000)
Ending inventory at retail			$ 200,000			$ 200,000
Cost-to-retail ratio	500,000 / 800,000	=	62.5%	600,000 / 1,000,000	=	60%
Ending inventory at cost						
200,000 x 0.625			$ 125,000			
200,000 x 0.60						$ 120,000

Note that the only difference in the two examples is the numbers used to calculate the cost-to-retail ratio.

As shown above, the lower of cost or market aspect of the retail method is a result of the treatment of net markups and net markdowns. **Net markups** (markups less markup cancellations) are net increases above the original retail price, which are generally caused by changes in supply and demand. **Net markdowns** (markdowns less markdown cancellations) are net decreases below the original retail price. An approximation of lower of cost or market is achieved by including net markups but excluding net markdowns from the cost-to-retail ratio.

To understand this approximation, assume that a toy is purchased for $6 and the retail price is set at $10. It is later marked down to $8. A cost-to-retail ratio including markdowns would be $6 divided by $8 or 75%, and ending inventory would be valued at $8 times 75%, or $6 (original cost). A cost-to-retail ratio excluding markdowns would be $6 divided by $10 or 60%, and ending inventory would be valued at $8 times 60%, or $4.80 (on a lower of cost or market basis). The write-down to $4.80 reflects the loss in utility that is evidenced by the reduced retail price.

The application of the lower of cost or market rule is illustrated for both the FIFO and average cost methods in the example below. Remember, if the markups and markdowns below had been included in the preceding example, **both** would have been included in the cost-to-retail ratio.

	FIFO cost (LCM)			*Average cost (LCM)*		
	Cost		*Retail*	*Cost*		*Retail*
Beginning inventory	$100,000		$ 200,000	$100,000		$ 200,000
Net purchases	500,000		800,000	500,000		800,000
Net markups	--		250,000	--		250,000
Total goods available for sale	$600,000		1,250,000	$600,000		1,250,000
Net markdowns			(50,000)			(50,000)
Sales at retail			(800,000)			(800,000)
Ending inventory at retail			$ 400,000			$ 400,000
Cost-to-retail ratio	500,000 / 1,050,000	=	47.6%	600,000 / 1,250,000	=	48%
Ending inventory at cost						
400,000 x 0.476			$ 190,400			
400,000 x 0.48						$ 192,000

Notice that under the FIFO (LCM) method all of the markups are considered attributable to the current period purchases. Although this is not necessarily accurate, it provides the most conservative estimate of the ending inventory.

There are a number of additional inventory topics and issues that affect the computation of the cost-to-retail ratio and, therefore, deserve some discussion. Purchase discounts and freight affect only the cost column in this computation. The sales figure that is subtracted from the adjusted cost of goods available for sale in the retail column must be gross sales after adjustment for sales returns. If sales are recorded at gross, deduct the gross sales figure. If sales are recorded at net, both the recorded sales and sales discount must be deducted to give the same effect as deducting gross sales (i.e., sales discounts are not included in the computation). Normal spoilage is generally allowed for in the firm's pricing policies, and for this reason it is deducted from the retail column after calculation of the cost-to-retail ratio. Abnormal spoilage, on the other hand, should be deducted from **both** the cost and retail columns **before** the cost-to-retail calculation, as it could distort the ratio. It is then generally reported as a loss separate from the cost of goods sold section. Abnormal spoilage is generally considered to arise from a major theft or casualty, while normal spoilage is usually due to shrinkage or breakage. These determinations and their treatments will vary depending on the firm's policies.

When applying the retail method, separate computations should be made for any departments that experience significantly higher or lower profit margins. Distortions arise in the retail method when a department sells goods with varying margins in a proportion different from that purchased, in which case the cost-to-retail percentage would not be representative of the mix of goods in ending inventory. Also, manipulations of income are possible by planning the timing of markups and markdowns.

The retail method is an acceptable method of valuing inventories for tax purposes in some, but not all, jurisdictions. The foregoing examples are not meant to imply that the method would be usable in any given jurisdiction; readers should ascertain whether or not it can be used.

LIFO retail method. As with other LIFO concepts, tax regulations are the governing force behind the LIFO retail method. Readers must ascertain whether regulations in their local jurisdictions permit application of this or any similar method.

The steps used in computing the value of ending inventory under the LIFO retail method are listed below and then applied to an example for illustrative purposes.

1. Calculate (or select) the current year conversion price index. Recall that in the base year this index will be 1.00.
2. Calculate the value of the ending inventory at both cost and retail. Remember, as with other LIFO methods, tax regulations do not permit the use of LCM, so both markups and markdowns are included in computation of the cost-to-retail ratio. However, the beginning inventory is excluded from goods available for sale at cost and at retail.
3. Restate the ending inventory at retail to base-year retail. This is accomplished by dividing the current ending inventory at retail by the current year index determined in step 1.
4. Layers are then treated in the same fashion as they were for the dollar-value LIFO example presented earlier. If the ending inventory restated to base-year retail exceeds the previous year's amount at base-year retail, a new layer is established.
5. The computation of LIFO cost is the last step and requires multiplying each layer at base-year retail by the appropriate price index and multiplying this product by the cost-to-retail ratio in order to arrive at the LIFO cost for each layer.

The following example illustrates a 2-year period to which the LIFO retail method is applied. The first period represents the first year of operations for the organization and, thus, is its base year.

Year 1

Step 1 -- Because this is the base year, there is no need to compute an index, as it will always be 1.00.

Step 2 --

	Cost	*Retail*
Beginning inventory	$ --	$ --
Purchases	582,400	988,600
Markups	--	164,400
Markdowns	--	(113,000)
Subtotal	$582,400	$1,040,000
Total goods available for sale		$1,040,000
Sales at retail		840,000
Ending year 1 inventory at retail		$ 200,000

Cost-to-retail index 582,400/1,040,000 = 56%
Ending inventory at cost
$200,000 x 0.56 $112,000

Step 3 -- Because this is the base year, the restatement to base-year cost is not necessary; however, the computation would be

$200,000/1.00 = $200,000.

Steps 4 and 5 -- The determination of layers is again unnecessary in the base year; however, the computation would take the following format.

	Ending inventory at base-year retail	*Conversion price index*	*Cost-to-retail ratio*	*LIFO cost*
Base year ($200,000/1.00)	$200,000	1.00	0.56	$112,000

Year 2

Step 1 -- The assumption is made that the computation of an internal index yields a result of 1.12 (obtained by double extending a representative sample).

Step 2 --

	Cost	*Retail*
Beginning inventory	$112,000	$ 200,000
Purchases	716,300	1,168,500
Markups	--	87,500
Markdowns	--	(21,000)
Subtotal	$716,300	$1,235,000
Total goods available for sale		$1,435,000
Sales at retail		1,171,800
Ending year 2 inventory at retail		$ 263,200

Cost-to-retail index 716,300/1,235,000 = 58%

Step 3 -- The restatement of ending inventory at current year retail to base-year retail is done using the index computed in step 1. In this case it is $263,200/1.12 = $235,000.

Steps 4 and 5 -- We know that there is a LIFO layer in year 2 because the $235,000 inventory at base-year retail exceeds the year 1 amount of $200,000.

The computation of the LIFO cost for each layer is shown below.

	Ending inventory at base-year retail	*Conversion price index*	*Cost-to-retail ratio*	*LIFO cost*
Base year ($200,000/1.00)	$200,000	1.00	0.56	$112,000
Year 2 layer	35,000	1.12	0.58	22,736
	$235,000			
Ending year 2 inventory at LIFO cost				$134,736

The treatment of subsequent increments and decrements is the same for this method as it is for the regular dollar-value method.

Gross profit method. The gross profit method is used to estimate ending inventory when a physical count is not possible or feasible. It can also be used to evaluate the reasonableness of a given inventory amount. The cost of goods available for sale is compared with the estimated cost of goods sold. For example, assume the following data:

Beginning inventory	$125,000
Net purchases	450,000
Sales	600,000
Estimated gross profit	32%

Ending inventory is then estimated as follows:

Beginning inventory	$125,000
Net purchases	450,000
Cost of goods available for sale	575,000
Cost of goods sold [$600,000 – (32% x $600,000)] or (68% x $600,000)	408,000
Estimated ending inventory	$167,000

The gross profit method is used for interim reporting estimates, analyses by auditors, and estimates of inventory lost in fires or other catastrophes. The method is generally not acceptable for either tax or annual financial reporting purposes (and is not in conformity with IAS 2). Thus, its major purposes are for internal and interim reporting.

Other Cost Topics

Base stock. The base stock method assumes that a certain level of inventory investment is necessary for normal business activities and is, therefore, permanent. The base stock inventory is carried at historical cost. Decreases in the base stock are considered temporary and are charged to cost of goods sold at replacement cost. Increases are carried at current year costs. The base stock approach is seldom used in practice and it is not allowed for tax purposes in many jurisdictions, and the LIFO method, which is more commonly permitted, gives similar results. Although the original IAS 2 permitted the base stock method, it has been proscribed by the revised IAS 2, which became effective for periods beginning in 1995.

Standard costs. Standard costs are predetermined unit costs used by many manufacturing firms for planning and control purposes. Standard costs are often incorporated into the accounts, and materials, work in process, and finished goods inventories are all carried on this basis of accounting. The use of standard costs in financial reporting is acceptable if adjustments are made periodically to reflect current conditions and if its use approximates one of the recognized cost flow assumptions.

Purchase commitments. Purchase commitments generally are not recorded in the accounts because they are executory in nature. However, footnote disclosure is required for firm purchase commitments that are material in amount in accordance with IAS 10.

Furthermore, and in conformity with the same standard, if losses have been incurred in connection with firm purchase commitments, the losses must be accrued if probable and reasonably estimable. Note that this results in recognition of loss before the asset is recognized on the books. Contingencies are discussed in detail in Chapter 11.

Inventories valued at selling price. In exceptional cases, inventories may be reported at sales price less disposal costs. Such treatment is justified when cost is difficult to determine, quoted market prices are available, marketability is assured, and units are interchangeable. IAS 2 stipulates that producers' inventories of livestock, agricultural and forest products, and mineral ores, to the extent that they are measured at net realizable value in accordance with well established practices, are to be valued in this manner. When inventory is valued above cost, revenue is recognized before the point of sale; full disclosure in the financial statements would, of course, be required.

Use of more than one cost method. IAS 2 did not address the question of whether a single reporting entity would be justified in using a multiplicity of costing methods for different components of its inventory. In practice, many reporting enterprises have used different methods; for example, the use of LIFO for raw materials and FIFO for work in process and finished goods inventories is fairly common. In other cases, conglomerate entities have certain operations or divisions which use one method, and others which employ alternative costing formulae.

While the issue was not raised, logic suggests that if a variety of costing methods were employed for essentially similar inventories by a single entity, it would make meaningful interpretation of the resulting financial statements more difficult for users. Accordingly, the newly constituted Standing Interpretations Committee (SIC) of the IASC has, as its maiden effort, addressed this matter. In reaching its conclusion that similar inventories must be costed by the same method, it weighed the guidance already contained in IAS 27 (on consolidated financial reporting) and IAS 16 (on property, plant, and equipment).

The existing standard on consolidations provides that uniform accounting policies are to be used for like transactions and other events in similar circumstances, The logic is to avoid adding "apples and oranges" to develop consolidated financial statements which are unintelligible as a consequence. The IASC's *Framework for the Preparation and Presentation of Financial Statements* similarly expresses the notion that measurement of like transactions and other events should be carried out in a consistent manner throughout an entity and over the time of its ongoing existence, for purposes of both separate and consolidated financial reporting.

IAS 16 permits the use of different methods of measurement for different classes of property and equipment. Thus, for example, buildings might be depreciated by the straight line method, and equipment may be depreciated using an accelerated method, it can be justified based on patterns of usage and other factors, such as likely incidence of repair and maintenance costs. However, the use of different methods for similar assets in similar modes of use would not be consistent with IAS.

Taking these matters into account, the logical conclusion would be that inventories used in similar fashion by a given entity, even differently sited or managed operations of a given enterprise, should be costed by the same formula or method. The SIC has officially endorsed this conclusion in its first interpretive release, which, if adopted, will become effective in 1999. In the authors' opinion, a careful reading of existing IAS and the *Framework* indicate that this is already the official response to this issue.

Disclosure Requirements

IAS 2 sets forth certain disclosure requirements relative to inventory accounting methods employed by the entity preparing the financial statements. According to this standard, the following must be disclosed:

1. The accounting policies adopted in measuring inventories, including the costing methods (e.g., FIFO, weighted average, or LIFO) employed
2. The total carrying amount of inventories and the carrying amount in classifications appropriate to the enterprise
3. The carrying amount of inventories carried at net realizable value

4. The amount of any reversal of any previous write-down that is recognized in earnings for the period
5. The circumstances or events that led to the reversal of a write-down of inventories to net realizable value
6. The carrying amount of inventories pledged as security for liabilities

The type of information to be provided concerning inventories held in different classifications is somewhat flexible, but traditional classifications, such as raw materials, work in progress, finished goods, and supplies, should normally be employed. In the case of service providers, inventories (which are really akin to unbilled receivables) can be described as work in progress.

When the cost of inventories is determined in accordance with the LIFO method, which is an available alternative under IAS 2, the financial statements must disclose the difference between the amount of inventories shown on the balance sheet and either (1) the cost determined in accordance with either the FIFO or weighted-average costing methods, subject to the net realizable value rule, or (2) the lower of current (i.e., replacement) cost as of the balance sheet date or net realizable value.

In addition to the foregoing, the financial statements should disclose either the cost of inventories recognized as an expense during the period (i.e., reported as cost of sales or included in other expense categories), or the operating costs, applicable to revenues, recognized as an expense during the period, categorized by their respective natures.

Costs of inventories recognized as expense includes, in addition to the costs inventoried previously and attaching to goods sold currently, the excess overhead costs charged to expense for the period because, under the standard, they could not be deferred to future periods.

7 CONSTRUCTION CONTRACTS

PERSPECTIVE AND ISSUES

Accounting for construction contracts involves questions as to when revenue should be recognized and how to measure the revenue to be recorded. The basic international GAAP underlying these questions is covered in IAS 11 (revised 1993), *Construction Contracts*. This standard, which became effective for periods beginning on or after January 1, 1995, superseded the original International Accounting Standard (IAS 11), *Accounting for Construction Contracts*, which was approved in 1978.

This standard uses the recognition criteria established by the IASC's *Framework for the Preparation and Presentation of Financial Statements* as the basis for the guidance it offers on accounting for construction contracts. This area of accounting is complicated by the need to rely on estimates of revenues, costs and progress toward completion, and by the principle of recognition of losses when apparent.

Sources of IAS
IAS 8, 11, 23

DEFINITIONS OF TERMS

Additional asset stipulation. A special provision in a construction contract which either gives the option to the customer to require construction of an additional asset or permits amendment to the construction contract so as to include an additional asset not envisioned by the original contract should be construed as a separate construction contract when

1. The additional asset differs significantly (in design, function, or technology) from the asset(s) covered by the original contract; or
2. The extra contract price fixed for the construction of the additional asset is negotiated without regard to the original contract price.

Back charges. Billings for work performed or costs incurred by one party that, in accordance with the agreement, should have been performed or incurred by the party billed.

Billings on long-term contracts. Accumulated billings sent to the purchaser at intervals as various milestones in the project are reached.

Change orders. Modifications of an original contract that effectively change the provisions of the contract without adding new provisions; synonymous with **variations**.

Claims. Amounts in excess of the agreed-on contract price that a contractor seeks to collect from a customer (or another party) for customer-caused delays, errors in specifications and designs, disputed variations in contract work, or other occurrences that are alleged to be the causes of unanticipated costs.

Combining (grouping) contracts. Grouping two or more contracts, whether with a single customer or with several customers, into a single profit center for accounting purposes, provided that

1. The group of contracts is negotiated as a single package;
2. The contracts combined are so closely interrelated that, in essence, they could be considered as a single contract negotiated with an overall profit margin; and
3. The contracts combined are either executed concurrently or in a sequence.

Construction contract. Contract specifically entered into for the construction of an asset or a combination of assets that are closely interrelated or interdependent in terms of their design, technology, and function or their end use or purpose.

Construction-in-progress (CIP). Inventory account used to accumulate the construction costs of the contract project. For the percentage-of-completion method, the CIP account also includes the gross profit earned to date.

Contract costs. Comprised of costs directly related to a specific contract, costs that are attributable to the contract activity in general and can be allocated to the contract, and other costs that are specifically chargeable to the customer under the terms of the contract.

Contract revenue. Comprised of initial amount of revenue stipulated by the contract plus any variations in contract work, claims, and incentive payments, provided that these extra amounts of revenue meet the recognition criteria set by the IASC's *Framework* (i.e., regarding the probability of future economic benefits flowing to the contractor and reliability of measurement).

Cost plus contract. Construction contract in which the contractor is reimbursed for allowable costs plus either a percentage of these costs or a fixed fee.

Cost-to-cost method. Percentage-of-completion method used to determine the extent of progress toward completion on a contract. The ratio of costs incurred through the end of the current year divided by the total estimated costs of the project is used to recognize income.

Estimated cost to complete. Anticipated additional cost of materials, labor, subcontracting costs, and indirect costs (overhead) required to complete a project at a scheduled time.

Fixed-price contract. Construction contract wherein the contract revenue is fixed either in absolute terms or is fixed in terms of unit rate of output; in certain cases both fixed prices being subject to any cost escalation clauses, if allowed by the contract.

Incentive payments. Any additional amounts payable to the contractor if specified performance standards are either met or surpassed.

Percentage-of-completion method. Method of accounting that recognizes income on a contract as work progresses by matching contract revenue with contract costs incurred based on the proportion of work completed. However, any expected loss, which is the excess of total incurred and expected contract costs over the total contract revenue, is recognized immediately irrespective of the stage of completion of the contract.

Precontract costs. Costs that are related directly to a contract and are incurred in securing a contract (e.g., architectural designs, purchase of special equipment, engineering fees, and start-up costs).They are included as part of contract costs if they can be identified separately and measured reliably and it is probable that the contract will be obtained.

Profit center. Unit for the accumulation of revenues and cost for the measurement of income.

Segmenting contracts. Dividing a single contract, which covers the construction of a number of assets, into two or more profit centers for accounting purposes, provided that

1. Separate proposals were submitted for each of the assets that are the subject matter of the single contract
2. The construction of each asset was the subject of separate negotiation wherein both the contractor and the customer were in a position to either accept or reject part of the contract pertaining to a single asset (out of numerous of assets contemplated by the contract)
3. The costs and revenues pertaining to each individual asset can be separately identified

Stage of completion. Proportion of the contract work completed, which may be determined using one of several methods that reliably measures it, including

1. Percentage-of-completion method
2. Surveys of work performed
3. Physical proportion of contract work completed

Subcontractor. Second-level contractor who enters into a contract with a prime contractor to perform a specific part or phase of a construction project.

Substantial completion. Point at which the major work on a contract is completed and only insignificant costs and potential risks remain.

Variation. Instruction by the customer for a change in the scope of the work envisioned by the construction contract.

CONCEPTS, RULES, AND EXAMPLES

Construction contract revenue may be recognized during construction rather than at the completion of the contract. This "as earned" approach to revenue recognition is justified because under most long-term construction contracts, both the buyer and the seller (contractor) obtain enforceable rights. The buyer has the legal right to require specific performance from the contractor and, in effect, has an ownership claim to the contractor's work in progress. The contractor, under most long-term contracts, has the right to require the buyer to make progress payments during the construction period. The substance of this business activity is that a continuous sale occurs as the work progresses.

IAS 11, as revised in 1993, recognizes the percentage-of-completion method as the only valid method of accounting for construction contracts. Prior to the revision of IAS 11, the international accounting standards recognized both the percentage-of-completion method and the completed-contract method as being acceptable alternative methods of accounting for long-term construction activities.

The thinking worldwide on this issue is equivocal and rather confusing. Many countries still recognize both the foregoing methods as being in accordance with generally accepted accounting principles (GAAP), although they may not be viewed as equally acceptable under given circumstances. The United States, Canada, and Japan are usually noted as protagonists of both GAAP methods on this subject. There is another set of countries whose GAAP is in line with the current IAS on the subject. The national accounting standards of the United Kingdom, Australia, China, and New Zealand recognize only the percentage-of-completion method. Germany, on the other hand, seems to have taken the extreme viewpoint as a supporter of only the completed-contract method. Although it may seem that the world is completely divided on this matter, a closer look into this contentious issue offers a better insight into the diversity in approaches.

Although Germany seems to be alone in the contest of alternative methods of accounting for long-term contracts, its position is more explicable when it is recalled that this country has traditionally been known for its conservative approach and its emphasis on creditor protection. Thus, it seems to have been guided primarily by the prudence concept in developing this accounting principle.

For countries that support both the methods, it is well-known that some also express a clear preference for the percentage-of-completion method. US GAAP, for instance, exemplifies this position. It recommends the percentage-of-completion method as preferable when estimates are reasonably dependable and the following conditions exist:

1. Contracts executed by the parties normally include provisions that clearly specify the enforceable rights regarding goods or services to be provided and received by the parties, the consideration to be exchanged, and the manner and terms of settlement.
2. The buyer can be expected to satisfy his obligations under the contract.
3. The contractor can be expected to perform its contractual obligations.

The Accounting Standards Division of the AICPA believes that these two methods should not be used as acceptable alternatives for the same set of circumstances. US GAAP states that in general, when estimates of costs to complete and extent of progress toward completion of long-term contracts are reasonably dependable, the percentage-of-completion method is preferable. When lack of dependable estimates or inherent hazards cause forecasts to be doubtful, the completed-contract method is preferable.

Percentage-of-Completion Method in Detail

A number of controversial issues are encountered when the percentage-of-completion method is used in practice. In the following paragraphs, the authors address a number of these, offering proposed approaches to follow for those matters that have not been authoritatively resolved, or, in many instances, even discussed by the international accounting standards.

Revised IAS 11 defines the percentage-of-completion method as follows:

> *The percentage of completion method recognizes income as work on a contract (or group of closely related contracts) progresses. The recognition of revenues and expenses is generally based on the stage of completion of the contract(s), except when a loss is expected, in which case immediate recognition of the loss is called (irrespective of the stage of completion). Under this method contract revenue is matched with the contract costs incurred in reaching the stage of completion, resulting in the reporting of contract revenue, contract costs and profit based on proportion of work completed.*

Under the percentage-of-completion method, the construction-in-progress (CIP) account is used to accumulate costs and recognized income. When the CIP exceeds billings, the difference is reported as a current asset. If billings exceed CIP, the difference is reported as a current liability. Where more than one contract exists, the excess cost or liability should be determined on a project-by-project basis, with the accumulated costs and liabilities being stated separately on the balance sheet. Assets and liabilities should not be offset unless a right of offset exists. Thus, the net debit balances for certain contracts should not ordinarily be offset against net credit balances for other contracts. An exception may exist if the balances relate to contracts that meet the criteria for combining.

Under the percentage-of-completion method, income should not be based on advances (cash collections) or progress (interim) billings. Cash collections and interim billings are based on contract terms that do not necessarily measure contract performance.

Costs and estimated earnings in excess of billings should be classified as an asset. If billings exceed costs and estimated earnings, the difference should be classified as a liability.

Contract costs. Contract costs comprise costs that are identifiable with a specific contract, plus those that are attributable to contracting activity in general and can be allocated to the contract and those that are contractually chargeable to a customer. Generally, contract costs would include all direct costs, such as direct materials, direct labor, and direct expenses and any construction overhead that could specifically be allocated to specific contracts.

Direct costs or costs that are identifiable with a specific contract include

1. Costs of materials consumed in the specific construction contract
2. Wages and other labor costs for site labor and site supervisors
3. Depreciation charges of plant and equipment used in the contract
4. Lease rentals of hired plant and equipment specifically for the contract
5. Cost incurred in shifting of plant, equipment, and materials to and from the construction site
6. Cost of design and technical assistance directly identifiable with a specific contract
7. Estimated costs of any work undertaken under a warranty or guarantee
8. Claims from third parties

With regard to claims from third parties, these should be accrued if they meet the criteria established under IAS 10 for the recognition of contingent losses as expenses (i.e., that it is probable that a liability has been incurred at the balance sheet date and a reasonable estimate of the amount of the resulting loss can be made). However, if either of the above-mentioned conditions is not met (and the possibility of the loss is not remote), this contingency will only be disclosed. Contingent losses are specifically required to be disclosed under IAS 11.

Contract costs may be reduced by incidental income if such income is not included in contract revenue. For instance, sale proceeds (net of any selling expenses) from the disposal of any surplus materials or from the sale of plant and equipment at the end of the contract may be credited or offset against these expenses. Drawing an analogy from this principle, it could be argued that if advances received from customers are invested by the contractor temporarily (instead of being allowed to lie idle in a current account), any interest earned on such investments could be treated as incidental income and used in reducing contract costs, which may or may not include borrowing costs (depending on how the contractor is financed, whether self-financed or leveraged). On the other hand, it may also be argued that instead of being subtracted from contract costs such interest income should be added to contract revenue.

In the authors' opinion, the latter argument may be valid if the contract is structured in such a manner that the contractor receives lump-sum advances at the beginning of the contract (or for that matter, even during the term of the contract, such that the advances at any point in time exceed the amounts due the contractor from the customer). In these cases, such interest income should in fact be treated as contract revenue and not offset against contract costs. The reasoning underlying treating this differently from the earlier instance (where idle funds resulting from advances are invested temporarily) is that such advances were envisioned by the terms of the contract and as such were probably fully considered in the negotiation process that preceded fixing contract revenue. Thus, since negotiated as part of the total contract price, this belongs in contract revenues. (It should be borne in mind that the different treatments for interest income will in fact have a bearing on the determination of the percentage or stage of completion of a construction contract.)

Indirect costs or overhead expenses should be included in contract costs provided that they are attributable to the contracting activity in general and could be allocated to specific contracts. Such costs include construction overhead, cost of insurance, cost of design, and technical assistance that is not related directly to specific contracts. They should be allocated using methods that are systematic and rational and are applied in a consistent manner to costs having similar features or characteristics. The allocation should be based on the normal level of construction activity, not on theoretical maximum capacity.

Example of contract costs

A construction company incurs $700,000 in annual rental expense for the office space occupied by a group of engineers and architects and their support staff. The company utilizes this group to act as the quality assurance team that overlooks all contracts undertaken by thc company. The company also incurs in the aggregate another $300,000 as the annual expenditure toward electricity, water, and maintenance of this office space occupied by the group. Since the group is responsible for quality assurance for all contracts on hand, its work, by nature, cannot be considered as being directed toward any specific contract but is in support of the entire contracting activity. Thus, the company should allocate the rent expense and the cost of utilities in accordance with a systematic and rational basis of allocation, which should be applied consistently to both types of expenditure (since they have similar characteristics).

Although the bases of allocation of this construction overhead could be many (such as the amounts of contract revenue, contract costs, and labor hours utilized in each contract) the basis of allocation that seems most rational is contract revenue. Further, since both expenses are similar in nature, allocating both the costs on the basis of the amount of contract revenue generated by each construction contract would also satisfy the consistency criteria.

Other examples of construction overhead or costs that should be allocated to contract costs are

1. Costs of preparing and processing payroll of employees engaged in construction activity
2. Borrowing costs that are capitalized under IAS 23 in conformity with the allowed alternative treatment

Certain costs are specifically excluded from allocation to the construction contract, as the standard considers them as not attributable to the construction activity. Such costs may include

1. General and administrative costs that are not contractually reimbursable
2. Costs incurred in marketing or selling
3. Research and development costs that are not contractually reimbursable
4. Depreciation of plant and equipment that is lying idle and not used in any particular contract

Types of contract costs. Contract costs can be broken down into two categories: costs incurred to date and estimated costs to complete. The **costs incurred to date** include precontract costs and costs incurred after contract acceptance. **Precontract costs** are costs incurred before a contract has been entered into, with the expectation that the contract will be accepted and these costs will thereby be recoverable through billings. The criteria for recognition of such costs are

1. They are capable of being identified separately.
2. They can be measured reliably.
3. It is probable that the contract will be obtained.

Precontract costs include costs of architectural designs, costs of learning a new process, cost of securing the contract, and any other costs that are expected to be recovered if the contract is accepted. Contract costs incurred after the acceptance of the contract are costs incurred toward the completion of the project and are also capitalized in the construction-in-progress (CIP) account. The contract does not have to be identified before the capitalization decision is made; it is only necessary that there be an expectation of the recovery of the costs. Once the contract has been accepted, the precontract costs become contract costs incurred to date. However, if the precontract costs are already recognized as an expense in the period in which they are incurred, they are not included in contract costs when the contract is obtained in a subsequent period.

Estimated costs to complete. These are the anticipated costs required to complete a project at a scheduled time. They would be comprised of the same elements as the original total estimated contract costs and would be based on prices expected to be in effect when the costs are incurred. The latest estimates should be used to determine the progress toward completion.

Although IAS 11 does not specifically provide instructions for estimating costs to complete, practical guidance can be gleaned from other international accounting standards, as follows: The first rule is that systematic and consistent procedures should be used. These procedures should be correlated with the cost accounting system and should be able to provide a comparison between actual and estimated costs. Additionally, the determination of estimated total contract costs should identify the significant cost elements.

A second important point is that the estimation of the costs to complete should include the same elements of costs included in accumulated costs. Additionally, the estimated costs should reflect any expected price increases. These expected price increases should not be blanket provisions for all contract costs, but rather, specific provisions for each type of cost. Expected increases in each of the cost elements such as wages, materials, and overhead items, should be taken into consideration separately.

Finally, estimates of costs to complete should be reviewed periodically to reflect new information. Estimates of costs should be examined for price fluctuations and should also be reviewed for possible future problems, such as labor strikes or direct material delays.

Accounting for contract costs is similar to accounting for inventory. Costs necessary to ready the asset for sale would be recorded in the construction-in-progress account, as incurred. CIP would include both direct and indirect costs but would usually not include general and administrative expenses or selling expenses since they are not normally identifiable with a particular contract and should therefore be expensed.

Subcontractor costs. Since a contractor may not be able to do all facets of a construction project, a subcontractor may be engaged. The amount billed to the contractor for work done by the subcontractor should be included in contract costs. The amount billed is directly traceable to the project and would be included in the CIP account, similar to direct materials and direct labor.

Back charges. Contract costs may have to be adjusted for back charges. Back charges are billings for costs incurred which the contract stipulated should have been performed by another party. These charges are often disputed by the parties involved.

Example of a back charge situation

The contract states that the subcontractor was to raze the building and have the land ready for construction; however, the contractor/seller had to clear away debris in order to begin construction. The contractor wants to be reimbursed for the work; therefore, the contractor back charges the subcontractor for the cost of the debris removal.

The contractor should treat the back charge as a receivable from the subcontractor and should reduce contract costs by the amount recoverable. If the subcontractor disputes the back charge, the cost becomes a **claim**. Claims are an amount in excess of the agreed contract price or amounts not included in the original contract price that the contractor seeks to collect. Claims should be recorded as additional contract revenue only if the requirements set forth in IAS 11 are met.

The subcontractor should record the back charge as a payable and as additional contract costs if it is probable that the amount will be paid. If the amount or validity of the liability is disputed, the subcontractor would have to consider the probable outcome in order to determine the proper accounting treatment.

Fixed-Price and Cost-Plus Contracts

IAS 11 recognizes two types of construction contracts which are distinguished based on their pricing arrangements: (1) fixed-price contracts and (2) cost-plus contracts.

Fixed-price contracts are contracts for which the price is not usually subject to adjustment because of costs incurred by the contractor. The contractor agrees to a fixed contract price or a fixed rate per unit of output. These amounts are sometimes subject to escalation clauses.

There are two types of **cost-plus contracts**.

1. **Cost-without-fee contract--**Contractor is reimbursed for allowable or otherwise defined costs with no provision for a fee. However, a percentage is added that is based on the foregoing costs.
2. **Cost-plus-fixed-fee contract--**Contractor is reimbursed for costs plus a provision for a fee. The contract price on a cost-type contract is determined by the sum of the reimbursable expenditures and a fee. The fee is the profit margin (revenue less direct expenses) to be earned on the contract. All reimbursable expenditures should be included in the accumulated contract costs account.

There are a number of possible variations of contracts which are based on a cost-plus-fee arrangement. These could include cost-plus-fixed-fee, under which the fee is a fixed monetary amount; cost-plus-award, under which an incentive payment is provided to the contractor, typically based on the project's timely or on-budget completion; and cost-plus-a-percentage-fee, under which a variable bonus payment will be added to the contractor's ultimate payment based on stated criteria.

Some contracts may have features of both a fixed-price contract and a cost-plus contract. A cost-plus contract with an agreed maximum price is an example of such a contract.

Recognition of Contract Revenue and Expenses

Percentage-of-completion accounting cannot be employed if the quality of information will not support a reasonable level of accuracy in the financial reporting process. Generally, only when the outcome of a construction contract can be estimated reliably, should the contract revenue and contract costs be recognized by reference to the stage of completion at the balance sheet date.

Different criteria have been prescribed by the standard for assessing whether the outcome can be estimated reliably for a contract, depending on whether it is a fixed-price contract or a cost-plus contract. The following are the criteria in each case:

1. If it is a fixed-price contract *(NOTE: **All** conditions should be satisfied)*:
    a. It meets the recognition criteria set by the IASC's *Framework*; that is
        (1) Total contract revenue can be measured reliably.
        (2) It is probable that economic benefits flow to the enterprise.
    b. Both the contract cost to complete and the stage of completion can be measured reliably.
    c. Contract costs attributable to the contract can be identified properly and measured reliably so that comparison of actual contract costs with estimates can be done.
2. If it is a cost-plus contract (*NOTE: **All** conditions should be satisfied*):
    a. It is probable that the economic benefits will flow to the enterprise.
    b. The contract costs attributable to the contract, whether or not reimbursable, can be identified and measured reliably.

When Outcome of a Contract Cannot Be Estimated Reliably

As stated above, unless the outcome of a contract can be estimated reliably, contract revenue and costs should not be recognized by reference to the stage of completion. IAS 11 establishes the following rules for revenue recognition in cases where the outcome of a contract cannot be estimated reliably:

1. Revenue should be recognized only to the extent of the contract costs incurred that are probable of being recoverable.
2. Contract costs should be recognized as an expense in the period in which they are incurred.

Any expected losses should, however, be recognized immediately.

It is not unusual that during the early stages of a contract, outcome cannot be estimated reliably. This would be particularly likely to be true if the contract represents a type of project with which the contractor has had limited experience in the past.

Contract Costs Not Recoverable Due to Uncertainties

Recoverability of contract costs may be considered doubtful in case of contracts that have any of the following characteristics:

1. The contract is not fully enforceable.
2. Completion of the contract is dependent on the outcome of pending litigation or legislation.
3. The contract relates to properties that are likely to be expropriated or condemned.
4. The contract is with a customer who is unable to perform its obligations, perhaps because of financial difficulties.
5. The contractor is unable to complete the contract or otherwise meet its obligation under the terms of the contract, as when, for example, the contractor has been experiencing recurring losses and is unable to get financial support from creditors and bankers and may be ready to declare bankruptcy.

In all such cases, contract costs should be expensed immediately. Although the implication is unambiguous, the determination that one or more of the foregoing conditions holds will be subject to some imprecision. Thus, each such situation needs to be assessed carefully on a case by case basis.

If and when these uncertainties are resolved, revenue and expenses should again be recognized on the same basis as other construction-type contracts (i.e., by the percentage-of-completion method). However, it is not permitted to restore costs already expensed in prior periods, since the accounting was not in error given the facts that existed at the time the earlier financial statements were prepared.

Revenue Measurement--Determining the Stage of Completion

The standard recognizes that the stage of completion of a contract may be determined in many ways and that an enterprise uses the method that measures reliably the work performed. The standard further stipulates that depending on the nature of the contract, one of the following methods may be chosen:

1. The proportion that contract costs incurred bear to estimated total contract cost (also referred to as the cost-to-cost method)
2. Survey of work performed method
3. Completion of a physical proportion of contract work (also called units-of-work-performed) method. (Note that progress payments and advances received from customers often do not reflect the work performed.)

Each of these methods of measuring progress on a contract can be identified as being either an input or an output measure. The **input measures** attempt to identify progress in a contract in terms of the efforts devoted to it. The cost-to-cost method is an example of an input measure. Under the cost-to-cost method, the percentage of completion would be estimated by comparing total costs incurred to date to total costs expected for the entire job. **Output measures** are made in terms of results by attempting to identify progress toward completion by physical measures. The units-of-work-performed method is an example of an output measure. Under this method, an estimate of completion is made in terms of achievements to date. Output measures are usually not considered to be as reliable as input measures.

When the stage of completion is determined by reference to the contract costs incurred to date, the standard specifically refers to certain costs that are to be excluded from contract costs. Examples of such costs are

1. Contract costs that relate to future activity (e.g., construction materials supplied to the site but not yet consumed during construction)
2. Payments made in advance to subcontractors prior to performance of the work by the subcontractor

Example of the percentage-of-completion method

The percentage-of-completion method works under the principle that "recognized income (should) be that percentage of estimated total income...that incurred costs to date bear to estimated total costs." The cost-to-cost method has become one of the most popular measures used to determine the extent of progress toward completion.

Under the cost-to-cost method, the percentage of revenue to recognize can be determined by the following formula:

$$\frac{\text{Cost to date}}{\text{Cumulative costs incurred} + \text{Estimated costs to complete}} \times \text{Contract price} - \text{Revenue previously recognized} = \text{Current revenue recognized}$$

By slightly modifying this formula, current gross profit can also be determined.

$$\frac{\text{Cost to date}}{\text{Cumulative costs incurred} + \text{Estimated costs to complete}} \times \text{Expected total gross profit} - \text{Gross profit previously recognized} = \text{Current gross profit}$$

Example of the percentage-of-completion (cost-to-cost) and completed-contract methods with profitable contract

Assume a $500,000 contract that requires 3 years to complete and incurs a total cost of $405,000. The following data pertain to the construction period:

	Year 1	*Year 2*	*Year 3*
Cumulative costs incurred to date	$150,000	$360,000	$405,000
Estimated costs yet to be incurred at year end	300,000	40,000	--
Progress billings made during year	100,000	370,000	30,000
Collections of billings	75,000	300,000	125,000

Completed-Contract and Percentage-of-Completion Methods

	Year 1		Year 2		Year 3	
Construction in progress	150,000		210,000		45,000	
Cash, payables, etc.		150,000		210,000		45,000
Contract receivables	100,000		370,000		30,000	
Billings on contracts		100,000		370,000		30,000
Cash	75,000		300,000		125,000	
Contract receivables		75,000		300,000		125,000

Completed-Contract Method Only

	Year 1		Year 2		Year 3	
Billings on contracts					500,000	
Cost of revenues earned					405,000	
Contracts revenues earned						500,000
Construction in progress						405,000

Percentage-of-Completion Method Only

	Year 1		Year 2		Year 3	
Construction in progress	16,667		73,333		5,000	
Cost of revenues earned	150,000		210,000		45,000	
Contract revenues Earned		166,667		283,333		50,000
Billings on contracts					500,000	
Construction in progress						500,000

Income Statement Presentation

	Year 1	Year 2	Year 3	Total
Percentage-of-completion:				
Contract revenues earned	$166,667*	$283,333**	$ 50,000***	$ 500,000
Cost of revenues earned	(150,000)	(210,000)	(45,000)	(405,000)
Gross profit	$ 16,667	$ 73,333	$ 5,000	$ 95,000
Completed-contract:				
Contract revenues earned	--	--	$ 500,000	$ 500,000
Cost of contracts completed	--	--	(405,000)	(405,000)
Gross profit	--	--	$ 95,000	$ 95,000

$$* \quad \frac{\$150{,}000}{450{,}000} \times 500{,}000 = \$166{,}667$$

$$** \quad \frac{\$360{,}000}{400{,}000} \times 500{,}000 - 166{,}667 = \$283{,}333$$

$$*** \quad \frac{\$405{,}000}{405{,}000} \times 500{,}000 - 166{,}667 - 283{,}333 = \$50{,}000$$

<u>*Balance Sheet Presentation*</u>

		Year 1	*Year 2*	*Year 3*
Percentage-of-completion:				
Current assets:				
Contract receivables		$ 25,000	$ 95,000	*
Costs and estimated earnings in excess of billings on uncompleted contracts				
Construction in progress	166,667**			
Less billings on long-term contracts	(100,000)	$ 66,667		
Current liabilities:				
Billings in excess of costs and estimated earnings on uncompleted contracts, year 2 ($470,000*** – 450,000****)			$ 20,000	
Completed-contract:				
Current assets:				
Contract receivables		$ 25,000	$ 95,000	*
Costs in excess of billings on uncompleted contracts				
Construction in progress	150,000			
Less billings on long-term contracts	(100,000)	$ 50,000		
Current liabilities:				
Billings in excess of costs on uncompleted contracts, year 2 ($470,000 – 360,000)			$110,000	

* *Since the contract was completed and title was transferred in year 3, there are no balance sheet amounts. However, if the project is complete but transfer of title has not taken place, there would be a balance sheet presentation at the end of the third year because the entry closing out the Construction-in-progress account and the Billings account would not have been made yet.*

** *$150,000 (Costs) + 16,667 (Gross profit)*

*** *$100,000 (Year 1 Billings) + 370,000 (Year 2 Billings)*

**** *$360,000 (Costs) + 16,667 (Gross profit) + 73,333 (Gross profit)*

Recognition of Expected Contract Losses

When the current estimate of total contract cost exceeds the current estimate of total contract revenue, a provision for the entire loss on the entire contract should be made. Provisions for losses should be made in the period in which they become evident under either the percentage-of-completion method or the completed-contract method. In other words, when it is probable that total contract costs will exceed total contract revenue, the expected loss should be recognized as an expense immediately. The loss provision should be computed on the basis of the total estimated costs to complete the contract, which would include the contract costs incurred to date plus estimated costs (use the same elements as contract costs incurred) to complete. The provision should be shown separately as a current liability on the balance sheet.

In any year when a percentage-of-completion contract has an expected loss, the amount of the loss reported in that year can be computed as follows:

Reported loss = Total expected loss + All profit previously recognized

Example of the percentage-of-completion and completed-contract methods with loss contract

Using the previous information, if the costs yet to be incurred at the end of year 2 were $148,000, the total expected loss is $8,000 [$500,000 – (360,000 + 148,000)], and the total loss reported in year 2 would be $24,667 ($8,000 + 16,667). Under the completed-contract method, the loss recognized is simply the total expected loss, $8,000.

Journal entry at end of year 2	*Percentage-of-completion*		*Completed-contract*	
Loss on uncompleted long-term contract	24,667		8,000	
Construction in progress (or estimated loss on uncompleted contract)		24,667		8,000

Profit or Loss Recognized on Contract
(Percentage-of-Completion Method)

	Year 1	*Year 2*	*Year 3*
Contract price	$500,000	$500,000	$500,000
Estimated total costs:			
Costs incurred to date	$150,000	$360,000	$506,000*
Estimated cost yet to be incurred	300,000	148,000	--
Estimated total costs for the 3-year period, actual for year 3	$450,000	$508,000	$506,000
Estimated income (loss), actual for year 3	$ 16,667	$ (8,000)	$ (6,000)
Less income (loss) previously recognized	--	16,667	(8,000)
Amount of estimated income (loss) recognized in the current period, actual for year 3	$ 16,667	$ (24,667)	$ 2,000

**Assumed*

Profit or Loss Recognized on Contract
(Completed-Contract Method)

	Year 1	*Year 2*	*Year 3*
Contract price	$500,000	$500,000	$500,000
Estimated total costs:			
Costs incurred to date	$150,000	$360,000	$506,000*
Estimated costs yet to be incurred	300,000	148,000	--
Estimated total costs for the 3-year period, actual for year 3	$ 50,000	$ (8,000)	$ (6,000)
Loss previously recognized	--	--	(8,000)
Amount of estimated income (loss) recognized in the current period, actual for year 3	$ --	$ (8,000)	$ 2,000

**Assumed*

Upon completion of the project during year 3, it can be seen that the actual loss was only $6,000 ($500,000 – 506,000); therefore, the estimated loss provision was overstated by $2,000. However, since this is a change of an estimate, the $2,000 difference must be handled prospectively; consequently, $2,000 of income should be recognized in year 3 ($8,000 previously recognized – $6,000 actual loss).

Combining and Segmenting Contracts

The profit center for accounting purposes is usually a single contract, but under some circumstances the profit center may be a combination of two or more contracts, a segment of a contract, or a group of combined contracts. Conformity with explicit criteria set forth in IAS 11 is necessary to combine separate contracts, or segment a single contract; otherwise, each individual contract is presumed to be the profit center.

For accounting purposes, a group of contracts may be combined if they are so closely related that they are, in substance, parts of a single project with an overall profit margin. A group of contracts, whether with a single customer or with several customers, should be combined and treated as a single contract if the group of contracts

1. Are negotiated as a single package
2. Require such closely interrelated construction activities that they are, in effect, part of a single project with an overall profit margin
3. Are performed concurrently or in a continuous sequence

Segmenting a contract is a process of breaking up a larger unit into smaller units for accounting purposes. If the project is segmented, revenues can be assigned to the different elements or phases to achieve different rates of profitability based on the relative value of each element or phase to the estimated total contract revenue. According to IAS 11, a contract may cover a number of assets. The construction of each asset should be treated as a separate construction contract when

1. The contractor has submitted separate proposals on the separate components of the project
2. Each asset has been subject to separate negotiation and the contractor and customer had the right to accept or reject part of the proposal relating to a single asset
3. The cost and revenues of each asset can be separately identified

Contractual Stipulation for Additional Asset--Separate Contract

The contractual stipulation for an additional asset is a special provision in the international accounting standard. IAS 11 provides that a contract may stipulate the construction of an additional asset at the option of the customer, or the contract may be amended to include the construction of an additional asset. The construction of the additional asset should be treated as a separate construction contract if

1. The additional asset significantly differs (in design, technology or function) from the asset or assets covered by the original contract
2. The price for the additional asset is negotiated without regard to the original contract price

Changes in Estimate

Since the percentage-of-completion method uses current estimates of contract revenue and expenses, it is normal to encounter changes in estimates of contract revenue and costs frequently. Such changes in estimate of the contract's outcome are treated on a par with changes in accounting estimate as defined by IAS 8, *Net Profit or Loss for the Period, Fundamental Errors and Changes in Accounting Policies.*

Disclosure Requirements Under IAS 11

A number of disclosures are prescribed by IAS 11; some of them are for all the contracts and others are only for contracts in progress at the balance sheet date. These are summarized below.

1. Disclosures relating to all contracts

   a. Aggregate amount of contract revenue recognized in the period
   b. Methods used in determination of contract revenue recognized in the period

2. Disclosures relating to contracts in progress

a. Methods used in determination of stage of completion (of contracts in progress)
b. Aggregate amount of costs incurred and recognized profits (net of recognized losses) to date
c. Amounts of advances received (as at balance sheet date)
d. Amount of retentions (as at balance sheet date)

Financial Statement Presentation Requirements Under IAS 11

Gross amounts due from customers should be reported as an asset. This amount is the net of

1. Costs incurred plus recognized profits, less
2. The aggregate of recognized losses and progress billings.

This represents, in the case of contracts in progress, excess of contract costs incurred plus recognized profits, net of recognized losses, over progress billings.

Gross amounts due to customers should be reported as a liability. This amount is the net of

1. Costs incurred plus recognized profits, less
2. The aggregate of the recognized losses and progress billings.

This represents, in the case of contract work in progress, excess of progress billings over contract costs incurred plus recognized profits, net of recognized losses.

APPENDIX A

ACCOUNTING UNDER SPECIAL SITUATIONS--GUIDANCE FROM US GAAP

A number of specialized situations that are fairly common in long-term construction contracting are not addressed by international accounting standards. To provide guidance on certain of these matters, the following interpretations are offered, based on existing practice under US GAAP.

Joint Ventures and Shared Contracts

Many contracts obtained by long-term construction companies are shared by more than one contractor. When the owner of the contract puts it up for bids, many contractors form syndicates or joint ventures to bid on and obtain a contract under which each contractor could not perform individually.

When this transpires, a separate set of books is maintained for the joint venture. If the percentages of interest for each venture are identical in more than one contract, the joint venture might keep its records almost like another construction company. Usually, the joint venture is for a single contract and ends on completion of that contract.

A joint venture is a form of a partnership, although a partnership for a limited purpose. An agreement of the parties and the terms of the contract successfully bid on will determine the nature of the accounting records. Income statements are usually cumulative statements showing all totals from the date of contract determination until the reporting date. Each venturer records its share of the amount from the venture's income statement less its previously recorded portion of the venture's income as a single line item similar to the equity method for investments. Similarly, balance sheets of the venture give rise to a single line asset balance of investment and advances in joint ventures. In most cases, footnote disclosure is similar to the equity method in displaying condensed financial statements of material joint ventures.

Accounting for Change Orders

Change orders are modifications of specifications or provisions of an original contract. Contract revenue and costs should be adjusted to reflect change orders that are approved by the contractor and customer. According to US GAAP, the accounting for the change order depends on the scope and price of the change. If the scope and price have both been agreed on by the customer and contractor, contract revenue and cost should be adjusted to reflect the change order.

According to US GAAP, accounting for unpriced change orders depends on their characteristics and the circumstances in which they occur. Under the completed-contract method, costs attributable to unpriced change orders should be deferred as contract costs if it is probable that total contract costs, including costs attributable to the change orders, will be recovered from contract revenues. Recovery should be deemed probable if the future event or events are likely to occur.

According to US GAAP, the following guidelines should be followed when accounting for unpriced change orders under the percentage-of-completion method:

1. Costs attributable to unpriced change orders should be treated as costs of contract performance in the period in which the costs are incurred if it is not probable that the costs will be recovered through a change in the contract price.
2. If it is probable that the costs will be recovered through a change in the contract price, the costs should be deferred (excluded from the cost of contract performance) until the parties have agreed on the change in contract price, or alternatively, they should be treated as costs of contract performance in the period in which they are incurred, and contract revenue should be recognized to the extent of the costs incurred.
3. If an adjustment to the contract price will be made in an amount which will exceed the costs attributable to the change order, this may be given recognition under certain circumstances. Specifically, if the amount of the excess can be reliably estimated, and if realization is probable, then the original contract price should be so adjusted. However, since the substantiation of the amount of future revenue is difficult, revenue in excess of the costs attributable to unpriced change orders should only be recorded in circumstances in which realization is assured beyond a reasonable doubt, such as circumstances in which an entity's historical experience provides such assurance or in which an entity has received a bona fide pricing offer from a customer and records only the amount of the offer as revenue.

Accounting for Contract Options

According to US GAAP, an addition or option to an existing contract should be treated as a separate contract if any of the following circumstances exist:

1. The product or service to be provided differs significantly from the product or service provided under the original contract.
2. The price of the new product or service is negotiated without regard to the original contract and involves different economic judgments.
3. The products or services to be provided under the exercised option or amendment are similar to those under the original contract, but the contract price and anticipated contract cost relationship are significantly different.

If the addition or option does not meet the foregoing circumstances, the contracts should be combined. However, if the addition or option does not meet the criteria for combining, they should be treated as change orders.

Accounting for Claims

These represent amounts in excess of the agreed contract price that a contractor seeks to collect from customers for unanticipated additional costs. The recognition of additional contract revenue relating to claims is appropriate if it is probable that the claim will result in additional revenue and if the amount can be estimated reliably. US GAAP specifies that all of the following conditions must exist for the probable and estimable requirements to be satisfied:

1. The contract or other evidence provides a legal basis for the claim; or a legal opinion has been obtained, stating that under the circumstances there is a reasonable basis to support the claim.
2. Additional costs are caused by circumstances that were unforeseen at the contract date and are not the result of deficiencies in the contractor's performance.
3. Costs associated with the claim are identifiable or otherwise determinable and are reasonable in view of the work performed.
4. The evidence supporting the claim is objective and verifiable, not based on management's "feel" for the situation or on unsupported representations.

When the foregoing requirements are met, revenue from a claim should be recorded only to the extent that contract costs relating to the claim have been incurred. When the foregoing requirements are not met, a contingent asset should be disclosed in accordance with US GAAP governing contingencies.

8 PROPERTY, PLANT, AND EQUIPMENT AND INTANGIBLE ASSETS

PERSPECTIVE AND ISSUES

Property, plant, and equipment and intangible assets (collectively referred to in this chapter as long-lived assets) are those that will provide an economic benefit to an enterprise for a number of future periods. GAAP regarding long-lived assets involves determination of the appropriate cost at which to record the assets initially, the amount at which to present the assets at subsequent reporting dates, and the appropriate method(s) to be used to allocate the cost or other recorded values over the periods being benefited. Under present international accounting standards, while historical cost is the defined benchmark treatment, revalued amounts may also be used for presenting long-lived assets in the statement of financial position, if certain conditions are met.

Long-lived assets are primarily operational in character, and they may be classified into two basic types: tangible and intangible. **Tangible assets** have physical substance and can be further categorized as follows:

1. Depreciable assets
2. Depletable assets
3. Other tangible assets

Intangible assets, on the other hand, have no physical substance. The value of an intangible asset is a function of the rights or privileges that its ownership conveys to the business enterprise. Intangible assets can be further categorized as being either

1. Identifiable, or
2. Unidentifiable (i.e., goodwill).

Identifiable intangibles include patents, copyrights, brand names, customer lists, trade names, and other specific rights that, typically, can be conveyed by an owner without necessarily also transferring related physical assets. **Goodwill**, on the other hand, cannot be meaningfully transferred to a new owner without also selling other assets.

Property (such as factory buildings) is often constructed by an enterprise over an extended period of time, and during this interval, when the property has yet to be placed in productive service, the enterprise will typically incur interest cost on borrowed funds used to finance the construction. IAS 23 provides, as an allowed alternative treatment, that such cost be added to the carrying value of the asset under construction. However, the benchmark treatment is to expense such costs as period costs, as they are incurred. A proposed IASC interpretation will stipulate that, once an enterprise adopts the allowed alternative as its accounting policy, interest costs should be added to the carrying value of all qualifying assets.

Research and development costs are also addressed in this chapter. Under the relevant international standard (IAS 9), research costs must be expensed as incurred, whereas development costs, as defined and subject to certain limitations, are to be classified as assets and amortized over the period to be benefited. The IASC agreed, in early 1997, to merge its guidance on research and development costs with that on other intangibles so that consistent guidance would be offered on all similar assets. When a new standard is finally issued, it is likely to include criteria for the capitalization and amortization of internally generated intangibles, including research and development costs, which will represent a significant change from the requirements of IAS 9, although an exposure draft has yet to be issued on this important proposal.

Long-lived assets are often acquired in nonmonetary transactions, either in exchanges of assets between the entity and another business, or when assets are contributed by shareholders to the enterprise. Although there are no specific standards on the accounting for these transactions under existing international GAAP, due to the fact that these are common occurrences, the accounting that may logically be applied to them is also considered in this chapter.

Sources of IAS

IAS 4, 9, 16, 23

Exposure Draft on Intangible Assets, E50
Exposure Draft on Impairment of Assets, E55

DEFINITIONS OF TERMS

Amortization. In general, the allocation of the cost of a long-term asset over its useful economic life; the term is also used specifically to define the allocation process for intangible assets.

Boot. Term commonly applied to monetary consideration given or received as a settle up in an asset exchange situation.

Carrying amount. Amount at which the asset is included in the balance sheet, that is cost (or other amount substituted for cost) less accumulated depreciation.

Cost. Amount of cash or cash equivalent paid or the fair value of other consideration given to acquire or construct an asset.

Depreciable amount. Cost of an asset or the other amount that has been substituted for cost, less the residual value of the asset.

Depreciation. Systematic and rational allocation of the depreciable amount of an asset over its economic life.

Exchange. Reciprocal transfer between an enterprise and another entity that results in the acquisition of assets or services, or the satisfaction of liabilities through a transfer of other assets, services, or other obligations.

Fair value. Amount that would be obtained for an asset in an arm's-length exchange transaction between knowledgeable, willing parties.

Fixed assets. Assets used in a productive capacity that have physical substance, are relatively long-lived, and provide future benefit that is readily measurable.

Intangible assets. Identifiable, nonmonetary assets that will provide economic benefit for more than one period but have no physical substance. Examples include goodwill, patents, and copyrights.

Monetary assets. Assets whose amounts are fixed in terms of units of currency. Examples are cash, accounts receivable, and notes receivable.

Nonmonetary assets. Assets other than monetary assets. Examples are inventories; investments in common stock; and property, plant, and equipment.

Nonmonetary transactions. Exchanges and nonreciprocal transfers that involve little or no monetary assets or liabilities.

Nonreciprocal transfer. Transfer of assets or services in one direction, either from an enterprise to its owners or another entity, or from owners or another entity to the enterprise. An enterprise's reacquisition of its outstanding stock is a nonreciprocal transfer.

Property, plant, and equipment. Tangible assets with an expected useful life of more than 1 year, that are held for use in the process of producing goods or services for sale, that are held for rental to others, or that are held for administrative purposes; also referred to commonly as fixed assets.

Recoverable amount. Amount expected to be obtainable through the future use of the asset, including the residual value thereof.

Residual value. Estimated amount expected to be obtained on ultimate disposition of the asset after its useful life has ended, net of estimated costs of disposal.

Similar productive assets. Productive assets that are of the same general type, that perform the same function, or that are employed in the same line of business.

Useful life. Period over which the asset will be employed in its productive capacity; measured either by time (number of years) or by productive period (number of units expected to be produced by use of the asset).

CONCEPTS, RULES, AND EXAMPLES

Property, Plant, and Equipment

Property, plant, and equipment (also variously referred to as plant, or fixed, assets, or as PP&E) is often used to denote tangible property to be used in a productive capacity that will benefit the enterprise for a period of greater than 1 year. This term is meant to distinguish these assets from intangibles, which are long-term, generally identifiable assets that do not have physical substance.

There are four concerns to be addressed in accounting for fixed assets.

1. The amount at which the assets should be recorded initially on acquisition
2. How value changes subsequent to acquisition should be reflected in the accounts, if at all
3. The rate at which the amount the assets are recorded should be allocated to future periods
4. The recording of the subsequent disposal of the assets

Initial measurement. All costs required to bring an asset into working condition should be recorded as part of the cost of the asset. Examples of such costs include sales or other nonrefundable taxes or duties, finders' fees, freight costs, site preparation and other installation costs, and setup costs. Thus, any reasonable cost incurred prior to using the asset in actual production involved in bringing the asset to the buyer is capitalized. These costs are **not** to be expensed in the period in that they are incurred, as they are deemed to add value to the asset and indeed were necessary expenditures to obtain the asset.

In certain cases, other costs will be incurred during the initial break-in period; these may, alternatively, be referred to as start-up or preproduction costs. Under the provisions of IAS 16, these costs are not to be added to the amount recorded for the asset unless they are absolutely necessary to bring the asset to a workable condition. Notwithstanding this rule, this remains an area of subjective judgment; under many circumstances there will be justification for adding certain costs, such as those associated with materials used in testing or adjusting the machinery or equipment in order to place it into actual production. If these amounts are significant and incurrence of the costs is a necessary precedent to using the asset, they should be added to the carrying amount of the asset. On the other hand, losses incurred in the early stages of actually employing the asset in its intended use cannot be capitalized but must be charged to expense as incurred, as these are not assets (i.e., these do not represent economic benefits that will later be received by the entity).

While interest costs incurred during the construction of certain assets may be added to the cost of the asset (as described in detail below), if an asset is purchased on deferred payment terms, the interest cost, whether made explicit or imputed, is not part of the cost of the asset. Accordingly, such costs should be expensed currently as interest charges. If the purchase price for the asset incorporates a deferred payment scheme, only the cash equivalent price should be capitalized as the initial carrying amount of the asset. If the cash equivalent price is not explicitly stated, the deferred payment amount should be reduced to present value by the application of an appropriate discount rate. This would normally be best approximated by use of the enterprise's incremental borrowing cost for debt having a maturity similar to the deferred payment term.

Administrative costs, as well as other categories of overhead, are not normally allocated to fixed asset acquisitions, despite the fact that some such costs, such as the salaries of the personnel who evaluate assets for proposed acquisitions, are in fact incurred as part of the acquisition process. As a general principle, administrative costs are expensed in the period incurred. On the other hand, truly incremental costs, such as a consulting fee or commission paid to an agent hired specifically to assist in the acquisition, may be treated as part of the initial amount to be recognized.

Initial recognition of self-constructed assets. Essentially the same principles that have been established for recognition of the cost of purchased assets also apply to self-constructed assets. All costs that must be incurred to complete the construction of the asset can be added to the amount to be recognized initially, subject only to the constraint that if these costs exceed the recoverable amount (as discussed fully later in this chapter), the excess must be expensed currently. This is necessary to avoid the gold-plated hammer syndrome, whereby a misguided or unfortunate asset construction project incurs excessive costs that then find their way onto the balance sheet, thereby overstating net worth as well as distorting future periods' earnings. Of course, internal (intracompany) profits cannot be allocated to construction costs.

Self-constructed assets may include, in addition to the range of costs discussed earlier, the cost of borrowed funds used during the period of construction. Capitalization of borrowing costs, as set forth by IAS 23, is discussed in a later section of this chapter.

The other issue that arises most commonly in connection with self-constructed fixed assets relates to overhead allocations. While capitalization of all direct costs (labor, materials, and variable overhead) is a well settled matter in accounting thought, a controversy exists regarding the proper treatment of fixed overhead. Two views of how to treat fixed overhead are

1. Charge the asset with its fair share of fixed overhead (i.e., use the same basis of allocation used for inventory).
2. Charge the fixed asset account with only the identifiable incremental amount of fixed overhead.

While international standards do not address this concern, it may be instructive to consider nonbinding guidance included in US GAAP. AICPA Accounting Research Monograph 1 has suggested that

> *...in the absence of compelling evidence to the contrary, overhead costs considered to have 'discernible future benefits' for the purposes of determining the cost of inventory should be presumed to have 'discernible future benefits' for the purpose of determining the cost of a self-constructed depreciable asset.*

The implication of this statement is that logic similar to what was applied to determining the acquisition costs that may be included in inventory might reasonably also be applied to the costing of fixed assets. Also consistent with the standards applicable to inventories, if the costs of fixed assets exceed realizable values, the excess costs should be written off to expense and not deferred to future periods.

Costs incurred subsequent to purchase or self-construction. Costs that are incurred subsequent to the purchase, such as those for repairs, maintenance, or betterments, are treated in one of the following ways:

1. Expensed
2. Capitalized
3. Recognized by a reduction of accumulated depreciation

Costs can be added to the carrying value of the related asset only when it is probable that future economic benefits, beyond those originally anticipated for the asset, will be received by the entity. For example, modifications to the asset made to extend its useful life (measured either in years or in units of potential production) or to increase its capacity (e.g., as measured by units per hour) would be capitalized. Similarly, if the expenditure results in an improved quality of output, or permits a reduction in other cost inputs (e.g., would result in labor savings), it is a candidate for capitalization. As with self-constructed assets, if the costs incurred exceed the defined threshold, they must be expensed currently.

It can be assumed that ordinary maintenance and repair expenditures will occur on a ratable basis over the life of the asset and should be charged to expense as incurred. Thus, if the purpose of the expenditure is either to maintain the productive capacity anticipated when the asset was acquired or constructed, or to restore it to that level, the costs are not subject to capitalization.

A partial exception is encountered if an asset is acquired in a condition that necessitates that certain expenditures be incurred in order to put it into the appropriate state for its intended use. For example, a deteriorated building may be purchased with the intention to restore and then use it. In such cases, costs that otherwise would be categorized as ordinary maintenance items might be subject to capitalization, subject, of course, to the constraint that the asset not be presented at a value that exceeds its recoverable amount. Once the restoration is completed, further expenditures of similar type would be viewed as being ordinary repairs or maintenance, and thus expensed as incurred.

Extraordinary repairs. In contrast to normal maintenance costs, extraordinary repairs or maintenance increase the value (utility) of the asset or increase the estimated useful life of the asset. IAS 16 does not stipulate whether such expenditures should be added to the gross carrying value of the asset or should be used to reduce the previously accumulated depreciation. However, there is a logical basis for increasing the asset account for those repairs that increase the value of the asset while decreasing the accumulated depreciation account for those repairs that extend the useful life of the asset. In effect, those that extend the life of the asset have recovered some of the depreciation recorded previously, and the asset will be depreciated again over its new, lengthier, lifetime. The chart on the following page summarizes the treatment of expenditures subsequent to acquisition consistent with the foregoing discussion.

Depreciation of fixed assets. In accordance with one of the more important basic accounting concepts, the matching principle, the costs of fixed assets are allocated to the periods benefited through depreciation. Whatever the method of depreciation chosen, it must result in the systematic and rational allocation of the cost of the asset (less its residual value) over the asset's expected useful life. The determination of the useful life must take a number of factors into consideration. These factors include technological change, normal deterioration, actual physical use, and legal or other limitations on the ability to use the property. The method of depreciation is based on whether the useful life is determined as a function of time (e.g., technological change or normal deterioration) or as a function of actual physical use.

Since depreciation accounting is intended as a strategy for cost allocation, it does not necessarily reflect changes in the value of the asset being amortized. Thus, with the exception of land, which has infinite life, all tangible fixed assets must be depreciated, even if (as sometimes occurs, particularly in periods of general price inflation) their nominal or real values increase.

Furthermore, if the recorded amount of the asset is allocated over a period of time (as opposed to units of production), it should be the expected period of usefulness to the entity, not the physical life of the property itself, that governs. Thus, such concerns as technological obsolescence, as well as normal wear and tear, must be addressed in the initial determination of the period over that to allocate the asset cost. The reporting entity's strategy for repairs and maintenance will also affect this computation, since the same physical asset might have a longer or shorter economic useful life in the hands of differing owners, depending on the care with which it is intended to be maintained.

Similarly, the same asset may have a longer or shorter economic life, depending on its intended use. A particular building, for example, may have a 50-year expected life as a facility for storing goods or for use in light manufacturing, but as a showroom would have a shorter period of usefulness, due to the disinclination of customers to shop at enterprises occupying older premises. Again, it is not physical life, but useful economic life, that should govern.

Costs Subsequent to Acquisition of Property, Plant, and Equipment

		Normal accounting treatment			
			Capitalize		
Type of expenditure	Characteristics	Expense when incurred	Charge to asset	Charge to accum. deprec.	Other
1. Additions	• Extensions, enlargements, or expansions made to an existing asset		x		
2. Repairs and maintenance a. Ordinary	• Recurring, relatively small expenditures				
	1. Maintain normal operating condition	x			
	2. **Do not** add materially to use value	x			
	3. **Do not** extend useful life	x			
b. Extraordinary (major)	• Not recurring, relatively large expenditures				
	1. Primarily increase the use value		x		
	2. Primarily extend the useful life			x	
3. Replacements and betterments	• Major component of asset is removed and replaced with the same type of component with comparable performance capabilities (replacement) or a different type of component having superior performance capabilities (betterment)				
a. Book value of old component is known					• Remove old asset cost and accum. deprec. • Recognize any loss (or gain) on old asset • Charge asset for replacement component
b. Book value of old component is not known	1. Primarily increase the use value		x		
	2. Primarily extend the useful life			x	
4. Reinstallations and rearrangements	• Provide greater efficiency in production or reduce production costs				
	1. Material costs incurred; benefits extend into future accounting periods		x		
	2. No measurable future benefit	x			

Compound assets, such as buildings containing such disparate components as heating plant, roofs, and other structural elements, are most commonly recorded in several separate accounts, to facilitate the process of amortizing the different elements over varying periods. Thus, a heating plant may have an expected useful life of 20 years, the roof a life of 15 years, and the basic structure itself a life of 40 years. Recordation in separate accounts eases the calculation of periodic depreciation in such situations, although for financial reporting purposes certain of these categories might be combined, based on materiality or other considerations.

IAS 16 has superseded IAS 4 concerning guidance on depreciation of property, plant, and equipment. IAS 4 remains effective for amortization of intangibles, although it might be obsoleted by the new standard on intangibles currently being developed. (The exposure draft on intangibles, E50, is discussed later in the chapter.)

Depreciation methods based on time.

1. Straight-line--Depreciation expense is incurred evenly over the life of the asset. The periodic charge for depreciation is given as

$$\frac{\text{Cost or amount substituted for cost, less residual value}}{\text{Estimate useful life of asset}}$$

2. Accelerated methods--Depreciation expense is higher in the early years of the asset's useful life and lower in the later years. IAS 16 only mentions one accelerated method, the diminishing balance method, but other methods have been employed in various countries under earlier or other contemporary accounting standards.

   a. Diminishing balance--A multiple of the straight-line rate times the net carrying value at the beginning of the year.

$$\text{Straight-line rate} = \frac{1}{\text{Estimated useful life}}$$

Example

Double-declining balance depreciation (if salvage value is to be recognized, stop when book value = estimated salvage value)

Depreciation = 2 x Straight-line rate x Book value at beginning of year

Another method to accomplish a diminishing charge for depreciation is the sum-of-the-years' digits method, that is commonly employed in the United States and certain other venues.

   b. Sum-of-the-years' digits (SYD) depreciation =

(Cost less salvage value) x Applicable fraction

$$\text{where applicable fraction} = \frac{\text{number of years of estimated life remaining as of the beginning of the year}}{\text{SYD}}$$

$$\text{and SYD} = \frac{n(n+1)}{2} \quad \text{and } n = \text{estimated useful life}$$

Example

An asset having a useful economic life of 5 years and no salvage value would have 5/15 (= 1/3) of its cost allocated to year 1, 4/15 to year 2, and so on.

3. Present value methods--A characteristic of this method of depreciation is that expense will be lower in the early years and higher in the later years. The effect of this pattern results in having the rate of return on the investment remain constant over the life of the asset. Time value of money formulas are used to effect this method of depreciation.

   a. Sinking fund method--Uses the future value of an annuity formula.
   b. Annuity fund method--Uses the present value of an annuity formula.

The present value approach is rarely encountered in practice, due to computational complexity, despite what many consider to be its theoretical validity. IAS 16 is silent regarding these methods, and the fact that the standard refers only to straight-line, diminishing balance, and sum-of-the-units methods may suggest that **increasing** charge methods would not be acceptable. However, the statement that a "variety of depreciation methods can be used to allocate the depreciable amount of an asset on a systematic and rational basis over its useful life" would at the same time seemingly support other unnamed methods.

Partial-year depreciation. Although IAS 16 is silent on the matter, when an asset is either acquired or disposed of during the year, the full year depreciation calculation should be prorated between the accounting periods involved. This is necessary to achieve proper matching. However, if individual assets in a relatively homogeneous group are regularly acquired and disposed of, one of several conventions can be adopted, as follows:

1. Record a full year's depreciation in the year of acquisition and none in the year of disposal.
2. Record one-half year's depreciation in the year of acquisition and one-half year's depreciation in the year of disposal.

Example of partial-year depreciation

Assume the following:

Taj Mahal Milling Co., a calendar year entity, acquired a machine on June 1, 1996 that cost $40,000 with an estimated useful life of 4 years and a $2,500 salvage value. The depreciation expense for each full year of the asset's life is calculated as follows:

	Straight-line	*Double-declining balance*					*Sum-of-years' digits*				
Year 1	37,500* ÷ 4 = 9,375	50%	x	40,000	=	20,000	4/10	x	37,500*	=	15,000
Year 2	9,375	50%	x	20,000	=	10,000	3/10	x	37,500	=	11,250
Year 3	9,375	50%	x	10,000	=	5,000	2/10	x	37,500	=	7,500
Year 4	9,375	50%	x	5,000	=	2,500	1/10	x	37,500	=	3,750

*(40,000 – 2,500).

Because the first full year of the asset's life does not coincide with the company's year, the amounts shown above must be prorated as follows:

	Straight-line	*Double-declining balance*					*Sum-of-years' digits*				
1996	7/12 x 9,375 = 5,469	7/12	x	20,000	=	11,667	7/12	x	15,000	=	8,750
1997	9,375	5/12	x	20,000	=	8,333	5/12	x	15,000	=	6,250
		7/12	x	10,000	=	5,833	7/12	x	11,250	=	6,563
						14,166					12,813
1998	9,375	5/12	x	10,000	=	4,167	5/12	x	11,250	=	4,687
		7/12	x	5,000	=	2,917	7/12	x	7,500	=	4,375
						7,084					9,062
1999	9,375	5/12	x	5,000	=	2,083	5/12	x	7,500	=	3,125
		7/12	x	2,500	=	1,458	7/12	x	3,750	=	2,188
						3,541					5,313
2000	5/12 x 9,375 = 3,906	5/12	x	2,500	=	1,042	5/12	x	3,750	=	1,562

Depreciation method based on actual physical use--Sum-of-the-units, or units of production, method. Depreciation may also be based on the number of units produced by the asset in a given year. IAS 16 identifies this as the sum-of-the-units method, but it is also commonly known as the units of production approach. It is best suited to those assets, such as machinery, that have an expected life that is most rationally defined in terms of productive output; in periods of reduced production (such as economic recession) the machinery is used less, thus extending its life when measured in units of time. It would not be rational to charge the same depreciation expense to such periods, as would be the case if straight-line or diminishing balance depreciation were used. Furthermore, if the deprcciation finds its way into inventory, the unit cost in periods of reduced production would be exaggerated and could even exceed net realizable value unless a units of production approach to depreciation were taken.

$$\text{Depreciation rate} = \frac{\text{Cost less residual value}}{\text{Estimated number of units to be produced by the asset over its estimated useful life}}$$

$$\text{Units of production depreciation} = \text{Depreciation rate} \times \text{Number of units produced during the period}$$

Other depreciation methods. Although IAS 16 does not discuss other methods of depreciation (nor even all the variations noted in the foregoing paragraphs), at different times and in various jurisdictions other methods have been used. Some of these are summarized as follows:

1. **Retirement method**--Cost of asset is expensed in period in which it is retired.
2. **Replacement method**--Original cost is carried in accounts and cost of replacement is expensed in the period of replacement.
3. **Group (or composite) method**--Averages the service lives of a number of assets using a weighted-average of the units and depreciates the group or composite as if it were a single unit. A group consists of similar assets, while a composite is made up of dissimilar assets.

$$\text{Depreciation rate} = \frac{\text{Sum of the straight-line depreciation of individual assets}}{\text{Total asset cost}}$$

$$\text{Depreciation expense} = \text{Depreciation rate} \times \text{Total group (composite) cost}$$

A peculiarity of the composite approach is that gains and losses are not recognized on the disposal of an asset, but rather, are netted into accumulated depreciation. This is because it is a presumption of this method that although dispositions of individual assets may yield proceeds greater than or less than their respective book values, the ultimate gross proceeds from a group of assets will not differ materially from the aggregate book value thereof, and accordingly, recognition of those individual gains or losses should be deferred and effectively netted out.

Residual value. Most depreciation methods discussed above require that a factor be applied to the net depreciable cost of the asset, where net depreciable cost is the historical cost or amount substituted therefor (i.e., fair value) less the estimated residual value of the asset. Although residual value is often not material and in practice is frequently ignored, the concept should nonetheless be understood, particularly since it is defined differently in the context of the benchmark and allowed alternative methods described by IAS 16.

If the benchmark method (historical cost) is used, residual value is defined as the expected worth of the asset, in present dollars (i.e., without any consideration of the impact of future inflation), at the end of its useful life. Residual value should, however, be net of any expected costs of disposition. In some cases, assets will have a negative residual value, as for example when the entity must incur out-ofpocket costs to dispose of the asset, or to return the property to an earlier condition, as in the case of certain operations, such as strip mines, that are subject to environmental protection or other laws. In such instances, periodic depreciation should total more than the asset's original cost, such that at the expected disposal date, an estimated liability has been accrued equal to the negative residual value.

If the alternative (revaluation) method is elected, residual value takes on a rather different meaning. Under this scenario, residual value must be assessed anew at the date of each revaluation of the asset. This is accomplished by using data on realizable values for similar assets, ending their respective useful lives at the time of the revaluation, after having been used for purposes similar to the asset being valued. Again, no consideration can be paid to anticipated inflation, and expected future values are not to be discounted to present values to give recognition to the time value of money. As with historical cost based accounting for plant assets, if a negative residual value is anticipated, this should be effectively recognized over the useful life of the asset by charging extra depreciation, such that the estimated liability will have been accrued by the disposal date.

Choice of depreciation method. While a number of different methods have been officially endorsed by international accounting standards, and others might be rationally supportable as well, in theory one method will be best in any given fact situation at reporting on the expiration of the service potential of the asset. Thus, straight-line presumes that the same economic value is obtained from use of the asset each period, while such accelerated approaches as the diminishing balance method are intended to combine decreasing periodic charges for depreciation with presumably increasing costs for repairs and maintenance as the asset ages, for an approximately level total cost of use across the years.

In practice, the amount of real support marshaled for the particular depreciation method employed will vary significantly, and it is very unusual for certifying (i.e., outside) accountants to dispute any entity's choice of method, as long as it is among those deemed to be GAAP. It is presumed that full disclosure of the methods used will permit the financial statement reader to interpret the financial statements meaningfully, in any event.

IAS 16 requires that the method of depreciation be critically reviewed periodically. If the expected pattern of utility of the asset has changed from when the method used was decided on, a different and more appropriate method should be selected. This change would be accounted for as a change in an accounting estimate and would affect financial reporting only on a prospective basis.

Useful lives. Irrespective of the method of depreciation used, the estimate of useful life must be revisited periodically. Useful life is defined in terms of expected utility to the enterprise, and as such may differ from both the physical life and economic life of the asset. Useful life is affected by such things as the entity's practices regarding repairs and maintenance of its assets, as well as the pace of technological change and the market demand for goods produced and sold by the entity using the assets as productive inputs. If it is determined that the estimated life is greater or less than previously believed, the change is handled as a change in accounting estimate, not as a correction of fundamental error. Accordingly, no restatement is made to previously reported depreciation; rather, the change is accounted for strictly on a prospective basis, being reflected in the period of change and all subsequent periods.

Example of estimating the useful life

To illustrate this concept, consider an asset costing $100,000 and originally estimated to have a productive life of 10 years. The straight-line method is used, and there was no residual value anticipated. After 2 years, management revises its estimate of useful life to a total of 6 years. Since the net carrying value of the asset is $80,000 after 2 years ($100,000 x 8/10), and the remaining expected life is 4 years (2 of the 6 revised total years having already elapsed), depreciation in years 3 through 6 will be $20,000 ($80,000/4) each.

Tax methods. The methods of computing depreciation discussed in the foregoing sections relate only to financial reporting under generally accepted accounting principles. Tax laws in different nations of the world vary widely in terms of the acceptability of depreciation methods, and it is not possible for a general treatise such as this to address those in any detail. However, to the extent that depreciation allowable for income tax reporting purposes differs from that required or permitted for financial statement purposes, deferred income taxes might have to be presented. Interperiod income tax allocation is discussed more fully in Chapter 14.

Revaluation of Fixed Assets

IAS 16 establishes two alternative approaches to accounting for fixed assets. The first of these is the benchmark (normal) treatment, under which acquisition or construction cost is used for initial recognition, subject to depreciation over the expected economic life and to possible write-down in the event of a permanent impairment in value. The allowed alternative treatment is to recognize revaluations.

The logic of recognizing revaluations relates to both the balance sheet and the measure of periodic performance provided by the income statement. Due to the effects of inflation (which even if quite moderate when measured on an annual basis can compound dramatically during the lengthy period over which fixed assets remain in use) the balance sheet can become a virtually meaningless agglomeration of dissimilar costs.

Furthermore, if income is determined by reference to historical costs of assets acquired in earlier periods, the replacement of those assets in the normal course of events may well require more resources than are provided by depreciation. Under these circumstances, even a nominally profitable enterprise might find that it has self-liquidated and is unable to continue in existence, at least, not with the same level of productive capacity, without new debt or equity infusions. In fact, a number of enterprises in many capital intensive industries have suffered just such a fate over the past generation.

At varying times the securities regulatory and other authorities and private sector standard setters in different nations have proposed or even required a range of alternative price level adjusted or current cost methods of accounting to address this problem. Notwithstanding these efforts, no uniform approach has ever gained the wide acceptance that would create a de facto standard. In certain jurisdictions, less complex and less useful methods have been tried to compensate crudely for the effects of inflation; accelerated depreciation methods (including 100% write-offs in the year of acquisition, in some cases) and LIFO inventory costing are the most prominent of these. Of course, these are not true substitutes for a comprehensive system of inflation-adjusted financial reporting.

Fair value. As a practical, yet reasonably effective alternative, IAS 16 promotes the concept of asset revaluation. The standard stipulates that fair value (defined as the amount for which the asset could be exchanged between knowledgeable, willing parties in an arm's-length transaction) be used in any such revaluations. Furthermore, the standard requires that, once an entity undertakes revaluations, they continue to be made with sufficient regularity such that the carrying amounts in any subsequent balance sheet are not materially at variance with fair value. In other words, if the reporting entity adopts the allowed alternative treatment, it cannot allow report balance sheets that contain obsolete fair values, since that would not only obviate the purpose of the allowed treatment but would actually make it impossible for the user to interpret the financial statements.

Fair value is defined in IAS 16 as generally being the market value of assets such as land and buildings, as determined by appraisers employing normal commercial valuation techniques. Market values can also be used for machinery and equipment, but since such items often do not have readily determinable market values, particularly if intended for specialized applications, they may instead be valued at depreciated replacement cost.

Estimates of the fair value of a given asset must be made in the context of the same type of service as it is used for at present. Thus, it would not be acceptable to assume an alternative use (e.g., a factory building could potentially be redeveloped into luxury housing units) when deriving the amounts to be reported on the balance sheet.

Alternative concepts of current value. A number of different concepts have been proposed over the years to achieve inflation accounting. Methods that address changes in specific prices, in contrast to those that attempt to adjust for general purchasing power changes have measured reproduction cost, replacement cost, sound value, exit value, entry value, and net present value.

In brief, **reproduction cost** refers to the actual current cost of exactly reproducing the asset, essentially ignoring changes in technology in favor of a strict bricks and mortar concept. Since the same service potential could be obtained currently, in many cases without a literal reproduction of the asset, this method fails to fully address the economic reality that accounting should ideally attempt to measure.

Replacement cost, in contrast, deals with the service potential of the asset, which is, after all, what creates value for its owner. An obvious example can be found in the realm of computers. While the cost to reproduce a particular mainframe machine exactly might be the same or somewhat lower today versus its original purchase price, the computing capacity of the machine might easily be replaced by one or a small group of microcomputers that could be obtained for a fraction of the cost of the larger machine. To gross up the balance sheet by reference to reproduction cost would be distorting, at the very least. Instead, the replacement cost of the service potential of the owned asset should be used to accomplish the revaluation contemplated by IAS 16.

Furthermore, even replacement cost, if reported on a gross basis, would be an exaggeration of the value implicit in the reporting entity's asset holdings, since the asset in question has already had some fraction of its service life expire. The concept of sound value addresses this concern. Sound value is the equivalent of the cost of replacement of the service potential of the asset, adjusted to reflect the relative loss in its utility due to the passage of time or the fraction of total productive capacity that has already been utilized.

Example of depreciated replacement cost (sound value)

An asset acquired January 1, 1994 at a cost of $40,000 was expected to have a useful economic life of 10 years. On January 1, 1997 it is appraised as having a gross replacement cost of $50,000. The sound value, or depreciated replacement cost, would be 7/10 x $50,000, or $35,000. This compares with a book, or carrying, value of $28,000 at that same date. Mechanically, to accomplish a revaluation at January 1, 1997, the asset should be written up by $10,000 (i.e., from $40,000 to $50,000 gross cost) and the accumulated depreciation should be proportionally written up by $3,000 (from $12,000 to $15,000). Under IAS 16, the net amount of the revaluation adjustment, $7,000, would be credited to revaluation surplus, an additional equity account.

An alternative accounting procedure is also permitted by the standard, under that the accumulated depreciation at the date of the revaluation is written off against the gross carrying value of the asset. In the foregoing example, this would mean that the $12,000 of accumulated depreciation at January 1, 1997, immediately prior to the revaluation, would be credited to the gross asset amount, $40,000, thereby reducing it to $28,000. Then the asset account would be adjusted to reflect the valuation of $35,000 by increasing the asset account by $7,000 ($35,000 – $28,000), with the offset again in stockholders' equity. In terms of total assets reported in the balance sheet, this has exactly the same effect as the first method.

However, many users of financial statements, including credit grantors and prospective investors, pay heed to the ratio of net property and equipment as a fraction of the related gross amounts. This is done to assess the relative age of the enterprise's productive assets and, indirectly, to estimate the timing and amounts of cash needs for asset replacements. There is a significant diminution of information under the second method. Accordingly, the first approach described above, preserving the relationship between gross and net asset amounts after the revaluation, is recommended as being the preferable alternative if the goal is meaningful financial reporting.

Application of revaluation to all assets in class. IAS 16 prudently requires that if any assets are revalued, all assets in those groupings or categories also be revalued. This is necessary to avert the presentation of a balance sheet that contains a mixture of historical costs and current values. Coupled with the requirement that revaluations take place with sufficient frequency to approximate fair values as of each balance sheet date, this preserves the integrity of the financial reporting process. In fact, given that a balance sheet prepared under the benchmark method of historical cost will, in fact, contain different historical costs (due to assets being acquired at varying times using dollars having different general and specific purchasing powers) the allowable alternative approach has the promise of providing even more consistent financial reporting. Offsetting this potential improvement somewhat, of course, is the greater subjectivity applied in determining fair values, vs. actual historical costs.

Although the requirement of IAS 16 is to revalue all assets in a given class, the standard recognizes that it may be more practical to accomplish this on a rolling, or cycle, basis. This would be done by, say, revaluing one-third of the assets in a given asset category, such as machinery, in each year, so that as of any balance sheet date one-third of the group is valued at current fair value, another one-third is valued at amounts that are 1 year obsolete, and another one-third are valued at amounts that are 2 years obsolete. Unless values are changing rapidly, it is likely that the balance sheet would not be materially distorted, and therefore this approach would in all likelihood be a reasonable means to facilitate the revaluation process.

Revaluation adjustments taken into income. While in general revaluation adjustments are to be shown directly in stockholders' equity as revaluation surplus, if a downward adjustment had previously been made to the asset and was recognized as an expense, the later upward revaluation would also be reported as income. Any revaluation receiving this treatment would be limited to the amount of expense recognized previously. As a practical matter, this should be a rare occurrence, since if the asset was revalued downward, the reference for that measurement would have been the estimated recoverable amount, and given what was judged to be a permanent impairment at an earlier date, it is very unlikely that there could be a later upward revaluation that could recover more than a minor portion of that impairment. However, in these unusual situations, a gain would be taken through the income statement.

The converse of the foregoing is also true: If an asset's carrying amount is decreased by recognition of a permanent impairment but the asset had previously been revalued upward by crediting revaluation surplus, the decline should be reported as a reduction of that surplus account rather than being reported as income. Any decline in value in excess of the amount previously recognized as an upward revaluation should be reported in earnings currently.

Example of revaluation and later downward adjustment

Consider the following example to illustrate the foregoing:

An asset was acquired January 1, 1994, for $10,000 and is expected to have a 5-year life. Straight-line depreciation will be used. At January 1, 1996, the asset is appraised as having a sound value (depreciated replacement cost) of $9,000. On January 1, 1998, the asset is appraised at a sound value of $1,500. The entries to reflect these events are as follows:

Date	Account	Debit	Credit
1/1/94	Asset	10,000	
	Cash, etc.		10,000
12/31/94	Depreciation expense	2,000	
	Accumulated depreciation		2,000
12/31/95	Depreciation expense	2,000	
	Accumulated depreciation		2,000
1/1/96	Asset	5,000	
	Accumulated depreciation		2,000
	Revaluation surplus		3,000
12/31/96	Depreciation expense	3,000	
	Accumulated depreciation		3,000
	Revaluation surplus	1,000	
	Retained earnings		1,000
12/31/97	Depreciation expense	3,000	
	Accumulated depreciation		3,000
	Revaluation surplus	1,000	
	Retained earnings		1,000
1/1/98	Accumulated depreciation	4,000	
	Revaluation surplus	1,000	
	Asset		5,000
	Loss from asset impairment	500	
	Accumulated depreciation		500

Certain of the entries in the foregoing example may need elaboration. The entries at 1994 and 1995 year ends are to record depreciation based on original cost, since there had been no revaluations through that point in time. On January 1, 1996 the revaluation is recorded; the appraisal of sound value ($9,000) suggests a 50% increase in value over depreciated historical cost ($6,000), which in turn means that the gross asset should be written up to $15,000 (a 50% increase over the historical cost, $10,000) and the accumulated depreciation should be written up proportionately (from $4,000 to $6,000). Had the appraisal revealed that the useful life of the equipment had also changed from its originally estimated amount, that would have been dealt with prospectively, as prescribed by IAS 8 (see Chapter 19 for a discussion of this matter).

In 1996 and 1997, depreciation must be provided on the new, higher value recorded at the beginning of 1996 (assuming that no additional appraisal is obtained in 1997). Since the asset has been written up by 50%, the periodic charge for depreciation must reflect the higher cost of doing business. However, while the income statements in each year must absorb greater depreciation expense, within the equity section of the balance sheet there will be an offsetting adjustment to transfer revaluation surplus to retained earnings, in the amount of the extra depreciation recognized each year.

As of January 1, 1998 the book value of the equipment is $3,000, which reflects the fact that the asset, having a gross replacement cost when last appraised of $15,000, is now 80% used up. A new appraisal reveals that the fair value is only $1,500 at this time. However, rather than charging the $1,500 decline in value ($3,000 – $1,500) to income, the portion of the decline that represents a retracing of the value increase previously recognized should be accounted for as a reversal of the revaluation surplus, not as a realized loss.

To effect the foregoing, the gross asset and related accumulated depreciation should be written down from amounts based on the 1996 appraisal (updated, in the case of accumulated depreciation, to the current balance) to original cost. Thus, the asset should be written down from $15,000 to $10,000, and the accumulated depreciation adjusted downward from $12,000 to $8,000. The further reduction in book value (from $2,000 to $1,500, as indicated by the latest appraisal) will be taken into income as a realized loss. The offset will be to accumulated depreciation, since the decline in value effectively means that the amount recognized as depreciation in prior periods had been understated; assuming no change in useful life, the depreciation charge for the final year (1998) will be $1,500, reducing the book value to zero at year end.

Exchanges of assets. IAS 16 discusses the accounting to be applied to those situations in which assets are exchanged for other similar or dissimilar assets, with or without the additional consideration of monetary assets. This topic is addressed later in this chapter, under the heading *Nonmonetary (Exchange) Transactions*.

Revisions to estimated residual value. Under the benchmark treatment prescribed by IAS 16, the amount estimated for residual value is made at the date of acquisition (or date a self-constructed asset is placed in service) and is not revised subsequently. In this regard the international standard departs from what has been the common practice of treating changes in estimated residual or salvage value as a change in an accounting estimate, and accounting for it prospectively by altering the annual depreciation charge for later years.

If the allowable alternative treatment is elected, at the date of each revaluation of the asset the expected residual amount should also be reassessed. The standard suggests that reference be made to actual residual values of similar assets reaching the end of their useful economic lives about the time the reevaluation is being conducted.

Impairment of Property, Plant, and Equipment

Current requirements. There is limited guidance under existing IAS addressing accounting for impairment of long-lived assets. In general, impairments are understood to mean permanent (or "other than temporary") declines in value, and these must be given recognition, although there is a notable lack of information on how this decline in utility is to be measured. IAS 16 states that recorded amounts of property, plant, and equipment should be periodically reviewed for impairment, which is deemed to have occurred when an asset's recoverable amount has declined below its carrying amount (which is generally depreciated cost, although if revaluations have been made the carrying amount will be higher). If impairment is detected, IAS 16 states that the decline in value is to be charged against income, except to the extent that upward revaluations were made previously, in which case the reversal of the write up would be charged directly to the equity account previously credited.

Proposed requirements. In its recent exposure draft E55, *Impairment of Assets*, the IASC has offered a comprehensive guide to accounting for impairments not only of plant assets, but of intangibles as well. While this proposal covers much of the same ground as the corresponding requirements under US GAAP (SFAS 121, effective in 1996), it reaches rather different conclusions and prescribes dissimilar methodologies. In general, it would be more likely that impairments would have to be recognized under a standard based on E55 than under US GAAP.

Bearing in mind that the currently outstanding proposal may well be altered before it becomes a final standard, the general outlines of this very important proposed set of requirements will be set forth in the following pages, as a guide to the readers who want to anticipate the impact it may have. However, care should be taken to review the new standard, if and when promulgated, for more detailed guidance.

E55 requires that a present value concept be applied, either implicitly or explicitly, to determine the value of long-lived assets and intangibles which may have been impaired. While not every asset would be so tested every reporting period, the proposed standard does set forth a range of indicators of possible impairment which are to be used to trigger the impairment test. Unlike the corresponding US GAAP standard, which prescribes a two-stage procedure (with a relatively simple initial threshold test for the existence of impairment, comparing undiscounted cash flows with carrying value), the proposed international accounting standard makes no use of undiscounted cash flow analysis. Since the test for the existence is unified with the calculation of the magnitude of impairment in E55, using discounted present values, if all other factors were held constant it would be more to conclude that impairment had occurred under the expected IAS than under the US rules.

Potentially impaired assets would be identified by reviewing, at each balance sheet date, whether any conditions exist which signal possible impairments. By reference to external conditions (such as known asset value decline, technological or legal environmental changes, or market and interest rate increases) and internal conditions (such as obsolescence, physical damage, manner in which the asset is used, or changed trends in performance), possible impairment of individual assets or groups of assets may be identified.

The new international standard will stipulate that assets should be reported at recoverable amounts, which will be defined as the greater of net selling price or value in use, when that is lower than carrying value. Net selling price is the amount which could be obtained in an arm's-length exchange, net of any incremental costs of disposition, while value in use equals the present value of expected future cash flows to be generated by the asset over the remainder of its useful economic life. Since in a smoothly functioning economy selling prices are indirectly determined by projected cash flows, both measures of recoverable amount are in fact dependent upon the application of present value concepts. In practice, for many classes of assets the value in use measure will be the operative definition of recoverable amount, since active markets for those assets will not exist, and subjective assessments of selling prices will prove to be too imprecise to employ.

E55 is quite detailed concerning the calculations needed for determining value in use. Management-developed cash flow projections are to be used for up to the next 5 years, with subsequent years (if any--cash flows cannot be projected for a time longer than the estimated depreciable life of the asset being considered) being extrapolated from the final forecaster year's data, but this must be constrained by a steady or declining growth rate, not to exceed the growth rate previously associated with the products, industries, or countries with which the assets are identified. Any net cash flow from the expected disposition of the asset at the end of its useful life is to be included as well (and this may even be negative), if the enterprise will have to pay for disposal or will incur cleanup or other costs. All cash flows are then to be discounted at a rate which reflects the time value of money when the computation is made, as well as the risk class of the asset being evaluated. Thus, changes in the interest rate environment alone could precipitate the recognition of an impairment or the recovery of a previously recognized impairment.

In general, recognition of impairment will involve a charge against earnings, which will affect the future pattern and amount of depreciation to be recognized and will also create a deductible temporary difference for which deferred taxes will have to be provided in most cases. However, if the reporting entity's policy is to account for plant assets at revalued amounts, as permitted under IAS 16, then the proposed standard will require that any impairment be treated as a revaluation decrease and charged against any previously provided revaluation surplus, with any further decline charged against earnings.

While the mandatory use of present value measurements may seem to represent an obstacle, in many cases it will be obvious that recoverable amounts exceed carrying values and this that detailed computations will not be needed. In some such circumstances, there will be no need to apply all the measurements suggested in E55.

The proposed standard also differs from the earlier US one in that it will require that previously recognized impairments be reversed, under certain defined conditions. The US standard holds that recognition of an impairment loss creates a new cost basis, from which increases in value may never be acknowledged. This difference in philosophy, of course, is further reflected in IAS 16, which permits the upward revaluation of property, plant, and equipment, which is prohibited under US GAAP.

Under the provisions of E55, if previously recognized impairments are later reversed, the credit in most cases will be to earnings. If the enterprise accounts for plant assets at revalued amounts, however, and the earlier impairment was treated as a revaluation decrease, then a later reversal of the impairment will be recorded again as a revaluation increase, as a credit to revaluation surplus rather than as income. Recognition of value increases will typically impact future depreciation patterns and amounts, and also will affect deferred taxes previously recognized. The proposal sets forth a series of conditions which would signal possible increases in recoverable amounts, and these largely mirror those defined as indicators of possible impairment. For example, decreases in interest rates and significant favorable changes in the technological or regulatory climate would suggest that a recovery in value may have taken place.

Earlier write-downs of goodwill will be more difficult to reverse, however, consistent with the general view that such apparent increases are really the result of internally generated goodwill, which is not to be given recognition under the IAS (the expected successor draft to E50, expected in late 1997, will preserve this rule). Only if the specific external condition which led to the earlier write-down of goodwill can be shown to have reversed will it be permissible to record the recovery in value.

In applying a proposed standard such as E55, or the existing US standard SFAS 121, a practical difficulty is identifying cash flows which relate to certain nonoperating assets, such as administrative headquarters and goodwill. Clearly, if the carrying values of these assets are excluded from the impairment testing process, the system would be flawed, since an entity cannot be deemed healthy if projected cash flows will just barely recover the carrying values of operating assets but contribute nothing to the recovery of possibly substantial carrying values of "overhead" assets. Accordingly, both E55 and SFAS 121 require that all plant assets and intangibles be assigned to business units which can be identified with cash flows. The guidance is fairly consistent: Aggregation of assets should be at the lowest level with which cash flows can be associated, and reasonable allocations should be made of such assets as corporate headquarters buildings. Goodwill should, whenever possible, be associated with the operating assets with which it was acquired (i.e., in a business combination), or otherwise reasonably allocated. If impairment is detected in an aggregation of assets (referred to as a cash-generating unit in the draft), any write-down should be taken first against goodwill, then against identifiable assets.

It is anticipated that, if adopted, the impairment standard will be effective beginning in 1999.

Retirements and Other Dispositions

In general, when an asset is no longer employed by an entity, it is removed from the balance sheet. In the case of fixed assets, both the asset and the related contra-asset, accumulated depreciation, should be eliminated. The difference between the net carrying amount and any proceeds received will be given immediate recognition as a gain or loss on the disposition.

If the allowed alternative treatment has been employed, the asset and the related accumulated depreciation account have been adjusted upward, and the asset is subsequently disposed of before the asset is fully depreciated, note that the gain or loss computed will be identical to what would have been determined had the benchmark treatment been used. That is because, at any point in time, the net amount of the revaluation (the step-up in gross asset amount less the present balance in the step-up in accumulated depreciation) will be offset exactly by the remaining balance in the revaluation surplus account. Elimination of the asset, contra-asset, and equity accounts will balance precisely, and there will be no gain or loss on this part of the disposition transaction. The gain or loss will be determined by the discrepancy between the net book value, based on historical cost, and the proceeds from the disposition.

Examples of accounting for asset disposition

On January 1, 1993, Zara Corp. acquired a machine at a cost of $12,000; it had an estimated life of 6 years, no residual value, and was expected to provide a level pattern of utility to the enterprise. Thus, straight-line depreciation in the amount of $2,000 was charged to operations. At the end of 4 years, the asset was sold for $5,000. Accounting in conformity with the IAS 16 benchmark approach was elected. The entries to record depreciation and to report the ultimate disposition on January 1, 1997 are as follows:

Date	Account	Debit	Credit
1/1/93	Machinery	12,000	
	Cash, etc.		12,000
12/31/93	Depreciation expense	2,000	
	Accumulated depreciation		2,000

Date	Account	Debit	Credit
12/31/94	Depreciation expense	2,000	
	Accumulated depreciation		2,000
12/31/95	Depreciation expense	2,000	
	Accumulated depreciation		2,000
12/31/96	Depreciation expense	2,000	
	Accumulated depreciation		2,000
1/1/97	Cash	5,000	
	Accumulated depreciation	8,000	
	Machinery		12,000
	Gain on asset disposition		1,000

Now assume the same facts as above, but that the allowed alternative method is used. At the beginning of year 4 (1996) the asset is revalued at a gross replacement cost of $15,000. A year later it is sold for $5,000. The entries are as follows (note in particular that the gain on the sale is identical to that reported under the benchmark approach):

Date	Account	Debit	Credit
1/1/93	Machinery	12,000	
	Cash, etc.		12,000
12/31/93	Depreciation expense	2,000	
	Accumulated depreciation		2,000
12/31/94	Depreciation expense	2,000	
	Accumulated depreciation		2,000
12/31/95	Depreciation expense	2,000	
	Accumulated depreciation		2,000
1/1/96	Machinery	3,000	
	Accumulated depreciation		1,500
	Revaluation surplus		1,500
12/31/96	Depreciation expense	2,500	
	Accumulated depreciation		2,500
	Revaluation surplus	500	
	Retained earnings		500
1/1/97	Cash	5,000	
	Accumulated depreciation	10,000	
	Revaluation surplus	1,000	
	Machinery		15,000
	Gain on asset disposition		1,000

Depletion

IAS 16 specifically excludes forests and other regenerative natural resources, as well as mineral rights and other nonregenerative resources, from applicability. No other international accounting standard addresses these matters, either. However, given the long-lived nature of those assets, the allocation of cost to periods benefited by a process similar to depreciation is an obvious necessity.

For example, under US GAAP, depletion is the annual charge for the use of natural resources. The depletion base includes all development costs, such as exploring, drilling, excavating, and other preparatory costs. The amount of the depletion base charged to income is determined by the following formula:

$$\frac{1}{\text{Total expected recoverable units}} \times \text{Depletion base} \times \text{Units sold}$$

The unit depletion rate is revised frequently due to the uncertainties surrounding the recovery of natural resources. The revision is made prospectively; the remaining undepleted cost is allocated over the remaining recoverable units.

Given the absence of an international standard on the matter of depletion, and given the need for rational allocation of the cost of long-lived mineral and other natural resource assets to the periods to be benefited, it is reasonable to follow the guidelines set forth above, which are based on US GAAP. For natural resource assets, which are typically harvested, mined, or otherwise placed into production or sold in patterns that are not stable over time (demand for commodities typically being far more volatile than demand for manufactured goods), the units of production method of depletion is almost always superior to straight-line methods.

Example of computing depletion costs

Assume that the rights to extract oil from a field are obtained for an initial payment of $2 million at the start of 1996, plus a commitment to restore the topography of the land, for an estimated cost of $1 million, after the extraction process has run its course. Geological surveys have suggested that the field contains 1,000,000 recoverable barrels of crude oil. Actual recoveries are 300,000 barrels in 1996 and 400,000 barrels in 1997. At the end of 1997, the estimated remaining recoverable crude oil was thought to be 400,000 barrels, and the cost to restore the condition of the land was now believed to be $900,000. Recovery in 1998 is 140,000 barrels, after which the field is abandoned and agreed-upon restoration is performed at a cost of $850,000 in early 1999. The entries to record these events are as follows:

1/1/96	Drilling rights	2,000,000	
	Cash		2,000,000
12/31/96	Depletion expense	900,000	
	Accumulated depletion		900,000
12/31/97	Depletion expense	1,200,000	
	Accumulated depletion		1,100,000
	Land restoration liability		100,000
12/31/98	Depletion expense	280,000	
	Land restoration liability		280,000
2/15/99	Land restoration liability	380,000	

Depletion expense	470,000	
Cash		850,000

The annual depletion costs in 1996 and 1997 are based on estimates of recoverable oil of 1,000,000 barrels and total costs of $3 million, including estimated land restoration (which is effectively negative salvage value). Depletion in 1998 is based on remaining accruable cost of $800,000 (the newly estimated land recovery cost of $900,000, less the already accrued $100,000) and revised recoverable oil of 400,000 barrels. When the facts ultimately become known in 1999 (that the recoverable oil was less than forecast and the restoration costs differ somewhat from the estimate made in 1998) the adjustment is really a change in an accounting estimate and thus must be reflected as an operating cost in 1999.

Intangible Assets

Definition of intangibles. Identifiable intangible assets include patents, copyrights, licenses, customer lists, brand names, import quotas, computer software, leasehold improvements, marketing rights, and specialized know-how. These items have in common the fact that there is no tangible substance to them (there may be tangible evidence of an asset's existence, such as a certificate indicating that a patent had been granted, but this does constitute the asset itself), they have an economic life of greater than 1 year, and they have a decline in utility over that period which can be measured or reasonably assumed. In many but not all cases, the asset is separable: That is, it could be sold or otherwise disposed of without simultaneously disposing of or diminishing the value of other assets held.

At the present time, there is no truly comprehensive international accounting standard governing intangible assets, although an exposure draft, E50, is now outstanding. Since the principles expounded by this draft are largely congruent with current practice and with US and other national standards, the proposed standard will be incorporated into the following discussion.

Identifiable intangibles have much similarity to tangible long-lived assets (property, plant, and equipment), and the accounting for them is accordingly also very similar. Key issues are

1. Whether the intangible asset has an identity separate from other aspects of the business enterprise
2. Whether the recoverable value can be ascertained with enough precision to warrant recordation as an asset

As to the former issue, the principal concern is to distinguish these intangibles from goodwill, the accounting for which is addressed by IAS 22. Goodwill is the residual cost of a business acquisition that cannot be assigned either to tangible assets, net of any liabilities assumed, or to identifiable intangibles. Unlike identifiable intangibles, goodwill cannot be separated from the assets (physical as well as intangible) it was acquired with. Since goodwill cannot be severed and sold, its real value is often questioned and the period over which it can be amortized is accordingly often made as brief as possible. Many users of financial statements recognize that goodwill is an accounting artifact arising in the context of business combinations, and implicitly, at least, will immediately deduct it from stockholders' equity.

Recognition criteria. To capitalize the cost of an intangible asset other than goodwill, it must have an independently observable existence and a cost that can be assigned to it. In the recent exposure draft, E50, it is proposed that an intangible asset be recognized only if future economic benefits associated therewith will flow to the reporting entity, and if the cost to the entity can be measured reliably. With regard to the former, it must be demonstrable that the intangible asset will enhance the expected inflow of benefits to the enterprise, that it in fact will be able to perform effectively in that role, and that the entity intends to use the intangible in the manner represented. Furthermore, the enterprise must be able to show that it has the other resources necessary to exploit the intangible asset's utility so as to reap the benefits that it possesses.

In many cases, these criteria will readily be satisfied. For example, if customer lists are purchased or if patents are acquired from other parties in arm's-length transactions, the benefits to be received will be understood, and the cost incurred will be known. In some situations, identifiable intangibles are acquired as part of a business combination or other bulk purchase transaction. Under GAAP, the aggregate purchase cost is to be allocated to assets acquired and liabilities assumed. If one or more of the assets are intangibles, the extent of judgment required in the allocation process becomes somewhat greater than would otherwise be the case; in extreme situations it may be impossible to determine how much, if any, of the aggregate cost should be allocated to intangibles. It is most likely to be determinable when the intangibles were actually negotiated for in the transaction rather than being thrown in to the deal. Furthermore, if the allocation of purchase price to individual assets is accomplished by applying discounted present value measures to future revenue streams, unless this same process is usable with regard to the intangibles, it is likely that any unallocated purchase price will have to be assigned to goodwill.

In the event that intangibles are internally generated (e.g., when patents are obtained following a period of research and development, or customer lists are developed) it may be possible to identify the relevant costs and thus to justify capitalization. (However, to the extent that these costs are more properly defined as research and development expenditures, they must be expensed currently according to IAS 9, except to the extent that capitalization of certain development costs is permitted by that standard.) For example, certain expenditures may be made to enhance brand names, such as image advertising campaigns, but these costs will also have ancillary benefits, such as promoting specific products that are being sold currently, and even boosting employee morale and performance. As a practical matter, it will be difficult to determine what portion of the expenditures relate to which achievement, and thus to ascertain how much, if any, of the cost may be capitalized as part of brand names. Thus, it is considered to be unlikely that threshold criteria for recognition can be met in such a case.

The more difficult issue relative to intangibles is whether recoverable value can be determined with any precision. Absent the ability to make this determination, even if the asset had been recorded properly on acquisition it would not be possible to justify continued presentation in the balance sheet, and thus immediate expensing would be prescribed under GAAP.

If expenditures on intangibles are treated as expenses because recognition criteria are not met, and later these criteria are satisfied, it is not permissible to restore any of the costs already expensed in prior periods. However, from the time that the recognition criteria first are met, further expenditures may be classified as intangible assets and amortized over the period to be benefited.

If, indeed, the cost of the intangible asset can be determined and its recoverable value can be reliably confirmed, it should be capitalized as an asset on acquisition or internal generation. E50 closely follows IAS 16 with regard to elements of cost that may be considered as part of the asset, and the need to recognize the cash equivalent price when the acquisition transaction provides for deferred payment terms. As with self-constructed tangible assets, elements of profit must be eliminated from amounts capitalized, but incremental administrative and other overhead costs can be allocated to the intangible and included in the asset's cost. Initial operating losses cannot be deferred by being added to the cost of the intangible, but must be expensed as incurred.

Intangibles acquired by means of governmental grants. If the intangible is acquired free of charge or by payment of nominal consideration, as by means of a governmental grant or similar program, and assuming the benchmark accounting treatment (historical cost) is employed, obviously there will be little or no amount reflected as an asset. If the asset is important to the reporting entity's operations, however, it must be adequately disclosed in the notes to the financial statements. If the allowed alternative (fair value) method is used, as discussed below, the intangible can be revalued periodically and reported on in the financial statements. However, given the probable lack of an active market, since governmental grants are generally not transferable, it is unlikely that this situation will be encountered.

Exchanges. These are addressed by E50 in a manner analogous to IAS 16 and are discussed in a later section of this chapter.

Subsequent costs added to intangible. As with tangible fixed assets, there may the necessity of incurring additional costs subsequent to the initial acquisition of an intangible asset. If these expenditures have the effect of increasing the utility of the asset in a measurable way, and this improvement can be related directly to the identifiable asset, they made be added to the asset's carrying value. The upper limit on the carrying amount of the intangible, of course, will be its recoverable amount.

For practical reasons, given the difficulty of making this assessment, capitalizing additional costs of intangibles is rather unlikely to occur.

Expensing the cost of intangibles. The criteria for recognition of intangible assets, as proposed by E50, are rather stringent, and many enterprises will find that expenditures either to acquire or to develop intangible assets will fail the test for capitalization. In such instances, all these costs must be expensed currently as incurred. Furthermore, once expensed, these costs cannot in a later period be resurrected and capitalized, even if the conditions for such treatment are later met (this is not meant, however, to preclude correction of an error made in an earlier period, if the conditions for capitalization were met but interpreted incorrectly by the reporting entity at that time).

In some cases, while certain of the criteria for capitalization as an intangible asset have not been met, thereby precluding recordation as an intangible asset, some or all of the costs at issue will be properly accounted for as deferred charges or prepaid expenses. Thus, expense recognition will be partially or fully deferred to later periods. For example, there may be uncertainty about the future economic benefits that will flow to the enterprise, as may be the case in the context of start-up costs for an entity or a product line. If such costs are properly reported as deferred charges in the particular jurisdiction, the criteria of E50 would not obviate such treatment.

Allowed alternative treatment--Revaluation. As with tangible assets under IAS 16, the proposed standard for intangibles would permit revaluation subsequent to original acquisition, with the asset being written up to fair value. Inasmuch as most of the particulars of E50 follow IAS 16 to the letter, these will not be repeated here. The unique features of E50 are as follows:

1. If the intangibles were not initially recognized (i.e., they were expensed rather than capitalized) it will not be possible to later recognize them at fair value.
2. Deriving fair value by applying a present value concept to projected cash flows (a technique that can be used in the case of tangible assets under IAS 16) is deemed to be too unreliable in the realm of intangibles, primarily because it would tend to commingle the impact of identifiable assets and goodwill. Accordingly, only actual transactions with third parties and the existence of active secondary markets can provide the needed fair value data in the instance of revaluation of intangibles. Active markets providing meaningful data are not expected to exist for such unique assets as patents and trademarks, and thus it is presumed that revaluation will not be applied to these types of assets in the normal course of business.
3. The mainstream accounting treatment for revaluation of fixed assets, involving the write-up of both gross asset carrying amount and accumulated depreciation to current amounts, thereby resulting in a net revaluation at the depreciated replacement cost (also known as sound value), is not available

for intangibles. E50 stipulates that any accumulated amortization at the date of revaluation is eliminated against the gross asset carrying amount and the net amount restated to fair value. This does not affect the actual result on the balance sheet and probably is meant to reflect the fact that, unlike tangible fixed assets, financial statements traditionally do not report gross and net amounts for intangibles, but rather, present only the net.

4. If an intangible is revalued using information obtained from an active secondary market, and the secondary market ceases to function, the carrying value should continue to be based on the last reliable market value, unless this is greater than the estimated recoverable amount. It is not required to revert to historical cost in such an instance.

As with plant, property, and equipment under IAS 16, if some assets in a given class are subjected to revaluation, all the assets in that class should be consistently accounted for, unless fair value information is not, or ceases to be, available.

Also in common with the requirements for tangible fixed assets, E50 would require that revaluations be taken directly to equity through the use of a revaluation surplus account, except to the extent that previous impairments had been recognized by a charge against income.

Example of revaluation of intangible assets

A patent right is acquired July 1, 1995, for $250,000; while it has a legal life of 15 years, due to rapidly changing technology, management estimates a useful life of only 5 years. Straight-line amortization will be used. At January 1, 1996, management is uncertain that the process can actually be made economically feasible, and decides to write down the patent to an estimated market value of $75,000. Amortization will be taken over 3 years from that point. On January 1, 1998, having perfected the related production process, the asset is now appraised at a sound value of $300,000. Furthermore, the estimate useful life is now believed to be 6 more years. The entries to reflect these events are as follows:

Date	Account	Debit	Credit
7/1/95	Patent	250,000	
	Cash, etc.		250,000
12/31/95	Amortization expense	25,000	
	Patent		25,000
1/1/96	Loss from asset impairment	150,000	
	Patent		150,000
12/31/96	Amortization expense	25,000	
	Patent		25,000
12/31/97	Amortization expense	25,000	
	Patent		25,000

1/1/98	Patent	275,000	
	Gain on asset value recovery		100,000
	Revaluation surplus		175,000

Certain of the entries in the foregoing example will now be explained further. The entry at year-end 1995 is to record depreciation based on original cost, since there had been no revaluations through that time; only a half-year amortization is provided ([$250,000/5] x 1/2). On January 1, 1996 the impairment is recorded by writing down the asset to the estimated value of $75,000, which necessitates a $150,000 charge to income (carrying value, $225,000, less fair value, $75,000).

In 1996 and 1997, depreciation must be provided on the new, lower value recorded at the beginning of 1996; furthermore, since the new estimated life was 3 years from January 1996, annual amortization will be $25,000.

As of January 1, 1998 the carrying value of the patent is $25,000; had the January 1996 revaluation not been made, the carrying value would have been $125,000 ($250,000 original cost, less 2.5 years amortization versus an original estimated life of 5 years). The new appraised value is $300,000, which will fully recover the earlier write-down and add even more asset value than the originally recognized cost. Under the guidance of the exposure draft E50, the recovery of $100,000 that had been charged to expense should be taken into income; the excess will be credited to stockholders' equity.

Amortization of intangibles. As with tangible assets subject to depreciation or depletion, the cost (or revalued carrying amount) of intangible assets is subject to rational and systematic amortization. Given that the useful economic life of many intangibles would be difficult to assess, the proposed rule is that a maximum 20-year life is permissible, with amortization being over a shorter useful life if known. The only exceptions would occur in those instances where the legal right has a life of greater than 20 years **and** either of the following conditions exist:

1. The intangible has an existence that is not separable from a **specific** tangible asset, the useful life of which can be reliably determined to exceed 20 years, or
2. There is an active secondary market for the intangible.

The thrust of these requirements is to make the 20-year life an upper limit for most intangibles.

Intangible assets may be amortized by the same systematic and rational methods that are used to depreciate tangible fixed assets. Thus, E50 would permit straight-line, diminishing balance, and units of production methods. These were explained earlier and will not be further elaborated on here. If a method other than straight-line is used, it must accurately mirror the expiration of the asset's economic service potential.

As is also true with depreciation and depletion, the annual charge is most commonly reflected as an expense. However, to the extent that it represents a cost of production of other long-term assets, or of inventory intended for sale to customers but that remains on hand at the end of the period, it will be capitalized as part of the other asset (property and equipment, or inventory) instead.

Residual value. Long-term assets subject to depreciation, depletion, or amortization should be written down, over their respective useful lives, to net residual values. As discussed earlier in this chapter, this residual may in fact be a negative amount, when costs of disposal or site restoration are anticipated. Tangible assets often have a positive residual value, before considering the disposal costs, because the item can generally be sold for scrap or possibly be transferred to another user that has less need for, or ability to afford, new assets of that type. Intangibles, on the other hand, lacking the physical attributes that would make scrap value a meaningful concept, often have little or no residual worth. Accordingly, E50 requires that a zero residual value be presumed unless an accurate measure of residual is possible.

Periodic review of useful life assumptions and amortization methods employed. As with fixed assets under IAS 16, the proposed standard on intangibles suggests that the amortization period be reconsidered at the end of each reporting period, and that the method of amortization also be reviewed at similar intervals. There is the expectation that due to their nature, intangibles are more likely to require revisions to one or both of these judgments. In either case, a change would be accounted for as a change in estimate, affecting current and future periods' reported earnings but not requiring restatement of previously reported periods.

Dispositions of intangible assets. The guidance of E50 virtually mirrors that of IAS 16, as discussed above. Gain or loss recognition will be prescribed for the difference between carrying amount (net, if applicable, of any remaining revaluation surplus) and the net proceeds from the sale.

Proposed revisions to accounting for intangibles. The foregoing discussion is based on the IASC's exposure draft, E50, issued in mid-1995 but never finalized as a standard. More recently, the committee has considered revisions to E50 which, among other things, would merge the guidance contained in IAS 9 on research and development costs (discussed later in this chapter) with that on other intangibles, including goodwill. While it does not appear that the guidance of E50 will be substantially altered as it relates to intangibles discussed in the preceding pages of this chapter, readers should be alert to the possibility that this might occur. The IASC is expected to produce a revised draft document prior to adoption of a comprehensive new standard--with the new requirements not expected before mid-1998.

Disclosure Requirements: Tangible and Intangible Assets

The disclosure rules set forth in IAS 16 for property, plant, and equipment, and those set forth in E50 for intangible assets, are largely identical, and both demand a large amount of detail in the financial statement notes.

For each class of tangible asset, disclosure is required of

1. The measurement basis used (benchmark or alternative approaches)
2. The depreciation method(s) used
3. Useful lives or depreciation rates used
4. The gross carrying amount and accumulated depreciation at both the beginning and end of the period
5. A reconciliation of the carrying amount at the beginning and end of the period, showing additions, dispositions, acquisitions by means of business combinations, increases or decreases resulting from revaluations, reductions to recognize impairments, amounts written back to recognize recoveries of prior impairments, depreciation, the net effect of translation of foreign entities' financial statements, and any other material items. (An example of such a reconciliation is presented below.)

In addition, the statements should also disclose the following facts:

1. Whether, in determining recoverable amounts, future projected cash flows have been discounted to present values
2. Any restrictions on titles and any assets pledged as security for debt
3. The accounting policy regarding restoration costs for items of plant, property, and equipment
4. The expenditures made for property, plant, and equipment, including any construction in progress
5. The amount of outstanding commitments for property, plant, and equipment acquisitions

With regard to intangibles, the disclosures are as follows:

1. The amortization method(s) used
2. Useful lives or amortization rates used
3. The gross carrying amount and accumulated amortization at both the beginning and end of the period
4. The carrying amount of any internally generated intangibles
5. A reconciliation of the carrying amount at the beginning and end of the period, showing additions, disposals, increases or decreases resulting from revaluations, reductions to recognize impairments, amounts written back to recognize recoveries of prior impairments, amortization, the net effect of translation of foreign entities' financial statements, and any other material items

In addition, the statements should also disclose the following facts:

1. If the amortization period for any intangibles exceed 20 years, the justification therefor
2. Whether, in determining recoverable amounts, future projected cash flows have been discounted to present values

3. Any restrictions on titles and any assets pledged as security for debt
4. The amount of outstanding commitments for property, plant, and equipment acquisitions

Example of reconciliation of asset carrying amounts

Date	Gross cost	Accumulated depreciation	Net book value
1/1/96	$4,500,000	$2,000,000	$2,500,000
Acquisitions	3,000,000		3,000,000
Disposals	(400,000)	(340,000)	(60,000)
Impairment		600,000	(600,000)
Depreciation		200,000	(200,000)
12/31/96	$7,100,000	$2,460,000	$4,640,000

Nonmonetary (Exchange) Transactions

Under US GAAP there exist very detailed rules (APB Opinion 29) governing accounting for nonmonetary transactions. By contrast, under international standards this topic is dealt with only superficially. Both IAS 16 and the proposed standard for intangibles, E50, note the accounting implications of exchanges of one item of property, plant, or equipment, or one intangible, for another of similar nature. The rules are simply that

1. The value is to be ascertained by reference to the asset received in the exchange, adjusted for any cash or equivalents paid or received.
2. If the exchange involves similar assets, to be used by the enterprise in essentially the same manner and for the same purpose as the item given up in the exchange, the exchange is not deemed to be the culmination of an earnings process, and accordingly, no gain or loss is recognized; the new asset will be recorded as the carrying amount of the asset given up, adjusted for any cash or equivalent given or received.
3. If dissimilar assets are exchanged, the cost of the item received is measured by reference to its fair value, which is generally the fair value of the asset given up, adjusted for any cash or cash equivalent received or given.

Dissimilar assets. An exchange is deemed to be the culmination of the earnings process when dissimilar assets are exchanged. The general rule is to value the transaction at the **fair market value** of the asset given received (unless the fair value of the asset given up is more clearly evident) and to recognize the gain or loss. If there is a settle-up paid or received in cash or cash equivalent, this is often referred to as **boot**.

Example of an exchange involving dissimilar assets and no boot

Assume the following:

1. Jamok, Inc. exchanges an automobile with a carrying value of $2,500 with Springsteen & Co. for a tooling machine with a fair market value of $3,200.
2. No boot is exchanged in the transaction.
3. The fair value of the automobile is not readily determinable.

In this case, Jamok, Inc. has recognized a gain of $700 ($3,200 – $2,500) on the exchange. Because the exchange involves dissimilar assets, the earnings process has culminated and the gain should be included in the determination of net income. The entry to record the transaction would be as follows:

Machine	3,200	
Automobile		2,500
Gain on exchange of automobile		700

Similar assets. Similar assets are those that are used for the same general purpose, are of the same general type, and are employed in the same line of business. Thus, it is not necessary to exchange identical assets. The treatment described applies to those assets that are exchanged as a result of technological advancement as well as to those that are exchanged as a result of wearing out. The general rule involving the exchange of similar assets involving a gain is to value the transaction at the book value of the asset given up. In this situation, the gain is effectively deferred over the life of the new asset by causing a lesser amount of annual depreciation to be charged to operations.

If cash or an equivalent is also included in the transaction, this suggests that the nonmonetary assets exchanged did not have equivalent values. If there is evidence that the asset given up was impaired as to value, as might be suggested if cash was needed to even up the trade, the impairment must be recognized. To fail to do this would result in an overstatement of the carrying amount of the new asset and excessive periodic depreciation charges over the term of its use.

Example of an exchange involving similar assets and boot

Assume the following:

1. Metronome exchanged a casting machine for a technologically newer model. The cost of the old machine was $75,000, and the accumulated depreciation was $5,000.
2. The fair value of the machine received was $90,000.
3. Boot was paid in the amount of $40,000.

A loss in the amount of $20,000 is recognized in connection with this transaction. This amount is the difference between the fair value of the asset received less the boot paid ($90,000 – $40,000 = $50,000) and the carrying value of the asset surrendered ($70,000). The entry required to record the transaction is as described below.

Loss on trade of machine	20,000	
New machine	90,000	
Accumulated depreciation	5,000	
Old machine		75,000
Cash		40,000

International accounting standards do not presently address the accounting for other types of nonmonetary exchanges that are nonreciprocal in nature. Under US GAAP, nonreciprocal transfers with owners and with nonowners are dealt with as described below.

Nonreciprocal transfers. Examples of nonreciprocal transfers with owners include dividends-in-kind, nonmonetary assets exchanged for common stock, split-ups, and spin-offs. An example of a nonreciprocal transaction with other than the owners is a donation of property either by or to the enterprise.

The valuation of most nonreciprocal transfers should be based on the fair market value of the asset given (or received, if the fair value of the nonmonetary asset is both objectively measurable and would be clearly recognizable). However, nonmonetary assets distributed to owners of an enterprise in a spin-off or other form of reorganization or liquidation should be based on the recorded amount. Where there is no asset given, the valuation of the transaction should be based on the fair value of the asset received.

Example of accounting for a nonreciprocal transfer

Assume the following:

1. XYZ donated property with a book value of $10,000 to a charity during the current year.
2. The property had a fair market value of $17,000 at the date of the transfer.

According to the US GAAP requirements, the transaction is to be valued at the fair market value of the property transferred, and any gain or loss on the transaction is to be recognized. Thus, XYZ should recognize a gain of $7,000 ($17,000 – $10,000) in the determination of the current period's net income. The entry to record the transaction would be as follows:

Charitable donations	17,000	
Property		10,000
Gain on transfer of property		7,000

Capitalization of Borrowing Costs

Logic, as well as promulgated GAAP, suggests that the cost of an asset should include all the costs necessary to get the asset set up and functioning properly for its intended use. For some years there has been a question of whether such costs should be included in the definition of all costs necessary or whether such costs should continue to be treated as purely a period expense. A corollary issue is whether an imputed cost of capital for equity financing should similarly be treated as a cost to be capitalized: The implicit argument being that the cost of a self-constructed asset, for example, should not differ between two entities simply because one finances it internally while another finances the asset with externally supplied (debt) capital.

This question was resolved in the United States with the promulgation of FASB Statement 34, which established US GAAP concerning the capitalization of interest. Borrowing costs, under defined conditions, are added to the cost of fixed assets (and inventory, in very limited circumstances), but the cost of equity capital may **not** be imputed.

The principal purposes to be accomplished by the capitalization of interest costs are as follows:

1. To obtain a more accurate original asset investment cost
2. To achieve a better matching of costs deferred to future periods with revenues of those future periods

International accounting standards differ from US GAAP in that both benchmark and allowed alternative treatments have been prescribed; the alternative treatment is very similar to that which is mandatory in the United States.

Benchmark treatment. The IAS 23 benchmark remains the method formerly universally followed in the United States and elsewhere. All borrowing costs are treated as period costs and expensed as incurred.

Alternative treatment. Interest actually incurred on borrowed funds used to finance the acquisition, construction, or production of a qualifying asset (defined below) is added to the carrying value of the asset. The amount of interest so accounted for depends on whether funds were borrowed specifically for the project in question or whether a pool of borrowed funds was deployed for a variety of projects, some of which may be subject to the interest capitalization rules.

Qualifying assets are those that normally take an extended period of time to prepare for their intended uses. While IAS 23 does not give further insight into the limitations of this definition, over 15 years of experience with FASB Statement 34 yields certain insights that may be germane to this matter. In general, interest capitalization has been applied to those asset acquisition and construction situations in which

1. Assets are being constructed for an entity's own use or for which deposit or progress payments are made.
2. Assets are produced as discrete projects that are intended for lease or sale.
3. Investments are being made that are accounted for by the equity method, where the investee is using funds to acquire qualifying assets for its principal operations which have not yet begun.

Generally, inventories and land that are not undergoing preparation for intended use are not qualifying assets. When land is in the process of being developed, it is a qualifying asset. If land is being developed for lots, the capitalized interest cost is added to the cost of the **land**. The related borrowing costs are then matched against revenues when the lots are sold. If, on the other hand, the land is being developed for a building, the capitalized interest cost should instead be added to the cost of the **building**. The interest is then matched against revenues as the building is depreciated.

The capitalization of interest costs would probably not apply to the following situations:

1. The routine production of inventories in large quantities on a repetitive basis
2. For any asset acquisition or self-construction, when the effects of capitalization would not be material, compared to the effect of expensing interest
3. When qualifying assets are already in use or ready for use
4. When qualifying assets are not being used and are not awaiting activities to get them ready for use
5. When qualifying assets are not included in a consolidated balance sheet
6. When principal operations of an investee accounted for under the equity method have already begun
7. When regulated investees capitalize both the cost of debt and equity capital
8. When assets are acquired with grants and gifts restricted by the donor to the extent that funds are available from those grants and gifts

If funds are borrowed specifically for the purpose of obtaining a qualified asset, the interest costs incurred thereon should be deemed eligible for capitalization, net of any interest earned from the temporary investment of idle funds. It is likely that there will not be a perfect match between funds borrowed and funds actually applied to the asset production process, at any given time, although in some construction projects funds are drawn from the lender's credit facility only as vendors' invoices, and other costs, are actually paid. Only the interest incurred on the project should be included as a cost of the project, however.

In other situations, a variety of credit facilities may be used to generate a pool of funds, a portion of which is applied to the asset construction or acquisition program. In those instances, the amount of interest to be capitalized will be determined by applying an average borrowing cost to the amount of funds committed to the project. Interest cost could include the following:

1. Interest on debt having explicit interest rates
2. Interest related to finance leases
3. Amortization of any related discount or premium on borrowings, or of other ancillary borrowing costs, such as commitment fees

The amount of interest to be capitalized is that portion that could have been avoided if the qualifying asset had not been acquired. Thus, the capitalized amount is the incremental amount of interest cost incurred by the entity to finance the acquired asset. A weighted-average of the rates of the borrowings of the entity should be used. The selection of borrowings to be used in the calculation of the weighted-average of rates requires judgment. In resolving this problem, particularly in the case of consolidated statements, the best criterion to use is the identification and determination of that portion of interest that could have been avoided if the qualifying assets had not been acquired.

The base (which should be used to multiply the rate by) is the average amount of accumulated net capital **expenditures incurred** for qualifying assets during the relevant time frame. Capitalized costs and expenditures are not the same terms. Theoretically, a capitalized cost financed by a trade payable for which no interest is recognized is not a capital expenditure to which the capitalization rate should be applied. Reasonable approximations of net capital expenditures are acceptable, however, and capitalized costs are generally used in place of capital expenditures unless there is a material difference.

If the average capitalized expenditures exceed the specific new borrowings for the time frame involved, the **excess** expenditures amount should be multiplied by the weighted-average of rates and not by the rate associated with the specific debt. This requirement more accurately reflects the interest cost incurred by the entity to bring the fixed asset to a properly functioning position.

The interest being paid on the debt may be simple or compound. Simple interest is computed on the principal alone, whereas compound interest is computed on principal and on any interest that has not been paid. Compounding may be yearly, monthly, or daily. Most fixed assets will be acquired with debt having interest compounded, and that feature should be considered when computing the amount of interest to be capitalized.

The total amount of interest actually incurred by the entity during the relevant time frame is the ceiling for the amount of interest cost capitalized. Thus, the amount capitalized cannot exceed the amount actually incurred during the period involved. On a consolidated basis, the ceiling is defined as the total of the parent's interest cost plus that of the consolidated subsidiaries. If financial statements are issued separately, the interest cost capitalized should be limited to the amount that the separate entity has incurred, and that amount should include interest on intercompany borrowings. The interest incurred is a gross amount and is not netted against interest earned except in rare cases, such as when there are externally restricted tax-exempt borrowings in certain jurisdictions.

Example of accounting for capitalized interest costs

Assume the following:

1. On January 1, 1996, Gemini Corp. contracted with Leo Company to construct a building for $2,000,000 on land that Gemini had purchased years earlier.
2. Gemini Corp. was to make 5 payments in 1996, with the last payment scheduled for the date of completion.
3. The building was completed December 31, 1996.
4. Gemini Corp. made the following payments during 1996:

January 1, 1996	$ 2,000,000
March 31, 1996	4,000,000
June 30, 1996	6,100,000
September 30, 1996	4,400,000
December 31, 1996	3,500,000
	$20,000,000

5. Gemini Corp. had the following debt outstanding at December 31, 1996:

a.	A 12%, 4-year note dated 1/1/96 with interest compounded quarterly. Both principal and interest due 12/31/99 (relates specifically to building project)	$8,500,000
b.	A 10%, 10-year note dated 12/31/92 with simple interest and interest payable annually on December 31	$6,000,000
c.	A 12%, 5-year note dated 12/31/94 with simple interest and interest payable annually on December 31	$7,000,000

The amount of interest to be capitalized during 1996 is computed as follows:

Average Accumulated Expenditures

Date	Expenditure	*Capitalization period**	*Average accumulated expenditures*
1/1/96	$ 2,000,000	12/12	$2,000,000
3/31/96	4,000,000	9/12	3,000,000
6/30/96	6,100,000	6/12	3,050,000
9/30/96	4,400,000	3/12	1,100,000
12/31/96	3,500,000	0/12	--
	$20,000,000		$9,150,000

**The number of months between the date when expenditures were made and the date on which interest capitalization stops (December 31, 1996).*

Potential Interest
Cost to be Capitalized

($8,500,000	x 1.12551)*	– $850,000	=	$1,066,840
650,000	x 0.1108**		=	72,020
$9,150,000				$1,138,860

* *The principal, $8,500,000, is multiplied by the factor for the future amount of $1 for 4 periods at 3% to determine the amount of principal and interest due in 1996.*
** *Weighted-average interest rate*

	Principal	Interest
10%, 10-year note	$ 6,000,000	$ 600,000
12%, 5-year note	7,000,000	840,000
	$13,000,000	$1,440,000

$$\frac{\text{Total interest}}{\text{Total principal}} = \frac{\$\ 1{,}440{,}000}{\$13{,}000{,}000} = 11.08\%$$

The actual interest is

12%, 4-year note [($8,500,000 x 1.12551) – $8,500,000]	=	$1,066,840
10%, 10-year note ($6,000,000 x 10%)	=	600,000
12%, 5-year note ($7,000,000 x 12%)	=	840,000
Total interest		$2,506,840

The interest cost to be capitalized is the lesser of $1,138,860 (avoidable interest) or $2,506,840 (actual interest). The remaining $1,367,980 ($2,506,840 – $1,138,860) would be expensed.

Determining the time period for interest capitalization. Three conditions must be met before the capitalization period should begin.

1. Expenditures for the asset are being incurred
2. Borrowing costs are being incurred
3. Activities that are necessary to prepare the asset for its intended use are in progress

As long as these conditions continue, interest costs can be capitalized.

Necessary activities are interpreted in a very broad manner. They start with the planning process and continue until the qualifying asset is substantially complete and ready to function as intended. These may include technical and administrative work prior to actual commencement of physical work, such as obtaining permits and approvals, and may continue after physical work has ceased. Brief, normal interruptions do not stop the capitalization of interest costs. However, if the entity intentionally suspends or delays the activities for some reason, interest costs should not be capitalized from the point of suspension or delay until substantial activities in regard to the asset resume.

If the asset is completed in a piecemeal fashion, the capitalization of interest costs stops for each part as it becomes ready to function as intended. An asset that must be entirely complete before the parts can be used as intended can continue to capitalize interest costs until the total asset becomes ready to function.

Suspension and cessation of capitalization. If there is an extended period during that there is no activity to prepare the asset for its intended use, capitalization of borrowing costs should be suspended. As a practical matter, unless the break in activity is significant, it is usually ignored. Also, if delays are normal and expected given the nature of the construction project (such as a suspension of building construction during the winter months) this would have been anticipated as a cost and would not warrant even a temporary cessation of borrowing cost capitalization.

Capitalization would cease when the project has been substantially completed. This would occur when the asset is ready for its intended use or for sale to a customer. The fact that routine, minor administrative matters still need to be attended to would not mean that the project had **not** been completed, however. The measure should be substantially complete, not absolutely finished, in other words.

Costs in excess of recoverable amounts. If the capitalization of borrowing costs causes the carrying value of the asset to exceed its recoverable value (if property, plant, or equipment) or its net realizable value (if an item held for resale), it will be necessary to record an adjustment to write the asset carrying value down. In the case of plant, property, and equipment, a later write-up may occur due to use of the allowed alternative (i.e., revaluation) treatment, recognizing fair value increases, in which case, as described earlier, recovery of a previously recognized loss will be reported in earnings.

Consistency of application. IAS 23 did not address the question of whether an entity would be justified in capitalizing interest costs (i.e., using the allowed alternative treatment) for some qualifying assets, while expensing currently, (i.e., applying the benchmark treatment) interest incurred in the acquisition, construction, or production of other qualifying assets. While the issue was not raised, logic suggests that if both methods were employed for qualifying assets by a single entity, it would make meaningful interpretation of the resulting financial statements more difficult for users. Accordingly, the recently constituted Standing Interpretations Committee (SIC) of the IASC has addressed this matter. In a currently outstanding draft interpretation, the SIC expresses its conclusion that if the allowed alternative method (i.e., capitalizing borrowing costs) is used for some qualifying assets, the method should be used for all such assets.

In reaching this conclusion, the committee weighed the guidance already contained in IAS 27 (on consolidated financial reporting) and the *Framework for the Preparation and Presentation of Financial Statements*. The existing standard on consolidations provides that uniform accounting policies are to be used for like transactions and other events in similar circumstances. The logic is to avoid having consolidated financial statements which are the summation of dissimilar measurements of like transactions or other economic phenomena. The IASC's *Framework for the Preparation and Presentation of Financial Statements* similarly expresses the notion that measurement of like transactions and other events should be carried out in a consistent manner throughout an entity and over the time of its ongoing existence, for purposes of both separate and consolidated financial reporting.

IAS 23 stipulates only one alternative methodology, capitalization of interest costs. The fact that only this single method is so sanctioned leads the SIC to conclude that the intention was to not leave the preparers with any further discretion. Accordingly, the conclusion is that it would not be appropriate to apply capitalization to some, but not all, qualifying assets. If adopted, this interpretation would become effective for 1998.

Disclosure requirements. With respect to an entity's accounting for borrowing costs, the financial statements must disclose which policy (benchmark or allowed alternative) is being utilized, as well as the actual borrowing costs capitalized during the period and the rate used to determine the amount of such costs eligible for capitalization. As noted above, this rate will be the weighted average of rates on all borrowings included in an allocation pool or the actual rate on specific debt identified with a given asset acquisition or construction project.

Research and Development Costs

Research and development (R&D) activities are defined in IAS 9 as follows:

- *a. Research is original and planned investigation undertaken with the prospect of gaining new scientific or technical knowledge and understanding.*
- *b. Development is the application of research findings or other knowledge to a plan or design for the production of new or substantially improved materials, devices, products, processes, systems or services prior to the commencement of commercial production or use.*

Research may include activities aimed at obtaining new knowledge, searching for applications for the findings of others, searching for product or process alternatives, and the formulation and design of possible new or improved product or process alternatives. Development connotes evaluation of product or process alternatives; design, construction, or testing of preproduction prototypes and models; design of tools and related items; and design, construction, and operation of pilot plants that are not intended for commercial operation.

Although the line between research and development may be difficult to discern in many instances, the distinction is more than academic. Under IAS 9 the accounting implications are rather different for development costs than for those associated with research.

The following are three of the ways that R&D costs may be incurred by a business:

1. Through an arrangement to develop R&D for other entities
2. Through the purchase of R&D from other entities
3. Through R&D activities conducted by and for the benefit of the enterprise

Costs incurred while conducting R&D for others. Accounting for R&D costs incurred as a result of contractual arrangements is dependent on the nature of the agreement. If the substance is that the risks and benefits are or will be transferred to the other entity, the costs incurred can be accumulated as inventory in accordance with IAS 2 or IAS 11, dealing with inventories in general and with construction contracts, respectively. On the other hand, if the risks and benefits are not to be transferred to others, the guidance of IAS 9 governs the accounting for these costs. This is as set forth in the following paragraphs.

In determining whether the risks and rewards remain with the entity incurring the costs or transfer to its customer, several factors should be considered. If the business receives funds from another party to perform R&D and is obligated to repay those funds regardless of the outcome, a liability must be recorded and the R&D costs expensed as incurred. Furthermore, even in the absence of a requirement to repay the advances, if repayment could be required at the other party's option, or if surrounding circumstances suggest that such repayment is probable, the same accounting result would obtain. In other words, to conclude that a liability does not exist, the transfer of the financial risk must be substantive and genuine.

Costs incurred through the purchase of R&D from others. If an enterprise engages another entity to perform research and development work on its behalf, the accounting implications are similar to what they would be if the work were performed by the enterprise itself. In general, research costs must be expensed as incurred, as must development costs incurred prior to the point when the criteria noted below are first satisfied. Since it is not appropriate to achieve indirectly an accounting result that could not be obtained directly, the costs paid to a contract R&D operation cannot be capitalized unless the same criteria are met.

Costs incurred while conducting R&D for the entity itself. Classification of costs will be important, since research expenditures will have to be expensed currently, while some development costs will be capitalized. Proper categorization should, however, be more readily achievable under this scenario, since the entity itself is directing the R&D efforts and would certainly know the nature of the costs incurred.

Accounting for research costs. Under revised IAS 9, all research costs must be expensed as incurred. This position is the result of the realization that the future economic value of such expenditures is highly questionable in most instances, and accordingly, a prudent and conservative stance is to avoid deferral of any expense recognition.

Accounting for development expenditures. Unlike research costs, some development expenditures are subject to deferral. The threshold issue is whether the efforts have advanced to a stage whereby each of a series of criteria has been met; if all the following have been satisfied, capitalization of development expenditures would be warranted:

1. The product or process is clearly defined and the costs attributable thereto can be identified separately and measured reliably.
2. Technological feasibility of the product or process can be demonstrated.
3. The entity intends to produce and market, or to use, the product or process.
4. The existence of a market for the product or process or, if to be used internally by the entity, its usefulness to it, can be demonstrated.
5. Adequate resources exist, or their availability can be shown, to complete the project and market or use the product or process.

As with other assets, the carrying amount of the capitalized development expenditures cannot exceed the recoverable amount; any excess costs would have to be written off to income as incurred. In determining recoverable amounts, the additional development costs expected to be incurred in obtaining the future economic benefits need to be considered. Selling prices and costs should be those prevailing at the time the estimate is being made, unless it is expected (as would be likely with technological advances and many other products) that selling prices in the future will be lower than those at present and the decline will not be offset by lower production costs.

The nature of development costs and the need to forecast future demand for products and processes is fraught with uncertainties that exceed those of many other accounting estimations. IAS 9 urges that a conservative approach be taken, while cautioning that deliberate understatement of assets is not to be countenanced.

Amortizing capitalized development expenditures. If development costs are capitalized, they are subject to systematic and rational amortization just as any other long-lived tangible or intangible asset would be. The nature of these costs suggests that amortization over a relatively brief period would be the norm. To the extent that these costs, through the amortization process, become part of the production costs of goods to be sold to others, the expenditures ultimately are recognized when the goods are in fact sold.

Impairment of capitalized development expenditures. Again in common with other classes of capitalized costs, there must be a periodic review of the deferred costs to assess whether ultimate recovery is likely. To the extent that the remaining unamortized balance, together with expected further development costs, production costs, and selling and administrative costs to be incurred directly in marketing the related product, exceeds the expected future economic benefits to be derived, the excess should be written off. In fact, as soon as any of the criteria noted are no longer met, the entire remaining balance of unamortized development costs should be expensed.

If, after the write-down or write-off of development costs occurs, there should be persuasive evidence that, due to new circumstances or events that are likely to persist for the foreseeable future, those costs are indeed recoverable, they should be written back as an asset. The upper limit would be the amount that would have been carried as an asset at the time of this adjustment had the write-down not occurred and had amortization continued consistent with prior accounting.

Required disclosures. IAS 9 stipulates the following required disclosures with regard to research and development expenditures:

1. The entity's accounting policies regarding these expenditures
2. The amount of R&D expenditures recognized as expense in the period being reported on
3. The amortization methods used
4. The useful lives or amortization methods used
5. A reconciliation of the balance of the unamortized research and development costs at the beginning and end of the year, noting the development costs recognized as an asset, development costs recognized as expense, development costs allocated to other asset accounts, and development costs written back after earlier recognition of impairment

Proposed changes to accounting for research and development costs. The IASC has decided to supersede its exposure draft on intangibles, E50, with a new proposal which will reportedly provide uniform guidance on all internally generated intangibles, including research and development costs. This would offer unified accounting for a range of intangibles which share certain key characteristics, and avoid the present situation in which certain expenditures which give rise to future economic benefits (such as research costs) are immediately expensed, whereas other expenditures (such as development costs) are often capitalized onto the balance sheet.

While an exposure draft has yet to be issued as of mid-1997 (and a final standard is not likely until mid-1998), the overall character of the proposal is reasonably clear. The Board's sentiment is that expenditures on internally generated intangibles should be reflected as assets if certain recognition criteria are met, and it appears that the new recognition criteria would contemplate capitalization of research costs under some conditions. Readers must be cautioned, however, that this position has yet to be officially endorsed, and many commentators have noted that the recognition criteria would be rather difficult to apply in practice; thus, there is a real possibility that the committee will modify these before reaching a consensus on an exposure draft.

Having offered the foregoing caveats, however, the current IASC thinking on a set of unified recognition criteria to be applied to all intangibles, including research and development costs, is as follows:

1. Capitalization would be prescribed if the asset were identifiable, that is, if the reporting entity could identify the resource that would generate future economic benefits.

2. An asset so recognized would have to be controlled by the reporting entity.
3. It would have to be probable that the benefit would be received (i.e., that the benefits would flow from the use of the asset) which could be confirmed if: the intangible asset's role can be defined; the asset's ability to perform the role effectively can be demonstrated; the intent to use the asset thusly can be explained; and the availability of adequate resources to enable the entity to reap the benefits can be shown; and
4. The cost of the intangible asset can be reliably measured.

The IASC has stressed that is it not the nature of the expenditure incurred, such as for research, but rather the output or result of the expenditure, such as new products, brands, or prototypes, which will govern whether the costs could be capitalized. The committee also has acknowledged that an all-inclusive list of qualifying costs could not be constructed, given the dynamic environment and growing importance of intellectual capital. As a method of operationalizing the intended standard, a further "filter" might be mandated: that the asset be separable (i.e., that it could be transferred to another unrelated entity) although possibly with the consequence of reducing the viability of the transferor. Work on this project is continuing.

9 INVESTMENTS

PERSPECTIVE AND ISSUES

Three important international accounting standards address several related aspects of accounting for investments. IAS 25 deals with the generic topic of investments in the debt and equity securities of other enterprises, for those situations where the investor is passive and does not exert significant influence over the investee. Such investments may be accounted for by a variety of permissible methods, depending on whether the investments are deemed to be current or long-term in nature. The existence of alternative measurement and reporting strategies means that financial statements of different entities might not be fully comparable, but the lack of consensus made it impossible to narrow the range of options allowed. Among the methods that are acceptable are historical cost, lower of cost or market, and pure market value--not all of which are appropriate in every circumstance, however.

IAS 28, which addresses investments in associates, is pertinent where the investor can be shown to possess significant influence over the investee. Whether significant influence in any given situation truly exists is a question of fact, but the standard does provide a mechanical rule to be employed in most circumstances. Under this standard, when an investor has more than 20% of the voting power, it generally will account for its investment by the equity method, whereby the proportional share of the investee's operating results will be reflected in the investor's financial statements. The equity method is sometimes described as being **one-line consolidation** since the same net effect on the investor's income and net assets will result as when consolidated financial statements are prepared (as described in Chapter 10), but without grossing up the income statement and balance sheet for all the investee's revenues, expenses, assets, and liabilities.

Finally, IAS 31 concerns the accounting by an investor for its interest in a joint venture arrangement. A **joint venture**, in which two or more entities have control jointly over the operations and/or assets of another enterprise, is a specialized type of investment situation, conceptually falling between significant influence and control. As with investments in general, there are several acceptable alternative accounting treatments for accounting for joint venture investments. However, one method, proportional consolidation, is designated as being preferred in this scenario, while the other defined technique, the equity method, is permitted as an allowed alternative.

Sources of IAS
IAS 25, 28, 31

DEFINITIONS OF TERMS

Associate. An enterprise over which an investor has significant influence but which is neither a subsidiary nor a joint venture of the investor company.

Control. The power to govern the financial and operating policies of an enterprise so as to obtain benefits from its activities.

Cost method. A method of accounting for investment whereby the investment is recorded at cost; the income statement reflects income from the investment only to the extent that the investor receives distributions from the investee's accumulated net profits arising after the date of acquisition.

Current investment. An investment that is, by its nature, readily realizable and is intended to be held for not more than 1 year.

Differential. The difference between the carrying value of common stock investment and the book value of underlying net assets of the investee; this should be allocated between excess (or deficiency) of fair value over (or under) book value of net assets and goodwill (a negative goodwill) and amortized appropriately against earnings from investee.

Equity method. A method of accounting whereby the investment is initially recorded at cost and subsequently adjusted for the post acquisition change in the investor's share of net assets of the investee. The investor's income statement reflects the investor's share of the investee's results of operations.

Fair value. The amount for which an asset could be exchanged between a knowledgeable, willing buyer and seller in an arm's-length transaction.

Goodwill. The excess of the cost of the acquired enterprise over the sum of the amounts assigned to identifiable assets acquired net of any liabilities assumed.

Investee. An enterprise that issued voting stock that is held by an investor.

Investee capital transaction. The purchase or sale by the investee of its own common shares, which alters the investor's ownership interest and is accounted for by the investor as if the investee were a consolidated subsidiary.

Investment. An asset held by an enterprise for purposes of accretion of wealth through distributions of interest, royalties, dividends, and rentals, or for capital appreciation or other benefits to be obtained.

Investment property. Investment in land and/or building that are not occupied substantially for use by, or in the operations of, the investor or an affiliate of the investor.

Investor. A business enterprise that holds an investment in the voting stock of another enterprise.

Joint control. The contractually agreed on joint sharing of control over the operations and/or assets of an economic activity.

Joint venture. A contractual arrangement whereby two or more parties undertake an economic activity subject to their joint control.

Long-term investment. An investment other than a current investment.

Market value. The amount obtainable from the sale of an investment in an active market.

Marketable. Assets for which there are active markets and from which market values, or other indicators that permit determination thereof, are available.

Significant influence. The power of the investor to participate in the financial and operating policy decisions of the investee; however, this is less than the ability to control those policies.

Subsidiary. An enterprise that is controlled by another enterprise (its parent).

Undistributed investee earnings. The investor's share of investee earnings in excess of dividends paid.

CONCEPTS, RULES, AND EXAMPLES

Accounting for Investments in Marketable Equity Securities

General background. The relevant international standard pertaining to accounting for investments is IAS 25, *Accounting for Investments.* This standard was reformatted in 1994 but has not otherwise been altered materially since it became effective in 1987. This standard applies to both debt and equity securities, whether being held as long-term or short-term investments, subject to certain defined limitations. It does not, however, apply to investments in subsidiaries (which are addressed by IAS 27, which is discussed in Chapter 10), or to investments in associates (IAS 28, covered later in this chapter), or investments in joint ventures (IAS 31, also covered later in this chapter). Furthermore, it does not address other categories of assets, such as patents or trademarks, finance leases, or retirement or other benefit plans.

In recent years there has been a trend away from imposing on accounting for investments requirements that are conditioned on the balance sheet classification of these assets. Rules established by some national standard-setting bodies have dispensed with this approach entirely. Most recently this has occurred in the United States, where FASB Statement 115 has established an entirely different classification scheme. Under that standard, investments in debt and equity securities are defined as being held to maturity, available for sale, or held for trading purposes. However, in the arena of international accounting, the pertinent standard continues to be governed by the current/noncurrent typology.

IAS 13 sets forth certain criteria to be applied when a reporting entity chooses to distinguish between current and noncurrent assets in its balance sheet. However, there is no requirement under generally accepted accounting principles that the balance sheet be presented on a classified basis, and in fact the discussion in IAS 13 offers compelling arguments why classification may be misleading in many circumstances. Furthermore, in certain industries it is traditional not to present classified balance sheets, either because regulatory authorities do not permit or encourage it, or because the distinction is not meaningful given the nature of the entity's operations.

An interesting aspect of IAS 25 is that the accounting implications of the current vs. noncurrent classification are operative even if the reporting entity does not present a classified balance sheet. Thus, a determination must be made for each investment as to whether or not it meets the criteria for being a current investment. If it does, the measurement strategies available for current investments are the available options, even though the investment will not be characterized as a current asset in the enterprise's balance sheet. Similarly, those investments that meet the criteria as being long-term investments will be measured according to one of the options prescribed for long-term investments, although they will not be described as noncurrent in the enterprise's balance sheet.

Current investments are deemed to be those that by their nature are readily realizable (i.e., marketable) and which are intended to be held for only a short time. Note that **both** criteria must be satisfied since many marketable investments will not be held with the intention of a sale in the near term and would accordingly not be candidates for accounting as current investments. Under the provisions of IAS 25, the reporting entity has a choice of using either pure market value or the lower of cost or market to account for current investments. These alternative accounting methods are offered as equally acceptable strategies, being denoted as neither the benchmark nor the available alternative.

Long-term equity investments may be accounted for in accordance with one of a number of alternative measurement strategies: historical cost, revalued amounts, or the lower of cost or market. Again, neither of these is denoted as being the benchmark treatment, and thus all are equally acceptable. Regardless of the valuation method utilized, however, permanent declines in value must be recognized.

The specific methodologies identified above will be explored in greater detail on the following pages.

Determining the cost of equity investments. The cost of any investment should include all associated acquisition charges, such as brokerage fees, duties, or other costs that must be incurred to obtain the investment asset in the condition and location desired. This basic principle applies to all assets that are acquired by an entity, of course, and is hardly unique to investments.

In some instances, an equity investment may be acquired in exchange for shares of stock in the investor entity. In such cases the measure of acquisition cost is given by the fair value of the shares surrendered, not by their nominal, par, or stated value, if any. In rare cases, the fair value of the equity shares acquired might be more objectively determinable than the value of the equity or other securities given up, and in such instances this alternative measurement tactic should be pursued.

In other situations, the equity investment will be acquired in exchange for other assets owned by the investor. Essentially the same rules apply as noted in the preceding discussion: The primary evidence of value will be the fair value of the assets given up; absent reliable data on this, the fair value of the assets acquired should be assessed directly.

In general, the historical cost of investments will not be modified having once been determined. Exceptions arise only in instances of permanent impairments (discussed later in this chapter) and liquidating dividends or returns of capital. Returns of capital occur when an investee makes distributions to investors from earnings that were accumulated prior to the date of the investment. In such instances the amounts received by the investor rightfully should not be deemed to be a return **on** the investment but must be recognized as being a partial return **of** the investment. As a practical matter, since a passive investor cannot know with certainty the investee's intention in making a distribution or whether the distribution is being made from preacquisition date earnings, and since that date will differ for each investor, the convention to be adopted is to treat distributions in excess of current earnings as returns of capital.

For example, if during the initial year an investment is held, earnings per share amount to $3.50 but dividends of $5.00 per share are paid, it would be reasonable to conclude that dividends in the amount of $1.50 per share are a return of capital. However, it is not necessary for dividends to exceed current earnings for there to be a return of capital, since it is common that only a fraction of annual earnings are paid out as dividends to stockholders. Thus, even distributions from earlier periods' earnings might not make the current total dividend exceed current earnings. In these instances, lacking specific knowledge that the intent was to pay out prior periods' earnings, it would be reasonable to account for these as normal distributions rather than returns of the funds invested.

Carrying amounts for current investments. IAS 25 offers financial statement preparers the option of using a pure market value approach or the more traditional lower of cost or market measurement scheme. Historically, lower of cost or market (LCM) has been viewed as an appropriate strategy because it adheres to the time honored accounting concepts of conservatism and realization. Conservatism demands that all losses be provided for at the earliest date of occurrence; while the realization concept stipulates that gains not be recognized until actually realized by the enterprise. LCM preserves the integrity of the historical cost based system of accounting except when economic losses have been incurred; in those instances, the losses are recognized and carrying value is reduced below historical cost. Under LCM, unrealized gains are not recognized under any circumstances.

The market value method, which is an equally acceptable accounting method under IAS 25, reflects the trend in recent years to move to a mark-to-market approach for some or all financial instruments. Although the international standards have not kept pace, to date, with the changes made under US GAAP, the trend is evident nonetheless. The belief is that for assets that are readily marketable, the most objective and meaningful measure is current fair value. This observation is particularly astute in the case of current investments in equity securities, since any temporary increase or decline in market value is less likely to be reversed prior to the disposition of the asset than would be true if the investment were to be held for the long term. Thus, a pure mark-to-market measurement approach to current investments can readily be endorsed from a theoretical perspective.

Accounting for changes in value. If current investments in equity securities are carried at LCM, declines in value are to be reflected currently in income. Later recoveries in value, not to exceed original cost, are also reported in current earnings.

On the other hand, if the investments are being accounted for purely on a market value basis, the reporting entity must elect an accounting policy (which, once chosen, may only be revised in accordance with the criteria established by IAS 8). The unrealized gains and losses resulting from recognition of market values may either be taken into income currently, or alternatively, the approach prescribed for long-term investments can be employed.

Under the latter strategy, increases in market value are credited to owners' equity, not income, and subsequent declines (but not in excess of unrealized gains recognized earlier) are offset against the revaluation surplus account. Any losses in excess of unrealized gains must be taken into earnings. If these losses are later reversed, the gains are also reflected in income. Put another way, under the alternative approach any **net** unrealized losses are reported in income (and thus eventually in retained earnings), while any **net** unrealized gains are reported in an additional equity account known as revaluation surplus.

Examples of accounting for investments under the lower of cost or market approach

Assume that Nirvana Corporation acquires the following investments on January 2, 1996:

1,000 shares Dubayy Trading Corp. common	$140,000
2,000 shares Kazakh Oil Drilling Co. common	320,000
Total cost	$460,000

Under the provisions of IAS 25, if the lower of cost or market method is utilized, the provision for market decline, if any, can be applied on the basis of individual securities, by categories of investments, or on a portfolio-wide basis. In the following sections, the individual investment and portfolio-wide approaches are illustrated, both with and without also reflecting the tax effects as prescribed by IAS 12 (for simplicity, an effective rate of 40% is presumed, and the distinctions between the deferral and liability approaches to interperiod income tax allocation will be ignored; these are fully described and illustrated in Chapter 14). In all the following, assume that the securities are valued at year end (December 31, 1996) as follows:

1,000 shares Dubayy Trading Corp. common	$128,000
2,000 shares Kazakh Oil Drilling Co. common	325,000
Total market value	$453,000

Also assume that the decline in value of the Dubayy Trading common stock does not represent an other than temporary loss in market worth.

Accounting for Investments Under IAS 25

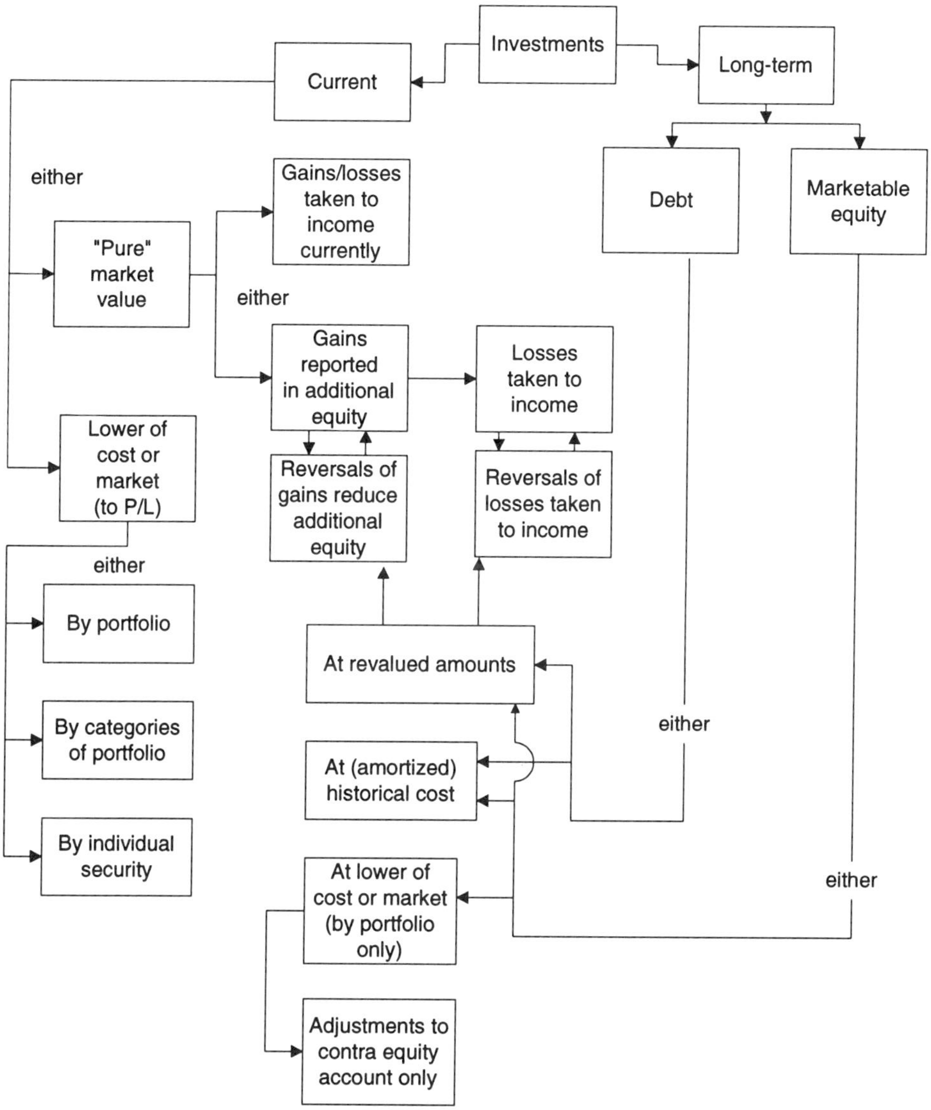

NOTE: The foregoing chart does not address other than temporary declines in value.

Example of computing the LCM adjustment on a portfolio-wide basis--Ignoring tax effects

The overall portfolio decline is $7,000 in this example; under IAS 25's rules, this should be credited not to any particular investment but to a valuation allowance (also known as a reserve or contra asset account). This is for two reasons. First, conceptually, if the portfolio is being valued as whole, the intent is not to adjust any particular securities' carrying values, as the expectation is that the overall portfolio will regain its value, even if a given security does not recover. Second, neither security declined in value by $7,000, but rather, one declined by more than this amount while another actually gained in value; however, LCM does not accept that any security will be written up to an amount in excess of historical cost.

The entry to record this adjustment would be as follows:

Loss on current investment portfolio	7,000	
Allowance for decline in market value of current investments		7,000

Including tax effects. In many jurisdictions, market value declines cannot be claimed as losses for tax purposes. Instead, the entity will be able to claim a loss only when the security is sold (i.e., when the loss is actually realized in an arm's-length transaction). However, under the provisions of IAS 12, tax effects are to be provided in the period the related gain or loss is reported in the income statement, under the concept of matching all costs associated with reported revenue in the same reporting period. In the present case, it is assumed that the effective tax rate is 40%; the entry to record the tax provision is

Deferred tax benefit	2,800	
Income tax expense (credit)		2,800

Example of computing the LCM adjustment on an individual security basis--Ignoring tax effects

While IAS 25 shows a clear preference for reporting the decline to LCM on a portfolio-wide or investment category basis, it does permit reporting LCM on an individual security basis. In fact, many believe that the portfolio-wide approach is a departure from the concept of LCM, since implicitly gains are being recognized on those components that had a value increase, thereby offsetting the declines which otherwise would have been recognized on those portfolio securities that did, in fact, decrease in value. In the present case, the Dubayy shares declined in value by $12,000, but this was offset by the $5,000 increase in value of the Kazakh shares. If the individual item approach were instead used, the full $12,000 decline would be recognized, while none of the $5,000 increase would be acknowledged. The entry to adjust to LCM at year end would be

Loss on current investment portfolio	12,000	
Investment in Dubayy Trading Corp.		12,000

Note that a contra asset or valuation account is not used in this case, since the loss can be directly associated with a particular investment security.

Including tax effects. As with the earlier illustration, tax effects are provided at 40%. The entry to record the tax provision is

Deferred tax benefit	4,800	
Income tax expense (credit)		4,800

Recoveries in value of investments accounted for at the lower of cost or market. As shown in the foregoing examples, downward adjustments to reflect the lower of cost or market must be taken directly to the income statement; these declines are not hidden in a contra account in the equity section of the balance sheet as is done in the case of certain long-term investments suffering declines in value. To be consistent, any later recoveries in value, but not to exceed the original carrying value, must also be reflected in income (and the deferred tax provision relating thereto will be reversed to tax expense, as well).

Examples of accounting for investments under the market value approach

Ignoring tax effects. IAS 25 also permits a pure market value approach to be applied to determine the financial statement presentation of current investments. The difference between LCM and market value is that under the former (subject to the observation that if applied on a portfolio-wide basis or on the basis of investment categories, some unrealized gains may implicitly be given recognition to the extent they offset unrealized losses), only declines in value and recoveries thereof can be reported, while under the latter both unrealized gains and losses are given recognition, without limitation.

IAS 25 provides a further complication if the market value method is elected: The reporting entity can adopt and consistently apply either of two rather distinct approaches to pure market value reporting. The first of these is to mark all the securities to market value, with all gains or losses reported in income currently. The second approach is to use the technique prescribed for long-term investments accounted for on the basis of revaluations (described below). Under this application, unrealized gains are reported in an additional equity account, and reversals of unrealized gains (but not in excess of previously reported increases) are adjusted to that account, with further declines reported in income. Also, if this technique is utilized, unrealized losses are reported as charges against earnings, and later recoveries (but not in excess of unrealized losses recognized previously) are also taken into income, with any further increases credited to an additional equity account.

To illustrate the accounting for current investments in securities, on the market value basis, using the method also prescribed for long-term investments (i.e., not taking all gains and losses immediately into income) as set forth in the preceding paragraph, consider these facts.

Assume that Utopia Corporation acquires the following investments on January 2, 1996:

1,000 shares Pan-Europe Trading Corp. common	$540,000
2,000 shares Transcontinental Co. common	230,000
Total cost	$770,000

At year end 1996, these investments have the following values:

1,000 shares Pan-Europe Trading Corp. common	$520,000
2,000 shares Transcontinental Co. common	310,000
Total cost	$830,000

At year end 1997, these investments have the following values:

1,000 shares Pan-Europe Trading Corp. common	$510,000
2,000 shares Transcontinental Co. common	165,000
Total cost	$675,000

IAS 25 stipulates that if the market value method is used, the adjustments should be made based on changes in values of specific, individual securities, not on a portfolio basis. Given that directive, it will be noted that the overall portfolio increase of $60,000 in 1996 actually is comprised of an unrealized loss of $20,000 on the Pan-European stock and an unrealized gain of $80,000 on the Transcontinental shares. The former must be reported in income, while the latter will be reported as an additional equity account, using the method chosen, and applied consistently, by Utopia Corporation. The entry in 1996 is as follows:

Loss on investment in Pan-Europe stock	20,000	
Investment in Transcontinental stock	80,000	
Investment in Pan-Europe stock		20,000
Unrealized gain on investment in Transcontinental stock (equity)		80,000

The decline in value of Pan-Europe shares continues in 1997, and further losses must be recognized as a charge against earnings. On the other hand, the Transcontinental shares also decline, fully reversing the gain of 1996 and ending 1997 below the original purchase cost. To the extent that the decline reverses the gain reported in an additional equity account, that account is reduced or eliminated; to the extent that the decline in value exceeds the previously recognized gain, the additional loss is reported in income. The entry for 1997 is therefore as follows:

Loss on investment in Pan-Europe stock	10,000	
Unrealized gain on investment in Transcontinental stock (equity)	80,000	
Loss on investment in Transcontinental stock	65,000	
Investment in Pan-Europe stock		10,000
Investment in Transcontinental stock		145,000

Including tax effects. The foregoing entries in 1996 and 1997 do not reflect the tax effects of the unrealized gains and losses recognized relative to the investments in Pan-Europe Trading Co. and Transcontinental Corp. shares. Again assuming that the local tax laws do not tax unrealized gains nor permit deductions for unrealized losses, the related tax entries in 1996 and 1997 would be as follows:

Deferred tax benefit	8,000	
Unrealized gain on investment in Transcontinental stock (equity)	32,000	
Income tax expense (credit)		8,000
Deferred tax liability		32,000

Note that the offset for the deferred tax liability recognized in connection with the unrealized gain on the Transcontinental stock is charged to the additional equity account, not to the tax provision in the income statement, since the gain was not reported in the income statement.

The entry in 1997 is as follows:

Deferred tax benefit	30,000	
Deferred tax liability	32,000	
Unrealized gain on investment in Transcontinental stock (equity)		32,000
Income tax expense (credit)		30,000

The charge to the deferred tax benefit account is made up of a $4,000 debit associated with the further $10,000 decline in value of Pan-Europe shares, that was taken as a charge to income, and a $26,000 charge relating to the $65,000 decline in value of Transcontinental **beyond** the reversal of the gain reported in the prior year. This excess loss was reported in income, and thus the tax effect must also be shown in the income statement. The tax effect of the $80,000 reversal of the earlier value increase is adjusted against the additional equity account.

Carrying amounts for long-term equity investments. Investments classified as long-term, or that would be categorized as noncurrent assets in a classified balance sheet, may be carried in the balance sheet under one of three available valuation approaches: original cost, revalued amounts, or lower of cost or market. The latter method is available only for investments in equity securities, and if utilized, must be applied on a portfolio basis.

IAS 25 states that long-term investments are usually carried at cost, absent a decline that is other than temporary in nature. The concept other than temporary represents a lower threshold than the term permanent would have, since there must be positive evidence to support a conclusion that a decline is only temporary in nature; absent that evidence, it would be presumed that any decline observed would be other than temporary. On the other hand, had the term "permanent" been invoked, this would have presented a rather higher threshold, which often could not be surmounted, leading to the conclusion that any given decline was other than permanent or temporary in nature. Thus, while neither term is unambiguous, it should be presumed that there must be positive evidence that a decline is indeed temporary to apply the accounting discussed below.

Reporting changes in value of long-term equity investments when the revaluation method is used. If the investment is being accounted for in accordance with the revaluation method, increases in value of long-term equity investments are reported in stockholders' (owners') equity as an additional equity account and are not first reflected in income. If later losses on the same investment are recognized, not in excess of the earlier gains, these are to be recognized by reducing the additional equity account, again without first passing through the income statement. Any further losses, however, must be reported as charges against earnings as incurred.

On the other hand, if losses are first recognized, these must be taken to the income statement. If market values later reverse, so that unrealized gains on the same investment are to be reported, these are also reflected in income, but only to the extent of previously recognized losses. Any further gains are taken to the additional equity account, not to income.

If this method is elected, revaluations should be made to fair value at regular intervals. The reporting entity would be required under these circumstances to adopt a firm policy regarding the frequency of revaluation, to prevent a capricious and possibly distorting use of this technique, such as to invoke fair value only during times of favorable changes in market prices. In addition to regularly timed revaluations, IAS 25 demands that all long-term investments be revalued essentially simultaneously, or that, at the minimum, entire categories be revalued together. The standard does not make clear its use of the term categories, but logically this might denote different risk classes and types of investments, such as corporate debt, government debt, and equity holdings. It might also imply that equity investments be further categorized (e.g., investments in public utilities, in blue chip industrial companies, in speculative high technology companies, etc.).

The examples presented above under the discussion of accounting for current investments on the pure market value method, are identical to the effects of accounting for long-term investments in equity securities on the revaluation method. Deferred taxes should, similarly, be provided for as demonstrated above, assuming that the tax laws do not permit tax recognition of unrealized gains or losses.

Accounting for long-term investments at cost. If this method is selected, no adjustments are made for later value changes, as long as these can be supported as being temporary in nature. If the changes are deemed to be other than temporary the declines must be charged against earnings immediately, and the written-down amount becomes the new cost basis, from which upward adjustments for later value increases cannot be made.

Accounting for long-term investments at the lower of cost or market. Under the third available alternative for accounting for long-term investments which is, however, applicable only in the case of equity investments, a lower of cost or market approach is applied. IAS 25 mandates that a portfolio-wide LCM methodology be used in the case of long-term investments, which is a more restrictive prescription than that given for current investments which are subject to evaluation on individual, category-wide, or full portfolio bases (although the portfolio approach is officially favored).

This requirement seemingly is intended to make downward adjustments in the portfolio carrying value less likely to occur, since unrealized gains on some investments in the portfolio will offset unrealized losses on other investments, so that the net effect of any declines will be moderated. Lower of cost or market cannot be applied to debt securities, even if readily marketable, or to nonmarketable equity investments.

Reductions to LCM are reported in a contra equity account rather than being reflected in income. Recoveries of previously recognized declines would reduce or eliminate this contra equity account. Under no circumstances could this account have a net credit balance, however.

Accounting for Investments in Debt Securities

Determining the cost of debt investments. As with investments in equity securities, the cost of any given investment in debt instruments should include any associated acquisition charges, such as brokerage fees, duties, or other costs. The essential difference between investments in debt and equity securities is that in the case of the former any variance between face or par value and the cost of acquisition, whether due to market forces or the fact that additional fees and costs were incurred, will affect the computed premium or discount on the investment. Depending on the method of accounting employed, as illustrated below, this premium or discount may need to be amortized over the expected holding period of the asset.

As with equity investments, investments in debt instruments may be acquired in exchange for shares of stock in the investor entity. The measure of acquisition cost is given by the fair value of the shares surrendered, not the face or par value of the debt. If the fair value of the debt acquired is more objectively determinable than the value of the equity or other securities given up, which is not expected to be the predominant situation, it should be used to record the transaction.

In other situations, the investment in debt securities will be acquired in exchange for other assets, such as land or equity in other investees. Again, primary evidence of value will be the fair value of the assets given up; in the absence of reliable data about this, the fair value of the debt instruments acquired should be determined directly.

With investments in debt, returns of capital will occur only when interest had been accrued, but unpaid, at the date of acquisition of the investment. When the interest due is paid later, it will not represent income to the investor, but merely return of a portion of the funds invested. Since normal accounting procedures are to record accrued interest as an asset distinct from the investment itself at the time the purchase is made, there will usually be little judgment required in properly accounting for the later collection of the amount owed.

Carrying amounts for current investments. The methods of accounting offered by IAS 25 for current equity investments apply equally to investments in debt.

Either a lower of cost or market approach or a pure market value approach are fully acceptable. The standard does not directly address the meaning of cost in the context of current investments, but presumably there would be little virtue in amortizing any premium or discount on acquisition of such investments since by definition the intent is to dispose of these in the near term. Thus, it is concluded that cost means original acquisition cost in this context.

If market value is defined as the exit value (i.e., the price that the investor would receive on a sale of the investment) it is likely that market would be lower than cost immediately on acquisition. The amount of this discrepancy would be equal to the spread between bid and ask prices, or would otherwise reflect normal transaction costs. However, notwithstanding this fact, it is unlikely that this difference would be a material amount, and therefore an immediate write-down to LCM would not be anticipated. Later price changes might necessitate such an adjustment, though.

The market value method is an equally acceptable accounting method under IAS 25 and reflects the trend in recent years to move to a mark-to-market approach for some, or all, financial instruments. Many accounting theoreticians, in fact, have argued that for all assets that are readily marketable and indeed, for debt obligations as well, the most objective and meaningful measure is current fair value. Investment in debt securities often have more objectively determinable fair market values, since there is an inverse mathematical relationship between market interest rates and prices for the securities in question, assuming that there are not also changes in other factors, such as the perceived credit risk of the debtor.

Changes in value of current investments in debt securities. If current investments in debt securities are carried at LCM, declines in value are to be reflected currently in income. Later recoveries in value, but not to exceed original cost, are also reported in current earnings.

If the debt investments are being accounted for on the basis of market value, the reporting entity will choose either to report unrealized gains and losses in income currently or to employ the approach prescribed for long-term investments. Under the latter strategy, increases in market value are credited to owners' equity, not income, and later declines (but not in excess of unrealized gains recognized earlier) are offset against the revaluation surplus account. Losses in excess of unrealized gains, however, must be taken into earnings. If these losses are later reversed, the gains are also reflected in income. Put another way, under the alternative approach any net unrealized losses are reported in income (and thus eventually in retained earnings), while any net unrealized gains are reported in the additional equity account, revaluation surplus.

Examples of accounting for current investments in debt securities

In the following illustrations, assume that Zanibar Mfg. Corp. has acquired, on January 2, 1996, $100,000 of Tralog Corp. bonds, bearing 8% coupons, for a price of 104 (bonds are quoted at percent of par or face value). The bonds are due to mature on

December 31, 1999, but Zanibar does not intend to hold them to that date; rather, it is the expectation that these will be liquidated to generate the cash needed to begin construction on a new factory building. The project is delayed, however, and 3 years pass without the investment being sold. The bonds are quoted on the market at 104.25 at December 31, 1996; 102 at December 31, 1997; and 100.5 at December 31, 1998.

Example of accounting for debt investments under the lower of cost or market approach

In 1996 the market value of the bonds increases; under the LCM approach, no unrealized gains are recognized, and therefore the investment is maintained at cost this year. In later years, market values decline, and these declines are fully reported in earnings under the LCM method. Note that with the due date approaching, it is only normal that the market value of bonds sold at a premium decline to par at maturity date, but this underlying reason makes no difference to the accounting to be applied. Since these bonds are classified as current, amortization of the premium (or of a discount, had there been any) is not affected. (Any deferred tax effects are ignored in this example.)

The entry at January 2, 1996 is as follows:

Current investment in bonds	104,000	
Cash		104,000

There is no entry at December 31, 1996.

The entry at December 31, 1997 is as follows:

Loss on decline in current investment in bonds	2,000	
Current investment in bonds		2,000

The entry at December 31, 1998 is as follows:

Loss on decline in current investment in bonds	1,500	
Current investment in bonds		1,500

Note that the offset to the loss is directly to the investment account, since the write-down is on the individual security. If the adjustment was for a decline in the entire portfolio, a valuation account would have been used instead.

Example of accounting for investments under the market value approach

The entry at January 2, 1996 is as follows:

Current investment in bonds	104,000	
Cash		104,000

The entry at December 31, 1996 is as follows:

Current investment in bonds	250	
Gain on increase in current investment in bonds		250

The entry at December 31, 1997 is as follows:

Loss on decline in current investment in bonds	2,250	
Current investment in bonds		2,250

The entry at December 31, 1998 is as follows:

Loss on decline in current investment in bonds	1,500	
Current investment in bonds		1,500

Note that on a pure market value basis, the gain in value in 1996 is taken into income and the losses in 1997 and 1998 are reflected in earnings.

Carrying amounts for long-term investments in debt securities. Debt investments classified as long-term, or which would be categorized as noncurrent assets in a classified balance sheet, may be carried in the balance sheet at either original cost or revalued amounts. The third method permitted by IAS 25 for equity investments, the lower of cost or market, is **not** available for investments in debt securities.

The standard states that long-term investments are usually carried at cost, absent a decline that is other than temporary in nature. The use of the term other than temporary rather than the simpler term permanent is intentional: The latter would imply a stricter standard of evidence to support an adjustment to the cost basis of the investment, since it would be necessary to support strongly the notion that the decline was permanent in nature. Under the other-than-temporary standard, there is, instead, a presumption that any material decline is not temporary, unless evidence (such as past market fluctuations) can be marshaled to suggest that a recovery is likely.

As applied to investments in debt securities, the term cost actually means amortized cost, since any premium or discount on acquisition must be charged or credited to interest income on a rational and systematic basis over the expected holding period. In most instances, there is no expectation that the investment will be liquidated before maturity, and therefore the premium or discount will be amortized to the maturity date (or, in the case of a premium, to an earlier call date).

Changes in value of long-term investments in debt securities. Increases in value of long-term debt investments are reported in stockholders' (owners') equity as an additional equity account and are not first reflected in income. If later losses on the same investment, not in excess of the earlier gains are incurred, these are to be recognized by reducing the additional equity account, again without first passing through the income statement. Any further losses in excess of earlier unrealized gains, however, must be reported as charges against earnings.

On the other hand, if losses are first incurred, these must be reported in the income statement. If market values later reverse, so that unrealized gains on the same investment are to be reported, these should also be reflected in income, but only to the extent of previously recognized losses. Any further gains are taken to the additional equity account, not to income.

Examples of accounting for long-term investments at revalued amounts

In the following illustrations, assume that Trafalgar Co. has acquired on January 2, 1996, $100,000 of Supercompute Corp. bonds, bearing 8% coupons, for a price of 104. The bonds are due to mature on December 31, 1999, and Trafalgar does intend to hold them to that date. Also on January 2, 1996, Trafalgar acquires $150,000 face value of Xenobe PLC 6% bonds due December 31, 2002, at a price of 89.5. The intention is also to hold these to maturity. The Supercompute bonds are quoted on the market at 104.25 at December 31, 1996; 102 at December 31, 1997; and 100.5 at December 31, 1998. The Xenobe bonds are quoted on the market at 89 at December 31, 1996; 94 at December 31, 1997; and 93 at December 31, 1998.

Ignoring tax effects. Under IAS 25, long-term investments are deemed to be individually important, and the unrealized gains or losses will be computed individually.

The entry at January 2, 1996 is as follows:

Investment in Supercompute bonds	104,000	
Investment in Xenobe bonds	134,250	
Cash		238,250

The entries at December 31, 1996 are as follows:

Investment in Supercompute bonds	250	
Additional equity from increase in value of Supercompute bonds		250

Loss on decline in Xenobe bonds	750	
Investment in Xenobe bonds		750

Note that the decline in value of Xenobe bonds is taken as a charge against earnings, while the increase in value of Supercompute bonds is credited to an additional equity account.

The entries at December 31, 1997 are as follows:

Additional equity from increase in value of Supercompute bonds	250	
Loss on decline in Supercompute bonds	2,000	
Investment in Supercompute bonds		2,250
Investment in Xenobe bonds	7,500	
Additional equity from increase in value of Xenobe bonds		6,750
Gain on recovery in Xenobe bonds		750

In the foregoing entries, the previously recognized unrealized gain of $250 in Supercompute bonds has been reversed, and a further decline in value amounting to $2,000 is now recognized as a charge against earnings. At the same time, a previously recognized loss in the value of Xenobe bonds, reported as charge against earnings in 1996, is reversed by a credit to income in 1997; a further gain in value, amounting to $6,750, is reported in an additional equity account.

The entries at December 31, 1998 are as follows:

Loss on decline in Supercompute bonds	1,500	
Investment in Supercompute bonds		1,500
Additional equity from increase in value of Xenobe bonds	1,500	
Investment in Xenobe bonds		1,500

In 1998 there is a further decline in Supercompute bonds' value, which is reported in earnings. There is also a decline in the value of Xenobe bonds, which represents a partial reversal of the unrealized gain reported in 1997 as a credit to additional equity and thus does not affect earnings.

Including tax effects. Assume the same facts as in the foregoing example, but now also assume that Trafalgar is taxed at a marginal rate of 40% and that unrealized gains or losses on long-term investments are not taxable or deductible. In addition to the entries shown above, the following entries relating to the deferred tax impact of the changes in the values of these investments are needed.

The entries at December 31, 1996 are as follows:

Additional equity from increase in value of Supercompute bonds	100	
Deferred tax liability		100
Deferred tax benefit	300	
Provision for income taxes--deferred		300

Note that the tax effect of the decline in value of Xenobe bonds is taken as a credit to earnings, since the loss in value was reported in the income statement, while the tax effect of the increase in value of Supercompute bonds is charged against the same additional equity account to which the gross value increase was credited.

The tax entries at December 31, 1997 are as follows:

Deferred tax liability	100	
Deferred tax benefit	800	
Additional equity from increase in value of Supercompute bonds		100
Provision for income taxes--deferred		800

Provision for income taxes--deferred	300	
Additional equity from increase in value of Xenobe bonds	2,700	
Deferred tax benefit		300
Deferred tax liability		2,700

In the foregoing entries, the $100 tax effect of the previously recognized unrealized gain in Supercompute bonds has been reversed, and the tax effect of a further decline in value, amounting to $800, is now recognized as a credit to earnings. Also, a previously recognized loss in the value of Xenobe bonds is reversed, necessitating a charge against income in 1997; the tax effect of the further gain in value, amounting to $2,700, is reported as a debit to additional equity account.

The entries at December 31, 1998 are as follows:

Deferred tax benefit	600	
Provision for income taxes--deferred		600

Deferred tax liability	600	
Provision for income taxes--deferred		600

In 1998 there is a further decline in Supercompute bonds' value, which is reported in earnings. The tax effect of this currently nondeductible loss is debited to deferred tax benefit and credited to tax expense. There is also a (coincidentally similar) decline in the value of Xenobe bonds, which represents a partial reversal of the unrealized gain reported in 1997; the tax effect of this is charged to the deferred tax liability provided previously.

Example of accounting for long-term investment at cost

If the historical cost method of accounting for long-term investments in debt securities is elected, the premium or discount should be amortized to interest income by the effective yield (constant return) method. If straight-line amortization produces results that are not materially different from the more precise effective yield method, it may be used (although, with wide use of computers, the formerly pragmatic decision to use a straight-line approximation is much less likely to serve as an excuse). In the present example, using the same facts as the foregoing illustration of the revaluation method, and ignoring tax effects, straight-line amortization will be employed.

The Supercompute bonds were purchased at a price of 104 when there were 4 years to maturity; absent an earlier call date, these will be amortized at a rate of $1,000 per year. The entries will be (each year)

Interest income	1,000	
Investment in Supercompute bonds		1,000

The Xenobe bonds were acquired at a discount of 10.5 points, which, given the 7 years to the maturity date, requires amortization of $2,250 per year (inasmuch as $150,000 face value were purchased). The entries will be

Investment in Xenobe bonds	2,250	
Interest income		2,250

Accounting for Other Types of Investments

In addition to addressing investments in debt and equity instruments, IAS 25 contemplates certain investments in properties, such as land or buildings, other than those being held for use. These may be accounted for either as property per se, in accordance with the applicable international accounting standards (as described in Chapter 8), or as investments. If the latter method is selected, depreciation will not be recorded, but instead the investment will be marked to fair value in a manner consistent with the guidelines of IAS 25. Changes in market value should be reflected in income or in equity in the same manner as are changes in value of other long term investments, as described in the earlier sections of this chapter.

Other-than-temporary impairments of investments. If long-term investments are being accounted for at cost but there has been a value decline that is deemed to be other than temporary in nature, this must be recognized by reducing the carrying value and taking a charge against earnings. A later recovery (which should be a rare event, given that the decline was thought to be permanent) would be reported in earnings also. (In this, the international standard differs from US and other GAAP, under which permanent declines in value cannot be recovered other than by an ultimate disposition.)

Determining which declines are temporary and which are other than temporary, of course, may not always be an exercise in the obvious. Certain indicators of permanent decline, such as a reorganization or bankruptcy filing by the investee, may be fairly clear, but in other instances (such as the lowering of ratings by credit agencies) it may be difficult to discern the probabilities for later recoveries. Various risk factors, as well as the size of the investor's stake in the investee, should be taken into account in making these determinations. Absent an ability to demonstrate that a decline is temporary, the conclusion must be that the loss in value is other than temporary, or permanent. Declines are measured at the individual security level, and thus, losses in one security's value cannot be offset by gains in another security's value.

The only exception to the requirement that other than temporary declines be reported in income arises if the security had previously been revalued upward, with the adjustment taken directly to a revaluation surplus account in owners' equity. In such a case, the write-down will be reported as a reversal of the unrealized gain recognized previously.

While the provisions of IAS 25 are not definitive (in recognition of the varying rules established by national standard-setting bodies), in general once a permanent impairment is recognized, the reduced carrying amount becomes the new cost basis from which other increases or decreases in value are measured. Under these circumstances, a clear statement of accounting policy will be needed, so that users of the financial statements can interpret them properly.

Transfers between current and long-term investments. Under the provisions of IAS 25, transfers of investments from the long-term category to the current will be accounted for in different ways, depending on what measurement strategy had previously been adopted.

If the investments will be accounted for by the LCM method once reclassed as current, the transfer should be made at the lower of cost or carrying amount. If the long-term investments being transferred had earlier been revalued upward, and there is a related balance in the revaluation surplus account in stockholders' equity, this must be written off at the time of transfer.

On the other hand, if the entity's policy is to account for current investments at market value, the transfer should be made at carrying value. Depending on the policy in effect for long-term investments, the carrying amount may be (amortized) cost, a revalued amount (probably market value), or (in the case of equity investments only) LCM, determined on a portfolio-wide basis. In any event, the current carrying value will become the initial cost basis for the investment as it is transferred to the current investment account. If the asset had been carried at a revalued amount and there is a balance in the revaluation surplus account at the date of transfer, **and** if the entity's policy is to recognize changes in market values of current investments in earnings, the balance of the revaluation surplus should be taken into income at this time.

For investments being transferred from the current to the long-term portfolio, the transfer should be at the lower of cost or market value, unless carried at pure market value, in which case they would be transferred at that value.

Switches of investments within a portfolio. IAS 25 addresses the situation in which a complex portfolio of investments is maintained, with periodic sales of selected individual holdings and purchases of new investments. A theory has been advanced to the effect that rather than viewing these sales as terminal transactions giving rise to recognition of gains or losses, the portfolio should be viewed as an integrated whole having an ongoing existence, and thus that there should be no gain or loss recognized on transactions in its individual components. Presumably, gain or loss would be recognizable only upon liquidation of the entire portfolio were this theory to be operationalized.

The standard does hold that the individual securities investments are the proper focus of accounting, and thus the preferred method is to measure gains or losses on the individual investment transactions. However, IAS 25 does permit the alternative treatment of recognizing gain or loss only on portfolio liquidation, but only in the very limited circumstance where the pure market value method of reporting investments is employed. Since under this method all gains and losses, whether realized or unrealized, are taken into income immediately, the use of a portfolio perspective has no practical effect at all.

For all intents and purposes, therefore, it is fair to state that gains and losses on investments are always measured at the individual investment level, whether they are accounted for at cost, lower of cost or market, or pure market value.

Accounting for Dispositions of Investments

Current investments. Current investments may, under the provisions of IAS 25, be carried at either market value or lower of cost or market (LCM). If carried at market, of course, in theory the selling price will be equal to the latest market price, which is already reflected in the carrying value, and thus there will be no further gain or loss on the actual sale transaction. As a practical matter, however, the accounting records will contain the market value as of the latest date on that the records were updated, or marked to market, which probably was the date the last interim or annual financial statement was prepared. Thus, the change in market value from that date until the actual transaction date would not yet have been reflected, and this amount would therefore be first recognized at the time of sale. The net result is the same in either case, of course.

If the investments to be disposed of had instead been accounted for under the LCM method, the impact on currently reported earnings of the sale will depend on whether LCM had been applied on an individual investment or portfolio basis. If the individual investment approach (which is the less preferred, per IAS 25) had been used, any gain or loss, determined as the difference between the carrying value of that individual investment and the proceeds realized on its disposition, would be reflected currently in earnings.

On the other hand, if the aggregate portfolio (or relevant portion of the portfolio) had been adjusted to LCM, that implicitly permitted some or all of the portfolio's unrealized gains to offset its unrealized losses, the gain or loss on the disposition of part of the portfolio should be determined with reference to the **cost** of the asset sold. That is, reference should be made to original cost, regardless of the unrealized gain or loss that subsequent to acquisition had been implicitly recognized as a part of the net LCM adjustments. The logic for this position is that accounting for these investments should be driven by the value of the entire portfolio (or a subpart of the portfolio if LCM is applied to categories of investments), and an occasional sale of one or another of the components of the portfolio would not immediately affect valuation of the entire portfolio. However, given the need to reassess the allowance for market decline at the time when the next balance sheet is being prepared, there will still be a partial reckoning of the real gain or loss on the transaction. Depending on how much unrealized gain had implicitly offset unrealized loss in the portfolio, the amount reported as a gain or loss on the trade, including the impact of any later reassessment of the LCM reserve, may still differ from the real gain or loss on the transaction itself.

Example of disposition of current investment, carried at lower of cost or market value

Assume that the company acquires the following investment portfolio during 1996 at the costs noted, and that the fair values are as shown as of year end:

Security description	*Acquisition cost*	*Year-end value*
1,000 shares Ball Steel common	$ 34,500	$ 37,000
2,000 shares Whammer Pfd. A	125,000	109,500
1,000 shares Hilltopper common	74,250	84,750
Total for portfolio	$233,750	$231,225

Using the lower of cost or market method, a valuation reserve of $2,525 is provided at year end 1996. Individual investments, however, are not adjusted; the net reserve effectively credits the unrealized gain on the investments in Ball Steel and Hilltopper as offsets against the decline in Whammer.

Now, assume that the investment in Whammer is sold in 1997 for $106,000, for an indicated loss of $3,500 versus its most recently measured market value ($109,500 at the end of 1996). However, under IAS 25, this is not used to measure the loss for financial reporting purposes. Rather, the comparison is made to cost, which in this case yields an indicated loss of $19,000. The transaction is reflected in the following journal entry:

Loss on sale of investment	19,000	
Cash	106,000	
Current investment in marketable securities		125,000

It is also necessary to reassess the allowance for the decline in the value of the portfolio when the composition of the portfolio changes. In the present example, assume that the value of the other components of the portfolio continue at their December 1996 amounts; in that case, the entire allowance ($2,525) needs to be reversed to income, since the remaining portfolio has a market value greater than cost, which, under the LCM method, will not be given recognition. Thus, the net loss recognized in the period of sale will be $19,000 – $2,525 = $16,475.

Long-term investments. Under the provisions of IAS 25, long-term investments may be carried at cost, at revalued amounts (market values), or (for marketable equity securities only) at LCM. The recognition of gain or loss on the disposition of a long-term investment depends on the method of accounting used.

If the investment had been accounted for at cost (or amortized cost, in the case of investments in debt securities), the gain or loss on disposition would simply be determined by reference to the difference between original (or amortized) cost and the selling price.

If the investment had been adjusted to a market value that was in excess of historical cost, and the revaluation was reflected in a revaluation surplus account, the question that arises on disposition of the investment is how to eliminate any remaining balance in this account. Under the provisions of IAS 25, the reporting entity is to adopt a policy of either transferring this balance to income, or else transferring it directly to retained earnings. Of these options, logically the former, recognizing the now realized (but previously unrealized) gain in income, would undeniably seem to be the more appropriate. From an accounting perspective, the only difference is whether this component of the realized gain is credited to current income or directly to retained earnings; the tax effect would need to be charged to tax expense or to retained earnings, for proper matching against the gain to which it relates.

If long-term investments in equity securities had been accounted for at the lower of cost or market, on a portfolio basis, gain or loss recognition on the sale of individual investments should follow the same general approach as outlined above, in the discussion of LCM applied to current investments. Accordingly, determination of gain or loss will be based on historical cost, not on carrying value. Any allowance for market decline (a contra asset account) would have to be reassessed at that time, with any adjustment thereto being made to the contra equity account.

Presentation and Disclosure Issues

Income statement presentation. For enterprises that engage in transactions in investments, periodic results of operations should include income arising from interest, royalties, dividends, and rentals on long-term and current investments, as well as profits or losses on the disposal of such investments. Depending on the policy adopted by the entity, unrealized gains and losses on current investments that are carried at market value may also be included in current income (the alternative would be to include these in an additional equity account). If the LCM method is used for current investments, any reductions to market value, and any reversals of such reductions, should be included in income. If other than temporary declines in the value of long-term investments have been given recognition, and if any of these declines have later been reversed, these should be explained to financial statement users. Finally, profits and losses on disposals of investments should be included in earnings.

Disclosures required. IAS 25 requires certain disclosures to be made in the income statement and in the balance sheet, if investments are held by the reporting entity or had been held and were sold during the reporting period.

Accounting policies, as defined in IAS 8, are to be disclosed. These should address the method of determining the carrying amounts of investments, recognition afforded to changes in the market value of current investments that are carried at market value, and the treatment of revaluation surplus in the event that a revalued investment is sold.

Disclosure is also required of significant amounts included in income for interest, royalties, dividends, and rentals on current and long-term investments; profits or losses on the disposal of current investments; and the changes in value of such investments.

If investments are not carried at market values, the market values must be shown in the footnote disclosures (or parenthetically in the balance sheet, if preferred). For other long-term investments, if the properties are not reported at fair value as permitted under the standard, the fair values are also to be disclosed.

If there are any material restrictions on the ability to realize the investments (i.e., to dispose of them freely and to obtain the proceeds therefrom), these matters need to be disclosed to readers of the financial statements. Any restrictions on the ability to collect income distributions on the investments must also be disclosed.

For long-term investments accounted for at revalued amounts, disclosure of the reporting entity's policy regarding the frequency of revaluation is required, as is the date of the most recent revaluation, the basis for the revaluation, and whether an external valuation expert's services were employed.

A reconciliation of the amount of the revaluation surplus account from the beginning to the end of the reporting period should be provided. Finally, for those enterprises for which the holding of investments is the primary business, an analysis of the investment portfolio is a required disclosure.

Optional disclosures. In addition to the disclosures enumerated above, IAS 25 identifies a number of useful, if not required, items of information that could assist in understanding the investments held by a reporting entity. These include an analysis of long-term investments by category, management's assessment of the fair values of nonmarketable investments, the methods used to value nonmarketable investments, the amount of revaluation surplus associated with assets disposed of during the period and converted to share capital (retained earnings), and information about any individually significant investments.

Specialized industry accounting practices. IAS 25 notes that in some countries investment companies are prohibited from distributing profits accumulated from the disposal of investments. For these entities, the distinction between interest and dividends, on the one hand, and gains or losses, on the other hand, is of great importance. Such enterprises are permitted to exclude from income realized and unrealized investment gains if investments are carried at fair value. Expanded disclosures of changes in investment values are required under these circumstances.

Equity Method of Accounting for Investments

In previous sections of this chapter the focus was on investments that are essentially passive in nature, where the investor has a small minority ownership interest (or, in the case of debt, no actual ownership interest at all) and accordingly, cannot control or materially influence decisions by management of the investee. In other situations (discussed in Chapter 10), an investor will have actual control over the actions taken by the management of the investee, or have joint control (discussed in a subsequent part of this chapter) over those decisions along with its co-investors. The third logical possibility is that the investor will have something less than control but will clearly also not be a passive investor. This is the issue of significant influence over an investee.

As GAAP has evolved over the past 30 years or so, it has become evident that investors having significant influence should not account for such investments on a cost basis, since to do so would permit deliberate manipulation of the financial reporting process and, more important, would not reflect economic reality. For example, if an investee has substantial income but the investor uses its influence to defer declaration of dividends, the cost method of accounting would result in the investor not reporting its share of the operating results, even though it had been in a position to cause a distribution of dividends, had it chosen to do so.

To respond to this set of real and potential reporting problems, GAAP has developed a number of proposed solutions. These include the equity method, the expanded equity method, and proportionate consolidation. International accounting standards and the various national standard-setting bodies have given differing levels of attention to these alternatives over the years, with the simple equity method being the one receiving the closest to a consensus of support.

The equity method, which has been referred to as one-line consolidation, permits an entity (the investor) owning a percentage of the common stock of another entity (the investee) to incorporate its pro rata share of the investee's operating results into its earnings. However, rather than include its share of each component of the investee's revenues, expenses, assets and liabilities into its financial statements, the investor should only include its share of the investee's **net** income as a separate line item in its income. The bottom-line impact on the investor's financial statements is **identical** whether the equity method or full consolidation is employed; only the amount of detail presented within the statements will differ.

Expanded equity method. Less commonly discussed are the expanded equity method and the proportionate consolidation method, which are effectively successive points along a continuum ranging from a pure cost basis to full consolidation. In contrast to the one-line consolidation approach of the simple equity method, the expanded equity method is an attempt to provide a bit more meaningful detail about the various assets and liabilities, and revenues and expenses in which the investor has an interest. Thus, the investor's interest in the investee's aggregate current assets would be presented, as a single number, in the current asset section of the investor's balance sheet. Similarly, the investor's share of the investee's noncurrent assets, current liabilities, and noncurrent liabilities would be captioned separately. On the income statement, the investor's share of significant items of revenue, expense, gains, and losses would be set forth separately. This would not extend to every item of the income statement, but would highlight the major ones.

A major advantage of this method is that the investor's financial statements will provide a more meaningful insight into the true economic scope of its operations, including indications of the volume of business being transacted. Furthermore, financial position will not be distorted by, for example, effectively merging the investee's current assets with the investor's noncurrent assets, which would be the result of placing equity in investee in the noncurrent asset section. As the amount of detail expands, this method edges into proportionate consolidation, however.

The expanded equity method has not been endorsed officially, although the equity method as defined by US standards setters (in Accounting Principles Board Opinion 18) does incorporate elements of this approach. Specifically, APB 18 mandates one-line consolidation for the balance sheet, but requires that certain elements of the investee's income statement (such as extraordinary items) retain their character when incorporated into the investor's income statement.

Proportionate consolidation. This is a more completely developed version of the expanded equity method, whereby the investor's share of each element of the investee's balance sheet and income statement is reported in the investor's statements. Although there is nonauthoritative GAAP in the United States supporting this method of accounting for investments in joint ventures, and under international accounting standards (as discussed later in the chapter) this method is prescribed optionally for joint ventures, it has not been widely advocated for investments in which the investor does not exercise, at a minimum, joint control.

Equity method as prescribed by IAS 28. The equity method is generally **not** a substitute for consolidation; it is employed where the investor has significant influence over the operations of the investee but lacks control. In general, significant influence is inferred when the investor owns between 20 and 50% of the investee's voting common stock. Any ownership percentage over 50% presumably gives the investor actual control, making full consolidation of financial statements necessary (or, if precisely 50% is owned in a joint venture, proportionate consolidation may be employed). The 20% threshold stipulated in IAS 28 is not absolute; circumstances may suggest that significant influence exists even though the investor's level of ownership is less than 20%, or that it is absent despite a level of ownership above 20%. The 20% lower threshold is identical to that prescribed under US GAAP.

In considering whether significant influence exists, IAS 28 identifies the following factors as evidence that such influence is present: (1) investor representation on the board of directors or its equivalent, (2) participation in policy making processes, (3) material transactions between the investor and investee, (4) interchange of managerial personnel, and (5) provision of essential technical information. There may be other factors present that suggest a lack of significant influence, such as organized opposition by the other shareholders, majority ownership by a small group of shareholders not inclusive of the investor, and inability to achieve representation on the board or to obtain information on the operations of the investee. Whether sufficient contrary evidence exists to negate the presumption of significant influence is a matter of judgment and requires a careful evaluation of all pertinent facts and circumstances, over an extended period of time in some cases.

When equity method is required. IAS 28 stipulates that the equity method should be employed by the investor for all investments in associates, unless the investment is acquired and held exclusively with a view to its disposal in the near term, or if it operates under severe long-term restrictions that would preclude making distributions to investors. In the latter cases, accounting by the cost method is preferred.

The standard does make something of a distinction between the accounting for investments in associates in consolidated financials versus that in separate financials of the investor. Most important, in separate financial statements of the investor, the investment may be carried at cost or at revalued amounts as prescribed by IAS 25 (discussed earlier in the chapter), as an alternative to the equity method. This mandate seemingly results from a view of separate statements of a parent entity, without consolidation of subsidiaries and without applying equity method accounting to associated entities, as reporting the financial position and results of operations of the enterprise on its own. This also is a consequence of the fact that the international standard-setting process is somewhat of a compromise approach, incorporating most, if not all, of the methods advocated by national standard-setting bodies worldwide. Thus, since different bodies have taken varying positions on such matters as consolidation and equity method accounting, this result has obtained.

In practice, many parent-only financial statements apply equity method accounting to subsidiaries and significant influence investees alike. This probably does provide the most meaningful reporting, avoiding detailed inclusion of any assets, liabilities, revenues, or expenses other than the parent company's own in its financial statements, while not distorting the bottom line measure of economic performance.

If the investment in the associate is presented in accordance with IAS 25 in these separate financial statements of the parent/investor, IAS 28 does require that there be disclosure of what would have been the effect had the equity method been applied.

Complications in applying equity method accounting. Complexities in the use of the equity method arise in two areas. First, the cost of the investment to the investor might not be equal to the fair value of the investor's share of investee net assets; this is analogous to the existence of goodwill in a purchase business combination. Or the fair value of the investor's share of the investee's net assets may not be equal to the book value thereof; this situation is analogous to the purchase cost allocation problem in consolidations. Since the ultimate income statement result from the use of equity method accounting must generally be the same as full consolidation, an adjustment must be made for each of these differentials.

The second major complexity relates to interperiod income tax allocation. The equity method causes the investor to reflect current earnings based on the investee's operating results; however, for income tax purposes the investor reports only dividends received and gains or losses on disposal of the investment. Thus, temporary differences result, and IAS 12 provides guidance as to the appropriate method of computing the deferred tax effects of these differences.

In the absence of these complicating factors, use of the equity method by the investor is straightforward: The original cost of the investment is increased by the investor's share of the investee's earnings and is decreased by its share of investee losses and by dividends received. The basic procedure is illustrated below.

Example of a simple case ignoring deferred taxes

Assume the following information:

On January 2, 1996, Regency Corporation (the investor) acquired 40% of Elixir Company's (the investee) voting common stock on the open market for $100,000. Unless demonstrated otherwise, it is assumed that Regency Corporation can exercise significant influence over Elixir Company's operating and financing policies. On January 2, Elixir's stockholders' equity is comprised of the following accounts:

Common stock, par $1, 100,000 shares authorized, 50,000 shares issued and outstanding	$ 50,000
Additional paid-in capital	150,000
Retained earnings	50,000
Total stockholders' equity	$250,000

Note that the cost of Elixir Company common stock was equal to 40% of the book value of Elixir's net assets. Assume also that there is no difference between the book value and the fair value of Elixir Company's assets and liabilities. Accordingly, the balance in the investment account in Regency's records represents exactly 40% of Elixir's stockholders' equity (net assets). Assume further that Elixir Company reported a 1996 net income of $30,000 and paid cash dividends of $10,000. Its stockholders' equity at year end would be as follows:

Common stock, par $1, 100,000 shares authorized, 50,000 shares issued and outstanding	$ 50,000
Additional paid-in capital	150,000
Retained earnings	70,000
Total stockholders' equity	$270,000

Regency Corporation would record its share of the increase in Elixir Company's net assets during 1996 as follows:

Investment in Elixir Company	12,000	
Equity in Elixir income ($30,000 x 40%)		12,000
Cash	4,000	
Investment in Elixir Company ($10,000 x 40%)		4,000

When Regency's balance sheet is prepared at December 31, 1996, the balance reported in the investment account would be $108,000 ($100,000 + $12,000 – $4,000). This amount represents 40% of the book value of Elixir's net assets at the end of the year (40% x $270,000). Note also that the equity in Elixir income is reported as one amount on Regency's income statement under the caption "Other income and expense."

IAS 12 established the requirement that deferred income taxes be provided for the tax effects of timing differences. Under this standard, which is discussed in detail in Chapter 14, a choice between two very different approaches to deferred tax accounting is permitted: the deferral method, which computes the tax effect when the timing difference is originated and does not later adjust the provision until the difference reverses; and the liability method, under which the provision is adjusted at each balance sheet date to reflect the current expectations regarding ultimate settlement amount.

Under either deferred tax accounting approach permitted under IAS 12, in computing the deferred tax effects of income recognized by the equity method, the investor must make an assumption regarding the means by which the undistributed earnings of the investee will be realized by the investor. The earnings can be realized either through later dividend receipts or by disposition of the investment at a gain, which, depending on tax jurisdiction, may result in differing tax implications. For example, in many jurisdictions the former assumption would result in taxes at the investor's marginal tax rate on ordinary income (net of any dividends received deduction or exclusion permitted by the local taxing authorities). The latter option would commonly be treated as a capital gain, which may be taxed at a different rate, or not at all.

Example of a simple case including deferred taxes

Assume the same information as in the example above. In addition, assume that Regency Corporation has a combined (federal, state, and local) marginal tax rate of 34% on ordinary income and that it anticipates realization of Elixir Company earnings through future dividend receipts. In Regency's tax jurisdiction, there is an 80% deduction for dividends received from nonsubsidiary investees, meaning that only 20% of the income is subject to ordinary tax. Regency Corporation's entries at year end 1996 will be as follows:

1.	Investment in Elixir Company	12,000	
	Equity in Elixir income		12,000
2.	Income tax expense	816	
	Deferred taxes		816

(Taxable portion of investee earnings to be received in the future as dividends times marginal tax rate: $12,000 x 20% x 34% = $816)

3.	Cash	4,000	
	Investment in Elixir Company		4,000

4.	Deferred taxes	272	
	Taxes payable--current		272

[Fraction of investee earnings currently taxed ($4,000/12,000) x 816 = $272]

If the liability method permitted under IAS 12 has been elected, the tax provision should be based on the projected tax effect of the temporary difference reversal, and this will be subsequently adjusted for a variety of reasons, including changed tax rates and altered management expectations (see Chapter 14 for a complete discussion). Notwithstanding this requirement, the actual tax effect of the temporary difference reversal may still differ from the deferred tax provided. This difference may occur because the actual tax effect is a function of the entity's other current items of income and expense in the year of reversal. It may also result from a realization of the investee's earnings in a manner other than anticipated (assuming that tax rates on ordinary income differ from those on capital gains).

To illustrate this last point, assume that in 1997, before any further earnings or dividends are reported by the investee, the investor sells the entire investment for $115,000. The tax impact is

Selling price	$115,000
Less cost	100,000
Gain	$ 15,000
Capital gain rate (marginal corporate rate)	x 34%
Tax liability	$ 5,100

The entries to record the sale, the tax thereon, and the amortization of deferred taxes provided previously on the undistributed 1996 earnings are as follows:

1.	Cash	115,000	
	Investment in Elixir Company		108,000
	Gain on sale of investment		7,000
2.	Income tax expense	4,556	
	Deferred tax liability		544
	Taxes payable--current		5,100

The income tax expense of $4,556 is the sum of two factors: (1) the capital gains rate of 34% applied to the actual book gain realized ($115,000 selling price less $108,000 carrying value), for a tax of $2,380, and (2) the difference between the capital gains tax rate (34%) and the effective rate on dividend income (20% x 34% = 6.8%) on the undistributed 1996 earnings of Elixir Company previously recognized as ordinary income by Regency Corporation [$8,000 x (34% – 6.8%) = $2,176].

Note that if the realization through a sale of the investment had been anticipated at the time the 1996 balance sheet was being prepared, the deferred tax liability account would have been adjusted (possibly to the entire $5,100 amount of the ultimate obligation), with the offsetting entry applied to 1996's ordinary tax expense. This approach, mandated by the liability approach under IAS 12, is radically different than that required by the deferral method under that same standard. The example above explicitly assumes that sale of the investment was not anticipated prior to 1997.

Accounting for a differential between cost and book value. The simple examples presented thus far avoided the major complexity of equity method accounting, the allocation of the differential between the cost to the investor and the investor's share in the net equity (net assets at book value) of the investee. Since the net impact of equity method accounting must equal that of full consolidation accounting, this differential must be analyzed into the following components and accounted for accordingly:

1. The difference between the book and fair values of the investee's net assets at the date the investment is made.
2. The remaining difference between the fair value of the net assets and the cost of the investment, that is generally attributable to goodwill.

According to IAS 28, any difference between the cost of the investment and the investor's share of the fair values of the net identifiable assets of the associate should be identified and accounted for in accordance with IAS 22 (as detailed in Chapter 10). Thus, the differential should be allocated to specific asset categories, and these differences will then be amortized to the income from investee account as appropriate, for example, over the economic lives of fixed assets whose fair values exceeded book values. The difference between fair value and cost will be treated like goodwill and, in accordance with the provisions of IAS 22, amortized over a period generally not to exceed 5 years, but potentially as long as 20 years.

Example of a complex case ignoring deferred taxes

Assume again that Regency Corporation acquired 40% of Elixir Company's shares on January 2, 1996, but that the price paid was $140,000. Elixir Company's assets and liabilities at that date had the following book and fair values:

	Book value	*Fair value*
Cash	$ 10,000	$ 10,000
Accounts receivable (net)	40,000	40,000
Inventories (FIFO cost)	80,000	90,000
Land	50,000	40,000
Plant and equipment (net of accumulated depreciation)	140,000	220,000
Total assets	$320,000	$400,000
Liabilities	(70,000)	(70,000)
Net assets (stockholders' equity)	$250,000	$330,000

The first order of business is the calculation of the differential, as follows:

Regency's cost for 40% of Elixir's common stock	$140,000
Book value of 40% of Elixir's net assets ($250,000 x 40%)	(100,000)
Total differential	$ 40,000

Next, the $40,000 is allocated to those individual assets and liabilities for which fair value differs from book value. In the example, the differential is allocated to inventories, land, and plant and equipment, as follows:

Item	*Book value*	*Fair value*	*Difference debit (credit)*	*40% of difference debit (credit)*
Inventories	$ 80,000	$ 90,000	$ 10,000	$ 4,000
Land	50,000	40,000	(10,000)	(4,000)
Plant and equipment	140,000	220,000	80,000	32,000
Differential allocated				$32,000

The difference between the allocated differential of $32,000 and the total differential of $40,000 is goodwill of $8,000. As shown by the following computation, goodwill represents the excess of the cost of the investment over the fair value of the net assets acquired.

Regency's cost for 40% of Elixir's common stock	$140,000
40% of the fair value of Elixir's net assets ($330,000 x 40%)	(132,000)
Excess of cost over fair value (goodwill)	$ 8,000

At this point it is important to note that the allocation of the differential is not recorded formally by either Regency Corporation or Elixir Company. Furthermore, Regency does not remove the differential from the investment account and allocate it to the respective assets, since the use of the equity method (one-line consolidation) does not involve the recording of individual assets and liabilities. Regency leaves the differential of $40,000 in the investment account, as part of the balance of $140,000 at January 2, 1996. Accordingly, information pertaining to the allocation of the differential is maintained by the investor, but this information is outside the formal accounting system, which is comprised of journal entries and account balances.

After the differential has been allocated, the amortization pattern is developed. To develop the pattern in this example, assume that Elixir's plant and equipment have 10 years of useful life remaining and that Elixir depreciates its fixed assets on a straight-line basis. Furthermore, assume that Regency amortizes goodwill over a 20-year period. Regency would prepare the following amortization schedule:

			Amortization		
Item	*Differential debit (credit)*	*Useful life*	*1996*	*1997*	*1998*
Inventories (FIFO)	$ 4,000	Sold in 1996	$4,000	$ --	$ --
Land	(4,000)	Indefinite	--	--	--
Plant and equipment (net)	32,000	10 years	3,200	3,200	3,200
Goodwill	8,000	20 years	400	400	400
Totals	$40,000		$7,600	$3,600	$3,600

Note that the entire differential allocated to inventories is amortized in 1996 because the cost flow assumption used by Elixir is FIFO. If Elixir had been using LIFO instead of FIFO, no amortization would take place until Elixir sold some of the inventory that existed at January 2, 1996. Since this sale could be delayed for many years under LIFO, the differential allocated to LIFO inventories would not be amortized until Elixir sold more inventory than it manufactured/purchased. Note also that the differential allocated to Elixir's land is not amortized, because land is not a depreciable asset.

The amortization of the differential is recorded formally in the accounting system of Regency Corporation. Recording the amortization adjusts the equity in Elixir's income that Regency recorded based on Elixir's income statement. Elixir's income must be adjusted because it is based on Elixir's book values, not on the cost that Regency incurred to acquire Elixir. Regency would make the following entries in 1996, assuming that Elixir reported net income of $30,000 and paid cash dividends of $10,000:

1. Investment in Elixir	12,000	
Equity in Elixir income ($30,000 x 40%)		12,000
2. Equity in Elixir income (amortization of differential)	7,600	
Investment in Elixir		7,600
3. Cash	4,000	
Investment in Elixir ($10,000 x 40%)		4,000

The balance in the investment account on Regency's records at the end of 1996 is $140,400 [$140,000 + $12,000 – ($7,600 + $4,000)], and Elixir's stockholders' equity, as shown previously, is $270,000. The investment account balance of $140,000 is not equal to 40% of $270,000. However, this difference can easily be explained, as follows:

Balance in investment account at December 31, 1996		$140,400
40% of Elixir's net assets at December 31, 1996		108,000
Difference at December 31, 1996		$ 32,400
Differential at January 2, 1996	$40,000	
Differential amortized during 1996	(7,600)	
Unamortized differential at December 31, 1996		$ 32,400

As the years go by, the balance in the investment account will come closer and closer to representing 40% of the book value of Elixir's net assets. After 20 years, the remaining difference between these two amounts would be attributed solely to the original differential allocated to land (a $4,000 credit). This $4,000 difference would remain until Elixir sold the property.

To illustrate how the sale of land would affect equity method procedures, assume that Elixir sold the land in the year 2016 for $80,000. Since Elixir's cost for the land was $50,000, it would report a gain of $30,000, of which $12,000 ($30,000 x 40%) would be recorded by Regency, when it records its 40% share of Elixir's reported net income, ignoring income taxes. However, from Regency's viewpoint, the gain on sale of land should have been $40,000 ($80,000 – $40,000) because the cost of the land from Regency's perspective was $40,000 at January 2, 1996. Therefore, besides the $12,000 share of the gain recorded above, Regency should record an additional $4,000 gain [($40,000 – $30,000) x 40%] by debiting the investment account and crediting the equity in Elixir income account. This $4,000 debit to the investment account will negate the $4,000 differential allocated to land on January 2, 1996, since the original differential was a credit (the fair market value of the land was $10,000 less than its book value).

Example of a complex case including deferred taxes

The impact of interperiod income tax allocation in the foregoing example is similar to that demonstrated earlier in the simplified example. However, a complication arises with regard to the portion of the differential allocated to goodwill, since in some jurisdictions amounts representing goodwill are not amortizable for tax purposes and, therefore, are a permanent (not a timing) difference that does not give rise to deferred taxes. The other components of the differential in this example are all generally defined as being timing differences.

The entries recorded by Regency Corporation in 1996 would be

		Debit	Credit
1.	Investment in Elixir	12,000	
	Equity in Elixir income		12,000
2.	Income tax expense	816	
	Deferred tax liability		
	($12,000 x 20% x 34%)		816
3.	Cash	4,000	
	Investment in Elixir		4,000
4.	Deferred tax liability	272	
	Taxes payable--current		
	($4,000/12,000 x 816)		272
5.	Equity in Elixir income	7,600	
	Investment in Elixir		7,600
6.	Deferred tax liability	490	
	Income tax expense		
	($7,200 x 20% x 34%)		490

Note that the tax effect of the amortization of the differential is based on $7,200, not $7,600, since the $400 goodwill amortization would not have been tax deductible.

Reporting disparate elements of the investee's income statement. As suggested earlier in this section, the expanded equity method would require that the major captions in the investee's income statement maintain their character when reported, pro rata, by the investor. IAS 28 does not mandate use of the expanded equity method, although it notes in its disclosure requirements that the investor's share of extraordinary and prior period items should be noted. Although the standard is silent on separate reporting on the face of the financial statements themselves, the authors are of the opinion that to the extent that certain items would be material part of the investor's income statement and thus have the potential to mislead users of those financial statements, it would be prudent and fully consistent with the spirit of IAS 28 to report these separately. For example, if the investee reports a correction of a fundamental error according to IAS 8, or an extraordinary gain or loss, it would be distortive to include the investor's share of these in equity in earnings of investee without signaling that these are not normal, recurring items of income or loss.

The solution, of course, is to include the investor's share of these items with similar items in the investor's financial statements. That is, the expanded equity method concept should be applied, judiciously, to the investor's income statement. This would not extend, however, to separate reporting of any items of operating income or expense (gross sales, salaries, depreciation, etc.)

Example of accounting for separately reportable items

Assume that both an extraordinary item and a prior period adjustment reported in an investee's income and retained earnings statements are individually considered material from the investor's viewpoint.

Investee's income statement:

Income before extraordinary item	$ 80,000
Extraordinary loss from earthquake (net of taxes of $12,000)	(18,000)
Net income	$ 62,000

Investee's retained earnings statement:

Retained earnings at January 1, 1996 as originally reported	$250,000
Add prior period adjustment--correction of an error made in 1995 (net of taxes of $10,000)	20,000
Retained earnings at January 1, 1996, as restated	$270,000

If an investor owned 30% of the voting common stock of this investee, the investor would make the following journal entries in 1996:

1. Investment in investee company	24,000	
Equity in investee income before extraordinary item ($80,000 x 30%)		24,000
2. Equity in investee extraordinary loss	5,400	
Investment in investee company ($18,000 x 30%)		5,400
3. Investment in investee company	6,000	
Equity in investee prior period adjustment ($20,000 x 30%)		6,000

The equity in the investee's prior period adjustment should be reported on the investor's retained earnings statement, and the equity in the extraordinary loss should be reported separately in the appropriate section on the investor's income statement.

Intercompany transactions between investor and investee. Transactions between the investor and the investee may require that the investor make certain adjustments when it records its share of the investee earnings. According to the realization concept, profits can be recognized by an entity only when realized through a sale to outside (unrelated) parties in arm's-length transactions (sales and purchases) between the investor and investee. Similar problems can arise when sales of fixed assets between the parties occur. In all cases, there is no need for any adjustment when the transfers are made at book value (i.e., without either party recognizing a profit or loss in its separate accounting records).

In preparing consolidated financial statements, all intercompany (parent-subsidiary) transactions are eliminated. However, when the equity method is used to account for investments, only the **profit component** of intercompany (investor-investee) transactions is eliminated. This is because the equity method does not result in the combining of all income statement accounts (such as sales and cost of sales) and therefore will not cause the financial statements to contain redundancies. In contrast, consolidated statements would include redundancies if the gross amounts of all intercompany transactions were not eliminated.

IAS 28 was not explicit regarding the percentage of unrealized profits on investor-investee transactions which were to be eliminated. Logical arguments can be made either to eliminate 100% of intercompany profits not realized through a subsequent transaction with unrelated third parties, which would follow the model of consolidated financial statements, or to eliminate only the percentage held by the investor. In a proposed interpretation recently exposed by the IASC's newly formed Standing Interpretations Committee, elimination of only the investor's percentage ownership is mandated. The logic is that in an investor-investee situation, the investor does not have control (as would be the case with a subsidiary), and thus the nonowned percentage is effectively realized through an arm's-length transaction. For joint ventures, IAS 31 prescribes proportionate consolidation, which implies likewise that profits on intercompany transactions be eliminated only to the extent of the investor's interest in the venture. However, to the extent that losses are indicative of impairment in the value of the investment, the rule that profit elimination be limited to the investor's ownership percentage would not apply.

Example of accounting for intercompany transactions

Continue with the same information from the previous example and also assume that Elixir Company sold inventory to Regency Corporation in 1997 for $2,000 above Elixir's cost. Thirty percent of this inventory remains unsold by Regency at the end of 1997. Elixir's net income for 1995, including the gross profit on the inventory sold to Regency, is $20,000; Elixir's income tax rate is 34%. Regency should make the following journal entries for 1997 (ignoring deferred taxes):

1. Investment in Elixir	8,000	
Equity in Elixir income ($20,000 x 40%)		8,000

2. Equity in Elixir income (amortization of differential)	3,600	
Investment in Elixir		3,600
3. Equity in Elixir income	158	
Investment in Elixir		158
($2,000 x 30% x 66% x 40%)		

The amount in the last entry needs further elaboration. Since 30% of the inventory remains unsold, only $600 of the intercompany profit is unrealized at year end. This profit, net of income taxes, is $396. Regency's share of this profit ($158) is included in the first ($8,000) entry recorded. Accordingly, the third entry is needed to adjust or correct the equity in the reported net income of the investee.

Eliminating entries for intercompany profits in fixed assets are similar to those in the examples above. However, intercompany profit is realized only as the assets are depreciated by the purchasing entity. In other words, if an investor buys or sells fixed assets from or to an investee at a price above book value, the gain would only be realized piecemeal over the asset's remaining depreciable life. Accordingly, in the year of sale the pro rata share (based on the investor's percentage ownership interest in the investee, regardless of whether the sale is upstream or downstream) of the unrealized portion of the intercompany profit would have to be eliminated. In each subsequent year during the asset's life, the pro rata share of the gain realized in the period would be added to income from the investee.

Example of eliminating intercompany profit on fixed assets

Assume that Radnor Co., that owns 25% of Empanada Co., sold to Empanada a fixed asset, having a 5-year remaining life, at a gain of $100,000. Radnor Co. is in the 34% marginal tax bracket. The sale occurred at the end of 1996; Empanada Co. will use straight-line depreciation to amortize the asset over the years 1997 through 2001.

The entries related to the foregoing are

1996:

1. Gain on sale of fixed asset	25,000	
Deferred gain		25,000
(To defer the unrealized portion of the gain)		
2. Deferred tax benefit	8,500	
Income tax expense		8,500
(Tax effect of gain deferral)		

Alternatively, the 1996 events could have been reported by this single entry.

Equity in Empanada income	16,500	
Investment in Empanada Co.		16,500

1997 through 2001 (each year):

1. Deferred gain	5,000	
Gain on sale of fixed assets		5,000
(To amortize deferred gain)		

2. Income tax expense	1,700	
Deferred tax benefit		1,700
(Tax effect of gain realization)		

The alternative treatment would be

Investment in Empanada Co.	3,300	
Equity in Empanada income		3,300

In the example above, the tax currently paid by Radnor Co. (34% x $25,000 taxable gain on the transaction) is recorded as a deferred tax benefit in 1996 since taxes will not be due on the book gain recognized in the years 1997 through 2001. Under provisions of IAS 12, deferred tax benefits should be recorded to reflect the tax effects of all deductible timing differences. Unless Radnor Co. could demonstrate that future taxable amounts arising from existing temporary differences exist, this deferred tax benefit might be offset by an equivalent valuation allowance in Radnor Co.'s balance sheet at year end 1996, because of the doubt that it will ever be realized. Thus, tne deferred tax benefit might not be recognizable, net of the valuation allowance, for financial reporting purposes unless other temporary differences not specified in the example provided future taxable amounts to offset the net deductible effect of the deferred gain. (*NOTE*: *The deferred tax impact of an item of income for book purposes in excess of tax is the same as a deduction for tax purposes in excess of book.*) This is discussed more fully in Chapter 14.

Accounting for a partial sale or additional purchase of the equity investment. This section covers the accounting issues that arise when the investor either sells some or all of its equity or acquires additional equity in the investee. The consequence of these actions could involve discontinuation of the equity method of accounting, or resumption of the use of that method.

Example of accounting for a discontinuance of the equity method

Assume that Plato Corp. owns 10,000 shares (30%) of Xenia Co. common stock for which it paid $250,000 10 years ago. On July 1, 1996, Plato sells 5,000 Xenia shares for $375,000. The balance in the Investment in Xenia Co. account at January 1, 1996, was $600,000. Assume that all the original differential between cost and book value has been amortized. To calculate the gain (loss) on this sale of 5,000 shares, it is necessary first to adjust the investment account so that it is current as of the date of sale. Assuming that the investee had net income of $100,000 for the 6 months ended June 30, 1996, the investor should record the following entries:

1. Investment in Xenia Co.	30,000	
Equity in Xenia income		30,000
($100,000 x 30%)		
2. Income tax expense	2,040	
Deferred tax liability		2,040
($30,000 x 20% x 34%)		

The gain on sale can now be computed, as follows:

Proceeds on sale of 5,000 shares	$375,000
Book value of the 5,000 shares ($630,000 x 50%)	315,000
Gain from sale of Xenia common	$ 60,000

Two entries will be needed to reflect the sale: one to record the proceeds, the reduction in the investment account, and the gain (or loss); the other to record the tax effects thereof. Recall that the investor must have computed the deferred tax effect of the undistributed earnings of the investee that it had recorded each year, on the basis that those earnings either would eventually be paid as dividends or would be realized as capital gains. When those dividends are ultimately received or when the investment is disposed of, the deferred tax liability recorded previously must be amortized.

To illustrate, assume that the investor in this example, Plato Corp., provided deferred taxes at an effective rate for dividends (considering the assumed 80% exclusion of intercorporate dividends) of 6.8%. The realized capital gain will be taxed at an assumed 34%. For tax purposes, this gain is computed as $375,000 – $125,000 = $250,000, giving a tax effect of $85,000. For accounting purposes, the deferred taxes already provided are 6.8% x ($315,000 – $125,000), or $12,920. Accordingly, an additional tax expense of $72,080 is incurred on the sale, due to the fact that an additional gain was realized for book purposes ($375,000 – $315,000 = $60,000; tax at 34% = $20,400) **and** that the tax previously provided for at dividend income rates was lower than the real capital gains rate [$190,000 x (34% – 6.8%) = $51,680 extra tax due]. The entries are as follows:

	Debit	Credit
1. Cash	375,000	
Investment in Xenia Co.		315,000
Gain on sale of Xenia Co. stock		60,000
2. Deferred tax liability	12,920	
Income tax expense	72,080	
Taxes payable--current		85,000

The gains (losses) from sales of investee stock are reported on the investor's income statement in the other income and expense section, assuming that a multistep income statement is presented.

According to IAS 28, an investor should discontinue use of the equity method when (1) it ceases to have significant influence in an associate while retaining some or all of its investment, or (2) the use of the equity method is no longer deemed to be appropriate because the associate is operating under severe and long-lasting restrictions that will limit its ability to transfer funds to the investor entity.

In the foregoing example, the sale of investee stock reduced the percentage owned by the investor to 15%. In such a situation, the investor should probably discontinue use of the equity method. The balance in the investment account on the date the equity method is suspended ($315,000 in the example) remains as an asset, subject to the applicable international accounting rules (i.e., historical cost, revalued amounts, or lower of cost or market, per IAS 25). This accounting principle change does not require computation of a cumulative effect or any retroactive disclosures in the investor's financial statements. In periods subsequent to this principles change, the investor records cash dividends received from the investment as dividend revenue. Any dividends received in excess of the investor's share of postdisposal earnings of the investee should be credited to the investment account rather than to income, as they would represent a return of capital.

If an entity has an investment in another enterprise's common stock that is below the level that would create a presumption of significant influence, and later increases that investment so that the threshold for application of the equity method is exceeded, the guidance of IAS 28 would suggest that at that time the difference between the carrying value of the investment and the fair value of the underlying net identifiable assets must be computed, as described earlier in the chapter. The carrying value of the investment will depend on which of the available alternative methods set forth in IAS 25 had been employed. Thus, if the investment had been carried at original cost, the variance between carrying value and underlying fair value will probably have changed by the time the threshold for applying the equity method will have been exceeded. On the other hand, if the investment had been adjusted to fair value on a regular basis, this variance will probably be somewhat less or even nonexistent.

Example of accounting for a return to the equity method of accounting

Continuing the same example, Xenia Co. reported earnings for the second half of 1996 and all of 1997, respectively, of $150,000 and $350,000; Xenia paid dividends of $100,000 and $150,000 in December of those years. During the period July 1996 through December 1997, Plato Corp. accounted for its investment in Xenia Co. as a long-term investment in marketable securities, using the revaluation method, with increases in carrying value being credited to an additional equity account. At December 31, 1996, the fair value of Plato's holding of Xenia's stock is assessed at $335,000; at December 31, 1997, the fair value is $365,000.

In January 1998, the Plato Corp. purchased 10,000 Xenia shares for $700,000, increasing its ownership to 45% and thereby necessitating a return for equity method accounting. The fair value of the underlying identifiable assets of Xenia at this date is $1,000,000. The relevant entries are as follows:

		Debit	Credit
1.	Cash	15,000	
	Income from Xenia dividends		15,000
	(To report dividends paid in 1996)		
2.	Investment in Xenia Corp.	20,000	
	Revaluation surplus		20,000
	(To reflect increased value of investment)		

		Debit	Credit
3.	Income tax expense	1,020	
	Revaluation surplus	6,800	
	Taxes payable--current		1,020
	Taxes payable--deferred		6,800
	(To record taxes on dividends at current effective tax rate [$15,000 x .068] and deferred taxes on value increase [$20,000 x .34] in 1996)		
4.	Cash	22,500	
	Income from Xenia dividends		22,500
	(To report dividends paid in 1997)		
5.	Investment in Xenia Corp.	30,000	
	Revaluation surplus		30,000
	(To reflect increased value of investment)		
6.	Income tax expense	1,530	
	Revaluation surplus	10,200	
	Taxes payable--current		1,530
	Taxes payable--deferred		10,200
	(To record taxes on dividends at current effective tax rate [$22,500 x .068] and deferred taxes on value increase [$30,000 x .34] in 1997)		
7.	Investment in Xenia Co.	700,000	
	Cash		700,000
	(To record additional investment in Xenia)		
8.	Revaluation surplus	33,000	
	Retained earnings		33,000
	(See explanation below)		

The last entry above is further explained as follows. IAS 28 does not suggest that a return to the equity method should result in a restatement of the investment account and the revaluation surplus and retained earnings accounts to catch up to what the balances would have been had the equity method not been discontinued earlier. Accordingly, the authors believe that the new cost basis of the investment at the time the equity method is reestablished should be the adjusted carrying amount immediately prior thereto. In the present example, the carrying amount was as follows:

Balance 6/30/96	$ 315,000
Adjust to fair value 12/96	20,000
Adjust to fair value 12/97	30,000
Balance, 12/97	$ 365,000
Additional investment, 1/98	700,000
Carrying value, 1/98	$1,065,000

The difference between the cost of $1,065,000 and Plato's equity in Xenia's net identifiable assets, $65,000, would be treated similar to goodwill and amortized over a maximum of 5 years (in limited circumstances, a maximum of 20 years), as illustrated earlier in the chapter.

The amount reflected in the revaluation surplus account, $33,000, would not be appropriate to carry forward, since the investment is no longer to be accounted for under IAS 25. Accordingly, this should be transferred to retained earnings, since it effectively has been realized by adoption or readoption of the equity method. Note that the $33,000 balance is the net of the $50,000 upward revaluation recognized, cumulatively, in 1996 and 1997, and the $17,000 tax provision, at capital gain rates (assumed in this example to be 34%), which was expected to affect the ultimate realization of this value increase. If the effective tax rate is expected to differ from the amount provided earlier, due to the effect of the significant influence over the investee's dividend decisions, then if the liability method under IAS 12 has been elected, there would also be an adjustment to the deferred tax provision.

To illustrate the latter point, assume that Plato now expects to realize all its income from Xenia in the form of dividends, to be taxed at an effective rate of 6.8%. The entry to adjust the deferred tax liability would be

Taxes payable--deferred	13,600	
Tax expense		13,600
(To record adjustment to deferred taxes)		

Note that the offset to the deferred tax adjustment is to current period (i.e., 1998) tax expense, under the rules of IAS 12, as described more fully in Chapter 14.

While the illustration above adjusts the revaluation surplus account directly to retained earnings, a good argument could be made that this should be reported in earnings instead, on the basis that this is an economic event occurring in 1998 and thus reportable in that period. Since IAS 28 is silent on this issue (as well as many others), the authors have elected to treat this in a manner analogous to a prior period adjustment (which is approximately equivalent to the treatment prescribed under US GAAP, which has been used as a benchmark), but with the understanding that adequate disclosure would have to be given in the financial statements to avoid any misunderstandings. The alternative treatment, reporting the adjustment in income, would also be acceptable, again with adequate explanations for financial statement users.

Investor accounting for investee capital transactions. IAS 28 does not address how the investor should reflect the impact of investee capital transactions that affect the worth of the investor's investment. However, given that the ultimate effects of equity method accounting are to be identical to full consolidation, it is logical that investee transactions of a capital nature that affect the investor's share of the investee's stockholders' equity should be accounted for as if the investee were a consolidated subsidiary. These transactions principally include situations where the investee purchases treasury stock from, or sells unissued shares or shares held in the treasury to, outside shareholders. (If the investor participates in these transactions on a pro rata basis, its percentage ownership will not change and no special accounting will be necessary.) Similar results will be obtained when holders of outstanding options or convertible securities acquire investee common shares.

When the investee engages in one of the foregoing capital transactions, the investor's ownership percentage is changed. This gives rise to a gain or loss, depending on whether the price paid (for treasury shares acquired) or received (for shares issued) is greater or lesser than the per share carrying value of the investor's interest in the investee. However, since no gain or loss can be recognized on capital transactions, these purchases or sales will affect paid-in capital and/or retained earnings directly, without being reflected in the investor's income statement. This method is consistent with the treatment that would be accorded to a consolidated subsidiary's capital transaction.

Example of accounting for an investee capital transaction

Assume that Roger Corp. purchases, on 1/2/96, 25% (2,000 shares) of Energetic Corp.'s outstanding shares for $80,000. The cost is equal to both the book and fair values of Roger's interest in Energetic's underlying net assets (i.e., there is no differential to be accounted for). One week later, Energetic Corp. buys 1,000 shares of its stock from other shareholders for $50,000. Since the price paid ($50/share) exceeded Roger Corp.'s per share carrying value of its interest, $40, Roger Corp. has in fact suffered an economic loss by the transaction. Also, its percentage ownership of Energetic Corp. has increased as the number of shares held by third parties has been reduced.

Roger Corp.'s new interest in Energetic's net assets is

$$\frac{\text{2,000 shares held by Roger Corp.}}{\text{7,000 shares outstanding in total}} \times \text{Energetic Corp. net assets}$$

$$.2857 \times (\$320{,}000 - \$50{,}000) = \$77{,}143$$

The interest held by Roger Corp. has thus been diminished by $80,000 – $77,143 = $2,857. Therefore, Roger Corp. should make the following entry:

Paid-in capital (or retained earnings)	2,857	
Investment in Energetic Corp.		2,857

Roger Corp. should charge the loss against paid-in capital if paid-in capital from past transactions of a similar nature exists; otherwise, the debit is to retained earnings. Had the transaction given rise to a gain, it would have been credited to paid-in capital only (never to retained earnings) following the GAAP principle that transactions in one's own shares cannot produce earnings.

Note that the amount of the charge to paid-in capital (or retained earnings) in the entry above can be verified as follows: Roger Corp.'s share of the posttransaction net equity (2/7) times the excess price paid ($50 – $40 = $10) times the number of shares purchased = 2/7 x $10 x 1,000 = $2,857.

Other-than-temporary impairment in value of equity method investments. IAS 28 provides that if there is a decline in value of an investment accounted for by the equity method which is determined to be other than temporary in nature, the carrying value of the investment should be adjusted downward. Other than temporary is used in the same sense as in IAS 25, described earlier in this chapter. This criterion must be applied on an individual investment basis.

Other disclosures required by IAS 28. The standard requires that there be disclosure of the percentage of ownership that is held by the investor in each investment and, if it differs, the percentage of voting rights that are controlled. The method of accounting that is being applied to each significant investment should also be identified.

In addition, there may have been certain assumptions or adjustments made in developing information so that the equity method was applied. For example, the investee may have used different accounting principles than the investor, for which the investor made allowances in determining its share of the investee's operating results. The reported results of an investee that used LIFO inventory accounting, for instance, may have been adjusted by the investor to conform to its FIFO costing method. Also, the investee's fiscal year may have differed from the investor's, and the investor may have converted this to its fiscal year by adding and subtracting stub period data. In any such case, if the impact is material, the fact of having made these adjustments should be disclosed, although it would be unusual to report the actual amount of such adjustments to users of the investor's financial statements.

If an associate has outstanding cumulative preferred stock, held by interests other than the investor, the investor should compute its equity interest in the investee's earnings after deducting dividends due to the preferred shareholders, whether or not declared. If material, this should be explained in the investor's financial statements.

Finally, if cumulative losses have been incurred by the investee such that under equity method accounting, the carrying value has been reduced to zero, normally no further share of the investee's losses will be reported. (The major exception to this rule: If the investor has guaranteed debt of the investee or otherwise indicated that it will stand behind the investee, it should record further losses and accordingly let the investment account go negative to reflect a liability on the investor's part.) However, disclosure should be made of the unrecorded negative equity, since this is a measure of the amount of future investee earnings that will have to be realized **before** any further income will be recognized by the investor.

Accounting for Investments in Joint Ventures

International accounting standards address accounting for interests in joint ventures as a topic separate from accounting for other investments. Joint ventures share many characteristics with investments that are accounted for by the equity method: The investor clearly has significant influence over the investee but does not have absolute control, and hence full consolidation is typically unwarranted. According to the provisions of IAS 31, two different methods of accounting are possible, although not as true alternatives for the same fact situations: the proportional consolidation method and the equity method.

Joint ventures can take many forms and structures. Joint ventures may be created as partnerships, as corporations, or as unincorporated associations. The standard identifies three distinct types, referred to as jointly controlled operations, jointly controlled assets, and jointly controlled entities. Notwithstanding the formal structure, all joint ventures are characterized by certain features: having two or more venturers that are bound by a contractual arrangement, and by the fact that the contractual agreement establishes joint control of the enterprise.

The contractual provision(s) establishing joint control most clearly differentiates joint ventures from other investment scenarios in which the investor has significant influence over the investee. In fact, in the absence of such a contractual provision, joint venture accounting would not be appropriate, even in a situation in which two parties each have 50% ownership interests in an investee. The actual existence of such a contractual provision can be evidenced in a number of ways, although most typically it is in writing and often addresses such matters as the nature, term of existence, and reporting obligations of the joint venture; the governing mechanisms for the venture; the capital contributions by the respective venturers; and the intended division of output, income, expenses, or net results of the venture.

The contractual arrangement also establishes joint control over the venture. The thrust of such a provision is to ensure that no venturer can control the venture unilaterally. Certain decision areas will be stipulated as requiring consent by all the venturers, while other decision areas may be defined as needing the consent of only a majority of the venturers. There is no specific set of decisions that must fall into either grouping, however.

Typically, one venturer will be designated as the manager or operator of the venture. This does not imply the absolute power to govern; however, if such power exists, the venture would be a subsidiary, subject to the requirements of IAS 27 and not accounted for properly under IAS 31.

Specific accounting guidance is dependent on whether the enterprise represents jointly controlled operations, jointly controlled assets, or a jointly controlled entity.

Jointly controlled operations. The first of three types of joint ventures, this is characterized by the assigned use of certain assets or other resources, in contrast to an establishment of a new entity, be it a corporation or partnership. Thus, from a formal or legal perspective, this variety of joint venture may not have an existence separate from its sponsors; from an economic point of view, however, the joint venture can still be said to exist, which means that it may exist as an accounting entity. Typically, this form of operation will utilize assets owned by the venture partners, often including plant and equipment as well as inventories, and the partners will sometimes incur debt on behalf of the operation. Actual operations may be conducted on an integrated basis with the partners' own, separate operations, with certain employees, for example, devoting a part of their efforts to the jointly controlled operation. The European Consortium Airbus may be a prototype of this type of enterprise.

IAS 31 is concerned not with the accounting by the entity conducting the jointly controlled operations, but by the venturers having an interest in the enterprise. Each venturer should recognize in its separate financial statements all assets of the venture that it controls, all liabilities that it incurs, all expenses that it incurs, and its share of any revenues produced by the venture. Often, since the assets are already owned by the venturers, they would be included in their respective financial statements in any event; similarly, any debt incurred will be reported by the partner even absent this special rule. Perhaps the only real challenge, from a measurement and disclosure perspective, would be the revenues attributable to each venturer's efforts, which will be determined by reference to the joint venture agreement and other documents.

Jointly controlled assets. In certain industries, such as oil and gas exploration and transmission and mineral extraction, jointly controlled assets are frequently employed. For example, oil pipelines may be controlled jointly by a number of oil producers, each of which uses the facilities and shares in its costs of operation. Certain informal real estate partnerships may also function in this fashion.

IAS 31 stipulates that in the case of jointly controlled asset, each venturer must report in its own financial statements its share of all jointly controlled assets, appropriately classified according to their natures. It must also report any liabilities that it has incurred on behalf of these jointly controlled assets, as well as its share of any jointly incurred liabilities. Each venturer will report any income earned from the use its share of the jointly controlled assets, along with the pro rata expenses and any other expenses it has incurred directly.

Jointly controlled entities. The major type of joint venture is the jointly controlled enterprise, which is really a form of partnership (although it may well be structured legally as a corporation) in which each partner has a form of control, rather than only significant influence. The classic example is an equal partnership of two partners; obviously, neither has a majority and either can block any important action, so the two partners must effectively agree on each key decision. Although this may be the model for a jointly controlled entity, it may in practice have more than two venturers and, depending on the partnership or shareholders' agreement, even minority owners may have joint control. For example, a partnership whose partners have 30%, 30%, 30%, and 10% interests, respectively, may have entered into a contractual agreement that stipulates that investment or financing actions may be taken only if there is unanimity among the partners.

Jointly controlled entities control the assets of the joint venture and may incur liabilities and expenses on its behalf. As a legal entity, it may enter into contracts and borrow funds, among other activities. In general, each venturer will share the net results in proportion to its ownership interest. As an entity with a distinct and separate legal and economic identity, the jointly controlled entity will normally produce its own financial statements and other tax and legal reports.

IAS 31 provides alternative accounting treatments that may be applied by the venture partners to reflect the operations and financial position of the venture. The objective is to report economic substance, rather than mere form, but there is not universal agreement on how this may best be achieved.

The benchmark treatment under the standard is the use of proportionate consolidation, which requires that the venture partner reflect its share of all assets, liabilities, revenues, and expenses on its financial statements as if these were incurred or held directly. In fact, this technique is very effective at conveying the true scope of an entity's operations, when those operations include interests in one or more jointly controlled entities. In this regard, the international accounting standards are more advanced than US, UK, or other national standards, which at best permit proportionate consolidation but do not mandate this accounting treatment.

If the venturer employs the proportionate consolidation method, it will have a choice between two presentation formats that are equally acceptable. First, the venture partner may include its share of the assets, liabilities, revenues, and expenses of the jointly controlled entity with similar items under its sole control. Thus, under this method, its share of the venture's receivables would be added to its own accounts receivable and presented as a single total on its balance sheet. Alternatively, the items that are undivided interests in the venture's assets, and so on, may be shown on separate lines of the venturer's financial statements, although still placed within the correct grouping. For example, the venture's receivables might be shown immediately below the partner's individually owned accounts receivable. In either case, the same category totals (aggregate current assets, etc.) will be presented; the only distinction is whether the venture-owned items are given separate recognition. Even if presented on a combined basis, however, the appropriate detail can still be shown in the financial statement footnotes, and indeed to achieve a fair presentation, this might be needed.

The proportionate consolidation method should be discontinued when the partner no longer has the ability to control the entity jointly. This may occur when the interest formerly held is disposed of, or when external restrictions are placed on the ability to exercise control. In some cases a partner will waive its right to control the entity, possibly in exchange for other economic advantages, such as a larger interest in the operating results.

Under the provisions of IAS 31, a second accounting method, the equity method, is also considered to be acceptable, although its designation as an allowed alternative signals that this is not the preferred treatment. The equity method in this context is as described in IAS 28 and as explained in the preceding section. As with the proportionate consolidation method, use of the equity method must be discontinued when the venturer no longer has joint control or significant influence over the jointly controlled entity.

Accounting for jointly controlled entities as passive investments. Although the expectation is that investments in jointly controlled entities will be accounted for by the proportionate consolidation or equity method (the benchmark and allowed alternative treatments, respectively), in certain circumstances the venturer should account for its interest following the guidelines of IAS 25, that is, as a passive investment. This would be the prescription when the investment has been acquired and is being held with a view toward disposition in the short term, or when the investee is operating under severe long-term restrictions that severely impair its ability to transfer funds to its venturer owners.

If the investment is seen as being strictly temporary, effectively it is being held for trading purposes in the same manner as a temporary investment in marketable securities would be. In such a situation it would not be logical to apply either the proportionate consolidation or equity method, since it would not be the venturer's share of the operating results of the venture that provided value to the venturer, but rather, the change in market value.

Similarly, if the venture were operating under such severe restrictions, expected to persist beyond a short time horizon, that transfers of funds from the jointly controlled entity to its venture parents were precluded, it would be misleading and conceptually invalid to treat the venture's operating results as bearing directly on the venture parents' earnings results. In such a case, an inability to transfer funds would mean that the venture partners would be unable to obtain any benefit, in the short run at least, from their investment in the jointly controlled entity.

Change from joint control to full control status. If one of the venturers' interest in the jointly controlled entity is increased, whether by an acquisition of some or all of another of the venturers' interest, or by action of a contractual provision of the venture agreement (resulting from a failure to perform by another venturer, etc.), the proportionate consolidation method of accounting ceases to be appropriate and full consolidation will become necessary. Guidance on preparation of consolidated financial statements is provided by IAS 27 and is discussed fully in Chapter 10.

Accounting for Transactions Between Venture Partner and Jointly Controlled Entity

Transfers at a gain to the transferor. A general, underlying principle of financial reporting is that earnings are to be realized only by engaging in transactions with outside parties. Thus, gains cannot be recognized by transferring assets (be they productive assets or goods held for sale in the normal course of the business) to a subsidiary, affiliate, or joint venture, to the extent this really would represent a transaction by an entity with itself. Were this not the rule, enterprises would establish a range of related entities to sell goods to, thereby permitting the reporting of profits well before any sale to real, unrelated customers ever took place. The potential for abuse of the financial reporting process in such a scenario is too obvious to need elaboration.

IAS 31 stipulates that when a venturer sells or transfers assets to a jointly controlled entity, it may recognize profit only to the extent that the venture is owned by the other venture partners, and then only to the extent that the risks and rewards of ownership has indeed been transferred to the jointly controlled entity. The logic is that a portion of the profit has in fact been realized, to the extent that the purchase was agreed on by unrelated parties that jointly control the entity making the acquisition. For example, if venturers A, B, and C jointly control venture D (each having a 1/3 interest), and A sells equipment having a book value of $40,000 to the venture for $100,000, only 2/3 of the apparent gain of $60,000, or $40,000, may be realized. In its balance sheet immediately after this transaction, A would report its share of the asset reflected in the balance sheet of D, 1/3 x $100,000 = $33,333, minus the unrealized gain of $20,000, for a net of $13,333. This is identical to A's remaining 1/3 interest in the pretransaction basis of the asset (1/3 x $40,000 = $13,333). Thus, there is no step up in the carrying value of the proportionate share of the asset reflected in the transferor's balance sheet.

If the asset is subject to depreciation, the deferred gain on the transfer (1/3 x $60,000 = $20,000) would be amortized in proportion to the depreciation reflected by the venture, such that the depreciated balance of the asset reported by A is the same as would have been reported had the transfer not taken place. For example, assume that the asset has a useful economic life of 5 years after the date of transfer to D. The deferred gain ($20,000) would be amortized to income at a rate of $4,000 per year. At the end of the first posttransfer year, D would report a net carrying value of $100,000 – $20,000 = $80,000; A's proportionate interest is 1/3 x $80,000 = $26,667. The unamortized balance of the deferred gain is $20,000 – $4,000 = $16,000. Thus the net reported amount of A's share of the jointly controlled entity's asset is $26,667 – $16,000 = $10,667. This amount is precisely what A would have reported the remaining share of its asset at on this date: 1/3 x ($40,000 – $8,000) = $10,667.

Of course, A has also reported a gain of $40,000 as of the date of the transfer of its asset to joint venture D, but this represents the gain that has been realized by the sale of 2/3 of the asset to unrelated parties B and C, the coventurers in D. In short, two-thirds of the asset has been sold at a gain, while one-third has been retained and is continuing to be used and depreciated over its remaining economic life and is reported on the cost basis in A's financial statements.

Transfers of assets at a loss. The foregoing illustration was predicated on a transfer to the jointly controlled entity at a nominal gain to the transferor, of which a portion was realized for financial reporting purposes. The situation when a transfer is at an amount below the transferor's carrying value is not analogous; rather, such a transfer is deemed to be confirmation of a permanent decline in value, which must be recognized by the transferor immediately rather than being deferred. This reflects the conservative bias in accounting: Unrealized losses are often recognized, while unrealized gains are deferred.

Assume that venturer C (a 1/3 owner of D, as described above) transfers an asset it had been carrying at $150,000 to jointly controlled entity D at a price of $120,000. If the decline is deemed to be other than temporary in nature (that presumptively it is, since C would not normally have been willing to engage in this transaction if the decline were expected to be reversed in the near term), C must recognize the full $30,000 at the time of the transfer. Subsequently, C will pick up its 1/3 interest in the asset held by D (1/3 x $120,000 = $40,000) as its own asset in its balance sheet, before considering any depreciation, and so on.

Accounting for Assets Purchased From a Jointly Controlled Entity

Transfers at a gain to the transferor. A similar situation arises when a venture partner acquires an asset from a jointly controlled entity: The venturer cannot reflect the gain recognized by the joint venture, to the extent that this represents its share in the results of the venture's operations. For example, again assuming that A, B, and C jointly own D, an asset having a book value of $200,000 is transferred by D to B for a price of $275,000. Since B has a 1/3 interest in D, it would (unless an adjustment were made to its accounting) report $25,000 of D's gain as its own, which would violate the realization concept under GAAP.

To avoid this result, B will record the asset at its cost, $275,000, less the deferred gain, $25,000, for a net carrying value of $250,000, which represents the transferor's basis, $200,000, plus the increase in value realized by unrelated parties (A and C) in the amount of $50,000.

As the asset is depreciated, the deferred gain will be amortized apace. For example, assume that the useful life of the asset in B's hands is 10 years. At the end of the first year, the carrying value of the asset is $275,000 – $27,500 = $247,500; the unamortized balance of the deferred gain is $25,000 – $2,500 = $22,500. Thus the net carrying value, after offsetting the remaining deferred gain, will be $247,500 – $22,500 = $225,000. This corresponds to the remaining life of the asset (9/10 of its estimated life) times its original net carrying amount, $250,000. The amortization of the deferred gain should be credited to depreciation expense to offset the depreciation charged on the nominal acquisition price and thereby to reduce it to a cost basis as required by GAAP.

Transfers at a loss to the transferor. If the asset was acquired by B at a loss to D, on the other hand, and the decline was deemed to be indicative of an other than temporary diminution in value, B should recognize its share of this decline. This contrasts with the gain scenario discussed immediately above, and as such is entirely consistent with the accounting treatment for transfers from the venture partner to the jointly controlled venture.

For example, if D sells an asset carried at $50,000 to B for $44,000, and the reason for this discount is an other-than-temporary decline in the value of said asset, the venture, D, records a loss of $6,000 and each venture partner will in turn recognize a $2,000 loss. B would report the asset at its acquisition cost of $44,000 and will also report its share of the loss, $2,000. This loss will not be deferred and will not be added to the carrying value of the asset in B's hands (as would have been the case if B treated only the $4,000 loss realized by unrelated parties A and C as being recognizable).

Disclosure Requirements

A venture partner is required to disclose in the notes to the financial statements its ownership interests in all significant joint ventures, including its ownership percentage and other relevant data. If the venturer uses proportionate consolidation and merges its share of the assets, liabilities, revenues, and expenses of the jointly controlled entity with its own assets, liabilities, revenues, and expenses, or if the venturer uses the equity method, the notes should disclose the amounts of the current and long-term assets, current and long-term liabilities, revenues, and expenses related to its interests in jointly controlled ventures.

Furthermore, the joint venture partner should disclose any contingencies that the venturer has incurred in relation to its interests in any joint ventures, noting any share of contingencies jointly incurred with other joint venturers. In addition, the venturer's share of any contingencies of the joint venture (as distinct from contingencies incurred in connection with its investment in the venture) for which it may be contingently liable must be reported. Finally, those contingencies that arise because the venturer is contingently liable for the liabilities of the other partners in the jointly controlled entity must be set forth. These disclosures are a logical application of the rules set forth in IAS 10, which is discussed in Chapter 11 of this book.

A venture partner should also disclose in the notes to its financial statements information about any commitments it has outstanding in respect to interests it has in joint ventures. These include any capital commitments it has itself and its share of any joint commitments it may have incurred with other venture partners, as well as its share of the capital commitments of the joint ventures themselves, if any.

10 BUSINESS COMBINATIONS AND CONSOLIDATED FINANCIAL STATEMENTS

PERSPECTIVE AND ISSUES

Regardless of its legal form, a business combination will be accounted for as either a uniting of interests or as an acquisition of one business by another, depending on the facts of the specific case. A uniting of interests presumes that the ownership interests of the combining entities continue essentially unchanged in the new combined enterprise. A series of restrictive criteria must be satisfied for a combination to be accounted for as a uniting of interests. Acquisition accounting is applicable when one entity acquires the assets, operations, or ownership interest from another enterprise or from its former owners. Most combinations are accounted for as acquisitions.

When a combination is to be accounted for as an acquisition, the assets acquired and liabilities assumed are recorded at their fair values, using purchase accounting. If the assets and liabilities total an amount other than the total acquisition price, the excess (or deficiency) is generally referred to as goodwill (negative goodwill). Goodwill can arise only in the context of a business combination that is an acquisition. In a uniting of interests, the assets and liabilities of the combining entities are carried forward at precombination book values, using the pooling method of accounting. This treatment is consistent with the theory that since a pooling does not result in the acquisition of one business entity by another, a new basis of accountability cannot be established.

When the acquired entity is **merged** into the acquiring entity or when both entities are **consolidated** into a new (third) entity, all assets and liabilities are recorded directly on the books of the surviving organization. Depending on whether the conditions stipulated by IAS 22 are met, the transaction will be treated as either a uniting of interests or an acquisition. However, when the acquirer obtains a majority (or all) of the common stock of the acquired entity (which maintains a separate legal existence), the assets and liabilities of the company acquired will not be recorded on the acquirer's books. In this case, GAAP normally requires that consolidated financial statements be prepared (i.e., that an accounting consolidation be effected, and either pooling or purchase accounting used, depending on the circumstances). In certain cases combined financial statements of entities under common control, neither of which is owned by the other, are also prepared. This process is very similar to an accounting consolidation using pooling accounting, except that the equity accounts of the combining entities are carried forward intact.

The major accounting issues in business combinations and consolidated or combined financial statement preparation are as follows:

1. The proper accounting basis for the assets and liabilities of the combining entities
2. The decision to treat a combination as a uniting of interests or as an acquisition
3. The elimination of intercompany balances and transactions in the preparation of consolidated or combined statements

Sources of IAS
IAS 22, 27

DEFINITIONS OF TERMS

Accounting consolidation. The process of combining the financial statements of a parent company and one or more legally separate and distinct subsidiaries.

Acquisition. A business combination in that one entity (the acquirer) obtains control over the net assets and operations of another (the acquiree) in exchange for the transfer of assets, incurrence of liability, or issuance of equity.

Business combination. The bringing together of separate enterprises into one economic entity as a result of one enterprise uniting with or obtaining control over the net assets and operations of another.

Combination. Any transaction whereby one enterprise obtains control over the assets and properties of another enterprise, regardless of the resulting form of the enterprise emerging from the combination transaction.

Combined financial statements. Financial statements presenting the financial position and/or results of operations of legally separate entities, related by common ownership, as if they were a single entity.

Consolidated financial statements. The financial statements of a group presented as those of a single enterprise.

Consolidation. A new enterprise is formed to acquire two or more other enterprises through an exchange of voting stock. The acquired enterprises then cease to exist as separate legal entities.

Control. The power to govern the financial and operating policies of an enterprise so as to obtain benefits from its activities.

Date of acquisition. The date on which control of the net assets and operations of the acquiree is effectively transferred to the acquirer.

Fair value. The amount for which an asset could be exchanged or a liability settled between knowledgeable, willing parties in an arm's-length transaction.

Goodwill. The excess of the cost of a business acquisition accounted for by the purchase method over the fair value of the net assets thereof; it must be amortized over a useful life of up to 20 years (available under defined circumstances only; the normal life is up to 5 years).

Group. A parent and all its subsidiaries.

Merger. One enterprise acquires all of the net assets of one or more other enterprises through an exchange of stock, payment of cash or other property, or the issue of debt instruments.

Minority interest. That part of the net results of operations and net assets of a subsidiary attributable to interests that are not owned, directly or indirectly through subsidiaries, by the parent.

Negative goodwill. This amount represents the net excess of fair value of the net assets of a business acquisition accounted for as a purchase, either determined after offsetting the maximum amount against the fair value of all nonmonetary assets acquired (the benchmark treatment) or without so offsetting (the alternative treatment).

Parent. An enterprise that has one or more subsidiaries.

Pooling-of-interests method. An accounting method used for a business combination that is predicated on a mutual exchange and continuation of ownership interests in the combining entities. It does not result in the establishing of a new basis of accountability. The pooling method is to be used for unitings of interests.

Purchase method. An accounting method used for a business combination that recognizes that one combining entity was acquired by another. It establishes a new basis of accountability for the acquiree. The purchase method is to be used for acquisitions.

Purchased preacquisition earnings. An account used to report the earnings of a subsidiary attributable to percentage ownership acquired at the interim date in the current reporting period.

Subsidiary. An enterprise that is controlled, directly or indirectly, by another enterprise.

Uniting of interests. A business combination in which the shareholders of the combining enterprises combine control over the whole, or effectively the whole, of their respective net assets and operations to achieve a continuing mutual sharing in the risks and benefits attaching to the combined entity such that neither party can be identified as the acquirer.

Unrealized intercompany profit. The excess of the transaction price over the carrying value of an item (usually inventory or plant assets) transferred from (or to) a parent to (or from) the subsidiary (or among subsidiaries) and not sold to an outside entity. For purposes of consolidated financial statements, recognition must be deferred until subsequent realization through a transaction with an unrelated party.

CONCEPTS, RULES, AND EXAMPLES

Introduction to Business Combinations

Business combinations occur under two different scenarios. By far, the most common type of combination is referred to as an acquisition, which is sometimes also known as a purchase or as a purchase business combination. The other business combinations, which represent a very small minority of cases, are effected in a manner known as a uniting of interests, which is also referred to as a pooling of interests or as a merger.

The aforenoted typology is independent of the legal form of the business combination. Thus, two entities may consolidate to create a new, third enterprise. Alternatively, one entity may purchase, for cash or for stock, the stock of another enterprise, which may or may not be followed by a formal merging of the acquired entity into the acquirer. In yet other cases, one entity may simply purchase the assets of another, with or without assuming the debts of that enterprise. The form of the combination does not define whether it will be viewed as an acquisition or a uniting of interests, however. Rather, it is the substance of the transaction, which will be explored in great detail in the following paragraphs, which will serve to define it. The accounting for acquisitions differs markedly from that prescribed for unitings of interests.

Uniting of Interests

In many countries it has long been accepted that some business combinations may be accounted for as unitings of interests. The practice actually precedes the naming of the accounting methodology used. For example, in the United States the pooling method has been used since at least the early 1930s, although the term was not applied until the mid-1940s. The earliest examples of transactions accounted for as poolings or unitings of interests generally involved affiliated entities (such as parents and subsidiaries), where the use of this method clearly made sense, since the mere act of formally joining previously affiliated entities would not seem to warrant establishing a new basis of accountability. Broader application of the method really began in the 1940s; initially, pooling treatment was accepted only for those mergers where the combining entities had roughly the same economic substance (so that it was difficult to discern which party was actually the acquirer). However, as time passed, pooling was accepted for a broad range of business combinations among economic unequals.

Official support for the method, in the form of a professional standard issued by the standard setters in the United States, first occurred in 1950. That standard permitted pooling accounting when the shareholders of each of the combining entities continued forward as participating owners of the new or surviving business. This criterion remains one of the clearest tests of whether a combination should be accorded pooling treatment. That standard also established comparable size and management continuity as criteria, but these terms were not quantitatively defined, and a wide range of combinations continued to be accounted for as poolings of interests.

Other US accounting standards addressing pooling accounting were promulgated during the following decade, with the eventual effect that pooling treatment became acceptable even when the size disparity among the combining entities was as great as 19:1. As a result, accounting for business combinations as poolings became extremely popular in the early and mid-1960s. The major reason was (and continues to be) that the true cost (as would be measured by the market value of the consideration, usually stock or debt instruments issued by the acquirer) of the acquisition was concealed, with the result that a lower basis of assets acquired would be carried forward, in turn producing lower amortization expense and higher reportable earnings in future periods. Also, the acquirer could incorporate the acquired entity's retained earnings (subject to some limitations) into its financial statements, thereby enhancing the appearance of the financial strength of the ongoing enterprise.

By the end of the decade of the 1960s, abuse of pooling of interests accounting in the United States had received so much attention that the standard setters imposed a new standard on accounting for business.

Recent evolution of uniting (pooling) of interests rules. Many standards-setting bodies now explicitly permit certain consolidations to be accounted for as poolings or unitings of interests. These independent, national accounting standards vary substantially in terms of the criteria that must be satisfied in order to employ this methodology. A minority of national accounting standards-setting bodies prohibit pooling accounting altogether, however, with France and Spain being two of the more important industrialized nations in this group.

In the United States, standards setters established perhaps the most complex criteria yet devised for determining if a business combination could be accounted for as a pooling of interests. The US Accounting Principles Board, in its Opinion 16, established 12 tests, all of which must be met for any given combination to be so treated. Some of these tests are indeed difficult to apply, and the overall effect is virtually to eliminate pooling treatment for any combination other than a pure stock swap between parties having roughly equal bargaining power, although, perhaps surprisingly, parity of size is not one of the 12 criteria.

Among the 12 criteria imposed in the United States are several that relate to the characteristics of the combining entities (being independent of each other as well as of any other enterprise, etc.), others that relate to the nature of exchange transaction (primarily a swap of voting common stock, effected in a single transaction, with continuity of interests by the combining parties in essentially the same proportions as prior to the merger, etc.), and yet another set that precludes planned-for postcombination transactions that would alter the relative ownerships of the combining groups.

International accounting standard for pooling. The international accounting standard, IAS 22, provides a rather more direct set of criteria for determining the appropriateness of pooling accounting treatment. Three tests must all be met, as follows:

1. The shareholders of the combining enterprises must achieve a continuing mutual sharing of the risks and benefits attaching to the combined enterprise.
2. The basis of the transaction must be principally an exchange of voting common shares of the enterprises involved.
3. The whole, or effectively the whole, of the net assets and operations of the combining enterprises are combined into one entity.

The first of these criteria relates to the continual sharing of risks and benefits by the combining shareholder groups. To achieve this, according to IAS 22, the following must occur:

1. The substantial majority, if not all, of the voting common shares of the combining enterprises are exchanged or pooled.
2. The fair value of one enterprise is not significantly different from that of the other enterprise.
3. The shareholders of each enterprise maintain substantially the same voting rights and interest in the combined entity, relative to each other, after the combination as before.

Thus, the international standards have effectively defined the essential characteristics of a true uniting of interests and have established tests that address these. In describing a uniting of interests, IAS 22 states that "…the shareholders of the combining enterprises join in a *substantially equal arrangement* to share control over the whole, or effectively the whole, of their net assets and operations." Furthermore, it states that to achieve such a mutual sharing of risks and benefits, "the fair value of one enterprise (cannot be) significantly different from that of the other." Although these words are perhaps suggestive of the notion that unitings cannot be said to occur unless the combining entities are virtually identical in size, the precise meaning is not made clear. Thus, it would appear that under these criteria the mergers of entities of at least somewhat differing sizes can continue to be accounted for as poolings if the other terms stated are met.

In addressing the "substantially equal arrangement" the IAS 22 approach is clearly not as ambiguous as the US standard, APB 16, which makes no reference to the relative sizes of the combining entities or their relative net worths. However, neither is it as restrictive as the recently proposed UK standard (FRED 6), which demands approximately equal size under what is virtually a "marriage of equals" doctrine.

While IAS 22 goes on to state that a "mutual sharing...is usually not possible without a substantially equal exchange of voting common shares..." this can be read to mean that the **relative** interests of the combining parties cannot be altered by the transaction. For example, if one combining entity has a fair value of two-thirds of that of the other entity, this would imply that after the combination the former shareholders of the smaller enterprise should control about 40% [= 2/3 ÷ (2/3 + 3/3)] of the new, combined entity. If this condition were not to be met, these shareholders would have either gained or lost **relative** voting power in the transaction, which would be strongly suggestive of an acquisition of one enterprise by the other. In practice, there will be many borderline circumstances in which judgment must be applied to ascertain if the terms of IAS 22 have indeed been met.

Indicators that a uniting has not occurred. The presence of certain attributes are presumptive evidence that a uniting of interests characterization would be inappropriate. These include

1. The relative equality in fair values of the combining enterprises is reduced and the percentage of voting common shares exchanged decreases.
2. The financial arrangements provide a relative advantage to one group of shareholders over the other shareholders; such arrangements may take effect either prior to or after the business combination occurs.
3. One party's share of the equity in the combined entity depends on how the business that it previously controlled performs subsequent to the business combination.

Accounting procedures in respect to unitings of interests. The pooling-of-interests method of accounting should be used to account for unitings of interest. Financial statements of the combining enterprises, for the period of the combination and for any comparative (i.e., earlier) periods shown, should include the assets, liabilities, revenues, and expenses of the combining enterprises as if they had always been combined in fact. No new basis of accounting is established; the bases of all assets and liabilities remains as before the uniting. These rules are essential to the concept of a uniting of interests, which represents that formerly separate entities have merely come together to do in the future as one enterprise what they did separately in the past, without either having acquired or been acquired by the other.

No goodwill or negative goodwill can be created in a uniting of interests. Goodwill is the excess of purchase price over the fair value of net identifiable assets acquired; absent an acquisition, there can be no new basis of accounting established and thus no goodwill. The same applies to negative goodwill, which is merely the excess of the fair value of the net identifiable assets acquired over the purchase price: Once again, no acquisition means no negative goodwill.

Although it is easiest to explain the accounting for a uniting of interests as resulting simply in the combining of all recorded assets, liabilities, and equities, in fact the equity sections of the combining enterprises' balance sheets may require certain adjustments. The reason is that, depending on the legal form of the uniting (e.g., one entity issuing shares for the shares of the other, or a new, third entity acquiring the shares of the combining parties) and the par or stated values of the shares of the combining entities, it may be necessary to capitalize some or all of the retained earnings of one or both of the combining companies. In no event, however, can a uniting of interests result in the creation of retained earnings: the immediate post-uniting combined balance of retained earnings will be equal to **or less than** the sum of the constituents' retained earnings. Put another way, any difference between the recorded capital accounts plus any additional consideration, and the recorded share capital acquired, should be adjusted against equity.

Any expenses incurred in consummating a uniting of interests should be recognized as expenses when incurred; they cannot be capitalized or adjusted against equity.

Basic example of uniting of interests

To illustrate the essential elements of the pooling-of-interests method of accounting, consider the following balance sheets of the combining entities:

Condensed Balance Sheets as of Date of Merger

	Company A	*Company B*	*Company C*
Assets	$30,000,000	$4,500,000	$6,000,000
Liabilities	$18,000,000	$1,000,000	$1,500,000
Common stock:			
$100 par	6,000,000	--	--
$10 par	--	3,000,000	--
$1 par	--	--	1,000,000
Additional paid-in capital	2,000,000	--	500,000
Retained earnings	4,000,000	500,000	3,000,000
Liabilities and stockholders' equity	$30,000,000	$4,500,000	$6,000,000

Company A will issue its shares for those of companies B and C, and both B and C will tender 100% of their common shares. A will give one of its shares for each 15 shares of B stock and one of its shares for each 25 shares of C stock. Thus, A will issue 20,000 shares to acquire B and 40,000 shares to acquire C.

In a uniting of interests, the historical basis of the assets and liabilities of the combining entities is continued. No new basis of accountability is established. The assets of the combined (postcombination) company A will total $40,500,000; total liabilities will be $20,500,000. Total equity (net assets) will, therefore, equal $20,000,000.

While the total stockholders' equity of the postcombination entity will equal the sum of the combining entities' individual equity accounts, the allocation between paid-in capital and retained earnings can vary. Total (postcombination) retained earnings can be equal to or less than the sum of the constituent entities' retained earnings but cannot be more than that amount. Consider the cases of companies B and C.

In the present example, company A issues 20,000 shares of its stock, or an aggregate par value of $2,000,000, to substitute for company B's $3,000,000 aggregate paid-in capital in effecting the merger with company B. Therefore, the combined (postacquisition) balance sheet will include $2,000,000 of par value capital stock, plus $1,000,000 of additional paid-in capital. Even though only $2,000,000 of stock was issued to replace company B's $3,000,000 of aggregate par, there can be no increase in retained earnings and no decrease in contributed capital as a consequence of the uniting.

The Company C merger presents the opposite situation: An aggregate of $4,000,000 of Company A stock is to be issued to supersede $1,000,000 of aggregate par and $500,000 of additional paid-in capital. To accomplish this, $2,500,000 of Company C retained earnings is capitalized, leaving only $500,000 of Company C retained earnings to be carried as retained earnings into the postacquisition balance sheet. In reality, such a situation would not exist. If the pooling of interests took place simultaneously, APB 16 requires only that the combined contributed capital of all entities not be reduced. Therefore, the issuance of 60,000 shares would create an entry on A's books as follows:

Net assets	8,000,000	
Additional paid-in capital	1,500,000	
Common stock		6,000,000
Retained earnings		3,500,000

Note that the additional paid-in capital on the books of Company A is reduced by an amount sufficient to make the total increase in contributed capital of A ($4,500,000), which equals the total contributed capital of both B ($3,000,000) and C ($1,500,000). In this way, all the retained earnings of B and C are transferred to A. This accounting would hold even if A, B, and C simultaneously transferred their net assets to a new entity, D (a consolidation). The opening entry on the books of D would look the same as the consolidated balance sheet of A after the merger, as presented below.

The balance sheet of Company A after the mergers are completed is as follows:

Assets	$40,500,000
Liabilities	$20,500,000
Common stock, $100 par	12,000,000
Additional paid-in capital	500,000
Retained earnings	7,500,000
Liabilities and stockholders' equity	$40,500,000

The historical basis of assets and liabilities is normally continued, but this rule has an exception: Where different accounting principles were employed by the combining entities, these principles should be conformed, where possible, by retroactive adjustment. Prior-period financial statements, when reissued on a pooled basis, should be restated for these changes.

If any combining entity has a deficit in its retained earnings, that deficit is continued in the combined entity (and may even be increased as a consequence of the par value changeover, as illustrated above for a nondeficit situation). It cannot be reduced or eliminated as a consequence of the combination.

Any expenses relating to a business combination accounted for as a pooling of interests (e.g., stock registration costs, finders' fees, and costs of preparing stockholders' prospectuses) must be charged against income in the period in which the combination is effected. No new assets can arise from a pooling.

Conforming accounting principles employed by the combining entities. The historical basis of assets and liabilities is normally continued, but this rule has an exception: Where different accounting principles were employed by the combining entities, these principles should be conformed, where possible, by retroactive adjustment. Prior-period financial statements, when reissued on a pooled basis, should be restated for these changes.

Reporting on the combined entity. When the pooling-of-interests method is used, it is necessary to report all periods presented on a combined basis. Thus, if only a single year is presented, the effect will be as if the combination occurred at the beginning of that year. If comparative statements are presented, the effect will be as if the combination occurred at the beginning of the earliest year being reported on. This is consistent with the concept of a pooling not being a discrete economic event, but rather as a combining of common interests, such that the most meaningful reporting, **after the date of the combination**, is to present the financial position and results of operations of those entities as if they had always been combined.

The combining entities may have had transactions with each other prior to the combination and may have had amounts due to or from each other at the end of earlier fiscal periods. To present combined statements of financial position and results of operations, all intercompany balances and transactions should be eliminated, to the extent that this is practical to accomplish.

Detailed example of uniting of interests using pooling method

To explain further the applicability of the criteria for applying uniting of interests accounting set forth earlier, a comprehensive example will be developed here and continued in the subsequent discussion of acquisition accounting.

Ahmadi Corporation (whose balance sheet is presented as Exhibit I) is about to merge with or acquire four other entities: Belfast (Exhibit II), Cairo (Exhibit III), Delhi (Exhibit IV), and Eyre (Exhibit V). Some of these business combinations may qualify for uniting of interests accounting; others will have to be treated as acquisitions.

1. The acquisitions will take place as follows:
    a. Belfast is acquired by exchanging one Ahmadi common share for each 15 of Belfast common shares.
    b. Cairo is acquired by exchanging one Ahmadi common share for each 75 of Cairo common shares.
    c. Delhi is acquired by paying $12,750,000 in 90-day demand notes to retire the $13.5 million bank loan, and by exchanging one Ahmadi share for each 20 of Delhi common shares (except as noted in 8. below).

d. Eyre is acquired by exchanging a new issue of $100 par, 7% preferred stock subject to a mandatory retirement plan (ending in 2000), plus common shares, for all Eyre common stock. Shareholders of Eyre will receive .35 share of Ahmadi preferred for each Eyre common share (total of 175,000 preferred shares), and one share of Ahmadi common for each four Eyre common shares (total of 125,000 common shares). Based on the dividend yield, the preferred stock has been appraised as having a fair market value of about $105.70 per share, or a total of $18,500,000.

2. The appraised value of each acquired firm is given as follows (amounts in thousands):

	Assets acquired	*Liabilities assumed*	*Net asset value (FMV)*
Belfast Corporation	$ 78,500	$ 2,500	$ 76,000
Cairo Company, Inc.	42,500	6,500	36,000
Delhi Corporation	111,000	7,500	103,500
Eyre, Inc.	168,000	78,000	90,000

In each case, current assets are appraised to be worth book values according to the acquired firms' balance sheets. Thus any excess fair value vs. the respective book values is due to values of the entities' plant assets.

3. Eyre originally issued 8% debentures on 1/1/92 at par value. Ahmadi purchased $20.0 million (face value) of these debentures on 1/1/95 at the market price of $97.60. The discount has been regularly amortized to earnings on a straight-line basis.
4. Investments by Belfast and Cairo in the common shares of Ahmadi Corporation were recorded at cost.
5. Each of the five corporations in question has been in business for at least 5 years, and none has ever been a subsidiary of each other or of any other entity.
6. The acquisition agreement with Cairo provides that if earnings of the acquired subsidiary exceed certain amounts in each or any of the following 5 years, additional shares of Ahmadi will be distributed to former Cairo shareholders. Specifically, for each 50% earnings advance over 1996 levels ($2,800,000 net), an additional 10% of shares are to be issued.
7. The agreement with Eyre provides that the purchase price of $80,000,000 (based on the market value of Ahmadi common shares received, plus the fair value of preferred stock received) is protected against market declines for 2 years subsequent to the merger (i.e., if the value of securities distributed to Eyre shareholders is below $80 million as of 12/31/98, additional Ahmadi Corporation common shares will be issued at that time, in an amount sufficient to bring the total value to the sum stipulated).
8. Holders of 5,000 shares of Delhi stock angrily dissented to the merger plan, and Ahmadi agreed to pay them $75 for each share tendered instead of issuing common stock.
9. Common stocks of the various firms were traded on stock exchanges or were quoted in the over-the-counter market in 1996 at these prices:

	High		*Low*		*Average*		*Ending*	
Ahmadi Corporation	$512		$388		$495		$492	
Belfast Corporation	51	7/8	28	1/2	35	1/4	35	3/4
Cairo Company, Inc.	8	3/4	7	1/2	8		8	1/8
Delhi Corporation	12	1/2	83	1/8	90	3/8	94	1/2
Eyre, Inc.	80	1/2	61		70	1/2	76	

10. Key management personnel of each of the merging entities, except for the directors and officers of Cairo Company, Inc., will continue in important management roles in the new, combined enterprise. The Cairo owners and managers have indicated their plans to retire and henceforth to be no more than passive investors in Ahmadi Corporation.

Exhibit I
Ahmadi Corporation
Condensed Balance Sheet
December 31, 1996

Sundry current assets		$ 75,000,000
Plant and equipment, net	$80,000,000	
Investment in Eyre 8% debentures	4,900,000	84,900,000
Total assets		$159,900,000
Sundry liabilities		$ 87,000,000
Common stock, $100 par	$22,500,000	
Additional paid-in capital	12,200,000	
Retained earnings	38,200,000	72,900,000
Total liabilities and stockholders' equity		$159,900,000

Exhibit II
Belfast Corporation
Condensed Balance Sheet
December 31, 1996

Sundry current assets		$ 3,900,000
Plant and equipment, net	$38,500,000	
Investment in Ahmadi common stock (11,250 shares)	9,800,000	48,300,000
Total assets		$52,200,000
Sundry liabilities		$ 2,500,000
Common stock, $10 par	$20,000,000	
Paid-in surplus	14,700,000	
Retained earnings	15,000,000	49,700,000
Total liabilities and stockholders' equity		$52,200,000

Exhibit III
Cairo Company, Inc.
Condensed Balance Sheet
December 31, 1996

Sundry current assets		$ 4,000,000
Plant and equipment, net	$17,400,000	
Investment in Acquisitive common stock (4,500 shares)	3,100,000	20,500,000
Total assets		$24,500,000
Sundry liabilities		$ 6,500,000
Common stock (no par), 3 million shares outstanding	$14,500,000	
Retained earnings	3,500,000	18,000,000
Total liabilities and stockholders' equity		$24,500,000

Exhibit IV
Delhi Corporation
Condensed Balance Sheet
December 31, 1996

Sundry current assets		$12,000,000
Plant and equipment, net		72,000,000
Total assets		$84,000,000
Sundry liabilities		$ 7,500,000
Bank term loan due 1999 (6%)		13,500,000
Common stock, $1 par	$ 1,000,000	
Premium on common stock	3,500,000	
Retained earnings	58,500,000	63,000,000
Total liabilities and stockholders' equity		$84,000,000

Exhibit V
Eyre, Inc.
Condensed Balance Sheet
December 31, 1996

Sundry current assets		$ 50,000,000
Plant and equipment, net		88,000,000
Total assets		$138,000,000
Sundry liabilities		$ 28,000,000
8% debentures due 1/1/2007		50,000,000
Common stock, $10 par	$ 5,000,000	
Paid-in capital	6,200,000	
Retained earnings	48,800,000	60,000,000
Total liabilities and stockholders' equity		$138,000,000

All the foregoing balance sheets are before recording the business combinations.

The first task is to determine which, if any, of the four business combinations qualify for uniting-of-interests treatment. The first company to be acquired, Belfast Corporation, is to be obtained in exchange for only the issuing corporation's shares (which suggests a uniting). Prior to the merger, Belfast does own some of Ahmadi Corporation's shares, but there is no requirement in IAS 22 that prevents some cross-ownership prior to an acquisition or a uniting of interests. In the present instance, Belfast owned 5% of Ahmadi's common stock prior to the transaction, which is not deemed to be a deterrent to pooling accounting.

Of more importance under IAS 22 are such matters as continuity of interests, sharing of risks and rewards, and relative size of the combining parties. In the case of the Ahmadi–Belfast merger, book values are discrepant but not dramatically so ($72.9 million vs. $49.7 million); market values based on recent stock prices are also similar, but a bit less so than book values would suggest ($111 million vs. $72 million). On the other hand, the book value of Ahmadi is very similar to Belfast's fair value ($72.9 million vs. $76 million), which provides some support for the notion that these entities do not have significantly different values. Although this area remains one to which a good deal of judgment must be applied, it would appear that in this instance the relative values are close enough to warrant consideration of the pooling method of accounting. Since Belfast management will remain in place and the transaction is essentially a common stock exchange (with Belfast owners having about 35% of the total shares after the swap, before considering the effects of the other mergers), the conclusion in this case will be to permit designation of this transaction as a uniting of interests.

The Cairo Company, Inc. case is somewhat easier to resolve. In terms of relative market values, there is great disparity between the participants to this transaction ($111 million vs. $24 million), and even if the assessed fair value of Cairo's assets ($36 million) is considered, the gulf is probably too wide to bridge, in terms of satisfying IAS 22 criteria. More obviously, the fact that none of the Cairo owners and managers will continue in active roles belies the notion that there will be true coming together of the constituent parties' interests. Thus, notwithstanding that the former Cairo shareholders will continue as passive investors in Ahmadi, their perspective on the investment will almost certainly differ from that of active participants in the daily affairs of the company.

The Cairo transaction also includes an element of contingent consideration, with former Cairo stockholders eligible to receive additional Ahmadi shares if future earnings are greater than forecast. This does suggest a disparity of risks and rewards as between the two groups of owners, which would make it questionable to use pooling accounting even if the other problems noted did not exist. For all of the foregoing reasons, the conclusion will be that this transaction must be accounted for as an acquisition, not a uniting of interests.

The Delhi Corporation merger involves both cash and stock, raising a possible red flag since unitings of interest are, generally, purely stock swaps among the parties to the combination. However, the "only-stock" rule relates only to that which is issued by the acquirer for the acquired entity's **voting** stock; cash or other means of payment may be given in exchange for other securities (nonvoting equity or debt) of the entity acquired. In this case, Ahmadi gives an interest-bearing note for preexisting debt of Delhi, which does not affect the uniting of interests criteria. Also, the fact that a small minority of Delhi shareholders (owning 0.5% of its shares) are bought out for cash does not have any negative consequences, since this normally occurs in many business combinations of this type. The relative sizes of the combining entities (in terms of market value of stock, $111 million vs. $95 million) are extremely favorable to uniting treatment. Finally, continuity of management makes this combination clearly eligible for uniting-of-interests treatment.

Finally, consider the Eyre, Inc. merger. Common shares of Eyre are being obtained in exchange for a package of preferred and common Ahmadi shares, and additional common shares may be issued in the future if the market value of the shares originally given falls below a specified threshold.

The issuance of preferred stock that is nonvoting is a clear violation of the concept of an exchange of voting interests among the parties to the transaction. Effectively, about one-fourth of the purchase is being made for preferred stock, with the remaining three-fourths being paid for with common stock (based on relative market values of the preferred and common shares). Whether this tainting is sufficient to preclude the use of uniting of interests accounting is a matter of professional judgment, however.

More significantly, the Eyre shareholders are to be given a form of price protection in this transaction. The arrangement is for a remeasurement of the value of the consideration paid (Ahmadi's preferred and common stock) to be made in 2 years, with additional payments owed if there has been a market decline. This effectively means that the Eyre shareholders are not facing the same set of risks and rewards as are the Ahmadi shareholders, and this discrepancy means that this transaction is probably an acquisition, not a uniting of interests.

Furthermore, the market value of Eyre ($38 million) is vastly lower than that of Ahmadi, meaning that these transacting parties are not equals in terms of economic power and will not be equals in future operations of the combined operations. All told, therefore, it is clear that this transaction must be accounted for as an acquisition.

The necessary entries to record the Belfast and Delhi mergers as poolings on Ahmadi's books are as follows:

		Debit	Credit
1.	Sundry current assets	3,900,000	
	Plant and equipment (net)	38,500,000	
	Treasury stock	9,800,000	
	Sundry liabilities		2,500,000
	Common stock, $100 par		13,333,300
	Additional paid-in capital		21,366,700
	Retained earnings		15,000,000
	(To record Belfast acquisition by pooling)		
2.	Paid-in capital	475,000	
	Sundry current assets	12,000,000	
	Plant and equipment (net)	72,000,000	
	Sundry current assets (cash)		375,000
	Sundry liabilities		7,500,000
	Demand note payable		12,750,000
	Gain on retirement of debt		750,000
	Common stock, $100 par		4,975,000
	Retained earnings		58,125,000

(To record Delhi acquisition by pooling)

If, instead of a merger, the combination (acquisition) form is utilized, whereby Ahmadi shares are exchanged directly for Belfast and Delhi shares held by the respective stockholders of those companies, Belfast and Delhi will continue their separate existence (albeit as wholly-owned subsidiaries of Ahmadi Corporation). The entries to record the transactions assuming a pooling are as follows:

1. Investment in Belfast common	49,700,000	
Common stock, $100 par		13,333,300
Additional paid-in capital		21,366,700
Retained earnings		15,000,000
(To record acquisition of Belfast shares)		

2. Investment in Delhi common	63,000,000	
Due from Delhi	13,500,000	
Paid-in capital	475,000	
Notes payable		12,750,000
Cash		375,000
Gain on retirement of debt		750,000
Common stock, $100 par		4,975,000
Retained earnings		58,125,000

(To record acquisition of Delhi stock, payment of bank loan and retirement of minority shares for cash)

The purchase accounting entries will be presented in the following section, after the basic elements of this method of accounting for business combinations are discussed. Disclosure requirements for both acquisitions and unitings are set forth later in this chapter.

Acquisition Accounting

In most business combinations, one enterprise gains control over another, and the identity of the acquirer can readily be determined. Generally, the combining enterprise that obtains more than one-half of the voting rights of the other combining enterprises is the acquirer. In exceptional cases, the party that is the acquirer does not obtain over one-half of the voting rights; but the identity of the acquirer will be the party that obtains power

1. Over more than one-half of the voting rights of the other enterprise by virtue of agreement with the other investors (e.g., voting trust arrangements or other contractual provisions)
2. To govern the financial and operating policies of the other enterprise, under a statute or agreement
3. To appoint and remove the majority of the board of directors or equivalent governing body of the other enterprise

4. To cast the majority of votes at meetings of the board of directors or equivalent body

Other indicators of which party was the acquirer in any given business combination are as follows (these are **suggestive** only, not conclusive):

1. The fair value of one entity is significantly greater than that of the other combining enterprises; in such a case, the larger entity would be deemed the acquirer.
2. The combination is effected by an exchange of voting stock for cash; the entity paying the cash would be deemed to be the acquirer.
3. Management of one enterprise is able to dominate selection of management of the combined entity; the dominant entity would be deemed to be the acquirer.

The major accounting issue relates to the allocation of the purchase cost to the various assets and liabilities acquired. Where the legal form of combination is a merger or a consolidation, the acquirer records all the assets and liabilities purchased at their fair market values (not the book values of the acquired entity). If the actual cost exceeds the fair value of the identifiable net assets acquired, this excess is recorded as an intangible asset (goodwill). A deficiency of cost under fair value is first used to reduce the fair values of all noncurrent nonmonetary assets acquired, with any balance remaining recorded as a deferred credit (erroneously called negative goodwill). Both goodwill and the deferred credit (negative goodwill) must be amortized, generally by the straight-line method, to earnings over not more than 20 years (usually over not more than 5 years), according to IAS 22.

If the acquisition form of combination is used, the acquired entity maintains a separate legal and accounting existence and all assets and liabilities remain at their premerger book values. However, when an accounting consolidation is performed (i.e., when consolidated financial statements are prepared), exactly the same results are obtained as those outlined above (i.e., assets and liabilities are adjusted to fair values, and goodwill is recorded). When less than 100% of the stock of the acquired entity is owned by the acquirer, a complication arises in the preparation of consolidated statements, and a minority interest (discussed below) must be computed.

The other major distinguishing characteristic of the purchase accounting method is that none of the equity accounts of the acquired entity (including its retained earnings) will appear on the acquirer's books or on consolidated financial statements. In other words, ownership interests of the acquired entity's shareholders are **not** continued after the merger, consolidation, or combination (acquisition) takes place.

Reverse acquisitions. IAS 22 establishes the notion of reverse acquisitions. These are characterized by an entity issuing shares in exchange for shares in its target acquiree, such that control passes to the acquiree due to the number of additional shares issued by the acquirer. In such cases, notwithstanding the nominal or legal identification of the acquirer and acquiree, for accounting purposes the enterprise whose shareholders now control the combined entity is the acquirer.

Accounting for acquisitions. The purchase method is to be used to report acquisitions; the transaction is to be recorded in a manner similar to that applied to other purchases of assets. That is, the purchase price must be allocated among the various assets that are obtained, net of any liabilities assumed in the transaction, commensurate with the fair values of those assets. If the price equals the fair value of the net assets, the allocation process will be straightforward, with each asset being recorded at fair value. If the price exceeds the fair value of the net identifiable assets, a goodwill issue must be addressed, as discussed below, since the individual identifiable assets cannot be recorded at amounts greater than their respective fair values. Similarly, if the fair values of the net identifiable assets acquired exceeds the price paid, negative goodwill exists; this is also discussed later in this chapter.

The acquisition should be recognized as of the date it is effected, since this form of business combination is a discrete transaction occurring at a point in time, caused by a change in ownership and resulting in changes in the bases of accountability. The standard suggests that the critical date is that when control of the net assets and operations of the acquired entity is effectively transferred to the acquirer. One important consequence of this rule is that results of operations of the acquiree are included only from the date of the transaction. Financial statements for earlier periods are not restated to reflect the combination (although pro forma results for earlier periods can, of course, be presented for purposes of supplementary analysis).

Acquisitions should be accounted for at the cost paid or incurred. Cost is the amount of cash paid or the fair value of other consideration given to the shareholders of the acquired entity. It includes transaction costs such as legal and accounting fees, investment banking charges, and so on. Depending on the terms of the acquisition agreement, it may include certain contingent consideration as well (discussed below).

Individual assets and liabilities should be recognized separately at the date acquired, if it is both probable that any associated economic benefits will flow to the enterprise, and a reliable measure of cost or fair value to the acquirer is available. In the case of most acquisitions, these conditions will readily be met, since in an arm's-length transaction the parties normally will have knowledge of the price paid and the acquirer would not have consummated the purchase unless all the attendant benefits would flow to it in subsequent periods.

If the fair value of the identifiable net assets acquired is lower than the price paid, the excess cost should be allocated to goodwill (excess of cost over fair value of net assets acquired). If the fair value of the identifiable net assets acquired is greater than the price paid, the excess value should be allocated to negative goodwill (excess of fair value of net assets acquired over cost).

Determining purchase price. In some acquisitions, a package consisting of different forms of consideration may be given. As is often stipulated in accounting rules, the primary measure should be the fair value of any assets given up in the transaction; these may include, in addition to cash, promissory notes, shares of stock, and even operating assets of the acquirer. Except when actual cash is exchanged, fair values may differ from book values. Thus, promissory notes may carry a rate of interest other than a market rate, in which case a premium or discount will be ascribed to the obligation. (For example, if a $10 million, 5% interest-bearing 2-year note is proffered in a business acquisition, in an environment where the buyer would normally pay 8% on borrowed funds, the actual purchase price will be computed as being somewhat lower than the nominal $10 million.)

Similarly, the acquirer's common stock will virtually always have a market value different from par or stated amounts. If there is an active market for the shares, reference should be made to the price quoted, although a small discount might be imputed to reflect the fact that a large offering of new shares would, in a perfect market, have a depressing effect on price. If the market price on any given day is not deemed to be a reliable indicator, the prices over a period of days before and after the announcement of the terms of the acquisition transaction should be considered. If the stock is thinly traded, or not traded at all, or if shares in a listed company are offered with restrictions (not salable for a fixed period of time, etc.), it would be necessary to ascertain a reasonable value, possibly in consultation with investment bankers or other experts. In extreme cases, the fair value of the proportionate interest in the acquired entity's net assets, or the fair value of the fraction of the acquirer's net assets represented by the shares issued would be used as a measure, whichever is more objectively determinable. If dissenting minority shareholders of the acquiree are paid in cash, the price paid may also serve as a reliable indicator of the value of the transaction. Of course, the parties to the transaction, being at arm's length, should also be able to place an objective value on the stock being exchanged, inasmuch as they had negotiated for this price.

If the acquirer exchanges certain of its assets, either operating assets that had been subject to depreciation, or investment securities or other investments assets, such as idle land, for the stock of the acquired entity, again an assessment of fair value must be made. Book value, even if the assets had been adjusted to fair value under the alternative treatment permitted by IAS 16, could not be taken as being fair value for purposes of accounting for the business combination, unless corroborated by other evidence.

If the acquisition is to be paid for on a deferred basis, the cost to be reflected will be the present value of the future payments, discounted at the acquiring entity's normal borrowing cost, given the terms of the arrangement.

Step acquisitions. In many instances, control over another entity is not achieved in a single transaction, but rather, after a series of such transactions. For example, one enterprise may acquire a 25% interest in another entity, followed by another 20% some time later, and then followed by another 10% at yet a later date. The last step gives the acquirer a 55% interest and thus control. The accounting concern is at what point in time the business combination took place and how to measure the cost of the acquisition.

IAS 22 stipulates that the cost of the acquisition is measured with reference to the cost and fair value data as of **each** exchange transaction. In the foregoing example, therefore, it would be necessary to look to the consideration paid for each of the three separate purchases of stock; if noncash, these would have to be valued as described earlier in this section. To the extent that the value of the consideration given differed from the fair value of the underlying net assets, measured at the date of the respective exchange, goodwill or negative goodwill would have to be recognized. Conceivably, successive purchases could be at premiums over and discounts from fair values.

In the example above, the first acquisition results in a 25% holding in the investee, which is over the threshold where significant influence is assumed to be exerted by the investor. Thus, the equity method should be employed beginning at the time of the first exchange and continuing through the second exchange (when a 45% ownership interest is achieved). Application of the equity method is explained in Chapter 9; one important aspect, however, is that the difference between cost and the fair value of the underlying interest in the net assets of the investee is to be treated as goodwill or negative goodwill and accounted for consistent with the provisions of IAS 22. Accordingly, this needs to be computed and then amortized as discussed in this chapter. The amount of unamortized goodwill (or negative goodwill) at the date of the next exchange transaction should not be merged into the next computation of goodwill, lest the amortization period for the first component be inadvertently extended beyond the limitations of the standard. In other words, each step in the transaction sequence should be accounted for as a separate acquisition.

The only exception to the foregoing requirements would occur if, as permitted under IAS 25, the entire investment is revalued to fair value at the dates of subsequent share purchases. Under this scenario, each revaluation must be accounted for as such, with the appropriate disclosures being made in the financial statements.

When control (majority ownership) is finally achieved (the third step acquisition in the example above), if an accounting consolidation is performed to produce consolidated financial statements, the fair values to be presented for the acquired entity's assets would be an appropriate blending of the fair values as of the various steps in the acquisition. In the present case, for example, using the benchmark treatment specified in IAS 22 (discussed in detail below), 25% of each asset would be reported at the fair value as of the date of the first exchange, another 20% at the fair value as of the date of the second exchange, and the final 10% at the fair value as of the date of the third exchange, with the remaining 45% of the asset stated at cost, that is, at the predecessor entity's carrying value.

Recording the Assets Acquired and Liabilities Assumed

The assets acquired and liabilities assumed in the business combination should be recorded at fair values. If the acquirer obtained a 100% interest in the acquired entity, or if a legal merger were effected, this process is straightforward. As suggested above, if the cost exceeds the fair value of the net assets acquired, the excess is deemed to be goodwill, and capitalized as an intangible asset, subject to amortization. If the fair value of net assets exceeds total cost, the difference is referred to as negative goodwill and is subjected to one of two treatments: either offset against nonmonetary assets, or credited to a liability account and later amortized (these are discussed in detail below).

Determining fair market values. The purchase method requires a determination of the fair market value for each of the acquired company's identifiable tangible and intangible assets and for each of its liabilities at the date of combination. The determination of these fair market values is crucial for proper application of the purchase method. The list below indicates how this is done for various assets and liabilities.

1. **Marketable securities**--Current market values.
2. **Nonmarketable securities**--Estimated fair values, determined on a basis consistent with relevant price-earnings ratios, dividend yields, and expected growth rates of comparable securities of entities having similar characteristics.
3. **Receivables**--Present values of amounts to be received determined by using current interest rates, less allowances for uncollectible accounts.
4. **Inventories**

   a. Finished goods and merchandise inventories--Estimated selling prices less the sum of the costs of disposal and a reasonable profit.
   b. Work-in-process inventories--Estimated selling prices of finished goods less the sum of the costs of completion, costs of disposal, and a reasonable profit.
   c. Raw material inventories--Current replacement costs.

5. **Plant and equipment**

   a. If expected to be used in operations--Current market value as determined by appraisal. Absent this evidence, because of the specialized nature or because of the infrequency of transactions other than as part of a continuing business, at depreciated replacement cost.
   b. If expected to be used only temporarily--At the lower of current replacement cost for similar productive capacity, or net realizable value.
   c. If to be sold--Current net realizable value.

6. **Identifiable intangible assets** (such as patents and licenses)--Estimated fair value.
7. **Net pension assets or obligations** for defined benefit plans--The actuarial present value of promised retirement benefits, net of the fair value of related assets. (Note that an asset can be recognized only to the extent that it would be available to the enterprise.)
8. **Tax assets and liabilities**--The amount of tax benefit arising from tax losses or the taxes payable in respect to net earnings or loss, assessed from the perspective of the combined entity or group resulting from the acquisition. The amount to be recorded is net of the tax effect of restating other identifiable assets and liabilities at fair values.
9. **Liabilities** (such as notes and accounts payable, long-term debt, warranties, claims payable)--Present value of amounts to be paid determined at appropriate current interest rates.
10. **Unfavorable contract obligations**--At the present value of the amounts to be disbursed, including any amounts (plant closures, etc.) arising incidental to the acquisition.

IAS 22 explicitly requires that in certain cases, such as for monetary liabilities, fair value be determined by the use of discounting. In other instances, such as for intangible assets, discounting is not explicitly prescribed. However, the standard permits the use of discounting in determining fair values of any identifiable assets and liabilities.

Since aggregate purchase cost is allocated to the identifiable assets (and liabilities) according to their respective fair values to the acquirer, assets having no value are assigned no cost. For example, facilities of the acquired entity that duplicate those of the acquirer and are to be disposed of should be assigned a cost equal to estimated net salvage value, or zero if no salvage is anticipated. In rare instances, however, a **negative** cost equal to the estimated costs of disposal is assigned. It could also be reasonably argued that holding costs should be allocated to assets to be disposed of when debt from the business acquisition is to be paid down from the proceeds of such asset sales. In effect, the value assigned to such assets to be sold would be the present value of the estimated selling price; interest incurred on debt used to finance these assets would then be charged to the asset rather than to interest expense until the disposition actually occurs. On the other hand, if facilities of the acquired entity duplicate and are superior to facilities of the purchaser, with the intention that the latter will be disposed of, fair value must be allocated to the former. Eventual disposition of the redundant facilities of the **acquirer** may later result in a recognized gain or loss. This would fall into the general category of indirect costs of acquisition, which are not capitalizable or allocable to assets acquired in the purchase business combination.

Allocation of Cost of Acquisition When the Acquirer Obtains Less Than 100% of the Acquiree's Voting Interest

When an acquirer obtains a majority interest, but not 100% ownership, in another entity, the process of recording the transaction will be more complicated. The portion of the acquired operation not owned by the acquirer, but claimed (in an economic sense) by outside interests, is referred to as **minority interest**. The accounting issue is whether, in a situation in which goodwill or negative goodwill will be reported, to value it with reference only to the price paid by the new (majority) owner, or whether to gross up the balance sheet for the minority's share as well. In general, an actual arm's-length transaction must take place before a new value can be placed on existing assets and operations (although under IAS 16 revaluations of plant assets can be made). Since the minority did not partake of the acquisition transaction, it can be argued that there is no basis on which to posit any recognition of goodwill for its share of the acquired entity.

The counterargument usually posed is that the majority change in ownership in such a situation is the most objective recent evidence of the value of the acquired enterprise. Furthermore, not to reflect the minority's interest at current market value would be to create a balance sheet having an amalgamation of dissimilar costs, some new, some old. In fact, in some countries the concept of push-down accounting (also known as new-basis accounting) had gained currency, and some regulatory authorities, including the US Securities and Exchange Commission (SEC), demand the application of this form of accounting within very narrowly defined circumstances. Due to the strength of arguments on both sides of this debate, the international accounting standards setters have decided to permit both approaches, as described further in the following paragraphs.

Benchmark treatment. Assets and liabilities recognized are measured at the aggregate of the fair value of the identifiable assets and liabilities acquired as of the date of the exchange transaction, to the extent of the acquirer's interest obtained in the transaction; plus the minority's proportion of the preacquisition carrying amounts of the assets and liabilities of the subsidiary (acquiree). This means that there will be no step up of the minority interest to reflect the valuation indirectly being placed on the enterprise being acquired by the new majority owner.

Under this benchmark approach, the minority interest shown in a consolidated balance sheet will be the minority percentage times the net assets of the subsidiary as reported in the subsidiary's stand-alone balance sheet. Goodwill will be reported to reflect only the excess paid by the majority owner in excess of the fair value of the net identifiable assets acquired. This is illustrated in an example later in the chapter.

The logic of this approach is its adherence to the cost principle. Since the new parent/majority owner has effectively acquired only a fraction of the acquired entity's assets and liabilities, only that fraction should logically be revalued to reflect the purchase price. The remaining fraction, representing the minority shareholders' interests, has not been acquired and therefore should not, under a cost concept approach, be revalued. This method of accounting treats business acquisitions like any other type of asset acquisition.

Allowed alternative treatment. All identifiable (i.e., excluding goodwill) assets and liabilities are recognized at their respective fair values, including those corresponding to the minority's ownership interest. This means that there is a step up in value to equal the valuation being placed on the enterprise indirectly by the new majority owner.

Under this approach, the minority interest shown in a consolidated balance sheet will be the minority percentage times the net assets of the subsidiary as reported in the parent's consolidated balance sheet. Goodwill will be reported, as under the benchmark treatment, to reflect only the excess paid by the majority owner in excess of the fair value of the net identifiable assets acquired. This, too, is illustrated in a later example.

This approach uses the purchase price for the majority interest as an indicator of the value of the entire acquired entity. The strength of this approach is that the acquired entity's assets and liabilities are valued on a consistent basis, presumably using the most recent, objectively determined valuation data. Since international accounting standards recognize the validity of revaluations of certain assets (see the discussion of IAS 16 in Chapter 8 and of IAS 25 in Chapter 9), this approach is not really a conceptual departure from accepted practice.

Example of accounting for a purchase

Continuing the Ahmadi Corporation example begun in the uniting of interests discussion earlier in this chapter, the journal entries to record the purchase of the Cairo Company, Inc. and Eyre, Inc. shares will be presented. Tax effects are ignored in these examples.

Using the fair market value information given earlier and assuming that a legal merger (or consolidation) form is used, Ahmadi makes these entries:

		Debit	Credit
1.	Sundry current assets	4,000,000	
	Plant and equipment	19,080,000	
	Treasury stock	3,100,000	
	Sundry liabilities		6,500,000
	Common stock, $100 par		4,000,000
	Additional paid-in capital		15,680,000
	(To record purchase of net assets of Cairo)		
2.	Sundry current assets	50,000,000	
	Plant and equipment	108,000,000	
	Sundry liabilities		28,000,000
	8% debentures		50,000,000
	Preferred stock, $100 par		17,500,000
	Premium on preferred		1,000,000
	Common stock, $100 par		12,500,000

Additional paid-in capital		49,000,000
(To record purchase of net assets of Eyre)		

The value of the Cairo purchase was determined by reference to the latest market value of the Ahmadi shares given ($492 per share). Notice that although the price paid (based on the market value of Ahmadi shares given up) was slightly greater than Cairo's net **book** value ($19.68 million vs. $18 million), it was considerably less than estimated fair value ($36 million, net). In other words, there was an excess of fair value over cost that, in accordance with the procedures specified by IAS 22, was allocated against plant and equipment (the only nonmonetary asset). Had this deficiency been large enough to reduce plant and equipment to zero, any remaining amount would have been recorded as a deferred credit (excess of fair value of net assets acquired over cost) and amortized systematically, like goodwill, over not more than 5 years, unless a longer life, not in excess of 20 years, could be justified. Implicitly, of course, by offsetting the negative goodwill against nonmonetary assets, it will be amortized over the depreciable lives of these assets.

The total value of the Eyre purchase was $80 million ($61.5 million of common shares, measured at the market value of $492 each multiplied by the 125,000 shares given, plus 175,000 shares of preferred having an approximate value of $105.70 each). The total price exceeded the net book value of Eyre's identifiable assets, although it was still lower than the fair value thereof, so here again there is an excess of fair value over cost (i.e., negative goodwill), and the noncurrent assets are recorded at less than their fair values.

If the shares are to be held by the parent as an investment instead (i.e., the companies are not to be legally combined), the entries by the parent company would be as follows:

1. Investment in Cairo common	19,680,000	
Common stock, $100 par		4,000,000
Additional paid-in capital		15,680,000
2. Investment in Eyre common	80,000,000	
Preferred stock, $100 par		17,500,000
Premium on preferred		1,000,000
Common stock, $100 par		12,500,000
Additional paid-in capital		49,000,000

Goodwill and Negative Goodwill

Goodwill. Goodwill represents the excess purchase price paid in a business acquisition over the fair value of the identifiable net assets obtained. Presumably, when an acquiring enterprise pays this premium price, it sees value that transcends the worth of the tangible assets and the identifiable intangibles, or else the deal would not have been consummated on such terms. Goodwill arising from acquisitions must be recognized as an asset and then amortized over a useful life not exceeding 5 years, unless a longer life can be demonstrated. A longer life, not to exceed 20 years, can sometimes be justified by reference to factors such as the foreseeable life of the business or industry; the effects of physical obsolescence, changes in demand, and other economic factors; the service life expectations of key individuals or groups of workers; any expected actions by competitors or potential competitors; and legal, regulatory, or contractual provisions affecting the useful life. In general, goodwill would have to be related closely to such identifiable assets as a patent or specific productive plant assets such as buildings, if a life longer than 5 years is to be supported. Because of the inherent uncertainty of the economic life of goodwill, however, the standards demand that in all cases a maximum life of 20 years be used. As of the date of this publication, the IASC has proposed that the 20-year limit on the amortization period for goodwill be lifted, consistent with the attempt to unify guidance in the standards on all intangible assets. According to the proposal, lives longer than 20 years will be permitted, but if a longer amortization period is specified, the asset will need to be tested for impairment annually, employing the methodology set forth in the IASC's draft on impairment, E55, which is discussed in Chapter 8.

The amortization of recorded goodwill should be accomplished using the straight-line method in most cases, since it would be unusual, although not inconceivable, to be able to demonstrate a different pattern of expiration of value. Furthermore, the balance in the goodwill account should be reviewed at each balance sheet date to determine whether the asset had suffered any impairment. If goodwill is no longer deemed probable of being fully recovered through the profitable operations of the acquired business, it should be partially written down or fully written off. Any write-off of goodwill must be charged to expense just as normal amortization is. Once written down, goodwill cannot later be restored as an asset, again reflecting the concern that the measurement of goodwill is difficult and proof of its existence almost impossible to develop.

Under the predecessor standard IAS 22 (issued in 1983 and superseded by revised IAS 22 in 1993), a permitted alternative treatment was to charge off goodwill against stockholders' equity immediately as of the date of the business combination. The logic of doing this was based on the aforementioned difficulty in demonstrating the existence of goodwill; thus, a more conservative approach that eliminated this questionable asset from the balance sheet immediately was advocated. However, in the interest of narrowing the range of acceptable alternatives to specific accounting issues, the revised IAS 22 has eliminated this option.

It should be noted that goodwill is recorded, in the case of acquisitions of less than 100%, only for the price paid by the new parent company in excess of the fair values of the net identifiable assets of the subsidiary. That is, no goodwill is imputed to the minority interests based on the price paid by the majority. While under the allowed alternative (see below) the net identifiable assets attributable to the minority may be written up to the values implied by the majority's purchase decision, goodwill will not be imputed for the minority share.

Negative goodwill from business acquisitions. Although the term **negative goodwill** sounds oxymoronic, since goodwill must be a positive good, in many business combinations there is an element of bargain purchase that gives rise to what has become popularly, and now officially, known as negative goodwill. This represents the shortfall of the purchase price paid in a business acquisition vs. the fair value of the net identifiable assets so obtained. It may be indicative of certain future costs that will have to be borne by the buyer to restore the profitability of the acquired operations, or may simply mean that the acquirer has achieved a favorable deal. In any event, this difference between cost and fair value must be accounted for in a manner analogous to (positive) goodwill.

Under the provisions of the original IAS 22 standard, three alternative treatments for negative goodwill were permitted. These included immediately writing off negative goodwill to equity (which would increase stockholders' equity), offsetting negative goodwill against the recorded amount of the nonmonetary assets acquired in the business combination, and amortizing negative goodwill in a manner akin to positive goodwill.

The logic of immediate write-off of negative goodwill is essentially the same as the immediate expensing of positive goodwill. Since the liability is as difficult to explain, if not more so, as the asset goodwill, many accountants and others in the business community believed it would be a more conservative approach to eliminate this item from the balance sheet. However, while immediate expensing of goodwill is conservative in the sense that it minimizes the reported net worth of the acquirer, immediate write-off of negative goodwill increases net worth, and thus can hardly be justified as a conservative accounting procedure.

A more intellectually appealing argument in support of immediately writing off negative goodwill was the capital from consolidation thesis. This held that since the acquiring entity had negotiated a bargain purchase, the financial reporting impact of that action should be reflected at once. The counterargument, however, is more impressive: Entities do not generate earnings or net worth by purchasing assets, but rather, by using those assets in a productive manner. Thus, if negative goodwill indeed represents the result of a bargain acquisition, it should be taken into earnings over the useful period of the acquired assets.

It was the latter argument that led directly to the second proposed method of accounting for negative goodwill--offsetting it against certain assets acquired in the business combination transaction. By reducing the carrying value of such assets, future periods would be relieved of some (or all) of the depreciation charges with which they would otherwise have been burdened. This conforms more closely to the matching concept, which is a basic underlying postulate of accrual basis accounting, as required under the international accounting standards. As originally promulgated, IAS 22 permitted negative goodwill to be offset against nonmonetary assets acquired in the business combination (other standards apply a slight variation to this: under US GAAP, the offset is against noncurrent assets); this continues under the revised standard.

The third alternative treatment is also easily understood, and essentially accomplishes the same matching goal as the second method, above. Just as positive goodwill is recorded as an asset, subject to amortization, negative goodwill is placed on the balance sheet and amortized. The difference is that negative goodwill, having a credit balance, must be grouped with the liabilities, when in fact this does not represent a real obligation at all. Analogies to deferred revenue can be made, and have been, but these have limited appeal, since other deferred revenues represent collections in advance from customers along with the concomitant obligation to perform future services for them or to deliver goods to them in the future. Notwithstanding this conceptual limitation, reporting negative goodwill as a liability and amortizing it over the useful period of the related identifiable assets does accomplish the goal of matching future revenues with related costs. It does so, however, at the price of having "grossed up" the balance sheet, which the previously noted approach has the virtue of avoiding.

The achievement of the revised IAS 22 is that the first-named method, immediately crediting negative goodwill to shareholders' interests (equity), has been eliminated. The other two methods, recording negative goodwill as a liability and amortizing it over a period of no more than 5 years, (or 20 years if convincing evidence can be accumulated to support that), or offsetting against nonmonetary assets obtained in the acquisition (with any excess recorded as a liability and amortized), remain allowable.

The benchmark treatment under IAS 22 is to reduce the carrying value of all nonmonetary assets acquired on a pro rata basis. Thus, it is not acceptable to select particular assets to absorb the negative goodwill: Assets that have a short life, such as inventories, will have to be credited with proportionately the same amount of negative goodwill as long-lived assets such as building and land. If the nonmonetary assets fully absorb the negative goodwill, any remaining balances in the assets will be accounted for normally. Thus, inventories will flow into cost of sales as the goods are disposed of, most plant assets will be depreciated over their respective useful economic lives, and some others, such as land, will be carried without modification (unless revaluation accounting is employed, as described in Chapter 8) until the asset is disposed of.

If the aggregate amount of nonmonetary assets, before absorbing negative goodwill, is less than the computed amount of negative goodwill from the business acquisition, these assets will be reduced to zero, and the remaining, unabsorbed negative goodwill will be accounted for as deferred income and amortized in the same manner as goodwill (see above).

IAS 22 also provides for an allowed alternative treatment, under which the negative goodwill is not offset against nonmonetary assets but is reported gross as deferred income. Negative goodwill is amortized as discussed above: generally on a straight-line basis, over no more than 5 years, unless a reason can be demonstrated to extent this to as long as 20 years. (Since amortization of negative goodwill **increases** reported earnings, there will be few reporting entities seeking support for a longer amortization period.)

The IASC has recently proposed to eliminate the benchmark treatment for negative goodwill. If this is done, the current alternative treatment, reporting the gross amount of negative goodwill as deferred income, to be amortized over a period currently established as a 20-year maximum, will become the required methodology. Other minor changes may also be made, and readers should be alert to the fact that this area is being currently reexamined.

Contingent Consideration

In some business combinations, the purchase price is not fixed at the time of the exchange, but is instead dependent on future events. There are two major types of future events that can be used to affect the purchase price: the performance of the acquired entity, and the market value of the consideration given for the acquisition.

If the amount of the contingent consideration is likely to be incurred and can be measured reliably at the date of the acquisition, it should be included in the cost of the acquisition. If the contingent consideration is not paid later, adjustments to certain amounts recorded need to be made: The usual effects are to adjust goodwill or negative goodwill, but other assets may need adjustment if negative goodwill was offset against nonmonetary assets according to the benchmark treatment. In other cases, resolution of an uncertainty after the date of the acquisition will necessitate recording contingent consideration, which should be recognized when probable and subject to reliable estimation.

The accounting for subsequent payment of the added consideration, if the effects had not been accrued at the date of the business combination as described above, depends on whether the contingency was related to the earnings of the acquired entity or to the market value of the original consideration package given by the acquirer.

In the former instance (exemplified by the purchase of Cairo Corp. in the example presented earlier), a later payment of added cash, stock, or any other valuable consideration will require revaluation of the purchase price. This revaluation could alter the amounts allocable to noncurrent assets (where cost in the original purchase transaction was less than fair value acquired and the difference was offset against those assets), or could result in an increased amount of goodwill being recognized. The effects of a revaluation are handled prospectively: The additional amortization of goodwill and/or fixed assets is allocated to the remaining economic lives of those items, without adjustment of any postacquisition periods' results already reported.

In the latter case (exemplified by the Eyre Co. merger in the earlier illustration), the event triggering the issuance of additional shares is a decline in market value of the original purchase package. The total value of the purchase ($80,000,000 in the Epsilon case) would not be changed and thus no alteration of allocated amounts would be needed. However, the issuance of extra shares of common stock will require that the allocation between the common stock and the additional paid-in capital accounts be adjusted. Had part of the original price been bonds or other debt, the reallocation could have affected the premium or discount on the debt, which would have an impact on future earnings as these accounts are subsequently amortized.

Consolidated Financial Statements

Requirements for consolidated financial statements. IAS 27 prescribes the requirements for the presentation of consolidated financial statements. Essentially, if one entity controls another enterprise, consolidated financial statements are required, unless certain, rarely met conditions are satisfied. Control is deemed to exist when the parent owns, directly or indirectly through subsidiaries, more than one-half of the voting power over an enterprise. It may also exist even absent this level of ownership if the parent has more than one-half the voting power as a result of a voting trust or similar arrangement; the power to govern the financial and operating policies of the enterprise by operation of law or by means of an agreement, the power to appoint or remove the majority of the directors or equivalent governing persons, or the power to cast a majority of votes at the meetings of the directors or its equivalent.

In limited circumstances, a majority owner may not have operating control over an enterprise, and consolidated financial reporting would not be deemed appropriate in such cases. This would be true when control is intended to be temporary, because the subsidiary was acquired with the definite intention to dispose of it in the near future. It would also be valid if the subsidiary operates under severe, long-term restrictions which limit its ability to remit funds to its parent entity. In either of these types of situations, the parent should account for its interest in the subsidiary as set forth in IAS 25 (discussed in Chapter 9).

It had previously been common to exclude subsidiaries from consolidated financial statements on the basis of nonhomogeneity of operations. For example, an integrated manufacturer might have excluded a financing subsidiary from its consolidated financial statements, since (it was argued) the operations were so dissimilar any resulting consolidated statements would have been impossible to interpret. IAS 27 makes it clear that such reasons are no longer acceptable; if the consolidated statements need further explanation for them to be meaningful, supplementary consolidating statements, showing details for each constituent entity, or detailed footnote schedules can be used to satisfy this need.

Intercompany transactions and balances. In preparing consolidated financial statements, any transactions among members of the group must be eliminated. For example, a parent may sell merchandise to its subsidiary, at cost or with a profit margin added, before the subsidiary ultimately sells the merchandise to unrelated parties in arm's-length transactions. Furthermore, any balances due to or from members of the consolidated group at the date of the balance sheet must also be eliminated. The reason for this requirement: to avoid grossing up the financial statements for transactions or balances that do not represent economic events with outside parties. Were this rule not in effect, a consolidated group could deliberately give the appearance of being a much larger enterprise than it is in truth, merely by engaging in multiple transactions with itself.

If assets have been transferred among the entities in the controlled group at amounts in excess of the transferor's cost, and they have not yet been further transferred to outside parties (e.g., inventories) or not yet consumed (e.g., plant assets subject to depreciation) by the date of the balance sheet, the amount of profit not yet realized through an arm's-length transaction must be eliminated. This is illustrated in the following examples.

Different fiscal periods of parent and subsidiary. A practical consideration in preparing consolidated financial statements is to have information on all constituent entities current as of the parent's year end. If the subsidiaries have different fiscal years, they may prepare updated information as of the parent's year end, to be used for preparing consolidated statements. Failing this, IAS 27 permits combining information as of different dates, as long as this discrepancy does not exceed 3 months. Of course, if this option is elected, the process of eliminating intercompany transactions and balances may become a bit more complicated, since reciprocal accounts (e.g., sales and cost of sales) will be out of balance for any events occurring after the earlier fiscal year end but before the later one.

Consistency of accounting policies. There is a presumption that all the members of the consolidated group should use the same accounting principles to account for similar events and transactions. However, in many cases this will not occur, as, for example, when a subsidiary is acquired that uses FIFO costing for its inventories while the parent has long employed the LIFO method. IAS 27 does not demand that one or the other entity change its method of accounting; rather, it merely requires that there be adequate disclosure of the accounting principles employed.

If a subsidiary was acquired during the period or was disposed of during the period, under the acquisition method of accounting, the results of the operations of the subsidiary should be included in consolidated financial statements only for the period it was owned. Since this may cause comparability with earlier periods presented to be impaired, there must be adequate disclosure in the accompanying footnotes to make it possible to interpret the information properly.

Example of consolidation workpaper (date of acquisition, 100% ownership)

The worksheet for the preparation of a consolidated balance sheet for Ahmadi Corp. and its four wholly-owned subsidiaries at the date of the acquisitions is shown below. Remember that it is presumed that Ahmadi (the parent) acquired the common stock of each subsidiary; had it acquired the net assets directly (through a legal merger or a consolidation), this **accounting consolidation** would not be necessary.

Except for Eyre, the entries are straightforward and need no further explanation, as they are necessary to eliminate the investment accounts of the parent and the equity accounts of the subsidiaries. Note that there are upward adjustments to the plant and equipment relative to the **acquisitions** of Cairo and Eyre. The **unitings** of Belfast and Delhi result in their book values being carried forward.

The elimination of the investment in Eyre debentures needs explanation. The parent paid $4,880,000 for debentures having a $5 million par on January 1, 1995. The discount has been properly amortized in 1995 and 1996, so that the carrying value at the date of acquisition of Eyre is $4,900,000. Therefore, on a consolidated basis, debt of $5 million has been extinguished at a cost of $4.9 million, for a gain on retirement of $100,000. Since the workpapers shown are only for the preparation of a consolidated balance sheet, the gain has been credited to retained earnings. This gain could also be recorded on the books of the parent, Ahmadi Corp., that would make its retained earnings equal to consolidated retained earnings.

Ahmadi Corporation and Subsidiaries
Workpapers for Consolidated Balance Sheet
As of December 31, 1996

	Ahmadi Corp.	*Belfast Corp.*	*Cairo Co., Inc.*	*Delhi Corp.*	*Eyre, Inc.*	*Elimination entries*	*Consolidated balance sheet*
Current assets	$ 74,625,000	$ 3,900,000	$ 4,000,000	$12,000,000	$ 50,000,000	$ --	$144,525,000
Plant and equipment	80,000,000	38,500,000	17,400,000	72,000,000	88,000,000	1,680,000 [c]	317,580,000
						5,000,000 [f]	
Investments:							
Eyre 8% debentures	4,900,000					(4,900,000) [g]	
Ahmadi stock		9,800,000	3,100,000			(9,800,000) [b]	
						(3,100,000) [d]	
Belfast Corp.	49,700,000					(49,700,000) [a]	
Cairo Co., Inc.	19,680,000					(19,680,000) [c]	
Delhi Corp.	76,500,000					(25,500,000) [e]	
Eyre, Inc.	80,000,000					(20,000,000) [f]	
	$385,405,000	$52,200,000	$24,500,000	$84,000,000	$138,000,000		$462,105,000
Current liabilities	$ 99,750,000	$ 2,500,000	$ 6,500,000	$21,000,000	$ 28,000,000	$(13,500,000) [e]	$144,250,000
8% debentures					50,000,000	(5,000,000) [g]	45,000,000
Preferred stock, $100 par	17,500,000						17,500,000
Premium on pfd. stock	1,000,000						1,000,000
Common stock:							
$100 par	57,308,300						57,308,300
$10 par		20,000,000				(20,000,000) [a]	
No par			14,500,000			(14,500,000) [c]	
$1 par				1,000,000		(1,000,000) [e]	

$10 par					5,000,000	(5,000,000) [f]	
Additional paid-in capital, etc.	97,771,700	14,700,000		3,500,000	6,200,000	(14,700,000) [a] (3,500,000) [e] (6,200,000) [f]	97,771,700
Retained earnings	112,075,000	15,000,000	3,500,000	58,500,000	48,800,000	(15,000,000) [a] (3,500,000) [c] (58,500,000) [e] (48,800,000) [f] 100,000 [g]	112,175,000
	$385,405,000	$52,200,000	$24,500,000	$84,000,000	$34,500,000		
Treasury stock (at cost)						(9,800,000) [b] (3,100,000) [d]	(12,900,000)
							$462,105,000

Consolidated Statements in Subsequent Periods, With Minority Interests

When a company acquires some, but not all, of the voting stock of another entity, the shares held by third parties represent a **minority interest** in the acquired company. This occurs when the acquisition form is employed. A legal merger or consolidation would give the acquirer a 100% interest in whatever assets it obtained from the selling entity. Under international accounting standards, if a parent company owns more than half of another entity, the two should be consolidated for financial statement purposes (unless to do so would mislead the statement users because control is temporary or the businesses are heterogeneous, etc.). The minority interest in the assets and earnings of the consolidated entity must also be accounted for.

When consolidated statements are prepared, the full amount of assets and liabilities (in the balance sheet) and income and expenses (in the income statement) of the subsidiary are generally presented. Accordingly, a contra must be shown for the portion of these items that does not belong to the parent company. In the balance sheet this contra is normally a credit item shown between total liabilities and stockholders' equity, representing the minority interest in consolidated net assets equal to the minority's percentage ownership in the net assets of the subsidiary entity. Although less likely, a debit balance in minority interest could result when the subsidiary has a deficit in its stockholders' equity and when there is reason to believe that the minority owners will make additional capital contributions to erase that deficit. This situation sometimes occurs where the entities are closely held and the minority owners are related parties having other business relationships with the parent company and/or its stockholders. In other circumstances, a debit in minority interest would be charged against parent company retained earnings under the concept that the loss will be borne by that company.

IAS 27 stipulates that minority interest be presented in the consolidated balance sheet separately from both liabilities and stockholders' equity. Accordingly, it will be shown in a separate caption after liabilities, but ahead of equity.

In the income statement, the minority interest in the income (or loss) of a consolidated subsidiary is shown as a deduction from (or addition to) the consolidated net income account. As above, if the minority interest in the net assets of the subsidiary has already been reduced to zero, and if a net debit minority interest will not be recorded (the usual case), the minority's interest in any further losses should not be recorded. (However, this must be explained in the footnotes.) Furthermore, if past minority losses have not been recorded, the minority's interest in current profits will not be recognized until the aggregate of such profits equals the aggregate unrecognized losses. This closely parallels the rule for equity method accounting recognition of profits and losses.

IAS 27 states that income attributable to minority interest be separately presented in the statement of earnings or operations. Generally, this is accomplished by presenting net income before minority interest, followed by the allocation to the minority, and then followed by net income.

Example of consolidation process involving a minority interest

Assume the following:

Alto Company and Bass Company
Balance Sheets at January 1, 1996
(before combination)

	Alto Company	*Bass Company*
Assets		
Cash	$ 30,900	$ 37,400
Accounts receivable (net)	34,200	9,100
Inventories	22,900	16,100
Equipment	200,000	50,000
Less accumulated depreciation	(21,000)	(10,000)
Patents	--	10,000
Total assets	$267,000	$112,600
Liabilities and stockholders' equity		
Accounts payable	$ 4,000	$ 6,600
Bonds payable, 10%	100,000	--
Common stock, $10 par	100,000	50,000
Additional paid-in capital	15,000	15,000
Retained earnings	48,000	41,000
Total liabilities and stockholders' equity	$267,000	$112,600

Note that in the foregoing, the net assets of Bass Company may be computed by one of two methods.

Method 1: Subtract the book value of the liability from the book values of the assets:

$112,600 – $6,600 = $106,000

Method 2: Add the book value of the components of Bass Company's stockholders' equity:

$50,000 + $15,000 + $41,000 = $106,000

At the date of the combination, the fair value of all the assets and liabilities were determined by appraisal, as follows:

Bass Company Item	*Book value (BV)*	*Fair market value (FMV)*	*Difference between BV and FMV*
Cash	$ 37,400	$ 37,400	$ --
Accounts receivable (net)	9,100	9,100	--
Inventories	16,100	17,100	1,000
Equipment (net)	40,000	48,000	8,000
Patents	10,000	13,000	3,000
Accounts payable	(6,600)	(6,600)	--
Totals	$106,000	$118,000	$12,000

When a minority interest exists, as in this example, the concept employed will determine whether the consolidated balance sheet reflects the full excess of fair market values over book values of the subsidiary's identifiable net assets, or only the parent company's percentage share thereof. Under the provisions of IAS 22, both approaches are acceptable. The benchmark treatment is to recognize a "step up" for only the share of the subsidiary's assets that have effectively been purchased by the parent; thus the subsidiary's assets as included in the parent's consolidated balance sheet will be comprised of a mixture of cost bases: the parent's cost for its share of identifiable assets, and the minority interest's predecessor cost basis for its share of the assets.

The allowed alternative treatment is to record all the assets and liabilities at their fair values as of the date of the acquisition, including the portion represented by the minority interest's ownership share. There will be no mixture of costs for the net identifiable assets acquired in the business combination on the consolidated balance sheet; all items will be presented at fair values as of the acquisition date. Goodwill, however, will be presented only to the extent that the acquirer paid more than the fair values of the net identifiable assets; there will not be any goodwill attributable to the minority interest.

In the present example, Bass's identifiable (i.e., before goodwill) net assets will be reported in the Alto consolidated balance sheet at either $116,800 or at $118,000, depending on whether the benchmark treatment or the allowed alternative treatment is used under IAS 22. These amounts are computed as follows:

Benchmark treatment		
Bass Company net assets, at FMV	$118,000	
90% thereof (majority interest)		$106,200
Bass Company net assets, at cost	106,000	
10% thereof (minority interest)		10,600
Total identifiable net assets		$116,800

Allowed alternative treatment

Bass Company net assets, at FMV	$118,000	
90% thereof (majority interest)		$106,200
Bass Company net assets, at FMV	118,000	
10% thereof (minority interest)		11,800
Total identifiable net assets		$118,000

The benchmark treatment will be utilized in the following discussion.

Assume that on January 1, 1996, Alto acquired 90% of Bass in exchange for 5,400 shares of $10 par common stock having a market value of $120,600. The purchase method is used to account for this transaction; any goodwill will be written off over 10 years.

Workpapers for the consolidated balance sheet as of the date of the transaction will be as shown below:

Alto Company and Bass Company Consolidated Working Papers
For Date of Combination--1/1/96

Purchase accounting
90% interest

	Alto Company	Bass Company	Adjustments and eliminations Debit	Adjustments and eliminations Credit	Minority interest	Consolidated balances
Balance sheet, 1/1/96						
Cash	$ 30,900	$ 37,400				$ 68,300
Accounts receivable	34,200	9,100				43,300
Inventories	22,900	16,100	$ 900b			39,900
Equipment	200,000	50,000	9,000b			259,000
Accumulated depreciation	(21,000)	(10,000)		$ 1,800b		(32,800)
Investment in stock of Bass Company	120,600			120,600a		
Difference between cost and book value			25,200a	25,200b		
Excess of cost over fair value (goodwill)			14,400b			14,400
Patents		10,000	2,700b			12,700
Total assets	$387,600	$112,600				$404,800
Accounts payable	$ 4,000	$ 6,600				$ 10,600
Bonds payable	100,000					100,000
Capital stock	154,000	50,000	45,000a		$ 5,000	154,000
Additional paid-in capital	81,600	15,000	13,500a		1,500	81,600
Retained earnings	48,000	41,000	36,900a		4,100	48,000
Minority interest					$10,600	10,600 MI
Total liabilities and equity	$387,600	$112,600	$147,600	$147,600		$404,800

Based on the foregoing, the consolidated balance sheet as of the date of acquisition will be as follows:

Alto Company and Bass Company
Consolidated Balance Sheet at January 1, 1996
(immediately after combination)

Assets	
Cash	$ 68,300
Accounts receivable, net	43,300
Inventories	39,900
Equipment	259,000
Less accumulated depreciation	(32,800)
Goodwill	14,400
Patents	12,700
Total assets	$404,800
Liabilities and stockholders' equity	
Accounts payable	$ 10,600
Bonds payable, 10%	100,000
Minority interest in Bass	10,600
Common stock, $10 par	154,000
Additional paid-in capital	81,600
Retained earnings	48,000
Total liabilities and stockholders' equity	$404,800

1. Investment on Alto Company's books

   The entry to record the 90% purchase-acquisition on Alto Company's books was

Investment in stock of Bass Company	120,600	
Capital stock		54,000
Additional paid-in capital		66,600

   (To record the issuance of 5,400 shares of $10 par stock to acquire a 90% interest in Bass Company)

   Although common stock is used for the consideration in our example, Alto Company could have used debentures, cash, or any other form of consideration acceptable to Bass Company's stockholders to make the purchase combination.

2. Difference between investment cost and book value

   The difference between the investment cost and the parent company's equity in the net assets of the subsidiary is computed as follows:

Investment cost		$120,600
Less book value % at date of combination		
Bass Company's		
Capital stock	$ 50,000	
Additional paid-in capital	15,000	
Retained earnings	41,000	
Total	$106,000	
Parent's share of ownership	x 90%	

Parent's share of book value	95,400
Excess of cost over book value	$ 25,200

This difference is due to several undervalued assets and to unrecorded goodwill. The allocation procedure is similar to that for a 100% purchase; however, in this case, the parent company obtained a 90% interest and thus will recognize 90% of the difference between the fair market values and book values of the subsidiary's assets, not 100%. The allocation of the cost differential was determined as follows:

	Difference between BV and FMV	*x 90%*
Cash	$ --	$ --
Accounts receivable	--	--
Inventories	1,000	900
Equipment, net	8,000	7,200
Patents	3,000	2,700
Accounts payable	--	--
Totals	$12,000	$10,800
Less differential between investment cost ($120,600) and 90% of Bass' book value ($106,000)		25,200
Net purchase cost allocated to goodwill		$14,400

The equipment has a book value of $40,000 ($50,000 less 20% depreciation of $10,000). An appraisal concluded that the equipment's replacement cost was $60,000 less 20% accumulated depreciation of $12,000, resulting in a net fair value of $48,000.

3. Elimination entries on workpaper

The basic reciprocal accounts are the investment in subsidiary account on the parent's books and the subsidiary's stockholder equity accounts. Only the parent's share of the subsidiary's accounts may be eliminated as reciprocal accounts. The remaining 10% portion is allocated to the minority interest. The entries below include documentation showing the company source for the information. The workpaper entry to eliminate the basic reciprocal accounts is as follows:

Capital stock--Bass Co.	45,000	
Additional paid-in capital--Bass Co.	13,500	
Retained earnings--Bass Co.	36,900*	
Differential	25,200	
Investment in stock of Bass Co.--Alto Co.		120,600

**($41,000 x 90% = $36,900)*

Note that only 90% of Bass Company's stockholders' equity accounts are eliminated. Also, an account called differential is debited in the workpaper entry. The differential account is a temporary account to record the difference between the cost of the investment in Bass Company from the parent's books and the book value of the parent's interest (90% in our case) from the subsidiary's books.

The next step is to allocate the differential to the specific accounts by making the following workpaper entry:

Inventory	900	
Equipment	9,000	
Patents	2,700	
Goodwill	14,400	
Accumulated depreciation		1,800
Differential		25,200

This entry reflects the allocations prepared in step 2 above and recognizes the parent's share of the asset revaluations.

The minority interest column is the 10% interest of Bass Company's net assets owned by outside third parties. Minority interest must be disclosed because 100% of the book values of Bass Company are included in the consolidated statements, although Alto Company controls only 90% of the net assets. An alternative method to prove minority interest is to multiply the net assets of the subsidiary by the minority interest share, as follows:

Stockholders' equity of Bass Company	x	Minority interest %	=	Minority interest
$106,000	x	10%	=	$10,600

The $10,600 would be reported on the credit side of the consolidated balance sheet between liabilities and stockholders' equity.

The benchmark treatment prescribed by IAS 22 was used above to prepare the consolidated balance sheet. If the allowed alternative treatment had been employed, minority interest would have been as follows:

Total fair market value of identifiable net assets of Bass Company	x	Minority percentage	=	Minority interest
$118,000	x	10%	=	$11,800

The example does not include any other intercompany accounts as of the date of combination. If any existed, they would be eliminated to present the consolidated entity fairly. Several examples of other reciprocal accounts will be shown later for the preparation of consolidated financial statements subsequent to the date of acquisition.

If the preceding example were accounted for on a push-down basis, Bass would record the following entry on its books:

Inventories	1,000	
Equipment	10,000	
Patents	3,000	
Accumulated depreciation		2,000
Paid-in capital		12,000

As a result, Alto would have an investment of $120,600 in a company whose net equity was $118,000. Then 90% x $118,000 or $106,200 contrasted with the cost of $120,600 would mean that the only number unaccounted for by Alto would be goodwill of $14,400. The elimination entry on the worksheet would change only with respect to the paid-in capital of Bass as follows:

Capital stock	45,000	
Paid-in capital	24,300	
Retained earnings	36,900	
Goodwill	14,400	
Investment		120,600

This would leave $5,000 of capital stock, $2,700 of paid-in capital, and $4,100 of retained earnings as minority interest or the same $11,800 as under the entity concept.

Example of consolidation for uniting involving minority interest

The foregoing entries are based on the combination being accounted for as an acquisition, using the purchase method of accounting. The same example will now be used to demonstrate the uniting of interests method, using the pooling method, applied to a minority interest situation. Assume the following:

1. On January 1, 1996, Alto Company acquired a 90% interest in Bass Company in exchange for 5,400 shares of $10 par value stock of Alto Company.
2. All criteria for a pooling have been met, and the combination is treated as a pooling of interests.

The workpaper for a consolidated balance sheet at the date of combination is presented below. Note that the first two columns are trial balances of Alto Company and Bass Company immediately after the combination was recorded by Alto Company.

1. Investment entry recorded on Alto Company's books

   The following entry was made by Alto Company to record its 90% acquisition-pooling of Bass Company:

Investment in stock of Bass Co.	95,400	
Capital stock, $10 par		54,000
Additional paid-in capital		4,500
Retained earnings		36,900

Alto Company and Bass Company Consolidated Working Papers
For Date of Combination--1/1/96

Purchase accounting
90% interest

	Alto Company	*Bass Company*	*Adjustments and eliminations* Debit	Credit	*Minority interest*	*Consolidated balances*
Balance sheet, 1/1/96						
Cash	$ 30,900	$ 37,400				$ 68,300
Accounts receivable	34,200	9,100				43,300
Inventories	22,900	16,100				39,000
Equipment	200,000	50,000				250,000
Accumulated depreciation	(21,000)	(10,000)				(32,800)
Investment in stock of Bass Company	95,400			95,400[a]		
Patents		10,000				10,000
Total assets	$362,400	$112,600				$379,600
Accounts payable	$ 4,000	$ 6,600				$ 10,600
Bonds payable	100,000					100,000
Capital stock	154,000	50,000	45,000[a]		$ 5,000	154,000
Additional paid-in capital	19,500	15,000	13,500[a]		1,500	19,500
Retained earnings	84,000[a]	41,000	36,900[a]		4,100	84,900
Minority interest					$10,600	10,600 MI
Total liabilities and equity	$362,400	$112,600	$95,400	$95,400		$362,400

The investment entry reflects the capital mix for a pooling of less than a 100% investment. The following schedule shows the mix for our 90% combination accomplished by the issuance of 5,400 shares of Alto Company's $10 par stock:

	Bass Company	*Alto Company's percentage share*	*Alto's share of Bass's equity*
Capital stock	$ 50,000	90%	$45,000
Additional paid-in capital	15,000	90%	13,500
Retained earnings	41,000	90%	36,900
	$106,000		$95,400

The $54,000 (5,400 shares x $10 par) in new capital issued by Alto Company represents $45,000 from Bass Company's capital stock and $9,000 of the $13,500 Bass Company's additional paid-in capital. Note that the remaining $4,500 of capital and $36,900 of Bass Company's retained earnings are carried over to Alto Company's books in the combination date entry. The $10,600 of Bass's capital that is not carried over to Alto will eventually be shown as minority interest on the consolidated balance sheet.

2. Elimination entry on workpaper

   Pooling accounting uses book values as a basis of valuation; therefore, no differential will ever occur in a pooling. The reciprocal accounts in a pooling consolidated balance sheet are in the investment in stock of Bass Company account from the parent's books and the stockholders' equity accounts from the subsidiary's books. Again, note that only 90% of the equity of Bass Company is being eliminated; the 10% remainder will be recognized as minority interest. The workpaper elimination entry is

Capital stock--Bass Co.	45,000	
Additional paid-in capital--Bass Co.	13,500	
Retained earnings--Bass Co.	36,900*	
Investment in stock of Bass Co.--Alto Co.		95,400

($41,000 x 90% = $36,900)

Consolidation process in periods subsequent to acquisition. Given the foregoing, the following additional information is available in the first year after the acquisition (1996):

1. Alto Company uses the partial equity method to record changes in the value of the investment account. The partial equity method means that the parent reports its share of earnings, and so on, of the subsidiary on its books using the equity method, but any differential between acquisition cost and underlying fair value of net assets, and so on, is not addressed on an ongoing basis; rather, these matters await the typical year-end accounting adjustment process.
2. During 1996, Alto Company sold merchandise to Bass Company that originally cost Alto Company $15,000, and the sale was made for $20,000. On December 31, 1996, Bass Company's inventory included merchandise purchased from Alto Company at a cost to Bass Company of $12,000.
3. Also during 1996, Alto Company acquired $18,000 of merchandise from Bass Company. Bass Company uses a normal markup of 25% above its cost. Alto Company's ending inventory includes $10,000 of the merchandise acquired from Bass Company.
4. Bass Company reduced its intercompany account payable to Alto Company to a balance of $4,000 as of December 31,1996, by making a payment of $1,000 on December 30. This $1,000 payment was still in transit on December 31, 1996.
5. On January 2, 1996, Bass Company acquired equipment from Alto Company for $7,000. The equipment was originally purchased by Alto Company for $5,000 and had a book value of $4,000 at the date of sale to Bass Company. The equipment had an estimated remaining life of 4 years as of January 2, 1996.
6. On December 31, 1996, Bass Company purchased for $44,000, 50% of the outstanding bonds issued by Alto Company. The bonds mature on December 31, 1999, and were originally issued at par. The bonds pay interest annually on December 31 of each year, and the interest was paid to the prior investor immediately before Bass Company's purchase of the bonds.

The worksheet for the preparation of consolidated financial statements as of December 31, 1996, is presented on the following pages, on the assumption that purchase accounting is used for the business combination.

The investment account balance at the statement date should be reconciled to ensure that the parent company made the proper entries under the method of accounting used to account for the investment. Since the partial equity method is used by Alto, the amortization of the excess of cost over book value will be recognized only on the worksheets.

An analysis of the investment account at December 31, 1996, is as presented below:

	Investment in Stock of Bass Company		
Original cost	120,600		
% of Bass Co.'s income ($9,400 x 90%)	8,460	3,600	% of Bass Co.'s dividends declared ($4,000 x 90%)
Balance, 12/31/96	125,460		

Any errors will require correcting entries before the consolidation process is continued. Correcting entries will be posted to the books of the appropriate company; eliminating entries are not posted to either company's books.

The difference between the investment cost and the book value of the net assets acquired was determined and allocated in the preparation of the date of combination consolidated statements presented earlier. The same computations are used in preparing financial statements for as long as the investment is owned.

The following adjusting and eliminating entries will be required to prepare consolidated financials as of December 31, 1996. Note that a consolidated income statement is required, and therefore, the nominal (i.e., income and expense) accounts are still open. The number or letter in parentheses to the left of the entry corresponds to the key used on the worksheets presented after the following discussion.

Step 1 -- Complete the transaction for any intercompany items in transit at the end of the year.

		Debit	Credit
(a)	Cash	1,000	
	Accounts receivable		1,000

This adjusting entry will now properly present the financial positions of both companies, and the consolidation process may be continued.

Step 2 -- Prepare the eliminating entries.

		Debit	Credit
(a)	Sales	38,000	
	Cost of goods sold		38,000

Total intercompany sales of $38,000 include $20,000 in a downstream transaction from Alto Company to Bass Company and

$18,000 in an upstream transaction from Bass Company to Alto Company.

(b)	Cost of goods sold	5,000	
	Inventory		5,000

The ending inventories are overstated because of the unrealized profit from the intercompany sales. The debit to cost of goods sold is required because a decrease in ending inventory will increase cost of goods sold to be deducted on the income statement. Supporting computations for the entry are as follows:

	In ending inventory of	
	Alto Company	*Bass Company*
Intercompany sales not resold, at selling price	$10,000	$12,000
Cost basis of remaining intercompany merchandise		
From Bass to Alto (÷ 125%)	(8,000)	
From Alto to Bass (÷ 133 1/3%)	______	(9,000)
Unrealized profit	$ 2,000	$ 3,000

Note: When preparing consolidated workpapers for 1997 (the next fiscal period), an additional eliminating entry will be required if the goods in 1996's ending inventory are sold to outsiders during 1997. The additional entry will recognize the profit for 1997 that was eliminated as unrealized in 1996. This entry is necessary since the entry at the end of 1996 was made only on the worksheet. The 1997 entry will be as follows:

Retained earnings--Bass Co., 1/1/97	2,000	
Retained earnings--Alto Co., 1/1/97	3,000	
Cost of goods sold, 1997		5,000

(c)	Accounts payable	4,000	
	Accounts receivable		4,000

This entry eliminates the remaining intercompany receivable/payable owed by Bass Company to Alto Company. This eliminating entry is necessary to avoid overstating the consolidated entity's balance sheet. The receivable/payable is not extinguished, and Bass Company must still transfer $4,000 to Alto Company in the future.

(d)	Gain on sale of equipment	3,000	
	Equipment		2,000
	Accumulated depreciation		250
	Depreciation expense		750

This entry eliminates the gain on the intercompany sale of the equipment, eliminates the overstatement of equipment, and removes the excess depreciation taken on the gain. Supporting computations for the entry are as follows:

	Cost	At date of intercompany sale accum. depr.	1996 depr. ex.	End-of-period accum. depr.
Original basis (to seller, Alto Co.)	$5,000	($1,000)	$ 1,000	($2,000)
New basis (to buyer, Bass Co.)	7,000	--	1,750	(1,750)
Difference	($2,000)		($ 750)	$ 250

If the intercompany sale had not occurred, Alto Company would have depreciated the remaining book value of $4,000 over the estimated remaining life of 4 years. However, since Bass Company's acquisition price ($7,000) was more than Alto Company's basis in the asset ($4,000), the depreciation recorded on the books of Bass Company will include part of the intercompany unrealized profit. The equipment must be reflected on the consolidated statements at the original cost to the consolidated entity. Therefore, the write-up of $2,000 in the equipment, the excess depreciation of $750, and the gain of $3,000 must be eliminated. The ending balance of accumulated depreciation must be shown at what it would have been if the intercompany equipment transaction had not occurred. In future periods, a retained earnings account will be used instead of the gain account; however, the other concepts will be extended to include the additional periods.

(e)	Bonds payable	50,000	
	Investment in bonds of Alto Company		44,000
	Gain on extinguishment of debt		6,000

This entry eliminates the book value of Alto Company's debt against the bond investment account of Bass Company. To the consolidated entity, this transaction must be shown as a retirement of debt even though Alto Company has the outstanding intercompany debt to Bass Company. SFAS 4 specifies that gains or losses on debt extinguishment, if material, should be shown as an extraordinary item. In future periods, Bass Company will amortize the discount, thereby bringing the investment account up to par value. A retained earnings account will be used in the eliminating entry instead of the gain account.

		Debit	Credit
(f)	Equity in subsidiary's income--Alto Co.	8,460	
	Dividends declared--Bass Co.		3,600
	Investment in stock of Alto Co.		4,860

This elimination entry adjusts the investment account back to its balance at the beginning of the period and also eliminates the subsidiary income account.

		Debit	Credit
(g)	Capital stock--Bass Co.	45,000	
	Additional paid-in capital--Bass Co.	13,500	
	Retained earnings--Bass Co.	36,900	
	Differential	25,200	
	Investment in stock of Bass Company--Alto Co.		120,600

This entry eliminates 90% of Bass Company's stockholders' equity at the beginning of the year, 1/1/96. Note that the changes during the year were eliminated in entry (f). The differential account reflects the excess of investment cost over the book value of the assets acquired.

		Debit	Credit
(h)	Inventory	900	
	Equipment	9,000	
	Patents	2,700	
	Goodwill	14,400	
	Accumulated depr.		1,800
	Differential		25,200

This entry allocates the differential (excess of investment cost over the book values of the assets acquired). Note that this entry is the same as the allocation entry made to prepare consolidated financial statements for January 1, 1996, the date of acquisition.

		Debit	Credit
(i)	Cost of goods sold	900	
	Depreciation expense	1,800	
	Other operating expenses--patent amortization	270	
	Other operating expenses--goodwill amortization	1,440	
	Inventory		900
	Accumulated depr.		1,800
	Patents		270
	Goodwill		1,440

The elimination entry amortizes the revaluations to fair market value made in entry (h). The inventory has been sold and therefore becomes part of cost of goods sold. The remaining revaluations will be amortized as follows:

	Revaluation	Amortization period	Annual amortization
Equipment (net)	$7,200	4 years	$1,800
Patents	2,700	10 years	270
Goodwill	14,400	10 years	1,440

The amortizations will continue to be made on future worksheets. For example, at the end of the next year (1997), the amortization entry (i) would be as follows:

Differential	4,410	
Depreciation expense	1,800	
Other operating expenses--patent amortization	270	
Other operating expenses--goodwill amortization	1,440	
Inventory		900
Accumulated depreciation		3,600
Patents		540
Goodwill		2,880

The initial debit of $4,410 to differential is an aggregation of the prior period's charges to income statement accounts ($900 + $1,800 + $270 + $1,440). During subsequent years, some accountants prefer reducing the allocated amounts in entry (h) for prior period's charges. In this case the amortization entry in future periods would reflect just that period's amortizations.

All the foregoing entries were based on the assumption that the acquisition was accounted for as a purchase. Had the pooling-of-interests method been used, however, book value rather than fair value would have been the basis for recording the accounting consolidation entries. Thus, entry (g) would be different, while entries (h) and (i) would not be made for a pooling. All other eliminating entries would be the same. The basic elimination entry (g) for a pooling, using the equity method of accounting for the investment, would be as follows:

Capital stock--Bass Co.	45,000	
Additional paid-in capital--Bass Co.	13,500	
Retained earnings--Bass Co.	36,900	
Investment in stock of Bass Co.		95,400

In adjusting for the minority interest in the consolidated entity's equity and earnings, the following guidelines should be observed:

1. Only the parent's share of the subsidiary's shareholders' equity is eliminated in the basic eliminating entry. The minority interest's share is presented separately.
2. The entire amount of intercompany reciprocal items is eliminated. For example, all receivables/payables and sales/cost of sales with a 90% subsidiary are eliminated.

3. For intercompany transactions in inventory and fixed assets, the possible effect on minority interest depends on whether the original transaction affected the subsidiary's income statement. Minority interest is adjusted only if the subsidiary is the selling entity. In this case, the minority interest is adjusted for its percentage ownership of the common stock of the subsidiary. The minority interest is not adjusted for unrealized profits on downstream sales. The effects of downstream transactions are confined solely to the parent's (i.e., controlling) ownership interests.

The minority interest's share of the subsidiary's income is shown as a deduction on the consolidated income statement since 100% of the sub's revenues and expenses are combined, even though the parent company owns less than a 100% interest. For our example, the minority interest deduction on the income statement is computed as follows:

Bass Company's reported income	$9,400
Less unrealized profit on an upstream inventory sale	(2,000)
Bass Company's income for consolidated financial purposes	$7,400
Minority interest share	x 10%
Minority interest on income statement	$ 740

The minority interest's share of the net assets of Bass Company is shown on the consolidated balance sheet between liabilities and controlling interest's equity. The computation for the minority interest shown in the balance sheet for our example is as follows:

Bass Company's capital stock, 12/31/96	$50,000	
Minority interest share	x 10%	$ 5,000
Bass Company's additional paid-in capital, 12/31/96	$15,000	
Minority interest share	x 10%	1,500
Bass Company's retained earnings, 1/1/96	$41,000	
Minority interest share	x 10%	4,100
Bass Company's 1996 income for consolidated purposes	$ 7,400	
Minority interest share	x 10%	740
Bass Company's dividends during 1996	$ 4,000	
Minority interest share	x 10%	(400)
Total minority interest, 12/31/96		$10,940

Alto Company and Bass Company Consolidated Working Papers
Year Ended December 31, 1996

Purchase Accounting
90% Owned Subsidiary
Subsequent Year, Partial Equity Method

	Alto Company	*Bass Company*	*Adjustments and eliminations* Debit	Credit	*Minority interest*	*Consolidated balances*
Income statements for year ended 12/31/96						
Sales	$750,000	$420,000	$ 38,000[a]			$1,132,000
Cost of sales	581,000	266,000	5,000[b]	$ 38,000[a]		814,900
			900[i]			
Gross margin	169,000	154,000				317,100
Depreciation and interest expense	28,400	16,200	1,800[i]	750[d]		45,650
Other operating expenses	117,000	128,400	1,710[i]			247,110
Net income from operations	23,600	9,400				24,340
Gain on sale of equipment	3,000		3,000[d]			
Gain on bonds				6,000[e]		6,000
Equity in subsidiary's income	8,460		8,460[f]			
Minority income ($7,400 x .10)					$ 740	(740)
Net income	$ 35,060	$ 9,400	$ 58,870	$ 44,750	$ 740	$ 29,600

	Alto Company	*Bass Company*	*Adjustments and eliminations* Debit	Credit	*Minority interest*	*Consolidated balances*
Statement of retained earnings for year ended 12/31/96						
1/1/96 retained earnings						
Alto Company	$ 48,000					$ 48,000
Bass Company		$ 41,000	$ 36,900[g]		$ 4,100	
Add net income (from above)	35,060	9,400	58,870	$ 44,750	740	29,600
Total	83,060	50,400			4,840	77,600
Deduct dividends	15,000	4,000		3,600[f]	400	15,000
Balance, 12/31/96	$ 68,060	$ 46,400	$ 95,770	$ 48,350	$ 4,440	$ 62,600

Balance sheet, 12/31/96						
Cash	$ 45,300	$ 6,400	$ 1,000[l]			$ 52,700
Accounts receivable (net)	43,700	12,100		$ 1,000[l]		50,800
				4,000[c]		
Inventories	38,300	20,750	900[h]	5,000[b]		54,050
				900[i]		
Equipment	195,000	57,000	9,000[h]	2,000[d]		259,000
Accumulated depreciation	(35,200)	(18,900)		250[d]		(57,950)
				1,800[h]		
				1,800[i]		
Investment in stock of Bass Company	125,460			4,860[f]		
				120,600[g]		
Differential			25,200[g]	25,200[h]		
Goodwill			14,400[h]	1,440[i]		12,960
Investment in bonds of Alto Company		44,000		44,000[e]		
Patents		9,000	2,700[h]	270[i]		11,430
	$412,560	$130,350				$382,990
Accounts payable	$ 8,900	$ 18,950	4,000[c]			$ 23,850
Bonds payable	100,000		50,000[e]			50,000
Capital stock	154,000	50,000	45,000[g]		$ 5,000	154,000
Additional paid-in capital	81,600	15,000	13,500[g]		1,500	81,600
Retained earnings (from above)	68,060	46,400	95,770	48,350	4,440	62,600
Minority interest					$10,940	10,940
	$412,560	$130,350	$261,470	$261,470		$382,990

The remainder of the consolidation process consists of the following worksheet techniques:

1. Take all income items across horizontally, and foot the adjustments, minority interest, and consolidated columns down to the net income line.
2. Take the amounts on the net income line (on income statement) in the adjustments, minority interest, and consolidated balances columns down to retained earnings items across the consolidated balances column. Foot and crossfoot the retained earnings statement.
3. Take the amounts of ending retained earnings in each of the four columns down to the ending retained earnings line in the balance sheet. Foot the minority interest column and place its total in the consolidated balances column. Take all the balance sheet items across to consolidated balances column.

Other Accounting Issues Arising in Business Combinations

Net operating loss carryforward of acquired entity. Depending on the tax jurisdiction, an acquirer may or may not succeed to the available tax loss benefits of acquired entity. International accounting standards (IAS 11, covered in detail in Chapter 14) permit two very different methods of accounting for the tax effects of temporary differences, including net operating loss carryforwards. If the liability method (the authors' preference) is employed, the amount to be recognized in the consolidated balance sheet should be the amount deemed most likely ultimately to be realized from these benefits. If the acquirer cannot use the tax losses of the acquired entity, no asset should be recognized. If the acquirer can only use these losses to offset future earnings of the acquired operations (a common restriction), the tax benefit should be recognized as an asset, but reduced by an allowance or reserve so that only the estimated net realizable amount is presented in the consolidated balance sheet.

Subsequent identification of, or changes in value of, assets and liabilities acquired. IAS 22 stipulates that individual assets and liabilities should be recorded in an acquisition to the extent that it is probable that any associated future economic benefits will flow to the acquirer and a reliable measure is available of the cost or fair values. In some cases, due to one or both of these criteria not being met at the date of the transaction, some assets or liabilities may not be recognized (which would normally have the ramification that goodwill or negative goodwill would be adjusted accordingly).

If new information becomes available after the date of the acquisition regarding the existence or the fair value of acquired assets or the amount of liabilities, it will be necessary to make an adjustment to some of the recorded amounts. IAS 22 sets as a time limit, however, the end of the first annual accounting period after the acquisition for any reallocation from goodwill or negative goodwill to other assets or liabilities. If such information becomes available after that date, the adjustment must be made to current period income or expense. The reason for this requirement is to avoid having changes made to goodwill or negative goodwill over an unlimited time horizon.

Changes in majority interest. The parent's ownership interest can change as a result of purchases or sales of the subsidiary's common shares by the parent or as a consequence of capital transactions of the subsidiary. The latter circumstance is generally handled precisely as demonstrated in the equity method discussion in Chapter 9. If the parent's relative book value interest in the subsidiary has changed, gains or losses are treated as incurred in an entity's own treasury stock transactions. Gains are credited to paid-in capital; losses are charged to any paid-in capital or to retained earnings created previously.

When the parent's share of ownership increases through a purchase of additional stock, simply debit investment and credit cash for the cost. A problem occurs with consolidated income statements when the change in ownership takes place in midperiod. Consolidated statements should be prepared based on the ending ownership level.

Example of a consolidation with a change in the majority interest

Assume that Alto Company increased its ownership of Bass Company from 90% to 95% on October 1, 1996. The investment was acquired at book value of $5,452.50 and is determined as follows:

Retained earnings at 10/1/96		$50,000
Additional paid-in capital, 10/1/96		15,000
Retained earnings at 10/1/96		
Balance, 1/1/96	$41,000	
Net income for 9 months ($9,400 x .75)	7,050*	
Preacquisition dividends	(4,000)	44,050
		$ 109,050
		x 5%
Book value acquired		$5,452.50

** Assumes income was earned evenly over the year.*

The consolidated net income should reflect a net of:

90%	x	$9,400	x	12/12	=	$8,460.00
5%	x	$9,400	x	3/12	=	117.50
95%						$8,577.50

The interim stock purchase will result in a new account being shown on the consolidated income statement. The account is **purchased preacquisition earnings**, which represents the percentage of the subsidiary's income earned, in this case, on the 5% stock interest from January 1, 1996, to October 1, 1996. The basic eliminating entries would be based on the 95% ownership as follows:

Equity in subsidiary's income--Alto Co.	8,577.50	
Dividends declared--Bass Co.		3,600.00
Investment in stock of Bass Co.		4,977.50
Capital stock--Bass Co.	47,500.00	
Additional paid-in capital--Bass Co.	14,250.00	
Retained earnings--Bass Co.	38,750.00**	
Purchased preacquisition earnings	352.50***	
Differential	25,200.00	
Investment in stock of Bass Co.--Alto Co.		126,052.50

*** 95% x $41,000 beginning 1996 balance*	*$38,950*
Less preacquisition dividend of 5% x $4,000	*(200)*
Retained earnings available, as adjusted	*$38,750*

**** 5% x $9,400 x 9/12 = $352.50*

Purchased preacquisition earnings is shown as a deduction, along with minority interest, to arrive at consolidated net income. Purchased preacquisition earnings are used only with interim acquisition under the purchase accounting method; all poolings are assumed to take place at the beginning of the period regardless of when, during the period, the acquisition was actually made.

Combined Financial Statements

When a group of entities is under common ownership, control, or management, it is often useful to present combined (or combining, showing the separate as well as the combined entities) financial statements. In this situation, the economic substance of the nominally independent entities' operations may be more important to statement users than is the legal form of those enterprises. When consolidated statements are not presented, combined statements may be used to show the financial position, or operating results, of a group of companies that are each subsidiaries of a common parent.

The process of preparing combined statements is virtually the same as consolidations employing the pooling-of-interests method. The major exception is that the equity section of the combined balance sheet will incorporate the paid-in capital accounts of each of the combining entities. However, only a single combined retained earnings account need be presented.

Example of a combined financial statement

Adams Corporation and Benbow Company, Inc.
Combined Balance Sheet
December 31, 1996

Stockholders' equity	
Capital stock:	
Preferred, $100 par, authorized 90,000 shares, issued 5,000 shares	$ 500,000
Common, $50 par, authorized 100,000 shares, issued 60,000 shares	3,000,000
Common, $10 par, authorized 250,000 shares, issued 100,000 shares	1,000,000
Additional paid-in capital	650,000
Retained earnings	3,825,000
	$8,975,000

Combinations of Entities Under Common Control

IAS 22 explicitly does **not** apply to entities under common control (brother-sister corporations, etc.). However, logic suggests that mergers among such affiliated entities must be accounted for "as if" poolings. This treatment is consistent with the concept of poolings as combinations of common shareholder interests. A question arises, however, when a parent (Company P) transfers ownership in one of its subsidiaries (Company B) to another of its subsidiaries (Company A) in exchange for additional shares of Company A. In such an instance, A's carrying value for the investment in B should be P's basis, not B's book value. Furthermore, if A subsequently retires the interests of minority owners of B, the transaction should be accounted for as a purchase, whether it is effected through a stock issuance by A or by a cash payment to the selling shareholders.

Furthermore, when a purchase transaction is closely followed by a sale of the parent's subsidiary to the newly acquired (target) entity, these two transactions should be viewed as a single transaction. Accordingly, the parent should recognize gain or loss on the sale of its subsidiary to the target company, to the extent of minority interest in the target entity. As a result, there will be a new basis (step up) not only for the target company's assets and liabilities, but also for the subsidiary company's net assets. Basis is stepped up to the extent of minority participation in the target entity to which the subsidiary company was transferred.

Accounting for Leveraged Buyouts

Possibly one of the most complex accounting issues to have arisen over the past decade has been the appropriate accounting for leveraged buyouts (LBO). At the center of this issue is the question of whether a new basis of accountability has been created by the LBO transaction. If so, a step up in the reported value of assets and/or liabilities is warranted. If not, the carryforward bases of the predecessor entity should continue to be reported in the company's financial statements.

International accounting standards do not address this issue directly. However, guidance can be obtained from the decisions made by the standard setters in the United States, which have dealt with this question. Although this guidance is not definitive, it is instructive.

The conclusion was that partial or complete new basis accounting is appropriate only when the transaction is characterized by a change in control of voting interest. A series of mechanical tests were developed by which this change in interest is to be measured. The EITF identified three groups of interests: shareholders in the newly created company, management, and shareholders in the old company (who may or may not also have an interest in the new company). Depending on the relative interests of these groups in the old entity (OLDCO) and in the new enterprise (NEWCO), there will be either (1) a finding that the transaction was a purchase (new-basis accounting applies), or (2) that it was a recapitalization or a restructuring (carryforward basis accounting applies).

Among the tests decreed to determine proper accounting for any given LBO transaction is the **monetary test**. This test requires that at least 80% of the net consideration paid to acquire OLDCO interests must be monetary. In this context, monetary means cash, debt, and the fair value of any equity securities given by NEWCO to selling shareholders of OLDCO. Loan proceeds provided by OLDCO to assist in the acquisition of NEWCO shares by NEWCO shareholders are excluded from this definition. If the portion of the purchase that is effected through monetary consideration is less than 80% but other criteria are satisfied, there will be a step up. This step up will be limited to the percentage of the transaction represented by monetary consideration.

US GAAP guidance also presents an extensive series of examples illustrating the circumstances that would and would not meet the purchase accounting criteria to be employed in LBO. These examples should be consulted as needed when addressing an actual LBO transaction accounting issue.

Spin-Offs

Occasionally, an entity disposes of a wholly or partially owned subsidiary or of an investee by transferring it unilaterally to the entity's shareholders. The proper accounting for such a transaction, generally known as a spin-off, depends on the percentage of the company that is owned.

If the ownership percentage is relatively minor, 25% for example, the transfer to stockholders would be viewed as a **dividend in kind** and would be accounted for at the fair value of the property (i.e., shares in the investee) transferred.

However, when the entity whose shares are distributed is majority or wholly-owned, the effect is not merely to transfer a passive investment but to remove the operations from the former parent and to vest them with the parent's shareholders. This transaction is a true spin-off transaction, not merely a property dividend. Although international accounting standards have not addressed this matter, as a point of reference, US GAAP requires that spin-offs and similar nonreciprocal transfers to owners be accounted for at the recorded book values of the assets and liabilities transferred.

If the operations (or subsidiary) being spun off are distributed during a fiscal period, it may be necessary to estimate the results of operations for the elapsed period prior to spin-off to ascertain the net book value as of the date of the transfer. Stated another way, the operating results of the subsidiary to be disposed of should be included in the reported results of the parent through the actual date of the spin-off.

In most instances, the subsidiary being spun off will have a positive net book value. This net worth represents the cost of the nonreciprocal transfer to the owners, and like a dividend, will be reflected as a charge against the parent's retained earnings at the date of spin-off. In other situations, the operations (or subsidiary) will have a net deficit (negative net book value). Since it is unacceptable to recognize a credit to the parent's retained earnings for other than a culmination of an earnings process, the spin-off should be recorded as a credit to the parent's paid-in capital. In effect, the stockholders (the recipients of the spun-off subsidiary) have made a capital contribution to the parent company by accepting the operations having a negative book value. As with other capital transactions, this would **not** be presented in the income statement, only in the statement of changes in stockholders' equity (and in the statement of cash flows).

Push-Down Accounting

Push-down accounting is an unresolved issue in accounting for an entity that has had a substantial change in the ownership of its outstanding voting shares. This technique reflects the revaluation of the assets and/or liabilities of the acquired company (on its books) based on the price paid for some or all of its shares by the acquirer. Push-down accounting has no impact on the presentation of consolidated financial statements or on the separate financial statements of the parent (investor) company. These financial statements are based on the price paid for the acquisition, not on the acquired entity's book value. However, the use of this accounting technique represents a departure in the way separate financial statements of the acquired entity are presented.

Advocates of push-down accounting point out that in a purchase business combination, a new basis of accounting is established. They believe that the new basis should be pushed down to the acquired entity and should be used when presenting its own separate financial statements.

While the push-down treatment has been used by a number of entities whose shares have been purchased by others, the entire area of push-down accounting remains controversial and without clear authoritative guidance. Although push-down makes some sense in the case where a major block of the investee's shares is acquired in a single free-market transaction, a series of step transactions would require continual adjustment of the investee's carrying values for assets and liabilities. Furthermore, the price paid for a fractional share of ownership of an investee may not always be meaningfully extrapolated to a value for the investee company as a whole.

Non-Sub Subsidiaries

An issue that has recently concerned accountants is the sudden popularity of what have been called **non-sub subsidiaries**. This situation arises when an entity plays a major role in the creation and financing of what is often a start-up or experimental operation but does not take an equity position at the outset. For example, the parent might finance the entity by means of convertible debt or debt with warrants for the later purchase of common shares. The original equity partner in such arrangements most often will be the creative or managerial talent, that generally exchanges its talents for a stock interest. If the operation prospers, the parent will exercise its rights to a majority voting stock position; if it fails, the parent presumably avoids reflecting the losses in its statements.

Although this strategy may seem to avoid the requirements of equity accounting or consolidation, the economic substance clearly suggests that the operating results of the subsidiary should be reflected in the financial statements of the real parent, even absent stock ownership. Until formal requirements are established in this area, an approach akin to the preparation of combined statements would seem reasonable.

Disclosure Requirements

Business combinations. For all business combinations, the following disclosures are required in the financial statements for the year in which the transaction occurs:

1. The name and descriptions of combining enterprises
2. The methods of accounting for the combinations
3. The effective date of the combinations, for accounting purposes
4. The identity of any operations resulting from the combination that are intended for disposition

For business combinations accounted for as acquisitions, the following disclosures are required:

1. The percentage of voting interests acquired
2. The cost of the acquisitions, and a description of consideration paid or contingently payable
3. The nature and amount of provisions for any restructuring or plant closure expenses arising as a result of any acquisitions, and recognized as of the date of the acquisitions

Furthermore, the financial statements should disclose the following:

1. The accounting treatment for goodwill and negative goodwill, including amortization periods
2. Justification for amortization periods greater than 5 years, if applicable
3. Description of and justification for amortization of goodwill or negative goodwill by other than the straight-line method
4. A reconciliation, with respect to both goodwill and negative goodwill, at the beginning and the end of the period, showing:
    a. The gross amount and accumulated amortization at the beginning of the period
    b. Any additional goodwill or negative goodwill recorded during the period
    c. Amortization recorded during the period
    d. Any adjustments resulting from the subsequent identification or changes in value of assets and liabilities
    e. Any other write-offs during the period
    f. The gross amount and accumulated amortization at year end

If the allocation of the purchase price to assets and liabilities is only made on a provisional basis, this fact must be disclosed, with the reasons therefor noted. When these matters are later resolved, this should also be disclosed.

For business combinations that are unitings of interests, the following disclosures are required in the period in which the event occurs:

1. A description of the shares issued, together with the percentages of each combining entity's voting shares exchanged to effect the uniting of interests
2. The amounts of assets and liabilities contributed by each constituent enterprise
3. Sales revenue, other operating revenues, extraordinary items, and net profit or loss of each enterprise prior to the date of the combination, which are included in the combined financial statements

If a business combination is effected **after** the balance sheet date, the foregoing disclosures should be made if practical, but the transaction should not be accounted for as if it had occurred prior to year end.

Consolidated financial statements. IAS 27 requires that for consolidated financial reporting, the names, countries of incorporation or residence, proportion of ownership interests, and if different, voting interests held be disclosed for all significant subsidiaries.

If any subsidiary is not included in the consolidated financial statements, the reasons must be set forth. If an entity over which the parent does not have majority voting control is included in the consolidated financial statements, the reasons for this must also be explained.

If a subsidiary was acquired or disposed of during the period, the effect of the event on the consolidated financial statements should be discussed. If parent-only financial statements are being presented (which is permitted, but not as a substitute for consolidated financial reporting), the method of accounting for interests in subsidiaries should be stated.

11 CURRENT LIABILITIES AND CONTINGENCIES

PERSPECTIVE AND ISSUES

The division of assets and liabilities into current and noncurrent allows working capital (current assets minus current liabilities) to be calculated. Working capital, which is the relatively liquid portion of total enterprise capital, can be used to determine the ability of an enterprise to repay obligations. Working capital assumes a going-concern concept. If the enterprise is to be liquidated in the near future, classification of assets and liabilities is inappropriate.

Current liabilities are those enterprise obligations whose liquidation is reasonably expected to require the use of existing resources properly classifiable as current assets or the creation of other current liabilities. This definition excludes from the current liability classification any currently maturing obligations that will be satisfied by using long-term assets and currently maturing obligations expected to be refinanced.

Offsetting of assets and liabilities is improper except where a right of setoff exists. A right of setoff is a debtor's legal right to discharge debt owed to another party by applying against the debt an amount the other party owes to the debtor.

The issue of contingencies (assets or liabilities whose ultimate outcome will be determined by future events) has been dealt with by IAS 10, which is soon to be modified by a new standard on provisions and contingencies (currently an exposure draft, E59). While the older standard largely mirrored the corresponding standard under US GAAP, with accrual mandated when the obligation was deemed to be "probable," the presumed replacement standard will set the recognition threshold at "more likely than not" which, while still subjectively determined, denotes a much lower level of probability. Accordingly, more contingent losses would be subject to accrual under E59 than under current IAS 10. Also, under the proposal contingent assets would be recognized when "virtually certain," which again is a lower threshold level than the standard it would replace. E59 furthermore addresses the broader topic of provisions, which are real liabilities (that is, existence is not contingent on future events) whose amount or timing is uncertain; these have also been commonly referred to as estimated liabilities.

Sources of IAS

IAS 1 (revised), superseding former *IAS* 5, 10, 13
E59, *Provisions, Contingent Liabilities, and Contingent Assets*

DEFINITIONS OF TERMS

Contingency. A condition arising from past events that exists at the balance sheet date, thus giving rise to an asset or liability, the outcome of which will be confirmed only on the occurrence or nonoccurrence of one or more future events which are outside the control of the reporting enterprise.

Current liabilities. Enterprise obligations whose liquidation is reasonably expected to require the use of existing resources properly classified as current assets or the creation of other current liabilities. Obligations that are due on demand or will be due on demand within 1 year or the operating cycle, if longer, are current liabilities.

Estimated liability. An obligation that is known to exist, although the obligee may not be known and the amount and timing of payment is subject to uncertainty.

Guarantee. A commitment to honor an obligation of another party in the event certain defined conditions are not met.

Indirect guarantee of indebtedness of others. A guarantee under an agreement that obligates one enterprise to transfer funds to a second enterprise upon the occurrence of specified events under conditions whereby (1) the funds are legally available to the creditors of the second enterprise, and (2) those creditors may enforce the second enterprise's claims against the first enterprise.

Operating cycle. The average length of time necessary for an enterprise to convert inventory to receivables to cash.

Possible loss. A contingent loss based on the occurrence of a future event or events whose likelihood of occurring is more than remote but less than likely.

Probable loss. A contingent loss based on the occurrence of a future event or events that are likely to occur.

Provision. Liabilities for which the amount or timing of the expenditure that will be undertaken is uncertain.

Remote loss. A contingent loss based on the occurrence of a future event or events whose likelihood of occurring is slight.

Restructuring. A program which is planned and controlled by management and which materially changes either the scope of business undertaken by the enterprise or the manner in which it is conducted.

CONCEPTS, RULES, AND EXAMPLES

Current Liabilities

Classification of balance sheets. Although balance sheets most often will present both assets and liabilities classified into current and noncurrent categories, there is no requirement under international accounting standards, nor indeed under national standards in the various countries, that this be done. The salient international standard, IAS 1 (revised 1997), notes that "when an enterprise supplies goods or services within a clearly identifiable operating cycle, separate classification of current and noncurrent assets and liabilities on the face of the balance sheet provides useful information by distinguishing the net assets that are continuously circulating as working capital from those used in the enterprise's long term operations. It also highlights assets that are expected to be realized within the current operating cycle, and liabilities that are due for settlement within the same period."

IAS 1 (revised) continues IAS 13's optional use of balance sheet classification into current and noncurrent, while clearly supporting such a presentation scheme. In practice, most manufacturing and distributing enterprises do present classified balance sheets, while financial institutions and certain other businesses engaging in long-term projects, such as construction companies, typically do not do so.

The presentation of a classified balance sheet reveals important information about liquidity, or the debt-paying ability of the enterprise. IAS 1 (revised) places substantial weight on this goal, as revealed by the requirement it imposes on entities which choose **not** to present classified balance sheets. Those enterprises must list assets and liabilities "broadly in order of their liquidity." Furthermore, the standard requires that there must be disclosure of assets expected to be recovered, and liabilities expected to be liquidated, more than 12 months after the date of the balance sheet. This does not necessarily require that these be placed in separate captions in the balance sheet, per se, although that can be done; rather, footnote disclosures can be used to accomplish this objective.

IAS 1 (revised) also makes explicit reference to the requirements imposed by IAS 32 concerning financial assets and liabilities. Since such common balance sheet items as trade and other receivables and payables are within the definition of financial instruments, information about maturity dates is already required under IAS. While most trade payables and accrued liabilities will be due within 30 to 90 days, and thus are understood by all financial statement readers to be current, this requirement would necessitate additional disclosure, either on the face of the balance sheet or in the footnotes thereto, when this assumption is not warranted.

The other purpose of presenting a classified balance sheet is to highlight those assets and obligations that are "continuously circulating" in the phraseology of IAS 1 (revised). That is, the goal is to identify specifically resources and commitments that are consumed or settled in the normal course of operating the business. In some types of businesses, such as certain construction enterprises, the normal operating cycle may exceed 1 year. Thus, some assets or liabilities might fail to be incorporated into a definition based on the first goal of reporting, providing insight into liquidity, but be included in one that meets the second goal.

As a compromise, if a classified balance sheet is indeed being presented, the convention for financial reporting purposes is to consider assets and liabilities current if they will be realized and liquidated within 1 year, or 1 operating cycle, whichever is longer. Because this may vary in practice from one reporting entity to another, however, it is important for users to read the accounting policies set forth in notes to the financial statements. The classification criterion should be set forth there, particularly if it is other than the rule most commonly employed, 1-year threshold.

Nature of current liabilities. Current liabilities are generally perceived to be those that are due within a brief time span. Convention is to use 1 year from the balance sheet date as the threshold for categorization as current, although for enterprises that have operating cycles longer than 1 year (e.g., certain types of construction projects), the longer period is often advocated as a more meaningful demarcation line. IAS 1 (revised 1997) states that liabilities are to be considered current when they are expected to be settled in the normal course of the entity's operating cycle, or are due to be settled within 12 months from the balance sheet date, whichever is longer. Examples of liabilities which are not be settled in the normal course of the operating cycle, but which, if due within 12 months would be deemed current, are current portions of long-term debt and bank overdrafts, dividends declared and payable, and various nontrade payables.

Current liabilities would almost always include not only obligations that are due on demand (typically including bank lines of credit, other demand notes payable, and certain overdue obligations for which forbearance has been granted on a day-to-day basis), but also the currently scheduled payments on longer-term obligations, such as installment notes. Also included in this group would be trade credit and accrued expenses, and deferred revenues and advances from customers, for which services are to be provided or product delivered within 1 year. If certain conditions are met (described below), short-term obligations that are intended to be refinanced may be excluded from current liabilities.

Like all liabilities, current liabilities may be known with certainty as to amount, due date, and payee, or one or more of these elements may be unknown or subject to estimation. Under the principles of accrual accounting, however, the lack of specific information on, say, the amount owed will not serve to justify a failure to record and report on such obligations. Estimated and contingent liabilities are discussed in detail later in this chapter.

Types of liabilities. Current obligations can be divided into those where

1. Both the amount and the payee are known
2. The payee is known but the amount may have to be estimated
3. The payee is unknown and the amount may have to be estimated

4. The liability has been incurred due to a loss contingency

These types of liabilities are discussed in the following sections.

Amount and Payee Known

Accounts payable arise primarily from the acquisition of materials and supplies to be used in the production of goods or in conjunction with the providing of services. Payables that arise from transactions with suppliers in the normal course of business, which customarily are due in no more than 1 year, may be stated at their face amount rather than at the present value of the required future cash flows.

Notes payable are more formalized obligations that may arise from the acquisition of materials and supplies used in operations or from the use of short-term credit to purchase capital assets. Although international accounting standards do not explicitly address the matter, it is widely agreed that monetary obligations, other than those due currently, should be presented at the present value of the amount owed, thus giving explicit recognition to the time value of money. However, most would agree that this exercise would not be needed to present current obligations fairly. (Of course, if the obligations are interest-bearing, at a reasonable rate determined at inception, this is not an issue.)

Dividends payable become a liability of the enterprise when the board of directors declares a cash dividend. Since declared dividends are usually paid within a short period of time after the declaration date, they are classified as current liabilities.

Unearned revenues or advances result from customer prepayments for either performance of services or delivery of product. They may be required by the selling enterprise as a condition of the sale or may be made by the buyer as a means of guaranteeing that the seller will perform the desired service or deliver the product. Unearned revenues and advances should be classified as current liabilities at the balance sheet date if the services are to be performed or the products are to be delivered within 1 year or the operating cycle, whichever is longer.

Returnable deposits may be received to cover possible future damage to property. Many utility companies require security deposits. A deposit may be required for the use of a reusable container. Refundable deposits are classified as current liabilities if the firm expects to refund them during the current operating cycle or within 1 year, whichever is longer.

Accrued liabilities have their origin in the end-of-period adjustment process required by accrual accounting. They represent economic obligations, even when the legal or contractual commitment to pay has not yet been triggered, and as such must be given recognition if the matching concept is to be adhered to. Commonly accrued liabilities include wages and salaries payable, interest payable, rent payable, and taxes payable.

Agency liabilities result from the legal obligation of the enterprise to act as the collection agent for employee or customer taxes owed to various federal, state, or local government units. Examples of agency liabilities include sales taxes, income taxes withheld from employee paychecks, and employee social insurance contributions, where mandated by law. In addition to agency liabilities, an employer may have a current obligation for the unemployment taxes. Payroll taxes typically are not legal liabilities until the associated payroll is actually paid, but in keeping with the concept of accrual accounting, if the payroll has been accrued, the associated payroll taxes should be as well.

Current maturing portion of long-term debt is shown as a current liability if the obligation is to be liquidated by using assets classified as current. However, if the currently maturing debt is to be liquidated by using other than current assets (i.e., by using a sinking fund that is properly classified as an investment), these obligations should be classified as long-term liabilities.

Obligations that, by their terms, are due on demand or will be due on demand within 1 year (or operating cycle, if longer) from the balance sheet date, even if liquidation is not expected to occur within that period, are classified as current liabilities. Although the international standards are not explicit on this point, it is also widely agreed that long-term obligations that contain call provisions are to be classified as current liabilities if as of the balance sheet date, one of the following occurs:

1. The debtor is in violation of the agreement, and this violation makes the obligation callable.
2. The debtor is in violation of the agreement, and such violation, unless cured within the grace period specified in the agreement, makes the obligation callable.

Note, however, that if circumstances arise that effectively negate the creditor's right to call the obligation, the obligation may be classified as long-term. Examples are

1. The creditor has waived the right to call the obligation caused by the debtor's violation, or the creditor has subsequently lost the right to demand repayment for more than 1 year (or operating cycle, if longer) from the balance sheet date.
2. Obligations contain a grace period for remedying the violation, and it is probable that the violation will be cured within the grace period. In these situations, the circumstances must be disclosed.

Short-term obligations expected to be refinanced may be classified as noncurrent liabilities if certain conditions are met. If an enterprise intends to refinance the currently maturing portion of long-term debt or intends to refinance callable obligations by replacing them with either new long-term debt or with equity securities, IAS 1 (revised) must be followed. IAS 1 (revised) states that an enterprise should reclassify currently maturing portions of long-term debt as long-term provided that the enterprise intends to refinance the obligation on a long-term basis and its intent is supported by any of the following:

1. **Original term greater than 12 months**. If the debt was originally scheduled for repayment within 1 year, a later agreement to extend it cannot, under new standard IAS 1 (revised), be reclassified as noncurrent, although once it is extended or refinanced the new or replacement debt will be classified according to its terms, and not be limited by the terms of the predecessor debt.
2. **The enterprise intends to refinance the debt on a long-term basis**. This intention must be present as of the balance sheet date in order to be useful in justifying a reclassification of the debt to noncurrent status.
3. **The intention to refinance is supported by an agreement to refinance, or to reschedule payments, which is completed before the financial statements are issued**. Absent an actual consummation of this agreement before the statements are issued, there can be no assurance that it will be successfully completed, and it would be foolish to permit reclassifying short-term obligations as being long-term under such a scenario. Given that there is often a lag between the date of the financial statements and the issuance thereof, an intention that existed as of the former should be consummated with an actual refinancing by the latter date. In some cases, release of the financial statements will be delayed until the refinancing is put into place, for the very reason that there is a strong desire to report the reclassified debt on the balance sheet.

Logic suggests that if short-term debt is classified as long-term due to the existence of a post-balance-sheet-date refinancing or a lender or investor commitment, the replacement debt should not be callable unless there is a violation of a provision of the agreement with which compliance is objectively determinable or measurable. As of the balance sheet date, the reporting enterprise should not be in violation of the terms of the agreement.

Furthermore, the amount of currently maturing debt to be reclassified should not exceed the amount raised by the actual refinancing, nor can it exceed the amount specified in the refinancing agreement. If the amount specified in the refinancing agreement can fluctuate, the maximum amount of debt that would be reclassified is equal to a reasonable estimate of the minimum amount expected to be available on any date from the maturing date of the maturing obligation to the end of the fiscal year. If no estimate can be made of the minimum amount available under the financing agreement, none of the maturing debt should be reclassified as long-term.

Finally, although again not stipulated overtly in IAS 1 (revised), a reasonable interpretation would be that if an enterprise uses current assets after the balance sheet date to liquidate a current obligation, and replaces those current assets by issuing either equity securities or long-term debt before the issuance of the balance sheet, the current obligation must still be classified as a current liability in the balance sheet. Without such a provision, it could be argued successfully that many current liabilities in fact are noncurrent, since these are paid off and then reinstated on a regular, sometimes monthly cycle.

Long-term debt subject to demand for repayment. What may be thought of as the polar opposite of short-term debt to be refinanced long-term is the situation in which an enterprise is obligated under a long-term (noncurrent) debt arrangement, where the lender has either the right to demand immediate or significantly accelerated repayment, or such acceleration rights vest with the lender upon the occurrence of certain events. For example, long-term (and even many short-term) debt agreements typically contain so-called covenants, which effectively are restrictions on the borrower as to undertaking further borrowings, paying dividends, maintaining specified levels of working capital, and so forth. If the covenants are breached by the borrower, the lender will have the right to call the debt or otherwise accelerate repayment.

In other cases, the lender will have certain "subjective acceleration clauses" inserted into the loan agreement, giving it the right to demand repayment if it perceives that its risk position has deteriorated as a result of changes in the borrower's business operations. liquidity, or other vaguely defined factors. Obviously this gives the lender great power and subjects the borrower to the real possibility that the nominally long-term debt will in fact be short-term.

IAS 1 (revised) addresses the matter of breach of loan covenants, but does not address the less common phenomenon of subjective acceleration clauses in loan agreements. As to the former, it provides that continued classification of the debt as noncurrent, when one or more of the stipulated default circumstances has occurred, is contingent upon meeting two conditions: First, the lender has agreed, prior to approval of the financial statements, not to demand payment as a consequence of the breach (this is known as a debt compliance waiver); and second, that it is considered not probable that further breaches will occur within 12 months of the balance sheet date. If one or both of these cannot be met, the debt must be reclassified to current status, if a classified balance sheet is presented.

Logic suggests that the existence of subjective acceleration clauses convert nominally long-term debt into currently payable debt. US GAAP, in fact, formally recognizes this reality. The authors therefore suggest that in the presence of such provisions, it would be misleading to categorize debt as noncurrent, regardless of the actual maturity date, since continued forbearance by the lender would be required, and this cannot be controlled by the enterprise reporting the debt. Such debt should be shown as current, with sufficient disclosure to inform the reader that the debt could effectively be "rolled over" until the nominal maturity date, at the sole discretion of the lender.

Payee Known But Amount May Have to Be Estimated

Under recently published exposure draft E59, *Provisions, Contingent Liabilities, and Contingent Assets*, those liabilities for which amount or timing of expenditure is uncertain are deemed to be **provisions**. While this term has been widely used informally (sometimes also being applied to contra asset accounts such as accumulated depreciation or allowance for uncollectible accounts receivable), it now has been given this precise definition (which explicitly excludes contra asset accounts). Although E59 is only in the exposure stage, final adoption with minimal changes is considered highly likely. Accordingly, the requirements of this proposed standard will be discussed as appropriate throughout the following sections of this chapter.

For all estimated liabilities which are included within the new definition of provisions, the amount to be recorded and presented on the balance sheet should be the best estimate as of the balance sheet date of the amount of expenditure which will be required to settle the obligation. This is often referred to as the "expected value" of the obligation, which is operationally defined as the amount the enterprise would pay, currently, to either settle the actual obligation or provide consideration to a third party to assume it. For estimated liabilities comprised of large numbers of relatively small, similar items, weighting by probability of occurrence can be used to compute the aggregate expected value; this is often used to compute accrued warranty reserves, for example. For those estimated liabilities comprised of only a few (or a single) discrete obligation, the most likely outcome may be used to measure the liability when there is a range of outcomes having roughly similar likelihoods, but if possible outcomes include amounts much greater (and lesser) than the most likely, it may be necessary to accrue a larger amount if there is a significant chance that the larger obligation will have to be settled, even if that is not the most likely outcome as such.

The exposure draft, E59, also addresses the use of discounting (i.e., presenting the estimated liability at present value, taking into account the time value of money). While the entire subject of present value measurement in accounting has been widely debated, and in practice there is a notable lack of consistency, with some standards requiring it, others prohibiting it, and many others remaining silent on the issue, the draft statement of principles on the provisions and contingencies project stated that discounting would be required if the effect was material. The exposure draft has stood fast on that principle, despite some opposition voiced in response and a plea for more guidance. The exposure draft requires the use of discounting when the effect would be material, so provisions estimated to be due farther into the future will have more need to be discounted than those due currently.

E59 states that the discount rate applied should be consistent with the estimation of cash flows (i.e., if cash flows are projected in nominal terms) that is, in the amount expected to be paid out, reflecting whatever price inflation occurs between the balance sheet date and the date of ultimate settlement of the estimated obligation, then a nominal discount rate should be used. If cash flows are projected in real terms, net of any price inflation, then a real interest rate should be applied. In either case, past experience must be used to ascertain likely timing of future cash flows, since discounting cannot otherwise be performed.

The following paragraphs discuss a range of common provisions, and the accounting treatment which is often applied to these particular items.

Taxes payable include federal or national, state or provincial, and local income taxes. Due to frequent changes in the tax laws, the amount of income taxes payable may have to be estimated. That portion deemed currently payable must be classified as a current liability. The remaining amount is classified as a long-term liability. Although estimated future taxes are broadly includable under the category "provisions," specific rules in IAS 12 (revised) prohibit discounting these amounts to present values.

Property taxes payable represent the unpaid portion of an entity's obligation to a state or other taxing authority that arises from ownership of real property. Often these taxes are levied in arrears, based on periodic reassessments of value and on governmental budgetary needs. Accordingly, the most acceptable method of accounting for property taxes is a monthly accrual of property tax expense during the fiscal period of the taxing authority for which the taxes are levied. The fiscal period of the taxing authority is the fiscal period that includes the assessment or lien date.

A liability for property taxes payable arises when the fiscal year of the taxing authority and the fiscal year of the entity do not coincide or when the assessment or lien date and the actual payment date do not fall within the same fiscal year. For example, XYZ Corporation is a calendar-year corporation that owns real estate in a state that operates on a June 30 fiscal year. In this state, property taxes are assessed and become a lien against property on July 1, although they are not payable until April 1 and August 1 of the next calendar year. XYZ Corporation would accrue an expense and a liability on a monthly basis beginning on July 1. At year end (December 31), the firm would have an expense for 6 months' property tax on their income statement and a current liability for the same amount.

Bonus payments may require estimation since the amount of the bonus payment may be affected by the amount of income taxes currently payable.

Compensated absences refer to paid vacation, paid holidays, and paid sick leave. IAS 1 (revised) does not address this topic explicitly, but consistent with the concept of accrual basis financial reporting, an employer should accrue a liability for employee's compensation of future absences if the employee's right to receive compensation for future absence is attributable to employee services already rendered, the right vests or accumulates, ultimate payment of the compensation is probable, and the amount of the payment can reasonably be estimated.

If an employer is required to compensate an employee for unused vacation, holidays, or sick days even if employment is terminated, the employee's right to this compensation is said to vest. Accrual of a liability for nonvesting rights depends on whether the unused rights expire at the end of the year in which earned or accumulated and are carried forward to succeeding years. If the rights expire, a liability for future absences should not be accrued at year end because the benefits to be paid in subsequent years would not be attributable to employee services rendered in prior years. If unused rights accumulate and increase the benefits otherwise available in subsequent years, a liability should be accrued at year end to the extent that it is probable that employees will be paid in subsequent years for the increased benefits attributable to the accumulated rights and the amount can reasonably be estimated.

Pay for employee leaves of absence that represent time off for past services should be considered compensation subject to accrual. Pay for employee leaves of absence that will provide future benefits and that are not attributable to past services rendered would not be subject to accrual. Although in theory such accruals should be based on expected future rates of pay, as a practical matter these are often computed on current pay rates, which may not materially differ and have the advantage of being known. Also, if the payments are to be made some time in the future, discounting of the accrual amounts would seemingly be appropriate, but again this may not often be done for practical considerations.

Similar arguments can be made to support the accrual of an obligation for post-employment benefits other than pensions if employees' rights accumulate or vest, payment is probable, and the amount can be reasonably estimated. If these benefits do not vest or accumulate, these would be deemed to be contingencies. Contingent obligations are discussed in IAS 10 and are considered later in this chapter.

Payee Unknown and the Amount May Have to Be Estimated

The following are further examples of estimated liabilities, which also will fall within the definition of provisions when a final standard consistent with the exposure draft E59 is issued, probably in early 1998. Accordingly, discounting should be applied to projected future cash flows to determine the amounts to be reported on the balance sheet, if the effect of discounting is material and if timing can be estimated sufficiently accurately to accomplish this process.

Premiums are usually offered by an enterprise to increase product sales. They may require the purchaser to return a specified number of boxtops, wrappers, or other proofs of purchase. They may or may not require the payment of a cash amount. If the premium offer terminates at the end of the current period but has not been accounted for completely if it extends into the next accounting period, a current liability for the estimated number of redemptions expected in the future period will have to be recorded. If the premium offer extends for more than one accounting period, the estimated liability must be divided into a current portion and a long-term portion.

Product warranties providing for repair or replacement of defective products may be sold separately or may be included in the sale price of the product. If the warranty extends into the next accounting period, a current liability for the estimated amount of warranty expense expected in the next period must be recorded. If the warranty spans more than the next period, the estimated liability must be partitioned into a current and long-term portion.

Offsetting assets against related liabilities. IAS 1 (revised) provides that current liabilities not be reduced by the deduction of a current asset (or vice versa), unless required or permitted by another IAS. In practice, there are few circumstances that would meet this requirement; certain financial institution transactions are the most commonly encountered exceptions.

Contingencies

While the currently effective definition of contingent losses is that contained in IAS 10, it will very likely be replaced soon by that set forth in the exposure draft E59, *Provisions, Contingent Liabilities, and Contingent Assets*. While these are not very different, the latter proposed standard sets a different and lower threshold for accrual, and since this is expected to supersede IAS 10 in 1998, the newer definition will be employed in the following discussion.

E59 defines a contingency as a condition arising from past events that exists at the balance sheet date, thus giving rise to an asset or liability, the outcome of which will be confirmed only on the occurrence or nonoccurrence of one or more future events which are outside the control of the reporting enterprise.

Contingencies must be distinguished from estimated liabilities, although both involve an uncertainty that will be resolved by future events. However, an estimate exists because of uncertainty about the amount of an event requiring an acknowledged accounting recognition. The event is known and the effect is known, but the amount itself is uncertain. For example, depreciation is an estimate, but not a contingency, because the actual fact of physical depreciation is acknowledged, although the amount is obtained by an assumed accounting method.

In a contingency, whether there will be an impairment of an asset or the occurrence of a liability is the uncertainty that will be resolved in the future. The amount is also usually uncertain, although that is not an essential characteristic. Collectibility of receivables is a contingency because both the amount of loss and the identification of which customer will not pay in the future is unknown. Similar logic would hold for obligations related to product warranties. Both the amount and the customer are currently unknown.

Assessing the likelihood of contingent events. It is tempting to express quantitatively the likelihood of the occurrence of contingent events (e.g., an 80%

probability), but this exaggerates the precision possible in the estimation process. For this reason, accounting standards have not been written to require quantification of the likelihood of contingent outcomes. Rather, qualitative descriptions, ranging along the continuum from remote to probable, have historically been prescribed. IAS 10, like the parallel US GAAP standard, required that contingent losses were to be formally recorded (that is, accrued) when they were deemed to be probable of occurrence, and the amount could be reasonably estimated. Although IAS 10 did not define these terms, the corresponding US standard, Financial Accounting Standards Board Statement 5, offered these useful definitions of these qualitative descriptors used in IAS 10.

1. **Probable**. The future event or events are likely to occur.
2. **Possible**. The chance of the future event or events occurring is more than remote but less than likely.
3. **Remote**. The chance of the future event or events occurring is slight.

Professional judgment is required to classify the likelihood of the future events occurring, as well as to assess the amount or range of amounts of possible outcomes. All relevant information that can be acquired concerning the uncertain set of circumstances needs to be obtained and used to determine the classification. In practice, most accountants believed that "probable" denoted a likelihood of something over 75-85%, while "possible" ranged down from the boundary of probable to a likelihood of about 20% or so.

Accrual of probable losses. IAS 10 states that a loss should be accrued by means of a charge against income if both of the following conditions are met:

1. It is probable that future events will confirm that an asset has been impaired or a liability has been incurred of the balance sheet date.
2. The amount of loss can reasonably be estimated.

Under IAS 10, it is not necessary that a single amount be identified. A range of amounts is sufficient to indicate that some amount of loss has been incurred and should be accrued. The amount accrued is the amount within the range that appears to be the best estimate. If there is no best estimate, the minimum amount in the range should be accrued since it is probable that the loss will be at least this amount. The maximum amount of loss should be disclosed. If future events indicate that the minimum loss originally accrued is inadequate, an additional loss should be accrued in the period when this fact becomes known. This accrual is a change in estimate, not a prior-period adjustment.

If IAS 10 is amended by a new accounting standard which results from E59, as is expected, the rules for accrual of contingent losses will change. E59 sets the threshold for accrual at "more likely than not," which most experts have defined as being very slightly over a 50% likelihood. Thus, if there is even a hint that the obligation is more likely to exist than to not exist, it will need to be formally recognized, if an amount can be reasonably estimated for it. The impact will be both to make it much less ambiguous when a contingency should be recorded, and to force recognition of far more of these obligations, at earlier dates than they are being given recognition at present.

When a loss is probable and no estimate is possible, these facts should be disclosed in the current period. The accrual of the loss should be made in the period in which the amount of the loss can be estimated. This accrual of a loss in future periods is a change in estimate. It is not a prior-period adjustment.

Possible losses. If the occurrence of the loss is possible, the facts and circumstances of the possible loss and an estimate of the amount, if determinable, should be disclosed. If the occurrence of the loss is remote, no accrual or disclosure is usually required. However, certain losses that are remote of occurrence have traditionally been disclosed, and this practice is ratified by IAS 10. Among these are guarantees of indebtedness (direct or indirect), obligations under standby letters of credit, guarantees to repurchase, and guarantees with similar circumstances. E59 continues this same threshold for disclosure, by stating that contingencies which have not been given formal recognition because they fail either part of the two-part test ("more likely than not" and reasonably estimable) should nonetheless be disclosed in the financial statements unless the possibility of a transfer of economic benefits is deemed remote. Thus, the new standard eschews the term "possible" but effectively uses this to describe the range of likelihood between "more likely than not" and "remote." What does change is the amount to be disclosed. E59 stipulates that the disclosure should be of the amount which is deemed to be the best estimate (i.e., the expected value), including the impact of discounting to present value, as of the date the financial statements are authorized for issuance (i.e., something later than the balance sheet date in most cases). If an estimate cannot be developed, that fact must be stated. In rare cases when such disclosures could harm the reporting entity (for example, in connection with some litigation matters), E59 provides that disclosure may be waived, although the general nature of the item and the rationale for nondisclosure is to be addressed.

Remote contingent losses. With the exception of the items mentioned above, contingent losses that are deemed remote in terms of likelihood of occurrence are not accrued or disclosed in the financial statements. For example, every business risks loss by fire, explosion, government expropriation, or guarantees made in the ordinary course of business. These are all contingencies because of the uncertainty surrounding whether the future event confirming the loss will or will not take place. The risk of asset expropriation exists, but this has become less common an occurrence in recent decades, and in any event, would be limited to less developed or politically unstable nations. Unless there is specific information about the expectation of such occurrences, which would thus raise the item to the possible category in any event, thereby making it subject to disclosure, these are not normally discussed in the financial statements.

Litigation. The most difficult area of contingencies is litigation. In some developed nations there is a great deal of commercial and other litigation, some of which exposes reporting entities to risks of material losses. Accountants must generally rely on attorneys' assessments concerning the likelihood of such events. Unless the attorney indicates that the risk of loss is remote or slight, or that the impact of any loss that does occur would be immaterial to the company, the accountant will require that the entity add explanatory material to the financial statements regarding the contingency. In cases where judgments have been entered against the entity, or where the attorney gives a range of expected losses or other amounts, certain accruals of loss contingencies for at least the minimum point of the range must be made. Similarly, if the reporting entity has made an offer in settlement of unresolved litigation, that offer would normally be deemed the lower end of the range of possible loss, and thus subject for accrual. In most cases, however, an estimate of the contingency is unknown and the contingency is reflected only in footnotes.

Expected recovery of loss from third parties. IAS 10 states that if an enterprise can avoid or reduce its exposure to a contingent loss by virtue of a related counterclaim or other claim against a third party, recovery of which is deemed to be probable, the recognition of a contingent loss by the entity will be net of this amount. This is actually a generous provision and must be approached carefully, since some counterclaims are no more than gain contingencies (discussed later) and would not be deemed subject to accrual under generally accepted accounting principles. Thus, an assessment would have to be made based on all the facts, to determine whether offsetting the expected recovery against the loss provision would be warranted.

For example, an enterprise may have been accused by the regulatory authorities of having violated an environmental protection rule by having dumped waste materials on a certain piece of land. The entity has certain insurance coverage against the cost of remediation of such damages, subject to having complied with certain rules. If the insurer disputes or questions the entity's previous compliance with those rules, and thus is challenging its obligation to perform under the terms of the insurance agreement, any recovery from the insurer would have to be deemed an unrecognizable gain contingency. On the other hand, if the insurer has acknowledged its obligation to the entity, the amount of the recovery, within the guidelines of the policy coverage, could be offset in estimating the loss to be accrued.

E59, which is expected to amend IAS 10 when it is ultimately adopted in 1998, continues the notion of treating a recovery of a contingent loss as a contingent asset, to be separately presented and evaluated. However, the threshold for recognition of contingent assets would apparently be lowered somewhat if E59 is adopted. This proposal states that a contingent asset should not be recognized until it is "virtually certain." IAS 10, on the other hand, stipulated that gain contingencies were not to be given recognition as assets in the financial statements, although disclosure in the notes to the statements was explicitly permitted. While the distinction is subtle, it is clear that some third party recoveries (such as from insurance companies) will be held to be "virtually certain" based upon reading of the contractual provisions or upon expert advice from legal counselors, and will thus, under E59, be recognized. Adding to the practical difficulty of implementing this (if adopted) is the fact that the term "virtual certainty" is not given an operational definition.

Unasserted claims or assessments. Unasserted claims are damages that another party has suffered for which the entity might be held responsible, of which the other party has not yet become aware, or for which responsibility has not been attributed to the entity. For example, if a company producing automobiles discovers that a certain model, sold widely over the past 2 years, contained a defect that could result in injury to its drivers, but no such accidents have been reported and no claims have been made against the company, this can be considered to be an unasserted claim. IAS 10 does not address these as distinct from other contingencies; however, logically it should not be necessary to disclose loss contingencies for an unasserted claim or assessment where there has been no manifestation of an awareness of possible claim or assessment by a potential claimant in normal circumstances. However, if it is deemed probable that a claim will be asserted and a reasonable possibility that an unfavorable outcome will occur, some discussion would appear to be warranted.

Gain contingencies. IAS 10 states that gain contingencies should not be accrued as income or as an asset in the financial statements. Although disclosure of contingent gains can be made in the notes to the statements, the standard warns against misleading implications regarding the likelihood of favorable outcomes.

Disclosure Requirements for Gain or Loss Contingencies

When loss contingencies are disclosed because they are deemed possible of occurrence or they are deemed probable but cannot be estimated as to amount, or when gain contingencies are disclosed, the following information should be provided:

1. The nature of the contingency
2. The uncertain factors that may affect the future outcome
3. An estimate of the financial effect, or a statement that such an estimate cannot be made

Under the provisions of E59, which will amend IAS 10 regarding loss and gain contingencies, either type of contingency, if not given formal recognition due to a failure to meet the respective recognition threshold criteria, will have to be disclosed unless the likelihood of outflows or inflows of economic benefits is judged to be remote. Those disclosures would include a description of the nature of the contingency, the types of uncertainties which might affect the ultimate outcomes, and an estimate of the potential financial effect as of the date the financial statements are authorized for issuance. Accordingly, the concepts of best estimate, expected value, and discounting would be brought to bear upon developing the disclosures to be made.

Contingencies arising from business combinations accounted for as acquisitions. It has been the practice that, when an enterprise makes an acquisition of another entity, to be accounted for under IAS 22, in some cases "contingency reserves" are recorded as liabilities. These are usually justified as being estimated costs of rationalizing operations between the acquirer's and acquiree's facilities, to eliminate duplication, dismiss excess or redundant staff, and so forth. Often these are vaguely defined but sometimes material amounts, and once accrued can be used to absorb various future costs. Furthermore, since the accounting impact of such accrual is to increase the amount to be allocated to goodwill, which is then amortized over as long as 20 years (that limit will probably be raised if E61, *Business Combinations*, is adopted as a final standard), the real result is that costs which would otherwise affect earnings in the short term if not recognized until incurred are instead amortized over a much longer period, thereby boosting earnings.

Due to the existence of this widespread practice problem, and to make the treatment of contingencies arising from business acquisitions consistent with that proposed by E59, the IASC has proposed, in E61, to ban the accrual of amounts which could be ascribed to future operating losses, reorganization costs and integration costs expected to be incurred in connection with acquisitions, but for which there is no present obligation. The IASC has argued that an acquirer cannot have an obligation to reorganize an entity over which it has not yet obtained control. Furthermore, management's intentions, even if entirely sincere, are not sufficient to support recognition of a liability; only when translated into actions that commit the entity (at least at a constructive or moral level, if not legally) does a real liability arise. Finally, the IASC concluded that the financial statements following an acquisition should reflect the acquired assets and liabilities that existed at the date of acquisition. Since reorganization and similar actions to improve profitability are postacquisition events, they are properly reportable in the income statements of the periods in which the actions take place.

12 LONG-TERM DEBT

PERSPECTIVE AND ISSUES

Long-term debt represents future sacrifices of economic benefits to be repaid over a period of more than 1 year or, if longer, the operating cycle. Long-term debt includes bonds payable, notes payable, lease obligations, pension and deferred compensation plan obligations, deferred income taxes, and unearned revenue. The accounting for bonds and long-term notes is covered in this chapter. Since at present, international accounting standards address only a few of these topics, the accounting recommendations herein are those of the authors, based on practices in many nations.

The proper valuation of long-term debt is the present value of future payments using the market rate of interest, either stated or implied in the transaction, at the date the debt was incurred. An exception to the use of the market rate of interest stated or implied in the transaction in valuing long-term notes occurs when it is necessary to use an imputed interest rate, if the debt is either noninterest-bearing or bears a clearly nonmarket rate of interest.

Sources of IAS
IAS 32

DEFINITIONS OF TERMS

Amortization. The process of allocating an amount to expense over the periods benefited.

Bond. A written agreement whereby a borrower agrees to pay a sum of money at a designated future date plus periodic interest payments at the stated rate.

Bond issue costs. Costs related to issuing a bond (i.e., legal, accounting, underwriting fees, and printing and registration costs).

Bonds outstanding method. The method of accounting for serial bonds that assumes the discount or premium applicable to each bond of the issue is the same dollar amount per bond per year.

Book value approach. The method of recording the stock issued from a bond conversion at the carrying value of the bonds converted.

Callable bond. A bond in that the issuer reserves the right to call and retire the bond prior to its maturity.

Carrying value. The face amount of a debt issue increased or decreased by the applicable unamortized premium or discount plus unamortized issue costs.

Collateral. Asset(s) pledged to settle the obligation to repay a loan, if not repaid.

Convertible debt. Debt that may be converted into common stock at the holder's option after specific criteria are met.

Covenant. A clause in a debt contract written for the protection of the lender that outlines the rights and actions of the parties involved when certain conditions occur (e.g., when the debtor's current ratio declines beyond a specified level).

Debenture. Long-term debt not secured by collateral.

Defeasance. Extinguishment of debt by creating a trust to service it.

Discount. Created when a debt instrument sells for less than face value and occurs when the stated rate on the instrument is less than the market rate at the time of issue.

Effective interest method. The method of amortizing the discount or premium to interest expense so as to result in a constant rate of interest when applied to the amount of debt outstanding at the beginning of any given period.

Effective rate. See market rate.

Face value. The stated amount or principal due on the maturity date.

Imputation. The process of interest rate approximation that is accomplished by examining the circumstances under which the note was issued.

Long-term debt. Probable future sacrifices of economic benefits arising from present obligations that are not currently payable within 1 year or the operating cycle of the business, whichever is longer.

Market rate. The current rate of interest available for obligations issued under the same terms and conditions.

Market value approach. The method of recording the stock issued from a bond conversion at the current market price of the bonds converted or the stock issued.

Maturity date. The date on which the face value (principal) of the bond or note becomes due.

Maturity value. See face value.

Premium. Created when a debt instrument sells for more than its face value and occurs when the stated rate on the instrument is greater than the market rate at the time of issue.

Principal. See face value.

Secured debt. Debt that has collateral to satisfy the obligation (i.e., a mortgage on specific property), if not repaid.

Serial bond. Debt whose face value matures in installments.

Stated rate. The interest rate written on the face of the debt instrument.

Straight-line method. The method of amortizing the premium or discount to interest expense such that there is an even allocation of interest expense over the life of the debt.

Take-or-pay contract. A contract in which a purchaser of goods agrees to pay specified fixed or minimum amounts periodically in return for products, even if delivery is not taken. It results from a project financing arrangement where the project produces the products.

Through-put agreement. An agreement similar to a take-or-pay contract except that a service is provided by the project under the financing arrangement.

Troubled debt restructure. Occurs when the creditor, for economic or legal reasons related to the debtor's financial difficulties, grants a concession to the debtor (deferment or reduction of interest or principal) that it would not otherwise consider.

Unconditional purchase obligation. An obligation to transfer a fixed or minimum amount of funds in the future or to transfer goods or services at fixed or minimum prices.

Yield rate. See market rate.

CONCEPTS, RULES, AND EXAMPLES

Notes and Bonds

Long-term debt generally takes one of two forms: notes or bonds. **Notes** represent debt issued to a single investor without intending for the debt to be broken up among many investors. Their maturity, usually lasting 1 to 7 years, tends to be shorter than that of a bond. **Bonds** also result from a single agreement. However, a bond is intended to be broken up into various subunits, typically $1,000 each, which can be issued to a variety of investors.

Notes and bonds share common characteristics: a written agreement stating the amount of the principal, the interest rate, when the interest and principal are to be paid, and the restrictive covenants, if any, that must be met. The interest rate is affected by many factors, including the cost of money, the business risk factors, and the inflationary expectations associated with the business.

Nominal vs. effective rates. The stated rate on a note or bond often differs from the market rate at the time of issuance. When this occurs, the present value of the interest and principal payments will differ from the maturity, or face value. If the market rate exceeds the stated rate, the cash proceeds will be less than the face value of the debt because the present value of the total interest and principal payments discounted back to the present yields an amount that is less than the face value. Because an investor is rarely willing to pay more than the present value, the bonds must be issued at a discount. The discount is the difference between the issuance price (present value) and the face, or stated value of the bonds. This discount is then amortized over the life of the bonds to increase the recognized interest expense so that the total amount of the expense represents the actual bond yield.

When the stated rate exceeds the market rate, the bond will sell for more than its face value (at a premium) to bring the effective rate to the market rate and will decrease the total interest expense. When the market and stated rates are equivalent at the time of issuance, no discount or premium exists and the instrument will sell at its face value. Changes in the market rate subsequent to issuance are irrelevant in determining the discount or premium or their amortization.

Notes are a common form of exchange in business transactions for cash, property, goods, and services. Most notes carry a stated rate of interest, but it is not uncommon for noninterest-bearing notes or notes bearing an unrealistic rate of interest to be exchanged. Notes such as these, which are long-term in nature, do not reflect the economic substance of the transaction since the face value of the note does not represent the present value of the consideration involved. Not recording the note at its present value will misstate the cost of the asset or services to the buyer as well as the selling price and profit to the seller. In subsequent periods, both the interest expense and revenue will be misstated.

While international accounting standards do not prescribe how to measure transactions such as described above, several different models are discussed. In describing one of the common methods of reporting the elements of financial statements in the IASC's *Framework for the Preparation and Presentation of Financial Statements,* it is stated that "liabilities are carried at the present discounted value of future net cash outflows..." In the authors' opinion, unless the obligations issued in nonmonetary transactions (e.g., acquisition of plant assets in exchange for long-term debt) are recorded at their discounted present values, using the borrowing entity's applicable marginal borrowing rate, the economic substance of the transaction will be misstated, possibly materially so.

Accordingly, it is suggested that all commitments to pay (and receive) money at a determinable future date be subjected to present value techniques and, if necessary, interest imputation, with the exceptions of the following:

1. Normal accounts payable due within 1 year
2. Amounts to be applied to purchase price of goods or services or that provide security to an agreement (e.g., advances, progress payments, security deposits, and retainages)
3. Transactions between parent and subsidiary
4. Obligations payable at some indeterminable future date (warranties)
5. Lending and depositor savings activities of financial institutions whose primary business is lending money
6. Transactions where interest rates are affected by prescriptions of a governmental agency (e.g., revenue bonds, tax exempt obligations, etc.)

Notes issued solely for cash. When a note is issued solely for cash, its present value is assumed to be equal to the cash proceeds. The interest rate is that rate which equates the cash proceeds to the amounts to be paid in the future (i.e., **no** interest rate is to be imputed). For example, a $1,000 note due in 3 years that sells for $889 has an implicit rate of 4% ($1,000 x .889, where .889 is the present value factor of a lump sum at 4% for 3 years). This rate is to be used when amortizing the discount.

Notes issued for cash and a right or privilege. Often when a note bearing an unrealistic rate of interest is issued in exchange for cash, an additional right or privilege is granted, such as the issuer agreeing to sell merchandise to the purchaser at a reduced rate. The difference between the present value of the receivable and the cash loaned should logically be regarded as an addition to the cost of the products purchased for the purchaser/lender and as unearned revenue to the issuer. This treatment stems from the desire to match revenue and expense in the proper periods and to differentiate between those factors that affect income from operations and income or expense from nonoperating sources. In the situation above, the discount (difference between the cash loaned and the present value of the note) will be amortized to interest revenue or expense, while the unearned revenue or contractual right is amortized to sales and inventory, respectively. The discount affects income from nonoperational sources, while the unearned revenue or contractual right affects the gross profit computation. This differentiation is necessary because the amortization rates used differ for the two amounts.

Example of accounting for a note issued for both cash and a contractual right

1. Miller borrows $10,000 via a noninterest-bearing 3-year note from Krueger.
2. Miller agrees to sell $50,000 of merchandise to Krueger at less than the ordinary retail price for the duration of the note.
3. The fair rate of interest on a note such as this is 10%.

As set forth in the discussion above, the difference between the present value of the note and the face value of the loan is to be regarded as part of the cost of the products purchased under the agreement. The present value factor for an amount due in 3 years at 10% is .75132. Therefore, the present value of the note is $7,513 ($10,000 x .75132). The $2,487 ($10,000 – $7,513) difference between the face value and the present value is to be recorded as a discount on the note payable and as unearned revenue on the future purchases. The following entries would be made to record the transaction:

Miller			*Krueger*		
Cash	10,000		Note receivable	10,000	
Discount on note payable	2,487		Contract right with supplier	2,487	
Note payable		10,000	Cash		10,000
Unearned revenue		2,487	Discount on note receivable		2,487

The discount on note payable (and note receivable) should be amortized using the effective interest (constant yield) method, while the unearned revenue account and contract right with supplier account are amortized on a pro rata basis as the right to purchase merchandise is used up. Thus, if Krueger purchased $20,000 of merchandise from Miller in the first year, the following entries would be necessary:

Miller			*Krueger*		
Unearned revenue	995*		Inventory (or cost of sales)	995	
Sales		995	Contract right with supplier		995
Interest expense	751		Discount on note receivable	751	
Discount on note payable		751**	Interest revenue		751

* *$2,487 x (20,000/50,000)*
** *$7,513 x 10%*

The amortization of unearned revenue and contract right with supplier accounts will fluctuate with the amount of purchases made. If there is a balance remaining in the account at the end of the loan term, it is amortized to the appropriate account in that final year.

Noncash transactions. When a note is issued for consideration such as property, goods, or services, and the transaction is entered into at arm's length, the stated interest rate is presumed to be fair unless (1) no interest rate is stated, (2) the stated rate is unreasonable, or (3) the face value of the debt is materially different from the consideration involved or the current market value of the note at the date of the transaction. As discussed above, it is recommended that when the rate on the note is not considered fair, the note is to be recorded at the fair market value of the property, goods, or services received or at an amount that reasonably approximates the market value of the note, whichever is the more clearly determinable. When this amount differs from the face value of the note, the difference is to be recorded as a discount or premium and amortized to interest expense.

Example of accounting for a note exchanged for property

1. Alpha sells Beta a machine that has a fair market value of $7,510.
2. Alpha receives a 3-year noninterest-bearing note having a face value of $10,000.

In this situation, the fair market value of the consideration is readily determinable and thus represents the amount at which the note is to be recorded. The following entry is necessary:

Machine	7,510	
Discount on notes payable	2,490	
Notes payable		10,000

The discount will be amortized to interest expense over the 3-year period using the interest rate **implied** in the transaction.

If the fair market value of the consideration or note is not determinable, the present value of the note must be determined using an **imputed** interest rate. This rate will then be used to establish the present value of the note by discounting all future payments on the note at this rate. General guidelines for imputing the interest rate include the prevailing rates of similar instruments from creditors with similar credit ratings and the rate the debtor could obtain for similar financing from other sources. Other determining factors include any collateral or restrictive covenants involved, the current and expected prime rate, and other terms pertaining to the instrument. The objective is to approximate the rate of interest that would have resulted if an independent borrower and lender had negotiated a similar transaction under comparable terms and conditions. This determination is as of the issuance date, and any subsequent changes in interest rates would be irrelevant.

Bonds represent a promise to pay a sum of money at a designated maturity date plus periodic interest payments at a stated rate. Bonds are used primarily to borrow funds from the general public or institutional investors when a contract for a single amount (a note) is too large for one lender to supply. Dividing up the amount needed into $1,000 or $10,000 units makes it easier to sell the bonds.

In most situations, a bond is issued at a price other than its face value. The amount of the cash exchanged is equal to the total of the present value of the interest and principal payments. The difference between the cash proceeds and the face value is recorded as a premium if the cash proceeds are greater or a discount if they are less. The journal entry to record a bond issued at a premium follows:

Cash	(proceeds)	
Premium on bonds payable	(difference)	
Bonds payable		(face value)

The premium will be recognized over the life of the bond issue. If issued at a discount, "Discount on bonds payable" would be debited for the difference. As the premium is amortized, it will reduce interest expense on the books of the issuer (a discount will increase interest expense). The premium (discount) would be added to (deducted from) the related liability when a balance sheet is prepared.

The **effective interest method** is the preferred method of accounting for a discount or premium arising from a note or bond, although some other method may be used (e.g., straight-line) if the results are not materially different. Although the effective interest method is not prescribed under international accounting standards as such, the profession has made the use of the effective interest method the only acceptable one. Under the effective interest method, the discount or premium is to be amortized over the life of the debt in such a way as to result in a constant rate of interest when applied to the amount outstanding at the beginning of any given period. Therefore, interest expense is equal to the market rate of interest at the time of issuance multiplied by this beginning figure. The difference between the interest expense and the cash paid represents the amortization of the discount or premium.

Where use of the straight-line amortization method does not result in a material distortion as compared to the effective interest method, it would also be acceptable. Interest expense under the **straight-line method** is equal to the cash interest paid plus the amortized portion of the discount or minus the amortized portion of the premium. The amortized portion is equal to the total amount of the discount or premium divided by the life of the debt from issuance in months multiplied by the number of months the debt has been outstanding that year. Formerly, the straight-line method was used because it eliminated the complicated calculations required by the effective interest method; however, the prevalence of computers and of programs that compute the interest accrual under the more accurate effective interest method have largely eliminated this reason.

Amortization tables are often created at the time of the bond's issuance to provide figures when recording the necessary entries relating to the debt issue. They also provide a check of accuracy since the final values in the unamortized discount or premium and carrying value columns should be equal to zero and the bond's face value, respectively.

Example of applying the effective interest method

1. A 3-year, 12%, $10,000 bond is issued at 1/1/94, with interest payments semiannually.
2. The market rate is 10%.

The amortization table would appear as follows:

Date	*Credit cash*	*Debit int. exp.*	*Debit prem.*	*Unam. prem. bal.*	*Carrying value*
1/1/94				$507.61	$10,507.61(a)
7/1/94	$ 600.00(b)	$ 525.38(c)	$ 74.62(d)	432.99(e)	10,432.99(f)
1/1/95	600.00	521.65	78.35	354.64	10,354.64
7/1/95	600.00	517.73	82.27	272.37	10,272.37
1/1/96	600.00	513.62	86.38	185.99	10,185.99
7/1/96	600.00	509.30	90.70	95.29	10,095.29
1/1/97	600.00	504.71(g)	95.29	--	$10,000.00
	$3,600.00	$3,092.39	$507.61		

(a)*PV of principal and interest payments*
$10,000(.74622) = $ 7,462.20
$ 600(5.07569) = 3,045.41
$10,507.61

(b)*$10,000.00 x .06*

(c)*$10,507.61 x .05*
(d)*$600.00 – $525.38*
(e)*$507.61 – $74.62*
(f)*$10,507.61 – $74.62*
(or $10,000 + $432.99)
(g)*Rounding error = $.05*

When the interest date does not coincide with the year end, an adjusting entry must be made. The proportional share of interest payable should be recognized along with the amortization of the discount or premium. Within the amortization period, the discount or premium can be amortized using the straight-line method, as a practical matter, or can be computed more precisely as described above.

If the bonds are issued between interest dates, discount or premium amortization must be computed for the period between the sale date and the next interest date. This is accomplished by "straight-lining" the period's amount calculated using the usual method of amortization. In addition, the purchaser prepays the seller the amount of interest that has accrued since the last interest date. This interest is recorded as a payable by the seller. At the next interest date, the buyer then receives the full amount of interest regardless of how long the bond has been held. This procedure results in interest being paid equivalent to the time the bond has been outstanding.

Costs may be incurred in connection with issuing bonds. Examples include legal, accounting, and underwriting fees; commissions; and engraving, printing, and registration costs. Although these costs should be classified as a deferred charge and amortized using the effective interest method, generally the amount involved is insignificant enough that use of the simpler straight-line method would not result in a material difference. These costs do not provide any future economic benefit and therefore should not be considered an asset. Since these costs reduce the amount of cash proceeds, they in effect increase the effective interest rate and probably should be accounted for the same as an unamortized discount. Short-term obligations that are expected to be refinanced and therefore classified as long-term debt according to IAS 13 are discussed in Chapter 11.

The following diagram illustrates the recommended accounting treatments for monetary assets (and liabilities).

Extinguishment of Debt

Early extinguishments. Management may reacquire or retire outstanding debt before its scheduled maturity. This decision is usually caused by changes in present or expected interest rates or in cash flows. One concern, however, is that in a period of rising rates, an entity can retire its debt early, at a discount (as rising rates cause a decline in the market value of fixed-rate debt instruments), that will be reported in the income statement as a gain, but then re-borrow at current market rates, thereby causing future periods to carry a heavier debt service burden. This is one example of "window dressing," which allows management to show favorable performance currently while affecting future results adversely.

Although accounting rules can prevent misleading reporting of certain forms of window dressing which are only sham transactions (such as nominal sales of investments under repurchase agreements, which in reality are only secured borrowings), other events are real transactions that must be given accounting recognition. The actual extinguishment of debt at a discount, giving rise to a gain, is one of the latter types of events; the only question is how best to make the users of the financial statements fully aware of the potential implications.

ACCOUNTING FOR MONETARY ASSETS AND LIABILITIES

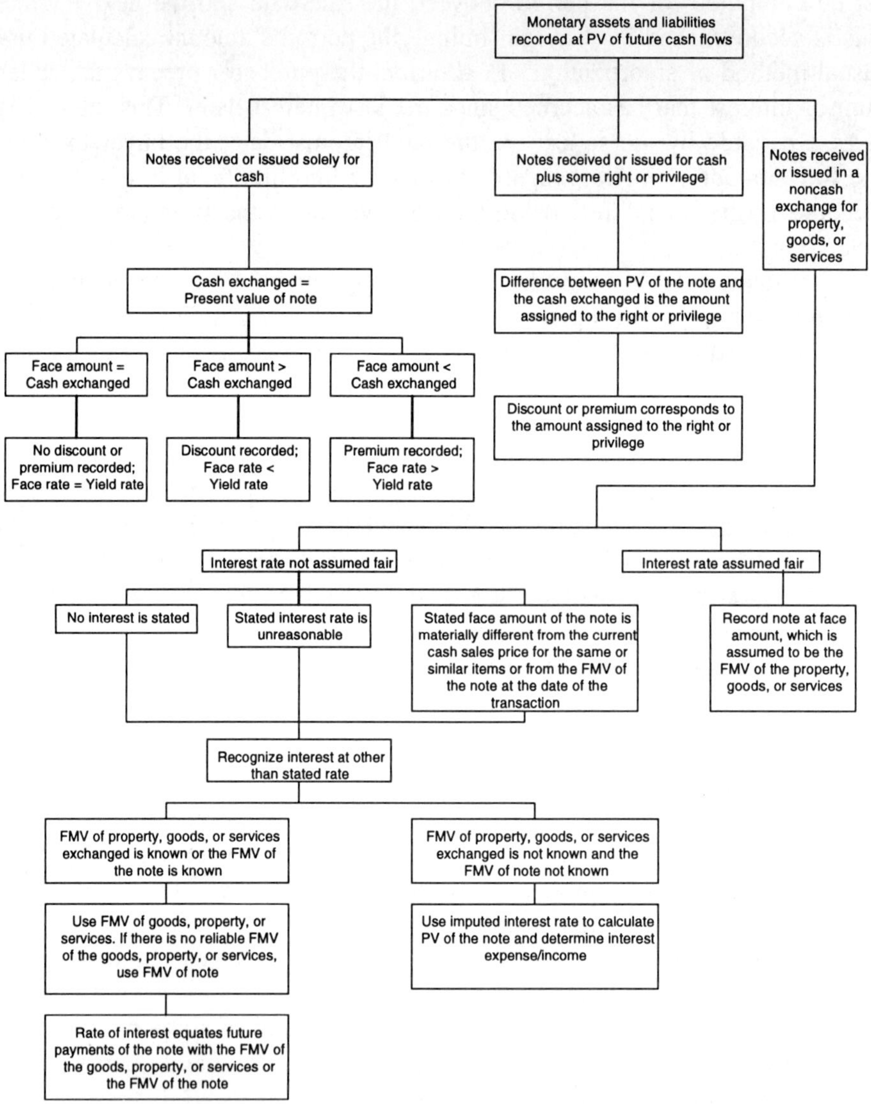

Although international standards have yet to address this, in the United States the accounting standard setters long ago mandated that gains or losses on debt extinguishment be given "extraordinary item" treatment in the statement of earnings. The purpose was merely to highlight such transactions, not to preclude the transactions themselves or to defer or avoid recognition of the resultant gains or losses.

Although gain or loss on debt extinguishment clearly does not meet the definition of an extraordinary item under US GAAP, a special rule established the requirement that such gains or losses be so accounted for.

International accounting standards establish (in IAS 8) a restrictive definition of extraordinary items. Clearly, this definition would not embrace such transactions as debt extinguishments, which are undertaken in the normal course of business by many entities. Therefore, the recommended, and only, recourse is to include adequate disclosure in the notes to the financial statements so that financial statement users are not mislead. This prescription is implied by IAS 5, which stipulates that the statements should include all information needed to make them not misleading.

Defeasance of debt. Another phenomenon that borders on window dressing is the relatively recent practice of engaging in **in-substance defeasance** of debt. Under this practice, certain assets are set aside in an irrevocable trust arrangement, to be used solely for the servicing and ultimate retirement of specific debt obligations. The concept is that since the assets are unavailable for any other purpose, both the assets and the debt obligations can validly be removed from the enterprise's balance sheet. Although this accounting treatment does not change the entity's reported net worth, it does alter the relationship between its reported debt and its equity. Since this is often viewed as being a key indicator of an entity's financial strength and long-term viability, this could have a material impact on how the entity is evaluated by investors and lenders.

International accounting standards do not address the matter of defeasance of debt. In the United States, defeasance has been a permitted accounting practice for over 10 years, although it is possible that with the promised promulgation of a new standard on derecognition of financial instruments (subject of a recent exposure draft) this practice may again become prohibited. The authors agree that the currently permitted treatment can result in distorting implications being drawn from the financial statements and urge that in-substance defeasances not be accounted for as true debt extinguishments.

Computing the gain or loss on debt extinguishments. The difference between the net carrying value and the acquisition price is to be recorded as a gain or loss. If the acquisition price is greater than the carrying value, a loss exists. A gain is generated if the acquisition price is less than the carrying value. These gains or losses are to be recognized in the period in which the retirement took place. Since, under international standards, these cannot be defined as extraordinary, logic suggests that they be reported as "other" income or expense, which is the same category in which interest expense is normally reported. It would **not** be appropriate, however, to include any gain or loss in the interest pool from which capitalized interest is computed under IAS 23 (discussed in Chapter 8).

The unamortized premium or discount and issue costs should be amortized to the acquisition date and recorded prior to determination of the gain or loss. If the extinguishment of debt does not occur on the interest date, the interest payable accruing between the last interest date and the acquisition date must also be recorded.

Example of accounting for the extinguishment of debt

1. A 10%, 10-year, $200,000 bond is dated and issued on 1/1/X4 at $98, with the interest payable semiannually.
2. Associated bond issue costs of $14,000 are incurred.
3. 4 years later, on 1/1/X8, the entire bond issue is repurchased at $102 per $100 face value and is retired.
4. The straight-line method of amortization is used since the result is not materially different from that when the effective interest method is used.

The gain or loss on the repurchase is computed as follows:

Reacquisition price [(102/100) x $200,000]		$204,000
Net carrying amount:		
Face value	$200,000	
Unamortized discount [2% x 200,000 x (6/10)]	(2,400)	
Unamortized issue costs [14,000 x (6/10)]	(8,400)	189,200
Loss on bond repurchase		$ 14,800

The loss on bond repurchase (debt extinguishment) is treated as another nonoperating item, in the same manner as interest expense. It should not be capitalized under IAS 23 as part of cost of plant assets, however.

Troubled Debt Restructurings

Another issue related to long-term debt is that of troubled debt restructurings. These usually involve situations where the creditor, for economic or legal reasons related to the debtor's financial difficulties, grants the debtor a concession that would otherwise not be granted. For example, the creditor may accept debtor assets having a market value less than the outstanding amount owed as full settlement of the obligation, or may offer extensions of time to pay or a reduction of either interest rate or face value, or both. These steps are taken because the creditor perceives the situation as being risky and deems it better to take "half a loaf" than to gamble on the outcome of a bankruptcy filing or other drastic action by the debtor.

Although no particular international accounting standards address these occurrences, there are some interesting accounting issues to be dealt with. If the debt restructuring is a settlement of the debt at less than the carrying amount, whether for cash of by an exchange of an asset, the debtor will have realized a gain and the creditor will have incurred a loss. The amount of the gain and the loss will be measured by the difference between the fair value (**not** the book value) of the asset transferred to settle the debt. For example, if a debtor transfers an asset having a $4.5 million book value and a $5.0 million fair market value to settle debt and accrued interest due in the amount of $6.0 million, a gain of $1.0 million has been enjoyed on the settlement and an asset carried at $4.5 million has been converted to its market value of $5.0 million, for another gain of $500,000. The creditor, meanwhile, has incurred a loss of $1.0 million.

The restructuring of troubled debt by modification of terms is more likely to cause accounting confusion than is an exchange of assets. For example, if the creditor prospectively waives some or all of the interest on the debt, so that, for example, a $4 million, 10% loan becomes a $4 million 2% debt obligation, there are some who would argue that this does not give rise to loss recognition by the creditor or gain recognition by the debtor, since it is only a modification of future terms. That is, under this view the creditor would realize less income in future periods but would not reflect a loss on the **agreement** to accept lower yield in later periods. Similarly, if the due date of the debt is extended, some have argued that this also is not a recognizable economic event, but rather, is to be reported only in later periods.

Notwithstanding these perspectives, it should be clear that an economic event has occurred by the very fact of the restructuring. Since the goal of accounting is to report on economic events, a more rational response would be to measure these events when they occur and include the effect in the creditor's and debtor's respective income statements at that time. The only meaningful way to accomplish this is to measure the present value of future cash flows under the restructured loan agreement, discounted by the **effective** rate on the original borrowing. (Effective rate is used to denote that if there were deferred fees or other costs, or a premium or discount, being amortized over the term of the loan, these should be taken into account and used instead of the nominal interest rate on the original debt.) Thus, the difference between the present value of the newly defined future cash flows and the carrying amount of the debt immediately prior to the restructuring should be the measure of the gain or loss to be recognized.

Example of restructuring with gain/loss recognized

Assume that a debtor owes on a 5% interest-bearing note payable in 5 years a remaining principal balance of $90,000 plus accrued interest of $10,000. The lender agrees to a restructuring to assist the debtor, which is in financial straits and threatening to declare bankruptcy. The interest rate is reduced to 4% by the lender, the principal is reduced to $72,500, and the accrued interest is forgiven entirely.

Future cash flows (after restructuring):	
Principal	$72,500
Interest (5 years x $72,500 x 4%)	14,500
Total cash to be received	$87,000

Note that it would **not** be meaningful simply to compare the new total expected cash flow from the loan, $87,000, to the carrying value of the loan ($100,000, including accrued interest), for an indicated loss of $13,000. This fails to consider the time value of money, since the $100,000 is owed to the creditor today, whereas the $87,000 will be collected over a 5 year period. Instead, it is necessary to compute the present value of future cash flows, using the effective rate of the original borrowing, 5%, as follows:

		5% 5 yrs. *PV factor*
Future cash flows (after restructuring):		
Principal	$56,806	($72,500 x 0.78353)
Interest	12,555	($ 2,900 x 4.32948)
Total present value	$69,361	

The difference between the amount owed immediately prior to the restructuring, $100,000, and the agreed-upon settlement, $69,361, is the measure of the economic loss, $30,639. The entries by the creditor would be as follows:

	Debit	Credit	
Beginning of Year 1			
Bad debt expense	30,639		
Interest receivable		10,000	
Valuation allowance		20,639	
End of Year 1			
Cash	2,900		
Valuation allowance	568		
Bad debt expense (or interest income)		3,468	(69,361 x .05)
End of Year 2			
Cash	2,900		
Valuation allowance	596		
Bad debt expense (or interest income)		3,496	(69,929 x .05)
End of Year 3			
Cash	2,900		
Valuation allowance	626		
Bad debt expense (or interest income)		3,526	(70,525 x .05)
End of Year 4			
Cash	2,900		
Valuation allowance	658		
Bad debt expense (or interest income)		3,558	(71,151 x .05)
End of Year 5			
Cash	2,900		
Valuation allowance	691		
Bad debt expense (or interest income)		3,591	(71,809 x .05)
Cash	72,500		
Valuation allowance	17,500		
Note receivable		90,000	

Entries to be made by the debtor would largely mirror those shown above.

Convertible Debt

Bonds are frequently issued with the right to convert them into common stock of the company at the holder's option when certain terms and conditions are met (i.e., a target market price is reached). Convertible debt is used for two reasons. First, when a specific amount of funds is needed, convertible debt often allows fewer shares to be issued (assuming conversion) than if the funds were raised by directly issuing the shares. Thus, less dilution occurs. Second, the conversion feature allows debt to be issued at a lower interest rate and with fewer restrictive covenants than if the debt were issued without it.

This dual nature of debt and equity, however, creates a question as to whether the equity element should receive separate recognition. Support for separate treatment is based on the assumption that this equity element has economic value. Since the convertible feature tends to lower the rate of interest, it can easily be argued that a portion of the proceeds should be allocated to this equity feature. On the other hand, a case can be made that the debt and equity elements are inseparable, and thus that the instrument is either all debt or all equity. International accounting standards had not previously addressed this matter directly, although the focus of *Framework for Preparation and Presentation of Financial Statements* on "true and fair presentation" could be said to support the notion that the proceeds of a convertible debt offering be allocated between debt and equity accounts. Recently, however, IAS 32 has been promulgated, defining convertible bonds (among others) as compound financial instruments, the component parts of which must be classified according to their separate characteristics.

Features of convertible debt. Features of convertible debt typically include: (1) a conversion price 15 to 20% greater than the market value of the stock when the debt is issued; (2) conversion features (price and number of shares) that protect against dilution from stock dividends, splits, and so on; and (3) a callable feature at the issuer's option that is usually exercised once the conversion price is reached (thus forcing conversion or redemption).

Convertible debt also has its disadvantages. If the stock price increases significantly after the debt is issued, the issuer would have been better off simply by issuing the stock. Additionally, if the price of the stock does not reach the conversion price, the debt will never be converted (a condition known as overhanging debt).

Accounting for compound instruments. IAS 32 establishes the notion that component parts of compound instruments, such as convertible bonds, must be accounted for separately, consistent with their separate characteristics, but does not prescribe specific methodologies to accomplish this. However, several measurement strategies are noted in the standard, and these are illustrated in the following paragraphs.

Residual allocation method. One method of allocating proceeds from the issuance of convertible debt would be allocate to the less easily measured component (probably the conversion feature) the residual after first assigning the market value to the more directly measured component (the debt, absent the conversion feature). To illustrate this approach, consider the following fact situation.

Example of the residual allocation method

Istanbul Corp. sells convertible bonds having aggregate par (face) value of $25 million to the public at a price of $98 on January 2, 1996. The bonds are due December 31, 2003, but can be called at $102 anytime after January 2, 1999. The bonds carry a coupon of 6% and are convertible into Istanbul Corp. common stock at an exchange ratio of 25 shares per bond (each bond having a face value of $1,000). Taking the discount on the offering price into account, the bonds were priced to yield about 6.3% to maturity.

The company's investment bankers have advised it that without the conversion feature, Istanbul's bonds would have had to have carried an interest yield of 8% to have been sold in the current market environment. Thus, the market price of a pure bond with a 6% coupon at January 2, 1996, would have been about $883.48 (the present value of a stream of semiannual interest payments of $30 per bond, plus a terminal value of $1,000, discounted at a 4% semiannual rate).

This suggests that of the $980 being paid for each bond, $883.48 is being paid for the pure debt obligation, and another $96.52 is being offered for the conversion feature. Given this analysis, the entry to record the original issuance of the $25 million in debt securities on January 2, 1996, would be as follows:

Cash	24,500,000	
Discount on bonds payable	2,913,000	
Bonds payable		25,000,000
Paid-in-capital--conversion feature		2,413,000

The discount should be amortized to interest expense, ideally by the effective yield method (constant return on increasing base) over the 8 years to the maturity date. For purposes of this example, however, straight-line amortization ($2,913,000 ÷ 16 periods = $182,000 per semiannual period) will be used. Thus, the entry to record the June 30, 1996 interest payment would be as follows:

Interest expense	932,000	
Discount on bonds payable		182,000
Cash		750,000

The paid-in capital account arising from the foregoing transaction would form a permanent part of the capital of Istanbul Corp. If the bonds are later converted, this would be transferred to the common stock accounts, effectively forming part of the price paid for the shares ultimately issued. If the bondholders decline to convert and the bonds are eventually paid off at maturity, the paid-in capital from the conversion feature will form a type of "donated capital" to the enterprise; the bondholders effectively have forfeited this capital that they had contributed to the company.

If the bonds are not converted, the discount on the bonds payable will continue to be amortized until maturity. However, if they are converted, the remaining unamortized balance in this account, along with the face value of the bonds, will constitute the "price" being paid for the stock to be issued. To illustrate this, assume the following:

On July 1, 1999, all the bonds are tendered for conversion to common stock of Istanbul Corp. The remaining book value of the bonds will be converted into common stock, which does not carry any par or stated value. The first step is to compute the book value of the debt.

Bonds payable		$25,000,000
Discount on bonds payable		
Original discount	$ 2,913,000	
Less amortization to date (4.4 yrs.)	(1,638,000)	1,275,000
Net book value of obligation		$23,725,000

The entry to record the conversion, given the foregoing information, is as follows:

Bonds payable	25,000,000	
Paid-in-capital--conversion feature	2,413,000	
Discount on bonds payable		1,275,000
Common stock, no par value		26,138,000

Note that in the foregoing entry, the effective price recorded for the shares being issued is the book value of the remaining debt, adjusted by the price previously recorded to reflect the sale of the conversion feature. In the present instance, given the book value at the conversion date (a function of when the conversion privilege was exercised), and given the conversion ratio of 25 shares per bond, an effective price of $41.82 per share is being paid for the stock to be issued. This is determined without any reference to the market value at the date of the conversion. Presumably, the market price is higher, as it is unlikely that the bondholders would surrender an asset earning 6%, with a fixed maturity date, for another asset having a lower value and having an uncertain future worth (although if the dividend yield were somewhat higher than the equivalent bond interest, an unlikely event, this might happen).

Another approach to the conversion would be to reflect the stock issuance at the then-current market value, reporting a gain or loss for the difference between the market value per share and the amount computed on the book value basis, as shown above. However, this can be criticized because it is not normally acceptable to report income statement events (the gain or loss) arising from capital transactions. For this reason, the book value approach is recommended.

Relative market value approach. The alternative to the residual value allocation method described above for assigning the proceeds from the sale of convertible debt would be to measure directly the market value of each component of the compound financial instrument. This may be more easily accomplished in some circumstances than in others. For example, if options on Istanbul stock are currently being traded on the open market at the time the convertible debt is offered for sale, it would be possible to assess the value of the conversion feature, although some judgment might be involved to adjust for the different features and limitations of exchange traded options and the conversion feature. Consider the following example.

Example of the relative market value approach

As in the example above, Istanbul Corp. sells convertible bonds having aggregate par (face) value of $25 million to the public at a price of $98 on January 2, 1996. The bonds are due December 31, 2003, but can be called at $102 anytime after January 2, 1999. The bonds carry a coupon of 6% and are convertible into Istanbul Corp. common stock at an exchange ratio of 25 shares per bond (each bond having a face value of $1,000). Taking the discount on the offering price into account, the bonds were priced to yield about 6.3% to maturity.

The company's investment bankers again have advised it that without the conversion feature, Istanbul's bonds would have had to have carried an interest yield of 8% to have been sold in the current market environment. Thus, the market price of a "pure" bond with a 6% coupon at January 2, 1996, would have been about $883.48. Now, however, assume also that options on Istanbul stock are being traded on the open market. The common stock is presently selling for $32 per share; options to buy the stock at $42 are trading at $3.50 each.

Since 625,000 shares will be issued if all the bonds are converted, this suggests a gross value of $2,187,500 due to the conversion feature, or an equivalent of $87.50 per bond. However, the actual conversion feature is at a lower price than is attached to the market-traded options ($40 vs. $42), and these have a longer life (8 years vs. a typical 2 years on market-traded options), so the investment bankers advise Istanbul management that the value per stock right would be $6, or an indicated value of $150 per bond (since each is convertible into 25 shares), for a total value of $3,750,000. Since the total indicated value of the conversion privilege ($3,750,000) plus the pure bonds ($883.48 x 25,000 bonds = $22,087,000) is greater (at $25,837,000) than the actual selling price of the bonds ($24,500,000), the amounts to be allocated to the debt and to the equity conversion feature should be pro rated, as follows:

22,087,000/25,837,000	x	24,500,000	=	$20,944,050 ($837.76 per bond)
3,750,000/25,837,000	x	24,500,000	=	$ 3,555,950 ($142.24 per bond)

This suggests that of the $980 being paid for each bond, $837.76 is being paid for the pure debt obligation, and another $142.24 is being offered for the conversion feature. Given this analysis, the entry to record the original issuance of the $25 million in debt securities on January 2, 1996, would be as follows:

Cash	24,500,000	
Discount on bonds payable	4,055,950	
Bonds payable		25,000,000
Paid-in-capital--conversion feature		3,555,950

As with the earlier example, the indicated discount would be amortized over the term to maturity of the debt, 8 years in this case, by the effective yield method, or by the straight-line method if this would not make a material difference in reported financial position and results of operations.

It might be noted that under present US GAAP, when convertible debt is issued no value is apportioned to the conversion feature when recording the issue. However, it is likely that US standards will eventually follow the path set by IAS 32 in this regard, since the issue of accounting for compound financial instruments has been debated for over 5 years and the existence of the newly promulgated international standard will doubtless put added pressure on US standard setters.

Induced Conversion of Debt

A special situation may occur in that the conversion privileges of convertible debt are modified after issuance of the debt. These modifications may take the form of reduced conversion prices or additional consideration paid to the convertible debt holder. The debtor offers these modifications or "sweeteners" to induce prompt conversion of the outstanding debt. This is in addition to the normal strategy of calling the convertible debt to induce the holders to convert, assuming the underlying economic values make this attractive (debtors often do this when only a small fraction of the originally issued convertible debt remains outstanding).

Logically, there are two ways to account for these sweeteners. The first would be to treat this as a reduction in the proceeds of the stock offering, thereby reducing paid-in capital from the transaction. The second possible accounting treatment would be to record these payments as an expense in the period of conversion. The former position is based on the notion that costs associated with the raising of equity capital are netted against the proceeds so generated; if a sweetener is deemed needed to raise the equity capital in a given situation, this should be accounted for as any other costs, such as underwriting fees, would be. The latter position springs from a recognition that if it had been part of the original arrangement, a change in the exchange ratio or other adjustment would have affected the allocation of the original proceeds between debt and equity, and the discount or premium originally recognized would have been different in amount, and hence periodic amortization would have differed as well.

There are no specific international standards on this matter, and the arguments for both treatments are impressive. Accordingly, both are illustrated here. The example that follows illustrates the calculation and recording of the debt conversion expense if the cost of the sweetener is deemed to be a period cost.

Example of debt conversion expense

1. January 1, 1995, Imag Company issued ten 8% convertible bonds at $1,000 par value without a discount or premium, maturing December 31, 2005.
2. The bonds are initially convertible into no-par common stock of Imag at a conversion price of $25.
3. On July 1, 1999, the convertible bonds have a market value of $600 each.
4. To induce the convertible bondholders to convert their bonds quickly, Imag reduces the conversion price to $20 for bondholders who convert before July 21, 1999 (within 20 days).

5. The market price of Imag Company's common stock on the date of conversion is $15 per share.

The fair value of the incremental consideration paid by Imag upon conversion is calculated as follows for each bond converted before July 21, 1999:

Value of securities issued to debt holders:	
Face amount	$1,000 per bond
÷ New conversion price	÷ $20 per share
Number of common shares issued upon conversion	50 shares
x Price per common share	x $15 per share
Value of securities issued	$ 750(a)

Value of securities issuable pursuant to the original conversion privileges:	
Face amount	$1,000 per bond
÷ Original conversion price	÷ $25 per share
Number of common shares issuable pursuant to original conversion privilege	40 shares
x Price per share	x $15 per share
Value of securities issuable pursuant to original conversion privileges	$ 600(b)
Value of securities issued	$ 750(a)
Value of securities issuable pursuant to the original conversion privileges	600(b)
Fair value of incremental consideration	$ 150

The entry to record the debt conversion for **each bond** is

Convertible debt	1,000	
Debt conversion expense	150	
Common stock--no par		1,150

If instead of the foregoing accounting treatment, it was decided to treat the sweetener as a cost of raising capital, in this fact situation the only change would be to credit common stock for $1,000 per bond rather than the market-determined $1,150. Depending on whether the stock carried a par or a stated value, it might have been necessary to make a slightly different entry, but the concept would be the same.

Debt Issued With Stock Warrants

Warrants are certificates enabling the holder to purchase a stated number of shares of stock at a certain price within a certain period. They are often issued with bonds to enhance the marketability of the bonds and to lower the bond's interest rate.

Detachable warrants are similar to other features, such as the conversion feature discussed earlier, which under IAS 32 make the debt a compound financial instrument and which necessitates that there be an allocation of the original proceeds among the constituent elements. Since warrants, which will often be traded in the market, are easier to value than are conversion features, the second method discussed above, pro rata allocation based on relative market values, is to be favored.

Example of accounting for a bond with a detachable warrant

1. A $1,000 bond with a detachable warrant to buy 10 shares of $10 par common stock at $50 per share is issued for $1,025.
2. Immediately after the issuance the bonds trade at $980 and the warrants at $60.
3. The market value of the stock is $54.

The relative market value of the bonds is 94% (980/1,040) and the warrant is 6% (60/1,040). Thus, $62 (6% x $1,025) of the issuance price is assigned to the warrants. The journal entry to record the issuance is

Cash	1,025	
Discount on bonds payable	37	
Bonds payable		1,000
Paid-in capital--warrants (or "Stock options outstanding")		62

The discount is the difference between the purchase price assigned to the bond, $963 (94% x $1,025), and its face value, $1,000. The debt itself is accounted for in the normal fashion.

The entry to record the subsequent future exercise of the warrant would be

Cash	500	
Paid-in capital--warrants	62	
Common stock		100
Paid-in capital		462 (difference)

Assuming the warrants are not exercised, the journal entry is

Paid-in capital--warrants	62	
Paid-in capital--expired warrants		62

13 ACCOUNTING FOR LEASES

PERSPECTIVE AND ISSUES

Entrepreneurs who experiment with innovative means of financing have long used leasing as a vehicle to finance acquisitions of business assets. During the past few decades, however, the business of leasing has experienced staggering growth. The tremendous popularity of leasing is quite understandable, as it offers great flexibility coupled with a range of economic advantages over ownership in many situations. The lessee (borrower) is typically able to obtain 100% financing with leasing, whereas under a credit purchase arrangement the buyer would generally have to make an initial payment that would not be financed. In many cases the leasing arrangement offers tax benefits through larger tax deductions compared to the purchasing option. Also, during the term of the lease, the lessor receives from the lessee the equivalent of interest in the form of lease payments and, at the end of the lease term, usually some residual value. Finally, leasing often protects the lessee from the risk of obsolescence.

The lease transaction derives its accounting complexity from the number of alternatives available to the parties involved. Leases can be structured to allow manipulation of the tax benefits associated with the leased asset. They can be used to transfer ownership of the leased asset, and they can be used to transfer the risk of ownership. In any event, the economic substance of the transaction dictates the accounting treatment. The accounting for lease transactions is probably the best example of the accounting profession's substance over form principle, as set forth in the IASC's *Framework for the Preparation and Presentation of Financial Statements*. If the transaction effectively transfers ownership to the lessee, the substance of the transaction is that of a sale and should be recognized as such even though the transaction takes the form of a lease.

IAS 17 remains the only promulgated standard on lease accounting under International Accounting Standards. IAS 17 became effective for years beginning on or after January 1, 1984, and has not been revised since that date. Although elimination of the free choice between two alternative income recognition methods permitted to lessors under finance leases had been considered as part of the IASC's comparability project in 1989, ultimately no changes were made at that time. Currently, however, an exposure draft, E56, is outstanding; one of its major changes would be to eliminate one of the methods now allowed. Other changes would strengthen certain disclosures. If enacted, E56 will replace existing standard IAS 17. The IASC has indicated that these changes are intended to improve lease accounting in the short term, but that further enhancements will likely be needed, and that a separate effort, after completion of the "core set of standards" project, will probably be undertaken. For example, a number of issues having narrower applicability have not been addressed. Topics such as leveraged leases need detailed guidance such as is provided under some nations' indigenous accounting standards.

In general, all kinds of leasing arrangements which satisfy the definition of a lease as contained in IAS 17 are covered by this standard. However, a scope limitation has been provided whereby the following specialized types of lease agreements are not covered by IAS 17, nor by exposure draft E56:

1. Lease agreements to explore for or use natural resources, such as oil, gas, timber, metals, and other mineral rights
2. Licensing agreements for such items as motion picture films, video recordings, plays, manuscripts, patents, and copyrights

While US GAAP also limits the applicability of its leasing standard to the foregoing leasing arrangements, the scope limitation under US GAAP is due to the fact that other pronouncements exist which deal specifically with those leasing arrangements; for instance, licensing agreements of the motion picture industry and the broadcasting industry, and for oil and gas producers, are covered by other promulgated standards. Under the International Accounting Standards however, to date, only licensing agreements for manuscripts, patents, and copyrights have been covered by a separate standard, namely E60, *Intangible Assets*, which is a recent exposure draft. E60 has superseded earlier (never enacted) exposure draft E50.

Sources of IAS
IAS 4, 5, 17, 24
Exposure Draft E55, 56, 60

DEFINITIONS OF TERMS

Bargain purchase option (BPO). A provision in the lease agreement allowing the lessee the option of purchasing the leased property for an amount that is sufficiently lower than the fair value of the property at the date the option becomes exercisable. Exercise of the option must appear reasonably assured at the inception of the lease.

Contingent rentals. Those lease rentals that are not fixed in amount but are based on a factor other than simply the passage of time; for example, based on percentage of sales, price indices, market rates of interest, or use of the leased asset.

Executory costs. Those costs such as insurance, maintenance, and taxes incurred for leased property, whether paid by the lessor or lessee. If paid by the lessee, the lessee's obligation to pay such costs are excluded from the minimum lease payments.

Fair value of leased property (FMV). The amount for which an asset could be exchanged between a knowledgeable, willing buyer and a knowledgeable, willing seller in an arm's-length transaction. When the lessor is a manufacturer or dealer, the fair value of the property at the inception of the lease will ordinarily be its normal selling price net of volume or trade discounts. When the lessor is not a manufacturer or dealer, the fair value of the property at the inception of the lease will ordinarily be its cost to the lessor unless a significant amount of time has lapsed between the acquisition of the property by the lessor and the inception of the lease, in which case fair value should be determined in light of market conditions prevailing at the inception of the lease. Thus, fair value may be greater or less than the cost or carrying amount of the property.

Finance lease. A lease that transfers substantially all the risks and rewards associated with the ownership of an asset. The risks related to ownership of an asset include the possibilities of losses from idle capacity or technological obsolescence and of variations in return due to changing economic conditions; rewards incidental to ownership of an asset include expectation of profitable operations over the asset's economic life and expectation of gain from appreciation in value or the ultimate realization of the residual value. Title may or may not eventually be transferred to the lessee.

Gross investment in the lease. The sum total of (1) the minimum lease payments under a finance lease (from the standpoint of the lessor), plus (2) any unguaranteed residual value accruing to the lessor.

Inception of the lease. The date of the written lease agreement or, if earlier, the date of a commitment by the parties to the principal provisions of the lease.

Initial direct costs. Initial direct costs, such as commissions and legal fees, incurred by lessors in negotiating and arranging a lease. These generally include (1) costs to originate a lease incurred in transactions with independent third parties that (a) result directly from and are essential to acquire that lease and (b) would not have been incurred had that leasing transaction not occurred; and (2) certain costs directly related to specified activities performed by the lessor for that lease, such as evaluating the prospective lessee's financial condition; evaluating and recording guarantees, collateral, and other security arrangements; negotiating lease terms; preparing and processing lease documents; and closing the transaction.

Lease. An agreement whereby a lessor conveys to the lessee in return for lease rentals the right to use an asset (property, plant, equipment, or land) for an agreed period of time. Other arrangements essentially similar to leases, such as hire-purchase contracts, bare-boat charters, and so on, are considered leases for purposes of the standard.

Lease term. The initial noncancelable period for which the lessee has contracted to lease the asset together with any further periods for which the lessee has the option to extend the lease of the asset, with or without further payment, which option it is reasonably certain (at the inception of the lease) that the lessee will exercise.

Lessee's incremental borrowing rate. The interest rate that the lessee would have to pay on a similar lease, or, if that is not determinable, the rate that at the inception of the lease the lessee would have incurred to borrow over a similar term (i.e., a loan term equal to the lease term), and with a similar security, the funds necessary to purchase the leased asset.

Minimum lease payments (MLP).

1. From the standpoint of the **lessee**. The payments over the lease term that the lessee is or can be required to make in connection with the leased property. The lessee's obligation to pay executory costs (e.g., insurance, maintenance, or taxes) are excluded from minimum lease payments. If the lease contains a bargain purchase option, the minimum rental payments over the lease term plus the payment called for in the bargain purchase option are included in minimum lease payments.

   If no such provision regarding a bargain purchase option is included in the lease contract, the minimum lease payments include the following:

   a. The minimum rental payments called for by the lease over the lease contract over the term of the lease (excluding any executory costs), plus
   b. Any guarantee of residual value, at the expiration of the lease term, to be paid by the lessee or a party related to the lessee.

2. From the standpoint of the **lessor**. The payments described above plus any guarantee of the residual value of the leased asset by a third party unrelated to either the lessee or lessor (provided that the third party is financially capable of discharging the guaranteed obligation).

Net cash investment in the lease. The difference between the following amounts:

1. Cash outflows in respect of the lease, including payments made to acquire the asset, tax payments (if any), interest and principal payments on outside financing (if any), but excluding payments relating to insurance, maintenance, and similar costs rechargeable to the lessee; and
2. Cash inflows in respect of the lease, including rental receipts, receipts from residual values, grants, tax credits, and other repayments arising from the lease. Exposure draft E56, which if enacted will replace original IAS 17, eliminates the lessor's option of computing finance lease income based on its net cash investment in the lease. Accordingly, E56 drops this term from its set of definitions.

Net investment in the lease. The difference between the lessor's gross investment in the lease and the unearned finance income.

Noncancelable lease. A lease that is cancelable only

1. On occurrence of some remote contingency
2. With the concurrence (permission) of the lessor
3. If the lessee enters into a new lease for the same or an equivalent asset with the same lessor
4. On payment by the lessee of an additional amount such that at inception, continuation of the lease appears reasonably assured

Nonrecourse (debt) financing. Lending or borrowing activities in which the creditor does not have general recourse to the debtor but rather has recourse only to the property used for collateral in the transaction or other specific property.

Operating lease. A lease that does not meet the criteria prescribed for a finance lease.

Penalty. Any requirement that is imposed or can be imposed on the lessee by the lease agreement or by factors outside the lease agreement to pay cash, incur or assume a liability, perform services, surrender or transfer an asset or rights to an asset, or otherwise forego an economic benefit or suffer an economic detriment.

Rate implicit in the lease. The discount rate that at the inception of the lease, when applied to the minimum lease payments, and the unguaranteed residual value accruing to the benefit of the lessor, causes the aggregate present value to be equal to the fair value of the leased property to the lessor, net of any grants and tax credits receivable by the lessor.

Related parties in leasing transactions. Entities that are in a relationship where one party has the ability to control the other party or exercise significant influence over the operating and financial policies of the related party. Examples include the following:

1. A parent company and its subsidiaries
2. An owner company and its joint ventures and partnerships
3. An investor and its investees

Significant influence may be exercised in several ways, usually by representation on the board of directors but also by participation in the policy making process, material intercompany transactions, interchange of managerial personnel, or dependence on technical information. The ability to exercise significant influence must be present before the parties can be considered related. Additional examples of significant influence in relation to leasing which are derived from US GAAP and which could be considered in interpretations under IAS 17 are

1. Significant influence may also be exercised through guarantees of indebtedness, extensions of credit, or through ownership of debt obligations, warrants, or other securities

2. If two or more entities are subject to the significant influence of a parent, owner, investor, or common officers or directors, those entities are considered related to each other

Renewal or extension of a lease. The continuation of a lease agreement beyond the original lease term, including a new lease where the lessee continues to use the same property.

Residual value of leased property. The fair value, estimated at the inception of the lease, that the enterprise expects to obtain from the leased property at the end of the lease term.

Sale and leaseback accounting. A method of accounting for a sale-leaseback transaction in which the seller-lessee records the sale, removes all property and related liabilities from its balance sheet, recognizes gain or loss from the sale, and classifies the leaseback in accordance with this section.

Unearned finance income. The excess of the lessor's gross investment in the lease over its present value.

Unguaranteed residual value. Part of the residual value of the leased asset (estimated at the inception of the lease) the realization of which by the lessor is not assured or is guaranteed by a party related to the lessor.

Useful life of leased property. The useful life refers to either the passage of time (the period over which the depreciable asset is expected to be used by an enterprise) or the amount of use (the number of production or similar units expected to be obtained from the leased asset). If adopted, E56 will replace the term "useful life" with "economic life," but otherwise will keep this definition intact.

CONCEPTS, RULES, AND EXAMPLES

Classification of Leases--Lessee

For accounting and reporting purposes the lessee has two alternatives in classifying a lease.

1. Operating
2. Finance

It should be observed that finance leases are referred to as a capital leases under US GAAP. Finance leases are those that essentially are alternative means of financing the acquisition of property or of substantially all the service potential represented by the property. The term **capital** is used because under accounting standards such leased property is treated as owned and accordingly, capitalized on the balance sheet. Since, due to the relative paucity of guidance on lease accounting under IAS there will be many issues on which informal direction will be taken from US GAAP, the terms **finance** and **capital** will be treated as synonymous in this chapter.

The proper classification of a lease is determined by the circumstances surrounding the leasing transaction. According to IAS 17, whether a lease is a finance lease or not will have to be judged based on the **substance** of the transaction, rather than the **form** of the contract. Further, if substantially all of the benefits and risks of ownership have been transferred to the lessee, the lease should be classified as a finance lease; such a lease is normally noncancelable and the lessor is assured of recovery of the capital invested plus a reasonable return on its investment. Substantially all of the risks or benefits of ownership are deemed to have been transferred if any one of the following criteria has been met:

1. The lease transfers ownership to the lessee by the end of the lease term.
2. The lease contains a bargain purchase option (an option to purchase the leased asset at a price that is expected to be substantially lower than the fair value at the date the option becomes exercisable) and it is reasonably certain that the option will be exercisable.
3. The lease term is for the major part of the useful life of the leased asset. Title **may or may not** eventually pass to the lessee.
4. The present value (PV), at the inception of the lease, of the minimum lease payments is greater than, or equal to substantially all of, the fair value of the leased asset, net of grants and tax credits to the lessor at that time. Title **may or may not** eventually pass to the lessee.

E56 adds to the foregoing set of indicators that a lease is to be accounted for as a finance lease by setting forth four additional criteria. If E56 is adopted, an evaluation of all eight criteria will be required to assess whether there is sufficient evidence to conclude that a given arrangement should be accounted for as a finance lease. The four new criteria are as follows:

5. If the lessee can cancel the lease, it must bear any associated losses.
6. Gains or losses due to fluctuations in the fair value of the residual accrue to the lessee.
7. At the lessee's option, the lease can be extended at a rental which is substantially below market rates
8. The leased assets are of a specialized nature such that major modifications would be needed by any other lessee.

The interest rate used to compute the present value should be the lessee's incremental borrowing rate unless it is practicable to determine the rate implicit in the lease, in which case that rate should be used. It is interesting to note that under US GAAP, in order to use the rate implicit in the lease to discount the minimum lease payments, this rate must be lower than the lessee's incremental borrowing rate. Logically, of course, if the lessee's incremental borrowing rate were lower than a rate offered implicitly in a lease, and the prospective lessee was aware of this fact, it would be more attractive to borrow and purchase, so the US rule may be somewhat superfluous. The IAS does not set this as a condition, however.

In general, if a lease agreement meets one of the four criteria set forth above, it is to be classified as a finance lease in the financial statements of the lessee under the existing standard. However, a further condition is established by IAS 17 for real estate leases: Unless there will be a title transfer by the end of the lease term (i.e., criterion 1 above should be met), the lease should normally **not** be deemed to be a finance lease.

The language used in the last two criteria for classifying leases makes them rather subjective and somewhat difficult to apply. In other words, given the same set of facts, it is possible for two enterprises to reach different conclusions regarding the classification of a given lease. The IAS 17 approach is quite distinct from that adopted by the corresponding US standard, SFAS 13. In that standard, a threshold of 75% of useful life is defined rather than the more vague "major portion of the useful life" of IAS 17; and threshold "present value of minimum lease payments" is set at 90% rather than the "greater than, or equal to substantially all of, the fair value of the leased asset" of the international standard. (Of course, in attempting to apply IAS 17, entities can look to SFAS 13 and other accounting literature for guidance, but these sources cannot be considered as definitive.)

In the absence of interpretation or direction from the IASC, it may be argued that the expression "major portion" represents 80% or 90% instead of 75% of the useful life, or that "substantially all" represents 95% or, for that matter, even 99%, instead of 90% of fair value at the inception of the lease. It is thus hoped that the IASC will address these issues when it revisits IAS 17, as it has agreed to do under its current work plan, since these have been difficult practical problems in applying the standard.

While existing standard IAS 17 does not address the alterations in lease terms which might call into question the classification of the original lease agreement, the exposure draft E56 provides for this contingency. Under the proposed standard's terms, if the parties agree to alter the terms of the lease, other than by renewing the lease or extending its term, in a manner which would have resulted in a different classification had the changed terms been in effect at inception of the lease, then the revised lease will be considered a new lease agreement.

Classification of Leases--Lessor

The lessor has the following alternatives in classifying a lease:

1. Operating lease
2. Finance lease
    a. Plain or regular finance lease, hereinafter referred to as direct financing lease, which is the term used by US GAAP

b. Finance lease by manufacturers or dealers, hereinafter referred to as sales-type lease, the term used by US GAAP
c. Leveraged lease, wherein financing is through a third-party creditor instead of the lessor

Consistent accounting by lessee and lessor. Since the events or transactions that take place between the lessor and the lessee are based on an agreement (the lease) that is common to both the parties, it is normally appropriate that the lease be classified in a consistent manner by both parties. Thus, if any one of the four criteria specified above for classification of a finance lease by the lessee is met, the lease should also be classified as a finance lease by the lessor. If the lease qualifies as a finance lease from the standpoint of the lessor, it would be classified either as a sales-type lease, a direct financing lease, or a leveraged lease, depending on the conditions present at the inception of the lease.

However, IAS 17 alludes to an exception to this general rule when it speaks about the "differing circumstances" sometimes leading to the same lease being classified differently by the lessor and lessee. The standard does not, unfortunately, expand on this matter, but once again reference can be made to US GAAP, which clearly sets forth the circumstances or factors which if not satisfied from the standpoint of the lessor would lead to different classifications by the lessor and the lessee. SFAS 13 stipulates that the following two conditions need to be satisfied **in addition** to the four criteria above before a lease could be classified as a finance lease (capital lease under US GAAP) from the standpoint of a lessor:

1. Collectibility of the minimum lease payments is reasonably predictable.
2. No important uncertainties surround the amount of nonreimbursable costs yet to be incurred by the lessor under the lease.

Under US GAAP, therefore, if a lease transaction does not meet the criteria for classification as a sales-type lease, a direct financing lease, or a leveraged lease as specified above, it is to be classified in the financial statements of the lessor as an operating lease. If the lessee has accounted for the lease as a capital lease, the asset being leased may appear on the balance sheets of both lessee and lessor.

Although guidance under IAS 17 does not establish additional conditions that must be fulfilled for the lessor to treat a lease as a financing transaction, as the US standard does, use of the "differing circumstances" language opens up the possibility that in any given situation, additional subjective considerations could be defined. This remains a matter for each enterprise to address on an individual basis, however.

Distinction Between Sales-Type, Direct Financing, and Leveraged Leases

A lease is classified as a sales-type lease when the criteria set forth above have been met and the lease transaction is structured such that the lessor (generally a manufacturer or dealer) recognizes a profit or loss on the transaction in addition to interest revenue. For this to occur, the fair value of the property, or if lower, the sum of the present values of the minimum lease payments and the estimated unguaranteed residual value, must differ from the cost (or carrying value, if different). The essential substance of this transaction is that of a sale, thus its name. Common examples of sales-type leases: (1) when an automobile dealership opts to lease a car to its customers in lieu of making an actual sale, and (2) the re-lease of equipment coming off an expiring lease.

A direct financing lease differs from a sales-type lease in that the lessor does not realize a profit or loss on the transaction other than interest revenue. In a direct financing lease, the fair value of the property at the inception of the lease is equal to the cost (or carrying value, if the property is not new). This type of lease transaction most often involves entities regularly engaged in financing operations. The lessor (a bank or other financial institution) purchases the asset and then leases the asset to the lessee. This transaction merely replaces the conventional lending transaction where the borrower uses the borrowed funds to purchase the asset.

There are many economic reasons why a lease transaction may be considered. These include

1. The lessee (borrower) is generally able to obtain 100% financing.
2. There may be tax benefits for the lessee.
3. The lessor receives the equivalent of interest as well as an asset with some remaining value at the end of the lease term (unless title transfers as a condition of the lease).
4. The lessee is protected from risk of obsolescence.

In summary, it may help to visualize the following chart when considering the classification of a lease:

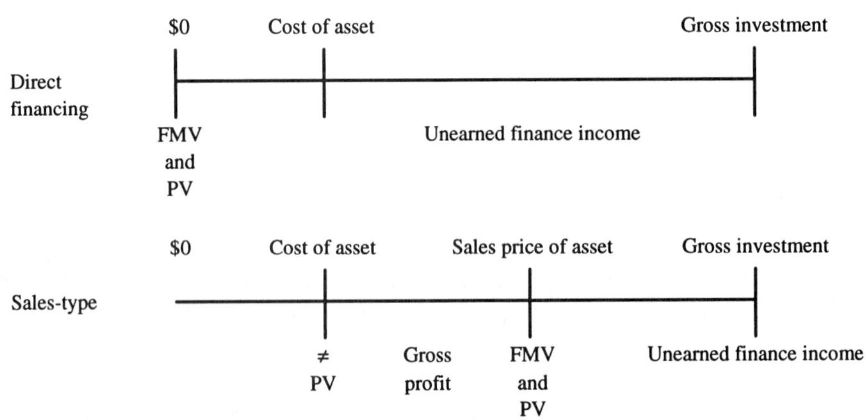

One specialized form of a direct financing lease is a **leveraged lease**. This type is mentioned separately both here and in the following section on how to account for leases because it is to receive a different accounting treatment by a lessor. A leveraged lease meets all the definitional criteria of a direct financing lease, but differs because it involves at least three parties: a lessee, a long-term creditor, and a lessor (commonly referred to as the **equity participant**). Other characteristics of a leveraged lease are as follows:

1. The financing provided by the long-term creditor must be without recourse as to the general credit of the lessor, although the creditor may hold recourse with respect to the leased property. The amount of the financing must provide the lessor with substantial leverage in the transaction.
2. The lessor's net investment declines during the early years and rises during the later years of the lease term before its elimination.

Accounting for Leases--Lessee

As discussed in the preceding section, there are two classifications that apply to a lease transaction in the financial statements of the lessee. They are as follows:

1. Operating
2. Finance

Operating leases. The accounting treatment accorded an operating lease is relatively simple; rental expense should be charged to income as the payments are made or become payable. IAS 17 stipulates that rental expense be "recognized on a systematic basis that is representative of the time pattern of the user's benefits, even if the payments are not on that basis." In case the lease payments are being made on a straight-line basis (i.e., equal payments per period over the lease term), recognition of the rental expense would normally be on a straight-line basis. However, if the lease agreement calls for either an alternative payment schedule or a scheduled rent increase over the lease term, in the absence of interpretations from the IASC it is recommended that the lease expense still be recognized on a straight-line basis unless another systematic and rational basis is a better representation of actual physical use of the leased property. In such an instance it will be necessary to create either a prepaid asset or a liability, depending on the structure of the payment schedule.

Additionally, if the lease agreement provides for a scheduled increase(s) in contemplation of the lessee's increased (i.e., more intensive) physical use of the leased property, the total amount of rental payments, including the scheduled increase(s), should be charged to expense over the lease term on a straight-line basis. On the other hand, if the scheduled increase(s) is due to additional leased property, recognition should be proportional to the leased property with the increased rents recognized over the years that the lessee has control over the use of the additional leased property. (These suggestions, and many other recommendations made in this chapter, are based on guidance from US GAAP, since the IAS does not address these matters at the present time.)

Notice that in the case of an operating lease there is no balance sheet recognition of the leased asset because the substance of the lease is merely that of a rental. There is no reason to expect that the lessee will derive any future economic benefit from the leased asset beyond the lease term. There may, however, be a deferred charge or credit on the balance sheet if the payment schedule under terms of the lease does not correspond with the expense recognition, as suggested in the preceding paragraph.

Finance leases. Recall that the classification of a lease must be determined prior to consideration of the accounting treatment. Therefore, it is necessary first to evaluate the lease transaction against the four criteria set forth in IAS 17 (transfer of title, bargain purchase option, major portion of useful life, or equal to or greater than substantially all net FMV). Assuming that the lease agreement satisfies one of these, it must be accounted for as a finance lease.

According to IAS 17, the lessee shall record a finance lease as an asset and an obligation (liability) at an amount equal to the lesser of (1) the fair value of the leased property at the inception of the lease, net of grants and tax credits receivable by the lessors, or (2) the present value of the minimum lease payments. For purposes of this computation, the minimum lease payments are considered to be the payments that the lessee is obligated to make or can be required to make, excluding executory costs such as insurance, maintenance, and taxes. The minimum lease payments generally include the minimum rental payments, any guarantee of the residual value made by the lessee or a party related to the lessee. If the lease includes a bargain purchase option (BPO), the amount required to be paid under the BPO is included in the minimum lease payments. The present value shall be computed using the incremental borrowing rate of the lessee unless it is practicable for the lessee to determine the implicit rate computed by the lessor.

(Under US GAAP, an important exception is made when the FMV of the leased asset is lower than the PV of the minimum lease payments, which exception has not yet been considered under IAS 17. In such a case an implicit rate is computed through a series of trial-and-error calculations. This rule is entirely logical, since it is well established in GAAP that assets are not to be recorded at amounts greater than fair value or net realizable value at acquisition. This exception has been illustrated in a numerical case study that follows.)

The lease term to be used in the present value computation is the fixed, noncancelable term of the lease, plus any further terms for which the lessee has the option to continue to lease the asset, with or without further payment, provided that it is reasonably certain, as of the beginning of the lease, that lessee will exercise such a renewal option.

Depreciation of leased assets. The depreciation of the leased asset will depend on how the lease qualified as a finance lease. If the lease transaction met the criteria as either transferring ownership or containing a bargain purchase option, the asset arising from the transaction is to be depreciated over the estimated useful life of the leased property. If the transaction qualifies as a finance lease because it met either the major part of useful life criteria, or the present value of MLP versus the fair-value criteria, the asset must be depreciated over the shorter of the lease term or the useful life of the leased property. The conceptual rationale for this differentiated treatment arises because of the substance of the transaction. Under the first two criteria, the asset actually becomes the property of the lessee at the end of the lease term (or on exercise of the BPO). In the latter situations, title to the property remains with the lessor.

Thus, the leased asset is to be depreciated (amortized) over the shorter of the lease term or its useful life if title does not transfer to the lessee, but when it is reasonably certain that the lessee will obtain ownership by the end of the lease term, the leased asset is to be depreciated over the asset's useful life. The manner in which depreciation is computed should be consistent with the lessee's normal depreciation policy for other depreciable assets owned by the lessee, recognizing depreciation on the basis set out in IAS 4, *Depreciation Accounting*, and IAS 16, *Property, Plant and Equipment*. Therefore, the accounting treatment and method used to depreciate (amortize) the leased asset is very similar to that used for an owned asset. The leased asset should not be depreciated (amortized) below the estimated residual value.

In some instances when the property is to revert back to the lessor, there may be a guaranteed residual value. This is an amount that the lessee guarantees to the lessor. If the fair value of the asset at the end of the lease term is greater than or equal to the guaranteed residual amount, the lessee incurs no additional obligation. On the other hand, if the fair value of the leased asset is less than the guaranteed residual value, the lessee must make up the difference, usually with a cash payment. The guaranteed residual value is often used as a device to reduce the periodic payments by substituting the lump-sum amount at the end of the term that results from the guarantee. In any event the depreciation (amortization) must still be based on the estimated residual value. This results in a rational and systematic allocation of the expense through the periods and avoids recognizing a large expense (or loss) in the last period as a result of the guarantee.

The annual (periodic) rent payments made during the lease term are to be apportioned between the reduction in the obligation and the finance charge (interest expense) in a manner such that the finance charge (interest expense) represents a constant periodic rate of interest on the remaining balance of the lease obligation. This is commonly referred to as the effective interest method. However, it is to be noted that IAS 17 also recognizes that an approximation of this pattern can be made, as an alternative.

At the inception of the lease the asset and liability (relating to future rental obligation) are recorded in the balance sheet of the lessee at the same amounts. However, since the depreciation charge for use of the leased asset and the finance expense during the lease term differ due to different policies being used to recognize them, as explained above, it is likely that the asset and related liability balances would not be equal in amount after inception of the lease.

The following examples illustrate the treatment described in the foregoing paragraphs:

Example of accounting for a finance lease--Asset returned to lessor

Assume the following:

1. The lease is initiated on 1/1/97 for equipment with an expected useful life of 3 years. The equipment reverts back to the lessor on expiration of the lease agreement.
2. The FMV of the equipment is $135,000.
3. Three payments are due to the lessor in the amount of $50,000 per year beginning 12/31/97. An additional sum of $1,000 is to be paid annually by the lessee for insurance.
4. Lessee guarantees a $10,000 residual value on 12/31/99 to the lessor.
5. Irrespective of the $10,000 residual value guarantee, the leased asset is expected to have only a $1,000 salvage value on 12/31/99.
6. The lessee's incremental borrowing rate is 10% (lessor's implicit rate is unknown).
7. The present value of the lease obligation is as follows:

PV of guaranteed residual value	=	$10,000 x 0.7513*	=	$ 7,513
PV of annual payments	=	$50,000 x 2.4869**	=	124,345
				$131,858

* *The present value of an amount of $1 due in three periods at 10% is 0.7513.*

** *The present value of an ordinary annuity of $1 for three periods at 10% is 2.4869.*

The first step in dealing with any lease transaction is to classify the lease. In this case, the lease term is for 3 years, which is equal to 100% of the expected useful life of the asset. Notice that the test of fair value versus present value is also fulfilled, as the PV of the minimum lease payments ($131,858) could easily be considered as being equal to substantially all the FMV ($135,000), being equal to 97.7% of the FMV. Thus, this lease should be accounted for as a finance lease.

In assumption 7 above the present value of the lease obligation is computed. Note that the executory costs (insurance) are not included in the minimum lease payments and that the incremental borrowing rate of the lessee was used to determine the present value. This rate was used because the implicit rate was not determinable. (*NOTE: To have used the implicit rate it would have to have been known to the lessee.*) The entry necessary to record the lease on 1/1/97 is:

Leased equipment	131,858	
Lease obligation		131,858

Note that the lease is recorded at the present value of the minimum lease payments, which in this case is less than the FMV. If the present value of the minimum lease payments had exceeded the FMV, the lease would be recorded at FMV.

The next step is to determine the proper allocation between interest and a reduction in the lease obligation for each lease payment. This is done using the effective interest method as illustrated below.

Year	Cash payment	Interest expense	Reduction in lease obligation	Balance of lease obligation
Inception of lease				$131,858
1	$50,000	$13,186	$36,814	95,044
2	50,000	9,504	40,496	54,548
3	50,000	5,452	44,548	10,000

The interest is calculated at 10% (the incremental borrowing rate) of the balance of the lease obligation for each period, and the remainder of the $50,000 payment is allocated to a reduction in the lease obligation. The lessee is also required to pay $1,000 for insurance on an annual basis. The entries necessary to record all payments relative to the lease for each of the 3 years are shown below.

	12/31/97	12/31/98	12/31/99
Insurance expense	1,000	1,000	1,000
Interest expense	13,186	9,504	5,452
Lease obligation	36,814	40,496	44,548
Cash	51,000	51,000	51,000

The leased equipment recorded as an asset must also be amortized (depreciated). The balance of this account is $131,858; however, as with any other asset, it cannot be depreciated below the estimated residual value of $1,000 (note that it is depreciated down to the actual estimated residual value, **not** the guaranteed residual value). In this case, the straight-line depreciation method is applied over a period of 3 years. This 3-year period represents the lease term, **not** the life of the asset, because the asset reverts back to the lessor at the end of the lease term. Therefore, the following entry will be made at the end of each year:

Depreciation expense	43,619	
Accumulated depreciation		43,619 [($131,858 – 1,000) ÷ 3]

Finally, on 12/31/99 we must recognize the fact that ownership of the property has reverted back to the owner (lessor). The lessee made a guarantee that the residual value would be $10,000 on 12/31/99; as a result, the lessee must make up the difference between the guaranteed residual value and the actual residual value with a cash payment to the lessor. The following entry illustrates the removal of the leased asset and obligation from the books of the lessee:

Lease obligation	10,000	
Accumulated depreciation	130,858	
Cash		9,000
Leased equipment		131,858

The foregoing example illustrated a situation where the asset was to be returned to the lessor. Another situation exists (under BPO or transfer of title) where the asset is expected to remain with the lessee. Remember that leased assets are amortized over their useful life when title transfers or a bargain purchase option exists. At the end of the lease, the balance of the lease obligation should equal the guaranteed residual value, the bargain purchase option price, or a termination penalty.

Example of accounting for a finance lease--Asset ownership transferred to lessee *and* fair market value of leased asset lower than present value of minimum lease payments

Assume the following:

1. A 3-year lease is initiated on 1/1/97 for equipment with an expected useful life of 5 years.
2. Three annual lease payments of $52,000 are required beginning on 1/1/97 (note that the payment at the beginning of the year changes the PV computation). The lessor pays $2,000 per year for insurance on the equipment.
3. The lessee can exercise a bargain purchase option on 12/31/99 for $10,000. The expected residual value at 12/31/00 is $1,000.
4. The lessee's incremental borrowing rate is 10% (lessor's implicit rate is unknown).
5. The fair market value of the property leased is $140,000.

Once again, the classification of the lease must take place prior to the accounting for it. This lease is classified as a finance lease because it contains a bargain purchase option (BPO). Note that in this case, the PV versus FMV test is also clearly fulfilled.

The PV of the lease obligation is computed as follows:

PV of bargain purchase option	=	$10,000	x 0.7513*	=	$ 7,513
PV of annual payments	=	($52,000 – 2,000)	x 2.7355**	=	136,755
					$144,288

* *The present value of an amount of $1 due in three periods at 10% is 0.7513.*

** *The present value of an annuity due of $1 for three periods at 10% is 2.7355.*

Notice that in the example above, the present value of the lease obligation is greater than the FMV of the asset. Also notice that since the lessor pays $2,000 a year for insurance, this payment is treated as executory costs and hence excluded from calculation of the present value of annual payments. In conclusion, since the PV is greater than the FMV, the lease obligation (as well as the leased asset) must be recorded at the FMV of the asset leased (being the lower of the two). The entry on 1/1/97 is as follows:

Leased equipment	140,000	
Obligation under capital lease		140,000

According to IAS 17, the apportionment between interest and principal is to be such that interest recognized reflects the use of a constant periodic rate of interest applied to the remaining balance of the obligation. As noted above, a special rule applies under

US GAAP (which are illustrated here) when the present value of the minimum lease payments exceeds the fair market value of the leased asset. When the PV exceeds the FMV of the leased asset, a new rate must be computed through a series of trial-and-error calculations. In this situation the interest rate was determined to be 13.265%. The amortization of the lease takes place as follows:

Date	*Cash payment*	*Interest expense*	*Reduction in lease obligation*	*Balance of lease obligation*
Inception of lease				$140,000
1/1/97	$50,000	$ --	$50,000	90,000
1/1/98	50,000	11,939	38,061	51,939
1/1/99	50,000	6,890	43,110	8,829
12/31/99	10,000	1,171	8,829	--

The following entries are required in years 1997 through 1999 to recognize the payment and depreciation (amortization).

		1997		*1998*		*1999*	
1/1	Operating expense	2,000		2,000		2,000	
	Obligation under capital lease	50,000		38,061		43,110	
	Accrued interest payable			11,939		6,890	
	Cash		52,000		52,000		52,000
12/31	Interest expense	11,939		6,890		1,171	
	Accrued interest payable		11,939		6,890		
	Obligation under capital lease						1,171
12/31	Depreciation expense	27,800		27,800		27,800	
	Accumulated depreciation ($139,000, 5 years)		27,800		27,800		27,800
12/31	Obligation under capital lease					10,000	
	Cash						10,000

Impairment of leased asset. IAS 17 did not address the issue of how impairments of leased assets are to be assessed or, if determined to have occurred, how they would need to be accounted for. The recent exposure draft, E56, does note that the provisions of E55, if and when adopted as a final standard, should be applied to leased assets in the same manner as they would be applied to owned assets. E55 is discussed more fully in Chapter 8.

Accounting for Leases--Lessor

As illustrated above, there are four classifications of leases with which a lessor must be concerned.

1. Operating
2. Sales-type
3. Direct financing
4. Leveraged

Operating leases. As in the case of the lessee, the operating lease requires a less complex accounting treatment than does a finance lease. The payments received by the lessor are to be recorded as rent income in the period in which the payment is received or becomes receivable. As with the lessee, if either the rentals vary from a straight-line basis or the lease agreement contains a scheduled rent increase over the lease term, the revenue is to be recorded on a straight-line basis unless an alternative basis of systematic and rational allocation is more representative of the time pattern of earning process contained in the lease. Additionally, if the lease agreement provides for a scheduled increase(s) in contemplation of the lessee's increased physical use of the leased property, the total amount of rental payments, including the scheduled increase(s), is allocated to revenue over the lease term on a straight-line basis. However, if the scheduled increase(s) is due to additional leased property, recognition should be proportional to the leased property, with the increased rents recognized over the years that the lessee has control over use of the additional leased property.

The lessor must show the leased property on the balance sheet under the caption "Investment in leased property." This account should be shown with or near the plant assets of the lessor and depreciated in the same manner as the rest of the lessor's plant assets. IAS 17 stipulates that "when a significant portion of the lessor's business comprises operating leases, the lessor should disclose the amount of assets by each major class of asset together with the related accumulated depreciation at each balance sheet date." Further, "assets held for operating are usually included as property, plant and equipment in the balance sheet."

In the case of operating leases, any initial direct (leasing) costs incurred by a lessor are either to be amortized over the lease term as the revenue is recognized (i.e., on a straight-line basis unless another method is more representative) or, alternatively, charged to expense as they are incurred.

Although there is no guidance on this matter under the international accounting standards, logically any incentives made by the lessor to the lessee are to be treated as reductions of rent and recognized on a straight-line basis over the term of the lease. This is also the position taken under US GAAP.

Depreciation of leased assets should be on a basis consistent with the lessor's normal depreciation policy for similar assets, and the depreciation expense should be computed on the basis set out in IAS 4, *Depreciation Accounting*, and IAS 16, *Property, Plant and Equipment*.

Sales-type leases. In the accounting for a sales-type lease, it is necessary for the lessor to determine the following amounts:

1. Gross investment
2. Fair value of the leased asset
3. Cost

From these amounts, the remainder of the computations necessary to record and account for the lease transaction can be made. The first objective is to determine the numbers necessary to complete the following entry:

Lease receivable	xx	
Cost of goods sold	xx	
Sales		xx
Inventory		xx
Unearned finance income		xx

The gross investment (lease receivable) of the lessor is equal to the sum of the minimum lease payments (excluding executory costs) from the standpoint of the lessor, plus the unguaranteed residual value accruing to the lessor. The difference between the gross investment and the present value of the two components of gross investment (i.e., minimum lease payments and unguaranteed residual value) is recorded as "unearned finance income" (also referred to as "unearned interest revenue"). The present value is to be computed using the lease term and implicit interest rate (both of which were discussed earlier).

IAS 17 stipulates that the resulting unearned finance income is to be amortized and recognized into income using the effective interest method, which will result in a constant periodic rate of return either on the "lessor's net investment" (which is the "lessor's gross investment" less the "unearned finance income") **or** the "net cash investment" outstanding in respect of the lease (which is the balance of the cash outflows and inflows in respect of the lease, excluding flows relating to insurance, maintenance, and similar costs rechargeable to the lessee). Further, the IAS requires that whichever basis (the "net investment outstanding" or the "net cash investment") is used for allocating unearned finance income over the lease term, such basis should be applied consistently to leases of a similar financial character. The basis used is also required to be disclosed and if more than one basis is used, the bases should be disclosed. (This free choice among two different bases of amortizing unearned finance income is **not** permitted under US GAAP, which requires amortization using the net investment basis. Furthermore, under the provisions of E56 this choice will be eliminated under international accounting standards as well, if the draft is adopted as a successor to current IAS 17, as expected.)

Consideration of "prudence" is called for by IAS 17 in recognizing finance income, which is in any event a qualitative characteristic or attribute of financial statements prepared under the IAS. The IASC's *Framework for Preparation and Presentation of Financial Statements* makes it incumbent on financial statement preparers to exercise prudence, in other words, it requires caution in the exercise of judgment. IAS 17 clarifies this in the context of spreading income on a systematic basis, by giving the example of recognition of uncertainties relative to collectibility of lease rentals or to fluctuation of interest rates in the future. For instance, the uncertainties surrounding collectibility of lease rentals usually increase with the lease term (i.e., the longer the lease term, the greater are the risks involved), and thus in keeping with the principle of prudence, modification of the pattern of income recognition may be required to compensate.

For example, a lessor may decide to delay the recognition of finance income into the later years in the case of leases with terms spread over, say, 20 years and above, as opposed to short-term leases with terms of 3 to 5 years, since predicting with certainty long-term collectibility, which depends on a number of factors, such as the future financial position of the lessee, is a very difficult task. Effectively, more of the earlier collections might be seen as returns on investment, rather than income, until longer-term viability has been demonstrated.

Recall that the fair market value (FMV) of the leased property is, by definition, equal to the normal selling price of the asset adjusted by any residual amount retained (this amount retained can be exemplified by an unguaranteed residual value, investment credit, etc.). According to IAS 17, the selling price to be used for a sales-type lease is equal to the fair value of the leased asset, or, if lower, the sum of the present values of the MLP and the estimated unguaranteed residual value accruing to the lessor, discounted at a commercial rate of interest. In other words, the normal selling price less the present value of the unguaranteed residual value is equal to the present value of the MLP. (Note that this relationship is sometimes used while computing the MLP when the normal selling price and the residual value are known; this is illustrated in a case study that follows.)

The cost of goods sold to be charged against income in the period of the sale is computed as the historical cost or carrying value of the asset (most likely inventory) plus any initial direct costs. Initial direct costs should be recognized as an expense at the inception of the lease, since these costs are related to earning the manufacturer's or dealer's profit.

The estimated unguaranteed residual values used in computing the lessor's gross investment in a lease should be reviewed regularly. In case of a permanent reduction (impairment) in the estimated unguaranteed residual value, the income allocation over the lease term is revised and any reduction with respect to amounts already accrued is recognized immediately.

To attract customers, manufacturer or dealer lessors sometimes quote artificially low rates of interest. This has a direct impact on the recognition of built-in profit, which is an integral part of the deal and is inversely proportional to the finance income generated from the deal. Thus, if finance income is artificially low, this results in recognition of excessive profit from the transaction at the time of the sale. Under such circumstances, the standard requires that selling profit be restricted to that which would have resulted had a commercial rate of interest been used in the deal. Thus, the substance of the transaction should be reflected in the financial statements.

The difference between the selling price and the amount computed as the cost of goods sold is the gross profit recognized by the lessor on the inception of the lease (sale). Manufacturer or dealer lessors often give an option to their customers of either leasing the asset (with financing provided by them) or buying the asset outright. Thus, a finance lease by a manufacturer or dealer lessor, also referred to as a sales-type lease, generates two types of revenue for the lessor.

1. The gross profit (or loss) on the sale, which is the equivalent to the profit (or loss) that would have resulted from an outright sale at normal selling prices.
2. The finance income or interest earned on the lease receivable to be spread over the lease term based on a pattern reflecting a constant periodic rate of return on either the lessor's net investment outstanding or the net cash investment outstanding in respect of the finance lease.

The application of these points is illustrated in the example below.

Example of accounting for a sales-type lease

XYZ Inc. is a manufacturer of specialized equipment. Many of its customers do not have the necessary funds or financing available for outright purchase. Because of this, XYZ offers a leasing alternative. The data relative to a typical lease are as follows:

1. The noncancelable fixed portion of the lease term is 5 years. The lessor has the option to renew the lease for an additional 3 years at the same rental. The estimated useful life of the asset is 10 years.
2. The lessor is to receive equal annual payments over the term of the lease. The leased property reverts back to the lessor on termination of the lease.
3. The lease is initiated on 1/1/97. Payments are due on 12/31 for the duration of the lease term.
4. The cost of the equipment to XYZ Inc. is $100,000. The lessor incurs cost associated with the inception of the lease in the amount of $2,500.
5. The selling price of the equipment for an outright purchase is $150,000.
6. The equipment is expected to have a residual value of $15,000 at the end of 5 years and $10,000 at the end of 8 years.
7. The lessor desires a return of 12% (the implicit rate).

The first step is to calculate the annual payment due to the lessor. Recall that the present value (PV) of the minimum lease payments is equal to the selling price adjusted for the present value of the residual amount. The present value is to be computed using the implicit interest rate and the lease term. In this case, the implicit rate is given as 12% and the lease term is 8 years (the fixed noncancelable portion plus the renewal period). Thus, the structure of the computation would be as follows:

Normal selling price – PV of residual value = PV of minimum lease payment

Or, in this case,

$150,000	–	(0.40388* x $10,000)	=	4.96764** x Minimum lease payment
$145,961.20	÷	4.96764	=	Minimum lease payment
		$29,382.40	=	Minimum lease payment

* *0.40388 is the present value of an amount of $1 due in eight periods at a 12% interest rate.*

** *4.96764 is the present value of an annuity of $1 for eight periods at a 12% interest rate.*

Prior to examining the accounting implications of a lease, we must determine the lease classification. In this example, the lease term is 8 years (discussed above) while the estimated useful life of the asset is 10 years; thus this lease qualifies as something other than an operating lease. (Note that it also meets the FMV versus PV criterion because the PV of the minimum lease payments of $145,961.20, which is 97% of the FMV [$150,000], could be considered to be equal to substantially all of the fair value of the leased asset.) Now it must be determined if this is a sales-type, direct financing, or leveraged lease. To do this, examine the FMV or selling price of the asset and compare it to the cost. Because the two are not equal, we can determine this to be a sales-type lease.

Next, obtain the figures necessary to record the entry on the books of the lessor. The gross investment is the total minimum lease payments plus the unguaranteed residual value, or

($29,382.40 x 8) + $10,000 = $245,059.20

The cost of goods sold is the historical cost of the inventory ($100,000) plus any initial direct costs ($2,500) less the PV of the unguaranteed residual value ($10,000 x 0.40388). Thus, the cost of goods sold amount is $98,461.20 ($100,000 + 2,500 – 4,038.80). Note that the initial direct costs will require a credit entry to some account, usually accounts payable or cash. The inventory account is credited for the carrying value of the asset, in this case $100,000.

The adjusted selling price is equal to the PV of the minimum payments, or $145,961.20. Finally, the unearned finance income is equal to the gross investment (i.e., lease receivable) less the present value of the components making up the gross investment (the minimum lease payment of $29,382.40 and the unguaranteed residual of $10,000). The present value of these items is $150,000 [($29,382.40 x 4.96764) + ($10,000 x 0.40388)]. Therefore, the entry necessary to record the lease is:

Lease receivable	245,059.20	
Cost of goods sold	98,461.20	
Inventory		100,000.00
Sales		145,961.20
Unearned finance income		95,059.20
Accounts payable (initial direct costs)		2,500.00

The next step in accounting for a sales-type lease is to determine proper handling of the payment. Both principal and interest are included in each payment. According to IAS 17, interest is recognized on a basis such that a constant periodic rate of return is earned over the term of the lease. This will require setting up an amortization schedule as illustrated below.

Year	*Cash payment*	*Interest*	*Reduction in principal*	*Balance of net investment*
Inception of lease				$150,000.00
1	$ 29,382.40	$18,000.00	$ 11,382.40	138,617.00
2	29,382.40	16,634.11	12,748.29	125,869.31
3	29,382.40	15,104.32	14,278.08	111,591.23
4	29,382.40	13,390.95	15,991.45	95,599.78
5	29,382.40	11,471.97	17,910.43	77,689.35
6	29,382.40	9,322.72	20,059.68	57,629.67
7	29,382.40	6,915.56	22,466.84	35,162.83
8	29,382.40	4,219.57	25,162.83	10,000.00
	$235,059.20	$95,059.20	$140,000.00	

A few of the columns need to be elaborated on. First, the net investment is the gross investment (lease receivable) less the unearned finance income. Notice that at the end of the lease term, the net investment is equal to the estimated residual value. Also note that the total interest earned over the lease term is equal to the unearned interest (unearned finance income) at the beginning of the lease term.

The entries below illustrate the proper treatment to record the receipt of the lease payment and the amortization of the unearned finance income in the first year.

Cash	29,382.40	
Lease receivable		29,382.40
Unearned finance income	18,000.00	
Interest revenue		18,000.00

Notice that there is no explicit entry to recognize the principal reduction. This is done automatically when the net investment is reduced by decreasing the lease receivable (gross investment) by $29,382.40 and the unearned finance income account by only $18,000. The $18,000 is 12% (implicit rate) of the net investment. These entries are to be made over the life of the lease.

At the end of the lease term the asset is returned to the lessor and the following entry is required:

Asset	10,000	
Leased receivable		10,000

If the estimated residual value has changed during the lease term, the accounting computations would have also changed to reflect this.

Direct financing leases. The accounting for a direct financing lease holds many similarities to that for a sales-type lease. Of particular importance is that the terminology used is much the same; however, the treatment accorded these items varies greatly. Again, it is best to preface our discussion by determining our objectives in the accounting for a direct financing lease. Once the lease has been classified, it must be recorded. To do this, the following amounts must be determined:

1. Gross investment
2. Cost
3. Residual value

As noted, a direct financing lease generally involves a leasing company or other financial institution and results in only interest revenue being earned by the lessor. This is because the FMV (selling price) and the cost are equal, and therefore no dealer profit is recognized on the actual lease transaction. Note how this is different from a sales-type lease, which involves both a profit on the transaction and interest revenue over the lease term. The reason for this difference is derived from the conceptual nature underlying the purpose of the lease transaction. In a sales-type lease, the manufacturer (distributor, dealer, etc.) is seeking an alternative means to finance the sale of his product, whereas a direct financing lease is a result of the consumer's need to finance an equipment purchase. Because the consumer is unable to obtain conventional financing, he or she turns to a leasing company that will purchase the desired asset and then lease it to the consumer. Here the profit on the transaction remains with the manufacturer while the interest revenue is earned by the leasing company.

Like a sales-type lease, the first objective is to determine the amounts necessary to complete the following entry:

Lease receivable	xxx	
Asset		xxx
Unearned finance income		xx

The gross investment is still defined as the minimum amount of lease payments (from the standpoint of a lessor) exclusive of any executory costs plus the unguaranteed residual value. The difference between the gross investment as determined above and the cost (carrying value) of the asset is to be recorded as the unearned finance income because there is no manufacturer's/dealer's profit earned on the transaction. The following entry would be made to record initial direct costs:

Initial direct costs	xx	
Cash		xx

Net investment in the lease is defined as the gross investment less the unearned income plus the unamortized initial direct costs related to the lease. Initial direct costs are defined in the same way that they were for purposes of the sales-type lease; however, the accounting treatment is different. Unlike under the sales-type lease, where these costs are required to be charged to expense immediately, under the direct finance lease there is an option available either

1. To amortize initial direct costs over the lease term, or
2. To charge them to expense immediately.

Thus, for a direct financing lease, when the first option is chosen, the unearned lease (i.e., interest) income and the initial direct costs will be amortized to income over the lease term so that a constant periodic rate is earned either on the lessor's net investment outstanding or on the net cash investment outstanding in the finance lease (i.e., the balance of the cash outflows and inflows in respect of the lease excluding executory costs chargeable to the lessee). Thus, the effect of the initial direct costs, in case the option to amortize is chosen, is to reduce the implicit interest rate, or yield, to the lessor over the life of the lease.

An example follows that illustrates the preceding principles.

Example of accounting for a direct financing lease

Emirates Refining needs new equipment to expand its manufacturing operation; however, it does not have sufficient capital to purchase the asset at this time. Because of this, Emirates Refining has employed Consolidated Leasing to purchase the asset. In turn, Emirates will lease the asset from Consolidated. The following information applies to the terms of the lease:

1. A 3-year lease is initiated on 1/1/98 for equipment costing $131,858, with an expected useful life of 5 years. FMV at 1/1/98 of equipment is $131,858.
2. Three annual payments are due to the lessor beginning 12/31/98. The property reverts back to the lessor on termination of the lease.
3. The unguaranteed residual value at the end of year 3 is estimated to be $10,000.
4. The annual payments are calculated to give the lessor a 10% return (the implicit rate).
5. The lease payments and unguaranteed residual value have a PV equal to $131,858 (FMV of asset) at the stipulated discount rate.
6. The annual payment to the lessor is computed as follows:

PV of residual value	=	$10,000 x .7513* = $7,513
PV of lease payments	=	Selling price – PV of residual value
	=	$131,858 – $7,513 = $124,345
Annual payment	=	$124,345 ÷ 2.4869** = $50,000

* *.7513 is the PV of an amount due in three periods at 10%.*

** *2.4869 is the PV of an ordinary annuity of $1 per period for three periods, at 10% interest.*

7. Initial direct costs of $7,500 are incurred by ABC in the lease transaction.

As with any lease transaction, the first step must be to classify the lease appropriately. In this case, the PV of the lease payments ($124,345) is equal to 94% of the FMV ($131,858), thus could be considered as equal to substantially all of the FMV of the leased asset. Next, determine the unearned interest and the net investment in lease.

Gross investment in lease [(3 x $50,000) + $10,000]	$160,000
Cost of leased property	131,858
Unearned finance income	$ 28,142

The unamortized initial direct costs are to be added to the gross investment in the lease, and the unearned finance income is to be deducted to arrive at the net investment in the lease. The net investment in the lease for this example is determined as follows:

Gross investment in lease	$160,000
Add:	
Unamortized initial direct costs	7,500
	$167,500
Less:	
Unearned finance income	28,142
Net investment in lease	$139,358

The net investment in the lease (Gross investment – Unearned finance income) has been increased by the amount of initial direct costs. Therefore, the implicit rate is no longer 10%. We must recompute the implicit rate, which is really the result of an internal rate of return calculation. We know that the lease payments are to be $50,000 per annum and that a residual value of $10,000 is available at the end of the lease term. In return for these payments (inflows) we are giving up equipment (outflow) and incurring initial direct costs (outflows), with a net investment of $139,358 ($131,858 + $7,500). The only way to obtain the new implicit rate is through a trial-and-error calculation as set up below.

$$\frac{50{,}000}{(1+i)^1} + \frac{50{,}000}{(1+i)^2} + \frac{50{,}000}{(1+i)^3} + \frac{10{,}000}{(1+i)^3} = \$139{,}358$$

Where: i = implicit rate of interest

In this case, the implicit rate is equal to 7.008%. Thus, the amortization table would be set up as follows:

	(a)	*(b)*	*(c)*	*(d)*	*(e)*	*(f)*
	Lease payments	*Reduction in unearned interest*	*PV x Implicit rate (7.008%)*	*Reduction in initial direct costs (b-c)*	*Reduction in PVI net investment (a-b + d)*	*PVI net investment in lease (f)(n+1) = (f)n – (e)*
0						$139,358
1	$ 50,000	$13,186 (1)	$ 9,766	$3,420	$ 40,234	99,124
2	50,000	9,504 (2)	6,947	2,557	43,053	56,071
3	50,000	5,455 (3)	3,929	1,526	46,071	10,000
	$150,000	$28,145*	$20,642	$7,503	$129,358	

**Rounded*

(b.1) $131,858 x 10% = $13,186
(b.2) [$131,858 – ($50,000 – 13,186)] x 10% = $9,504
(b.3) [$95,044 – ($50,000 – 9,504)] x 10% = $5,455

Here the interest is computed as 7.008% of the net investment. Note again that the net investment at the end of the lease term is equal to the estimated residual value.

The entry made initially to record the lease is as follows:

Lease receivable** [($50,000 x 3) + 10,000]	160,000	
Asset acquired for leasing		131,858
Unearned lease finance income		28,142

When the payment (or obligation to pay) of the initial direct costs occurs, the following entry must be made:

Initial direct costs	7,500	
Cash		7,500

Using the schedule above, the following entries would be made during each of the years indicated:

	Year 1		*Year 2*		*Year 3*	
Cash	50,000		50,000		50,000	
Lease receivable**		50,000		50,000		50,000
Unearned finance income	13,186		9,504		5,455	
Initial direct costs		3,420		2,557		1,526
Interest income		9,766		6,947		3,929

Finally, when the asset is returned to the lessor at the end of the lease term, it must be recorded on the books. The necessary entry is as follows:

Used asset	10,000	
Lease receivable**		10,000

***Also commonly referred to as the "gross investment in lease."*

Leveraged leases. Leveraged leases are discussed in detail in Appendix B of this chapter, because of the complexity involved in the accounting treatment based on guidance available under US GAAP, where this topic has been given extensive coverage. Under International Accounting Standards, this concept has been defined, but with only a very brief outline of the treatment to be accorded to this kind of lease. A leveraged lease is defined in IAS 17 as a finance lease, which is structured such that there are at least three parties involved: the lessee, the lessor, and one or more long-term creditors who provide part of the acquisition finance for the leased asset, usually without any general recourse to the lessor. Succinctly, this type of a lease is given the following unique accounting treatment:

1. The lessor records his or her investment in the lease net of the nonrecourse debt and the related finance costs to the third-party creditor(s).
2. The recognition of the finance income is based on the lessor's net cash investment outstanding in respect of the lease.

Sale-Leaseback Transactions

Sale-leaseback describes a transaction where the owner of property (seller-lessee) sells the property and then immediately leases all or part of it back from the new owner (buyer-lessor). These transactions may occur when the seller-lessee is experiencing cash flow or financing problems or because there are tax advantages in such an arrangement in the lessee's tax jurisdiction. The important consideration in this type of transaction is recognition of two separate and distinct economic transactions. However, it is important to note that there is not a physical transfer of property. First, there is a sale of property, and second, there is a lease agreement for the same property in which the original seller is the lessee and the original buyer is the lessor. This is illustrated as follows:

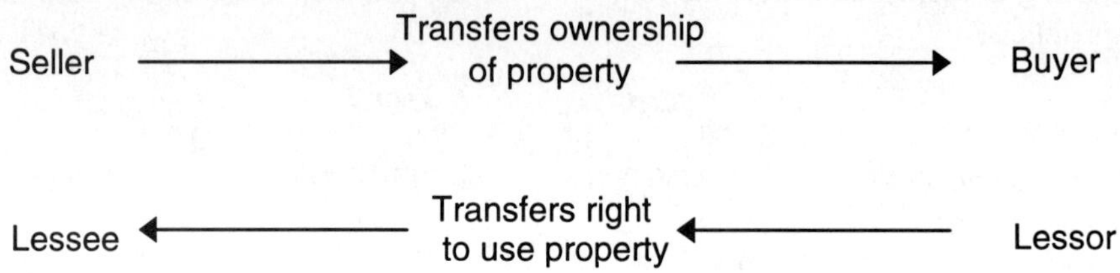

A sale-leaseback transaction is usually structured such that the sales price of the asset is greater than or equal to the current market value. The result of this higher sales price is a higher periodic rental payment over the lease term. The transaction is usually attractive because of the tax benefits associated with it, and because it provides financing to the lessee. The seller-lessee benefits from the higher price because of the increased gain on the sale of the property and the deductibility of the lease payments, which are usually larger than the depreciation that was previously being taken. The buyer-lessor benefits from both the higher rental payments and the larger depreciable basis.

Under IAS 17, the accounting treatment depends on whether the sale and leaseback results in a finance lease or an operating lease. If it results in a finance lease, any excess of sale proceeds need not immediately be recognized as income in the financial statements of the seller-lessee. If such an excess is recognized, it should be deferred and amortized over the lease term.

If a sale and leaseback transaction results in an operating lease

1. If it is evident that the transaction is established at fair value, any profit or loss should be recognized immediately.
2. If sale price is not established at fair value
    a. If sale price is below fair value, any profit or loss should be recognized immediately, except that when a loss is to be compensated by below fair market future rentals, the loss should be deferred and amortized in proportion to the rental payments over the period the asset is expected to be used.
    b. If the sale price is above fair value, the excess over fair value should be deferred and amortized over the period for which the asset is expected to be used.

IAS 17 stipulates that in case of operating leases, if at the time of the sale and leaseback transaction the fair value is less than the carrying amount of the leased asset, the difference between the fair value and the carrying amount should immediately be recognized.

However, in case the sale and leaseback result in a finance lease, no such adjustment is considered necessary unless there has been an impairment in value, in which case the carrying value should be reduced to the recoverable amount in accordance with the provisions of IAS 16, *Property, Plant and Equipment*.

Additional guidance. Sale-leaseback transactions can be rather complex, and the guidance offered by IAS 17 is limited. Therefore, to provide further insight into this common type of financing arrangement, additional commentary is offered, based on the rules and interpretations under US GAAP.

The accounting treatment from the seller-lessee's perspective will depend on the degree of rights to use retained by the seller-lessee. The degree of rights to use retained may be categorized as follows:

1. Substantially all
2. Minor
3. More than minor but less than substantially all

The guideline for the determination substantially all is based on the classification criteria presented for the lease transaction. For example, a test based on the 90% recovery criterion seems appropriate. That is, if the present value of fair rental payments is equal to 90% or more of the fair value of the sold asset, the seller-lessee is presumed to have retained substantially all the rights to use the sold property. The test for retaining minor rights would be to substitute 10% or less for 90% or more in the preceding sentence.

If substantially all the rights to use the property are retained by the seller-lessee and the agreement meets at least one of the criteria for capital lease treatment, the seller-lessee should account for the leaseback as a capital lease, and any profit on the sale should be deferred and either amortized over the life of the property or treated as a reduction of depreciation expense. If the leaseback is classified as an operating lease, it should be accounted for as one, and any profit or loss on the sale should be deferred and amortized over the lease term. Any loss on the sale would also be deferred unless the loss were perceived to be a real economic loss, in which case the loss would be recognized immediately and not deferred.

If only a minor portion of the rights to use are retained by the seller-lessee, the sale and the leaseback should be accounted for separately. However, if the rental payments appear unreasonable based on the existing market conditions at the inception of the lease, the profit or loss should be adjusted so that the rentals are at a reasonable amount. The amount created by the adjustment should be deferred and amortized over the life of the property if a capital lease is involved or over the lease term if an operating lease is involved.

If the seller-lessee retains more than a minor portion but less than substantially all the rights to use the property, any excess profit on the sale should be recognized on the date of the sale. For purposes of this paragraph, excess profit is derived as follows:

1. If the leaseback is classified as an operating lease, the excess profit is the profit that exceeds the present value of the minimum lease payments over the lease term. The seller-lessee should use its incremental borrowing rate to compute the present value of the minimum lease payments. If the implicit rate of interest in the lease is known, it should be used to compute the present value of the minimum lease payments.
2. If the leaseback is classified as a capital (i.e., finance) lease, the excess profit is the amount greater than the recorded amount of the leased asset.

When the fair value of the property at the time of the leaseback is less than its undepreciated cost, the seller-lessee should immediately recognize a loss for the difference. In the example below, the sales price is less than the book value of the property. However, there is no economic loss because the FMV is greater than the book value.

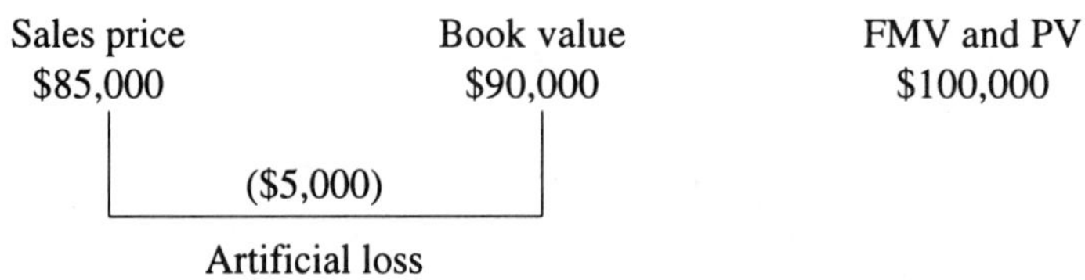

The artificial loss must be deferred and amortized as an addition to depreciation.

The following diagram summarizes the accounting for sale-leaseback transactions.

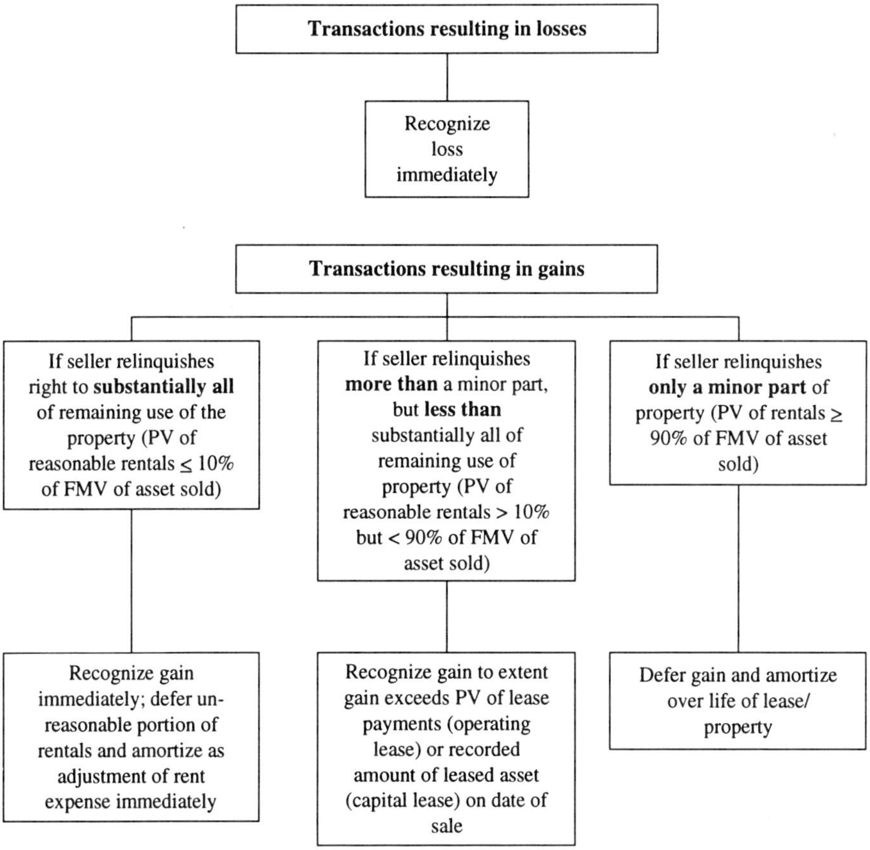

In the foregoing circumstances, when the leased asset is land only, any amortization should be on a straight-line basis over the lease term, regardless of whether the lease is classified as a capital or an operating lease.

Executory costs are not to be included in the calculation of profit to be deferred in a sale-leaseback transaction. The buyer-lessor should account for the transaction as a purchase and a direct financing lease if the agreement meets the criteria of **either** a direct financing lease **or** a sales-type lease. Otherwise, the agreement should be accounted for as a purchase and an operating lease.

Sale-leaseback involving real estate. Under US GAAP, three requirements are necessary for a sale-leaseback involving real estate (including real estate with equipment) to qualify for sale-leaseback accounting treatment. Those sale-leaseback transactions not meeting the three requirements should be accounted for as a deposit or as a financing. The three requirements are

1. The lease must be a normal leaseback.

2. Payment terms and provisions must adequately demonstrate the buyer-lessor's initial and continuing investment in the property.
3. Payment terms and provisions must transfer all the risks and rewards of ownership as demonstrated by a lack of continuing involvement by the seller-lessee.

A normal leaseback involves active use of the leased property in the seller-lessee's trade or business during the lease term.

The buyer-lessor's initial investment is adequate if it demonstrates the buyer-lessor's commitment to pay for the property and indicates a reasonable likelihood that the seller-lessee will collect any receivable related to the leased property. The buyer-lessor's continuing investment is adequate if the buyer is contractually obligated to pay an annual amount at least equal to the level of annual payment needed to pay that debt and interest over no more than (1) 20 years for land, and (2) the customary term of a first mortgage loan for other real estate.

Any continuing involvement by the seller-lessee other than normal leaseback disqualifies the lease from sale-leaseback accounting treatment. Some examples of continuing involvement other than normal leaseback include

1. The seller-lessee has an obligation or option (excluding the right of first refusal) to repurchase the property.
2. The seller-lessee (or party related to the seller-lessee) guarantees the buyer-lessor's investment or debt related to that investment or a return on that investment.
3. The seller-lessee is required to reimburse the buyer-lessor for a decline in the fair value of the property below estimated residual value at the end of the lease term based on other than excess wear and tear.
4. The seller-lessee remains liable for an existing debt related to the property.
5. The seller-lessee's rental payments are contingent on some predetermined level of future operations of the buyer-lessor.
6. The seller-lessee provides collateral on behalf of the buyer-lessor other than the property directly involved in the sale-leaseback.
7. The seller-lessee provides nonrecourse financing to the buyer-lessor for any portion of the sales proceeds or provides recourse financing in which the only recourse is the leased asset.
8. The seller-lessee enters into a sale-leaseback involving property improvements or integral equipment without leasing the underlying land to the buyer-lessor.
9. The buyer-lessor is obligated to share any portion of the appreciation of the property with the seller-lessee.
10. Any other provision or circumstance that allows the seller-lessee to participate in any future profits of the buyer-lessor or appreciation of the leased property.

Example of accounting for a sale-leaseback transaction

To illustrate the accounting treatment in a sale-leaseback transaction, suppose that Lessee Corporation sells equipment that has a book value of $80,000 and a fair value of $100,000 to Lessor Corporation, and then immediately leases it back under the following conditions:

1. The sale date is January 1, 1997, and the equipment has a fair value of $100,000 on that date and an estimated useful life of 15 years.
2. The lease term is 15 years, noncancelable, and requires equal rental payments of $13,109 at the beginning of each year.
3. Lessee Corp. has the option annually to renew the lease at the same rental payments on expiration of the original lease.
4. Lessee Corp. has the obligation to pay all executory costs.
5. The annual rental payments provide the lessor with a 12% return on investment.
6. The incremental borrowing rate of Lessee Corp. is 12%.
7. Lessee Corp. depreciates similar equipment on a straight-line basis.

Lessee Corp. should classify the agreement as a capital lease since the lease term exceeds 75% (which is deemed to be a major part) of the estimated economic life of the equipment, and because the present value of the lease payments is greater than 90% (deemed to be substantially all) of the fair value of the equipment. Assuming that collectibility of the lease payments is reasonably predictable and that no important uncertainties exist concerning the amount of nonreimbursable costs yet to be incurred by the lessor, Lessor Corp. should classify the transaction as a direct financing lease because the present value of the minimum lease payments is equal to the fair market value of $100,000 ($13,109 x 7.62817).

Lessee Corp. and Lessor Corp. would normally make the following journal entries during the first year:

Upon Sale of Equipment on January 1, 1997

Lessee Corp.			*Lessor Corp.*		
Cash	100,000		Equipment	100,000	
Equipment*		80,000	Cash		100,000
Unearned profit on sale-leaseback		20,000			
Leased equipment	100,000		Lease receivable ($13,109 x 15)	196,635	
Lease obligations		100,000	Equipment		100,000
			Unearned interest		96,635

**Assumes new equipment*

To Record First Payment on January 1, 1997

Lessee Corp.			*Lessor Corp.*		
Lease obligations	13,109		Cash	13,109	
Cash		13,109	Lease receivable		13,109

To Record Incurrence and Payment of Executory Costs

Lessee Corp.			*Lessor Corp.*
Insurance, taxes, etc.	xxx		(No entry)
Cash (accounts payable)		xxx	

To Record Depreciation Expense on the Equipment, December 31, 1997

Lessee Corp.			*Lessor Corp.*
Depreciation expense	6,667		(No entry)
Accum. depr. -- capital leases ($100,000 ÷ 15)		6,667	

To Amortize Profit on Sale-Leaseback by Lessee Corp., December 31, 1997

Lessee Corp.			*Lessor Corp.*
Unearned profit on sale-leaseback	1,333		(No entry)
Depr. expense ($20,000 ÷ 15)		1,333	

To Record Interest for 1997, December 31, 1997

Lessee Corp.			*Lessor Corp.*		
Interest expense	10,427		Unearned interest income	10,427	
Accrued interest payable		10,427	Interest income		10,427

Partial Lease Amortization Schedule

Date	*Cash payment*	*Interest expense*	*Reduction of obligation*	*Lease obligation*
Inception of lease				$100,000
1/1/97	$13,109	$ --	$13,109	86,891
1/1/98	13,109	10,427	2,682	84,209

Leases Involving Land and Buildings--Guidance Under IAS 17

IAS 17 stipulates rules relating to leases of land and building. In general, the treatment of such leases is to be the same as for leases of other assets. However, since land has an indefinite useful life, if title is not expected to pass to the lessee at the end of the lease term, such leases are to be classified as operating leases. Were the lessee to capitalize such a lease arrangement, the fact that no periodic depreciation would be reported would inevitably result in a write-off of the asset at the termination of the lease, which clearly would not contribute to meaningful financial reporting.

Similarly, IAS recognizes the fact that buildings have useful lives that extend well beyond the lease terms, and often, long-term leases for buildings contain provisions whereby rents are regularly adjusted upward to market rates. Thus, if title is not expected to pass to the lessee at the end of the lease term or if rents are adjusted upward regularly to reflect market rates, the lessor retains a significant part of the risks and rewards incidental to ownership, and hence such leases should

normally be classified as operating leases. However, whether or not to capitalize the building in the financial statements of the lessee is a question of facts and circumstances, and to do so is not absolutely prohibited by the standard.

Leases Involving Real Estate--Guidance Under US GAAP

Again, the guidance under IAS 17 is limited, and the practice under US GAAP is instructive. Under those standards, leases involving real estate can be divided into the following four categories:

1. Leases involving land only
2. Leases involving land and building(s)
3. Leases involving real estate and equipment
4. Leases involving only part of a building

Leases Involving Land Only

Lessee accounting. If the lease agreement transfers ownership or contains a bargain purchase option, the lessee should account for the lease as a capital lease and record an asset and related liability in an amount equal to the present value of the minimum lease payments. If the lease agreement does not transfer ownership or contain a bargain purchase option, the lessee should account for the lease as an operating lease.

Lessor accounting. If the lease gives rise to dealer's profit (or loss) and transfers ownership (i.e., title), the standards require that the lease shall be classified as a sales-type lease and accounted for under the provisions of the US standard dealing with sales of real estate, in the same manner as would a seller of the same property. If the lease transfers ownership, both the collectibility and the no material uncertainties criteria are met, but if it does not give rise to dealer's profit (or loss), the lease should be accounted for as a direct financing or leveraged lease, as appropriate. If the lease contains a bargain purchase option and both the collectibility and no material uncertainties criteria are met, the lease should be accounted for as a direct financing, leveraged, or operating lease as appropriate. If the lease does not meet the collectibility and/or no material uncertainties criteria, the lease should be accounted for as an operating lease.

Leases Involving Land and Building

Lessee accounting. If the agreement transfers title or contains a bargain purchase option, the lessee should account for the agreement by separating the land and building components and capitalize each separately. The land and building elements should be allocated on the basis of their relative fair market values measured at the inception of the lease. The land and building components are accounted for separately because the lessee is expected to own the real estate by the end of the lease term. The building should be depreciated over its estimated useful life without regard to the lease term.

When the lease agreement neither transfers title nor contains a bargain purchase option, the fair value of the land must be determined in relation to the fair value of the aggregate properties included in the lease agreement. If the fair value of the land is less than 25% of the fair value of the leased properties in aggregate, the land is considered immaterial. Conversely, if the fair value of the land is 25% or greater of the fair value of the leased properties in aggregate, the land is considered material.

When the land component of the lease agreement is considered immaterial (FMV land $<$ 25% total FMV), the lease should be accounted for as a single lease unit. The lessee should capitalize the lease if one of the following occurs:

1. The term of the lease is 75% or more of the economic useful life of the real estate
2. The present value of the minimum lease payments equals 90% or more of the fair market value of the leased real estate less any lessor tax credits

If neither of the two criteria above is met, the lessee should account for the lease agreement as a single operating lease.

When the land component of the lease agreement is considered material (FMV land $\geq$ 25% total FMV), the land and building components should be separated. By applying the lessee's incremental borrowing rate to the fair market value of the land, the annual minimum lease payment attributed to land is computed. The remaining payments are attributed to the building. The division of minimum lease payments between land and building is essential for both the lessee and lessor. The lease involving the land should **always** be accounted for as an operating lease. Under US GAAP, the lease involving the building(s) must meet either the 75% (of useful life) or 90% (of fair value) test to be treated as a capital lease. If neither of the two criteria is met, the building(s) will also be accounted for as an operating lease.

Lessor accounting. The lessor's accounting depends on whether the lease transfers ownership, contains a bargain purchase option, or does neither of the two. If the lease transfers ownership and gives rise to dealer's profit (or loss), US GAAP requires that the lessor classify the lease as a sales-type lease and account for the lease as a single unit under the provisions of SFAS 66 in the same manner as a seller of the same property. If the lease transfers ownership, meets both the collectibility and no important uncertainties criteria, but does not give rise to dealer's profit (or loss), the lease should be accounted for as a direct financing or leveraged lease as appropriate.

If the lease contains a bargain purchase option and gives rise to dealer's profit (or loss), the lease should be classified as an operating lease. If the lease contains a bargain purchase option, meets both the collectibility and no material uncertainties criteria, but does not give rise to dealer's profit (or loss), the lease should be accounted for as a direct financing lease or a leveraged lease, as appropriate.

If the lease agreement neither transfers ownership nor contains a bargain purchase option, the lessor should follow the same rules as the lessee in accounting for real estate leases involving land and building(s).

However, the collectibility and the no material uncertainties criteria must be met before the lessor can account for the agreement as a direct financing lease, and in no such case may the lease be classified as a sales-type lease (i.e., ownership must be transferred).

The treatment of a lease involving both land and building can be illustrated in the following examples.

Example of accounting for land and building lease containing transfer of title

Assume the following:

1. The lessee enters into a 10-year noncancelable lease for a parcel of land and a building for use in its operations. The building has an estimated useful life of 12 years.
2. The FMV of the land is $75,000, while the FMV of the building is $310,000.
3. A payment of $50,000 is due to the lessor at the beginning of each of the 10 years of the lease.
4. The lessee's incremental borrowing rate is 10%. (Lessor's implicit rate is unknown.)
5. Ownership will transfer to the lessee at the end of the lease.

The present value of the minimum lease payments is $337,951 ($50,000 x 6.75902*). The portion of the present value of the minimum lease payments that should be capitalized for each of the two components of the lease is computed as follows:

FMV of land	$ 75,000
FMV of building	310,000
Total FMV of leased property	$385,000

Portion of PV allocated to land	$337,951 x	75,000 / 385,000 =	$ 65,835
Portion of PV allocated to building	$337,951 x	310,000 / 385,000 =	272,116
Total PV to be capitalized			$337,951

The entry made to record the lease initially is as follows:

Leased land	65,835	
Leased building	272,116	
Lease obligation		337,951

**6.75902 is the PV of an annuity due for ten periods at 10%.*

Subsequently, the obligation will be decreased in accordance with the effective interest method. The leased building will be amortized over its expected useful life.

Example of accounting for land and building lease without transfer of title or bargain purchase option

Assume the same facts as in the previous example except that title does not transfer at the end of the lease.

The lease is still a capital lease because the lease term is more than 75% of the useful life. Since the FMV of the land is less than 25% of the leased properties in aggregate, (75,000/385,000 = 19%), the land component is considered immaterial and the lease will be accounted for as a single lease. The entry to record the lease is as follows:

Leased property	337,951	
Lease obligation		337,951

Assume the same facts as in the previous example except that the FMV of the land is $110,000 and the FMV of the building is $275,000. Once again, title does not transfer.

Because the FMV of the land exceeds 25% of the leased properties in aggregate (110,000/385,000 = 28%), the land component is considered material and the lease would be separated into two components. The annual minimum lease payment attributed to the land is computed as follows:

$$\frac{\text{FMV of land}}{\text{PV factor}} \quad \frac{\$110{,}000}{6.75902^*} = \$16{,}275$$

The remaining portion of the annual payment is attributed to the building.

Annual payment	$50,000
Less amount attributed to land	(16,275)
Annual payment attributed to building	$33,725

The present value of the minimum annual lease payments attributed to the building is then computed as follows:

Minimum annual lease payment attributed to building	$ 33,725
PV factor	x 6.75902*
PV of minimum annual lease payments attributed to building	$227,948

The entry to record the capital portion of the lease is as follows:

Leased building	227,948	
Lease obligation		227,948

**6.75902 is the PV of an annuity due for ten periods at 10%.*

There would be no computation of the present value of the minimum annual lease payment attributed to the land since the land component of the lease will be treated as an operating lease. For this reason, each year, $16,275 of the $50,000 lease payment will be recorded as land rental expense. The remainder of the annual payment ($33,725) will be applied against the lease obligation using the effective interest method.

Leases involving real estate and equipment. When real estate leases also involve equipment or machinery, the equipment component should be separated and accounted for as a separate lease agreement by both lessees and lessors. According to US GAAP, "the portion of the minimum lease payments applicable to the equipment element of the lease shall be estimated by whatever means are appropriate in the circumstances." The lessee and lessor should apply the capitalization requirements to the equipment lease independently of accounting for the real estate lease(s). The real estate leases should be handled as discussed in the preceding two sections. In a sale-leaseback transaction involving real estate with equipment, the equipment and land are not separated.

Leases involving only part of a building. It is common to find lease agreements that involve only part of a building, as, for example, when a floor of an office building is leased or when a store in a shopping mall is leased. A difficulty that arises in this situation is that the cost and/or fair market value of the leased portion of the whole may not be determinable objectively.

Lessee accounting. If the fair value of the leased property is objectively determinable, the lessee should follow the rules and account for the lease as described in "leases involving land and building." If the fair value of the leased property cannot be determined objectively but the agreement satisfies the 75% test, the estimated economic life of the building in which the leased premises are located should be used. If this test is not met, the lessee should account for the agreement as an operating lease.

Lessor accounting. From the lessor's position, both the cost and fair value of the leased property must be objectively determinable before the procedures described under "leases involving land and building" will apply. If either the cost or the fair value cannot be determined objectively, the lessor should account for the agreement as an operating lease.

DISCLOSURE REQUIREMENTS UNDER IAS 17

Lessee Disclosures

1. Disclosure should be made of the amounts of assets that are subject of finance leases at each balance sheet date. Liabilities related to these assets should be shown separately from other liabilities, differentiating between current and noncurrent portions. Preparers of financial statements are encouraged to present on the asset side leased assets capitalized by major class of assets. It is not appropriate for the liabilities to be as a deduction from the leased assets. On the liability side the aggregate amount of obligations under finance lease should be shown either as

   a. The total gross minimum lease payments along with deduction for future finance charges, or
   b. The net present value of the lease obligations presented as a single amount with disclosure in summary form the interest rates used in discounting the minimum lease payments.

2. Commitments toward minimum lease payments under finance leases and under noncancelable operating leases, with terms extending over 1 year, should be disclosed in summary form, giving the amounts and the periods in which the payments will become due.
3. Disclosure is also required of significant financing restrictions, renewal or purchase options, contingent rentals, and other contingencies arising from leases.

In addition to (or where appropriate, instead of) the foregoing, if the exposure draft E56 is adopted as a successor to the existing standard IAS 17, the following new disclosures will be mandated:

1. For each major class of asset, the gross carrying amount, accumulated depreciation, and accumulated impairment losses at the balance sheet date, and the depreciation charged on the income statement.
2. The total present value of lease liabilities as of the balance sheet date, categorized into those due in 1 year or less, those due in more than 1 but no more than 5 years, and those due in more than 5 years.
3. The amount of finance charges included in profit or loss of the period.
4. Contingent rents included in profit or loss for the period.
5. The total of minimum sublease payments to be received in the future under noncancellable subleases as of the balance sheet date.
6. A general description of the lessee's significant leasing arrangements including, but not necessarily limited to, the basis for determining contingent rentals, the existence and terms of renewal or purchase options and escalation clauses, and restrictions imposed such as on dividend or assumptions of further debt.

Furthermore, the exposure draft E56 clarifies that the requirements of IAS 32 also are applicable to finance leases. E56 also sets forth in greater detail the disclosure requirements which will be applicable to lessees under operating leases. While some of these were suggested under original IAS 17 or are implicitly needed to provide adequate disclosure under general concept, the proposal will offer preparers more explicit guidance. The following disclosures are therefore established:

1. Noncancellable future minimum lease payments, categorized into those due in 1 year or less, those due in more then 1 but no more than 5 years, and those due in more than 5 years.

2. The total of minimum lease payments to be received under noncancellable subleases.
3. Rent expense included in profit or loss for the period, with separate amounts of minimum and contingent rents, and for sublease rents.
4. A general description of the lessee's significant leasing arrangements including, but not necessarily limited to, the basis for determining contingent rentals, the existence and terms of renewal or purchase options and escalation clauses, and restrictions imposed such as on dividends or assumption of further debt.

Lessor Disclosures

1. Disclosure is required at each balance sheet date of the "gross investments" in leases reported as finance leases, and the related "unearned finance income" and "unguaranteed residual values" of the leased assets.

   Preparers are encouraged to disclose, as an indicator of growth, the gross investment net of unearned finance income from new business added during the accounting period, after deducting the relevant amounts for canceled leases. Disclosure is also encouraged of the lessor's general leasing arrangements and of the future minimum payments to be received for specified periods in future.
2. Disclosure is required of the basis used in allocating income over the lease term so as to produce a constant periodic rate of return as required by the standard. Indication is required of whether the return relates to:

   a. Net investment outstanding, or
   b. Net cash investment outstanding in the lease.

   (If more than one basis has been used, the bases should be disclosed.)
3. In case a significant portion of the lessor's business comprises operating leases, the lessor should disclose, at each balance sheet date

   a. The amount of assets leased under operating leases by each major class of asset
   b. The related accumulated depreciation thereon

It is encouraged to disclose the lessor's general leasing arrangements, the amounts of rental income from operating leases, and the minimum future rentals on noncancelable leases both in aggregate and in a specified future period.

In addition to the foregoing items, exposure draft E56 would require enhanced disclosures which would include the following for lessors under finance leases:

1. The present value of future minimum lease payments receivable as of the balance sheet date, categorized into those due in 1 year or less, those due in more than 1 year but not more than 5 years, and those due beyond 5 years.

2. The accumulated allowance for uncollectible minimum lease payments receivable.
3. Total contingent rentals included in income.
4. A general description of the lessor's significant leasing arrangements.

For operating leases, E56 prescribed the following expanded disclosures:

1. Accumulated impairment losses by class of asset at the balance sheet date.
2. Depreciation recognized on assets held for operating lease use during the period.
3. Minimum future lease payments under noncancellable operating leases, in the aggregate and classified into those due in no more than 1 year, those due in more than 1 but not more than 5 years, and those due in more than 5 years.
4. Total contingent rentals included in income for the period.
5. A general description of leasing arrangements to which it is a party.

APPENDIX A

SPECIAL SITUATIONS NOT YET ADDRESSED BY IAS 17 BUT WHICH HAVE BEEN INTERPRETED UNDER US GAAP

In the following section, a number of interesting and common problem areas that have not been addressed by the international standards are briefly considered. The guidance found in US GAAP is referenced, as this is likely to represent the most comprehensive source of insight into these matters. However, it should be understood that this constitutes only possible approaches and is not authoritative guidance.

Change in the Provisions of a Lease

In the case of either a sales-type or direct financing lease where there is a change in the provisions of a lease, the lease should be accounted for by the lessor as discussed below. The principal concern is with changes in the provisions that affect the amount of the remaining minimum lease payments. When a change such as this occurs, one of the following three things can happen:

1. The change does not give rise to a new agreement. A new agreement is defined as a change which, if in effect at the inception of the lease, would have resulted in a different classification.
2. The change does give rise to a new agreement that would be classified as a direct financing lease.
3. The change gives rise to a new agreement classified as an operating lease.

If either (1) or (2) occurs, the balance of the minimum lease payments receivable and the estimated residual value (if affected) is adjusted to reflect the effect of the change. The net adjustment is to be charged (or credited) to the unearned income account and the accounting for the lease adjusted to reflect the change.

If the new agreement is an operating lease, the remaining net investment (lease receivable less unearned income) is to be removed from the books and the leased asset recorded at the lower of its cost, present fair value, or carrying value. The net adjustment resulting from these entries is charged (or credited) to the income of the period. Thereafter, the new lease is accounted for as any other operating lease.

Termination of a Lease

The lessor shall remove the remaining net investment from his or her books and record the leased equipment as an asset at the lower of its original cost, present fair value, or current carrying value. The net adjustment is reflected in the income of the current period.

TREATMENT OF SELECTED ITEMS IN ACCOUNTING FOR LEASES UNDER US GAAP

	Lessor: Operating	Lessor: Direct financing and sales-type	Lessee: Operating	Lessee: capital
Initial direct costs	Capitalize and amortize over lease term in proportion to rent revenue recognized (normally SL basis)	Direct financing: Record in separate account Add to net investment in lease Compute new effective rate that equates gross amt. of min. lease payments and unguar. residual value with net invest. Amortize so as to produce constant rate of return over lease term Sales-type: Expense in period incurred	N/A	N/A
Investment tax credit retained by lessor	N/A	Reduces FMV of leased asset for 90% test	N/A	Reduces FMV of leased asset for 90% test
Bargain purchase option	N/A	Include in: Minimum lease payments 90% test	N/A	Include in: Minimum lease payments 90% test
Guaranteed residual value	N/A	Include in: Minimum lease payments 90% test Sales-type: Include PV in sales revenues	N/A	Include in: Minimum lease payments 90% test
Unguaranteed residual value	N/A	Include In: "Gross Investment in Lease" Not included in: 90% test Sales-type: Exclude from sales revenue Deduct PV from cost of sales	N/A	Include in: Minimum lease payments 90% test
Contingent rentals	Revenue in period earned	Not part of minimum lease payments; revenue in period earned	Expense in period incurred	Not part of minimum lease payments; expense in period incurred
Amortization period	Amortize down to estimated residual value over estimated economic life of asset	N/A	N/A	Amortize down to estimated residual value over lease term or estimated economic life[c]
Revenue (expense)[a]	Rent revenue (normally SL basis) Amortization depreciation expense)	Direct financing: Interest revenue on net investment in lease (gross investment less unearned interest income) Sales-type: Dealer profit in period of sale (sales revenue less cost of leased asset) Interest revenue on net investment in lease	Rent expense (normally SL basis)[b]	Interest expense and depreciation expense

[a]*Elements of revenue (expense) listed for the items above are not repeated here (e.g., treatment of initial direct costs).*

[b]*If payments are not on a SL basis, recognize rent expense on a SL basis unless another systematic and rational method is more representative of use benefit obtained from the property, in which case, the other method should be used.*

[c]*If lease has automatic passage of title or bargain purchase option, use estimated economic life; otherwise, use the lease term.*

The lessee is also affected by the terminated agreement because he or she has been relieved of the obligation. If the lease is a capital lease, the lessee should remove both the obligation and the asset from his or her accounts and charge any adjustment to the current period income. If accounted for as an operating lease, no accounting adjustment is required.

Renewal or Extension of an Existing Lease

The renewal or extension of an existing lease agreement affects the accounting of both the lessee and the lessor. US GAAP specifies two basic situations in this regard: (1) the renewal occurs and makes a residual guarantee or penalty provision inoperative, or (2) the renewal agreement does not do the foregoing and the renewal is to be treated as a new agreement. The accounting treatment prescribed under the latter situation for a lessee is as follows:

1. If the renewal or extension is classified as a capital lease, the (present) current balances of the asset and related obligation should be adjusted by an amount equal to the difference between the present value of the future minimum lease payments under the revised agreement and the (present) current balance of the obligation. The present value of the minimum lease payments under the revised agreement should be computed using the interest rate that was in effect at the inception of the original lease.
2. If the renewal or extension is classified as an operating lease, the current balances in the asset and liability accounts are removed from the books and a gain (loss) recognized for the difference. The new lease agreement resulting from a renewal or extension is accounted for in the same manner as other operating leases.

Under the same circumstances, US GAAP prescribes the following treatment to be followed by the lessor:

1. If the renewal or extension is classified as a direct financing lease, then the existing balances of the lease receivable and the estimated residual value accounts should be adjusted for the changes resulting from the revised agreement. (*NOTE: Remember that an upward adjustment of the estimated residual value is not allowed.*) The net adjustment should be charged or credited to an unearned income account.
2. If the renewal or extension is classified as an operating lease, the remaining net investment under the existing sales-type lease or direct financing lease is removed from the books and the leased asset recorded as an asset at the lower of its original cost, present fair value, or current carrying amount. The difference between the net investment and the amount recorded for the leased asset is charged to income of the period. The renewal or extension is then accounted for as for any other operating lease.

3. If the renewal or extension is classified as a sales-type lease **and** it occurs at or near the end of the existing lease term, the renewal or extension should be accounted for as a sales-type lease. (*NOTE: A renewal or extension that occurs in the last few months of an existing lease is considered to have occurred at or near the end of the existing lease term.*)

If the renewal or extension causes the guarantee or penalty provision to be inoperative, the lessee adjusts the current balance of the leased asset and the lease obligation to the present value of the future minimum lease payments (according to the relevant standard, "by an amount equal to the difference between the PV of future minimum lease payments under the revised agreement and the present balance of the obligation"). The PV of the future minimum lease payments is computed using the implicit rate used in the original lease agreement.

Given the same circumstances, the lessor adjusts the existing balance of the lease receivable and estimated residual value accounts to reflect the changes of the revised agreement (remember, no upward adjustments to the residual value). The net adjustment is charged (or credited) to unearned income.

Leases Between Related Parties

Leases between related parties are classified and accounted for as though the parties are unrelated, except in cases where it is clear that the terms and conditions of the agreement have been influenced significantly by the fact of the relationship. When this is the case, the classification and/or accounting is modified to reflect the true economic substance of the transaction rather than the legal form.

If a subsidiary's principal business activity is leasing property to its parent or other affiliated companies, consolidated financial statements are presented. The US GAAP standard on related parties requires that the nature and extent of leasing activities between related parties be disclosed.

Accounting for Leases in a Business Combination

A business combination, in and of itself, has no effect on the classification of a lease. However, if, in connection with a business combination, the lease agreement is modified to change the original classification of the lease, it should be considered a new agreement and reclassified according to the revised provisions.

In most cases, a business combination that is accounted for by the pooling-of-interest method or by the purchase method will not affect the previous classification of a lease unless the provisions have been modified as indicated in the preceding paragraph.

The acquiring company should apply the following procedures to account for a leveraged lease in a business combination accounted for by the purchase method:

1. The classification of leveraged lease should be kept.
2. The net investment in the leveraged lease should be given a fair market value (present value, net of tax) based on the remaining future cash flows. Also, the estimated tax effects of the cash flows should be given recognition.
3. The net investment should be broken down into three components: net rentals receivable, estimated residual value, and unearned income.
4. Thereafter, the leveraged lease should be accounted for as described above in the section on leveraged leases.

Accounting for Changes in Lease Agreements Resulting From Refunding of Tax-Exempt Debt

If, during the lease term, a change in the lease results from a refunding by the lessor of tax-exempt debt (including an advance refunding) and (1) the lessee receives the economic advantages of the refunding and (2) the revised agreement can be classified as a capital lease by the lessee and a direct financing lease by the lessor, the change should be accounted for as follows:

1. If the change is accounted for as an extinguishment of debt

    a. **Lessee accounting**. The lessee should adjust the lease obligation to the present value of the future minimum lease payments under the revised agreement. The present value of the minimum lease payments should be computed by using the interest rate applicable to the revised agreement. Any gain or loss should be recognized currently as a gain or loss on the extinguishment of debt in accordance with the provisions of SFAS 4.
    b. **Lessor accounting**. The lessor should adjust the balance of the lease receivable and the estimated residual value, if affected, for the difference in present values between the old and revised agreements. Any resulting gain or loss should be recognized currently.

2. If the change is not accounted for as an extinguishment of debt

    a. **Lessee accounting**. The lessee should accrue any costs in connection with the debt refunding that is obligated to be refunded to the lessor. These costs should be amortized by the interest method over the period from the date of refunding to the call date of the debt to be refunded.
    b. **Lessor accounting**. The lessor should recognize any reimbursements to be received from the lessee, for costs paid in relation to the debt refunding, as revenue. This revenue should be recognized in a systematic manner over the period from the date of refunding to the call date of the debt to be refunded.

Sale or Assignment to Third Parties--Nonrecourse Financing

The sale or assignment of a lease or of property subject to a lease that was originally accounted for as a sales-type lease or a direct financing lease will not affect the original accounting treatment of the lease. Any profit or loss on the sale or assignment should be recognized at the time of transaction except under the following two circumstances:

1. When the sale or assignment is between related parties, apply the provisions presented above under "related parties."
2. When the sale or assignment is with recourse, it should be accounted for using the provisions of the US standard on sale of receivables with recourse.

The sale of property subject to an operating lease should not be treated as a sale if the seller (or any related party to the seller) retains "substantial risks of ownership" in the leased property. A seller may retain substantial risks of ownership by various arrangements. For example, if the lessee defaults on the lease agreement or if the lease terminates, the seller may arrange to do one of the following:

1. Acquire the property or the lease
2. Substitute an existing lease
3. Secure a replacement lessee or a buyer for the property under a remarketing agreement

A seller will not retain substantial risks of ownership by arrangements where one of the following occurs:

1. A remarketing agreement includes a reasonable fee to be paid to the seller
2. The seller is not required to give priority to the releasing or disposition of the property owned by the third party over similar property owned by the seller

When the sale of property subject to an operating lease is not accounted for as a sale because the substantial risk factor is present, it should be accounted for as a borrowing. The proceeds from the sale should be recorded as an obligation on the seller's books. Rental payments made by the lessee under the operating lease should be recorded as revenue by the seller even if the payments are paid to the third-party purchaser. The seller shall account for each rental payment by allocating a portion to interest expense (to be imputed in accordance with the provisions of APB 21), and the remainder will reduce the existing obligation. Other normal accounting procedures for operating leases should be applied except that the depreciation term for the leased asset is limited to the amortization period of the obligation.

The sale or assignment of lease payments under an operating lease by the lessor should be accounted for as a borrowing as described above.

Nonrecourse financing is a common occurrence in the leasing industry whereby the stream of lease payments on a lease is discounted on a nonrecourse basis at a financial institution with the lease payments collateralizing the debt. The proceeds are then used to finance future leasing transactions. Even though the discounting is on a nonrecourse basis, US GAAP prohibits the offsetting of the debt against the related lease receivable unless a legal right of offset exists or the lease qualified as a leveraged lease at its inception.

Money-Over-Money Lease Transactions

In cases where a lessor obtains nonrecourse financing in excess of the leased asset's cost, a technical bulletin states that the borrowing and leasing are separate transactions and should not be offset against each other unless a right of offset exists. Only dealer profit in sales-type leases may be recognized at the beginning of the lease term.

Acquisition of Interest in Residual Value

Recently, there has been an increase in the acquisition of interests in residual values of leased assets by companies whose primary business is other than leasing or financing. This generally occurs through the outright purchase of the right to own the leased asset or the right to receive the proceeds from the sale of a leased asset at the end of its lease term.

In instances such as these, the rights should be recorded by the purchaser at the fair value of the assets surrendered. Recognition of increases in the value of the interest in the residual (i.e., residual value accretion) to the end of the lease term are prohibited. However, a nontemporary write-down of the residual value interest should be recognized as a loss. This guidance also applies to lessors who sell the related minimum lease payments but retain the interest in the residual value. Guaranteed residual values also have no effect on this guidance.

Leases Involving Government Units

Leases that involve government units (i.e., airport facilities, bus terminal space, etc.) usually contain special provisions that prevent the agreements from being classified as anything but operating leases. These special provisions include the governmental body's authority to abandon a facility at any time during lease term, thus making its economic life indeterminable. These leases also do not contain a BPO or transfer ownership. The fair market value is generally indeterminable because neither the leased property nor similar property is available for sale.

However, leases involving government units are subject to the same classification criteria as those of nongovernment units, except when the following six criteria are met. (*NOTE: If all six conditions are met, the agreement should be classified as an operating lease by both lessee and lessor.*)

1. A government unit or authority owns the leased property
2. The leased property is part of a larger facility operated by or on behalf of the lessor
3. The leased property is a permanent structure or part of a permanent structure that normally cannot be moved to another location
4. The lessor, or a higher governmental authority, has the right to terminate the lease at any time under the lease agreement or existing statutes or regulations
5. The lease neither transfers ownership nor allows the lessee to purchase or acquire the leased property
6. The leased property or similar property in the same area cannot be purchased or leased from anyone else

Accounting for a Sublease

A sublease is used to describe the situation where the original lessee re-leases the leased property to a third party (the sublessee), and the original lessee acts as a sublessor. Normally, the nature of a sublease agreement does not affect the original lease agreement, and the original lessee/sublessor retains primary liability.

The original lease remains in effect, and the original lessor continues to account for the lease as before. The original lessee/sublessor accounts for the lease as follows:

1. If the original lease agreement transfers ownership or contains a bargain purchase option and if the new lease meets any one of the four criteria specified in US GAAP (i.e., transfers ownership, BPO, the 75% test, or the 90% test) and both the collectibility and uncertainties criteria, the sublessor should classify the new lease as a sales-type or direct financing lease; otherwise, as an operating lease. In either situation, the original lessee/sublessor should continue accounting for the original lease obligation as before.
2. If the original lease agreement does not transfer ownership or contain a bargain purchase option, but it still qualified as a capital lease, the original lessee/sublessor should (with one exception) apply the usual criteria set by US GAAP in classifying the new agreement as a capital or operating lease. If the new lease qualifies for capital treatment, the original lessee/sublessor should account for it as a direct financing lease, with the unamortized balance of the asset under the original lease being treated as the cost of the leased property. The one exception arises when the circumstances surrounding the sublease suggest that the sublease agreement was an important part of a predetermined plan in which the original lessee played only an intermediate role between the original lessor and the sublessee. In this situation, the sublease should be classified by the 75% and 90% criteria as well

as collectibility and uncertainties criteria. In applying the 90% criterion, the fair value for the leased property will be the fair value to the original lessor at the inception of the original lease. Under all circumstances, the original lessee should continue accounting for the original lease obligation as before. If the new lease agreement (sublease) does not meet the capitalization requirements imposed for subleases, the new lease should be accounted for as an operating lease.

3. If the original lease is an operating lease, the original lessee/sublessor should account for the new lease as an operating lease and account for the original operating lease as before.

APPENDIX B

LEVERAGED LEASES

One of the more complex accounting subjects regarding leases is the accounting for a leveraged lease. Once again, as with both sales-type and direct financing, the classification of the lease by the lessor has no effect on the accounting treatment accorded the lease by the lessee. The lessee simply treats it as any other lease and thus is interested only in whether the lease qualifies as an operating or a capital lease. The lessor's accounting problem is substantially more complex than that of the lessee.

To qualify as a leveraged lease, a lease agreement must meet the following requirements, and the lessor must account for the investment tax credit (when in effect) in the manner described below. (*NOTE: Failure to do so will result in the lease being classified as a direct financing lease.*)

1. The lease must meet the definition of a direct financing lease. (The 90% of FMV criterion does not apply.)*
2. The lease must involve at least three parties.
    a. An owner-lessor (equity participant)
    b. A lessee
    c. A long-term creditor (debt participant)
3. The financing provided by the creditor is nonrecourse as to the general credit of the lessor and is sufficient to provide the lessor with substantial leverage.
4. The lessor's net investment (defined below) decreases in the early years and increases in the later years until it is eliminated.

The last characteristic (item 4) poses the accounting problem.

The leveraged lease arose as a result of an effort to maximize the tax benefits associated with a lease transaction. To accomplish this, it was necessary to involve a third party to the lease transaction (in addition to the lessor and lessee), a long-term creditor. The following diagram illustrates the existing relationships in a leveraged lease agreement:

---

* *A direct financing lease must have its cost or carrying value equal to the fair value of the asset at the inception of the lease. Thus, even if the amounts are not significantly different, leveraged lease accounting should not be used.*

The leveraged lease arrangement*

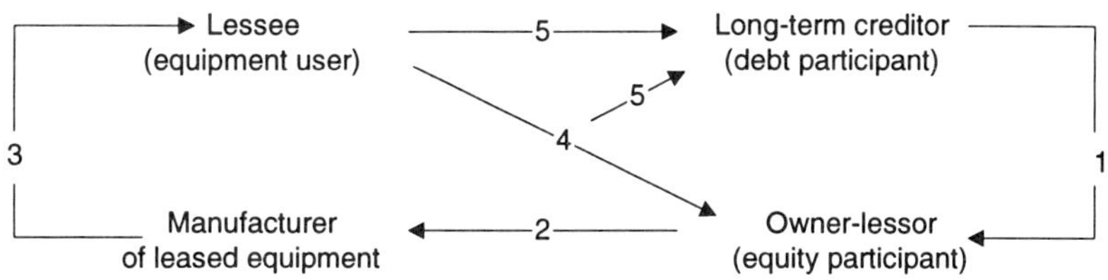

1. The owner-lessor secures long-term financing from the creditor, generally in excess of 50% of the purchase price. US GAAP indicates that the lessor must be provided with sufficient leverage in the transaction; thus the 50%.
2. The owner then uses this financing along with his or her own funds to purchase the asset from the manufacturer.
3. The manufacturer delivers the asset to the lessee.
4. The lessee remits the periodic rent to the lessor.
5. The debt is guaranteed by either using the equipment as collateral, the assignment of the lease payments, or both, depending on the demands established by the creditor.

The FASB concluded that the entire lease agreement be accounted for as a single transaction and not a direct financing lease plus a debt transaction. The feeling was that the latter did not readily convey the net investment in the lease to the user of the financial statements. Thus, the lessor is to record the investment as a net amount. The gross investment is calculated as a combination of the following amounts:

1. The rentals receivable from the lessee, net of the principal and interest payments due to the long-term creditor
2. A receivable for the amount of the investment tax credit (ITC) to be realized on the transaction (repealed in the United States but may yet exist in other jurisdictions)
3. The estimated residual value of the leased asset
4. The unearned and deferred income, consisting of
   a. The estimated pretax lease income (or loss), after deducting initial direct costs, remaining to be allocated to income
   b. The ITC remaining to be allocated to income over the remaining term of the lease

The first three amounts described above are readily obtainable; however, the last amount, the unearned and deferred income, requires additional computations. To derive this amount, it is necessary to create a cash flow (income) analysis by

**Adapted from "A Straightforward Approach to Leveraged Leasing" by Pierce R. Smith, The Journal of Commercial Bank Lending, July 1973, pp. 40-47.*

year for the entire lease term. As described in item 4 above, the unearned and deferred income consists of the pretax lease income (Gross lease rentals – Depreciation – Loan interest) and the unamortized investment tax credit. The total of these two amounts for all the periods in the lease term represents the unearned and deferred income at the inception of the lease.

The amount computed as the gross investment in the lease (foregoing paragraphs) less the deferred taxes relative to the difference between pretax lease income and taxable lease income is the net investment for purposes of computing the net income for the period. To compute the periodic net income, another schedule must be completed that uses the cash flows derived in the first schedule and allocates them between income and a reduction in the net investment.

The amount of income is first determined by applying a rate to the net investment. The rate to be used is the rate that will allocate the entire amount of cash flow (income) when applied in the years in which the net investment is positive. In other words, the rate is derived in much the same way as the implicit rate (trial and error), except that only the years in which there is a positive net investment are considered. Thus, income is recognized only in the years in which there is a positive net investment.

The income recognized is divided among the following three elements:

1. Pretax accounting income
2. Amortization of investment tax credit
3. The tax effect of the pretax accounting income

The first two are allocated in proportionate amounts from the unearned and deferred income included in calculation of the net investment. In other words, the unearned and deferred income consists of pretax lease accounting income and any investment tax credit. Each of these is recognized during the period in the proportion that the current period's allocated income is to the total income (cash flow). The last item, the tax effect, is recognized in the tax expense for the year. The tax effect of any difference between pretax lease accounting income and taxable lease income is charged (or credited) to deferred taxes.

When tax rates change, all components of a leveraged lease must be recalculated from the inception of the lease using the revised after-tax cash flows arising from the revised tax rates.

If, in any case, the projected cash receipts (income) are less than the initial investment, the deficiency is to be recognized as a loss at the inception of the lease. Similarly, if at any time during the lease period the aforementioned method of recognizing income would result in a future period loss, the loss shall be recognized immediately.

This situation may arise as a result of the circumstances surrounding the lease changing. Therefore, any estimated residual value and other important assumptions must be reviewed on a periodic basis (at least annually). Any change is to be incorporated into the income computations; however, there is to be no upward revision of the estimated residual value.

The following example illustrates the application of these principles to a leveraged lease:

Example of simplified leveraged lease

Assume the following:

1. A lessor acquires an asset for $100,000 with an estimated useful life of 3 years in exchange for a $25,000 down payment and a $75,000 3-year note with equal payments due on 12/31 each year. The interest rate is 18%.
2. The asset has no residual value.
3. The PV of an ordinary annuity of $1 for 3 years at 18% is 2.17427.
4. The asset is leased for 3 years with annual payments due to the lessor on 12/31 in the amount of $45,000.
5. The lessor uses the ACRS method of depreciation for tax purposes and elects to reduce the ITC rate to 4%, as opposed to reducing the depreciable basis.
6. Assume a constant tax rate throughout the life of the lease of 40%.

Chart 1 analyzes the cash flows generated by the leveraged leasing activities. Chart 2 allocates the cash flows between the investment in leveraged leased assets and income from leveraged leasing activities. The allocation requires finding that rate of return, which when applied to the investment balance at the beginning of each year that the investment amount is positive, will allocate the net cash flow fully to net income over the term of the lease. This rate can be found only by a computer program or by an iterative trial-and-error process. The example that follows has a positive investment value in each of the 3 years, and thus the allocation takes place in each time period. Leveraged leases usually have periods where the investment account turns negative and is below zero.

Allocating principal and interest on the loan payments is as follows:

$75,000 ÷ 2.17427 = $34,494

Year	*Payment*	*Interest 18%*	*Principal*	*Balance*
Inception of lease	$ --	$ --	$ --	$75,000
1	34,494	13,500	20,994	54,006
2	34,494	9,721	24,773	29,233
3	34,494	5,261	29,233	--

Chart 1

	A	B	C	D	E	F	G	H	I
	Rent	Depr.	Interest on loan	Taxable income (A-B-C)	Income tax payable (rcvbl.) Dx40%	Loan principal payments	ITC	Cash flow (A+G-C -E-F)	Cumulative cash flow
Initial	$ --	$ --	$ --	$ --	$ --	$ --	$ --	$(25,000)	$(25,000)
Year 1	45,000	25,000	13,500	6,500	2,600	20,994	4,000	11,906	(13,094)
Year 2	45,000	38,000	9,721	(2,721)	(1,088)	24,773	--	11,594	(1,500)
Year 3	45,000	37,000	5,261	2,739	1,096	29,233	--	9,410	7,910
Total	$135,000	$100,000	$28,482	$ 6,518	$ 2,608	$75,000	$4,000	$ 7,910	

The chart below allocates the cash flows determined above between the net investment in the lease and income. Recall that the income is then allocated between pretax accounting income and the amortization of the investment for credit. The income tax expense for the period is a result of applying the tax rate to the current periodic pretax accounting income.

The amount to be allocated in total in each period is the net cash flow determined in column H above. The investment at the beginning of year 1 is the initial down payment of $25,000. This investment is then reduced on an annual basis by the amount of the cash flow not allocated to income.

Chart 2

	1	2	3	4	5	6	7
	Cash flow assumption				Income analysis		
	Investment beginning of year	Cash flow	Allocated to investment	Allocated to income	Pretax income	Income tax expense	Investment tax credit
Year 1	$25,000	$11,906	$ 7,964	$3,942	$3,248	$1,300	$1,994
Year 2	17,036	11,594	8,908	2,686	2,213	885	1,358
Year 3	8,128	9,410	8,128	1,282	1,057	423	648
		$32,910	$25,000	$7,910	$6,518	$2,608	$4,000

Rate of return = 15.77%

1. Column 2 is the net cash flow after the initial investment, and columns 3 and 4 are the allocation based on the 15.77% rate of return. The total of column 4 is the same as the total of column H in Chart 1.
2. Column 5 allocates column D in Chart 1 based on the allocations in column 4. Column 6 allocates column E in Chart 1, and column 7 allocates column G in Chart 1 in the same basis.

The journal entries below illustrate the proper recording and accounting for the leveraged lease transaction. The initial entry represents the cash down payment, investment tax credit receivable, the unearned and deferred revenue, and the net cash to be received over the term of the lease.

The remaining journal entries recognize the annual transactions that include the net receipt of cash and the amortization of income.

	Year 1		*Year 2*		*Year 3*	
Rents receivable [Chart 1 (A-C-F)]	31,518					
Investment tax credit receivable	4,000					
Cash		25,000				
Unearned and deferred income		10,518				
[Initial investment, Chart 2 (5+7) totals]						
Cash	10,506		10,506		10,506	
Rent receivable		10,506		10,506		10,506
[Net for all cash transactions, Chart 1 (A-C-F) line by line for each year]						
Income tax receivable (cash)	4,000					
Investment tax credit receivable		4,000				
Unearned and deferred income	5,242		3,571		1,705	
Income from leveraged leases		5,242		3,571		1,705
[Amortization of unearned income, Chart 2 (5+7) line by line for each year]						

The following schedules illustrate the computation of deferred income tax amount. The annual amount is a result of the temporary difference created due to the difference in the timing of the recognition of income for book and tax purposes. The income for tax purposes can be found in column D in Chart 1, while the income for book purposes is found in column 5 of Chart 2. The actual amount of deferred tax is the difference between the tax computed with the temporary difference and the tax computed without the temporary difference. These amounts are represented by the income tax payable or receivable as shown in column E of Chart 1 and the income tax expense as shown in column 6 of Chart 2. A check of this figure is provided by multiplying the difference between book and tax income by the annual rate.

Year 1

Income tax payable	$ 2,600	
Income tax expense	(1,300)	
Deferred income tax (Dr)		$1,300
Taxable income	$ 6,500	
Pretax accounting income	(3,248)	
Difference	$ 3,252	
$3,252 x 40% = $1,300		

Year 2

Income tax receivable	$ 1,088	
Income tax expense	885	
Deferred income tax (Cr)		$1,973
Taxable loss	$ 2,721	
Pretax accounting income	2,213	
Difference	$ 4,934	
$4,934 x 40% = $1,973		

Year 3

Income tax payable	$ 1,096	
Income tax expense	(423)	
Deferred income tax (Dr)		$ 673
Taxable income	$ 2,739	
Pretax accounting income	(1,057)	
Difference	$ 1,682	
$1,682 x 40% = $673		

14 ACCOUNTING FOR INCOME TAXES

PERSPECTIVE AND ISSUES

The substitution of the liability method of computing deferred tax assets and liabilities for the venerable deferral method has been long foretold. As the balance sheet has reasserted primacy over the income statement over the past two decades, the accurate depiction of entities' financial positions has become the supreme goal of financial reporting, and ever-stricter compliance with definitions of assets and liabilities has been demanded. As a consequence, certain measurement concepts, particularly the matching principle which was so important in the era of income statement dominance, have faded in significance. Income tax accounting provides the most striking example of this change in philosophy.

The use of the deferral method had been required under the rules imposed by a number of national standard-setting bodies, most notably by the U.S. Accounting Principles Board (in Opinion 11, issued in 1967,) and was justified largely by the matching principle. The deferral method was optional under the earlier international accounting standard, IAS 12. However, the deferral method was often difficult to apply, and it had the unfortunate tendency of resulting in debits or credits on the balance sheet which bore little relationship to future tax benefits or obligations. The liability method, which was also permitted under IAS 12, is balance sheet oriented and is much more consistent with the conceptual definitions of assets and liabilities adopted by IASC, FASB, and others. In more recent years, the liability method has been mandated by the US Financial Accounting Standards Board (first in Statement 96, and then in its successor, 109) and other major standard-setting bodies.

The International Accounting Standards Committee in 1989 adopted the *Framework for the Preparation and Presentation of Financial Statements*, which offered definitions of assets and liabilities which served notice that the deferral method of accounting for interperiod tax allocation would no longer be conceptually tolerable. An initial proposal for a replacement for IAS 12 was exposed in 1989 as E33. This proposal, which was not enacted, prohibited the deferral method and mandated a version of the liability approach. A substantially revised exposure draft, E49, followed in 1994. The new international standard, IAS 12 (revised), adopted in late 1996 for application in 1998, embraces an approach which largely emulates SFAS 109, albeit with some distinctions.

Under the new standard, deferred assets and liabilities are to be presented at the amounts which are expected to flow to or from the reporting entity when the benefits are ultimately realized or the obligations are settled. Revised IAS 12 makes no significant distinction between operation losses and other types of deductible temporary differences, and requires that both be given recognition when realization is deem to be probable. Discounting of these amounts to present values is not permitted. Both tax assets and liabilities are measured by reference to expected tax rates, which in general are the enacted, effective rates as of the balance sheet date. The new standard also alters the criteria for recordation of the tax effects of temporary differences arising from ownership interest in investees and subsidiaries, and for the accounting related to goodwill and negative goodwill arising from business acquisitions. Presentation of deferred tax assets or liabilities as current assets or liabilities is prohibited, and a somewhat lengthier list of additional disclosures has also been mandated by the new rules.

Sources of IAS
IAS 12 *(revised)*

DEFINITIONS OF TERMS

Accounting profit. Net profit or loss for the reporting period before deducting income tax expense.

Current tax expense. The amount of income taxes payable (recoverable) in respect of the taxable profit (tax loss) for a period.

Deductible temporary differences. Temporary differences that result in amounts that are deductible in determining taxable profit when the carrying amount of the asset or liability is recovered or settled.

Deferred tax asset. The amounts of income taxes recoverable in future periods in respect of deductible temporary differences, carryforwards of unused tax losses, and carryforwards of unused tax credits.

Deferred tax expense. The change during a reporting period in the deferred tax liabilities and deferred tax assets of an entity.

Deferred tax liability. The amounts of income taxes payable in future periods in respect of taxable temporary differences.

Gains and losses included in nonowner movements in equity but excluded from net income. Certain items which, under GAAP, are events occurring currently but which are reported directly in equity, such as changes in market values of noncurrent portfolios of marketable equity securities.

Interperiod tax allocation. The process of apportioning income tax expense among reporting periods without regard to the timing of the actual cash payments for taxes. The objective is to reflect fully the tax consequences of all economic events reported in current or prior financial statements and, in particular, to report the expected tax effects of the reversals of temporary differences existing at the reporting date.

Intraperiod tax allocation. The process of apportioning income tax expense applicable to a given period between income before extraordinary items and those items required to be shown net of tax such as extraordinary items and prior period adjustments.

Operating loss carryback or carryforward. The excess of tax deductions over taxable income. To the extent that this results in a carryforward, the tax effect thereof is included in the entity's deferred tax asset, unless not expected to be realized.

Permanent differences. Differences between accounting profit and taxable profit as a result of the treatment accorded certain transactions by the income tax regulations which differs from the accounting treatment. Permanent differences will not reverse in subsequent periods, and accordingly, do not create a need for deferred tax recognition.

Tax basis. The amount attributable (explicitly or implicitly) to an asset or liability by the taxation authorities in determining taxable profit.

Tax credits. Reductions in the tax liability as a result of certain expenditures accorded special treatment under the tax regulations.

Tax expense. The aggregate of current tax expense and deferred tax expense for a reporting period.

Tax planning strategy. A representation by management of a planned transaction or series of transactions that would affect the particular future years in which temporary differences will result in taxable or deductible amounts.

Taxable profit (loss). The profit (loss) for a taxable period, determined in accordance with the rules established by the taxation authorities, on which income taxes are payable (recoverable).

Taxable temporary differences. Temporary differences that result in taxable amounts in determining taxable profit of future periods when the carrying amount of the asset or liability is recovered or settled.

Temporary differences. The differences between tax and financial reporting bases of assets and liabilities that will result in taxable or deductible amounts in future periods. Temporary differences include "timing differences" as defined by prior GAAP as well as certain other differences, such as those arising from business combinations. Some temporary differences cannot be associated with particular assets or liabilities, but nonetheless, do result from events that received financial statement recognition and will have tax effects in future periods.

Unrecognized tax benefits. Deferred tax benefits that have not been recognized because they are not deemed probable of being realized.

CONCEPTS, RULES, AND EXAMPLES

Basic Concepts of Interperiod Income Tax Allocation

Over the years, a number of theories have been advanced regarding the computation of income tax expense when timing (or temporary--the distinction will be explained shortly) differences exist. The most popular of these have been the deferral method and the liability method. A third approach, the net of tax method (more accurately thought of as a variation on the other two methods, which focuses on the manner of displaying the tax debit or credit in the balance sheet), for a time received a moderate amount of academic support but was far less widely employed (or understood) by practitioners.

Although the deferral method was soundly based on the matching principle and was never promoted as being balance sheet oriented, in practice it suffered from some complexity and sometimes also resulted in material distortion of the balance sheet. This was considered acceptable during the late 1960s and 1970s, a time when most attention was being directed to the income statement, but as the focus in more recent years shifted again to the meaningful reporting of an entity's financial position, these issues have received renewed scrutiny. Following the adoption of the IASC's *Framework for the Preparation and Presentation of Financial Statements*, it was inevitable that substantial changes in accounting for income taxes would be made. The deferred charges and credits created by the application of the deferral method, permitted by the original IAS 12, were generally not true assets or liabilities as defined in the *Framework*, and accordingly do not belong on the balance sheet. The deferral method, as a consequence, could no longer be supported as being representative of generally accepted accounting principles.

Another longstanding debate relating to interperiod income tax allocation has been among proponents of no allocation (reporting only the amount of taxes currently payable as income tax expense), partial allocation (providing deferred taxes only for those timing differences whose ultimate reversal could be reasonably predicted), and comprehensive allocation. Taken together with the contest between the deferred and the liability methods, either of which could be applied in conjunction with the comprehensive or partial allocation approaches, the result was that a number of distinct measurement strategies could be applied to timing differences, yielding very different financial statement results.

IAS 12, adopted effective 1979, essentially favored comprehensive allocation, albeit with exceptions for certain items for which the tax effects were deemed not likely to reverse within 3 years. More significantly, however, IAS 12 permitted the application of either the deferral or the liability method, which are diametrically opposed theories regarding the determination of deferred taxes. Although that standard required full disclosure of whatever method was used, tax expense could be computed in very different manners for two otherwise identical entities, for which the standard was widely criticized. It is unlikely that many users of financial statements information would have been able to compute the adjustments necessary to make otherwise noncomparable reports comparable.

Under IAS 12, timing differences referred to items of income or expense that entered into the determination of taxable income in periods different than financial reporting income. Common examples of timing differences were depreciation, deferred compensation, prepaid income, bad debt reserves, and cash versus accrual accounting. These items are included in the broader concept of temporary differences as defined by revised IAS 12. However, the newer term is more inclusive than the one it replaces. It also connotes the effects of asset basis reductions for tax credits taken, asset basis increases resulting from inflation indexing, certain intercompany transfers among entities for which consolidated financial statements but not consolidated tax returns are prepared, and certain effects of accounting for purchase business combinations.

While the requirement for comprehensive interperiod tax allocation appears to be well understood in practice, the appropriate measurement of tax expense, including the tax effects of temporary differences, is less clear. This is addressed in the following section.

Measurement of Tax Expense

Current tax expense. Income tax expense for an entity is comprised of current tax expense and deferred tax expense. Either of these can be a benefit (that is, a credit), rather than an expense (a debit), depending on whether there is taxable profit or loss for the period. For convenience, the term "tax expense" will be used to denote either an expense or a benefit. Current tax expense is easily understood as the tax effect of the entity's reported taxable income or loss for the period, as determined by relevant rules of the various taxing authorities to which it is subject. Deferred tax expense, on the other hand, is more complicated: Depending on the theory being applied, it may be based on the current period difference between taxable and financial statement income, or it may be based on a projection of changes in the future implications of differences between certain tax and financial statement amounts.

Deferred tax expense under the deferral method. The deferral method permitted under original IAS 12 computed deferred tax expense by reference to the difference between taxable income and accounting income (referred to as accounting profit under revised IAS 12). Simply put, the deferral method determines the income tax expense for the period based on the accounting income, while the current liability is based on taxable income. The difference between the actual current liability and the income tax expense is treated as either a deferred charge or credit that is amortized ratably as the timing difference reverses. Timing differences that originate during the period are referred to as originating differences, while the reversal of tax effects arising from differences which originated in prior periods are referred to as reversing differences.

Thus, the deferral method was income statement oriented, since deferred tax expense was computed on income statement amounts. Once computed, with the offset to deferred tax expense being placed on the balance sheet as a deferred tax asset or liability, this amount was never revisited or revised, until ultimately it would be reversed when the underlying timing differences themselves were reversed. The fact that the amounts presented on the balance sheet might not truly represent future benefits to be received (i.e., tax savings) or obligations to be satisfied (i.e., tax liabilities) was not a concern.

When the deferral method was used, tax expense could be computed by a "shortcut" technique by applying the effective tax rate times pretax accounting income (accounting profit). The difference between the amount thus computed and current tax expense would then be the net change in the deferred tax asset or liability for the year.

Deferred tax expense under the liability method. Under the liability method the current period's total income tax expense cannot be computed directly. Rather, it must be calculated as the sum of the two components: current tax expense and deferred tax expense. This total will not, in general, equal the current tax rate times accounting profit. The reason is that deferred tax expense is defined as the change in the deferred tax asset and liability accounts in the current period, and this change may encompass more than the current tax rate times the net temporary differences occurring in the present reporting period.

It is generally agreed that IAS 12 permitted, and the aborted proposal E33 would have required, an income statement oriented version of this methodology, while revised IAS 12 has mandated a balance sheet oriented approach, much like that imposed by SFAS 109 under US GAAP. Depending on which variation on the liability method is employed, the precise amount of deferred tax assets and liabilities may vary somewhat. Nonetheless, either variant of the liability method would include in current period deferred tax expense the effects of changing tax rates on as-yet unreversed temporary differences. Thus, current period tax expense would include not merely the tax effects of currently reported revenue and expense items, but also certain tax effects of items reported previously.

Although the primary objective of income tax accounting under the liability method is no longer the proper matching of revenue and expense, the matching principle remains very important. Therefore, the tax effects of items excluded from the income statement, such as corrections of fundamental errors, are also excluded from the income statement.

Liability Method in Detail

Overview. The liability method is balance sheet oriented, in contrast to the deferral method, which is income statement oriented. (This is true for both the variant of the liability method advocated by IAS 12 and by the proposed, but not adopted, draft to replace IAS 12, E33, which computed deferred taxes by reference to the net changes in timing differences, as well as for the method adopted by revised IAS 12, which computes deferred taxes by reference to the changes in temporary differences.) The primary goal of the liability method is to present the estimated actual taxes to be payable in future periods as the income tax liability on the balance sheet. To accomplish this goal it is necessary to consider the effect of certain enacted future changes in the tax rates when computing the current period's tax provision. The computation of the amount of deferred taxes is based on the rate expected to be in effect when the temporary differences reverse. The annual computation is considered a tentative estimate of the liability (or asset) that is subject to change as the statutory tax rate changes or as the taxpayer moves into other tax rate brackets.

The *Framework for the Preparation and Presentation of Financial Statements* defines liabilities as obligations resulting from past transactions and involving "giving up resources embodying economic benefits in order to satisfy the claim of [another] party." Assets are defined as "the potential to contribute, directly or indirectly, to the flow of cash . . . to the enterprise." As the background paper to revised IAS 12 made clear, the deferred debits and credits generated through the use of the deferral method do not meet the definitions of assets and liabilities prescribed by the *Framework.* This lack of consistency was one of the primary reasons for the IASC's reconsideration of IAS 12, which culminated in the issuance of revised IAS 12 in 1996.

Application of the liability method is, in concept at least, relatively simple when compared to the deferral method. Unlike under the deferral method, there is no need to maintain a historical record of the timing of origination of the various unreversed differences, since the effective rates at which the various components were established is not relevant. As the liability method is strictly a balance sheet approach, the primary concern is to state the obligation for taxes payable as accurately as possible, based on expected tax impact of future reversals. This is accomplished by multiplying the aggregate unreversed temporary differences, including those originating in the current period, by the tax rate expected to be in effect in the future to determine the expected future liability. This expected liability is the amount presented on the balance sheet at the end of the period. The difference between this amount and the amount on the books at the beginning of the period, simply put, is the deferred tax expense or benefit for the current reporting period.

An example of application of the liability method of deferred income tax accounting follows.

Simplified example of interperiod allocation using the liability method

Ghiza International has no permanent differences in either years 1998 or 1999. The company has only two temporary differences, depreciation and prepaid rent. No consideration is given to the nature of the deferred tax account (i.e., current or long-term) as it is not considered necessary for purposes of this example. Ghiza has a credit balance in its deferred tax account at the beginning of 1998 in the amount of $180,000. This balance consists of $228,000 ($475,000 depreciation temporary difference x 48% tax rate) of deferred taxable amounts and $48,000 ($100,000 prepaid rent temporary difference x 48% tax rate) of deferred deductible amounts.

For purposes of this example, it is assumed that there was a constant effective 48% tax rate in all periods prior to 1998. The pretax accounting income and the temporary differences originating and reversing in 1998 and 1999 are as follows:

Ghiza International

			1998		*1999*
Pretax accounting income			$800,000		$1,200,000
Timing differences:					
Depreciation:	originating	$(180,000)		$(160,000)	
	reversing	60,000	(120,000)	100,000	(60,000)
Prepaid rental income:	originating	75,000		80,000	
	reversing	(25,000)	50,000	(40,000)	40,000
Taxable income			$730,000		$1,180,000

The tax rates for years 1998 and 1999 are 46% and 38%, respectively. These rates are assumed to be independent of one another, and the 1999 change in the rate was not known until it took place in 1999.

Computation of tax provision--1998:		
Balance of deferred tax account, 1/1/98		
Depreciation ($475,000 x 48%)		$228,000
Prepaid rental income ($100,000 x 48%)		(48,000)
		$180,000
Aggregate temporary differences, 12/31/98		
Depreciation ($475,000 + $120,000)	$ 595,000	
Prepaid rental income ($100,000 + $50,000)	(150,000)	
	$ 445,000	
Expected future rate (1998 rate)	x 46%	
Balance required in the deferred tax account, 12/31/98		204,700
Required addition to the deferred tax account		$ 24,700
Income taxes currently payable ($730,000 x 46%)		335,800
Total tax provision		$360,500

Computation of tax provision--1999		
Balance of deferred tax account, 1/1/99		
Depreciation ($595,000 x 46%)		$273,700
Prepaid rental income ($150,000 x 46%)		(69,000)
		$204,700
Aggregate timing differences, 12/31/99		
Depreciation ($595,000 + $60,000)	$ 655,000	
Prepaid rental income ($150,000 + $40,000)	(190,000)	
	$ 465,000	
Expected future rate (1999 rate)	x 38%	

Balance required in the deferred tax account, 12/31/99	176,700
Required reduction in the deferred tax account	$ (28,000)
Income taxes currently payable ($1,180,000 x 38%)	448,400
Total tax provision	$420,400

Liability Method Explained in Detail

While conceptually the liability method is rather straightforward, in practice there are a number of complexities to be addressed. In the following pages, these measurement and reporting issues are discussed in greater detail.

1. Nature of temporary differences
2. Treatment of operating loss carryforwards
3. Measurement of deferred tax assets and liabilities
4. Valuation allowance for deferred tax assets that are not assured of realization
5. Effect of tax law changes on previously recorded deferred tax assets and liabilities
6. Effect of tax status changes on previously incurred deferred tax assets and liabilities
7. Tax effects of business combinations
8. Intercorporate income tax allocation
9. Exceptions to the general rules of revised IAS 12

Detailed examples of deferred income tax accounting under revised IAS 12 are presented throughout the following discussion of these issues.

Nature of Temporary Differences

The majority of the typical reporting entity's transactions are treated identically for tax and financial reporting purposes. Some transactions and events, however, will have different tax and accounting implications. In many of these cases, the difference relates to the period in which the income or expense will be recognized. Under IAS 12, the latter differences were referred to as "timing differences" and were said to **originate** in one period and to **reverse** in a later period. Common timing differences include those relating to depreciation methods, deferred compensation plans, percentage-of-completion accounting for long-term construction contracts, and cash vs. accrual accounting.

Revised IAS 12 introduces the concept of temporary differences, which is rather more comprehensive than that of timing differences. Temporary differences include all the categories of the earlier concept, plus a number of additional items as well. Temporary differences include all differences between the tax and financial reporting bases of assets and liabilities if those differences will result in taxable or deductible amounts in future years.

Examples of temporary differences that were also deemed to be timing differences under the original IAS 12 are the following:

1. **Revenue recognized for financial reporting purposes before being recognized for tax purposes**. Examples include revenue accounted for by the installment method for tax purposes, but reflected in income currently; certain construction-related revenue recognized on a completed-contract method for tax purposes, but on a percentage-of-completion basis for financial reporting; earnings from investees recognized by the equity method for accounting purposes but taxed only when later distributed as dividends to the investor. These are taxable temporary differences, which give rise to deferred tax liabilities.
2. **Revenue recognized for tax purposes prior to recognition in the financial statements**. These include certain types of revenue received in advance, such as prepaid rental income and service contract revenue. Referred to as deductible temporary differences, these items give rise to deferred tax assets.
3. **Expenses that are deductible for tax purposes prior to recognition in the financial statements**. This results when accelerated depreciation methods or shorter useful lives are used for tax purposes, while straight-line depreciation or longer useful economic lives are used for financial reporting; and when there are certain preoperating costs and certain capitalized interest costs that are deductible currently for tax purposes. These items are taxable temporary differences and give rise to deferred tax liabilities.
4. **Expenses that are reported in the financial statements prior to becoming deductible for tax purposes**. Certain estimated expenses, such as warranty costs, as well as such contingent losses as accruals of litigation expenses, are not tax deductible until the obligation becomes fixed. These are deductible temporary differences, and accordingly give rise to deferred tax assets.

In addition to these familiar and well understood timing differences, temporary differences include a number of other categories that also involve differences between the tax and financial reporting bases of assets or liabilities. These are

1. **Reductions in tax deductible asset bases arising in connection with tax credits**. Under tax provisions in certain jurisdictions, credits are available for certain qualifying investments in plant assets. In some cases, taxpayers are permitted a choice of either full accelerated depreciation coupled with a reduced investment tax credit, or a full investment tax credit coupled with reduced depreciation allowances. If the taxpayer chose the latter option, the asset basis is reduced for tax depreciation, but would still be fully depre-

ciable for financial reporting purposes. Accordingly, this election would be accounted for as a taxable timing difference, and give rise to a deferred tax liability.

2. **Increases in the tax bases of assets resulting from the indexing of asset costs for the effects of inflation**. Occasionally, proposed and sometimes enacted by taxing jurisdictions, such a tax law provision allows taxpaying entities to finance the replacement of depreciable assets through depreciation based on current costs, as computed by the application of indices to the historical costs of the assets being remeasured. This reevaluation of asset costs gives rise to deductible temporary differences that would be associated with deferred tax benefits.
3. **Certain business combinations accounted for by the acquisition method**. Under certain circumstances, the costs assignable to assets or liabilities acquired in purchase business combinations will differ from their tax bases. The usual scenario under which this arises is when the acquirer must continue to report the predecessor's tax bases for tax purposes, although the price paid was more or less than book value. Such differences may be either taxable or deductible and, accordingly, may give rise to deferred tax liabilities or assets. These differences were in fact treated as timing differences under the original IAS 12, and will now be recognized as temporary differences by revised IAS 12.
4. **Assets which are revalued for financial reporting purposes although the tax bases are not affected**. This is analogous to the matter discussed in the preceding paragraph. Under certain international accounting standards (such as IAS 16, *Property, Plant, and Equipment*, and IAS 15, *Accounting for Investments*), assets are written up to fair value although for tax purposes these adjustments are ignored until and unless the assets are disposed of. The discrepancies between the adjusted book carrying values and the tax bases are temporary differences under revised IAS 12, and deferred taxes are to be provided on these variations. This is required even if there is no intention to dispose of the assets in question, or if, under tax laws, exchanges for other, similar assets (or reinvestment of proceeds of sales in similar assets) would effect a postponement of the tax obligation.

Items that would not have been deemed timing differences under IAS 12 but are temporary differences under revised IAS 12 include the following:

1. **Assets and liabilities acquired in transactions that are not business combinations which are not deductible or taxable in determining taxable profit.** In some tax jurisdictions, certain assets are never deductible in computing taxable profit. Depending on jurisdiction, buildings, intangibles, and other assets may be nondeductible. Thus, the asset in question has a differing accounting basis than tax basis, which defines a temporary differ-

ence. Similarly, certain liabilities may not be recognized for tax purposes. While revised IAS 12 agrees that these represent temporary differences (since the tax basis of zero differs from the book basis in each instance) and that, under the principles of tax accounting using the liability method, this should result in the recognition of deferred tax liabilities or assets, the decision was made to not permit this. The reason given is that the new result would be to "gross up" the recorded amount of the asset or liability to offset the recorded deferred tax liability or benefit, and this would make the financial statements "less transparent." It could also be argued that, when as asset has as one of its attributes nondeductibility for tax purposes, the price paid for this asset has been affected accordingly, so that any such "gross up" would cause the asset to be reported at an amount in excess of fair value.

2. **Assets and liabilities acquired in business combinations**. When assets and liabilities are valued at fair value, as required under IAS 22, but the tax basis is not adjusted (i.e., there is a carryforward basis for tax purposes), there will be differences between the tax and financial reporting bases of these assets and liabilities which constitute temporary differences. Deferred tax benefits and obligations need to be recognized for these differences.
3. **Goodwill that cannot be amortized (deducted) for tax purposes**. In some jurisdictions, goodwill cannot be deducted for tax purposes. Conceptually, when goodwill is carried on the balance sheet but cannot be amortized for tax purposes, the tax basis of this asset is zero, which thus differs from the financial reporting basis and which would therefore require that deferred taxes be assessed thereon. However, since goodwill or negative goodwill is a residual amount, any attempt to compute the deferred tax effect of the difference between tax and book bases would result in grossing up that very account (goodwill or negative goodwill, as the case may be). Although such a presentation could be rationalized, it would be of dubious usefulness to the readers of the financial statements. For this reason, revised IAS 12 has ruled that no deferred taxes be provided on the difference between the tax and book bases of nondeductible goodwill or nontaxable negative goodwill.

Measurement of Deferred Tax Assets and Liabilities

The procedure to compute the gross deferred tax provision (i.e., before addressing whether the deferred tax asset is probable of being realized and therefore should be recognized) is as follows:

1. Identify all temporary differences existing as of the reporting date.
2. Segregate the temporary differences into those that are taxable and those that are deductible. This step is necessary because under revised IAS 12

only those deferred tax benefits which are probable of being realized are recognized, whereas all deferred obligations are given full recognition.

3. Accumulate information about the deductible temporary differences, particularly the net operating loss and credit carryforwards that have expiration dates or other types of limitations.
4. Measure the tax effect of aggregate taxable temporary differences by applying the appropriate expected tax rates (federal plus any state, local, and foreign rates that are applicable under the circumstances).
5. Similarly, measure the tax effects of deductible temporary differences, including net operating loss carryforwards.

It should be emphasized that separate computations should be made for each tax jurisdiction, since in assessing the propriety of recording the tax effects of deductible temporary differences it is necessary to consider the entity's ability to absorb deferred tax benefits against tax liabilities. Inasmuch as benefits in one tax jurisdiction will not reduce taxes payable in another jurisdiction, separate calculations will be needed. Also, for purposes of balance sheet presentation (discussed below in detail), offsetting of deferred tax assets and liabilities is permissible only within jurisdictions, since there would never be a legal right to offset obligations due to, and from, different taxing authorities. Similarly, separate computations should be made for each taxpaying component of the business: If a parent company and its subsidiaries are consolidated for financial reporting purposes but file separate tax returns, the reporting entity comprises a number of components, and the tax benefits of any one will be unavailable to reduce the tax obligations of the others.

The principles set forth above are illustrated by the following examples.

Basic example of the computation of deferred tax liability and asset

Assume that Noori Company has pretax financial income of $250,000 in 1998, a total of $28,000 of taxable temporary differences, and a total of $8,000 of deductible temporary differences. There are no operating loss or tax credit carryforwards. The tax rate is a flat (i.e., not graduated) 40%. Also assume that there were no deferred tax liabilities or assets in prior years.

Taxable income is computed as follows:

Pretax financial income	$250,000
Taxable temporary differences	(28,000)
Deductible temporary differences	8,000
Taxable income	$230,000

The journal entry to record required amounts is

Current income tax expense	92,000	
Deferred tax asset	3,200	
Income tax expense--deferred	8,000	
Deferred tax liability		11,200
Income taxes currently payable		92,000

Current income tax expense and income taxes currently payable are each computed as taxable income times the current rate ($230,000 x 40%). The deferred tax asset of $3,200 represents 40% of deductible temporary differences of $8,000. The deferred tax liability of $11,200 is calculated as 40% of taxable temporary differences of $28,000. The deferred tax expense of $8,000 is the **net** of the deferred tax liability of $11,200 and the deferred tax asset of $3,200.

In 1999, Noori Company has pretax financial income of $450,000, aggregate taxable and deductible temporary differences are $75,000 and $36,000, respectively, and the tax rate remains a flat 40%. Taxable income is $411,000, computed as pretax financial income of $450,000 minus taxable differences of $75,000 plus deductible differences of $36,000. Current income tax expense and income taxes currently payable each are $164,400 ($411,000 x 40%).

Deferred amounts are calculated as follows:

	Deferred tax liability	*Deferred tax asset*	*Income tax expense--deferred*
Required balance at 12/31/99			
$75,000 x 40%	$30,000		--
$36,000 x 40%		$14,400	--
Balances at 12/31/98	11,200	3,200	--
Adjustment required	$18,800	$11,200	$7,600

The journal entry to record the deferred amounts is

Deferred tax asset	11,200	
Income tax expense--deferred	7,600	
Deferred tax liability		18,800

Because the **increase** in the liability in 1999 is larger (by $7,600) than the increase in the asset for that year, the result is a deferred tax **expense** for 1999.

Considerations for Recognition of Deferred Tax Assets

Although the case for presentation in the financial statements of any amount computed for deferred tax liabilities is clear, it can be argued that deferred tax assets should be included in the balance sheet only if they are, in fact, very likely to be realized in future periods. Since realization will almost certainly be dependent on the future profitability of the reporting entity, it may become necessary to ascertain the likelihood that the enterprise will be profitable. Absent convincing evidence of that, the concepts of conservatism and realization would suggest that the asset be treated as a contingent gain, and not accorded recognition until and unless ultimately realized.

In revised IAS 12, the IASC has adopted a posture which holds that deferred tax assets resulting from temporary differences and from tax loss carryforwards are to be given recognition only if realization is deemed to be **probable**. To operationalize this concept, the standard sets forth several criteria, which variously apply to deferred tax assets arising from temporary differences and from tax loss carryforwards. The standard establishes that

1. It is probable that future taxable profit will be available against which a deferred tax asset arising from a deductible temporary difference can be utilized when there are sufficient taxable temporary differences relating to the same taxation authority which will reverse either (a) in the same period as the reversal of the deductible temporary difference, or (b) in periods into which the deferred tax asset can be carried back or forward; or
2. If there are insufficient taxable temporary differences relating to the same taxation authority, it is probable that the enterprise will have taxable profits in the same period as the reversal of the deductible temporary difference or in periods to which the deferred tax can be carried back or forward, or there are tax planning opportunities available to the enterprise that will create taxable profit in appropriate periods.

Thus, there will be a modest element of judgment required in making an assessment about how probable the realization of the deferred tax asset is, in circumstances in which there is not a balance of deferred tax liability equal to or greater than the amount of the deferred tax asset. If it cannot be concluded that realization is probable, the deferred tax asset is not given recognition. The revised IAS 12 methodology is somewhat different than that which is applied under current US GAAP, which is prescribed by SFAS 109. In conformity with that standard, all deferred tax assets are first recorded, after which a valuation allowance or reserve is established to offset that portion which is not deemed to be "more likely than not" realizable. The net effect is similar under either approach, however, although the consensus opinion is that the US GAAP realization threshold, "more likely than not," represents a somewhat lower boundary than does IAS 12's "probable." While the former implies a probability of just slightly over 50%, the latter is thought to connote a likelihood in the range of 75-80% or even higher. Worded yet another way, it would be more challenging to support the existence of a valid deferred tax asset under the IAS standard than under US GAAP rules as they now exist.

Future temporary differences as a source for taxable profit to offset deductible differences. In some instances, an entity may have deferred tax assets that will be realizable when future tax deductions are taken, but it cannot be concluded that there will be sufficient taxable profits to absorb these future deductions. However, the enterprise can reasonably predict that, if it continues as a going concern, it will generate other temporary differences such that taxable profits will be created. It has often been argued that the going concern assumption underlying much of accounting theory is sufficient rationale for the recognition of deferred tax assets in such circumstances.

However, revised IAS 12 makes it clear that this is not valid reasoning. The reason is that the taxable temporary differences anticipated for future periods will themselves reverse in even later periods; these cannot do "double duty" by also being projected to be available to absorb currently existing deductible temporary differences. Thus, in evaluating whether realization of currently outstanding deferred tax benefits is probable, it is appropriate to consider the currently outstanding taxable temporary differences, but not taxable temporary differences which are projected to be created in later periods.

Tax planning opportunities that will help realize deferred tax assets. When an entity has deductible temporary differences and taxable temporary differences pertaining to the same tax jurisdiction, there is a presumption that realization of the relevant deferred tax assets is probable, since the relevant deferred tax liabilities should be available to offset these. However, before concluding on this it is necessary to consider further the **timing** of the two sets of reversals. If the deductible temporary differences will reverse, say, in the very near term, and the taxable differences will not reverse for many years, it is a concern that the tax benefits created by the former occurrence may expire unused prior to the latter event. Thus, when the availability of deferred tax obligations is the basis for recognition of deferred tax assets, it is also necessary to consider whether, under pertinent tax regulations, the benefit carryforward period is sufficient to assure that it will not be lost to the reporting enterprise.

For example, if the deductible temporary difference is projected to reverse in 2 years but the taxable temporary difference is not anticipated to occur for another 10 years, and the tax jurisdiction in question offers only a 5-year tax loss carryforward, then (absent other facts suggesting that the tax benefit is probable of realization) the deferred tax benefit could not be given recognition.

However, the entity might have certain tax planning opportunities available to it, such that the pattern of taxable profits could be altered to make the deferred tax benefit, which might otherwise be lost, probable of realization. For example, again depending on the rules of the salient tax jurisdiction, an election might be made to tax interest income on an accrual rather than a cash received basis, which might accelerate income recognition such that it would be available to offset or absorb the deductible temporary differences. Also, claimed tax deductions might be deferred to later periods, similarly boosting taxable profits in the short term.

More subtly, a reporting entity may have certain assets, such as buildings, which have appreciated in value. It is entirely feasible, in many situations, for an enterprise to take certain steps, such as selling the building to realize the taxable gain thereon and then either leasing back the premises or acquiring another suitable building, to salvage the tax deduction that would otherwise be lost to it due to the expiration of a loss carryforward period. If such a strategy is deemed to be reasonably available, even if the entity does not expect to have to implement it (for example, because it expects other taxable temporary differences to be originated in the interim), it may be used to justify recognition of the deferred tax benefits.

Consider the following example of how an available tax planning strategy might be used to support recognition of a deferred tax asset that otherwise might have to go unrecognized.

Example of the impact of a qualifying tax strategy

Assume that Kirloski Company has a $180,000 operating loss carryforward as of 12/31/97, scheduled to expire at the end of next year. Taxable temporary differences of $240,000 exist that are expected to reverse in approximately equal amounts of $80,000 in 1998, 1999, and 2000. Kirloski Company estimates that taxable income for 1998 (exclusive of the reversal of existing temporary differences and the operating loss carryforward) will be $20,000. Kirloski Company expects to implement a qualifying tax planning strategy that will accelerate the total of $240,000 of taxable temporary differences to 1998. Expenses to implement the strategy are estimated to approximate $30,000. The applicable expected tax rate is 40%.

In the absence of the tax planning strategy, $100,000 of the operating loss carryforward could be realized in 1998 based on estimated taxable income of $20,000 plus $80,000 of the reversal of taxable temporary differences. Thus, $80,000 would expire unused at the end of 1998 and the net amount of the deferred tax asset at 12/31/97 would be recognized at $40,000, computed as $72,000 ($180,000 x 40%) minus the valuation allowance of $32,000 ($80,000 x 40%).

However, by implementing the tax planning strategy, the deferred tax asset is calculated as follows:

Taxable income for 1998:	
Expected amount without reversal of taxable temporary differences	$ 20,000
Reversal of taxable temporary differences due to tax planning strategy, net of costs	210,000
	230,000
Operating loss to be carried forward	(180,000)
Operating loss expiring unused at 12/31/98	$ -0-

The deferred tax asset to be recorded at 12/31/97 is $54,000. This is computed as follows:

Full benefit of tax loss carryforward		
	$180,000 x 40% =	$72,000
Less:	Net-of-tax effect of anticipated expenses related to implementation of the strategy $30,000 – ($30,000 x 40%) =	18,000
Net		$54,000

Kirloski Company will also recognize a deferred tax liability of $96,000 at the end of 1997 (40% of the taxable temporary differences of $240,000).

Revised expectations that a deferred tax benefit is realizable. It may happen that in a reporting period a deferred asset is deemed not probable of being realized and accordingly is not recognized, but in a later reporting period the judgment is made that the amount in fact is realizable. If this change in expectation occurs, the deferred tax asset previously not recognized will now be recorded. This does not constitute a prior-period adjustment, but instead is included in earnings, consistent with other changes in accounting estimates, in the current period. Thus, the tax provision in the period when the estimate is revised will be affected.

Similarly, if a deferred tax benefit provision is made in a given reporting period, but later events suggest that the amount is, in whole or in part, not probable of being realized, the provision should be partially or completely reversed. Again, this adjustment will be included in the tax provision in the period in which the estimate is altered. Under either scenario the footnotes to the financial statements will need to offer sufficient information to the users to permit meaningful interpretations to be made, since the amount of tax expense will bear an unusual relationship to the accounting profit for the period.

If the deferred tax provision in a given period is misstated due to a clerical error such a miscalculation of the effective expected tax rate, this would constitute a fundamental error, and the effect of the correction may be reflected in opening retained earnings. This should be distinguished from a change in an accounting estimate. Fundamental errors are discussed in Chapter 19.

Determining the extent to which the deferred tax asset is realizable. Assume that Zacharias Corporation has a deductible temporary difference of \$60,000 at December 31, 1997. The applicable tax rate is a flat 40%. Based on available evidence, management of Zacharias Corporation concludes that it is probable that all sources will not result in future taxable income sufficient to realize more than \$15,000 (i.e., 25%) of the deductible temporary difference. Also, assume that there were no deferred tax assets in previous years and that prior years' taxable income was inconsequential.

At 12/31/97 Zacharias Corporation records a deferred tax asset in the amount of \$6,000 (\$60,000 x 25% x 40%). The journal entry at 12/31/97 is:

Deferred tax asset	6,000	
Income tax benefit--deferred		6,000

The deferred income tax benefit of \$6,000 represents the tax effect of that portion of the deferred tax asset (25%) that is probable of being realized. In 1998 assume that Zacharias Corporation's results are

Pretax financial loss	\$(32,000)
Reversing deductible differences from 1997	(10,000)
Loss carryforward for tax purposes	\$(42,000)

The total of the loss carryforward (\$42,000, as computed above) plus the amount of deductible temporary differences from 1997 not reversing in 1998 (\$50,000) equals \$92,000. Before considering how much of the benefit is probable of being realized, a deferred tax asset of $36,800 ($92,000 x 40%) is computed at the end of 1998. However, the management of Zacharias Corporation has to consider what portion of this deferred tax asset is probable of being realized. It concludes that it is probable that $25,000 of the tax loss carryforward will **not** be realized. Thus, the net tax loss carryforward that is **probable** of being realized is $92,000 – $25,000 = $67,000, which yields a tax benefit of $26,800 ($67,000 x 40%).

Since the balance in the deferred tax asset account had been $6,000, the adjustment needed is now as follows. The journal entry at 12/31/98 is

Deferred tax asset	20,800	
Income tax benefit--deferred		20,800

While the common sense meaning of the **probable** criterion is clear enough, there can be a practical difficulty of assessing whether or not this threshold test is net in a given standard. Revised IAS 12 states that deferred tax assets can be recognized when there are sufficient taxable temporary differences relating to the same taxation authority and the same taxable entity which are expected to reverse in the same period as the expected reversal of the deductible temporary difference or in periods into which a tax loss arising from the deferred tax asset can be carried back or forward. The standard also suggests that, if there is an insufficiency of taxable temporary differences to absorb the deductible temporary differences, but it is deemed probable that sufficient taxable income will otherwise be earned, or that tax planning strategies are available to the entity, this can be used as a basis for concluding that it is probable that the benefits will be received.

As a practical matter, there are a number of positive and negative factors which may be evaluated in reaching a conclusion as to amount of the deferred tax asset to be recognized. Positive factors (those suggesting that the full amount of the deferred tax asset associated with the gross temporary difference should be recorded) might include

1. Evidence of sufficient future taxable income, exclusive of reversing temporary differences and carryforwards, to realize the benefit of the deferred tax asset
2. Evidence of sufficient future taxable income arising from the reversals of existing taxable temporary differences (deferred tax liabilities) to realize the benefit of the tax asset
3. Evidence of sufficient taxable income in prior year(s) available for realization of an operating loss carryback under existing statutory limitations
4. Evidence of the existence of prudent, feasible tax planning strategies under management control which, if implemented, would permit the realization of the tax asset. These are discussed in greater detail below.
5. An excess of appreciated asset values over their tax bases, in an amount sufficient to realize the deferred tax asset. This can be thought of as a sub-

set of the tax strategies idea, since a sale or sale/leaseback of appreciated property is one rather obvious tax planning strategy to salvage a deferred tax benefit which might otherwise expire unused.

6. A strong earnings history exclusive of the loss that created the deferred tax asset. This would, under many circumstances, suggest that future profitability is likely and therefore that realization of deferred tax assets are probable.

Although the foregoing may suggest that the reporting entity will be able to realize the benefits of the deductible temporary differences outstanding as of the balance sheet date, certain negative factors should also be considered in determining whether realization of the full amount of the deferred tax benefit is probable under the circumstances. These factors could include

1. A cumulative recent history of accounting losses. Depending on extent and length of time over which losses were experienced, this could reduce the assessment of likelihood of realization below the important "probable" threshold.
2. A history of operating losses or of tax operating loss or credit carryforwards that have expired unused
3. Losses that are anticipated in the near future years, despite a history of profitable operations

Thus, the process of determining how much of the computed gross deferred tax benefit should be recognized involves the weighing of both positive and negative factors to determine whether, based on the preponderance of available evidence, it is probable that the deferred tax asset will be realized. Revised IAS 12 notes that a history of unused tax losses should be considered "strong evidence" that future taxable profits might prove elusive. In such cases, it would be expected that primary reliance would be placed on the existence of taxable temporary differences which, upon reversal, would provide taxable income to absorb the deferred tax benefits that are candidates for recognition in the financial statements. Absent those taxable temporary differences, recognition would be much more difficult.

To illustrate this computation in a more specific fact situation, assume the following facts:

1. Malpasa Corporation reports on a calendar year and adopted revised IAS 12 in 1998.
2. As of the December 31, 1998 balance sheet, Malpasa has taxable temporary differences of $85,000 relating to depreciation, deductible temporary differences of $12,000 relating to deferred compensation arrangements, a net operating loss carryforward (which arose in 1996) of $40,000, and a capital loss carryover of $10,000.
3. Malpasa's expected tax rate for future years is 40% for ordinary income, and 25% for net long-term capital gains. Capital losses cannot be offset against ordinary income.

The first steps are to compute the required balances of the deferred tax asset and liability accounts, without consideration of whether the tax asset would be probable of realization. The computations would proceed as follows:

Deferred tax liability:	
Taxable temporary difference (depreciation)	$85,000
Effective tax rate	x 40%
Required balance	$34,000
Deferred tax asset:	
Deductible temporary differences:	
Deferred compensation	$12,000
Net operating loss	40,000
	$52,000
Effective tax rate	x 40%
Required balance (a)	$20,800
Capital loss	$10,000
Effective tax rate	x 25%
Required balance (b)	$ 2,500
Total deferred tax asset:	
Ordinary (a)	$20,800
Capital (b)	2,500
Total required balance	$23,300

The next step would be to consider whether realization of the deferred tax asset is probable. Malpasa management must evaluate both positive and negative evidence to determine this matter. Assume now that management identifies the following factors which may be relevant:

1. Before the net operating loss deduction, Malpasa reported taxable income of $5,000 in 1998. Management believes that taxable income in future years, apart from NOL deductions, should continue at about the same level experienced in 1998.
2. The taxable temporary differences are not expected to reverse in the foreseeable future.
3. The capital loss arose in connection with a transaction of a type that is unlikely to recur. The company does not generally engage in activities that have the potential to result in capital gains or losses.
4. Management estimates that certain productive assets have a fair value exceeding their respective tax bases by about $30,000. The entire gain, if realized for tax purposes, would be a recapture of depreciation previously taken. Since the current plans call for a substantial upgrading of the company's plant assets, management feels that it could easily accelerate those actions to realize taxable gains, should it be desirable to do so for tax planning purposes.

Based on the foregoing information, Malpasa Corporation management concludes that a $2,500 adjustment to deferred tax assets is required. The reasoning is as follows:

1. There will be some taxable operating income generated in future years ($5,000 annually, based on the earnings experienced in 1998), which will absorb a modest portion of the reversal of the deductible temporary difference ($12,000) and net operating loss carryforward ($40,000) existing at year end 1998.
2. More important, the feasible tax planning strategy of accelerating the taxable gain relating to appreciated assets ($30,000) would certainly be sufficient, in conjunction with operating income over several years, to permit Malpasa to realize the tax benefits of the deductible temporary difference and NOL carryover.
3. However, since capital loss carryovers are only usable to offset future capital gains and Malpasa management is unable to project future realization of capital gains, the associated tax benefit accrued ($2,500) will **probably** not be realized, and thus cannot be recognized.

Based on this analysis, deferred tax benefits in the amount of $20,800 should be recognized.

Effect of Tax Law Changes on Previously Recorded Deferred Tax Assets and Liabilities

The balance sheet oriented measurement approach of revised IAS 12 necessitates the reevaluation of the deferred tax asset and liability balances at each year end. Although revised IAS 12 does not directly address the question of changes to tax rates or other provisions of the tax law (e.g., deductibility of items) which may be enacted that will affect the realization of future deferred tax assets or liabilities, the effect of these changes should be reflected in the year end deferred tax accounts in the period the changes are enacted. The offsetting adjustments should be made through the current period tax provision.

When revised tax rates are enacted, they may affect not only the unreversed effects of items which were originally reported in the continuing operations section of the income statement, but also the unreversed effects of items first presented as extraordinary items or in other income statement captions. Although it might be conceptually superior to report the effects of tax law changes on such unreversed temporary differences in these same income statement captions, as a practical matter the complexities of identifying the diverse treatments of these originating transactions or events would make such an approach unworkable. Accordingly, remeasurements of the effects of tax law changes should generally be reported in the tax provision associated with continuing operations.

Example of the computation of a deferred tax asset with a change in rates

Assume that the Fanuzzi Company has $80,000 of deductible temporary differences at the end of 1997, which are expected to result in tax deductions of approximately $40,000 each on tax returns for 1998-1999. Enacted tax rates are 50% for the years 1993-1997, and 40% for 1998 and thereafter.

The deferred tax asset is computed at 12/31/97 under each of the following independent assumptions:

1. If Fanuzzi Company expects to offset the deductible temporary differences against taxable income in the years 1998-1999, the deferred tax asset is $32,000 ($80,000 x 40%).
2. If Fanuzzi Company expects to realize a tax benefit for the deductible temporary differences by loss carryback refund, the deferred tax asset is $40,000 ($80,000 x 50%).

Assume that Fanuzzi Company expects to realize a tax asset of $32,000 at the end of 1997. Also assume that taxes payable in each of the years 1994-1996 were $8,000 (or 50% of taxable income). Realization of $24,000 of the $32,000 deferred tax asset is assured through carryback refunds even if no taxable income is earned in the years 1998-1999. Whether some or all of the remaining $8,000 will be recognized depends on Fanuzzi Company's assessment of the levels of future taxable earnings (i.e., whether the probable threshold is exceeded).

The foregoing estimate of the **certain** tax benefit, based on a loss carryback to periods of higher tax rates than are statutorily in effect for future periods, should be utilized only when future losses (for tax purposes) are expected. This restriction applies since the benefit thus recognized exceeds benefits that would be available in future periods, when tax rates will be lower.

Reporting the Effect of Tax Status Changes

Changes in the tax status of the reporting entity should be reported in a manner that is entirely analogous to the reporting of enacted tax changes. When the tax status change becomes effective, the consequent adjustments to deferred tax assets and liabilities are reported in current tax expense, as part of the tax provision relating to continuing operations.

The most commonly encountered changes in status are those attendant to an election, where permitted, to be taxed as a partnership or other "flow through" enterprise. (This means that the corporation will not be treated as a taxable entity but rather as an enterprise that "flows through" its taxable income to the owners on a current basis. This favorable tax treatment is available to encourage small businesses, and often will be limited to entities having sales revenue under a particular threshold level, or to entities having no more than a maximum number of shareholders.) Enterprises subject to such optional tax treatment may also request that a previous election be terminated. When a previously taxable corporation becomes a nontaxed corporation, the stockholders become personally liable for taxes on the company's earnings, whether the earnings are distributed to them or not (similar to the relationship among a partnership and its partners).

Although revised IAS 12 does not address the accounting for a change in tax status, given the balance sheet oriented determination of deferred tax assets and liabilities under this standard, a logical approach would be to eliminate deferred taxes by reversal through current period tax expense when a formerly taxable entity becomes nontaxable. For example, if an entity having a net deferred tax liability elects nontaxed corporation status, it will report a tax benefit in its tax current provision.

Similarly, if a previously nontaxed corporation becomes a taxable entity, the effect is to assume a net tax benefit or obligation for unreversed temporary differences existing at the date the change becomes effective. Accordingly, the financial statements for the period of such a change will report the effects of the event in the current tax provision. If the entity had at that date many taxable temporary differences as yet unreversed, it would report a large tax expense in that period. Conversely, if it had a large quantity of unreversed deductible temporary differences, a substantial deferred tax benefit (if probable of realization) would need to be recorded, with a concomitant credit to the current period's tax provision in the income statement. Whether eliminating an existing deferred tax balance or recording an initial deferred tax asset or liability, the income tax footnote to the financial statements will need to fully explain the nature of the events that transpired.

In some jurisdictions, nontaxed corporation elections are automatically effective when filed. In such a case, if a reporting entity makes an election before the end of the current fiscal year, it is logical that the effects be reported in current year income to become effective at the start of the following period. For example, an election filed in December 1997 would be reported in the 1997 financial statements to become effective at the beginning of the company's next fiscal year, January 1, 1998. No deferred tax assets or liabilities would appear on the December 31, 1997 balance sheet, and the tax provision for the year then ended would include the effects of any reversals that had previously been recorded. Practice varies, however, and in some instances the effect of the elimination of the deferred tax assets and liabilities would be reported in the year the election actually becomes effective.

Reporting the Effect of Accounting Changes Made for Tax Purposes

Occasionally, an entity will initiate or be required to adopt changes in accounting that affect income tax reporting but will not affect financial statement reporting. For example, in certain jurisdictions at varying times, the following changes have been mandated: use of the direct write-off method of bad debt recognition instead of providing an allowance for bad debts, while continuing to use the reserve method as required by GAAP for financial reporting; the "full costing" method of computing inventory valuations for tax purposes (adding some items that are administrative costs to overhead), while continuing to expense currently those costs not inventoriable under GAAP; and use of accelerated capital recovery (depreciation) methods for tax reporting while continuing to use normal methods for financial reporting. Often, these changes really involve two distinct temporary differences. The first of these is the one-time, catch-up adjustment which either immediately or over a prescribed time period affects the tax basis of the asset or liability in question (net receivables or inventory, in the examples above), and which then reverses as these assets or liabilities are later realized or settled and are eliminated from the balance sheet. The second change is the ongoing differential in the amount of newly acquired assets or incurred liabilities being recognized for tax and accounting purposes; these differences also eventually reverse. This second type of change is the normal temporary difference which has already been discussed. It is the first change that differs from those previously discussed earlier in the chapter.

As an example, consider that Leipzig Corporation has, at December 31, 1997, gross receivables of $12,000,000 and an allowance for bad debts in the amount of $600,000. Also assume that expected future taxes will be at a 40% rate. Effective January 1, 1998, the tax law is revised to eliminate deductions for accrued bad debts, with existing allowances required to be taken into income ratably over 3 years (a "3-year spread"). A balance sheet of Leipzig Corporation prepared on January 1, 1998, would report a deferred tax benefit in the amount of $240,000 (i.e., $600,000 x 40%, which is the tax effect of future deductions to be taken when specific receivables are written off and bad debts are incurred for tax purposes); a current tax liability of $80,000 (one-third of the tax obligation); and a noncurrent tax liability of $160,000 (two-thirds of the tax obligation). Under the requirements of revised IAS 12, the deferred tax benefit must be entirely reported as noncurrent in classified balance sheets, inasmuch as no deferred tax benefits or obligations can be shown as current.

Implications of Changes in Tax Rates and Status Made in Interim Periods

Tax rate changes may occur during an interim reporting period. International accounting standards have not heretofore addressed reporting issues which arise in financial statements which are intended to cover interim periods. However, this topic is one of the items included in the "core set of standards" project due for completion by mid-1998, and in late 1996 the IASC did issue a Draft Statement of Principles (DSOP) on interim financial reporting, the first step toward promulgating a standard on this topic. While this is discussed in greater detail in Chapter 18, a brief summary is offered here as this will significantly impact on income tax accounting.

The key conceptual issue for interim reporting is whether the interim period (which could be a month, quarter, etc.) should be treated as a stand-alone period subject to the same rules, such as those regarding accounting accruals and deferrals, as would a full-year reporting period, or whether the shorter period should be subject to special rules in recognition of the fact that the interim periods are subsets of the full year. The former position, known as the "discrete view," has now essentially been embraced by the IASC. In doing so, the committee has rejected the long-held preference of the US standard setters, among others, for the so-called "integral view."

The integral view, first espoused by a US standard-setting body in 1973, holds that the interim period must be viewed as only a component part of the full year to which it belongs. Under this view, one of the major goals of interim period reporting is to provide information from which an informed estimate of full-year results can be constructed. This leads naturally to the position that certain departures from "full year accounting principles" should be entertained, as these will serve to make the reported interim results more effective in achieving that objective.

The difference between financial statements prepared in accordance with the discrete and integral views depends on the nature of revenue and expense items incurred by the reporting enterprise. In many cases, there will be no differences at all, or they will be immaterial in significance; under other circumstances, however, the discrepancies could be very substantial.

A particular concern is with income taxes. In many jurisdictions enterprises are subject to graduated income tax rates (e.g., 15% on the first $50,000 of taxable income, then 25% on the next $100,000, etc.). Corporation taxation laws are based on annual, not interim, reporting, and thus it is the enterprise's full-year earnings which will determine what tax bracket it ultimately finds itself in. If each interim period is strictly treated as a discrete period, the early months or quarters could report earnings as if the entity were subject to, say, only a 15% tax rate, and later periods could create the impression that the tax rate was much higher, when obviously the tax laws do not dictate that late-in-the-year earnings are taxed differently than early-in-the-year profits. Under the integral approach, it is required that a "blended" or expected rate for the full year be computed, and that taxes on each interim period's earnings be calculated at that rate, subject to revision as the year progresses and actual results vary from forecasted amounts. By contrast, a purely discrete approach would apply different rates to different interim periods, as the entity's income carries into successively higher brackets over the course of the year.

The use of the discrete approach raises the risk that interim period financial reports, particularly statements of operations, could be distorted; the shorter the interim period, the greater the probability that this could occur, since there would be less opportunity for other randomly occurring events to "smooth out" periodic results. The IASC has seemingly recognized this problem while nevertheless not endorsing the integral approach. Thus, DSOP recognizes that income taxes are inherently an annual expense, and accordingly mandates the use of a projected effective annual (i.e., blended) rate in all interim periods, clearly departing from the discrete view. This lack of strict conformity with the IASC's normally preferred theory of interim reporting, the discreet approach, is troubling to some observers.

There are other complexities which are created by interim financial reporting, as well. The most common practice is to report the effects of changes in tax rates or tax status in the interim period in which enactment occurs. Furthermore, the effects of the changes are most often included in the tax provision applicable to continuing operations, despite the source of the temporary differences impacted currently by the tax law change.

For example, if an entity accrued a loss relating to an extraordinary item in the first fiscal quarter, which under relevant tax law will not be tax deductible until paid, the tax effect would be shown in the extraordinary item section of the income statement for the first quarter. If tax rates are changed in the third quarter of the same year, the deferred tax benefit recognized in connection with the extraordinary item would now need to be adjusted upward or downward, based on the newly enacted tax rate schedule.

Practice varies with regard to where in the income statement for the third quarter, in this example, the effect of the change in tax rates would be reported. Some report such items in the tax provision applicable to income from continuing operations, while others include this in extraordinary items. Furthermore, some would not include the full effect in the third quarter at all, but rather would account for the change in rates by the prospective application of a revised effective tax rate to income being reported for remaining interim periods of the year during which enactment took place. Hopefully these and other questions will be resolved when the IASC completes its consideration of the interim financial reporting issue sometime in 1998.

Accounting for Income Taxes in Business Combinations

One of the more complex aspects of interperiod income tax accounting occurs when business combinations, treated as acquisitions as defined by IAS 22, are consummated. The principal complexity relates to the recognition, at the date of the purchase, of the deferred tax effects of the differences between the tax and financial reporting bases of assets and liabilities acquired. Further difficulties arise in connection with the recognition of goodwill and negative goodwill. If the reporting entity expects that the ultimate tax allocation will differ from the initial one (such as when disallowance by the tax authorities of an allocation made to identifiable intangibles is anticipated by the taxpayer), yet another complex accounting matter must be dealt with.

Under the provisions of revised IAS 12, the tax effects of any differences in tax and financial reporting bases are to be reflected, from the date of the purchase, as deferred tax assets and liabilities. The same rules that apply to the recognition of deferred tax assets and liabilities arising under other circumstances (i.e., the origination of temporary differences by the reporting entity) are equally applicable to such instances, except for the initial recognition of an asset or liability in a transaction other than a business combination when, at the time of the transaction, neither accounting profit nor taxable profit is affected. Accordingly, if deferred tax assets are not deemed to be probable of ultimate realization, they are not recognized in any of these circumstances.

Depending on the tax jurisdiction in which they occur, acquisitions can be either taxable or nontaxable in nature. In a taxable acquisition, the total purchase price paid will be allocated to assets and liabilities for both tax and financial reporting purposes, although under some circumstances the specifics of these allocations may differ, and to the extent the allocation is made to nondeductible goodwill there will be differences in future periods' taxable and accounting profit. In a nontaxable acquisition, the predecessor entity's tax bases for the various assets and liabilities will be carried forward, while for financial reporting the purchase price will be allocated to the assets and liabilities acquired. Thus, in most cases, there will be significant differences between the tax and financial reporting bases. For this reason, both taxable and nontaxable acquisitions can involve the application of deferred income tax accounting.

Accounting for Purchase Business Combinations at Acquisition Date

Revised IAS 12 requires that the tax effects of the tax-book basis differences of all assets and liabilities generally be presented as deferred tax assets and liabilities as of the acquisition date. In general, this grossing up of the balance sheet is a straightforward matter. An example, in the context of the business acquisition of Windlass Corp., follows:

1. The income tax rate is a flat 40%.
2. The acquisition of a business is effected at a cost of $500,000.
3. The fair values of assets acquired total $750,000.
4. The carryforward tax bases of assets acquired total $600,000.
5. The fair and carryforward tax bases of the liabilities assumed in the purchase are $250,000.
6. The difference between the tax and fair values of the assets acquired, $150,000, consists of taxable temporary differences of $200,000 and deductible temporary differences of $50,000.
7. There is no doubt as to the realizability of the deductible temporary differences in this case.

Based on the foregoing facts, allocation of the purchase price is as follows:

Gross purchase price	$ 500,000
Allocation to identifiable assets and (liabilities):	
Assets other than goodwill and deferred tax benefits	750,000
Deferred tax benefits	20,000
Liabilities, other than deferred tax obligations	(250,000)
Deferred tax obligations	(80,000)
Net of the above allocations	440,000
Allocation to goodwill	$ 60,000

Goodwill and negative goodwill. Goodwill arises when part of the price paid in a business combination accounted for as a purchase cannot be allocated to identifiable assets; negative goodwill results from bargain purchases. Goodwill may be tax deductible, depending on tax jurisdiction, or may be nondeductible. If deductible, the mandated amortization period may differ from that prescribed by IAS 22. Since under GAAP goodwill is to be amortized over its expected economic life (not to exceed 20 years, and generally not over 5 years), a temporary difference will often develop. Since negative goodwill is offset against all nonmonetary assets for financial reporting (if the benchmark treatment is employed), differences between tax and book depreciation will result in many situations.

If goodwill or negative goodwill is not deductible or taxable, respectively, in a given tax jurisdiction, in theory its tax basis is zero, and thus there is a difference between tax and financial reporting bases, to which one would logically expect deferred taxes would be attributed. However, given the residual nature of goodwill or negative goodwill, recognition of deferred taxes would in turn create yet more goodwill, and thus more deferred tax, etc. There would be little purpose achieved by loading up the balance sheet with more goodwill and related deferred tax in such circumstances, and the computation itself would be quite challenging. Accordingly, revised IAS 12 prohibits "grossing up" goodwill in such a fashion. Similarly, if there is negative goodwill which is not allocated to the cost of assets, but rather which is presented as a deferred credit items and which is not taxable, no deferred tax benefit will be computed and presented.

It is important to understand the slight inconsistency of the rules of revised IAS 12 as they relate to goodwill.

1. If positive goodwill is nondeductible for tax purposes, no deferred tax liability should be associated with it; but
2. No negative goodwill reported as a deferred revenue account in the financial statements should have a deferred tax benefit associated with it.

The accounting for a taxable purchase business combination is essentially similar to that for a nontaxable one. However, unlike the previous example, in which there were numerous assets with different tax and financial reporting bases, there are likely to be only a few differences in the case of taxable purchases. In jurisdictions in which goodwill is not deductible, attempts are often made for tax purposes to allocate excess purchase cost to tangible assets as well as to other intangibles, such as covenants not to compete. (Such attempts may or not survive review by the tax authorities, of course.) In jurisdictions where goodwill is deductible, presumably this is not a motivation, although because goodwill is often viewed as a suspect asset, entities will still be more comfortable if purchase cost can be attributed to "real" assets, even when goodwill can be amortized for tax purposes.

Accounting for Purchase Business Combinations After the Acquisition

Under the provisions of the original IAS 12, net deferred tax benefits were not to be carried forward as assets unless there was a reasonable expectation they would be realized. Under revised IAS 12 the criterion has evolved slightly; the new standard is that deferred tax assets must be probable of being realized. The assessment of this probability was discussed earlier in the chapter.

In the example above, it was specified that all deductible temporary differences were fully realizable, and therefore the deferred tax benefits associated with those temporary differences were recorded as of the acquisition date. In other situations, there may be substantial doubt concerning realizability; that is, it may not be **probable** that the benefits will be realized, and accordingly, the deferred tax asset would not be recognized, under revised IAS 12, at the date of the business acquisition. If so, the allocation of the purchase price would have to reflect that fact, and more of the purchase cost would be allocated to goodwill than would otherwise be the case. If at a later date, it is decided that some or all of the deferred tax asset not recognized at the time of the acquisition is, in fact, probable of being ultimately realized, the effect of that reevaluation will be taken into tax expense (benefit) in the period in which the reevaluation is made. Furthermore, the portion of the extra goodwill recognized at the time of the business acquisition that remains unamortized at the date of the reevaluation must be written off to expense.

To illustrate this last concept, assume that a business acquisition is made on January 1, 1997, and the deferred tax assets of $100,000 are **not** recognized at that time, due to an assessment that realization is not probable. The unrecognized tax benefit is implicitly allocated to goodwill. Also assume that the goodwill is being amortized over 5 years. On January 1, 1999, the likelihood of ultimately realizing the tax benefit is reassessed as being probable, and all of these are projected for later years. The entries at that date are as follows:

Deferred tax benefits	100,000	
Income tax expense (benefit)		100,000
Amortization of goodwill	60,000	
Goodwill		60,000

Note that only the remaining **unamortized** balance of goodwill associated with the original nonrecognition of the deferred tax benefit is charged to expense at the date the deferred tax benefit is reassessed.

In some situations, the amount of deferred tax benefits upon reassessment will exceed the balance in the goodwill account, or there may have been no goodwill recognized in connection with the business acquisition at all. Revised IAS 12 stipulates that, as a result of this reassessment, negative goodwill cannot be recognized, nor can any existing negative goodwill be increased. The implication is that, while negative goodwill could have been first recognized at the time of a business acquisition which involved recognition of deferred assets, it would not be possible to later recognize deferred tax benefits under such circumstances.

A related issue arises when the acquirer, rather than the acquiree, had not previously recognized deferred tax benefits prior to the acquisition, due to imposition of the "probable" test. If as a result of the acquisition, this asset becomes probable of realization (e.g., if under relevant tax laws the earnings of the acquired entity will provide the acquirer with an opportunity to utilize the deductible temporary differences), it will be given recognition, with the result that the goodwill otherwise recorded in the transaction will be reduced, or negative goodwill will be increased or first given recognition.

Unitings of Interests

In unitings of interests, the combining entities generally do not adjust carrying values of assets and liabilities. Reissued or comparative financial statements of periods before the effective date of the combination are restated on a combined basis. Although revised IAS 12 does not address the question, one issue that may arise is if one of the combining entities had an unrecognized deferred tax benefit (i.e., the deferred tax benefit was not deemed to be probable of realization), the restated financials may or may not reflect the benefits. That is, the deferred tax benefits may be restored on a retrospective basis.

This treatment depends on whether the combined entity will be able, under provisions of the tax laws, to utilize the operating loss and tax credit carryforwards of the merged companies. If it can do so, the deferred tax benefits should be recognized in any restated prior-period financial statements. If, under the law, the benefits cannot be utilized in a consolidated tax return or if a consolidated return is not expected to be filed, the tax benefits would not be recognized in financial statements restated for the uniting of interests.

Under some circumstances, unitings of interests may be taxable, meaning that for tax purposes there will be a step-up of the net assets of one of the merged entities. The differences between the new, stepped-up tax bases and the carryforward book values utilized for financial reporting purposes are temporary differences giving rise to deferred tax benefits. Whether these benefits are given recognition depends on whether realization is deemed to be probable. If the deferred tax benefit is not recognized at inception, and it is later partially or fully recognized when it is determined that the likelihood of ultimate realization is probable, the effect of this accounting recognition should be reflected in tax expense for the current period.

Tax Allocation for Business Investments

As noted in Chapter 9, there are two basic methods of accounting for investments in the common stock of other corporations: (1) the cost method and (2) the equity method. The **cost method** requires that the investing corporation (investor) record the investment at its purchase price, and no additional entry is made to the account over the life of the asset (this does not include any valuation contra accounts). The cost method is used in instances where the investor is not considered to have significant influence over the investee. The ownership threshold generally used is 20% of ownership. This figure is not considered an absolute, but it will be used to identify the break between application of the cost and equity methods. Under the cost method, ordinary income is recognized as dividends are declared by the investee, and capital gains (losses) are recognized on disposal of the investment. For tax purposes, no provision is made during the holding period for the allocable undistributed earnings of the investee. Deferred tax computation is not necessary when using the cost method because there is no temporary difference.

The **equity method** is generally used whenever an investor owns more than 20% of an investee or has significant influence over its operations. The equity method calls for recording the investment at cost and then increasing this carrying amount by the allocable portion of the investee's earnings. The allocable portion of the investee's earnings is then included in the pretax accounting income of the investor. Dividend payments are no longer included in pretax accounting income but are considered to be a reduction in the carrying amount of the investment. However, for tax purposes, dividends are the only revenue realized. As a result, the investor needs to recognize deferred income tax expense on the undistributed earnings of the associate that will be taxed in the future.

IAS 28 distinguishes between an associate and a subsidiary and prescribes different accounting treatments for each. An associate is considered to be a corporation whose stock is owned by an investor who holds more than 20% but no greater than 50% of the outstanding stock. An association situation occurs when the investor has significant influence but not control over the corporation invested in. A subsidiary, on the other hand, exists when one enterprise exerts control over another, which is presumed when it holds more than 50% of the stock of the other entity.

Under revised IAS 12, two conditions must both be satisfied to justify **not** reflecting deferred taxes in connection with the earnings of a subsidiary (a control situation), branches and associates (significant influence), and joint ventures. These are (1) that the parent, investor or venturer is able to control the timing of the reversal of the temporary difference, and (2) it is probable that the difference will not reverse in the foreseeable future. Unless both conditions are met, the tax effects of these temporary differences must be given recognition.

When a parent company that has the ability to control the dividend and other policies of its subsidiary determines that dividends will not be declared, and thus that the undistributed profit of the subsidiary will not be taxed at the parent company level, no deferred tax liability is to be recognized. If this intention is later altered, the tax effect of this change in estimate would be reflected in the current period's tax provision.

On the other hand, an investor, even one having significant influence, cannot absolutely determine the associate's dividend policy. Accordingly, it has to be presumed that earnings will eventually be distributed and that these will create taxable income at the investor company level. Therefore, deferred tax liability must be provided for reporting entity's share of all undistributed earnings of its associates for which it is accounting by the equity method, unless there is binding agreement for the earnings of the investee to be not distributed within the foreseeable future.

In the case of the joint ventures, there are a wide range of possible relationships between the venturers, and in some cases the reporting entity has the ability to control the payment of dividends. As in the foregoing, if the reporting entity has the ability to exercise this level of control and it is probable that distributions will not be made within the foreseeable future, no deferred tax liability will be reported.

In all these various circumstances, it will be necessary to assess whether distributions within the foreseeable future are probable. The standard does not define "foreseeable future" and thus this will remain a matter of subjective judgment. The criteria of revised IAS 12, while subjective, are less ambiguous than under the original IAS 12, which permitted nonrecognition of deferred tax liability when it was "reasonable to assume that (the associates's) profits will not be distributed."

To illustrate the application of these concepts, assume that Parent Company owns 30% of the outstanding common stock of Investee Company and 70% of the outstanding common stock of Subsidiary Company. Additional data for the year 1997 are as follows:

	Investee Company	*Subsidiary Company*
Net income	$50,000	$100,000
Dividends paid	20,000	60,000

How the foregoing data are used to recognize the tax effects of the stated events is discussed below.

Income Tax Effects from Investee Company

The 1998 accounting profit of Parent Company will include equity in its associate's income equal to $15,000 ($50,000 x 30%). Parent's taxable income, however, will include dividend income of $6,000 ($20,000 x 30%), and, under applicable tax law, a credit of 80% of the $6,000, or $4,800, will also be allowed for the dividends received. This 80% dividends received deduction is a permanent difference between accounting and taxable profits.

The amount of the deferred tax credit in 1998 depends on the expectations of Parent Company as to the manner in which the $9,000 of undistributed income will be received. In many tax jurisdictions, the effective tax rate will differ based on method of realization; dividend income may be taxed at a different rate than capital gains (achieved on the sale of an investment in an associate, for example). If the expectation of receipt is via dividends, the temporary difference is 20% of $9,000, or $1,800, and the deferred tax credit for this originating temporary difference in 1996 is the current tax rate times $1,800. However, if the expectation is that receipt will be through future sale of the investment, the gain on which would be fully taxed, the temporary difference is $9,000 and the deferred tax credit is the current capital gains rate times the $9,000.

The entries below illustrate these alternatives. A tax rate of 34% is used for both ordinary income and for capital gains. Note that the amounts in the entries below relate only to Investee Company's incremental impact on Parent Company's tax accounts.

	Expectations for undistributed income			
	Dividends		*Capital gains*	
Income tax expense	1,020		2,208	
Deferred tax liability		612[b]		1,800[c]
Income taxes payable		408[a]		408[a]

[a]Computation of income taxes payable:

Dividend income--30% x ($20,000)	$6,000
Less 80% dividends received deduction	(4,800)
Amount included in Parent's taxable income	$1,200
Tax liability--34% x ($1,200)	$ 408

[b]Computation of deferred tax liability (dividend assumption):

Originating temporary difference:	
Parent's share of undistributed income-- 30% x ($30,000)	$ 9,000
Less 80% dividends received deduction	(7,200)
Originating temporary difference	$ 1,800
Deferred tax liability--34% x ($1,800)	$ 612

[c]Computation of deferred tax liability (capital gain assumption):

Originating temporary difference: Parent's share of undistributed income--30% x ($30,000)	$9,000
Deferred tax liability--20% x ($9,000)	$1,800

Income Tax Effects from Subsidiary Company

The accounting profit of Parent Company will also include equity in Subsidiary income of $70,000 (70% x $100,000). This $70,000 will be included in pretax consolidated income if Parent and Subsidiary issue consolidated financial statements. Depending on the rules of the particular tax jurisdiction, it may be that for tax purposes, Parent and Subsidiary will not file a consolidated tax return (e.g., because the prescribed minimum level of control, that is, 80%, is not present). In the present example, assume that it will not be possible to file consolidated tax returns. Consequently, the taxable income of Parent will include dividend income of $42,000 (70% x $60,000). Assume further that there will be an 80% dividends received deduction, which will amount to $33,600. The originating temporary difference results from Parent's equity ($28,000) in the Subsidiary's undistributed earnings of $40,000.

The amount of the deferred tax credit in 1998 depends on the expectations of Parent Company as to the manner in which this $28,000 of undistributed income will be received. The same expectations can exist as discussed previously, for Parent's equity in Investee's undistributed earnings (i.e., through future dividend distributions or capital gains).

The entries below illustrate these alternatives. A marginal tax rate of 34% is assumed. The amounts in the entries below relate only to Subsidiary Company's incremental impact on Parent Company's tax accounts.

	Expectations for undistributed income			
	Dividends		*Capital gains*	
Income tax expense	4,760		12,376	
Deferred tax liability		1,904[b]		9,520[c]
Income taxes payable		2,856[a]		2,856[a]

[a]Computation of income taxes payable:

Dividend income--70% x ($60,000)	$42,000
Less 80% dividends received deduction	(33,600)
Amount included in Parent's taxable income	$ 8,400
Tax liability--34% x ($8,400)	$ 2,856

[b]Computation of deferred tax liability (dividend assumption):

Originating temporary difference:	
Parent's share of undistributed income--70% x ($40,000)	$28,000
Less 80% dividends received deduction	(22,400)
Originating temporary difference	$ 5,600
Deferred tax liability--34% x ($5,600)	$ 1,904

[c]Computation of deferred tax liability (capital gain assumption):

Originating temporary difference: Parent's share of undistributed income--70% x ($40,000)	$28,000
Deferred tax liability--34% x ($28,000)	$ 9,520

If a parent company owns a large enough percentage of the voting stock of a subsidiary and the parent, so that it may consolidate the subsidiary for both financial and tax reports, no temporary differences exist between pretax consolidated income and taxable income. Under the rules in some jurisdictions, it may be possible to submit separate tax returns even if consolidated returns could alternatively be filed; in such circumstances, there may be a tax rule that grants a 100% dividends received deduction, to avoid incurring double taxation. If, in the circumstances noted above, consolidated financial statements are prepared but a consolidated tax return is not, it would be the case that a dividends received deduction of 100% would be allowed. Accordingly, the temporary difference between pretax consolidated income and taxable income is zero if the parent assumes that the undistributed income will be realized in dividends.

Tax Effects of Compound Financial Instruments

IAS 32, *Financial Instruments: Disclosure and Presentation,* established the important notion that when financial instruments are compound, the separately identifiable components are to be accounted for according to their distinct natures. For example, when an enterprise sells convertible debt instruments, those instruments have characteristics of both debt and equity securities, and accordingly the issuance proceeds should be allocated among those components in the ratio which the fair values bear to the total proceeds. A problem arises, however, because the taxing authorities may not agree that a portion of the proceeds should be allocated to a secondary instrument. For example, when convertible bonds are sold, for tax reporting purposes the entire proceeds are considered to be the basis of the debt instrument in most jurisdictions, with no basis being allocated to the conversion feature. Accordingly this will create a temporary difference between the interest expense to be recognized for financial reporting purposes and interest to be recognized for income tax purposes, which in turn will have deferred tax implications.

Consider the following scenario. Tamara Corp. issues 6% convertible bonds due in 10 years with a face value of $3,000,000, with the bonds being convertible into Tamara common stock at the holders' option. Proceeds of the offering amount to $3,200,000, for an effective yield of approximately 5.13% at a time when "straight" debt with similar risks and time to maturity is yielding just under 6.95% in the market. Since the fair value of the debt component is thus $2.8 million out of the actual proceeds of $3.2 million, the convertibility feature is seemingly worth $400,000 in the financial marketplace. Thus the ratio of fair values is as follows:

Debt portion: $2,700,000 + $3,200,000 = .875 (i.e., 87.5%)
Equity portion: $400,000 + $3,200,000 = .125 (i.e., 12.5%)

If these ratios are then applied to the actual proceeds of the offering of the convertible debt, $3 million, the resulting computed amounts are used to record the transaction under the guidance of IAS 32, as follows:

Account	Debit	Credit
Cash	3,000,000	
Unamortized net discount	375,000	
Debt payable		3,000,000
Equity--paid in capital account		375,000

The unamortized debt discount will be amortized as additional interest cost over the life of the bonds (10 years, in this example) for financial reporting purposes, but for tax purposes the deductible interest cost will be limited, typically, to the actual interest paid in this instance. The "originating" phase of the temporary difference will be when the compound security is first sold; the "reversing" of this temporary difference will occur as the debt discount is amortized until the net carrying value of the debt equals the face value.

To illustrate, assume that the tax rate is 30%, and for simplicity, also assume that the debt discount will be amortized on a straight-line basis over the 10-year term ($375,000 ÷ 10 = $47,500 per year), although in practice amortization using the "effective yield" method is preferred. The entries to establish deferred tax liability accounting at inception, and to reflect interest accrual and reversal of the deferred tax account are as follows:

At inception (in addition to the entry shown above)

Account	Debit	Credit
Equity - paid in capital account	112,500	
Deferred tax payable		1112,500

Each year thereafter

Account	Debit	Credit
Interest expense	217,500	
Interest expense		180,000
Unamortized debt discount		37,500
Deferred tax payable	11,250	
Tax expense--deferred		11,250

Note that the offset to deferred tax liability at inception is a charge to equity, in effect reducing the credit to paid-in capital for the equity portion of the compound financial instrument to a net of tax basis, since allocating a portion of the proceeds to the equity component caused the creation of a nondeductible deferred charge, debt discount. When the deferred charge is later amortized, however, the reversing of the temporary difference leads to a reduction in tax expense to better "match" the higher interest expense reported in the financial statements than on the tax return.

Accounting for Income Taxes: Intraperiod Tax Allocation

While revised IAS 12 is concerned predominantly with the requirements of **interperiod** income tax allocation (deferred tax accounting), it also addresses the questions of **intraperiod** tax allocation. Intraperiod tax allocation relates to the matching in the income (or other financial) statement of various categories of comprehensive income or expense (continuing operations, extraordinary items, corrections of fundamental errors, etc.) with the tax effects of those items. The general principle is that tax effects should follow the items to which they relate. The computation of the tax effects of these items is, however, complicated by the fact that many, if not most, jurisdictions feature progressive tax rates. For that reason, a question arises as to whether overall "blended" rates should be apportioned across all the disparate elements (ordinary income, corrections of errors, etc.) or whether the marginal tax effects of items other than ordinary income should be reported instead.

Revised IAS 12 does not answer this question or, in fact, even address it. It might, however, be instructive to consider the two approaches, since this will affect the presentation of the income statement and, in the case of fundamental errors, the statement of retained earnings as well.

The blended rate approach would calculate the average, or effective, rate applicable to all an entity's taxable earnings for a given year (including the deferred tax effects of items that will be deductible or taxable in later periods, but that are being reported in the current year's financial statements). This effective rate is then used to compute income taxes on each of the individually reportable components. For example, if an entity has an effective blended rate of 46% in a given year, after considering the various tax brackets and any available credits against the gross amount of the tax computed, this rate is used to calculate the taxes on ordinary income, extraordinary income, the results of discontinued operations, the correction of fundamental errors, and the effects of changes in accounting principles, if any.

The alternative to the blended rate approach is what can be called the marginal tax effect approach. Using this computational technique, a series of "with and without" calculations will be made to identify the marginal, or incremental, effects of items other than those arising from ordinary, continuing operations. This is essentially the approach dictated under US GAAP (SFAS 109 and its various predecessors) and is the primary approach employed under UK GAAP as well. Since the prescription of this with-and-without method is detailed most extensively in current US GAAP, that explanation is referred to extensively in the following discussion.

Prior to the promulgation of current US GAAP, the with-and-without technique was applied under prior US standards in a step-by-step fashion proceeding down the face of the income statement. For example, an entity having continuing operations, discontinued operations, and extraordinary items would calculate tax expense as follows:

1. Tax would be computed for the aggregate results and for continuing operations. The difference between the two amounts would be allocated to the total of discontinued operations and extraordinary items.
2. Tax expense would be computed on discontinued operations. The residual amount (i.e., the difference between tax on the discontinued operations and

the tax on the total of discontinued operations and extraordinary items) would then be allocated to extraordinary items.

Thus, the amount of tax expense allocated to any given classification in the statement of income (and the other financial statements, if relevant) was partially a function of the location in which the item was traditionally presented in the income and retained earnings statements.

Under current US GAAP, total income tax expense or benefit for the period is allocated among continuing operations, discontinued operations, extraordinary items, and stockholders' equity. The standard creates a few anomalies, however, since, as defined in current US GAAP, the tax provisions on income from continuing operations include not only taxes on the income earned from continuing operations, as expected, but also a number of other tax effects, including the following:

1. The impact of changes in tax laws and rates, which includes the effects of such changes on items that were previously reflected directly in stockholders' equity
2. The impact of changes in tax status
3. Changes in estimates about whether the tax benefits of deductible temporary differences or net operating loss or credit carryforwards are probable of realization. (*NOTE: Under current US GAAP the actual criterion is "more likely than not," which differs from IAS's "probable" criterion.*)

Under current US GAAP, stockholders' equity is charged or credited with the initial tax effects of items that are reported directly in stockholders' equity, including that related to corrections of the effects of accounting errors of previous periods, which under the international standards are known as fundamental errors. The effects of tax rate or other tax law changes on items for which the tax effects were originally reported directly in stockholders' equity are reported in continuing operations if they occur in any period after the original event. This approach was adopted by current US GAAP because of the presumed difficulty of identifying the original reporting location of items that are affected possibly years later by changing rates; the expedient solution was to require all such effects to be reported in the tax provision allocated to continuing operations.

Example of intraperiod allocation using the with-and-without approach

Assume that there were $50,000 in deductible temporary differences at 12/31/97; these remain unchanged during the current year, 1998.

Income from continuing operations	$400,000
Loss from discontinued operations	(120,000)
Extraordinary gain on involuntary conversion	60,000
Correction of fundamental error:	
understatement of depreciation in 1997	(20,000)
Tax credits	5,000

Tax rates are: 15% on first $100,000 of taxable income; 20% on next $100,000; 25% on next $100,000; 30% thereafter.

Expected future tax rates were 20% at December 31, 1997, but are judged to be 28% at December 31, 1998.

Retained earnings at December 31, 1997, totaled $650,000.

Intraperiod tax allocation proceeds as follows:

Step 1 -- Tax on total taxable income of $320,000 ($400,000 – $120,000 + $60,000 – $20,000) is **$61,000** ($66,000 based on rate structure, less tax credit of $5,000).

Step 2 -- Tax on income from continuing operations of $400,000 is **$85,000**, net of tax credit.

Step 3 -- The difference, $24,000, is allocated pro rata to discontinued operations, extraordinary gain, and correction of the error in prior year depreciation.

Step 4 -- Adjustment of the deferred tax asset, amounting to a $4,000 increase due to an effective tax rate estimate change [$50,000 x (.28 – .20)] is allocated to continuing operations, regardless of the source of the temporary difference.

A summary combined income and retained earnings statement is presented below.

Income from continuing operations, before income taxes		$400,000
Income taxes on income from continuing operations:		
Current	$90,000	
Deferred	(4,000)	
Tax credits	(5,000)	81,000
Income from continuing operations, net		319,000
Loss from discontinued operations, net of tax benefit of $36,000		(84,000)
Extraordinary gain, net of tax of $18,000		42,000
Net income		277,000
Retained earnings, January 1, 1997		650,000
Correction of fundamental error, net of tax effects of $6,000		(14,000)
Retained earnings, December 31, 1997		$913,000

Applicability to international accounting standards. Since revised IAS 12 is silent on the method to be used to compute the tax effects of individual captions in the statement of income and the statement of retained earnings, financial statement preparers have the option of using essentially a with-and-without or blended rate approach. Both can be rationalized from either practical or theoretical perspectives. The blended rate method would clearly be easier to apply, since only one set of computations using progressive tax rates would be needed. The blended rate method also avoids the implication that items other than income from continuing operations represented the "last dollars" earned, since the rates applicable to those items would not be the highest marginal rates. On the other hand, the with-and-without method averts the situation where the blended rate applied to income from continuing operations is subject to wide variation due simply to the occasional existence of extraordinary and other unusual items.

On balance, and given the lack of a prescribed methodology in revised IAS 12, the authors slightly favor the blended rate approach. Whichever methodology is employed, however, it is vital that the notes to the financial statements clearly describe how the computation was made and disclose the tax effects of the various components presented. Revised IAS 12 does, however, permit the tax effects of all extraordinary items to be presented in one amount, if computation of each extraordinary item is not readily accomplished.

Classification of Deferred Taxes

E49, which was the antecedent to revised IAS 12, stipulated that an enterprise that presents a classified balance sheet will categorize its deferred tax liabilities and assets as either current or noncurrent (1) consistent with the probable time of the recovery or settlement of the asset or liability with respect to assets and liabilities arising from current tax expense, and (2) based on the probable time of reversal of the underlying temporary differences with respect to deferred tax liabilities and assets arising from temporary differences. The final standard, however, has disavowed this approach.

Revised IAS 12 states that, when an enterprise prepares a classified balance sheet (separating current from noncurrent assets and liabilities), deferred tax assets and liabilities are never to be included in the current category. The standard does not explain the logic for this prohibition, but it may be that the prospect of requiring entities to assess the amount and pattern of temporary difference reversals proved daunting. In fact, the extent of this scheduling would have been rather limited, since the only concern would have been to assess whether the expected reversals would occur before or after the 1-year threshold. With an absolute rule, however, revised IAS 12 is undeniably easier to apply.

Deferred tax assets pertaining to certain tax jurisdictions may be fully or partially recognizable, while other such assets may not be recognized at all, based on application of the "probable" criterion to the expected timing and availability of taxable temporary differences and other items entering into the determination of taxable profit in each jurisdiction.

Tax assets and liabilities should not be offset in the balance sheet, except to the extent that they pertain to taxes levied by the same taxing authority and are similarly classified in the balance sheet (i.e., both being current or both being noncurrent).

Finally, when entities included in consolidated financial statements are taxed separately, a tax asset recognized by one member of the group should not be offset against a liability recognized by another member of the same group, unless a legal right of offset is enforceable. For example, in some jurisdictions the tax loss carryforward of an acquired affiliate entity cannot be used to reduce taxable profit of another member of the group, even if consolidated tax returns are being prepared. In such a case, the deferred tax asset recognized in connection with the tax loss carryforward cannot be offset against a deferred tax liability of another member of the consolidated group. Further, in evaluating whether realization of the tax asset is probable, the existence of the tax liability could not be considered.

Financial Statement Disclosures

Revised IAS 12 mandates a number of disclosures, including some which have not been required under earlier practice. The purpose of these disclosures, of course, is to provide the user with an understanding of the relationship between accounting profit and the related tax effects, as well as to aid in predicting future cash inflows or outflows related to tax effects of assets and liabilities already reflected in the balance sheet. Newly imposed disclosures are intended to provide greater insight into the relationship between deferred tax assets and liabilities recognized, the related tax expense or benefit recognized in earnings, and the underlying natures of the related temporary differences resulting in those items. There is also enhanced disclosure for discontinued operations under revised IAS 12. Finally, when deferred tax assets are given recognition under defined conditions, there will be disclosure of the nature of the evidence supporting recognition. The specific disclosures are presented in the following paragraphs in greater detail.

Balance sheet disclosures. A reporting entity is required to disclose the amount of a deferred tax asset and the nature of evidence supporting its recognition, when

1. Utilization of the deferred tax asset is dependent on future taxable profits in excess of the profits arising from the reversal of the existing taxable temporary differences; **and**
2. The enterprise has suffered a loss in the same tax jurisdiction to which the deferred tax assets relate in either the current or preceding period.

Income statement disclosures. Revised IAS 12 places primary emphasis on disclosure of the components of income tax expense or benefit. The following information must be disclosed about the components of tax expense for each year for which an income statement is presented.

The components of tax expense or benefit, which may include some or all of the following:

1. Current tax expense or benefit

2. Any adjustments recognized in the current period for taxes of prior periods
3. The amount of deferred tax expense or benefit relating to the origination and reversal of temporary differences
4. The amount of deferred tax expense or benefit relating to changes in tax rates or the imposition of new taxes
5. The amount of the tax benefit arising from a previously unrecognized tax loss, tax credit, or temporary difference of a prior period that is used to reduce current period tax expense
6. The amount of the tax benefit from a previously unrecognized tax loss, tax credit, or temporary difference of a prior period that is used to reduce deferred tax expense
7. Deferred tax expense arising from the write-down of a deferred tax asset because it is no longer deemed probable of realization
8. The amount of tax expense relating to changes in accounting policies and fundamental errors accounted for in accordance with the allowed alternative treatment stipulated by IAS 8 (i.e., by inclusion in income of the current period)

In addition to the foregoing, revised IAS 12 also requires that disclosures be made of the following items which are to be separately stated:

1. The aggregate current and deferred tax relating to items that are charged or credited to equity
2. Tax expense related to extraordinary items recognized during the period
3. The relationship between tax expense or benefit and accounting profit or loss either (or both) as
    a. A numerical reconciliation between tax expense or benefit and the product of accounting profit or loss times the applicable tax rate(s), with disclosure of how the rate(s) was determined; or
    b. A numerical reconciliation between the average effective tax rate and applicable rate, also with disclosure of how the applicable rate was determined
4. An explanation of changes in the applicable rate vs. the prior reporting period
5. The amount and date of expiration of unrecognized tax assets relating to deductible temporary differences, tax losses and tax credits
6. The aggregate amount of any temporary differences relating to investments in subsidiaries, branches, and associates and interests in joint ventures for which deferred liabilities have not been recognized.
7. For each type of temporary difference, including unused tax losses and credits, disclosure of

a. The amount of the deferred tax assets and liabilities included in each balance sheet presented; and
b. The amount of deferred income or expense recognized in the income statement, if not otherwise apparent from changes in the balance sheets

8. Regarding discontinued operations, disclosure of the tax expense or benefit related to
   a. The gain or loss on discontinuance; and
   b. The profit or loss from the ordinary activities of the discontinued operation for the period and all prior periods presented.

Finally, in a new requirement, disclosure must be made of the amount of deferred tax asset and the evidence supporting its presentation in the balance sheet, when both these conditions exist: Utilization is dependent upon future profitability beyond that assured by the future reversal of taxable temporary differences, **and** the enterprise has suffered a loss in either the current period or the preceding period in the jurisdiction to which the deferred tax asset relates.

Examples of informative disclosures about income tax expense

The disclosure requirements imposed by revised IAS 12 are extensive and in some instances complicated. The following examples have been adapted from the standard itself, with some modifications.

Note: Income tax expense

Major components of the provisions for income taxes are as follows:

	1998	1999
Current tax expense	$75,500	$82,450
Deferred tax expense (benefit), relating to the origination and reversal of temporary differences	12,300	(16,275)
Effect on previously provided deferred tax assets and liabilities resulting from increase in statutory tax rates	--	7,600
Total tax provision for the period	$87,800	$73,775

The aggregate current and deferred income tax expense (benefit) which was charged (credited) to stockholder's equity for the periods

	1998	1999
Current tax, related to correction of fundamental error	$(5,200)	$ --
Deferred tax, related to revaluation of investments	--	45,000
Total	$(5,200)	$45,000

The relationship between tax expense and accounting profit is explained by the following reconciliations (*NOTE: Only one required*):

	1998	*1999*
Accounting profit	$167,907	$132,398
Tax at statutory rate (43% in 1998; 49% in 1999)	$ 72,200	$ 64,875
Tax effect of expenses which are not deductible:		
Charitable contributions	600	1,300
Civil fines imposed on the entity	15,000	
Effect on previously provided deferred tax assets and liabilities resulting from increase in statutory rates	--	7,600
Total tax provision for the period	$87,800	$73,775

	(%)	
	1998	*1999*
Statutory tax rate	43.0	49.0
Tax effect of expenses which are not deductible:		
Charitable contributions	0.4	1.0
Civil fines imposed on the entity	8.9	--
Effect on previously provided deferred tax assets and liabilities resulting from increase in statutory rates	--	5.7
Total tax provision for the period	52.3	55.7

In 1999, the federal government imposed a 14% surcharge on the income tax, which has affected 1999 current tax expense as well as the recorded amounts of deferred tax assets and liabilities, since when these benefits are ultimately received or settled, the new, higher tax rates will be applicable.

Deferred tax assets and liabilities included in the accompanying balance sheets as of December 31, 1998 and 1999 are as follows, as classified by categories of temporary differences:

	1998	*1999*
Accelerated depreciation for tax purposes	$ 26,890	$ 22,300
Liabilities for postretirement health care that are deductible only when paid	(15,675)	(19,420)
Product development costs deducted from taxable profits in prior years	2,500	--
Revaluation of fixed assets, net of accumulated depreciation	--	2,160
Deferred tax liability, net	$ 13,715	$ 5,040

APPENDIX

ACCOUNTING FOR INCOME TAXES IN INTERIM PERIODS

Interim Reporting

Under presently enacted international accounting standards, there are no specific rules applicable to interim financial reporting. However, as noted in the main body of this chapter, the IASC has produced a draft statement of principles (DSOP) in anticipation of promulgating a new standard on interim financial reporting as part of its current "core set of standards" program. The DSOP does address, among other topics, the matter of income tax accounting in interim reporting periods. However, this is essentially limited to the important question of whether taxes should be accrued based on a projected effective tax rate for the full year, or on the rates applicable to the earning to date; it does not address other issues which arise in connection with tax allocation to interim periods. In the absence of official guidance on these matters, the following is offered based on current practices and guidelines which have been provided by other standard-setting bodies.

The general consensus is that the appropriate perspective for interim period reporting is to view the interim period as an integral part of the year rather than as a discrete period. For purposes of computing income tax provisions, this objective is usually achieved by projecting income for the full annual period, computing the tax thereon, and applying the effective rate to the interim period income or loss, with quarterly (or monthly) revisions to the expected annual results and the tax effects thereof, as necessary.

Notwithstanding this general principle, however, there are certain complexities that arise only in the context of interim financial reporting. Included in this group of issues are (1) recognizing the tax benefits of losses based on expected earnings of later interim or annual periods, (2) reporting the benefits of net operating loss carryforwards in interim periods, and (3) reporting the effects of tax law changes in interim periods. Other matters requiring interpretation include the classification of deferred taxes on interim balance sheets and the allocation of interim period tax provisions between current and deferred expense.

Basic example of interim period accounting for income taxes

Andorra Woolens, Inc. estimates that accounting profit for the full fiscal year ending June 30, 1998, will be $400,000. The company expects amortization of goodwill for the year to be $30,000, the annual premium on an officer's life insurance policy is $12,000, and dividend income (from a less than 20% ownership interest) is expected to be $100,000. Under pertinent tax rules, goodwill is not amortizable and premiums paid on officer's life insurance is not an expense. Furthermore, there is a dividends received deduction of 70% for intercorporate investments of under 20%.

The company recognized income of $75,000 in the first quarter of the year. The deferred tax liability arises solely in connection with depreciation temporary differences;

these differences totaled $150,000 at the beginning of the year and are projected to equal $280,000 at year end. The effective rate expected to apply to the reversal at both year beginning and year end is 34%. The change in the taxable temporary difference during the current interim period is $30,000.

Andorra Woolens must first calculate its estimated effective income tax rate for the year. This rate is computed using all the tax planning alternatives available to the company (e.g., tax credits, foreign rates, capital gains rates, etc.).

Estimated pretax accounting income		$ 400,000
Permanent differences:		
Add: Nondeductible officer's life insurance premium	$12,000	
Nondeductible amortization of organization costs	30,000	42,000
		442,000
Less: Dividends received deduction ($100,000 x 70%)		(70,000)
Estimated "book" taxable income		372,000
Less: Change in taxable temporary difference		(130,000)
Estimated taxable income for the year		$ 242,000
Tax on estimated taxable income (see below)		$ 70,530
Effective tax rate for **current** tax provision [$70,530/(400,000 – 130,000)]		26.1%

Tax rate schedule				
At least	*Not more than*	*Rate*	*Taxable income*	*Tax*
$ --	$50,000	15%	$ 50,000	$ 7,500
50,000	75,000	25%	25,000	6,250
75,000	--	34%	167,000	56,780
				$70,530

The deferred tax provision for the interim period should be based on the actual change in the temporary difference (depreciation, in this example) during the interim period. In this case the depreciation temporary difference grew by $30,000 during the period, and the expected tax rate that will apply to the reversal, in future years, is the marginal rate of 34%. Accordingly, the tax provision for the period is as follows:

"Ordinary" income for the interim period	$75,000
Less: Change in temporary difference	30,000
Net "ordinary" income	45,000
Applicable tax rate	26.1%
Current tax provision	$11,755
Tax effect of temporary difference ($30,000 x 34%)	10,200
Total provision	$21,955

Therefore, the entry necessary to record the income tax expense at the end of the first quarter is as follows:

Income tax expense	21,955	
Income taxes payable--current		11,755
Deferred tax liability		10,200

The financial statement presentation would remain the same as has been illustrated in prior examples.

In the second quarter, Andorra Woolens, Inc. revises its estimate of income for the full fiscal year. It now anticipates only $210,000 of book income, including only $75,000 of dividend income, because of dramatic changes in the national economy. Other permanent differences are still expected to total $42,000.

Estimated pretax accounting income		$ 210,000
Permanent differences:		
Add: Nondeductible officer's life insurance premium	$12,000	
Nondeductible amortization of organization costs	30,000	42,000
		252,000
Less: Dividends received deduction ($75,000 x 70%)		(52,500)
Estimated "book" taxable income		199,500
Less: Change in taxable temporary difference		(130,000)
Estimated taxable income for the year		$ 69,500
Tax on estimated taxable income (see below)		$ 12,375
Effective tax rate for **current** tax provision [$12,375/(210,000 – 130,000)]		15.5%

Tax rate schedule				
At least	*Not more than*	*Rate*	*Taxable income*	*Tax*
$ --	$50,000	15%	$50,000	$ 7,500
50,000	75,000	25%	19,500	4,875
				$12,375

The actual earnings for the second quarter were $22,000, and the change in the temporary difference was only $10,000. The tax provision for the second quarter is computed as follows:

"Ordinary" income for the half year	$97,000
Less: Change in temporary difference	40,000
Net ordinary income	57,000
Applicable tax rate	15.5%
Current tax provision	$ 8,835
Tax effect of temporary difference ($40,000 x 34%)	13,600
Total provision	$22,435

Under the general principle that changes in estimate are reported prospectively, the results of prior quarters are not restated for changes in the estimated effective annual tax rate. Given the provision for current and deferred income taxes that was made in the first interim period, shown above, the following entry is required to record the income taxes as of the end of the second quarter:

Income tax expense	480	
Income taxes payable--current	2,920	
Deferred tax liability		3,400

The foregoing illustrates the basic problems encountered in applying the promulgated GAAP to interim reporting. In the following paragraphs, we discuss some items requiring modifications to the approach described above.

Net Operating Losses in Interim Periods

The tax effects of operating losses are treated no differently than any other temporary differences; if probable of being realized, the tax effects are reflected as deferred tax benefits in the period the loss is incurred. If not deemed probable, no tax effects are recognized; if the estimation of realizability changes in a later period, the deferred tax benefit is then recorded, with the offset being included in current period tax expense. However, given the desire to treat interim periods as integral parts of the annual period of which they are a component, the accounting treatment of net operating losses raises a number of issues. These include (1) calculation of the expected annual tax rate for purposes of interim period income tax provisions, and (2) recognition of an asset for the tax effects of a loss carryforward.

Carryforward from prior years. Loss carryforward benefits from prior years first given recognition (i.e., by recordation of a deferred tax benefit when none had been recognized in the period the loss was incurred) in interim periods are included in the ordinary tax provision. Common practice is to compute the expected annual effective tax rate on **ordinary** income at each interim reporting date, and use this rate to provide income taxes on ordinary income on a cumulative basis at each interim date. The tax effects of extraordinary items, discontinued operations, and other nonoperating categories were excluded from this computation; those tax effects are typically separately determined on a with-and-without basis, as explained later in this appendix.

Recognition of a previously unrecognized tax benefit should be included as a credit in the tax provision of the interim period when there is a reevaluation of the likelihood of future tax benefits being realized. Similarly, a reduction of the deferred tax benefit resulting from a revised judgment that the benefits are not probable of being realized would cause a catch-up adjustment to be included in the current interim period's ordinary tax provision. In either situation, the effect is **not** prorated to future interim periods by means of the effective tax rate estimate. To illustrate, consider the following example.

Example of carryforward from prior years

Dacca Corporation has a previously unrecognized $50,000 net operating loss carryforward; a flat 40% tax rate for current and future periods is assumed. Income for the full year (before NOL) is projected to be $80,000; in the first quarter a pretax loss of $10,000 will be reported.

Projected annual income	$80,000
x Tax rate	40%
Projected tax liability	$32,000

Accordingly, in the income statement for the first fiscal quarter, the pretax operating loss of $10,000 will give rise to a tax **benefit** of $10,000 x 40% = $4,000.

In addition, a tax benefit of $20,000 ($50,000 loss carryforward x 40%) is given recognition and is included in the current interim period tax provision relating to continuing operations. Thus, total tax benefit for the first fiscal quarter will be $24,000 (= $4,000 + $20,000).

If Dacca's second quarter results in a pretax operating income of $30,000, and the expectation for the full year remains unchanged (i.e., operating income of $80,000), the second quarter tax provision is $12,000 ($30,000 x 40%).

The tax provision for the fiscal first half-year will be a benefit of $12,000, as follows:

Cumulative pretax income through second quarter ($30,000 – $10,000)	$ 20,000
x Effective rate	40%
Tax provision before recognition of NOL carryforward benefit	$ 8,000
Benefit of NOL carryforward first recognized in first quarter	(20,000)
Total tax provision (benefit)	$(12,000)

The foregoing example assumes that during the first quarter, Dacca's judgment changed as to the full realizability of the previously unrecognized benefit of the $50,000 loss carryforward. Were this **not** the case, however, the benefit would have been recognized only as actual tax liabilities were incurred (through current period earnings) in amounts to offset the NOL benefit.

To illustrate the latter situation, assume the same facts about earnings for the first two quarters, and assume now that Dacca's judgment about realizability of prior-period NOL does not change. Tax provisions for the first quarter and first half are as follows:

	First quarter	*First half-year*
Pretax income (loss)	$(10,000)	$20,000
x Effective rate	40%	40%
Tax provision before recognition of NOL carryforward benefit	$(4,000)	$ 8,000
Benefit of NOL carryforward recognized	-0-	(8,000)
Tax provision (benefit)	$(4,000)	$ -0-

Notice that recognition of a tax benefit of $4,000 in the first quarter is based on the expectation of at least a breakeven full year's results. That is, the benefit of the first quarter's loss was deemed probable of realization. Otherwise, no tax benefit would have been reported in the first quarter.

Estimated loss for the year. When the full year is expected to be profitable, it will be irrelevant that one or more interim periods results in a loss, and the expected effective rate for the full year should be used to record interim period tax benefits, as illustrated above. However, when the full year is expected to produce a loss, computation of the expected annual tax benefit rate must logically take into account the extent to which a deferred tax asset will be recordable at year end. For the first set of examples, below, assume that the realization of tax benefits related to operating loss carryforwards are not entirely probable. That is, only a portion of the benefits will be recognized.

For each of the following examples we assume that the L'avventura Corporation is anticipating a loss for the fiscal year of $150,000. A deferred tax liability of $30,000 is currently recorded on the company's books; all of the credits will reverse in the 15-year carryforward period permitted by applicable tax law. Assume that future taxes will be at a 40% rate.

Example 1

Assume that the company can carry back the entire $150,000 to the preceding 3 years. The tax potentially refundable by the carryback would (remember, this is only an estimate until year end) amount to $48,000 (an assumed amount). The effective rate is then 32% ($48,000/150,000).

	Ordinary income (loss)		*Tax (benefit) expense*		
Reporting period	*Reporting period*	*Year-to-date*	*Year-to-date*	*Less previously provided*	*Reporting period*
1st qtr.	$ (50,000)	$ (50,000)	$(16,000)	$ --	$(16,000)
2nd qtr.	20,000	(30,000)	(9,600)	(16,000)	6,400
3rd qtr.	(70,000)	(100,000)	(32,000)	(9,600)	(22,400)
4th qtr.	(50,000)	(150,000)	(48,000)	(32,000)	(16,000)
Fiscal year	$(150,000)				$(48,000)

Note that both the income tax expense (2nd quarter) and benefit are computed using the estimated annual effective rate. This rate is applied to the year-to-date numbers just as in the previous examples, with any adjustment being made and realized in the current reporting period. This treatment is appropriate because the accrual of tax benefits in the first, third, and fourth quarters is consistent with the effective rate estimated at the beginning of the year; in contrast to those circumstances in which a change in estimate is made in a quarter relating to the realizability of tax benefits not provided previously (or provided for only partially).

Example 2

In this case assume that L'avventura Corporation can carry back only $50,000 of the loss and that the remainder must be carried forward. Realization of income to offset the loss is not deemed to be probable. The estimated carryback of $50,000 would generate a tax refund of $12,000 (again assumed). The company is assumed to be in the 40% tax bracket (a flat rate is used to simplify the example). The benefit of the operating loss carryforward is recognized only to the extent that it is deemed to be probable of realization. In this example, management has concluded that only one-fourth of the gross benefit will be realized in future years. Accordingly, only $10,000 of estimated tax benefit related to the carryforward of the projected loss is recordable. Considered in conjunction with the carryback of $12,000, the company will obtain a $22,000 tax benefit relating to the projected current year loss, for an effective tax benefit rate of 14.7%. The calculation of the estimated annual effective rate is as follows:

Expected net loss			$150,000
Tax benefit from carryback		$12,000	
Benefit of carryforward ($100,000 x 40%)	$40,000		
Portion not deemed to be probable of realization	(30,000)	10,000	
Total recognized benefit			$22,000
Estimated annual effective rate ($22,000 ÷ 150,000)			14.7%

	Ordinary income (loss)		Tax (benefit) expense			
			Year-to-date			
Reporting period	Reporting period	Year-to-date	Computed	Limited to	Less previously provided	Reporting period
1st qtr.	$ 10,000	$ 10,000	$ 1,470	$ --	$ --	$ 1,470
2nd qtr.	(80,000)	(70,000)	(11,733)	--	1,470	(10,263)
3rd qtr.	(100,000)	(170,000)	(14,667)	(22,000)	(10,263)	(4,404)
4th qtr.	20,000	(150,000)	(22,000)	--	(22,000)	--
Fiscal year	$(150,000)					$(22,000)

In the foregoing, the tax expense (benefit) is computed by multiplying the year-to-date income or loss by the estimated annual effective rate, and then subtracting the amount of tax liability or benefit provided in prior interim periods. It makes no difference if the current period indicates an income or a loss, assuming of course that the full-year estimated results are not being revised. However, if the cumulative loss for the interim periods to date exceeds the projected loss for the full year on which the effective tax benefit rate had been based, no further tax benefits can be recorded, as illustrated above in the provision for the third quarter.

Operating loss occurring during an interim period. An instance may occur in which the company expects net income for the year and incurs a net loss during one of the reporting periods. In this situation, the estimated annual effective rate, which was calculated based on the expected net income figure, is applied to the year-to-date income or loss to arrive at a total year-to-date tax provision. The amount previously provided is subtracted from the year-to-date figure to arrive at the provision for the current reporting period. If the current period operations resulted in a loss, the tax provision for the period will reflect a tax benefit.

Tax Provision Applicable to Discontinued Operations or Extraordinary Items Occurring in Interim Periods

Extraordinary items. Extraordinary items and discontinued operations are to be shown net of their related tax effects. The interim treatment accorded these items does not differ from the fiscal year-end reporting required by GAAP. However, common practice is not to include these items in computation of the estimated annual tax rate. These items are generally recognized in the interim period in which they occur; that is, they are not annualized. Recognition of the tax effects of a loss due to any of the aforementioned situations would be made if the benefits are expected to be realized during the year or if they will be recognizable as a deferred tax asset at year end under the provisions of revised IAS 12.

If a situation arises where realization is not probable in the period of occurrence but becomes assured in a subsequent period in the same fiscal year, the previously unrecognized tax benefit should be reported in income from continuing operations until it reduces the tax provision to zero, with any excess reported in other categories of income (e.g., discontinued operations) that provided a means of realization for the tax benefit.

The following examples illustrate the treatment required for reporting extraordinary items. Again, these items are **not** to be used in calculating the estimated annual tax rate. For income statement presentation purposes, extraordinary items are shown net of their applicable tax provision.

The following data apply to the next two examples:

1. Dynamix Company expects fiscal year ending June 30, 1998, income to be $96,000 and net permanent differences to reduce taxable income by $25,500.
2. Dynamix Company also incurred a $30,000 extraordinary loss in the second quarter of the year.

Example 1

In this case, assume that the loss can be carried back to prior periods, and therefore the realization of any tax benefit is assured. Based on the information given earlier, the estimated annual effective tax rate can be calculated as follows:

Expected pretax accounting income	$96,000
Anticipated permanent differences	(25,500)
Expected taxable income	$70,500

Tax Calculation "Excluding" Extraordinary Item

$50,000	x	0.15	=	$ 7,500
20,500	x	0.25	=	5,125
$70,500				$12,625

Effective annual rate = 13.15% ($12,625 ÷ 96,000)

No adjustment in the estimated annual effective rate is required when the extraordinary, unusual, or infrequent item occurs. The tax (benefit) applicable to the item is computed using the estimated fiscal year ordinary income and an analysis of the incremental impact of the extraordinary item. The method illustrated below is applicable when the company anticipates operating income for the year. When a loss is anticipated but realization of benefits of loss carryforwards is not probable, the company computes its estimated annual effective rate based on the amount of tax to be refunded from prior years. The tax (benefit) applicable to the extraordinary item is then the decrease (increase) in the refund to be received.

Computation of the tax applicable to the extraordinary item is as follows:

Estimated pretax accounting income	$96,000
Permanent differences	(25,500)
Extraordinary item	(30,000)
Expected taxable income	$40,500

Tax Calculation "Including" Extraordinary Item

$40,500 x 0.15 = $6,075

Tax "excluding" extraordinary item	$12,625
Tax "including" extraordinary item	6,075
Tax benefit applicable to extraordinary item	$ 6,550

			Tax (benefit) applicable to				
			Ordinary income (loss)		Extraordinary item		
Reporting period	*Ordinary income (loss)*	*Extraordinary item*	*Reporting period*	*Year-to-date*	*Year-to-date*	*Previously provided*	*Reporting period*
1st qtr.	$10,000	$ --	$ 1,315	$ 1,315	$ --	$ --	$ --
2nd qtr.	(20,000)	(30,000)	(2,630)	(1,315)	(6,550)	--	(6,550)
3rd qtr.	40,000	--	5,260	3,945	(6,550)	(6,550)	--
4th qtr.	66,000	--	8,680	12,625	(6,550)	(6,550)	--
Fiscal year	$96,000	$(30,000)	$12,625				$(6,550)

Example 2

Again, assume that Dynamix Company estimates net income of $96,000 for the year with permanent differences of $25,500 that reduce taxable income. The extraordinary loss of $30,000 cannot be carried back and the ability to carry it forward is not probable. Because no deferred tax credits exist, the only way that the loss can be deemed to be realizable is to the extent that current year ordinary income offsets the effect of the loss. As a result, realization of the loss is assured only as, and to the extent that, there is ordinary income for the year.

			Tax (benefit) applicable to				
			Ordinary income (loss)		*Extraordinary item*		
Reporting period	*Ordinary income (loss)*	*Extraordinary item*	*Reporting period*	*Year-to-date*	*Year-to-date*	*Previously provided*	*Reporting period*
1st qtr.	$ 5,000	$ --	$ 658	$ 658	$ --	$ --	$ --
2nd qtr.	20,000	(30,000)	2,630	3,288	(3,288)[a]	--	(3,288)
3rd qtr.	(10,000)	--	(1,315)	1,973	(1,973)[a]	(3,288)	1,315
4th qtr.	81,000	--	10,652	12,625	(6,550)[a]	(1,973)	(4,577)
Fiscal year	$96,000	$(30,000)	$12,625				$(6,550)

[a]*The recognition of the tax benefit to be realized relative to the extraordinary item is limited to the lesser of the total tax benefit applicable to the item or the amount available to be realized. Because realization is based on the amount of tax applicable to ordinary income during the period, the year-to-date figures for the tax benefit fluctuate as the year-to-date tax expense relative to ordinary income fluctuates. Note that at no point does the amount of the tax benefit exceed what was calculated above as being applicable to the extraordinary item.*

Discontinued operations in interim periods. The computations described for extraordinary items will also apply to the income (loss) from the discontinued segment, including any provisions for operating gains (losses) subsequent to the measurement date.

If the decision to dispose of operations occurs in any interim period other than the first period, the operating income (loss) applicable to the discontinued segment has already been used in computing the estimated annual effective tax rate. Therefore, a recomputation of the **total tax** is not required. However, the total tax is to be divided into two components.

1. That tax applicable to ordinary income (loss)
2. That tax applicable to the income (loss) from the discontinued segment

This division is accomplished as follows: A revised estimated annual effective rate is calculated for the income (loss) from ordinary operations. This recomputation is then applied to the ordinary income (loss) from the preceding periods. The total tax applicable to the discontinued segment is then composed of two items.

1. The difference between the total tax originally computed and the tax recomputed on remaining ordinary income
2. The tax computed on unusual, infrequent, or extraordinary items as described above

Example

Realtime Corporation anticipates net income of $150,000 during the fiscal year. The net permanent differences for the year will be $10,000. The company also anticipates tax credits of $10,000 during the fiscal year. For purposes of this example, we assume a flat statutory rate of 50%. The estimated annual effective rate is then calculated as follows:

Estimated pretax income	$150,000
Net permanent differences	(10,000)
Taxable income	140,000
Statutory rate	50%
Tax	70,000
Anticipated credits	(10,000)
Total estimated tax	$ 60,000
Estimated effective rate ($60,000 ÷ 150,000)	40%

The first two quarters of operations were as follows:

	Ordinary income (loss)		*Tax provision*		
Reporting period	*Reporting period*	*Year-to-date*	*Year-to-date*	*Less previously provided*	*Reporting period*
1st qtr.	$30,000	$30,000	$12,000	$ --	$12,000
2nd qtr.	25,000	55,000	22,000	12,000	10,000

In the third quarter, Realtime made the decision to dispose of Division X. During the third quarter, the company earned a total of $60,000. The company expects the disposal to result in a one-time charge to income of $50,000 and estimates that operating losses subsequent to the disposal will be $25,000. The company estimates revised ordinary income in the fourth quarter to be $35,000. The two components of pretax accounting income (discontinued operations and revised ordinary income) are shown below.

		Division X	
Reporting period	*Revised ordinary income*	*Loss from operations*	*Provision for loss on disposal*
1st qtr.	$ 40,000	$(10,000)	$ --
2nd qtr.	40,000	(15,000)	--
3rd qtr.	80,000	(20,000)	(75,000)
4th qtr.	35,000	--	--
Fiscal year	$195,000	$(45,000)	$(75,000)

Realtime must now recompute the estimated annual tax rate. Assume that all the permanent differences are related to the revised continuing operations. However, $3,300 of the tax credits were applicable to machinery used in Division X. Because of the discontinuance of operations, the credit on this machinery would not be allowed. Any recapture of prior-period credits must be used as a reduction in the tax benefit from either operations or the loss on disposal. Assume that the company must recapture $2,000 of investment tax credit which is related to Division X.

The recomputed estimated annual rate for continuing operations is as follows:

Estimated (revised) ordinary income	$195,000
Less net permanent differences	(10,000)
	$185,000
Tax at statutory rate of 50%	$ 92,500
Less anticipated credits from continuing operations	(6,700)
Tax provision	$ 85,800
Estimated annual effective tax rate ($85,800 ÷ 195,000)	44%

The next step is then to apply the revised rate to the quarterly income from continuing operations as illustrated below.

	Ordinary income		*Estimated annual*	*Tax provision*		
Reporting period	*Reporting period*	*Year-to-date*	*effective rate*	*Year-to-date*	*Less previously provided*	*Reporting period*
1st qtr.	$ 40,000	$ 40,000	44%	$17,600	$ --	$17,600
2nd qtr.	40,000	80,000	44%	35,200	17,600	17,600
3rd qtr.	80,000	160,000	44%	70,400	35,200	35,200
4th qtr.	35,000	195,000	44%	85,800	70,400	15,400
Fiscal year	$195,000					$85,800

The tax benefit applicable to the operating loss from discontinued operations and the loss from the disposal must now be calculated. The first two quarters are calculated on a differential basis as shown below.

	Tax applicable to ordinary income		*Tax (benefit) expense*
Reporting period	*Previously reported*	*Recomputed (above)*	*applicable to Division X*
1st qtr.	$12,000	$17,600	$ (5,600)
2nd qtr.	10,000	17,600	(7,600)
			$(13,200)

The only calculation remaining applies to the third quarter tax benefit pertaining to the operating loss and the loss on disposal of the discontinued segment. The calculation of this amount is made based on the revised estimate of annual ordinary income, both including and excluding the effects of the Division X losses. This is shown below.

	Loss from operations of Division X	*Provision for loss on disposal*
Estimated annual income from continuing operations	$195,000	$195,000
Net permanent differences	(10,000)	(10,000)
Loss from Division X operations	(45,000)	--
Provision for loss on disposal of Division X	--	(75,000)
Total	$140,000	$110,000

Tax at the statutory rate of 50%	$ 70,000	$ 55,000
Anticipated credits (from continuing operations)	(6,700)	(6,700)
Recapture of previously recognized tax credits as a result of disposal	--	2,000
Taxes after effect of Division X losses	63,300	50,300
Taxes computed on estimated income before the effect of Division X losses	85,800	85,800
Tax benefit applicable to Division X	(22,500)	(35,500)
Amounts recognized in quarters one and two ($5,600 + $7,600)	(13,200)	--
Tax benefit to be recognized in the third quarter	$ (9,300)	$(35,500)

The quarterly tax provisions can be summarized as follows:

	Pretax income (loss)			*Tax (benefit) applicable to*		
Reporting period	*Continuing operations*	*Operations of Division X*	*Provision for loss on disposal*	*Continuing operations*	*Operations of Division X*	*Provision for loss on disposal*
1st qtr.	$ 40,000	$(10,000)	$ --	$17,600	$ (5,600)	$ --
2nd qtr.	40,000	(15,000)	--	17,600	(7,600)	--
3rd qtr.	80,000	(20,000)	(75,000)	35,200	(9,300)	(35,500)
4th qtr.	35,000	--	--	15,400	--	--
Fiscal year	$195,000	$(45,000)	$(75,000)	$85,800	$(22,500)	$(35,500)

The following income statement shows the proper financial statement presentation of these unusual and infrequent items. The notes to the statement indicate which items are to be included in the calculation of the annual estimated rate.

Income Statement

Net sales*		$xxxx
Other income*		xxx
		xxxx
Costs and expenses		
Cost of sales*	$xxxx	
Selling, general, and administrative expenses*	xxx	
Interest expense*	xx	
Other deductions*	xx	
Unusual items	xxx	
Infrequently occurring items	xxx	xxxx
Income (loss) from continuing operations before income taxes and other items listed below		xxxx
Provision for income taxes (benefit)**		xxx
Income (loss) from continuing operations before items listed below		xxxx

Discontinued operations:		
Income (loss) from operations of discontinued Division X (less applicable income taxes of $xxxx)	xxxx	
Income (loss) on disposal of Division X, including provision of $xxxx for operating losses during phase-out period (less applicable taxes of $xxxx)	xxxx	xxxx
Income (loss) before extraordinary items and cumulative effect of a change in accounting principle		xxxx
Extraordinary items (less applicable income taxes of $xxxx)		xxxx
Cumulative effect on prior years of a change in accounting principle (less applicable income taxes of $xxxx***)		xxxx
Net income (loss)		$xxxx

* *Components of ordinary income (loss).*

** *Consists of total income taxes (benefit) applicable to ordinary income (loss), unusual items, and infrequent items.*

*** *This amount is shown net of income taxes. Although the income taxes are generally disclosed (as illustrated), this is not required.*

15 ACCOUNTING FOR PENSIONS

PERSPECTIVE AND ISSUES

IAS 19, the current international standard on accounting for pension costs, was issued in 1993 and became effective for years beginning in 1995. It replaced an earlier standard, also called IAS 19, which was issued in 1983. The revised standard is far more specific than its antecedent and significantly narrows the range of acceptable practice. However, when contrasted to the corresponding US standards, IAS 19 still permits a surprisingly wide range of practice. For this reason, further reform of the pension cost accounting rules under the IAS has long been expected, and recently published Exposure Draft E54, which will be discussed later in this chapter, offers vastly more precise guidance than is contained in the current standard.

Under revised IAS 19, both the accrued benefit and the projected benefit valuation methods are permitted (the former being the benchmark treatment, the latter the available alternative), and in the common situation where compensation trends upward, enterprises accounting for the cost of pension programs under these options will report notably different magnitudes of periodic charges; in some cases, these charges will differ materially. The acceptability of these two very different measurement models has been widely cited as the most glaring deficiency of revised IAS 19. On the other hand, there is reasonable theoretical support for each of these approaches.

IAS 19 applies to all pension schemes, whether formal or informal, and also is to be utilized in developing the accounting for similar types of benefit programs. The standard is not very precise in defining the extent to which components of pension cost are to be disclosed in the financial statements and also gives a fair amount of latitude to preparers when it comes to amortizing certain cost elements, such as those associated with plan amendments.

Of the two major classes of pension plans, defined contribution and defined benefit, accounting for the latter is by far the more difficult. Given the central role that accounting estimates play in the accounting for defined benefit plans, some diversity will always be implicit in financial reporting, and full disclosure of key assumptions and methods is the best prescription to prevent misleading financial statement users. Due to the long-term nature of employee benefit plans, IAS 19 provides for delayed recognition of certain cost components, such as those resulting from changes in actuarial estimates (i.e., changes are not recognized immediately but are recognized subsequently in a gradual and systematic way). Estimates and averages may be used as long as material differences do not result. Explicit assumptions and estimates of future events should be used for each specified variable included in pension costs.

The principal emphasis of IAS 19 is on calculation of the present value of the pension obligation, with somewhat less attention being directed toward determining the fair value of plan assets and structuring the disclosure of the elements of periodic pension costs. The main accounting problems revolve around the amount to be expensed on the income statement and the amount to be accrued on the balance sheet.

IAS 19 also establishes requirements for disclosures to be made by employers when defined contribution or defined benefit pension plans are settled, curtailed, or terminated. Some previously unrecognized amounts are required to be recognized immediately under such circumstances.

Although there are some major differences in terminology and measurement, accounting for other postemployment benefits basically follows the fundamental framework established for pension accounting. The most commonly encountered postretirement benefit is healthcare benefits granted either without charge or at reduced cost to retirees. IAS 19 does not address these concerns at any great length, but it does clearly suggest that these benefits constitute a form of deferred compensation and require accrual accounting. The expected costs should be attributed to the period that employees render services. The employer's obligation for postemployment benefits should be fully accrued when the employee attains full eligibility for all expected benefits.

Exposure Draft E54, if adopted, will significantly expand the requirements under IAS for accounting for the cost of not only pensions but of a range of other postemployment benefits commonly offered to employees or mandated by laws and regulations. Briefly, this would entirely replace existing IAS 19, and it would both narrow the current range of acceptable alternatives and enlarge the set of informative disclosures. Among other important changes, the new standard will eliminate all projected benefit valuation methods and permit only one version of the accrued benefit valuation method, create a "corridor" approach to recognition of actuarial gains and losses, demand annual valuations vs. the current triennial requirement, and address past service cost recognition and other matters never dealt with by the earlier standards. Per E54, implementation of a new standard would be phased in over as long as 3 years.

Sources of IAS

IAS 19

Exposure Draft E54

DEFINITIONS OF TERMS

Accrued benefit obligation. Actuarial present value of benefits (whether vested or nonvested) attributed by the pension benefit formula to employee service rendered before a specified date and based on employee service and compensation (if applicable) prior to that date. The accrued benefit obligation may differ from the projected benefit obligation in that it may include no assumption about future compensation levels. For plans with flat-benefit or no-pay-related pension benefit formulas, the accrued benefit obligation and the projected benefit obligation are the same.

Accrued benefit valuation methods. Actuarial valuation methods that reflect retirement benefits based on service rendered by employees to the date of the valuation. Assumptions about projected salary levels to the date of retirement must be incorporated.

Accrued pension cost. Cumulative net pension cost accrued in excess of the employer's contributions.

Accrued postretirement benefit obligation. The actuarial present value of benefits attributed to employee service rendered to a particular date. Prior to an employee's full eligibility date, the accrued postretirement benefit obligation as of a particular date for an employee is the portion of the expected postretirement benefit obligation attributed to that employee's service rendered to that date. On and after the full eligibility date, the accrued and expected postretirement benefit obligations for an employee are the same.

Actuarial present value. Value, as of a specified date, of an amount or series of amounts payable or receivable thereafter, with each amount adjusted to reflect (1) the time value of money (through discounts for interest) and (2) the probability of payment (by means of decrements for events such as death, disability, withdrawal, or retirement) between the date specified and the expected date of payment.

Actuarial valuation. The process used by actuaries to estimate the present value of benefits to be paid under a retirement plan and the present values of plan assets and sometimes also of future contributions.

Amortization. Usually refers to the process of reducing a recognized liability systematically by recognizing revenues or reducing a recognized asset systematically by recognizing expenses or costs. In pension accounting, amortization is also used to refer to the systematic recognition in net pension cost over several periods of previously unrecognized amounts, including unrecognized prior service cost and unrecognized net gain or loss.

Attribution. Process of assigning pension benefits or cost to periods of employee service.

Career-average-pay formula (career-average-pay plan). Benefit formula that bases benefits on the employee's compensation over the entire period of service with the employer. A career-average-pay plan is a plan with such a formula.

Contributory plan. Pension plan under which employees contribute part of the cost. In some contributory plans, employees wishing to be covered must contribute; in other contributory plans, employee contributions result in increased benefits.

Current service cost. The cost to the employer under a retirement benefit plan for the services rendered by employees during the period, exclusive of cost elements identified as past service cost, experience adjustments, and the effects of changes in actuarial assumptions.

Curtailment. Event that significantly reduces the expected years of future service of present employees or eliminates for a significant number of employees the accrual of defined benefits for some or all of their future services. Curtailments include (1) termination of employee's services earlier than expected, which may or may not involve closing a facility or discontinuing a segment of a business, and (2) termination or suspension of a plan so that employees do not earn additional defined benefits for future services. In the latter situation, future service may be counted toward vesting of benefits accumulated based on past services.

Defined benefit pension plan. Retirement benefit plans under which amounts to be paid as retirement benefits are determinable, usually by reference to employees' earnings and/or years of service.

Defined contribution pension plan. Benefit plans under which amounts to be paid as retirement benefits are determined by the contributions to a fund together with accumulated investment earnings thereon.

Expected long-term rate of return on plan assets. Assumption as to the rate of return on plan assets reflecting the average rate of earnings expected on the funds invested or to be invested to provide for the benefits included in the projected benefit obligation.

Expected postretirement benefit obligation. The actuarial present value as of a particular date of the benefits expected to be paid to or for an employee, the employee's beneficiaries, and any covered dependents pursuant to the terms of the postretirement benefit plan.

Expected return on plan assets. Amount calculated as a basis for determining the extent of delayed recognition of the effects of changes in the fair value of assets. The expected return on plan assets is determined based on the expected long-term rate of return on plan assets and the market related value of plan assets.

Experience adjustments. Adjustments to benefit costs arising from the differences between the previous actuarial assumptions as to future events and what actually occurred.

Fair value. Amount that a pension plan could reasonably expect to receive for an investment in a current sale between a willing buyer and a willing seller (i.e., in other than a forced or liquidation sale).

Final-pay plan. A defined benefit plan that promises benefits based on the employee's remuneration at or near the date of retirement. It may be the compensation of the final year, or of a specified number of years near the end of the employee's service period.

Flat-benefit formula (flat-benefit plan). Benefit formula that bases benefits on a fixed amount per year of service, such as $20 of monthly retirement income for each year of credited service. A flat-benefit plan is a plan with such a formula.

Fund. Used as a verb, to pay over to a funding agency (as to fund future pension benefits or to fund pension cost). Used as a noun, assets accumulated in the hands of a funding agency for the purpose of meeting pension benefits when they become due.

Funding. The irrevocable transfer of assets to an entity separate from the employer's enterprise, to meet future obligations for the payment of retirement benefits.

Gain or loss. Change in the value of either the projected benefit obligation or the plan assets resulting from experience different from that assumed or from a change in an actuarial assumption.

Gain or loss component (of net periodic pension cost). Sum of (1) the difference between the actual return on plan assets and the expected return on plan assets and (2) the amortization of the unrecognized net gain or loss from previous periods. The gain or loss component is the net effect of delayed recognition of gains and losses (the net change in the unrecognized net gain or loss) except that it does not include changes in the projected benefit obligation occurring during the period and deferred for later recognition.

Interest cost component (of net periodic pension cost). Increase in the accrued or projected benefit obligation due to the passage of time.

Measurement date. Date as of which plan assets and obligations are measured.

Mortality rate. Proportion of the number of deaths in a specified group to the number living at the beginning of the period in which the deaths occur. Actuaries use mortality tables, which show death rates for each age, in estimating the amount of pension benefits that will become payable.

Net periodic pension cost. Amount recognized in an employer's financial statements as the cost of a pension plan for a period. Components of net periodic pension cost are service cost, interest cost (which is implicitly presented as part of service cost), actual return on plan assets, gain or loss, amortization of unrecognized prior service cost, and amortization of the unrecognized net obligation or asset existing at the date of initial application of IAS 19.

Past service cost. The actuarially determined cost arising on the introduction of a retirement benefit plan, on the making of improvements to such a plan, or on the completion of minimum service requirements for eligibility in such a plan, all of which give employees credit for benefits for service prior to the occurrence of one or more of these events.

Pay-as-you-go. A method of recognizing the cost of retirement benefits only at the time that cash payments are made to employees on or after retirement.

Plan amendment. Change in terms of an existing plan or the initiation of a new plan. A plan amendment may increase benefits, including those attributed to years of service already rendered.

Postretirement benefits. All forms of benefits, other than retirement income, provided by an employer to retirees. Those benefits may be defined in terms of specified benefits, such as health care, tuition assistance, or legal services, that are provided to retirees as the need for those benefits arises, or they may be defined in terms of monetary amounts that become payable on the occurrence of a specified event, such as life insurance benefits.

Prepaid pension cost. Cumulative employer contributions in excess of accrued net pension cost.

Prior service cost. Cost of retroactive benefits granted in a plan amendment.

Projected benefit obligation. The actuarial present value as of a date of all benefits attributed by the pension benefit formula to employee service rendered prior to that date. The projected benefit obligation is measured using assumptions as to future compensation levels if the pension benefit formula is based on those future compensation levels (pay-related, final-pay, final-average-pay, or career-average-pay plans).

Projected benefit valuation methods. Actuarial valuation methods that reflect retirement benefits based on service both rendered and to be rendered by employees, as of the date of the valuation. Contrasted with accumulated benefit valuation methods, projected benefit valuation methods will result in a more level assignment of costs to the periods of employee service, although this will not necessarily be a straight-line allocation. Assumptions about projected salary levels must be incorporated.

Retirement benefit plans. Formal or informal arrangements whereby employers provide benefits for employees on or after termination of service, when such benefits can be determined or estimated in advance of retirement from the provisions of a document or from the employers' practices.

Retroactive benefits. Benefits granted in a plan amendment (or initiation) that are attributed by the pension benefit formula to employee services rendered in periods prior to the amendment. The cost of the retroactive benefits is referred to as prior service cost.

Service. Employment taken into consideration under a pension plan. Years of employment before the inception of a plan constitute an employee's past service;

years thereafter are classified in relation to the particular actuarial valuation being made or discussed. Years of employment (including past service) prior to the date of a particular valuation constitute prior service.

Settlement. Transaction that (1) is an irrevocable action, (2) relieves the employer (or the plan) of primary responsibility for a pension benefit obligation, and (3) eliminates significant risks related to the obligation and the assets used to effect the settlement. Examples include making lump-sum cash payments to plan participants in exchange for their rights to receive specified pension benefits and purchasing nonparticipating annuity contracts to cover vested benefits.

Terminal funding. A method of recognizing the projected cost of retirement benefits only at the time an employee retires.

Unrecognized prior service cost. Portion of prior service cost that has not been recognized as a part of net periodic pension cost.

Vested benefits. Those benefits, the rights to which, under the conditions of a retirement benefit plan, are not conditional on continued employment.

CONCEPTS, RULES, AND EXAMPLES

Importance of Pension Accounting

For a variety of cultural, economic, and political reasons, the existence of private pension plans has increased tremendously over the past 30 years, and these arrangements are the most common "fringe benefit" offered by employers in many nations. For many employers, pension costs have become a very material component of compensation paid to employees and can be an even bigger fraction of net operating results. Unlike the case with wages, the timing of the payment of cash, to either the plan's administrators or its beneficiaries, can vary substantially from the underlying economic event. This creates the possibility of misleading financial statement presentation of the true costs of conducting business. For this reason, accounting for the cost of pension plans and similar schemes (postretirement benefits other than pensions, etc.) has received a great deal of attention from national and international standards setters.

Basic Objectives of Accounting for Pension Costs

Need for pension accounting rules. The principal objectives of pension accounting are to measure the compensation cost associated with employees' benefits and to recognize that cost over the employees' service period. The relevant international accounting standard, IAS 19, is concerned only with the accounting aspects of pensions; the funding of pension benefits is considered to be a financial management matter and accordingly is not addressed by this pronouncement.

When an entity provides benefits, the amounts of which can be estimated in advance, to its retired employees and their beneficiaries, the arrangement is deemed to be a pension plan. The typical plan is written and the amount of benefits can be determined by reference to the plan documents. However, the plan and its provisions can also be implied from unwritten but established past practices. The accounting for most types of retirement plans is suggested by, if not heavily detailed in, IAS 19. Plans may be unfunded, insured, trust fund, defined contribution and defined benefit plans, and deferred compensation contracts, if equivalent. Independent (not employer sponsored) deferred profit sharing plans and pension payments made to selected employees on a case-by-case basis, are not considered pension plans.

The establishment of a pension plan represents a long-term commitment to employees. Although some entities manage their own plans, this commitment usually takes the form of contributions that are made to an independent trustee or, in some countries, to a governmental agency. These contributions are used by the trustee to acquire plan assets of various kinds, although the available types of investments may be restricted by governmental regulations in certain jurisdictions. Plan assets are used to generate a return, which typically consists of earned interest and/or appreciation in asset value.

The earnings from the plan assets (and occasionally, the proceeds from their liquidation) provides the trustee with cash to pay the benefits to which the employees become entitled. These benefits, in turn, are defined by the terms of the pension plan, which is known as the plan's benefit formula. In the case of defined benefit plans, the benefit formula incorporates many factors, including employee compensation, employee service longevity, employee age, and so on, and is considered to provide the best indication of pension obligations and costs. It is used as the basis for determining the pension cost recognized each fiscal year.

Income statement vs. balance sheet objectives. As the accounting requirements for pensions and other forms of postemployment benefits have evolved over the years, the primary objective has been to assign the periodic costs of such plans properly to the periods in which the related benefits are received by the employers incurring these costs. These benefits are obviously received when the workers are productively working on their jobs, not during the later years when they are enjoying their retirements. For that reason, accounting long ago recognized that the "pay-as-you-go" method of expense recognition, under which expense recognition would be deferred until the benefit payments to retirees were actually made, would cause an unacceptable mismatching of costs and benefits and a distortion of the income statement. The probable result of this mismatching would be the overstating of earlier years' results of operations and understating those of later years when large retirement payments are being made. As pensions and other fringe benefits expanded over the past generation to become a material and ever-increasing fraction of workers' compensation, this problem could no longer be ignored by accounting standards setters.

The reason that pay-as-you-go accounting was not eliminated completely long ago is that many pension plans and similar employee benefit plan arrangements are rather complex, and the accounting necessary to report on them properly is also difficult. Most significantly, in the case of defined benefit plans, actual costs may not be known for many years, even decades, since a variety of future events (employee turnover, performance of investments, salary increases, etc.) will affect the ultimate burden on the employer. Accordingly, the measurement of expense on a current basis demands that many complicated estimates be made, some involving actuarial computations, and accountants have often been reluctant to anchor the financial statements to estimates that are potentially very imprecise. Only when the impact of this method of accounting became unacceptably distortive, due to the growing occurrence and magnitude of these benefit plans, were professional standards revised to prohibit continued use of pay-as-you-go accounting.

As pensions became an almost universal fixture of the employment landscape (in some nations, private pensions are mandated by law; in other countries, participation in government-sponsored plans is required), the failure to require such accounting became an impediment to meaningful financial reporting. Notwithstanding the limitations of actuarial and other estimates, financial statements incorporating the accrual of pension costs are vastly more accurate and useful than those based on a pay-as-you-go approach.

Evolution of international accounting standards on pension costs. About 30 years ago, major accounting standard-setting bodies began urging that pension costs be accrued properly in financial statements. At first, a wide range of actuarial methods were permitted, each of which could produce more meaningful results than the pay-as-you- go method, but over time the range of options permitted has been narrowed in major jurisdictions.

As presently constituted, pension accounting rules have tended to focus overwhelmingly on the income statement. That is, the dominant objective has been to match income and expense properly on a current basis, so that the periodic measurement of operating performance is within the bounds of material accuracy.

It has been less clear that the meaningful presentation of the balance sheet has been a priority, however. Thus, even when an employer has retained full responsibility for the ultimate payment of pension benefits (as with defined benefit plans), the employer's statement of financial position has usually excluded a complete representation of the assets and obligations of the pension scheme. This has been due partly to the fact that various "smoothing" approaches have been made to expense measurement, causing the balance sheet (given the rigors of double-entry bookkeeping) to become the repository for the resulting deferred charges and credits and thus making the overall picture from the balance sheet side less meaningful. Furthermore, accountants have been genuinely ambivalent about the validity of presenting information about the assets and obligations of the pension plan on the face of the employer's balance sheet, believing that the pension plan constitutes a separate economic and reporting entity.

The evolution of accounting thought concerning reporting employer's pension costs and obligations can be illustrated by reference to the standards developed in the United States. The first modern US standard on pension accounting, APB Opinion 8 (promulgated in 1966), required that the principles of accrual accounting be employed for pension costs. Although this prescription hardly seems newsworthy today, it was significant at the time, since pay-as-you-go accounting had been the most prevalent previous practice. However, while APB 8 demanded that "matching" of some sort be accomplished, it left the methodology of accomplishing this worthy goal undefined.

APB 8, accordingly, was widely criticized for permitting the use of too great a variety of costing methods, making it very difficult to compare results across enterprises. Also, under APB 8 the financial statements did not contain a meaningful disclosure about the amount of the entity's actual future obligation (particularly in the case of defined benefit plans, which were then utilized predominantly by large enterprises). This limitation was largely alleviated with the promulgation of SFAS 36, which mandated a series of footnote disclosures about the actuarial position of the plan itself in the financial statements of the sponsor. Although this did not place the plan's assets and obligations on the employers' balance sheets, it did for the first time give users of financial statements the ability to assess such concerns as underfunding.

The experience under international accounting standards has mirrored that of the United States. The original IAS 19, released in 1983, permitted either accrued benefit or projected benefit valuation methods to be used in determining periodic pension cost. However, the standard prohibited use of pay-as-you-go or other methods that did not have as goals the matching of the costs of future pension benefits against the proper periods in which the workers earned those payments. Neither of the two major approaches to the measurement of periodic pension cost, accrued benefit and projected benefit, was identified as being conceptually superior. In this regard, the rule was very similar to that adopted in the United Kingdom, where both valuation methodologies were (and still are) viewed as being equally acceptable.

APB 8 and SFAS 36 were superseded in the United States in 1986 by SFAS 87 (and its companion standard, SFAS 88, addressing plan curtailments and related matters). SFAS 87 was, in many respects, the role model for the recent revision of IAS 19. However, IAS 19 (revised) differs from SFAS 87 in a number of important regards: It does not require extensive footnote disclosures (but does not prohibit them, either); is not as prescriptive in defining how many of the cost factors (e.g., plan amendments, actuarial gains and losses) are to be allocated; and does not identify a single actuarial method to be used to compute pension costs. Nonetheless, this newly revised standard does in fact borrow heavily from SFAS 87. The expected replacement for existing IAS 19, as set forth in the currently outstanding Exposure Draft E54, will conform the international standards much more closely to the US GAAP rules, greatly expand the required disclosures, and for the first time offer guidance on accounting for the cost of other postemployment benefits.

Comparison to requirements of other standard-setting bodies. SFAS 87, the relevant US GAAP standard, requires that periodic pension cost be measured with reference to the **projected** benefit obligation, which take into account future salary progression for those plans that determine pension benefits with reference to final pay or career average pay levels. That is, the pension costs recognized in the current year include a component that reflects the pay increases which are projected to occur in later years and which will affect the ultimate pension benefits to be paid. This feature was one of the more controversial features of the standard when it was proposed: Not only does this greatly complicate the determination of periodic pension cost, but it can be argued that it is improper to consider possible future decisions, such as salary adjustments which may or may not be granted, in the computation of current period expense.

The validity of the first-named objection can readily be conceded: It clearly is more difficult to consider future salary progression than to ignore it. However, for most entities that operate in major industries, there is usually sufficient history and experience to enable actuaries to forecast salary progressions meaningfully. Furthermore, the relative sensitivity of the computed pension expense to such assumptions and projections can be conveyed to financial statements users, such as by reporting the dollar impact of a 1% change in the underlying salary progression assumption, although few reporting entities have thus far chosen to do this.

The latter objection is more difficult to dismiss. A reasonable argument can be made that the current period's pension cost should be based on those facts and circumstances existing in the current period. Thus, it can be held that the salaries in effect, including any scheduled increases, such as under union or management contracts in effect at the balance sheet date, which will be enacted automatically, should be used in this computation, without attempting to speculate about other possible future changes in compensation. This approach would hold that the venerable "matching principle" would best be served by deferring recognition of future cost increases caused by decisions made in future periods to these later periods. Thus, under this theory, if management grants wage increases in 1998 that will affect pension benefits, financial statement recognition of those actions should be delayed to 1998 and subsequent years.

The opposing argument is that given a long tradition of wage inflation, it is more than mere speculation to project future cost increases. This position holds that the compliance with the spirit of the matching principle demands that all reasonably anticipated costs necessary to generate the current period's revenues be given recognition. Since the cost of future pension benefits will probably include the effects of increases to be granted in later years, proper matching will not be achieved if these are deferred. Even though these future benefit increases are not a contractual obligation, if the past behavior of management makes these cost increases at least likely to occur and subject to reasonable estimation, then in the interest of accurate financial reporting these should be given appropriate current recognition.

The UK rule contrasts with that in the United States. The pertinent standard, SSAP 24, does not prescribe a particular valuation method, but only dictates that pension cost be recognized on a systematic and rational basis over the working lives of the employees participating in the plan. Both accrued benefit and projected benefit approaches are thus permitted, and indeed both are popular. Furthermore, a variety of specific actuarial costing methods are employed under each of these approaches. As a consequence, the comparability of financial reporting by entities complying with UK GAAP is inferior to that under the current US GAAP.

Basic Principles of IAS 19

Benefit plans addressed by the standard. IAS 19 is applicable to all retirement benefits regardless of the forms of plans, be they formal or informal, written or verbal, defined contribution or defined benefit, funded or unfunded. The standard also covers employer participation in multiemployer plans and contributions made to national or other plans. Finally, the standard is applicable to employment termination agreements, to the extent that these meet the technical definition of retirement benefit plans.

Implicitly, the principles set forth in IAS 19 apply also to other forms of employee remuneration plans, including other postemployment benefit plans (such as those providing continuing health insurance coverage after retirement), other forms of health and welfare programs, and extended leave plans. Although the standard does not address these directly, it is clear that the same underlying concepts, to achieve proper matching of the cost of these employment arrangements with the periods in which the services are provided, are applicable. The expected replacement for IAS 19 will be much more explicit in addressing the accounting for the costs associated with other types of postemployment and postretirement benefit plans.

Although there are myriad types of plans in existence, the most critical distinction is between defined contribution and defined benefit plans. The former promises retirees only those benefits that can be financed from the accumulated assets in the plan, which resulted from employer contributions (usually based on a formula related to wages paid currently), employee contributions (often voluntary, but sometimes required by company policy or local law), and the earnings that have been amassed thereon. Often, typically under terms of "self-directed" plans, the workers will be given a choice of investments in which their respective shares of the contributions can be placed, and they will individually enjoy the rewards of wise picks or suffer the consequences of poor selections.

Defined benefit plans, on the other hand, are quite different in terms of investment policy and ultimate risk. Employees are promised certain benefits upon retirement, and it is the employer's task to generate the assets necessary to fund those payments. The investments in the retirement fund may or may not be adequate to meet these commitments, but the sufficiency or lack thereof should be completely transparent to the beneficiaries. In fact, it is not even necessary for the plan to be funded at all; the employer can simply wait until the employees retire to make these payments out of its own treasury. Since the employer bears the full risk, workers will typically not have any voice in how the pension contributions are invested.

Although an accounting strategy based on pension plan contributions currently made might reasonably approximate the actual cost (properly determined) when defined contribution plans are employed, the very different characteristics of defined benefit plans makes such an approach completely unacceptable. Thus, for defined benefit plans, real accrual basis accounting is an absolute necessity.

Cost recognition distinguished from funding practices. Although sound management practice may be to fund retirement benefit plans on a current basis, in some jurisdictions the requirement to do this is either limited or absent entirely. Furthermore, in some jurisdictions the currently available tax deduction for contributions to pension plans may be limited, reducing the incentive to make such contributions until such time as the funds are actually needed for making payouts to retirees. Since the objective of periodic financial reporting is to match costs and revenues properly on a current basis, the pattern of funding is obviously not a useful guide to proper accounting for pension costs.

Accrued benefit vs. projected benefit valuation methods. For defined benefit plans, there are two major approaches to computing an entity's pension obligation at any given point in time. The first of these, employing what are referred to as **accrued** (or **accumulated**) **benefit methods**, are based on services provided by employees through the date of valuation, without considering future services to be rendered by them. Periodic pension cost is a function, accordingly, of services that are provided in the current period. Since the obligation for future pension payments is computed as the discounted present value of the amounts to be paid in later years, accrued benefit methods will calculate increasing charges (even if wage levels are constant) as employees approach retirement, since the present values of future payments will increase as the time to retirement shortens. Periodic charges also increase, in most actual instances, because attrition rates (employees who leave, thereby forfeiting their rights to retirement payments) decline over time, since older employees show less inclination to change employment. While wages will typically increase over time as employees age, both due to compensation increases due to seniority and performance improvements, and as a result (if the past is any guide) of ongoing wage inflation, this should not be the cause of increasing pension costs as time to retirement grows shorter, since even accrued benefit valuation methods must be based on assumptions about future salary progression. While obviously, over time, these assumptions and expectations cannot be precisely accurate, the presumption should be that "estimation errors" will be randomly distributed, and that over the long run good-faith estimates of salary progression, and the resultant effects on periodic pension costs, will be fairly accurate. Consequently, periodic pension costs should not drift upward as employees age because of wage increases.

The second approach, the **projected** benefit valuation method, uses actuarial estimation techniques that consider both the services already rendered as well as those to be rendered by the employees. The goal is to allocate the entire retirement cost smoothly over each employee's respective working life. The pension obligation at any point in time is computed as the present value of the aggregate future payments earned to the balance sheet date. As with accrued benefit valuation methods, future salary progression must be taken into account in determining periodic pension costs over the working lives of employees. The difference, however, is that future costs are spread more evenly over the full period of employment (although this does not imply that straight-line allocation is an absolute requirement), as compared to the accrued benefit valuation methods, and, in particular, pension related costs will not show the constantly increasing pattern exhibited by the alternative approach simply due to the shortening time horizon as retirement dates draw near.

As already noted, proponents of accrued and projected benefit valuation approaches have claimed that the matching concept underlies their preferred method. For large employers having a work force comprised of individuals of all ages, and which typically replace older retiring workers with younger ones, pension costs will be similar under either method on an aggregate basis. While pension costs relative to older workers will be higher, and costs relating to younger workers will be lower, if the accrued benefit valuation method is used vs. what would be reflected if the projected benefit valuation method were used, with a stable mix of ages of workers, this will not significantly vary. For smaller employers, or those with a work force skewed toward younger or older workers, then holding all other considerations constant, the periodic pattern of pension costs will diverge under these two methods.

The original international accounting standard on pension costs, issued in 1983 as IAS 19, did not stipulate any specific actuarial valuation method or even indicate a preference for one. Revised IAS 19, issued in 1993 for application beginning in 1995, designated the accrued benefit valuation method as the "benchmark treatment," with the projected benefit valuation method also endorsed as the "allowed alternative" method. Under the provisions of E54, however, projected benefit valuation methods would be eliminated entirely from the realm of acceptability, and only one accrued benefit valuation method, the "projected unit credit method," would be allowed, thus conforming to the requirement under current US GAAP. Since Exposure Draft E54 proposes that the new standard, if adopted, be phased in over 3 years, the currently available alternative methods of determining periodic pension cost will remain important for some time to come.

The accrued and projected benefit methods are discussed and illustrated in greater detail later in this chapter.

Net Periodic Pension Cost

General discussion. Absent specific information to the contrary, it is assumed that a company will continue to provide retirement benefits well into the future. The accounting for the plan's costs should be reflected in the financial statements and these amounts should not be discretionary. All pension costs should be charged against income. No amounts should be charged directly to retained earnings.

The benefits earned and costs recognized over the employees' service period must be attributed by the pension plan's benefit formula. The amount of expense to be recognized currently depends largely on two matters: (1) whether the plan in substance is a defined contribution or a defined benefit plan, and (2) if a defined benefit plan, whether an accrued benefit or a projected benefit approach to valuation, will be taken.

Periodic measurement of cost for defined contribution plans. Under the terms of a defined contribution plan (in some cases referred to as a "money purchase" plan), the employer will be obligated for fixed or determinable contributions in each period, often computed as a percentage of the wage and salary base paid to the covered employees during the period. For one example, contributions might be set at 4% of each employee's wages and salaries, up to $50,000 wages per annum. Generally, the contributions must actually be made by a specific date, such as 90 days after the end of the enterprise's fiscal year, consistent with local law. The expense must be accrued for accounting purposes in the year the cost is incurred, whether the contribution is made currently or not.

Employers may make further, discretionary contributions to benefit plans in certain periods. For example, if the entity enjoys a particularly profitable year, the board of directors may vote to grant another 2% of wages as a bonus contribution to the employees' benefit plan. The extent to which this is done will depend, among other factors, on the tax laws of the relevant jurisdiction. Normally, an enterprise making such a discretionary contribution does not do so simply to reward past performance by its workers. Rather, it does so in the belief that the gesture will cause its employees to be motivated to be more productive and loyal in the forthcoming years.

For this reason, IAS 19 stipulates that the cost of any extra, discretionary contributions are to be recognized as expense over the periods to be benefited, which may conceivably include future periods as well as the current one. The standard does not address the question of how such costs are to be allocated, however. For example, if management believes that the current and the following 5 years will be benefited, the discretionary contribution should presumably be expensed one-sixth currently, with the remaining balance amortized one-fifth per year. Arguably, however, the "halo effect" of a bonus contribution in the current year will persist for only a few years, with the positive motivational effects declining each year, which might suggest that a "declining balance" method of amortization might be more appropriate. This would seemingly be acceptable under the standard, but the assumptions underlying such an unorthodox methodology would need to be documented carefully, and the possibility of additional disclosure in the financial statements would have to be considered.

Example of disclosure for defined contribution pension plan

> Panhellenic Tours contributes 5% of employee qualifying salaries to a defined contribution pension program each year. These contributions are included in compensation expense currently. Furthermore, in 1996 the company made a further 2% contribution to the plan, in appreciation of the outstanding efforts of its employees during the period. Based on past experience, management believes that this added, discretionary contribution will benefit the company for 4 years; accordingly, one-fourth of this contribution is included in compensation cost in 1996; the remainder will be expensed ratably in 1997, 1998, and 1999.

Past service costs arise when a plan is amended retroactively, so that additional contributions are made with respect to services rendered in past years. For example, if a plan formerly required contributions of 5% of salaries and is amended retroactively to provide for contributions of 6%, an extra 1% of each employee's aggregate salary for all prior years will be transferred to the employee's pension account. When plans are amended in this fashion, it is generally management's belief that it will provide an incentive for greater efforts in the future. Past service costs incurred in connection with defined contribution plans are accounted for in the same manner as additional, discretionary contributions. Generally, the costs should be amortized over each employee's expected remaining service (working) life; the use of reasonable averages would be acceptable for this purpose. To the extent that some of the past service costs are incurred with respect to retired employees, however, those costs would need to be fully expensed in the current period. It should be noted that E54 has proposed that past service costs, such as those which result from plan amendments which grant retroactive benefit increases, be either amortized over the remaining working lives of affected employees or charged to expense immediately; the IASC has indicated that, based on response it receives to the draft, one of these methods will be selected for mandatory application. Under both current and proposed rules, however, retroactive amendments affecting former employees who have already retired must be expensed immediately, since there can be no argument that the employer will reap any goodwill or other benefits by granting such increases to workers no longer on duty.

Terminations of defined contribution plans generally provide no difficulties from an accounting perspective, since costs had been recognized currently in most instances. However, if certain costs, such as those associated with past services and with discretionary bonus contributions made in past years, have not yet been fully amortized, the remaining unrecognized portions of those costs must be expensed in the period when it becomes probable that the plan is to be terminated. This should be the period when the decision to terminate is made, which on occasion may precede the actual termination of the plan.

Periodic measurement of cost for defined benefit plans. Defined benefit plans present a far greater challenge to accountants than do defined contribution plans, since the amount of expense to be recognized currently will need to be determined on an actuarial basis. This will be the case whether the benchmark treatment (using the accrued benefit valuation method) or the allowed alternative treatment (using the projected benefit valuation method) is utilized. Both of these methods are discussed at length in the following sections of this chapter.

Conceptually, net periodic pension cost will consist of the sum of the following six components:

1. Current (pure) service cost
2. Interest cost for the current period on the accrued or projected benefit obligation
3. Past service costs
4. Experience adjustments
5. Effects of changes in actuarial assumptions
6. Amortization of unrecognized net asset or net obligation existing at date of initial application of IAS 19

IAS 19 does not separately address each of these elements; in particular, interest cost is dealt with implicitly as part of current service cost. However, for purposes of explaining the accounting for defined benefit plans, these will be made explicit in the following discussion. It is interesting to note, furthermore, that if the proposed changes incorporated in E54 are adopted, these pension cost elements will have to be presented in the footnote disclosures, in a manner very similar to what is now required under US GAAP (SFAS 87).

Current service cost. Current service cost must be determined by an actuarial valuation method and will be affected by assumptions such as expected turnover of staff, average retirement age, the plan's vesting schedule, and life expectancy after retirement. If the projected benefit method is used, the probable progression of wages over the employees' remaining working lives will also have to be taken into consideration if retirement benefits will be affected by levels of compensation in later years. Under the accrued benefit valuation method, on the other hand, future salary increases not presently contractually guaranteed are typically ignored, but the other factors noted above will be considered.

Under IAS 19, current service cost also implicitly incorporates a factor for interest on the accrued or projected benefit obligation. This occurs because the actuarial present value of future benefits at the current reporting date is compared to the equivalent amount a year earlier, with the difference being denoted as current period service cost. Thus, the passage of time is automatically incorporated as a computational element, but conceptually this is a separate matter. (Under US GAAP, for example, service cost and interest cost are treated explicitly as different components of pension cost.) For clarity, it is addressed separately in this chapter while recognizing that for financial reporting purposes it may be merged with service cost.

To explain the concept of service cost, assume a single employee who is promised a pension of $1,000 per year for each year worked before retirement, for life, upon retirement at age 60 or thereafter. Further assume that this is the worker's first year on the job, and he is 30 years of age. The consulting actuary determines that if the worker, in fact, retires at age 60, he will have a life expectancy of 15 years, and at the present value of the required benefits ($1,000/yr x 15 years = $15,000) discounted at the appropriate settlement rate for a commercial annuity policy, 8%, equals $8,560. In other words, based on the work performed thus far (1 year's worth), this employee has earned the right to a lump sum settlement of $8,560 at age 60. Since this is 30 years into the future, this amount must be reduced to present value, which at 8% is a mere $851, which is the pension cost to be recognized currently (this assumes the benchmark treatment, the accrued benefit method, as discussed further below).

In year 2, this worker earns the right to yet another annuity stream of $1,000 per year upon retirement, which has, again, a present value of $8,560 at the projected retirement age of 60. However, since age 60 is now only 29 years hence, the present value of that promised benefit at the end of the current (second) year is $919, which represents the service cost in year 2. This pattern will continue: As the employee ages, the current cost of pension benefits grows apace, with (for example) the cost in the final working year being $8,560, before considering interest on the previously accumulated obligation--which would, however, add another $18,388 of expense, for a total cost for this one employee in his final working year of $26,948. It should be noted, however, that in "real life" situations, for employee groups in the aggregate, this may not hold, since new, younger employees will be added as older employees die or retire, which will tend to smooth out the annual cost of the plan.

There is one other aspect to the current pension cost, however. The $851 obligation recorded in the first year of the example above will have grown to $919 by the end of the second year. IAS 19 does not address this directly, unlike the corresponding US standard, SFAS 87 (discussed immediately below). The implication is that this $68 increase in the obligation for future benefits, due to the passage of time, is under IAS 19 included in current pension cost in year 2. Thus, current pension cost of $987 ($919 + $68) would be reported in year 2.

If the allowed alternative (projected benefit) approach were employed in the foregoing example, greater cost would be recognized in the early years of the employee's working life, since the actuarial determination will now be based on service provided and service to be provided. In the present example, it will be projected that the employee will remain on the job for 30 years, thereby earning an annual pension of $30,000, which will have a discounted present value at retirement of $256,800. This amount would be spread evenly over the employee's working life, for an annual cost of about $8,560. That is, the pension cost associated with this worker would be $8,560 in the first year of his working life and every year thereafter. (There are a number of actuarial valuation methods, and this simplified illustration is intended only to contrast the benchmark treatment with the allowed alternative.)

Interest on the accrued or projected benefit obligation. As noted, since the actuarial determination of current period cost is the present value of the future pension benefits to be paid to retirees by virtue of their service in the current period, the longer the time until the expected retirement date, the lower will be the service cost recognized. However, over time this accrued cost must be further increased, until at the employees' respective retirement dates the full amounts of the promised payments have been accreted. In this regard, the accrued pension liability is much like a sinking fund that grows from contributions plus the earnings thereon.

Under IAS 19, the interest component is effectively included in current service cost, although conceptually these are separate elements. That is, what is referred to as current service cost includes not only the "pure" current service cost for benefits earned during the reporting period, but also the growth in previously accumulated pension costs during the current period, due to the mere passage of time. There is no requirement to present these components of pension expense separately, either in the income statement itself or in the accompanying footnotes. Under the provisions of E54, however, interest cost will be explicitly presented as a component of pension cost.

Other elements of benefit cost. IAS 19 presents only a brief description of the elements of pension cost other than current service cost. The standard notes that the other cost components, which include past service costs, experience adjustments, the effects of changes in actuarial assumptions, and the effects of plan amendments, should generally be recognized as expense (or, in some cases, as income) systematically over the expected remaining working lives of the employees. The standard does not suggest how these costs should be recognized; that is, whether straight-line amortization should be used in all cases, or whether some form of "front end loading" might be advisable or even justifiable. However, if expenses are expected to benefit the employer over a shorter period, that should be used to determine the amount of periodic expense.

The only exceptions to the foregoing, where recognition of costs would be over a period other than the expected remaining working lives of the employees, arise in the case of plan terminations and some plan amendments. Regarding plan terminations, logic would suggest that any remaining deferrals of experience adjustments and other pension cost elements should be charged immediately to pension expense when it becomes probable that a defined benefit plan will be terminated or substantially curtailed, since there will be few or no future periods over which these costs could be amortized. (Settlements and curtailments are discussed further below.)

Plan amendments. Plan amendments are similar to discretionary contributions made to defined contribution plans: Management's expectation would normally be that the workers to whom the bonuses were distributed would be more productive in the future. Realistically, the periods to be benefited in such cases might be few in number. Accordingly, amortization over the entire remaining working lives of the employees granted such a plan amendment would not be an accurate reflection of the real underlying economics, and amortization over a much shorter period might instead be warranted. The length of the period is a matter of management judgment, but IAS 19 does suggest that the length of time until the next expected plan amendment (when there is a basis for defining such an expectation) would be a maximum amortization period. E54, as written, would require that past service costs, such as from plan amendments, be either amortized over the remaining working lives of affected employees or charged to expense immediately; but the IASC has indicated that, based on the response it receives to the draft, only one of these methods will be selected and application will be mandatory. Under both current and proposed rules, however, retroactive amendments affecting former employees who have already retired must be expensed immediately, since there can be no argument that the employer will reap any goodwill or other benefits by granting such increases to workers no longer employed.

Past service costs. Past service costs refer to the credit given, upon the adoption of a pension program, to employees for work done prior to that date. Unless otherwise directed by local laws, employers need not credit years of service accumulated before a plan is initiated, but often they will grant this benefit so that employees with lengthy service will not be resentful of the benefits that younger workers will eventually receive. Conceptually, it could be argued that the costs associated with prior service are "sunk costs" having no future benefit to the entity. However, while it is not possible to demonstrate empirically the future utility associated with prior service costs, the existence of future value is suggested indirectly by the fact that without the expectation of receiving a benefit, management would not make such contributions. Accordingly, past service costs are deferred and recognized over a period of time equal to the average remaining service lives of those workers employed at the date the plan is implemented.

IAS 19 does not distinguish plan amendments from past service costs arising from the initial adoption of a pension scheme. The latter refers only to the accumulated benefits assigned to existing employees at the date the plan is first adopted, while the former is the equivalent situation arising from later plan amendments. (In the United States, although APB 8 did make a distinction between past service cost and prior service cost, as the effects of plan amendments were then known, the later

SFAS 87 eliminated the distinction.) While past service costs arising from the adoption of a new plan can only be an expense item, plan amendments can give rise to either expense or income, depending on whether benefits are being expanded or trimmed back. However, as a practical matter, amendments that reduce the benefits to be granted to existing workers may occur only infrequently, such as when an entity is in economic difficulty and the employees have agreed to assist to solve its problems.

Experience adjustments. Experience adjustments are made to recognize the fact that actual employee turnover, retirement ages, and other events will almost always develop differently from expectations. As a consequence, contributions to the plans will have to be adjusted over time, and similarly the amounts to be recognized as pension expense will need to be modified. IAS 19 states that these adjustments are to be smoothed out by amortizing over the remaining working lives of the employees. However, the standard does not stipulate precisely how this is to be accomplished. Thus, a question remains whether each year's experience adjustment must be accounted for separately, and amortized over the average remaining working lives of the employees at work on that date, or whether a "rolling average" approach can be taken as an expedient.

Experience adjustments also would include, for funded plans, the effect of investments that earn at rates different from what had been anticipated. For example, plan trustees may have expected that its portfolio would gain an average of 8% in value per year, but after a period of time it becomes apparent that the real annual earnings rate is only 5%. This means that larger contributions will have to be made to the plan, over time, to accumulate the funds needed to service the retirement benefits that have been promised. This also means that the amounts to be recognized as pension expense will have to be increased. Since it is inevitable that actual earnings on plan assets will differ from assumptions, these adjustments will occur regularly. IAS 19 states that these are to be amortized to expense over the working lives of the employees active when the discrepancies are computed.

It should be noted that the approach taken under US GAAP seems to be helpful in the latter regard. Under SFAS 87 the accumulated experience adjustments (which are referred to as "unrecognized gains and losses" in that standard) are deferred but amortized only if they exceed a threshold level (a condition referred to as "exceeding the corridor"). The logic is that, over time, the gains and losses will tend to offset and, effectively, cancel each other out, without the need for recognition in pension expense. Only when this natural offsetting is not occurring (which under the US standard is signaled when the unrecognized gain or loss exceeds 10% of the amount of plan assets or the actuarially determined projected benefit obligation, whichever is greater) will amortization of the excess amount begin. The advantage of the US GAAP approach is that, in most cases, unrecognized gains or losses will not be subjected to amortization, thereby reducing the computational complexity of pension cost determination.

In connection with this matter, IAS 19 states that "experience adjustments are *usually* allocated." This has caused some to question whether amortization is always required or whether a methodology analogous to that prescribed under US GAAP could properly be applied. Since the standard does not further discuss this and offers no overt support for a corridor approach, the authors conclude that to conform to the spirit of IAS 19, amortization is required without exception. On the other hand, it would appear to be defensible not to recompute the average of the remaining working lives each year, but rather, absent a material change about which management is aware, to employ an approximation, subject to a redetermination made at regular intervals (such as the triennial actuarial determinations otherwise mandated by the standard) that over time the accounting for these adjustments continues to be reasonable. E54 proposes a recognition threshold for actuarial gains and losses much like the US GAAP approach, with a 10% corridor within which such gains or losses would not be currently recognized, in the hope that future offsetting losses or gains will eliminate the deferred amount. However, the US GAAP requirement is that amounts in excess of the 10% corridor would be subject to amortization, whereas the IASC exposure draft calls for immediate full recognition of the amount falling outside the corridor.

Changes in actuarial assumptions arise from the periodic reevaluation of certain factors affecting the ultimate pension costs to be borne by the enterprise, including expected long-term return on invested amounts and the effective discount rate to be applied to future benefit obligations in computing current service cost. For example, in periods of rising interest rates, there will be a favorable impact on the current service costs accumulated up to the present balance sheet date, since the present value of a future obligation falls as rates rise. (Of course, the charge to expense for the interest component will grow correspondingly in future years, but this will be addressed by future actuarial determinations of current period expense.) IAS 19 states that the effects of changes in actuarial assumptions should also be amortized to pension cost over the working lives of current employees.

Transition adjustment. The final element of periodic pension cost under IAS 19 relates to the effect of first adopting the accounting standard. The transitional provisions of IAS 19 offer a choice of two methods. First, consistent with IAS 8's provisions concerning changes in accounting policies, the provisions of IAS 19 may be applied retrospectively. The effect is to record an asset or a liability for the cumulative effect of the change, depending on whether or not the cumulative amount of pension cost recognized in prior periods was more or less than would have been recognized had the provisions of IAS 19 been applied, respectively. This transitional asset or liability will be amortized to pension expense over future periods, although the standard is silent as to how this is to be accomplished.

Second, rather than to record the transitional asset or liability formally, as prescribed by IAS 8, IAS 19 permits merely disclosing the amount of the unrecognized cumulative effect in the period of adoption, and disclosing any remaining unrecognized amounts each subsequent period for which financial statements are prepared. Amortization over a period no longer than the remaining working lives of participating employees is prescribed in this case (and logically would be the correct approach if the transitional asset or liability were formally recorded, as well).

Effect of change in actuarial valuation method used. As discussed above, IAS 19 permits two very different valuation methods to be used in determining the amount of pension obligation at the balance sheet date and thus the pension expense for the period then ended. As noted, the accrued benefit obligation method computes the present value of future benefits earned as a result of services already rendered, while the projected benefit obligation approach calculates the present value of future benefits earned and to be earned. The principal distinction between the methods relates to the impact of future likely salary increases when the benefit formula is based on final pay or average pay.

Although the accrued benefit method has been denoted the benchmark treatment and the projected benefit method the available alternative treatment, entities can change from one method to another. When that occurs, IAS 19 stipulates that the effect of the change should be accounted for, and disclosed as, a change in accounting policy in accordance with IAS 8. That standard (discussed in greater detail in Chapter 19) provides both benchmark and alternative treatments.

The benchmark treatment is to account for the change on a retrospective basis, with the adjustment taken to retained earnings as of the beginning of the earliest year being presented, and comparative periods being restated accordingly. The available alternative treatment is to apply the new method of accounting retrospectively as well, but to include the effect of the change in the current period's income statement (as a special item, the cumulative effect of a change in an accounting principle). Prior periods are not restated if presented for comparative purposes, although disclosure, on a pro forma basis, is required unless impracticable to do so.

Specific Actuarial Methods Permitted by the Standard

IAS 19 permits either accrued benefit or projected benefit valuation methods to be used, and a number of specific actuarial methods have been developed in making the computation of pension cost under either of these broad approaches. However, not all methods used by actuaries would be deemed to be consistent with the requirements of the standard. In particular, certain methods (which are entirely valid from the perspective of actuarial science, it should be stressed) do not separately address past service cost and/or experience adjustments, but rather, include these implicitly in current service cost. The effect is that IAS 19's prescription that past service cost and experience adjustments be amortized over the remaining working lives of the employees affected could not be met. For that reason, these actuarially valid methods would not be useful in computing periodic pension cost in accordance with the standard.

The principal accrued benefit method in use, which conforms with the requirements of IAS 19, is the "projected unit credit method." Acceptable projected benefit methods include the "entry age normal" and "attained age normal" methods. Projected benefit methods which are probably not consistent with the requirements of IAS 19 include the "individual level premium" and "aggregate" methods, as these do not distinguish past service costs from current benefit costs. Details on these computational techniques are not presented here, as these are the province of actuaries, not accountants. However, the accountant must ascertain that one of the acceptable methods is being used if actuarial data are being employed to determine the accounting for (rather than merely the funding of) the plan.

Of course, if the proposals in E54 are enacted, none of the currently allowable projected benefit valuation methods will be usable, and only the projected unit credit version of the accrued valuation benefit method will be permitted as a means of computing periodic pension cost. This will conform IAS to US GAAP and, more importantly, eliminate a source of wide variations in the amounts being reported as pension cost. This change, if it occurs, will take as long as 3 years to be implemented, so the methods discussed earlier will continue to be of interest for some time into the future.

Employer's Liabilities and Assets

IAS 19 has as its primary, possibly sole, concern the measurement of periodic expense incurred in connection with pension plans of employers. One source of dissatisfaction with the standard is its failure to address the assets or liabilities that may be recognized on the employers' balance sheets as a consequence of expense recognition, which may include deferral of certain items (e.g., past service costs). In fact, the amounts that may find their way onto the balance sheet will often not meet the strict definition of assets or liabilities, but rather, will be "deferred charges or credits." This will consist of the cumulative difference between the amount funded and the amount expensed over the life of the plan.

IAS 19 has been criticized for not requiring, under appropriate circumstances, recognition of an additional, or minimum, liability when plans are materially underfunded. The point of comparison is SFAS 87, which does demand that this minimum liability, which results when the accumulated (accrued) benefit obligation exceeds the fair value of plan assets and a liability in the amount of the difference is not already recorded as unfunded accrued pension cost. Under the corresponding US standard, SFAS 87, the additional minimum liability is recognized by an offset to an intangible asset up to the amount of unrecognized prior service cost. Any additional debit needed is considered a loss and is shown net of tax benefits as a separate component reducing equity. If E54 is adopted, the balance sheet will reflect the net debit or credit associated with the plan assets and obligations. The amount to be presented as an asset or liability will be computed as the net, as of the balance sheet date, of the present value of the benefit obligation, any unrecognized actuarial gains or losses (i.e., those falling inside the 10% "corridor"), any unrecognized past service cost with respect to current employees (being amortized over their respective working lives), and the market value of plan assets. This approach will differ markedly from the method used under US GAAP, where a so-called "minimum liability" is computed with reference only to the shortfall of plan assets vs. what SFAS 87 calls the accumulated benefit obligation, which is the present value of future benefits less the portion which is expected to result from salary progression. E54 does not have a parallel concept, but will go much further towards putting the totality of plan assets and obligations on the employer's balance sheet.

Other Pension Considerations

If an entity has more than one plan, IAS 19 provisions should be applied separately to each plan. Offsets or eliminations are not allowed unless there clearly is the right to use the assets in one plan to pay the benefits of another plan.

Participation in a multiemployer plan (to which two or more unrelated employers contribute) requires that the contribution for the period be recognized as net pension cost and that any contributions due and unpaid be recognized as a liability. Assets in this type of plan are usually commingled and are not segregated or restricted. A board of trustees usually administers these plans, and multiemployer plans are generally subject to a collective bargaining agreement. If there is a withdrawal from this type of plan and if an arising obligation is either probable or reasonably possible, the provisions of international accounting standards that address contingencies (IAS 10) apply.

Some plans are, in substance, a pooling or aggregation of single employer plans and are ordinarily without collective-bargaining agreements. Contributions are usually based on a selected benefit formula. These plans are not considered multiemployer, and the accounting is based on the respective interest in the plan.

Business combinations. When an entity that sponsors a single employer defined benefit plan is purchased in a manner that must be accounted for as an acquisition under the provisions of IAS 22, the purchaser should assign part of the purchase price to an asset if plan assets exceed the projected benefit obligation or to a liability if the projected benefit obligation exceeds plan assets. The projected benefit obligation should include the effect of any expected plan curtailment or termination. This assignment eliminates any existing unrecognized components, and any future differences between contributions and net pension cost will affect the asset or liability recognized when the purchase took place.

Plan terminations. IAS 19 addresses plan terminations in general terms only, primarily to emphasize that certain costs, such as prior service costs incurred in connection with plan amendments, must be recognized immediately when there is an expectation that the plan will be terminated. It is interesting to note that under the corresponding US rules, there is a separate statement, SFAS 88, which was issued concurrent with the pension costing standard, SFAS 87, and which is far more detailed with regard to the accounting implications of plan settlements, curtailments, and other forms of terminations.

The US standard distinguishes curtailments from settlements. Settlements include both the purchase of nonparticipating annuity contracts and lump-sum cash payments. The following three criteria must all be met to constitute a pension obligation settlement under that standard:

1. It must be irrevocable
2. It must relieve the obligor of primary responsibility
3. It must eliminate significant risks associated with elements used to effect it

A defeasance strategy does not constitute a settlement.

Under an annuity contract settlement, an unrelated insurance company unconditionally accepts an obligation to provide the required benefits. The following criteria must be met for this type of settlement:

1. It must be irrevocable
2. It must involve transfer of material risk to the insurance company

There can be no reasonable doubt as to the ability of the insurance company to meet its contractual obligation. The substance of any participating annuity contract must relieve the employer of most of the risks and rewards or it does not meet the criteria.

Curtailments include early discontinuance of employee services or cessation or suspension of a plan. Additional benefits may not be earned, although future service time may be counted toward vesting. Curtailments must meet the following criteria:

1. It must materially diminish present employees' future service, or
2. It must stop or materially diminish the accumulation of benefits by a significant number of employees.

A curtailment and a settlement can occur separately or together.

The accounting for settlements and curtailments is detailed in SFAS 88 for those complying with US GAAP. Under international accounting standards (IAS 19), the procedures are less complex: Any deferred cost (such as discretionary contributions which are being amortized over a number of years) should be expensed immediately, and of course any additional costs being incurred in connection with the transaction (legal fees, etc.) would be expensed currently.

Termination benefits. Under certain circumstances enterprises find that they must offer special inducements to employees to take early retirement. Such termination benefits should be accounted for in accordance with IAS 10. Special short time period benefits require that a loss and a liability be recognized when the offer is accepted and the amount can reasonably be estimated. Contractual termination benefits require that a loss and a liability be recognized when it is probable that employees will receive the benefits and the amount can reasonably be estimated. The cost of these benefits is the cash paid and the present value of future payments. Termination benefits and curtailments can occur together.

The failure of IAS 19 to comprehensively address termination, curtailment, and settlement issues was the cause for substantial criticism of that standard. The proposed replacement, set forth in E54, pays much more attention to these matters and provides extended guidance regarding measurement, presentation, and disclosure of such costs and obligations. Settlements and curtailments are defined similarly to under US GAAP, and all related gains or losses are to be recognized when the event occurs. The gain or loss would consist of any resulting change in the present value of the obligation, any resulting change in the market value of the plan's assets, and any related actuarial gains or losses and past service costs which remained unrecognized at that time. Termination benefits would be recognized as a liability and an expense when the entity first had a demonstrable obligation to terminate a group of employees or provide benefits as a result of an offer made to encourage early retirements by staff members.

Disclosure of Pension Costs

For defined contribution plans, IAS 19 requires the following disclosures:

1. A general description of each plan, identifying the employee groups covered
2. The amount of expense recognized in the period being reported on
3. Any other significant matters related to retirement benefits that affect comparability with the previous period reported on

For defined benefit plans, as would be expected, there are more disclosures mandated. These include

1. A general description of each plan, identifying the employee groups covered
2. The accounting policies adopted for benefit costs, including a general description of the actuarial methods used, consistent with the accounting policy disclosures required under IAS 1
3. A statement as to whether or not the plan is funded
4. The amount of expense recognized in the period being reported on
5. The actuarial present value of promised retirement benefits as of the date of the most recent actuarial valuation (IAS 19 requires that these be updated at least every 3 years)
6. If the plan is funded, the fair value of plan assets as of the date of the most recent actuarial valuation
7. If the amounts funded since inception differ from the aggregate amount of expense recognized over that period, the amount of the resulting asset or

liability and the funding approach that has been adopted (if more than one plan, with both related asset and liability amounts, these cannot be netted)

8. The principal actuarial assumptions used in determining the cost of retirement benefits and any significant changes in those assumptions
9. The date of the most recent actuarial valuation, and the frequency with which such valuations are conducted
10. Any other significant matters related to retirement benefits, including the effects of any plan terminations, curtailments, or settlements, that might affect comparability with the previous period's financial statements

If E54 is enacted, the required disclosures for defined benefit plans will be expanded somewhat to include analyses of significant amounts recognized as assets and liabilities on the balance sheet. These would set forth, at a minimum, the present value of the unfunded defined benefit obligations, the present value of the funded defined benefit obligations, the market value of plan assets, the net actuarial gains or losses not recognized as of the balance sheet date, the past service cost not recognized in the balance sheet, and the total recognized assets and liabilities. Also to be disclosed would be the market value of each class of the employer's (i.e., the reporting entity's) financial instruments included in the reported market value of plan assets. For each income statement, the amounts of current service cost, interest cost, expected return on plan assets, actuarial gains and losses, past service costs, and effects of any curtailments and settlements included in earnings would need to be set forth. Other information would be similar to current requirements, if somewhat more detailed: the principal actuarial assumptions used, including discount rates, expected return on assets, expected salary cost progression, medical cost trend rates, and so forth.

Although it is not required that when an entity has more than one plan, the foregoing information be presented separately for each plan, it is recognized that when plans having deficits are combined with those having surpluses, the value of the disclosure may be impaired. IAS 19 permits presenting one consolidated set of disclosures, separate disclosures for each plan, or some intermediate degree of aggregation of disclosures, as the preparer deems appropriate.

Postretirement Benefits Other Than Pensions

IAS 19 is meant to establish standards for employers' accounting for other (than pension) postretirement benefits, although these are not addressed explicitly by that standard. The following discussion is intended to analogize from IAS 19.

Logic suggests that the principles set forth in IAS 19 should apply to all forms of postretirement benefits, although the most material benefit is usually postretirement healthcare. IAS 19 would presumably require that accrual accounting be employed in recognizing these costs, based on the three primary characteristics of pension accounting.

1. Delayed recognition (changes are not recognized immediately but are subsequently recognized in a gradual and systematic way)
2. Reporting net cost (aggregates of various items are reported as one net amount)
3. Offsetting assets and liabilities (assets and liabilities are sometimes shown net)

Accounting for postretirement benefits. The accrued postretirement benefit obligation is the actuarial present value as of a specific date of the benefits expected to be paid to the employee, beneficiaries, and covered dependents based on services provided to the entity through the balance sheet date. Measurement of this obligation should be based on the following:

1. Expected amount and timing of future benefits
2. Expected future costs
3. Extent of cost sharing (contributions, deductibles, coinsurance provisions, etc.) between employer, employee, and others (e.g., government). The actuarial present value of employee contributions reduce the actuarial present value of the benefit obligation. Obligations to return employee contributions, plus interest if applicable, should be recognized as a component of benefit obligation.

Consistent with the other provisions of IAS 19, the computed benefit obligation may or may not include an assumed salary progression for a pay-related plan. If a projected benefit approach is taken, future compensation levels should be the best estimate after considering the individual employees involved, general price levels, seniority, productivity, promotions, indirect effects, and so on.

Net periodic postretirement benefit costs include the following components:

1. Service cost--Accrued obligation for benefits attributable to the current period (i.e., the portion of the obligation earned this period)
2. Interest cost--Interest on the accrued benefit obligation
3. Actual return on plan assets, if the plan is funded
4. Gain or loss due to actuarial changes, and so on
5. Amortization of unrecognized prior service cost, if any
6. Amortization of the transition asset or obligation

Service costs and interest costs should be defined and measured in the same manner by as for pension plans.

While IAS 19 did not explicitly address the matter of accounting for other postemployment or postretirement benefits, the proposed new standard, E54, does include all such benefit plans under the same umbrella of accounting guidance. This would apply to programs such as long-term compensated absences, profit sharing or bonus arrangements, and deferred compensation payable 12 months or longer after being earned. The amount to be presented on the balance sheet would be the net of the present value of the plan's obligations and the market value of any assets held by the plan. Periodic expense related to such benefit plans would consist of current service cost, interest cost, expected return on plan assets, actuarial gains or losses if outside the 10% "corridor," past service costs, and the effects of any curtailments or settlements.

Assumptions. Assumptions underlying cost recognition for postemployment benefits other than pensions should be the best estimate available of the plan's future experience, solely with regard to the individual assumption under consideration. Plan continuity can be presumed unless there is evidence to the contrary. Principal actuarial assumptions include discount rates, present value factors, retirement age, participation rates (contributory plans), salary progression (pay-related plans), and probability of payment (turnover, dependency status, mortality). Present value factors for health care obligations include cost trend rates, national health insurance reimbursement rates, and per capita claims cost by age.

Current interest rates, as of the measurement date, should be used for discount rates in present value calculations. Examples include high quality fixed income investments with similar amounts and timing and interest rates at which the postretirement benefit obligations could be settled. The benefit obligation, service cost, and interest cost components use assumed discount rates.

The expected long-term rate of return on plan assets should be the average rate of earnings on contributions during the period and on qualifying existing plan assets. Current returns on plan assets and reinvestment returns should be given consideration in arriving at the rate to be used. Related income taxes, if applicable, should reduce the rate. Expected return on plan assets and the market-related value of plan assets use this rate in their calculation.

Deferred compensation contracts. Some entities establish deferred compensation arrangements for key executives or, in some cases, for all employees. If the aggregate deferred compensation contracts with individual employees are equivalent to a pension plan, the contracts should be accounted for according to IAS 19. If not, the amounts to be accrued should not be less than the present value of the estimated payments to be made under each such arrangement. This estimated amount should be accrued in a systematic and rational manner. When elements of both current and future employment are present, only the portion attributable to the current services should be accrued. All requirements of the contract, such as the continued employment for a specified period and availability for consulting services and agreements not to compete after retirement, need to be met for the employee to receive future payments.

One benefit that may be found in a deferred compensation contract is the period payments to employees or their beneficiaries for life, with provisions for a minimum lump-sum settlement in the event of early death of one or all of the beneficiaries. The estimated amount to be accrued should be based on the life expectancy of each person concerned or on the estimated cost of an annuity contract, not on the minimum amount payable in the event of early death.

Stock-based compensation arrangements. The proposed replacement for IAS 19 would also address, to a limited extent, equity compensation benefits such as share options and other instruments issued to employees at less than fair value as well as cash payments which depend on the future market value of shares (such as phantom stock plans). While the proposal addresses these plans as being benefits which conceptually could be dealt with in a manner analogous to pensions, it then states that insofar as there is a lack of consensus on how these should be accounted for, no prescriptions are offered. Of course, as the recent experience in the US (where a logical and comprehensive proposal was effectively scuttled by a concerted effort by corporate managers wishing to avoid having earnings impacted by recognition of costs incurred in connection with such plans) clearly shows, this is a very difficult area for accounting standards setters to deal with. Accordingly, even if E54 is enacted, the matter of accounting for the cost of stock based compensation schemes will have to wait for a later solution.

16 STOCKHOLDERS' EQUITY

PERSPECTIVE AND ISSUES

The IASC's *Framework for the Preparation and Presentation of Financial Statements* defines equity as the residual interest in the assets of an enterprise after deducting all its liabilities. Stockholders' equity is comprised of all capital contributed to the entity (including share premium, also referred to as capital paid-in in excess of par value) plus retained earnings (i.e., the entity's accumulated earnings less any distributions that have been made therefrom).

Stockholders' equity (referred to as equity in IAS 1 [revised]) also includes reserves, such as statutory or legal reserves, general reserves and contingency reserves, and revaluation surplus. IAS 1 (revised) categorizes stockholders' interests into three broad subdivisions: issued capital, reserves, and accumulated profits or losses. This newly revised standard also sets forth requirements for disclosures about the details of share capital for corporations and the various capital accounts of other types of enterprises.

Stockholders' equity represents an interest in the net assets (i.e., assets less liabilities) of the entity. It is not a claim on those assets in the sense that liabilities are. On liquidation of the business, an obligation arises for the entity to distribute any remaining assets to the shareholders after the creditors are paid.

Earnings are not generated by transactions in an entity's own equity (e.g., by the issuance, reacquisition, or reissuance of its common or preferred shares). Depending on the laws of the jurisdiction of incorporation, distributions to shareholders may be subject to various limitations, such as to the amount of retained (accounting basis) earnings.

A major objective of the accounting for stockholders' equity is the adequate disclosure of the sources from which the capital was derived. For this reason, a number of different paid-in capital accounts may be presented in the balance sheet. The rights of each class of shareholder must also be disclosed. Where shares are reserved for future issuance, such as under the terms of stock option plans, this fact must also be made known.

Sources of IAS

IAS 1 (revised), 8, 16, 25, 32

CONCEPTS, RULES, AND EXAMPLES

The international accounting standards (IAS), including the statement of principles, deal only with presentation and disclosure requirements relating to stockholders' equity. IAS have yet to address the accounting for the various components of stockholders' equity. There are numerous complex accounting issues relating to the various components of stockholders' equity, some of which have been and others are still being tackled by standard-setting bodies worldwide. The absence of any international accounting standard dealing with the accounting treatment of equity transactions is an impediment to uniform and appropriate accounting by international conglomerates, multinational corporations and other companies that comply with IAS. Given the absence of any promulgated international GAAP on this highly complex and important area, this chapter makes extensive use of the guidance under US GAAP.

Presentation and Disclosure Requirements Under IAS

Stockholders' equity (referred to as equity in IAS 1 [revised]) also includes reserves such as statutory or legal reserves, general reserves and contingency reserves, and revaluation surplus. IAS 1 (revised) categorizes stockholders' interests in three broad subdivisions: issued capital, reserves, and accumulated profits or losses. This newly revised standard also sets forth requirements for disclosures about the details of share capital for corporations and the various capital accounts of other types of enterprises.

Disclosures Relating to Share Capital

1. **The number or amount of shares authorized, issued, and outstanding.** It is required that a company disclose information relating to the number of shares authorized, issued, and outstanding. Each of these has a different connotation. Authorized share capital is the maximum number of shares that a company is permitted to issue, according to its articles of association or its charter or bylaws (these being given different names in different countries). The number of shares issued and outstanding could vary, based on the fact that a company could have acquired its own shares and is holding them as treasury stock (discussed below under reacquired shares).

2. **Capital not yet paid in**. In an initial public offering (IPO), subscribers may be asked initially to pay in only a portion of the par value, with the balance due in installments, which are known as **calls**. Thus, it is likely that on the date of the balance sheet, a certain portion of the share capital is not yet paid in. For instance, while the gross amount of the stock subscription increases capital, if the due date of the last and final call falls on February 7, 1997, following the accounting year end of December 31, 1996, the amount of capital not yet paid in should be shown as a deduction from stockholders' equity. In this manner, only the net amount (of capital) received up to the date of the balance sheet will be properly included in net stockholders' equity. IAS 1 (revised) requires that a distinction be made between shares which have been issued and fully paid, on the one hand, and those which have been issued but not fully paid, on the other hand. The number of shares outstanding at the beginning and at the end of each period presented must also be reconciled.
3. **Par value per share**. This is also generally referred to as legal value or face value per share. The par value of shares is specified in the corporate charter or bylaws and referred to in other documents, such as the share application and prospectus. Par value is the smallest unit of share capital that can be acquired unless the prospectus permits fractional shares (which is very unusual for commercial enterprises). In certain countries, including the United States, it is also permitted for corporations to issue no-par stock (i.e., stock that is not given any par value). In such cases, again depending on local corporation laws, sometimes a stated value is determined by the board of directors, which is then accorded effectively the same treatment as par value. IAS (revised) requires disclosure of par values or of the fact that the shares were issued without par values.

   Traditionally, companies often issued shares at par value in cases where shares are issued immediately on incorporation or soon thereafter. However, when a well-established company with a proven track record issues shares, it may issue new shares at a premium. As a practical matter, par values have had a much diminished importance as corporation laws have been modernized in many jurisdictions, and often the par values will be trivial, such as $1 or even $0.01 per share. In such cases, issuance prices even at inception of a new corporation will be substantially above par value.
4. **Movements in share capital accounts during the year**. This information is usually disclosed in the footnotes to the financial statements, generally in a statement format, although in some circumstances merely described in a narrative in the footnotes. This statement, referred to as the Statement of Changes in Stockholders' Equity, highlights the changes during the year in the various components of stockholders' equity. It also serves the purpose of reconciling the beginning and the ending balances of stockholders' eq-

uity, as shown in the balance sheet. Under the provisions of IAS 1 (revised), enterprises must now present either a statement showing the changes in all the equity accounts (including issued capital, reserves and accumulated profit or loss), or a statement reporting changes in equity other than those arising from transactions with, or distributions to, owners.

5. **Rights, preferences, and restrictions with respect to the distribution of dividends and to the repayment of capital**. When there is more than one class of share capital with varying rights, adequate disclosure of the rights, preferences, and restrictions attached to each such class of share capital will enhance understandability of the information provided by the financial statements.
6. **Cumulative preference dividends in arrears**. If a company does not pay dividends on the preference shares for a certain number of years, it is required by statute (corporate law worldwide requires this) to make up these arrears in later years, if the shares have a cumulative feature. These dividends have to be paid before any dividends are paid on other equity shares. Although practice varies, most preference shares are cumulative in nature; preference shares that do not have this feature are called **noncumulative preference shares**.
7. **Reacquired shares**. Shares that are reacquired by a company are referred to as **treasury stock**. In those jurisdictions where the corporate or company law of the country permits the repurchase of shares, such shares, on acquisition by the company or its consolidated subsidiary, become legally available for reissue or resale without further authorization. **Shares outstanding** refers to shares other than those held as treasury stock. Treasury stock does not reduce the number of shares issued but affects the number of shares outstanding. It is to be noted that certain countries prohibit companies from purchasing their own shares, since to do so is considered as a reduction of share capital that can be achieved only with the express consent of the shareholders in an extraordinary general meeting and then only under certain conditions.

   In the United Kingdom, traditionally companies were prohibited from purchasing their own shares. However, the UK Companies Act of 1981 relaxed this prohibition by allowing this practice, subject of course to certain conditions. Even in the United States, for that matter, not all states recognize treasury stock, and in those states the reacquired shares are to be treated as having been retired. Normally, treasury stock is shown as a reduction of stockholders' equity. Under very rare circumstances it may be presented as an asset, and shown on the asset side of the balance sheet, provided that adequate disclosure is made of this. Accounting for treasury stock is discussed further, in detail, in the latter part of this chapter.

8. **Shares reserved for future issuance under options and sales contracts, including the terms and amounts**. Companies issue stock options that grant the holder of these options rights to a specified number of shares at a certain price. A good example of a stock option is an option granted under an employee stock ownership plan (ESOP). Stock options are an increasingly popular means of employee remuneration, and usually top management is offered such noncash perquisites as part of its remuneration package. If a company has shares reserved for future issuance under option plans or sales contracts, it is necessary to disclose the number of shares, including terms and amounts, so reserved.

   The accounting for stock options is dealt with later in this chapter and presents many intriguing and complex issues, most of which the accounting profession has already addressed. However, by looking at the number of technically complex issues in this area, the impression may be had that the profession is still unable to come to grips fully with this topic. Under US GAAP, for example, a number of pronouncements have been issued only in the area of ESOP, but the new standard issued in 1993 is not mandatorily applicable to shares held as of that date; instead, employers may continue to use the prior accounting methods for shares purchased prior to that time. Significant changes in the authoritative literature have recently been promulgated on the matter of accounting for stock-based compensation (options, appreciation rights, etc.). These changes are also discussed later in this chapter.

Disclosures Relating to Other Equity

1. **Capital paid in excess of par value.** This is the amount received on the issuance of shares that is the excess over the par value. It is called additional paid-in capital in the United States, while in some other countries, including the United Kingdom, it is referred to as "share premium."
2. **Revaluation reserve**. When a company carries property, plant, and equipment at other than historical costs, as is permitted by IAS 16 (i.e., it does not follow the benchmark treatment but, instead, follows the allowed alternative treatment, and revalues property, plant, and equipment to fair value), the difference between the historical costs (net of accumulated depreciation) and the fair values is credited to the revaluation reserve. Under IAS 25, long-term investments could also be carried at revalued amounts. Thus, revaluation reserve could arise not only from revaluations of property, plant, and equipment but even from revaluations of long-term investments.

   The standard requires that movements of this reserve during the period (year) be disclosed, which is usually done in the footnotes. Also, restrictions as to any distributions of this reserve to shareholders should be disclosed.

3. **Reserves.** Reserves include capital as well as revenue reserves. Also, statutory reserves and voluntary reserves are included under this category. Finally, special reserves, including contingency reserves, are included herein.

   Statutory reserves (or legal reserves, as they are called in some jurisdictions) are created based on the requirements of the law or the statute under which the company is incorporated. For instance, most corporate statutes in Middle Eastern countries require that companies set aside 10% of their net income for the year as a "statutory reserve," with such appropriations to continue until the balance in this reserve account equals 50% of the company's equity capital.

   Sometimes a company's articles, charter, or bylaws may require that the company set aside each year a certain percentage of its net profit (income) by way of a contingency or general reserve. Unlike statutory or legal reserves, contingency reserves are based on the provisions of corporate bylaws. Apparently, the rationale behind creation of such reserves is to make the company strong by requiring that each year a stipulated percentage of profits be plowed back into equity instead of being distributed to shareholders.

   The standard requires that movements during the period (year) in these reserves be disclosed, along with the nature and purpose of each reserve presented within owners' equity.

4. **Retained earnings.** By definition, retained earnings represents a corporation's accumulated profits (losses) less any distributions that have been made therefrom. However, based on provisions contained in the international accounting standards, other adjustments are also made to the amount of retained earnings. IAS 8 (revised 1993), *Net Profit or Loss for the Period, Fundamental Errors and Changes in Accounting Policies*, requires the following to be shown as adjustments to retained earnings:

   a. Under the benchmark treatment, correction of fundamental errors that relate to prior periods should be reported by adjusting the opening balance of retained earnings. Comparative information should be restated, unless it is impracticable to do so.
   b. Under the benchmark treatment, the resulting adjustment from a change in accounting policy which is to be applied retrospectively should be reported as an adjustment to the opening balance of retained earnings. Comparative information should be restated unless it is impracticable to do so.

When dividends have been proposed but not formally approved, and hence when such intended dividends have not yet become reportable as a liability of the enterprise, disclosure is required by IAS 1 (revised). Also, the amount of any cumulative preference dividends not recognized as charges against accumulated profits must be disclosed, whether parenthetically or in the footnotes.

Classification Between Liabilities and Equity

IAS 32 requires that the issuer of a financial instrument should classify the instrument, or its components, as a liability or as equity, according to the substance of the contractual arrangement on initial recognition. The crux of the issue is the differentiation between a financial liability and an equity instrument.

The standard defines a financial liability as a contractual obligation:

1. To deliver cash or another financial asset to another enterprise, or
2. To exchange financial instruments with another enterprise under conditions that are potentially unfavorable.

An equity instrument, on the other hand, has been defined by the standard as any contract that evidences a residual interest in the assets of an enterprise after deducting all its liabilities.

Compound financial instruments. Increasingly, it is not uncommon for corporations to issue financial instruments that have attributes of both equity and liabilities. IAS 32 stipulates that an enterprise that issues such financial instruments, which are technically known as compound instruments, should classify the component parts of the financial instrument separately as equity or liability as appropriate. (For a detailed discussion on financial instruments, refer to Chapter 5.)

APPENDIX A

ILLUSTRATION OF FINANCIAL STATEMENT PRESENTATION

This appendix provides an illustration of the various financial statements that **may** be required to be presented and are related to the stockholders' equity section of the balance sheet.

Stockholders' Equity Section of a Balance Sheet

Capital stock:		
Preferred stock, $100 par, 7% cumulative, 30,000 shares authorized, issued, and outstanding		$ 3,000,000
Common stock, no par, stated value $10 per share, 500,000shares authorized, 415,000 shares issued		4,150,000
Total capital stock		$ 7,150,000
Additional paid-in capital:		
Issued price in excess of par value--preferred	$ 150,000	
Issued price in excess of stated value--common	845,000	995,000
Total paid-in capital		$ 8,145,000
Donated capital		100,000
Retained earnings:		
Appropriated for plant expansion	$2,100,000	
Unappropriated	2,275,000	4,375,000
Total capital and retained earnings		$12,620,000
Less 10,000 common shares held in treasury, at cost		(120,000)
Total stockholders' equity		$12,500,000

Retained Earnings Statement

Balance at beginning of year, as reported	$ 3,800,000
Prior period adjustment--correction of an error in method of depreciation (less tax effect of $77,000)	115,000
Balance at beginning of year, restated	$ 3,915,000
Net income for the year	748,000
Cash dividends declared during the year	
Preferred stock	(210,000)
Common stock	(78,000)
Balance at end of year	$ 4,375,000

Statement of Changes in Stockholders' Equity (including Retained Earnings Statement)

	Preferred stock		*Common stock*		*Additional paid-in*	*Donated*	*Retained*	*Treasury stock*	*Total stockholders'*
	Shares	*Amount*	*Shares*	*Amount*	*capital*	*capital*	*earnings*	*(common)*	*equity*
Balance, 12/31/X5, as reported	--	--	400,000	$4,000,000	$840,000	$100,000	$3,800,000	$(120,000)	$ 8,620,000
Correction of an error in method of depr.	--	--	--	--	--	--	115,000	--	115,000
Balance, 12/31/X4, restated	--	--	400,000	$4,000,000	$840,000	$100,000	$3,915,000	$(120,000)	$ 8,735,000
Preferred stock issued in public offering	30,000	$3,000,000	--	--	150,000	--	--	--	3,150,000
Stock options exercised	--	--	15,000	150,000	5,000	--	--	--	155,000
Net income	--	--	--	--	--	--	748,000	--	748,000
Cash dividends declared:									
Preferred, $7.00 per share	--	--	--	--	--	--	(210,000)	--	(210,000)
Common, $.20 per share	--	--	--	--	--	--	(78,000)	--	(78,000)
Balance, 12/31/X6	30,000	$3,000,000	415,000	$4,150,000	$995,000	$100,000	$4,375,000	$(120,000)	$12,500,000

APPENDIX B

ADDITIONAL GUIDANCE UNDER US GAAP

As noted in the main portion of this chapter, international accounting standards have not addressed a number of complex and interesting issues that do arise in connection with financial reporting by enterprises in many countries. Although the material in this appendix is not authoritative, it is being provided with the intent that it be instructive as additional guidance. Since these are matters that are not addressed by IAS, the treatments illustrated herein are not prohibited for application to financial statements prepared in conformity with international accounting standards.

DEFINITIONS OF TERMS

Additional paid-in capital. Amounts received at issuance in excess of the par or stated value of capital stock and amounts received from other transactions involving the entity's stock and/or stockholders. It is classified by source.

Allocated shares. ESOP shares assigned to individual participants. These shares are usually based on length of service, compensation, or a combination of both.

Appropriation (of retained earnings). A segregation of retained earnings to communicate the unavailability of a portion for dividend distributions.

Authorized shares. The maximum number of shares permitted to be issued by a corporation's charter and bylaws.

Callable. An optional characteristic of preferred stock allowing the corporation to redeem the stock at specified future dates and at specific prices. The call price is usually at or above the original issuance price.

Cliff vesting. A condition of an option or other stock award plan which provides that the employee becomes fully vested at a single point in time.

Combination plans. Compensation plans under which employees receive two or more components, such as options and stock appreciation rights, all of which can be exercised. Thus, each component is actually a separate plan and is accounted for as such.

Committed-to-be-released shares. ESOP shares that will be allocated to employees for service performed currently. They are usually released by payment of debt service.

Compensatory plan. A stock option plan including elements of compensation that are recognized over the service period.

Compensatory stock option plans. Plans that do not meet the criteria for noncompensatory plans. Their main purpose is to provide additional compensation to officers and employees.

Constructive retirement method. Method of accounting for treasury shares that treats the shares as having been retired. The shares revert to authorized but unissued status. The stock and additional paid-in capital accounts are reduced, with a debit to retained earnings or a credit to a paid-in capital account for the excess or deficiency of the purchase cost over or under the original issuance proceeds.

Contributed capital. The amount of equity contributed by the corporation's shareholders. It consists of capital stock plus additional paid-in capital.

Convertible. An optional characteristic of preferred stock allowing the stockholders to exchange their preferred shares for common shares at a specified ratio.

Cost method. Method of accounting for treasury shares that presents aggregate cost of reacquired shares as a deduction from the total of paid-in capital and retained earnings.

Cumulative. An optional characteristic of preferred stock. Any dividends of prior years not paid to the preferred shareholders must be paid before any dividends can be distributed to the common shareholders.

Date of declaration. The date on which the board of directors votes that a dividend be paid. A legal liability (usually current) is created on this date in the case of cash, property, and scrip dividends.

Date of grant. The date on which the board of directors awards the stock to the employees in stock option plans.

Date of payment. The date on which the shareholders are paid the declared dividends.

Date of record. The date on which ownership of the shares is determined. Those owning stock on this date will be paid the declared dividends.

Deficit. A debit balance in the retained earnings account. Dividends may not generally be paid when this condition exists. Formally known as accumulated deficit.

Discount on capital stock. Occurs when the stock of a corporation is originally issued at a price below par value. The original purchasers become contingently liable to creditors for this difference.

Employee stock ownership plan (ESOP). A form of defined contribution employee benefit plan whereby the employer facilitates the purchase of shares of stock in the company for the benefit of the employees, generally by a trust established by the company. The plan may be leveraged by borrowings either from the employer-sponsor or from third-party lenders.

Fixed options. Options that grant the holder the rights to a specified number of shares at fixed prices. It is not dependent on achievement of performance targets.

Graded vesting. A vesting process whereby the employee becomes entitled to a stock-based award fractionally over a period of years.

Issued stock. The number of shares issued by the firm and owned by the shareholders and the corporation. It is the sum of outstanding shares plus treasury shares.

Junior stock. Shares with certain limitations, often as to voting rights, which are granted to employees pursuant to a performance compensation program. Such shares are generally convertible to ordinary shares on achievement of defined goals.

Legal capital. The aggregate par or stated value of stock. It represents the amount of owners' equity that cannot be distributed to shareholders. It serves to protect the claims of the creditors.

Liquidating dividend. A dividend distribution that is not based on earnings. It represents a return of contributed capital.

Measurement date. The date on which the price used to compute compensation under stock-based compensation plans is fixed.

Noncompensatory stock options. Options which, under current GAAP, do not include an element of compensation being paid to the participants. Under proposed GAAP all stock plans would include an element of compensation to be measured and allocated over the service periods of the employees.

Noncompensatory stock option plans. Plans whose primary purpose is widespread ownership of the firm among its employees and officers. They must meet four criteria (see APB 25, para 7, or the section on stock options).

No-par stock. Stock that has no par value. Sometimes a stated value is determined by the board of directors. In this case the stated value is accorded the same treatment as par value stock.

Outstanding stock. Stock issued by a corporation and held by shareholders (i.e., issued shares that are not held in the treasury).

Par value method. A method of accounting for treasury shares that charges the treasury stock account for the aggregate par or stated value of the shares acquired and charges the excess of the purchase cost over the par value to paid-in capital and/or retained earnings. A deficiency of purchase cost is credited to paid-in capital.

Participating. An optional characteristic of preferred stock whereby preferred shareholders may share ratably with the common shareholders in any profit distributions in excess of a predetermined rate. Participation may be limited to a maximum rate or may be unlimited (full).

Performance based options. Options that are granted to employees conditional on the achievement of defined goals.

Phantom stock plan. A type of stock compensation arrangement that gives employees the right to participate in the increase in value of the company's shares (book value or market value, as stipulated in the plan) without actually being required to purchase the shares initially.

Quasi reorganization. A procedure that reclassifies amounts from contributed capital to retained earnings to eliminate a deficit in that account. All the assets and liabilities are first revalued to their current values. It represents an alternative to a legal reorganization in bankruptcy proceedings.

Retained earnings. The undistributed earnings of a firm.

Service period. The period over which a stock-based compensation award is earned by the recipient. If not otherwise defined in the plan, it is the vesting period.

Stock-based compensation. Any of a wide variety of compensation arrangements under which employees receive shares of stock, options to purchase shares, or other equity instruments, or under which the employer incurs obligations to the employees based on the price of the company's shares.

Stock options. Enables officers and employees of a corporation to purchase shares in the corporation.

Stock rights. Enables present shareholders to purchase additional shares of stock of the corporation. It is commonly used if a preemptive right is granted to common shareholders by some state corporation laws.

Suspense shares. ESOP shares that usually collateralize ESOP debt. They have not been allocated or committed to be released.

Tandem options. Compensation plans under which employees receive two or more components, such as options and stock appreciation rights, whereby the exercise of one component cancels the other(s). The accounting is based on the component that is more likely to be exercised.

Treasury stock. Shares of a corporation that have been repurchased by the corporation. This stock has no voting rights and receives no cash dividends. Some states do not recognize treasury stock. In such cases, reacquired shares are treated as having been retired.

Vesting. The process whereby the recipient of a stock-based compensation award earns the right to control or exercise the award.

CONCEPTS, RULES, AND EXAMPLES

Legal Capital and Capital Stock

Legal capital typically relates to that portion of the stockholders' investment in a corporation that is permanent in nature and represents assets that will continue to be available for the satisfaction of creditor's claims. Traditionally, legal capital was comprised of the aggregate par or stated value of common and preferred shares issued. In recent years, however, many states have eliminated the requirement that corporate shares have a designated par or stated value. Some states have adopted provisions of a model act that completely eliminated the distinction between par value and the amount contributed in excess of par.

Ownership interest in a corporation is made up of common and, optionally, preferred shares. The common shares represent the residual risk-taking ownership of the corporation after the satisfaction of all claims of creditors and senior classes of equity.

Preferred stock. Preferred shareholders are owners who have certain rights superior to those of common shareholders. These rights will pertain either to the earnings or the assets of the corporation. Preferences as to earnings exist when the preferred shareholders have a stipulated dividend rate (expressed either as a dollar amount or as a percentage of the preferred stock's par or stated value). Preferences as to assets exist when the preferred shares have a stipulated liquidation value. If a corporation were to liquidate, the preferred holders would be paid a specific amount before the common shareholders would have a right to participate in any of the proceeds.

In practice, preferred shares are more likely to have preferences as to earnings than as to assets. Some classes of preferred shares may have both preferential rights. Preferred shares may also have the following features: participation in earnings beyond the stipulated dividend rate; a cumulative feature, affording the preferred shareholders the protection that their dividends in arrears, if any, will be fully satisfied before the common shareholders participate in any earnings distribution; and convertibility or callability by the corporation. Whatever preferences exist must be disclosed adequately in the financial statements, either on the face of the balance sheet or in the notes.

In exchange for the preferences, the preferred shareholders' rights or privileges are limited. For instance, the right to vote may be restricted to common shareholders. The most important right denied to the preferred shareholders, however, is the right to participate without limitation in the earnings of the corporation. Thus, if the corporation has exceedingly large earnings for a particular period, these earnings would tend to accrue to the benefit of the common shareholders. This is true even if the preferred stock is participating (a fairly uncommon feature) because even participating preferred stock usually has some upper limitation placed on its degree of participation.

Occasionally, as discussed in the chapter, several classes of stock will be categorized as common (e.g., Class A common, Class B common, etc.). Since there can be only one class of shares that represents the true residual risk-taking investors in a corporation, it is clear that the other classes, even though described as common shareholders, must in fact have some preferential status. Typically, these preferences relate to voting rights. The rights and responsibilities of each class of shareholder, even if described as common, must be fully disclosed in the financial statements.

Issuance of shares. The accounting for the sale of shares by a corporation depends on whether the stock has a par or stated value. If there is a par or stated value, the amount of the proceeds representing the aggregate par or stated value is credited to the common or preferred stock account. The aggregate par or stated value is generally defined as legal capital not subject to distribution to shareholders. Proceeds in excess of par or stated value are credited to an additional paid-in capital account. The additional paid-in capital represents the amount in excess of the legal capital which may, under certain defined conditions, be distributed to shareholders. A corporation selling stock below par value credits the capital stock account for the par value and debits an offsetting discount account for the difference between par value and the amount actually received.

If there is a discount on original issue capital stock, it serves to notify the actual and potential creditors of the contingent liability of those investors. As a practical matter, corporations avoided this problem by reducing par values to an arbitrarily low amount. This reduction in par eliminated the chance that shares would be sold for amounts below par. Where corporation laws make no distinction between par value and amounts in excess of par, the entire proceeds from the sale of stock may be credited to the common stock account without distinction between the stock and the additional paid-in capital accounts. The following entries illustrate these concepts:

Facts: A corporation sells 100,000 shares of $5 par common stock for $8 per share cash.

Cash	800,000	
Common stock		500,000
Additional paid-in capital		300,000

Facts: A corporation sells 100,000 shares of no-par common stock for $8 per share cash.

Cash	800,000	
Common stock		800,000

Preferred stock will often be assigned a par value because in many cases the preferential dividend rate is defined as a percentage of par value (e.g., 10%, $25 par value preferred stock will have a required annual dividend of $2.50). However, the dividend can be stated as a dollar amount per year, thereby obviating the need for par values.

Stock issued for services. If the shares in a corporation are issued in exchange for services or property rather than for cash, the transaction should be reflected at the fair value of the property or services received. If this information is not readily available, the transaction should be recorded at the fair value of the shares that were issued. Where necessary, appraisals should be obtained to properly reflect the transaction. As a final resort, a valuation by the board of directors of the stock issued can be utilized. Stock issued to employees as compensation for services rendered should be accounted for at the fair value of the services performed, if determinable, or the value of the shares issued.

If shares are given by a major shareholder directly to an employee for services performed for the entity, this exchange should be accounted for as a capital contribution to the company by the major shareholder and as compensation expense incurred by the company. Only when accounted for in this manner will there be conformity with the general principle that all costs incurred by an entity, including compensation, should be reflected in its financial statements.

Issuance of stock units. In certain instances, common and preferred shares may be issued to investors as a unit (e.g., a unit of one share of preferred and two shares of common can be sold as a package). Where both of the classes of stock are publicly traded, the proceeds from a unit offering should be allocated in proportion to the relative market values of the securities. If only one of the securities is publicly traded, the proceeds should be allocated to the one that is publicly traded based on its known market value. Any excess is allocated to the other. Where the market value of neither security is known, appraisal information might be used. The imputed fair value of one class of security, particularly the preferred shares, can be based on the stipulated dividend rate. In this case, the amount of proceeds remaining after the imputing of a value of the preferred shares would be allocated to the common stock.

The foregoing procedures would also apply if a unit offering were made of an equity and a nonequity security such as convertible debentures.

Stock Subscriptions

Occasionally, particularly in the case of a newly organized corporation, a contract is entered into between the corporation and prospective investors, whereby the latter agree to purchase specified numbers of shares to be paid for over some installment period. These stock subscriptions are not the same as actual stock issuances, and the accounting differs.

The amount of stock subscriptions receivable by a corporation is sometimes treated as an asset on the balance sheet and is categorized as current or noncurrent in accordance with the terms of payment. However, most subscriptions receivable are shown as a reduction of stockholders' equity in the same manner as treasury stock. Since subscribed shares do not have the rights and responsibilities of actual outstanding stock, the credit is made to a stock subscribed account instead of to the capital stock accounts.

If the common stock has par or stated value, the common stock subscribed account is credited for the aggregate par or stated value of the shares subscribed. The excess over this amount is credited to additional paid-in capital. No distinction is made between additional paid-in capital relating to shares already issued and shares subscribed for. This treatment follows from the distinction between legal capital and additional paid-in capital. Where there is no par or stated value, the entire amount of the common stock subscribed is credited to the stock subscribed account.

As the amount due from the prospective shareholders is collected, the stock subscriptions receivable account is credited and the proceeds are debited to the cash account. Actual issuance of the shares, however, must await the complete payment of the stock subscription. Accordingly, the debit to common stock subscribed is not made until the subscribed shares are fully paid for and the stock is issued.

The following journal entries illustrate these concepts:

1. 10,000 shares of $50 par preferred are subscribed at a price of $65 each; a 10% down payment is received.

Cash	65,000	
Stock subscriptions receivable	585,000	
Preferred stock subscribed		500,000
Additional paid-in capital		150,000

2. 2,000 shares of no par common shares are subscribed at a price of $85 each, with one-half received in cash.

Cash	85,000	
Stock subscriptions receivable	85,000	
Common stock subscribed		170,000

3. All preferred subscriptions are paid, and one-half of the remaining common subscriptions are collected in full and subscribed shares are issued.

Cash [$585,000 + ($85,000 x 0.50)]	627,500	
Stock subscriptions receivable		627,500
Preferred stock subscribed	500,000	
Preferred stock		500,000
Common stock subscribed	127,500	
Common stock ($170,000 x 0.75)		127,500

When the company experiences a default by the subscriber, the accounting will follow the provisions of the state in which the corporation is chartered. In some jurisdictions, the subscriber is entitled to a proportionate number of shares based on the amount already paid on the subscriptions, sometimes reduced by the cost incurred by the corporation in selling the remaining defaulted shares to other stockholders. In other jurisdictions, the subscriber forfeits the entire investment on default. In this case the amount already received is credited to an additional paid-in capital account that describes its source.

Additional Paid-in Capital

Additional paid-in capital represents all capital contributed to a corporation other than that defined as par or stated value. Additional paid-in capital can arise from proceeds received from the sale of common and preferred shares in excess of their par or stated values. It can also arise from transactions relating to the following:

1. Sale of shares previously issued and subsequently reacquired by the corporation (treasury stock)
2. Retirement of previously outstanding shares
3. Payment of stock dividends in a manner that justifies the dividend being recorded at the market value of the shares distributed

4. Lapse of stock purchase warrants or the forfeiture of stock subscriptions, if these result in the retaining by the corporation of any partial proceeds received prior to forfeiture
5. Warrants that are detachable from bonds
6. Conversion of convertible bonds
7. Other gains on the company's own stock, such as that which results from certain stock option plans

When the amounts are material, the sources of additional paid-in capital should be described in the financial statements.

Donated Capital

Donated capital should also be adequately disclosed in the financial statements. Donated capital can result from an outright gift to the corporation (e.g., a major shareholder donates land or other assets to the company in a nonreciprocal transfer) or may result when services are provided to the corporation. Under current US GAAP, such nonreciprocal transactions will be recognized as revenue in the period the contribution is received.

In these situations, historical cost is not adequate to reflect properly the substance of the transaction, since the historical cost to the corporation would be zero. Accordingly, these events should be reflected at fair market value. If long-lived assets are donated to the corporation, they should be recorded at their fair value at the date of donation, and the amount so recorded should be depreciated over the normal useful economic life of such assets. If donations are conditional in nature, they should not be reflected formally in the accounts until the appropriate conditions have been satisfied. However, disclosure might still be required in the financial statements of both the assets donated and the conditions required to be met.

Retained Earnings

Legal capital, additional paid-in capital, and donated capital collectively represent the contributed capital of the corporation. The other major source of capital is retained earnings, which represents the accumulated amount of earnings of the corporation from the date of inception (or from the date of reorganization) less the cumulative amount of distributions made to shareholders and other charges to retained earnings (e.g., from treasury stock transactions). The distributions to shareholders generally take the form of dividend payments but may take other forms as well, such as the reacquisition of shares for amounts in excess of the original issuance proceeds.

Retained earnings are also affected by action taken by the corporation's board of directors. Appropriation serves disclosure purposes and serves to restrict dividend payments but does nothing to provide any resources for satisfaction of the contingent loss or other underlying purpose for which the appropriation has been made. Any appropriation made from retained earnings must eventually be returned to the retained earnings account. It is not permissible to charge losses against the appropriation account nor to credit any realized gain to that account. The use of appropriated retained earnings has diminished significantly over the years.

An important rule relating to retained earnings is that transactions in a corporation's own stock can result in a reduction of retained earnings (i.e., a deficiency on such transactions can be charged to retained earnings) but cannot result in an increase in retained earnings (any excesses on such transactions are credited to paid-in capital, never to retained earnings).

If a series of operating losses have been incurred or distributions to shareholders in excess of accumulated earnings have been made and if there is a debit balance in retained earnings, the account is generally referred to as accumulated deficit.

Dividends

Dividends are the pro rata distribution of earnings to the owners of the corporation. The amount and the allocation between the preferred and common shareholders is a function of the stipulated preferential dividend rate, the presence or absence of (1) a participation feature, (2) a cumulative feature, and (3) arrearages on the preferred stock, and the wishes of the board of directors. Dividends, even preferred stock dividends, where a cumulative feature exists do not accrue. Dividends become a liability of the corporation only when they are declared by the board of directors.

Traditionally, corporations were not allowed to declare dividends in excess of the amount of retained earnings. Alternatively, a corporation could pay dividends out of retained earnings and additional paid-in capital but could not exceed the total of these categories (i.e., they could not impair legal capital by the payment of dividends). States that have adopted the Model Business Corporation Act grant more latitude to the directors. Corporations can now, in certain jurisdictions, declare and pay dividends in excess of the book amount of retained earnings if the directors conclude that, after the payment of such dividends, the fair value of the corporation's net assets will still be a positive amount. Thus, directors can declare dividends out of unrealized appreciation, which, in certain industries, can be a significant source of dividends beyond the realized and recognized accumulated earnings of the corporation. This action, however, represents a major departure from traditional practice and demands both careful consideration and adequate disclosure.

Three important dividend dates are:

1. The declaration date
2. The record date
3. The payment date

The declaration date governs the incurrence of a legal liability by the corporation. The record date refers to that point in time when a determination is made as to which specific registered stockholders will receive dividends and in what amounts. Finally, the payment date relates to the date when the distribution of the dividend takes place. These concepts are illustrated in the following example:

Example of payment of dividends

On May 1, 1994, the directors of River Corp. declare a $.75 per share quarterly dividend on River Corp.'s 650,000 outstanding common shares. The dividend is payable May 25 to holders of record May 15.

May 1	Retained earnings (or Dividends)	487,500	
	Dividends payable		487,500
May 15	No entry		
May 25	Dividends payable	487,500	
	Cash		487,500

If a dividends account is used, it is closed directly to retained earnings at year end.

Dividends may be made in the form of cash, property, or scrip, which is a form of short-term note payable. Cash dividends are either a given dollar amount per share or a percentage of par or stated value. Property dividends consist of the distribution of any assets other than cash (e.g., inventory or equipment). Finally, scrip dividends are promissory notes due at some time in the future, sometimes bearing interest until final payment is made.

Occasionally, what appear to be disproportionate dividend distributions are paid to some but not all of the owners of closely held corporations. Such transactions need to be analyzed carefully. In some cases these may actually represent compensation paid to the recipients. In other instances, these may be a true dividend paid to all shareholders on a pro rata basis, to which certain shareholders have waived their rights. If the former, the distribution should not be accounted for as a dividend but as compensation or some other expense category and included on the income statement. If the latter, the dividend should be grossed up to reflect payment on a proportional basis to all the shareholders, with an offsetting capital contribution to the company recognized as having been effectively made by those to whom payments were not made.

Property dividends. If property dividends are declared, the paying corporation may incur a gain or loss. Since the dividend should be reflected at the fair value of the assets distributed, the difference between fair value and book value is recorded at the time the dividend is declared and charged or credited to a loss or gain account.

Scrip dividends. If a corporation declares a dividend payable in scrip that is interest bearing, the interest is accrued over time as a periodic expense. The interest is not a part of the dividend itself.

Liquidating dividends. Liquidating dividends are not distributions of earnings, but rather, a return of capital to the investing shareholders. A liquidating dividend is normally recorded by the declarer through charging additional paid-in capital rather than retained earnings. The exact accounting for a liquidating dividend is affected by the laws where the business is incorporated, and these laws vary from state to state.

Stock dividends. Stock dividends represent neither an actual distribution of the assets of the corporation nor a promise to distribute those assets. For this reason, a stock dividend is not considered a legal liability or a taxable transaction.

Despite the recognition that a stock dividend is not a distribution of earnings, the accounting treatment of relatively insignificant stock dividends (defined as being less than 20 to 25% of the outstanding shares prior to declaration) is consistent with it being a real dividend. Accordingly, retained earnings are debited for the fair market value of the shares to be paid as a dividend, and the capital stock and additional paid-in capital accounts are credited for the appropriate amounts based on the par or stated value of the shares, if any. A stock dividend declared but not yet paid is classified as such in the stockholders' equity section of the balance sheet. Since such a dividend never reduces assets, it cannot be a liability.

The selection of 20 to 25% as the threshold for recognizing a stock dividend as an earnings distribution is arbitrary, but it is based somewhat on the empirical evidence that small stock dividends tend not to result in a reduced market price per share for outstanding shares. In theory, any stock dividend should result in a reduction of the market value of outstanding shares in an inverse relationship to the size of the stock dividend. The aggregate value of the outstanding shares should not change, but the greater number of shares outstanding after the stock dividend should necessitate a lower per share price. As noted, however, the declaration of small stock dividends tends not to have this impact, and this phenomenon supports the accounting treatment.

On the other hand, when stock dividends are larger in magnitude, it is observed that per share market value declines after declaration of the dividend. In such situations it would not be valid to treat the stock dividend as an earnings distribution. Rather, it should be accounted for as a split. The precise treatment depends on the legal requirements of the state of incorporation and on whether the existing par value or stated value is reduced concurrent with the stock split.

If the par value is not reduced for a large stock dividend and if state law requires that earnings be capitalized in an amount equal to the aggregate of the par value of the stock dividend declared, the event should be described as a stock split effected in the form of a dividend, with a charge to retained earnings and a credit to the common stock account for the aggregate par or stated value. When the par or stated value is reduced in recognition of the split and state laws do not require treatment as a dividend, there is no formal entry to record the split but merely a notation that the number of shares outstanding has increased and the per share par or stated value has decreased accordingly.

Treasury Stock

Treasury stock consists of a corporation's own stock that has been issued, subsequently reacquired by the firm and not yet reissued or canceled. Treasury stock does not reduce the number of shares issued but does reduce the number of shares outstanding, as well as total stockholders' equity. These shares are not eligible to receive cash dividends. Treasury stock is not an asset, although in some circumstances, it may be presented as an asset if adequately disclosed. Reacquired stock that is awaiting delivery to satisfy a liability created by the firm's compensation plan or reacquired stock held in a profit sharing trust is still considered outstanding and would not be considered treasury stock. In each case, the stock would be presented as an asset with the accompanying footnote disclosure.

Three approaches exist for the treatment of treasury stock: the cost, par value, and constructive retirement methods.

Cost method. Under the cost method, the gross cost of the shares reacquired is charged to a contra equity account (treasury stock). The equity accounts that were credited for the original share issuance (common stock, paid-in capital in excess of par, etc.) remain intact. When the treasury shares are reissued, proceeds in excess of cost are credited to a paid-in capital account. Any deficiency is charged to retained earnings (unless paid-in capital from previous treasury share transactions exists, in which case the deficiency is charged to that account, with any excess charged to retained earnings). If many treasury stock purchases are made, a cost flow assumption (e.g., FIFO or specific identification) should be adopted to compute excesses and deficiencies on subsequent share reissuances. The advantage of the cost method is that it avoids identifying and accounting for amounts related to the original issuance of the shares and is, therefore, the simpler, more frequently used method. The cost method is most consistent with the one-transaction concept. This concept takes the view that the classification of stockholders' equity should not be affected simply because the corporation was the middle "person" in an exchange of shares from one stockholder to another. In substance, there is only a transfer of shares between two stockholders. Since the original balances in the equity accounts are left undisturbed, its use is most acceptable when the firm acquires its stock for reasons other than retirement, or when its ultimate disposition has not yet been decided.

Par value method. Under the second approach, the par value method, the treasury stock account is charged only for the aggregate par (or stated) value of the shares reacquired. Other paid-in capital accounts (excess over par value, etc.) are relieved in proportion to the amounts recognized on the original issuance of the shares. The treasury share acquisition is treated almost as a retirement. However, the common (or preferred) stock account continues at the original amount, thereby preserving the distinction between an actual retirement and a treasury share transaction.

When the treasury shares accounted for by the par value method are subsequently resold, the excess of the sale price over par value is credited to paid-in capital. A reissuance for a price below par value does not create a contingent liability for the purchaser. It is only the original purchaser who risks this obligation to the entity's creditors.

Constructive retirement method. The constructive retirement method is similar to the par value method except that the aggregate par (or stated) value of the reacquired shares is charged to the stock account rather than to the treasury stock account. This method is superior when (1) it is management's intention not to reissue the shares within a reasonable time period, or (2) the state of incorporation defines reacquired shares as having been retired.

The two-transaction concept is most consistent with the par value and constructive retirement methods. First, the reacquisition of the firm's shares is viewed as constituting a contraction of its capital structure. Second, the reissuance of the shares is the same as issuing new shares. There is little difference between the purchase and subsequent reissuance of treasury shares and the acquisition and retirement of previously issued shares and the issuance of new shares.

Treasury shares originally accounted for by the cost method can subsequently be restated to conform to the constructive retirement method. If shares were acquired with the intention that they would be reissued and it is later determined that such reissuance is unlikely (due for example, to the expiration of stock options without their exercise), it is proper to restate the transaction.

Example of accounting for treasury stock

1. 100 shares ($50 par value) that were sold originally for $60 per share are later reacquired for $70 each.
2. All 100 shares are subsequently resold for a total of $7,500.

To record the acquisition, the entry is:

Cost method			*Par value method*			*Constructive retirement method*		
Treasury stock	7,000		Treasury stock	5,000		Common stock	5,000	
Cash		7,000	Additional paid-in capital--common stock	1,000		Additional paid-in capital--common stock	1,000	
			Retained earnings	1,000		Retained earnings	1,000	
			Cash		7,000	Cash		7,000

To record the resale, the entry is:

Cost method			*Par value method*			*Constructive retirement method*		
Cash	7,500		Cash	7,500		Cash	7,500	
Treasury stock		7,000	Treasury stock		5,000	Common stock		5,000
Additional paid-in capital--treasury stock		500	Additional paid-in capital--common stock		2,500	Additional paid-in capital--common stock		2,500

If the shares had been resold for $6,500, the entry is:

Cost method			*Par value method*			*Constructive retirement method*		
Cash	6,500		Cash	6,500		Cash	6,500	
*Retained earnings	500		Treasury stock		5,000	Common stock		5,000
Treasury stock		7,000	Additional paid-in			Additional paid-in		
			capital--common			capital--common		
			stock		1,500	stock		1,500

* *"Additional paid-in capital--treasury stock" or "Additional paid-in capital--retired stock" of that issue would be debited first to the extent it exists.*

Alternatively, under the par or constructive retirement methods, any portion of or the entire deficiency on the treasury stock acquisition may be debited to retained earnings without allocation to paid-in capital. Any excesses would always be credited to an "Additional paid-in capital--retired stock" account.

The laws of some states govern the circumstances under which a corporation may acquire treasury stock and they may prescribe the accounting for the stock. For example, a charge to retained earnings may be required in an amount equal to the treasury stock's total cost. In such cases, the accounting according to state law prevails. Also, some states define excess purchase cost of reacquired (i.e., treasury) shares as being "distributions" to shareholders which are no different in nature than dividends. In such cases, the financial statement presentation should adequately disclose the substance of these transactions (e.g., by presenting both dividends and excess reacquisition costs together in the retained earnings statement).

When a firm decides to retire the treasury stock formally, the journal entry is dependent on the method used to account for the stock. Using the original sale and reacquisition data from the illustration above, the following entry would be made:

Cost method			*Par value method*		
Common stock	5,000		Common stock	5,000	
Additional paid-in			Treasury stock		5,000
capital--common stock	1,000				
*Retained earnings	1,000				
Treasury stock		7,000			

* *"Additional paid-in capital--treasury stock" may be debited to the extent that it exists.*

If the constructive retirement method were used to record the treasury stock purchase, no additional entry would be necessary on formal retirement of the shares.

After the entry is made, the pro rata portion of all paid-in capital existing for that issue (i.e., capital stock and additional paid-in capital) will have been eliminated. If stock is purchased for immediate retirement (i.e., not put into the treasury) the entry to record the retirement is the same as that made under the constructive retirement method.

In the case of donated treasury stock, the intentions of management are important. If the shares are to be retired, the capital stock account is debited for the par or stated value of the shares, "Donated capital" is credited for the fair market value, and "Additional paid-in capital--retired stock" is debited or credited for the difference. If the intention of management is to reissue the shares, three methods of accounting are available. The first two methods, cost and par value, are analogous to the aforementioned treasury stock methods except that "Donated capital" is credited at the time of receipt and debited at the time of reissuance. Under the cost method, the current market value of the stock is recorded (an apparent contradiction), whereas under the par value method, the par or stated value is used. Under the last method, only a memorandum entry is made to indicate the number of shares received. No journal entry is made at the time of receipt. At the time of reissuance, the entire proceeds are credited to "Donated capital." The method actually used is generally dependent on the circumstances involving the donation and the preference of the firm.

Other Equity Accounts

There are other adjustments to balance sheet accounts that are accumulated and reflected as separate components of stockholders' equity. Under current US GAAP, these include unrealized gains or losses on available-for-sale portfolios of debt and marketable equity securities, accumulated gain or loss on translation of foreign currency-denominated financial statements, and the net loss not recognized as pension cost.

Stock Options

The subject of accounting for stock options has long been controversial in the United States. A rule made more than 20 years ago decreed that most stock options would not result in recognition of compensation expense if the option exercise price were at least equal to the market price at the date of the granting of the options. Although this defied logic (if such options were not valuable compensation, executives would not negotiate these as part of their total compensation programs) it had long been traditional that this accounting would be applied. However, as long as 10 years ago the profession's top standards setters concluded that most such plans should indeed give rise to the recognition of compensation cost, and then began a long, controversial project to develop the appropriate accounting procedures.

The standards-setting body ultimately did propose a new standard that would have required a fairly complicated measurement strategy for compensation cost for most such option arrangements. A great, orchestrated outcry arose from many sectors of industry, particularly from those enterprises, such as technology companies, which traditionally make great use of this technique of compensating executives. The ultimate result was that a final standard was promulgated which recommended, but did not require, use of this technique. Supplemental disclosures are required for entities that decline to adopt the suggested method, however, which effectively results in presentation of an alternative income amount as if the recommended technique had been employed.

Since this situation is still not fully resolved and is unique, at the present time, to the United States, detailed presentation of the very complex methodology is omitted here.

Stock Appreciation Rights

Another type of stock-based compensation program gives the employees the opportunity to participate in any increase in value of the company's stock without having to incur the cost of actually purchasing the shares themselves. Such plans are often referred to as phantom stock plans, stock appreciation rights, or variable stock award programs. A wide variety of such plans have been devised in practice. Some provide for the payment of cash to the employees, while others reward participants with shares of the sponsoring company's stock. Often such plans are granted together with compensatory stock option plans as either combination plans or as tandem plans: the former give the employees the rights to both the options and the phantom stock, while the latter require the employees to choose which they will exercise (simultaneously forfeiting the other).

Under US GAAP, compensation cost incurred in connection with stock appreciation rights or other variable awards is determined prospectively until full vesting is achieved, with future increases or decreases in market price resulting in charges or credits to periodic compensation expense. Total compensation cost is allocated ratably (if cliff vesting is provided by the plan) or proportionally (if graded vesting is provided). When an employee forfeits options or rights for which compensation had previously been accrued, the accrual is to be reversed against compensation expense in the period of the forfeiture.

Performance-based stock compensation plans often provide for payment in shares instead of cash. For example, a stock appreciation rights plan may contain a provision that the increase in value will be distributed to the participant in the form of sufficient shares of the sponsor's stock to have an aggregate fair market value equal to the amount of the award. If the plan provides only for payment in shares (a plan that most often is referred to as a phantom stock plan), the offset to the periodic charge for compensation cost should be to paid-in capital accounts. If the award is payable at the participant's choice in either cash or stock, a liability should be accrued, since the sponsor cannot control the means by which the obligation will be settled. If the payment will be made in cash or stock at the option of the company, the offset to compensation should be either to a liability account or to equity accounts, based on the best available information concerning the sponsor's intentions. As these intentions change from one period to another, the amounts should be reclassified as necessary.

Accounting for stock appreciation rights has been altered by the recent standard on stock-based compensation. Furthermore, there are many variations in these plans and thus the precise accounting cannot be stipulated in general terms. Further discussion of this topic is beyond the scope of this book.

Convertible Preferred Stock

The treatment of convertible preferred stock at its issuance is no different from that of nonconvertible preferred. When it is converted, the book value approach is used to account for the conversion. Use of the market value approach would entail a gain or loss for which there is no theoretical justification, since the total amount of contributed capital does not change when the stock is converted. When the preferred stock is converted, the "Preferred stock" and related "Additional paid-in capital--preferred stock" accounts are debited for their original values when purchased, and "Common stock" and "Additional paid-in capital--common stock" (if an excess over par or stated value exists) are credited. If the book value of the preferred stock is less than the total par value of the common stock being issued, retained earnings is charged for the difference. This charge is supported by the rationale that the preferred shareholders are offered an additional return to facilitate their conversion to common stock. Many states require that this excess instead reduce additional paid-in capital from other sources.

Preferred Stock with Mandatory Redemption

A mandatory redemption clause requires the preferred stock to be redeemed (retired) at a specified date(s). This feature is in contrast to callable preferred stock, which is redeemed at the issuing corporation's option. When combined with a cumulative dividend preference, the mandatory redemption feature causes the preferred stock to have the characteristics of debt, especially when the stock is to be redeemed in 5 to 10 years. The dividend payments represent interest, and redemption is the repayment of principal. However, there is one important difference. The dividend payments do not receive the same tax treatment as do interest payments. They are not deductible in determining taxable income.

Despite these debt-like characteristics, this class of preferred stock currently receives no special treatment under GAAP. It is treated as any other stock on issuance, and on redemption, the stock is treated as an ordinary retirement. (It should be noted that this conflicts with the requirements under the international standard, IAS 32, which does demand that a "substance over form" analysis be conducted and that items such as mandatorily redeemable stock be treated as debt. This is one instance, but not the only one, in which the international standards have progressed beyond the US standards.)

For disclosure purposes under US GAAP, the stock is treated as equity and is presented within the stockholders' equity portion of the balance sheet. Disclosure of the amounts and timing of any redemption payments for each of the 5 years following the balance sheet date is required as footnote disclosure, however.

Book Value Stock Plans

Another type of stock purchase plan, the book value plan, is intended also to be a compensation program for participating employees, although there are important secondary motives in many such plans, such as the desires to generate capital and to tie employees to the employer. Under the terms of typical book value plans, employees (or those attaining some defined level, such as manager) are given the opportunity or, in some cases, they are required to purchase shares in the company, which then must be sold back to the company on termination of employment.

Under US GAAP, if the employees participating in a nonpublic company's book value stock plan have substantive investments in the company that are at risk, the increases in book value during the period of ownership are not to be treated as compensation. However, if the employees are granted options to purchase shares at book value, compensation is to be recognized for value increases, presumably because under the latter scenario the employee has no investment at risk and is only being given an "upside" opportunity. This interpretation is also applicable to book value options granted to employees of publicly held companies.

For accounting purposes, shares issued at book value to employees are simply recorded as a normal stock sale. To the extent that book value exceeds par or stated value, additional paid-in capital accounts may also be credited.

For such plans in publicly owned companies, GAAP states that these plans are performance plans akin to stock appreciation rights, and accordingly, results in compensation expense recognition. This conclusion was reached at least in part due to pressure from the US securities regulators.

Junior Stock

Another category of stock-based compensation program involves junior stock. Typically, such shares are subordinate to normal shares of common stock with respect to voting rights, dividend rate, or other attributes, and are convertible into regular common shares if and when stipulated performance goals are achieved. Like stock appreciation rights, grants of junior stock represent a performance-based program, in contrast to fixed stock options.

An interpretation under US GAAP holds that compensation cost incurred in connection with grants of junior stock is generally to be accrued. However, compensation is to be recognized only when it is deemed to be probable (as that term is defined by the accounting literature dealing with contingencies) that the performance goals will be achieved. It may be that achievement is not deemed probable at the time the junior stock is issued, but it later becomes clear that such achievement is indeed likely. In other circumstances, the ability to convert junior stock to regular stock is dependent on the achievement of more than a single performance goal, and it is not probable that all such goals can be achieved, although some of them are deemed probable of achievement. In both scenarios, full accrual of compensation cost may be delayed until the estimated likelihood of achievement improves.

The rule specifies that the measure of compensation is derived from the comparison of the market price of ordinary common stock with the price to be paid, if any, for the junior stock. Since the junior stock will be convertible to ordinary common stock if the defined performance goals are achieved, the compensation to be received by the employees participating in the plan is linked to the value of unrestricted common shares.

Put Warrant

A detachable put warrant can either be put back to the debt issuer for cash or can be exercised to acquire common stock. US GAAP holds that these instruments should be accounted for in the same manner as mandatorily redeemable preferred stock. The proceeds applicable to the put warrant ordinarily are to be classified as equity. In the case of a warrant with a put price substantially higher than the value assigned to the warrant at issuance, however, the proceeds should be classified as a liability since it is likely that the warrant will be put back to the company.

The original classification should not be changed because of subsequent economic changes in the value of the put. The value assigned to the put warrant at issuance, however, should be adjusted to its highest redemption price, starting with the date of issuance until the earliest date of the warrants. Changes in the redemption price before the earliest put dates are changes in accounting estimates, and changes after the earliest put dates should be recognized in income. If the put is classified as equity, the adjustment should be reported as a charge to retained earnings, and if the put is classified as a liability, the adjustment is reported as interest expense.

Accounting for Stock Issued to Employee Stock Ownership Plans

Increasingly, US corporations have been availing themselves of favorable tax regulations that encourage the establishment of employee stock ownership plans. Employee stock ownership plans (ESOP) are defined contribution employee benefit plans in which shares of the sponsoring entity are given to employees as additional compensation.

In brief, ESOP are created by a sponsoring corporation that either funds the plan directly (unleveraged ESOP) or, as is more often the case, facilitates the borrowing of money either directly from an outside lender (directly leveraged ESOP) or from the employer, who in turn will borrow from an outside lender (indirectly leveraged ESOP). Borrowings from outside lenders may or may not be guaranteed by the sponsor. Since effectively the only source of funds for debt repayment are future contributions by the sponsor, US GAAP requires that the ESOP's debt be considered debt of the sponsor. Depending on the reasons underlying the creation of the

ESOP (estate planning by the controlling shareholder, expanding the capital base of the entity, rewarding and motivating the workforce, etc.), the sponsor's shares may be contributed to the plan in annual installments, in a block of shares from the sponsor, or shares from an existing shareholder may be purchased by the plan.

Direct or indirect borrowings by the ESOP must be reported as debt in the sponsor's balance sheet. An offset to a contra equity account, not to an asset, is also reported since the plan represents a commitment (morally, if not always legally) to make future contributions to the plan and not a claim to resources. This results in a "double hit" to the sponsor's balance sheet (i.e., the recording of a liability and the reduction of net stockholders' equity), which is often an unanticipated and unpleasant surprise. This contra equity account was called "unearned compensation" under prior accounting rules but is now referred to as "unearned ESOP shares." If the sponsor lends funds to the ESOP without a "mirror" loan from an outside lender, this loan should not be reported in the employer's balance sheet as debt, although the debit should still be reported as a contra equity account.

As the ESOP services the debt (using contributions made by the sponsor and/or dividends received on sponsor shares held by the plan) the sponsor reflects the reduction of the obligation by reducing the debt and the contra equity account on its balance sheet. Simultaneously, income and thus retained earnings will be affected as the contributions to the plan are reported in the sponsor's current results of operations. Thus, the double hit is eliminated, but net worth continues to reflect the economic fact that compensation costs have been incurred. US GAAP requires that the interest cost component be separated from the remaining compensation expense, that is, that the sponsor's income statement should reflect the true character of the expenses being incurred rather than aggregating the entire amount into a category such as "ESOP contribution."

In a leveraged ESOP, shares held serve as collateral for the debt and are not allocated to employees until the debt is retired. In general, shares must be allocated by the end of the year in which the debt is repaid; however, to satisfy the tax laws, the allocation of shares may take place at a faster pace than retirement of the principal portion of the debt.

The cost of ESOP shares allocated is measured (for purposes of reporting compensation expense in the sponsor's income statements) based on the fair value on the release date, in contrast to the actual historical cost of the shares to the plan. Dividends paid on unallocated shares (i.e., shares held by the ESOP) are reported in the sponsor's income statement as compensation cost and/or as interest expense.

Example of accounting for ESOP transactions

Assume that Intrepid Corp. establishes an ESOP, which then borrows $500,000 from Second Interstate Bank. The ESOP then purchases 50,000 shares of Intrepid no-par shares from the company; none of these shares are allocated to individual participants. The entries would be

Cash	500,000	
Bank loan payable		500,000
Unearned ESOP shares (contra equity account)	500,000	
Common stock		500,000

The ESOP then borrows an additional $250,000 from the sponsor, Intrepid, and uses the cash to purchase a further 25,000 shares, all of which are allocated to participants.

Compensation	250,000	
Common stock		250,000

Intrepid Corp. contributes $50,000 to the plan, which the plan uses to service its bank debt, consisting of $40,000 principal reduction and $10,000 interest cost. The debt reduction causes 4,000 shares to be allocated to participants at a time when the average market value had been $12 per share.

Interest expense	10,000	
Bank loan payable	40,000	
Cash		50,000
Compensation	48,000	
Additional paid-in capital		8,000
Unearned ESOP shares		40,000

Dividends of $0.10 per share are declared (only the ESOP shares are represented in the following entry, but dividends are paid equally on all outstanding shares).

Retained earnings	2,900	
Compensation	4,600	
Dividends payable		7,500

Note that in all the foregoing illustrations the effect of income taxes is ignored. Since the difference between the cost and fair values of shares committed to be released is analogous to differences in the expense recognized for tax and accounting purposes with regard to stock options, the same treatment should be applied. That is, the tax effect should be reported directly in stockholders' equity rather than in earnings.

Corporate Bankruptcy and Reorganizations

Entities operating under and emerging from protection of the bankruptcy laws. The going concern assumption is one of the basic postulates underlying generally accepted accounting principles and is responsible for, among other things, the historical cost convention in financial reporting. For entities that have entered bankruptcy proceedings, however, the going concern assumption will no longer be of central importance.

Traditionally, the basic financial statements (balance sheet, income statement, and statement of cash flows) presented by going concerns were seen as less useful for entities undergoing reorganization. Instead, the statement of affairs, reporting assets at estimated realizable values and liabilities at estimated liquidation amounts, was recommended for use by such organizations. In more recent years, use of the statement of affairs has not frequently been encountered in practice. About 5 years ago, a new standard was promulgated, setting forth certain financial reporting standards for entities undergoing, and emerging from, reorganization under the bankruptcy laws.

Under GAAP, assets are presented at estimated realizable values. Liabilities are set forth at the estimated amounts to be allowed in the balance sheet and liabilities subject to compromise are to be distinguished from those that are not. Furthermore, US GAAP requires that in both statements of income and cash flows, normal transactions be differentiated from those that have occurred as a consequence of the entity's being in reorganization. While certain allocations to the latter category are rather obvious, such as legal and accounting fees incurred, others are less clear. For example, the standard suggests that if the entity in reorganization earns interest income on funds that would normally have been used to settle obligations owed to creditors, such income will be deemed to be income arising as a consequence of the bankruptcy action.

Another interesting aspect of this standard is the accounting to be made for the emergence from reorganization (known as "confirmation of the plan of reorganization"). GAAP now provides for "fresh start" financial reporting in such instances. This accounting is similar to that applied to purchase business combinations, with the total confirmed value of the entity on its emergence from reorganization being analogous to the purchase price in an acquisition. In both cases, this total value is to be allocated to the identifiable assets and liabilities of the entity, with any excess being allocated to goodwill. In the case of entities emerging from bankruptcy, goodwill ("reorganization value in excess of amounts allocable to identifiable assets") is measured as the excess of liabilities existing at the plan confirmation date, computed at present value of future amounts to be paid, over the "reorganization value of assets. Reorganization value is calculated with reference to a number of factors, including forecasted operating results and cash flows of the new entity.

This standard applies only to entities undergoing formal reorganization under the bankruptcy code. Less formal procedures may still be accounted for under preexisting quasi reorganization accounting procedures.

Quasi reorganizations

Generally, this procedure is applicable during a period of declining price levels. It is termed "quasi" since the accumulated deficit is eliminated at a lower cost and with less difficulty than a legal reorganization. Under the provisions of US GAAP, the procedures in a quasi reorganization involve

1. Proper authorization from stockholders and creditors where required.
2. Revaluation of assets to their current values. All losses are charged to retained earnings, thus increasing any deficit.
3. Elimination of any deficit by charging paid-in capital
   a. Additional paid-in capital to the extent it exists
   b. Capital stock when additional paid-in capital is insufficient. The par value of the stock is reduced, creating the extra additional paid-in capital to which the remaining deficit is charged.

No retained earnings may be created by a reorganization. Any excess created by the reduction of par value is credited to "Paid-in capital from quasi reorganization." Retained earnings must be dated for 10 years (less than 10 years may be justified under exceptional circumstances) after a quasi reorganization takes place. Disclosure similar to "since quasi reorganization of June 30, 19XX" is appropriate.

17 EARNINGS PER SHARE

PERSPECTIVE AND ISSUES

Earnings per share (EPS) is a ratio (or index) that is widely used by both present and prospective investors to gauge the profitability of a corporation. Its purpose is to indicate, in an easily understood and readily comparable manner, how effective an enterprise has been in using the resources provided by the holders of its equity shares. At its simplest, EPS is computed by dividing net income (loss) by the number of shares of outstanding equity shares. The EPS computation becomes more complicated with the existence of potential ordinary shares; that is, securities which are not presently equity shares but which have the potential of causing additional equity shares to be issued in future. Examples of this class of instrument include convertible preference shares or convertible debt, and options or warrants. The accounting profession recognized many years ago that if earnings per share were to be calculated while ignoring these potentially dilutive securities, there would be a great possibility that the computed amount would be misleading. In addition, a lack of standardization in the precise manner in which these securities are included in the EPS computation would tend to make comparisons among corporations more difficult and potentially quite misleading as well. For these reasons, there have been attempts to prescribe the EPS computation by various standards setters over the past 40 years.

Possibly due to the ever-growing complexity of financial reporting (due, in turn, to the more complicated nature of business transactions and relationships), users of financial statements have long sought a concise, meaningful statistic which would capture succinctly the reporting enterprise's success or failure for the period being reported on. The concept of earnings per share evolved as an obvious candidate for this data element. The reaction of the accounting profession, first in the United States and later in the United Kingdom, was one of caution and concern, since it was feared that users would begin to use this summary statistic as a surrogate for the vastly more informative full set of financial statements; clearly, no summary element of data can convey even a small fraction of the information contained in a more expansive document, such as a balance sheet or income statement.

Later, however, faced with an overwhelming clamor for such a statistic, the profession attempted to provide guidance on appropriate methods of computation and communication of earnings per share information, coupled with a prohibition against using other appealing but more misleading indexes, particularly cash flow per share. After a period of evolution, the long-standing US requirements (set forth in APB Opinion 15) were finally promulgated in the late 1960s. A similar UK standard followed a few years later. Both of these have been subject to much criticism on the basis of complexity and arbitrariness, but largely endured (with minor amendments) for 25 years. Most recently, the US standard has been superseded by SFAS 128, which essentially mirrors the new international accounting standard and which eliminates much of the complexity for which its venerable predecessor had been disparaged. The UK Accounting Standards Board (ASB) followed suit and also issued an exposure draft, FRED 16, in mid-1997. This closely follows IAS 33 and if adopted will make the new concept of basic earnings per share a virtually universal financial reporting requirement.

Rules governing the computation of earnings per share had never been a part of international accounting standards, but the need to develop an official position on this topic provided a welcome opportunity for joint research by national and international standard-setting bodies. The result is that the new international standard, IAS 33, is almost entirely replicated by the US standard, SFAS 128. This result should further the goals of internationalization of commerce and will probably also reinforce the emerging leadership role of international accounting standards.

The International Accounting Standards Committee issued IAS 33, *Earnings Per Share*, in early 1997, to become operative for financial statements covering periods beginning on or after January 1, 1998. The objective of IAS 33 is to prescribe the ground rules for the determination and presentation of earnings per share. It is interesting to note that the objectives of the standard were expanded from the time the Exposure Draft, E52, was issued until the final version of IAS 33 was promulgated. IAS 33 emphasizes the **denominator** of the earnings per share calculation and notes that even though EPS calculations have limitations, because different accounting policies typically can be used in the determination of earnings, which is in the **numerator** of the equation, **a consistently determined denominator enhances financial reporting**.

IAS 33 states that the standard should be applied to both enterprises whose ordinary shares or potential ordinary shares are publicly traded, and enterprises that are **in the process of issuing** ordinary shares or potential ordinary shares in public securities markets. The standard's antecedent, E52, did not mandate that the rules should be applied in this manner, by contrast. The standard's applicability to entities which have not yet issued shares but which are only in the process of doing so may introduce an element of subjectivity in attempting to apply IAS 33 in actual practice. Perhaps this will ultimately have to be clarified by the newly constituted Standing Interpretations Committee of the IASC.

In case of those enterprises whose shares are **not publicly traded** but which voluntarily choose to disclose EPS figures anyway, the IAS 33 makes it incumbent on these enterprises to calculate and disclose EPS in accordance with the provisions of this standard. Thus, while IAS 33 does not require presentation of EPS data by all enterprises, it does prescribe the computational methods to be used by all enterprises that choose to make such disclosures.

In situations when both parent company and consolidated financial statements are presented, IAS 33 requires that the information called for by this standard need only be presented based on the consolidated information. The reasoning given for this rule is that users of financial statements of a parent company are interested in the results of operations of the group as a whole as opposed to the parent company on a stand-alone basis. Of course, nothing prevents the enterprise from also presenting the parent-only information, including EPS, should it choose to do so.

Sources of IAS
IAS 33

DEFINITIONS OF TERMS

A number of terms used in a discussion of earnings per share have special meanings in that context. When used, they are intended to have the meanings given in the following definitions.

Antidilution. An increase in earnings per share or reduction in net loss per share, resulting from the inclusion of a potentially dilutive security, in EPS calculations.

Basic earnings per share. The amount of net profit or loss for the period that is attributable to each ordinary share that is outstanding during all or part of the period.

Call price. The amount at which a security may be redeemed by the issuer at the issuer's option.

Common stock. A stock that is subordinate to all other stocks of the issuer. Also known as ordinary shares.

Common stock equivalent. This expression is used under the US GAAP to denote a security which, because of its terms or the circumstances under which it was issued, is in substance equivalent to common stock. There is no equivalent concept under the proposed international accounting standards.

Contingent issuance. A possible issuance of ordinary (equity) shares that is dependent on the exercise of conversion rights, options, or warrants, the satisfaction of certain conditions, or similar arrangements.

Conversion price. The price that determines the number of ordinary (equity) shares into which a security is convertible. For example, $100 face value of debt convertible into five ordinary (equity) shares would be stated to have a conversion price of $20.

Conversion rate. The ratio of (1) the number of common shares issuable on conversion to (2) a unit of convertible security. For example, a preference share may be convertible at the rate of three ordinary shares for each preference share.

Conversion value. The current market value of the common shares obtainable on conversion of a convertible security, after deducting any cash payment required on conversion.

Diluted earnings per share. The amount of net profit for the period per share, reflecting the maximum dilutions that would have resulted from conversions, exercises, and other contingent issuances that individually would have decreased earnings per share and in the aggregate would have had a dilutive effect.

Dilution. A reduction in earnings per share or an increase in net loss per share, resulting from the assumption that convertible securities have been converted or that options and warrants have been exercised, or other contingent shares have been issued on the fulfillment of certain conditions. Securities that would cause such earnings dilution are referred to as dilutive securities.

Dual presentation. The presentation with equal prominence of two different earnings per share amounts on the face of the income statement: One is basic earnings per share; the other is diluted earnings per share.

Earnings per share. The amount of earnings for a period attributable to each ordinary (equity) share (common stock). For convenience, the term is used in IAS 33 to refer to either net income (earnings) per share or net loss per share. It should be used without qualifying language (e.g., diluted) only when no potentially dilutive convertible securities, options, warrants, or other agreements providing for contingent issuances of ordinary (equity) shares are outstanding.

Exercise price. The amount that must be paid for a ordinary (equity) share on exercise of a stock option or warrant.

If-converted method. A method of computing earnings per share data that assumes conversion of convertible securities as of the beginning of the earliest period reported (or at time of issuance, if later). This method was mandated under US GAAP.

Option. The right to purchase ordinary (equity) shares in accordance with an agreement upon payment of a specified amount, including but not limited to options granted to and stock purchase agreements entered into with employees.

Ordinary shares. Those shares that are subordinate to all other stocks of the issuer. Also known as common stock.

Redemption price. The amount at which a security is required to be redeemed at maturity or under a sinking-fund arrangement.

Senior security. This is an expression used under US GAAP and refers to a security having preferential rights and which is neither an ordinary (equity) share nor a common stock equivalent (as defined above). A nonconvertible preference share is an example of a senior security.

Time of issuance. The time of issuance generally is the date when agreement as to terms has been reached and announced, even though such agreement is subject to certain further actions, such as directors' or stockholders' approval.

Treasury stock method. A method of recognizing the use of proceeds that would be obtained on exercise of options and warrants in computing earnings per share. It assumes that any proceeds would be used to purchase ordinary (equity) shares at current market prices. The proposed international standard does not prescribe this method but uses a different calculation to achieve the same result.

Warrant. A security giving the holder the right to purchase shares of common stock in accordance with the terms of the instrument, usually on payment of a specified amount.

Weighted-average number of shares. The number of shares determined by relating (1) the portion of time within a reporting period that a particular number of shares of a certain security has been outstanding to (2) the total time in that period. For example, if 100 shares of a certain security were outstanding during the first quarter of a fiscal year and 300 shares were outstanding during the balance of the year, the weighted-average number of outstanding shares would be 250 [(100 x 1/4) + (300 x 3/4)].

CONCEPTS, RULES, AND EXAMPLES

Background

Investors and other interested parties have always sought a simple means of assessing a company's progress and performance. What on the surface looks like the ultimate distillation of an enterprise's financial data is the summary statistic known as earnings per share (EPS), which presents in a single number the net result of a period's operations from the perspective of the owner of its common, or ordinary, shares. Over the years, the accounting profession has attempted to discourage reliance on this measure or any other single condensed indicator which would omit much of the detail information that was deemed necessary to truly understand the entity's operations, but eventually, when the demand for such a criterion became irresistible, accountants attempted to develop guidelines that would at least ensure that any such benchmark measure would be valid and consistently applied.

In the United States, the profession's first attempt to provide guidance in this area was through Accounting Research Bulletin (ARB) 49 (1958). However, this pronouncement was generally ignored, and most enterprises still computed EPS simplistically, by dividing net income minus preferred stock dividends by a weighted-average of the number of common shares outstanding and ignoring the potential impact of other dilutive securities (which fortunately were typically not significant in those less complicated times). However, the distortion inherent in an

EPS number computed without regard for potentially dilutive securities was exacerbated during the merger and acquisition activity of the 1960s. Many of these mergers, which resulted in higher reported earnings for the combined entity, were accomplished by the issuance of convertible securities, options, or warrants and by the retirement of the common stock of the merged company. Thus, an entity that disregarded outstanding dilutive securities when computing EPS could show an increase in EPS without a corresponding increase in profitability. The increase was due to larger combined earnings being divided by a smaller number of common shares.

In the US, the next official pronouncement on the subject was the Accounting Principles Board (APB) Opinion 9 (1966), which advised corporations with potentially dilutive securities (convertible preferred stock, convertible debt, or outstanding options or warrants) that if "potential dilution was material, supplementary pro forma computations of earnings per share should be furnished, showing what the earnings would be if conversions or contingent issuances took place." This standard suffered from some of the same weaknesses as its predecessor, and compliance, if marginally better than with ARB 49, was still not satisfactory.

The most significant development occurred when the Accounting Principles Board (APB) published Opinion 15 (1969), which expanded the definition of those securities that have the potential to dilute EPS, and which provided much more specific guidance in computational matters, as well as clearly delineating the reporting and disclosure requirements. This pronouncement was not applicable to nonprofit corporations, government-owned corporations, registered investment companies, mutual companies without common stock or common stock equivalents, or (in a major change which occurred almost a decade after the original issuance of APB 15) nonpublic enterprises, as was later defined in FASB Statement 21. However, the standard required that if any of these exempted entities did voluntarily present EPS information, it had to have been prepared and displayed in conformity with the requirements of APB 15.

Although the standard established by APB 15 has been implemented universally over the past 25 years, it has been subject to severe criticism, most of which has focused on the complex and arbitrary nature by which potentially dilutive securities are treated. As a result, in mid-1993 the FASB began the process of looking for ways to revise APB 15 by inviting comment letters on the subject. A large majority of letters indicated a need to revise the denominator used in the EPS calculation. The board then initiated an earnings per share project and released an exposure draft of a new standard in mid-1996.

In the United Kingdom, the first accounting standard to be issued on the subject was SSAP 3, *Earnings Per Share*, which was issued in 1972 and prescribed not only minimum disclosure requirements relating to EPS but also dealt with the basis of calculating the ratio. Subsequently, the Accounting Standards Board (ASB) in the United Kingdom came to realize that a great deal of emphasis was being placed on reported EPS figures, which led to the promulgation of a different interpretation in a later standard (FRS 3), which attempted to simplify EPS reporting and requires that EPS be calculated based on earnings after extraordinary items. It should be noted, however, that despite the ASB's stipulation in FRS 3 to present the EPS numbers in a standardized and simple manner, it also allows the companies in the United Kingdom to present additional EPS figures prepared on other bases as well, which have to be reconciled to the EPS number required by FRS 3. This, in the opinion of many authorities on the subject, has made the EPS reporting in the United Kingdom much more volatile and in reality only a starting point for further analyses.

Given the recent promulgation of virtually identical and essentially simplified standards by both the FASB and the IASC, there is reason to hope that, at least on this one rather narrow topic, it may be possible to develop a single solution for a financial reporting problem which all preparers can accept as being correct.

Simple Capital Structure

A simple capital structure may be said to exist either when the capital structure consists solely of ordinary (equity) shares or when it includes no potential ordinary shares, which could be in the form of options, warrants, or other rights, that on conversion or exercise could, in the aggregate, dilute earnings per share. Dilutive securities are essentially those that exhibit the rights of debt or other senior security holders (including warrants and options) and which have the potential on their issuance to reduce the earnings per share.

Computational guidelines. In its simplest form, the EPS calculation is net income divided by the weighted-average number of ordinary shares outstanding. The objective of the EPS calculation is to determine the amount of earnings available to each ordinary share. Complexities arise because net income does not necessarily represent the earnings available to the ordinary shareholder, and a simple weighted-average of ordinary shares outstanding does not necessarily reflect the true nature of the situation. Adjustments can take the form of manipulations of the numerator or of the denominator of the formula used to compute EPS, as discussed in the following paragraphs.

Numerator. The net income figure used as the numerator in any of the EPS computations must reflect any claims against it by holders of senior securities. The justification for this reduction is that the claims of the senior securities must be satisfied before any income is available to the common shareholder. These securities are usually in the form of preference shares, and the deduction from income is the amount of the dividend declared during the year on the preference shares. If the preference shares are cumulative, the dividend is to be deducted from income (or added to the loss), whether it is declared or not. If preference shares do not have a cumulative right to dividends and current period dividends have been omitted, such dividends should not be deducted in computing EPS. Cumulative dividends in arrears that are paid currently do not affect the calculation of EPS in the current period, since such dividends have already been considered in prior periods' EPS computations. However, the amount in arrears should be disclosed, as should all of the effects of the rights given to senior securities on the EPS calculation.

Denominator. The weighted-average number of ordinary shares outstanding is used so that the effect of increases or decreases in outstanding shares on EPS data is related to the portion of the period during which the related consideration affected operations. The difficulty in computing the weighted-average exists because of the effect that various transactions have on the computation of ordinary shares outstanding. Although it is impossible to analyze all the possibilities, the following discussion presents some of the more common transactions affecting the number of ordinary shares outstanding. The theoretical construct set forth in these relatively simple examples can be followed in all other situations.

If a company reacquires its own shares (referred to as treasury stock), in countries where it is legally permissible to do so, the number of shares reacquired should be excluded from EPS calculations as of the date of acquisition. The same theory holds for the issuance of ordinary shares during the period. The number of shares newly issued is included in the computation only for the period after their issuance date. The logic for this treatment is that the consideration for the shares was not available to generate earnings until the shares were issued. This same logic applies to the reacquired shares because the consideration relative to those shares was no longer available to generate earnings after the acquisition date.

A stock dividend (bonus issue) or a stock (share) split does not generate additional resources or consideration, but it does increase the number of shares outstanding. The increase in shares as a result of a stock split or dividend, or decrease in shares as a result of a reverse split, should be given retroactive recognition as an appropriate equivalent charge for all periods presented. Thus, even if a stock dividend or split occurs at the end of the period, it is considered outstanding for the entire period of each period presented. The reasoning is that a stock dividend or split has no effect on the ownership percentage of the common stockholder. As such, to show a dilution in the EPS reported would erroneously give the impression of a decline in profitability when in fact it was merely an increase in the shares outstanding due to the stock dividend or split.

IAS 33 carries this logic one step further by requiring the disclosure of pro forma (adjusted) amounts of basic and diluted earnings per share for the period in case of issue of shares with no corresponding change in resources (e.g., stock dividends or splits) occurring **after** the balance sheet date, but before the issuance of the financial statements. The reason given is that the nondisclosure of such transactions would affect the ability of the users of the financial statements to make proper evaluations and decisions. It is to be noted, however, that the EPS numbers as presented on the face of the income statement are not required by IAS 33 to be retroactively adjusted, as is the case under US GAAP, because such transactions do not reflect the amount of capital used to produce the net profit or loss for the period.

Complications also arise when a business combination occurs during the period. The treatment of the additional shares depends on the nature of the combination. If the business combination is recorded as a uniting of interests, the additional shares are assumed to have been issued at the beginning of the year regardless of when the combination occurred. Conversely, if the combination is accounted for as an acquisition, the shares are considered issued and outstanding as of the date of acquisition. The reason for this varied treatment lies in the income statement treatment accorded a uniting of interests vs. an acquisition. In a uniting of interests, the income of the acquired company is included in the statements for the entire year, whereas in an acquisition, the income is included only for the period after acquisition.

IAS 33 recognizes that in certain countries it is permissible for ordinary shares to be issued in partly paid form, and the standard accordingly stipulates that partly paid instruments should be included as ordinary share equivalents to the extent to which they carry rights (during the financial reporting year) to participate in dividends vis-à-vis fully paid shares. Further, in the case of contingently issuable shares (i.e., ordinary shares issuable on fulfillment of certain conditions, say, on achieving a certain level of profits or sales), IAS 33 requires that such shares be considered outstanding and included in the computation of basic earnings per share only when all the required conditions have been satisfied.

IAS 33 gives examples of situations where ordinary shares may be issued, or the number of shares outstanding may be reduced, without causing corresponding changes in resources of the corporation. Such examples include bonus issues, a bonus element in other issues such as a rights issue (to existing shareholders), a share split, a reverse share split, and a capital reduction without a corresponding refund of capital. In all such cases the number of ordinary shares outstanding before the event is adjusted, as if the event had occurred at the beginning of the earliest period reported. For instance, in a three-to-one bonus issue the number of shares outstanding prior to the issue is multiplied by a factor of 4. These and other situations are summarized in the tabular list that follows.

In case of rights shares, the number of ordinary shares to be used in calculating basic EPS is the number of ordinary shares outstanding prior to the issue, multiplied by the following factor:

$$\frac{\text{Fair value immediately prior to the exercise of the rights}}{\text{Theoretical ex-rights fair value}}$$

There are several ways to compute the theoretical value of the shares on an ex-rights basis. IAS 33 suggests that this be derived by adding the aggregate fair value of the shares immediately prior to exercise of the rights to the proceeds from the exercise, and dividing the total by the number of shares outstanding after exercise. To illustrate, consider that the entity currently has 10,000 shares outstanding, with a market value of $15 per share, when it offers each holder rights to acquire one new share at $10 for each four shares held. The theoretical value ex-rights would be given as follows:

$$\frac{(10{,}000 \text{ x } \$15) + (2{,}500 \text{ x } \$10)}{12{,}500} = \frac{175{,}000}{12{,}500} = \$14$$

Thus, the ex-rights value of the ordinary shares is $14 each.

Weighted-Average (W/A) Computation

Transaction	*Effect on W/A computation*
Common stock outstanding at the beginning of the period	Increase number of shares outstanding by the number of shares
Issuance of common stock during the period	Increase number of shares outstanding by the number of shares issued times the portion of the year outstanding
Conversion into common stock	Increase number of shares outstanding by the number of shares converted times the portion of the year outstanding
Company reacquires its stock	Decrease number of shares outstanding by number of shares reacquired times portion of the year outstanding
Stock dividend or split	Increase number of shares outstanding by number of shares issued or increased due to the split
Reverse split	Decrease number of shares outstanding by decrease in shares
Pooling of interest	Increase number of shares outstanding by number of shares issued
Purchase	Increase number of shares outstanding by number of shares issued times portion of year since acquisition

The foregoing do not characterize all possible complexities arising in the EPS computation; however, most of the others occur under a complex structure which is considered in the following section of this chapter. The illustration below applies the foregoing concepts to a simple capital structure.

Example of EPS computation--Simple capital structure

Assume the following information:

	Numerator information			*Denominator information*	
a.	Income from ordinary activities before extraordinary items	$130,000	a.	Common shares outstanding 1/1/97	100,000
b.	Extraordinary loss (net of tax)	30,000	b.	Shares issued for cash 4/1/97	20,000
c.	Net income	100,000	c.	Shares issued in 10% stock dividend declared in July 1997	12,000
d.	6% cumulative preference shares, $100 par, 1,000 shrs. issued and outstanding	100,000	d.	Shares of treasury stock purchased 10/1/97	10,000

When calculating the numerator, the claims of senior securities (i.e., preference shares) should be deducted to arrive at the earnings attributable to ordinary (equity) shareholders. In this example the preference shares are cumulative. Thus, regardless of whether or not the board of directors declares a preference dividend, holders of the preference shares have a claim of $6,000 (1,000 shares x $100 x 6%) against 1997 earnings. Therefore, $6,000 must be deducted from the numerator to arrive at the net income attributable to the holders of ordinary shares. Note that any cumulative preference dividends in arrears are ignored in computing this period's EPS since they would have been incorporated into previous periods' EPS calculations. Also note that this $6,000 would have been deducted for noncumulative preferred only if a dividend of this amount had been declared during the period. The EPS calculations follow.

Earnings per common share

On income from continuing operations before extraordinary items = ($130,000 – 6,000) ÷ Ordinary shares outstanding = $1.00

On net income = ($100,000 – 6,000) ÷ Ordinary shares outstanding = $0.76

The computation of the denominator is based on the weighted-average number of ordinary shares outstanding. Recall that a simple weighted-average is not considered appropriate because of the various complexities. The table below illustrates one way of computing the weighted-average number of shares outstanding.

Item	Number of shares actually outstanding	Fraction of the year outstanding	Shares times fraction of the year
Number of shares as of beginning of the year 1/1/97	110,000 [100,000 + 10%(100,000)]	12/12	110,000
Shares issued 4/1/97	22,000 [20,000 + 10%(20,000)]	9/12	16,500
Treasury shares purchased 10/1/97	(10,000)	3/12	(2,500)
Weighted-average number of common shares outstanding			124,000

Recall that the stock dividend declared in July is considered to be retroactive to the beginning of the year. Thus, for the period 1/1 through 4/1, 110,000 shares are considered to be outstanding. When shares are issued, they are included in the weighted-average beginning with the date of issuance. The stock dividend applicable to these newly issued shares is also assumed to have existed for the same period. Thus, we can see that of the 12,000 share dividend, 10,000 shares relate to the beginning balance and 2,000 shares to the new issuance (10% of 100,000 and 20,000, respectively). The purchase of the treasury stock requires that these shares be excluded from the calculation for the remainder of the period after their acquisition date. The figure is subtracted from the calculation because the shares were purchased from those outstanding prior to acquisition. To complete the example, we divided the previously derived numerator by the weighted-average number of common shares outstanding to arrive at EPS.

On income from continuing operations before extraordinary items = ($130,000 – 6,000) ÷ 124,000 common shares = $1.00

On net income = ($100,000 – 6,000) ÷ 124,000 common shares = $0.76

Reporting a $0.24 loss per share ($30,000 ÷ 124,000) due to the extraordinary item is optional. The numbers computed above for the EPS based on net income is the only presentation required on the face of the income statement.

Complex Capital Structure

The computation of EPS under a complex capital structure involves all of the complexities discussed under the simple structure and many more. By definition, a complex capital structure is one that has dilutive potential ordinary shares which have the potential to be exercised and reduce EPS. The effects of any antidilutive potential ordinary shares (those that increase EPS) is not to be included in the computation of diluted earnings per share.

Note that a complex structure requires dual presentation of both basic EPS and diluted EPS unless the basic earnings per share is a loss per share. In case the basic EPS is a loss per share, IAS 33 does not prohibit an enterprise from disclosing the figure for the diluted EPS (which was, however, the position taken by the Exposure Draft, E52).

For the purposes of calculating diluted EPS, the net profit attributable to ordinary shareholders and the weighted-average number of shares outstanding should be adjusted for the effects of all the dilutive potential ordinary shares.

According to IAS 33, the numerator, representing the net profit attributable to the ordinary shareholders for the period, should be adjusted by the after-tax effect, if any, of the following items:

1. Interest recognized in the period for the dilutive potential ordinary shares
2. Any dividends recognized in the period for the dilutive potential ordinary shares, where those dividends have been deducted in arriving at net profit attributable to ordinary shareholders
3. Any other changes in income or expenses that would result from the conversion of the dilutive potential ordinary shares

For instance, conversion of debentures into ordinary shares will reduce interest expense, which will cause an increase in the profit for the period. This will have a consequential effect on contributions based on the profit figure, say, employer's contribution to an employee profit sharing plan. The effect of such consequential changes on the bottom line should be considered in the computation of the numerator of the diluted EPS ratio.

The denominator, which has the weighted number of ordinary shares, should be adjusted (increased) by the weighted-average number of ordinary shares that would have been outstanding assuming the conversion of all dilutive potential ordinary shares.

Contingent Issuances of Ordinary Shares

As in the computation of the basic EPS, shares whose issuance is contingent on the occurrence of certain events are considered outstanding and included in the computation of diluted EPS only if the stipulated conditions have been met (the event has occurred). Issuances that are dependent on certain conditions being met can be illustrated through the following example. For instance, there may be a condition or requirement in a contract to increase earnings over a period of time to a certain stipulated level and that upon attainment of this level of earnings, the issuance of shares to take place; this is regarded as a contingent issuance of shares. These securities are included in the computation of diluted EPS.

There are basically two methods used to incorporate the effects of potential ordinary shares, popularly referred to as

1. The treasury stock method
2. The if-converted method

These terms were first popularized by the former US GAAP requirements set forth in APB 15. IAS 33 does not specifically refer to the methods it has prescribed by the foregoing names, but does mention, in the case of the method of accounting for share warrants and options that, in effect, the method prescribed by it produces the same results as the treasury stock method.

Treasury stock method. The treasury stock method, which is used to account for the hypothetical exercise of most warrants or options, requires that EPS be computed as if the options or warrants were exercised at the beginning of the period (or date of issuance, if later) and that the funds obtained from the exercise were used to purchase common stock at the average market price for the period.

For example, if a corporation has warrants outstanding for 1,000 shares of common stock exercisable at $10 per share and the average market price of the common stock is $16 per share, the following would hypothetically occur: The company would receive $10,000 (1,000 x $10) and issue 1,000 shares from the exercise of the warrants that would enable it to purchase 625 shares ($10,000 ÷ $16) in the open market. The net increase in the denominator (which effects a dilution in EPS) is 375 shares (1,000 issued less 625 repurchased). Under the terminology of IAS 33, those 375 shares are deemed to have been issued "for no consideration." In all cases where the exercise price is lower than the market price, assumed exercise will be dilutive and some portion of the shares will be deemed issued for no consideration. If the exercise price is greater than the average market price, the exercise should not be assumed since the result of this would be antidilutive.

Treasury Stock Method

Denominator must be increased by net dilution, as follows:

Net dilution = Shares issued – Shares repurchased

where

Shares issued = Proceeds received/Exercise price

Shares repurchased = Proceeds received/Average market price per share

If-converted method. The if-converted method is used for those securities that are currently sharing in the earnings of the company through the receipt of interest or dividends as senior securities but have the potential for sharing in the earnings as ordinary shares. The if-converted method logically recognizes that the convertible security can only share in the earnings of the company as one or the other, not as both. Thus, the dividends or interest less tax effects applicable to the convertible security as a senior security are not recognized in the net income figure used to compute EPS, and the weighted-average number of shares is adjusted to reflect the conversion as of the beginning of the year (or date of issuance, if later). See the example of the if-converted method for illustration of treatment of convertible securities when they are issued during the period and therefore were not outstanding for the entire year.

Example of the if-converted method

Assume a net income of $50,000 and a weighted-average number of common shares outstanding of 10,000. The following information is provided regarding the capital structure.

1. 7% convertible debt, 200 bonds each convertible into 40 ordinary shares. The bonds were outstanding the entire year. The income tax rate is 40%. The bonds were issued at par ($1,000 per bond). No bonds were converted during the year.
2. 4% convertible, cumulative preferred stock, par $100, 1,000 shares issued and outstanding. Each preferred share is convertible into 2 common shares. The preferred shares were issued at par and were outstanding the entire year. No shares were converted during the year.

The first step is to compute the basic EPS, that is, assuming only the issued and outstanding ordinary shares. This figure is simply computed as $4.60 ($50,000 – 4,000 preferred dividends) ÷ (10,000 ordinary shares outstanding). The diluted EPS must be less than this amount for the capital structure to be considered complex and for a dual presentation of EPS to be necessary.

To determine the dilutive effect of the preferred stock, an assumption (generally referred to as the if-converted method) is made that all of the preferred stock is converted at the earliest date that it could have been during the year. In this example, the date would be January 1. (If the preferred had been first issued during the year, the earliest late conversion could have occurred would have been the issuance date.) The effects of this assumption are twofold: (1) if the preferred is converted, there will be no preferred dividends of $4,000 for the year; and (2) there will be an additional 2,000 shares of common outstanding during the year (the conversion rate is 2 for 1 on 1,000 shares of preferred). Diluted EPS is computed, as follows, reflecting these two assumptions:

$$\frac{\text{Net income}}{\begin{array}{c}\text{Weighted-average of common shares}\\ \text{outstanding + Shares issued upon}\\ \text{conversion of preferred}\end{array}} = \frac{\$50{,}000}{12{,}000 \text{ shares}} = \$4.17$$

The convertible preferred is dilutive because it reduced EPS from $4.60 to $4.17. Accordingly, a dual presentation of EPS is required.

In the example, the convertible bonds are also assumed to have been converted at the beginning of the year. Again, the effects of the assumption are twofold: (1) if the bonds are converted, there will be no interest expense of $14,000 (7% x $200,000 face value), and (2) there will be an additional 8,000 shares (200 bonds x 40 shares) of common stock outstanding during the year. One note of caution, however, must be mentioned; namely, the effect of not having $14,000 of interest expense will increase income, but it will also increase tax expense. Consequently, the net effect of not having interest expense of $14,000 is $8,400 [(1 – 0.40) x $14,000]. Diluted EPS is computed as follows, reflecting the dilutive preferred and the effects noted above for the convertible bonds.

Computations of Primary and Fully Diluted Earnings Per Share

$$\frac{\text{Net income + Interest expense (net of tax)}}{\text{Weighted-average of common shares outstanding + Shares issued upon conversion of preferred and conversion of bonds}} = \frac{\$50,000 + 8,400}{20,000 \text{ shares}} = \$2.92$$

The convertible debt is also dilutive, as it reduces EPS from $4.17 to $2.92. Together the convertible bonds and preferred reduced EPS from $4.60 to $2.92. The following table summarizes the computations made for this example.

Computations of Primary and Fully Diluted Earnings Per Share

	EPS on outstanding common stock (the "benchmark" EPS)		*Basic*		*Diluted*	
Items	*Numerator*	*Denominator*	*Numerator*	*Denominator*	*Numerator*	*Denominator*
Net income	$50,000		$50,000		$50,000	
Preferred dividend	(4,000)					
Common shs. outstanding		10,000 shs.		10,000 shs.		10,000 shs.
Conversion of preferred				2,000		2,000
Conversion of bonds					8,400	8,000
Totals	$46,000	÷ 10,000 shs.	$50,000	÷ 12,000 shs.	$58,400	÷ 20,000 shs.
EPS	$4.60		$4.17		$2.92	

The foregoing example was simplified to the extent that none of the convertible securities were, in fact, converted during the year. In most real situations, some or all of the securities may have been converted, and thus actual reported earnings (and basic EPS) would already have reflected the fact that preferred dividends were paid for only part of the year and/or that interest on convertible debt was accrued for only part of the year. These factors would need to be taken into consideration in developing a "time-weighted" numerator and denominator for the EPS equations.

Furthermore, the sequence followed in testing the dilution effects of each of several series of convertible securities may affect the outcome, although this is not always true. It is best to perform the sequential procedures illustrated above by computing the impact of each issue of potential ordinary shares from the most dilutive to the least dilutive. This rule also applies if convertible securities (for which the if-converted method will be applied) and options (for which the treasury stock approach will be applied) are outstanding simultaneously.

Finally, if some potential ordinary shares are only issuable on the occurrence of a contingency, conversion should be assumed for EPS computation purposes only to the extent that the conditions were met as of the balance sheet date. In effect, the end of the reporting period should be treated as if it were also the end of the contingency period.

No antidilution. No assumptions of conversion should be made if the effect would be antidilutive. As in the discussion above, it may be that the sequence in which the different issues or series of convertible or other instruments that are potentially ordinary shares are considered will affect the ultimate computation. The goal in computing diluted EPS is to calculate the maximum dilutive effect. The individual issues of convertible securities, options, and other items should be dealt with from the most dilutive to the least dilutive to effect this result.

Modified Treasury Stock Method

Numerator

Net income recomputed to reflect retirement of debt or income from investments

- Add interest expense less tax effects
- Add income from investments less tax effects

- -

Denominator

Common stock outstanding + Number of shares not acquired with proceeds from options and warrants

Disclosure Requirements Under IAS 33

1. Enterprises should present both basic EPS and diluted EPS on the face of the income statement for each class of ordinary shares that has a different right to share in the net profit for the period. Equal prominence should be given to both the basic EPS and diluted EPS figures for all periods presented.
2. Enterprises should present basic EPS and diluted EPS even if the amounts disclosed are negative. In other words, the standard mandates disclosure of not just **earnings per share** but even **loss per share** figures.
3. Enterprises should disclose amounts used as the numerator in calculating basic EPS and diluted EPS along with a reconciliation of those amounts to the net profit or loss for the period. Disclosure is also required of the weighted-average number of ordinary shares used as the denominator in calculating basic EPS and diluted EPS along with a reconciliation of these denominators to each other.
4. a. In addition to the disclosure of the figures for basic EPS and diluted EPS, as required above, if an enterprise chooses to disclose per share amounts using a reported component of net profit, other than net profit or loss for the period attributable to ordinary shareholders, such amounts should be calculated using the weighted-average number of

ordinary shares determined in accordance with the requirements of IAS 33; this will ensure comparability of the per share amounts disclosed;

b. In cases where an enterprise chooses to disclose the above per share amounts using a component of net profit not reported as a line item in the income statement, a reconciliation is mandated by the standard, which should reconcile the difference between the component of net income used with a line item reported in the income statement; and

c. When additional disclosure is made by an enterprise of the above per share amounts, basic and diluted per share amounts should be disclosed with equal prominence (just as basic EPS and diluted EPS figures are given equal prominence).

5. Enterprises are encouraged to disclose the terms and conditions of financial instruments or contracts generating potential ordinary shares since such terms and conditions may determine whether or not any potential ordinary shares are dilutive and, if so, the effect on the weighted-average number of shares outstanding and any consequent adjustments to the net profit attributable to the ordinary shareholders.
6. If changes (resulting from a bonus issue or share split, etc.) in the number of ordinary or potential ordinary shares occur, after the balance sheet date but before issuance of the financial statements, and the per share calculations reflect such changes in the number of shares, such a fact should be disclosed.
7. Enterprises are also encouraged to disclose a description of ordinary share transactions or potential ordinary share transactions, other than capitalization issues and share splits, occurring after the balance sheet date and which are of such importance that nondisclosure would affect the ability of the

18 INTERIM AND SEGMENT REPORTING

INTERIM REPORTING

PERSPECTIVE AND ISSUES

Interim reporting is financial reporting covering periods of less than a year. Most commonly, such reports will be for a period of either 1 month or 3 months (the latter being referred to as quarterly reporting), although in many jurisdictions tradition calls for semiannual reporting. The purpose of quarterly or other interim reports is to provide financial statement users with more timely information for investment and credit decisions, based on an ability to project full-year results from interim performance. Additionally, interim reports can yield significant information concerning trends affecting the business and seasonality effects, both of which could be "buried" in annual reports.

The basic objective of interim reporting is to provide frequent and timely assessments of enterprise performance. However, interim reporting has inherent limitations. As the reporting period is shortened, the effects of errors in estimation and allocation are magnified. The proper allocation of annual operating expenses is a significant concern. Because the progressive tax rates of most jurisdictions are applied to total annual income and various tax credits may arise, the determination of interim income tax expense is often difficult. Other annual operating expenses are often concentrated in one interim period, yet benefit the entire year's operations. Examples include advertising expenses and major repairs or maintenance of equipment. The effects of seasonal fluctuations and temporary market conditions further limit the reliability, comparability, and predictive value of interim reports. Because of this reporting environment, the issue of independent auditor association with interim financial reports is subject to continuing controversy.

While some national standards had long existed regarding interim financial reporting, most notably in the United States, where the pertinent requirements were established in 1973, international accounting standards on this topic had been totally absent until very recently. The IASC released a draft statement of principles in late 1996, after having solicited views on the topic by means of an issues paper earlier that year, and it is expected to codify its views in a new financial reporting standard sometime before mid-1998. The discussion presented in this chapter is heavily weighted toward the positions which the IASC has taken in its DSOP, but readers should be alert to the possibility that the final standard, if and when produced, may vary from some of these positions.

Two distinct views of interim reporting have been advocated, particularly by US and UK standard setters, but others believe that the distinction is less meaningful than it appears at first blush. The first view holds that the interim period is an integral part of the annual accounting period (the integral view), while the second views the interim period as a discrete accounting period of its own (the discrete view). Depending on which view is accepted, expenses would either be recognized as incurred or would be allocated to the interim periods based on forecasted annual activity levels such as sales volume. The integral approach would require more use of estimation, and forecasts of full-year performance would be necessary antecedents for the preparation of interim reports.

Sources of IAS
DSOP, Interim Financial Reporting

DEFINITIONS OF TERMS

Discrete view. An approach to measuring interim period income by viewing each interim period separately.

Estimated annual effective tax rate. An expected annual tax rate which reflects estimates of annual earnings, tax rates, tax credits, etc.

Integral view. An approach to measuring interim period income by viewing each interim period as an integral part of the annual period. Expenses are recognized in proportion to revenues earned through the use of special accruals and deferrals.

Interim reporting. Financial reporting for a period of less than a year, generally for a period of 3 months.

Last-12-months reports. Financial reporting for the 12-month period which ends on a given interim date.

Liquidation of LIFO inventories. The situation which occurs when quarterly sales exceed purchases and base-period costs are released into cost of goods sold.

Seasonality. The normal, expected occurrence of a major portion of revenues or costs in one or two interim periods.

Year-to-date reports. Financial reporting for the period which begins on the first day of the fiscal year and ends on a given interim date.

CONCEPTS, RULES, AND EXAMPLES

Alternative Concepts of Interim Reporting

The argument is often made that interim reporting is generically different than financial reporting for a full fiscal year. Two distinct views of interim reporting have developed. Under the first view, the interim period is considered to be an integral part of the annual accounting period. Annual operating expenses are estimated and then allocated to the interim periods based on forecasted annual activity levels such as sales volume. When this approach is employed, the results of subsequent interim periods must be adjusted to reflect estimation errors.

Under the second view, the interim period is considered to be a discrete accounting period with status equal to a fiscal year. Thus, there are no estimations or allocations different from those used for annual reporting. The same expense recognition rules apply as under annual reporting, and no special interim accruals or deferrals are applied. Annual operating expenses are recognized in the interim period in which they are incurred, irrespective of the number of interim periods benefited.

Proponents of the integral view argue that the unique expense recognition procedures are necessary to avoid creating possibly misleading fluctuations in period-to-period results. Using the integral view results in interim earnings which are indicative of annual earnings and, thus, useful for predictive purposes. Proponents of the discrete view argue that the smoothing of interim results for purposes of forecasting annual earnings has undesirable effects. For example, a turning point in an earnings trend which occurred during the year may be obscured.

Yet others have noted that the distinction between the integral and the discrete approaches is arbitrary and, in fact, rather meaningless. These critics note that interim periods bear the same relationship to full years as fiscal years do to longer intervals in the life cycle of a business, and that all periodic financial reporting necessitates the making of estimates and allocations. Direct costs and revenues are best accounted for as incurred and earned, respectively, which equates to a discrete approach in most instances, while many indirect costs are more likely to require that an allocation process be applied, which is suggestive of an integral approach. In short, a mix of methods will be necessary as dictated by the nature of the cost or revenue item being reported upon, and neither a pure integral nor a pure discrete approach could be utilized in practice. The DSOP on interim financial reporting does, in fact, nominally adopt a discrete view, but also includes many aspects of the integral view, as described more fully below.

Objectives of Interim Reporting: The IASC Perspective

The purpose of interim reporting is to provide information which will be useful in making economic decisions (as, of course, is annual financial information). Furthermore, interim financial reporting is expected to provide information specifically about the financial position, performance, and change in financial position of an enterprise. The objective is general enough to embrace the preparation and presentation of either full financial statements or condensed information.

While accounting is often criticized for looking at an entity's performance "through the rear-view mirror," in fact it is well understood by standards setters that to be useful, such information must provide insights into future performance. In the IASC's draft statement of principles on interim reporting, the Committee states that the purpose of interim period reporting is to provide interested parties with an understanding of the enterprise's earnings generating capacity and cash flow generating capacity, which are clearly future-oriented. Furthermore, the interim data is expected to give interested parties not only insights into such matters as seasonal volatility or irregularity, and provide timely notice about changes in patterns or trends, both as to income or cash generating behavior, but also into such balance sheet-based phenomena as liquidity.

In reaching the positions set forth in the DSOP, the IASC has considered the importance of interim reporting in identifying the "turning points" in an enterprise's earnings or liquidity. In the Committee's opinion, the integral approach to interim reporting can mask these turning points, and thereby prevent users of the financial statements from taking appropriate actions. If this observation is correct, this would be an important reason to endorse the discrete view. In fact, the extent to which application of an integral approach masks "turning points" is probably related to the extent of "smoothing" applied to revenue and expense data; it seems quite feasible that interim reporting in accordance with the integral view, if done sensitively, would reveal turning points as well as reports prepared under the contrary approach. As proof of this, one can consider national economic statistics, which are most commonly reported on "seasonally adjusted" bases, which is analogous to the consequence of utilizing an integral approach to interim reporting of enterprise financial information. Such economic data is often quite effective at highlighting so-called "turning points" and is employed far more typically than is unadjusted monthly data, for example.

While the objectives of interim reporting are highly consistent with those of annual financial reporting, there are, in the IASC's view, further concerns. These have been identified in the DSOP as involving matters of cost and timeliness, as well as questions of materiality and measurement accuracy. In general, the conclusion is that to be truly useful, the information must be produced in a more timely fashion than is often the case with annual reports (although other research suggests that users' tolerance for delayed information is markedly declining in all arenas), and that some compromises in terms of accuracy may be warranted in order to achieve greater timeliness.

Basic Conclusions About Application of Accounting Principles to Interim Financial Reports

The draft statement of principles takes a firm stand on the side of the discrete view of the financial reporting process as it applies to interim periods. As noted, this holds that the same measurement concepts applicable to full-year financial reporting should be applied to each interim period on a "stand alone" basis. Most noteworthy is the fact that this is diametrically opposed to the position under US GAAP (APB 28), which mandates the integral view. However, neither position is pure in the sense that all measures are consistent with the stated overall philosophy. For example, while in the DSOP the discrete view is endorsed, the method of accounting for income taxes prescribed is clearly compliant with the integral view, not the discrete view.

The DSOP states that interim financial data should be prepared in conformity with accounting policies used in the most recent annual financial statements. The only exception noted is for the situation when a change in accounting principle has been adopted since the last year-end financial report was issued. The statement also stipulates that the definitions of assets, liabilities, income and expenses for the interim period are to be identical to those applied in annual reporting situations.

While the foregoing are not radical notions, and in fact are not unlike similar statements found in national GAAP standards addressing interim reporting, there is one very important omission. The DSOP does **not** condition the foregoing definitions by stating, as does the corresponding US GAAP standard, that some principles and practices might need to be modified to better serve the goal of interim reporting; namely, so that reported results for interim periods might better relate to the results of operations for the annual period. Thus, the DSOP appears to be quite committed to a pure discrete view of interim financial reporting.

Further evidence of this last noted observation comes in the context of cost deferrals. The DSOP states that deferral of costs at interim reporting dates is only acceptable if those same costs could be deferred at the end of a full fiscal year, given like circumstances. This clearly suggests that no loosening of the deferral guidelines would be permissible, in contrast with US GAAP which states that costs be "allocated among interim periods, . . .using appropriate. . .accruals and deferrals." While for many, if not most, categories of costs and expenses, the results of applying the two approaches may not differ materially in most circumstances, there would be some situations in which the DSOP approach would expense some costs which could justifiably be deferred during interim periods, even if not at year end, under US GAAP. For example, a major repair incurred early in the year, and which is clearly expected to benefit the full year (if not even a longer term) could not be partially deferred under the guidelines of the DSOP, while US GAAP seemingly permits, and even encourages, deferral and amortization over subsequent interim periods of the same year.

While the DSOP is quite forthright about declaring its allegiance to the discrete view of interim financial reporting, it does incorporate a number of important exceptions to the principle. These matters are discussed in greater detail below.

Statements and Disclosures to be Presented in Interim Financial Reports

Minimum requirements. The DSOP sets forth the minimum requirements which would pertain to interim financial reports. Essentially, the standard would, if promulgated consistent with the DSOP, mandate that only the basic financial statements (balance sheet, income statement, and cash flow statement) be presented, in condensed format, with a reduced set of informative (i.e., footnote) disclosures. The interim cash flow statement would only need to display the three subtotals (operating, investing, and financing) which are commonly reported, plus the reconciliation of cash for the period. The DSOP would not have required presentation of what was then being called the "statement of nonowner movements in equity"--the term used in the then-outstanding E53, which has been obsoleted by the issuance of IAS 1 (revised), which has modified that aspect of the proposed standard on presentation and disclosure. Presumably, a final standard based on this DSOP will not require interim presentation of the statement reporting all movements in equity or changes in equity other than those arising from transactions with, or distributions to, owners, even in a condensed format.

Regarding the condensed balance sheet and income statement, the DSOP does stipulate that the major captions found on the corresponding annual financial statements be included on the interims. For the balance sheet, this could mean that the presentation set forth only, as an illustration, current assets, plant property and equipment, and other assets; current and noncurrent liabilities; and stockholders' equity. As to the income statement, the minimum presentation might include revenue, major captions of expenses (e.g., cost of sales, administrative costs, selling expenses, etc.), and little else. However, present thinking would be to require presentation of earnings per share (as recently prescribed by IAS 33) even in interim statements, but, of course, this would only apply to enterprises which are subject to this rule for annual reporting purposes also.

The document is not completely clear regarding the separate presentation of captions requiring special disclosure in the context of annual financial statements, such as extraordinary items, or routine items which due to magnitude or nature could be significant in explaining the performance of the entity during the period. For example, adjustments to write down the carrying value of receivables or plant assets to realizable or recoverable amounts, or litigation settlements, are cited in the context of annual reporting as items which typically may need expanded disclosure, either through the use of captions in the income statement or by means of footnote narratives. The DSOP states that, given the constraints likely to affect the precision of interim reporting, the use of expanded disclosures might actually be more important in that arena than is the case for annual reporting. However, it does not provide an example of the criteria which might be applied in making a determination of whether a specific disclosure is necessary in a given situation.

Informative disclosures. The DSOP also addresses the informative disclosures required to accompany the condensed interim financial statements. While a number of notes would potentially be required, there could clearly be far less disclosure than is presently prescribed under enacted IAS. A total of six mandatory disclosures (to be made only if warranted under the circumstances) are set forth in the draft statement. These are

1. A discussion of any differences in accounting principles or methods of computation applied in the interim financial statements vs. the annual statements
2. Explanatory comments about seasonality or cyclicality of interim operations
3. The nature and magnitude of significant items affecting interim results that are unusual because of nature, size, or incidence
4. Dividends paid, either in the aggregate or on a per share basis, presented separately for ordinary (common) shares and other classes of shares
5. Revenue and operating result for business segments or geographical segments, whichever has been the entity's primary mode of segment reporting
6. Any significant events occurring subsequent to the end of the interim period

The DSOP also urges that certain additional information be presented if available and not prohibited or restricted under relevant local laws. This would include what is often referred to as "soft" information which is not as susceptible to objective, independent verification as is traditional financial statement data. The draft statement identifies discussions of significant changes in business trends (such as product demand, market shares, prices and costs), descriptions of significant new commitments (as for capital projects), and expectations for the full fiscal year's performance. Some of these items might be viewed as sensitive by management, and depending on the local litigation climate, there may be a fear of legal action if, for example, the full year results vary materially from what was alluded to as being likely in the interim statements. Thus, it might well be that some time will have to elapse after (and if) the interim reporting standard is finalized before meaningful disclosures of this type of information becomes commonplace.

Interestingly, while the discrete view of interim reporting is endorsed by the draft statement of principles, there is no attempt to make the interim reports self-sufficient as financial documents. The view of the IASC is that users of interim financial statements will, in all likelihood, have access to the most recent annual report issued by the enterprise, and thus there will be no need to repeat much of the routine disclosures which are mandatory in annual reports presented in conformity with IAS. Undoubtedly, this position was intended to help reduce the cost of preparing interim reports, as well as in making their issuance more timely.

Comparative financial statements. The draft statement endorses the concept of comparative reporting, which is generally acknowledged to be more useful than is the presentation of information about only a single period. This is consistent with the position taken by the accounting profession for many decades, although comparative reports are often not an absolute requirement. The IASC furthermore will encourage not only comparative condensed statements (e.g., the second quarter of 1998 together with the second quarter of 1997), but also the inclusion of year-to-date reports (e.g., the first half of 1998 and also for the first half of 1997) as well. Thus, a complete presentation could involve four columns of data.

Furthermore, the IASC has noted that, for highly seasonal businesses in particular, the inclusion of condensed income statements for the 12 months ending on the date of the most recent interim report (often known as "rolling 12-month" statements) would be very useful. The objective of rolling 12-month statements is that seasonality concerns are eliminated, since by definition each rolling period contains all the seasons of the year. (Rolling statements cannot correct for cyclicality that encompasses more than 1 year, such as business recessions.) Companies affected by seasonality are urged to consider including these additional statements, which could result in a condensed interim income statement comprised of six or more columns of data.

Accounting Policies in Interim Periods

Consistency. The DSOP logically states that interim period financial statements should be prepared using the same accounting principles which had been employed in the most recent annual financial statements. This is consistent with the idea that the latest annual report provides the frame of reference which will be employed by users of the interim information. The fact that interim data is expected to be useful in making projections of the forthcoming full year's reported results of operations makes consistency of accounting principles between the interim period and prior year important, since the projected results for the current year will undoubtedly be evaluated in the context of year-earlier performance. Unless the accounting principles applied in both periods are consistent, any such comparison is likely to be less than fully valid.

The decision to require consistent application of accounting principles across interim periods and in comparison with the earlier fiscal year is not only an implication of the view of interim reporting as being largely a means of predicting the coming fiscal year results. It is also driven by the conclusion that each interim reporting period "stand alone," rather than being merely an integral portion of the full year. In the IASC's view, when an interim period is seen as an integral part of the full year, it is easier to rationalize applying different accounting principles to the interims, if doing so will more meaningfully present the results of the portion of the full year within the boundaries of the annual reporting period. For example, deferral of certain costs at interim balance sheet dates, notwithstanding the fact that such costs could not validly be deferred at year end, might serve the theoretically legitimate purpose of providing a more accurate predictor of full year results.

On the other hand, if each interim period is seen as a discrete unit to be reported upon without having to serve the higher goal of providing an accurate prediction of the full year's expected outcome, then a decision to depart from previously applied accounting principles is less easily justified. Given the IASC's stated clear preference for the discrete view of interim financial reporting, its proposed requirement regarding consistency of accounting principles is entirely logical.

Notwithstanding the presumption that accounting principles will be consistently applied, there is a recognition that interim reporting will necessitate a greater use of estimates and even a less precise methodology of measurement. The possible lack of precision is not equivalent to a departure from consistency in application of accounting principles, however. The willingness of the IASC to explicitly excuse a lesser degree of precision in interim reporting contrasts with the position taken in the equivalent US GAAP standard (APB 28, which was issued more than 25 years ago); that rule, while recognizing that estimates may need to be employed, nevertheless does not imply that a lesser degree of precision would be acceptable as a result. In any event, with the evolution of information systems technology now occurring at a rapid rate, the issue of precision in measurements is likely to fade in the foreseeable future as a constraining influence on interim reporting.

Consolidated reporting requirement. The draft statement also requires that, if the enterprise's most recent annual financial statements were prepared on a consolidated basis, then the interim financial reports in the immediate subsequent year should also be. This is entirely in keeping with the notion of consistency of application of accounting principles. The rule would not, however, preclude publishing supplementary "parent company only" interim reports, even if the most recent annual financial statements did not include such additional data.

Materiality as Applied to Interim Financial Statements

Materiality is, of course, one of the most fundamental concepts underlying financial reporting. At the same time, it has largely been resistant to attempts to define it. A number of accounting standards do require that items be disclosed if material; for example, under IAS 8, material extraordinary items are to be separately stated. However, performing an arithmetical calculation of a threshold for materiality is not prescribed in that (or any other) accounting standard, but rather is left to the devices of each individual charged with responsibility for financial reporting.

The DSOP on interim reporting puts forward the notion that materiality for interim reporting purposes will differ from that defined in the context of an annual period. This follows from the decision to endorse the discrete view of interim reporting, of course. Thus, for example, discontinued operations and extraordinary items would have to be evaluated for disclosure against whatever benchmark, such as gross revenue, is deemed appropriate, as that item is being reported in the interim financial statements, and not in the prior year's or expected coming year's full period results. The effect would normally be to lower the threshold level for reporting such items: Some items separately set forth in the interim financials might not be so presented in the full annual report which later includes that same interim period. The objective is to not mislead the user of the information by failing to include a disclosure which **might** appear to be material within the context of the interim report, since that is the user's immediate frame of reference. If later the threshold is raised and items previously presented are no longer deemed worthy of such attention, this is not thought to create a risk of misleading the user, in contrast to a failure to disclose an item in the interim statements which, measured against the performance parameters of the interim period, might appear significant.

To illustrate, assume that Xanadu Corp. has gross revenues of $2.8 million in the first fiscal quarter, and will in fact go on to earn revenues of $12 million for the full year. Traditionally, materiality is defined as 5% of revenues. If in the first quarter an extraordinary gain of $200,000 is incurred, this should be separately set forth in the quarterly financial statements, since it exceeds the defined 5% threshold for materiality. If there are no other extraordinary losses for the balance of the year, it might validly be concluded that disclosure in the year-end financials may be omitted, since a $200,000 loss is not material in the context of $12 million of revenues. Thus, Xanadu's first quarter report might include an item defined as extraordinary which is later redefined as not being extraordinary.

Recognition Issues

General concepts. The draft statement of principles holds that definitions of assets, liabilities, income and expense should be the same for interim period reporting as at year end. These items, as well as other related ones (gains and losses, etc.), are defined in the IASC's *Framework for the Preparation and Presentation of Financial Statements*. The effect of stipulating that the same definitions apply to interim reporting is to further underscore the concept of interim periods being discrete units of time upon which the statements report. For example, given the definition of assets as resources generating future economic benefits for the enterprise, expenditures which could not be capitalized at year end, because of a failure to meet this definition, could similarly not be given deferred recognition at interim dates. Thus, by applying the same definitions at interim dates, the IASC has mandated the same recognition rules as are applicable at the end of full annual reporting periods.

However, while the overall implication is that identical recognition and measurement rules are to be applied to interim financial statements, the draft statement does go on to set forth a number of modifications to the general rule. Some of these are in simple acknowledgement of the limitations of certain measurement techniques, and the recognition that applying those definitions at interim dates might necessitate interpretations different from those useful for annual reporting. In other cases, the DSOP clearly departs from its own absolute commitment to the discrete view, even though the authors fully agree that such departures are not only wise, but probably fully necessary. These specific recognition and measurement issues are addressed below.

Recognition of annual costs incurred unevenly during the year. It is frequently observed that some types of costs are incurred in uneven patterns over the course of a fiscal year, while not being driven strictly by variations in volume of sales activity. For example, major expenditures on advertising may be prepaid at the inception of the campaign; tooling for new product production will obviously be heavily weighted to the preproduction and early production stages. Certain discretionary costs, such as research and development, will not bear any predictable pattern or necessary relationship with other costs or revenues. Contributions to pension funds may be made annually, often in arrears, and payroll and other taxes may be paid quarterly or monthly.

If an integral view approach had been elected by the IASC, there would be potent arguments to be made in support of the accrual or deferral of certain costs. For instance, if a major expenditure for overhauling equipment is scheduled to occur during the final interim period, logic could well suggest that the expenditure should be anticipated in the earlier interim periods of the year. Under the discrete view adopted in the DSOP, however, such an accrual would be seen as an inappropriate attempt to smooth the operating results over all the interim periods constituting the full fiscal year. Accordingly, such anticipation of future expenses is prohibited, unless, of course, the future expenditure gives rise to a true liability in the current period or meets the test of being a contingency which is probable and the magnitude of which is reasonably estimable.

For example, many business enterprises grant bonuses to managers only after the annual results are known; even if the relationship between the bonuses and the earnings performance is fairly predictable from past behavior, these remain discretionary in nature and need not be given. Such a bonus arrangement would not give rise to a liability during earlier interim periods, inasmuch as the management has yet to declare that there is a commitment which will be honored. (Compare this with the situation where managers have contracts specifying a bonus plan, which clearly would give rise to a liability during the year, albeit one which might involve complicated estimation problems.)

Another example involves contingent lease arrangements. Often in operating leases the lessee will agree to a certain minimum or base rent, plus an amount which is tied to some variable such as sales revenue. This is typical, for instance, in retail rental contracts, such as for space in shopping malls, since it encourages the landlord to maintain the facilities in an appealing fashion such that tenants are successful in attracting customers. Only the base amount of the periodic rental is a true liability, however, unless and until the higher rent becomes payable as sales targets are achieved. If contingent rents are on a sliding scale (e.g., 1% of sales volume up to $500,000, then 2% of amounts up to $1.5 million, etc.), the projected level of full-year sales should not be used to compute rental accruals in the early periods. Rather, only the contingent rents payable on the actual sales levels already achieved should be so recorded. Again, a different prescription would be made if the integral view were to be strictly adhered to, but since the IASC has endorsed the opposite discrete view, this is not an issue.

While the foregoing examples were clearly categories of costs which, while often fairly predictable, would not constitute a legal obligation of the reporting enterprise until the associated conditions were fully met, there are other examples which are more ambiguous. Paid vacation time and holiday leave would often be enforceable as legal commitments, and if so, provision for these should be made in interim financial statements. In other cases, as when accrued vacation time is lost if not used by the end of a defined reporting year, such costs might not be subject to accrual under the discrete view. The facts of each such situation would have to be carefully analyzed to make such a determination.

Revenues received seasonally, cyclically, or occasionally. The draft statement is clear that revenues such as dividends and interest receipts cannot be anticipated or deferred at interim dates, unless such would be acceptable at year end. Thus, interest is typically accrued for, since it is well established that this represents a contractual commitment. Dividends, on the other hand, are not recognized until declared since even when highly predictable based on past experience, these are not obligations of the paying corporation until actually declared.

Furthermore, seasonality factors should not be "smoothed" out of the financial statements. For example, retail stores typically have a high percentage of annual revenues occurring in the holiday shopping period, and the quarterly or other interim financial statements should fully reflect such seasonality. It would be difficult, in fact, to come to any other conclusion about reporting such revenues, even if the integral view were zealously embraced (which of course the DSOP does not do, even tepidly). Given the endorsement of the discrete view, there is no basis for reaching the alternative judgement.

Income taxes. Notwithstanding the impeccable logic used by the IASC to establish rules for the recognition of most items of revenue or expense consistent with the philosophy espoused by the draft statement, the DSOP departs from the strict application of the discrete view when the subject of income taxes is addressed. The fact that income taxes are assessed annually by the taxing authorities is the primary reason for reaching the conclusion that taxes are to be accrued based on the expected effective tax rate for the full fiscal year. Further, if rate changes have been enacted to take effect later in the fiscal year (while some rate changes take effect in midyear, more likely this would be an issue if the enterprise reports on a fiscal year and the new tax rates become effective at the start of a calendar year), the expected effective rate should take into account the rate changes as well as the anticipated pattern of earnings to be experienced over the course of the year. Thus, the rate to be applied to interim period earnings (or losses, as discussed further below) will take into account the expected level of earnings for the entire forthcoming year, as well as the effect of enacted changes in the tax rates to become operative later in the fiscal year.

Most enterprises are subject to a multiplicity of taxing jurisdictions, and in some instances the amount of income subject to tax will vary from one to the next, since different laws will include and exclude disparate items of income or expense from the tax base. For example, interest earned on government issued bonds may be exempted from tax by the jurisdiction which issued them, but be defined as fully taxable by other tax jurisdictions the entity is subject to. To the extent feasible, the appropriate expected effective tax rate should be separately ascertained for each taxing jurisdiction, so that the most accurate estimate of income taxes can be developed at each interim reporting date. In general, an overall estimated effective tax rate will not be as satisfactory for this purpose as would a more carefully constructed set of estimated rates, since the pattern of taxable and deductible items will fluctuate from one period to the next.

In computing an expected effective tax rate for a given tax jurisdiction, all relevant features of the tax regulations should be taken into account. Jurisdictions may provide for tax credits based on new investment in plant assets, expansions of payrolls, relocation of facilities, research and development expenditures, levels of export sales, and so forth, and the expected credits against the tax for the full year should be given consideration in the derivation of an expected effective tax rate. Thus, the tax effect of new plant investment, when the local taxing body offers an investment credit for qualifying investment in tangible productive assets, will be reflected in all the interim periods of the fiscal year in which the new investment occurs (assuming it can be forecast to occur later in a given fiscal year), and not merely in the period in which the new investment occurs. This is consistent with the underlying concept that taxes are strictly an annual phenomenon, but it is at variance with the purely discrete view of interim financial reporting.

The interim reporting DSOP notes that, although tax credits and similar modifying elements are to be taken into account in developing the expected effective tax rate to apply to interim earnings, tax benefits which will relate to one-time events are to be reflected in the interim period when those events take place. This is perhaps most likely to be encountered in the context of capital gains taxes incurred in connection with occasional dispositions of investments and other capital assets; since it is not feasible to project the rate at which such transactions will occur over the course of a year, the tax effects should be recognized only as the underlying events transpire.

While in most cases tax credits are to be handled as suggested in the foregoing paragraphs, in some jurisdictions tax credits, particularly those which relate to export revenue or capital expenditures, are in effect government grants. The accounting for government grants is set forth in IAS 20; in brief, grants are recognized in income over the period necessary to properly match them to the costs which the grants are intended to offset or defray. Thus, compliance with both IAS 20 and the interim reporting DSOP would necessitate that tax credits be carefully analyzed to identify those which are in substance grants, and then accounting for the credit consistent with its true nature.

When an interim period loss gives rise to a tax loss carryback, it should be fully reflected in that interim period. Similarly, if a loss in an interim period produces a tax loss carryforward, it should be recognized immediately, but only if the criteria set forth in revised IAS 12, are met. Specifically, it must be deemed probable that the benefits will be realizable before the loss benefits can be given formal recognition in the financial statements. In the case of interim period losses, it may be necessary to assess not only whether the enterprise will be profitable enough in future fiscal years to utilize the tax benefits associated with the loss, but, furthermore, whether interim periods later in the same year will provide earnings of sufficient magnitude to absorb the losses of the current period. (It should be noted that the DSOP was published prior to the enactment of revised IAS 12, and accordingly applies the "assured beyond a reasonable doubt" criterion of the original IAS 12. However, if a final standard on interim financial reporting is promulgated by the IASC, it will be conformed to revised IAS 12 as well as any other new or revised standards which are established in the intervening period.)

Revised IAS 12 provides that changes in expectations regarding the realizability of benefits related to net operating loss carry forwards should be reflected currently in tax expense. Similarly, if a tax loss carryforward benefit is not deemed probable of being realized until the interim (or annual) period when it in fact becomes realized, the tax effect will be included in tax expense of that period. Appropriate explanatory material must be included in the notes to the financial statements, even on an interim basis, to provide the user with an understanding of the unusual relationship between pretax accounting income and the provision for income taxes.

Volume rebates or other anticipated price changes in interim reporting periods. In what some may view as yet another departure from the conceptually pure "discrete view" approach to interim reporting, the DSOP prescribes that where volume rebates or other contractual changes in the prices of goods and services are anticipated to occur over the annual reporting period, these should be anticipated in the interim financial statements for periods within that year. The logic is that the effective cost of materials, labor, or other inputs will be altered later in the year as a consequence of the volume of activity during earlier interim periods, among others, and it would be a distortion of the reported results of those earlier periods if this were not taken into account. Clearly this must be based on estimates, since the volume of purchases, etc., in later portions of the year may not materialize as anticipated. As with other estimates, however, as more accurate information becomes available this will be adjusted on a prospective basis, meaning that the results of earlier periods should not be revised or corrected.

The requirement to take volume rebates and similar adjustments into effect in interim period financial reporting applies equally to vendors or providers, as well as to customers or consumers of the goods and services. In both instances, however, it must be deemed probable that such adjustments have been earned or will occur, before giving recognition to them in the financials. This high of a threshold has been set because the definitions of assets and liabilities in the IASC's *Framework for the Preparation and Presentation of Financial Statements* require that they be recognized only when it is probable that the benefits will flow into or out from the enterprise. Thus, accrual would only be appropriate for contractual price adjustments and related matters. Discretionary rebates and other price adjustments, even if typically experienced in earlier periods, would not be given formal recognition in the interim financials.

Depreciation and amortization in interim periods. The rule regarding depreciation and amortization in interim periods is more consistent with the DSOP's stated discrete view of interim reporting. Charges to be recognized in the interim periods are to be related to only those assets actually employed during the period; planned acquisitions for later periods of the fiscal year are not to be taken into account.

While this rule seems entirely logical, it can give rise to a problem which is not encountered in the context of most other types of revenue or expense items. This occurs when the tax laws or financial reporting conventions permit or require that special allocation formulas be used during the year of acquisition (and often disposition) of an asset. In such cases, depreciation or amortization will be an amount other than the amount which would be computed purely based on the fraction of the year the asset was in service. For example, say that convention is that one-half year of depreciation is charged during the year the asset is acquired, irrespective of how many months it is in service. Further assume that a particular asset is acquired at the inception of the fourth quarter of the year. Under the DSOP's direction, the first three quarters would not be charged with any depreciation expense related to this asset (even if it was known in advance that the asset would be place in service in the fourth quarter). However, this would then necessitate charging fourth quarter operations with one-half year's (i.e., two quarters') depreciation, which arguably would distort that final period's results of operations.

The draft statement does address this problem area. It states that an adjustment should be made in the final interim period so that the sum of interim depreciation and amortization equals an independently computed annual charge for these items. However, since there is no requirement that financial statements be separately presented for a final interim period (and most enterprises, in fact, do not report for a final period), such an adjustment might be implicit in the annual financials, and presumably would be explained in the notes if material (the DSOP does not explicitly require this, however).

The alternative financial reporting strategy, that is, projecting annual depreciation, including the effect of asset dispositions and acquisitions planned for or reasonably anticipated to occur during the year, and then allocating this ratably to interim periods, has been rejected. Such an approach might have been rationalized in the same way that the use of the effective annual tax rate was in assigning tax expense or benefits to interim periods, but this has not been done.

Inventories. Inventories represent a major category for most manufacturing and merchandising enterprises, and some inventory costing methods pose unique problems for interim financial reporting. In general, however, the same inventory costing principles should be utilized for interim reporting as for annual reporting. However, the use of estimates in determining quantities, costs and net realizable values at interim dates will be more pervasive. The DSOP make it clear that, while measurement precision may be reduced at interim dates, measurement principles should not vary from those appropriate to full year financial reporting.

Three particular difficulties are addressed in the draft statement. These are the matters of determining net realizable values at interim dates, the use of the LIFO costing method, and the allocation of manufacturing variances.

Regarding net realizable value determination, the statement expresses the belief that the determination of NRV at interim dates should be based on selling prices and costs to complete at those dates. Projections should not, therefore, be made regarding conditions which possibly might exist at the time of the fiscal year end. Furthermore, write-downs to NRV taken at interim reporting dates should be reversed in subsequent interim reporting periods only to the extent that this would have been permissible had the decline occurred in one fiscal year and the recovery had occurred in a subsequent year.

LIFO inventory costing poses unique problems because it is almost solely driven by tax regulations (although in a few industries a case can be made that the physical flow of goods follows a last-in, first-out pattern) which provide an economic incentive to use the method. As a tax-driven accounting procedure, annual measurement is usually prescribed, and certain adjustments required at year end can potentially interfere with meaningful financial reporting if made at interim dates. The most commonly encountered issue is that of liquidation of lower cost LIFO layers at interim dates, only to have the physical quantity restored before year end.

To avoid distorting the operating results of the interim period in which the liquidation occurs (overstating interim profits by expensing lower cost inventory through cost of sales), as well as that of the later period when the inventory volume is restored (having the reverse effect), common practice has long been to provide a "reserve" for temporary liquidations of inventory, effectively charging current period cost of sales for the higher level of costs which, it is expected, will be incurred when the temporary liquidation is reversed. This is the method sanctioned under US GAAP, for example. It would have seemed as logical to prescribe this methodology as it is to require use of an estimated effective annual tax rate to compute income tax provisions at interim reporting dates, since both are rooted in the fact that income taxes are annual determinations, including the impact of inventory costing methods.

However, the IASC has apparently chosen to strictly enforce the "discrete view" approach as it relates to LIFO inventory costing at interim dates. Accordingly, the DSOP states that a reduction in the quantity of LIFO inventories should be reflected in inventory valuations at interim reporting dates, even when reversal by year end is anticipated. This rule would be effective even in the face of involuntary liquidations such as those caused by natural disasters, strikes or temporary materials shortages.

The last of the special issues related to inventories which are addressed by the DSOP concerns allocation of variances at interim dates. When standard costing methods are employed, the resulting variances are typically allocated to cost of sales and inventories in proportion to the dollar magnitude of those two captions, or according to some other rational system. Some have deferred this process to year end, on the basis that some of the variances will tend to offset over the course of a full fiscal year, particularly if the result of volume fluctuations due to seasonal factors. When variance allocation is thus deferred, the full balance of the variances are placed onto the balance sheet, typically as additions to or deductions from the inventory accounts. However, the DSOP expresses a preference that these variances be disposed of at interim dates, since to not do so could result in reporting inventory at interim dates at more or less than actual cost.

Foreign Currency Translation Adjustments at Interim Dates

Given the IASC's adoption of the discrete view regarding interim reporting, it is not surprising that the same approach to translation gains or losses as is mandated at year end would be proposed in the DSOP for interim reporting. IAS 21 provides for deferral of the effects of translating the assets and liabilities of foreign subsidiaries and other consolidated entities at one rate (the closing rate) but translating the income statement accounts at another rate (typically, the average rate for the period). The DSOP stipulates that precisely the same approach be applied to interim reporting situations. This can give rise to potential discontinuity between the interim periods and the full year's reporting, since typically the average rate for the year will not equal an average of the average rates for the interim periods, largely due to the fact that revenues and expenses will not occur ratably throughout all the periods and weighted average rates will not be employed at a sufficiently precise level.

The DSOP does not make explicit a suggested mechanism for dealing with this potential anomaly, but logic suggests that this may be effectively handled in a manner similar to that prescribed for depreciation and amortization. That is, the annual financial statements should be based on applying the principles of IAS 21 to annual financial data, and any adjustment to compensate for interim computations would flow through the final interim period's earnings. If material, these should be set forth separately or explained in the notes; if a separate final interim period is not reported on, any necessary explanation would be made in the annual financial statements, to the extent this has a material effect.

Adjustments to Previously Reporting Interim Data

While year-to-date financial reporting is not required, although the DSOP does recommend it in addition to normal interim period reporting, the concept finds some expression in the draft statement's position that adjustments not be made to earlier interim periods' results. By measuring income and expense on a year-to-date basis, and then effectively "backing into" the most recent interim period's presentation by deducting that which was reported in earlier interim periods, the need for retrospective adjustment of information which was reported earlier is obviated. However, there may be the need for disclosure of the effects of such measurement strategies when this results effectively in including adjustments in the most current interim period's reported results.

Accounting Changes in Interim Periods

The benchmark treatment for voluntary accounting principles changes (i.e., those which are not mandated by statute or imposed by accounting standards setters) is to restate all periods being presented retrospectively for application of the new method. This is preferred because of the salutary effects on comparability of financial data for the current and preceding years. While IAS 8 does not address interim reporting, the same benefits would be achieved if earlier interim periods were restated for the effects of any voluntarily made changes in accounting principle in interim periods other than the first. Accordingly, the DSOP states that all such changes must be reflected in the first interim period of the reporting year, and not in later interim periods.

Furthermore, the draft stipulates that changes in accounting policy or correction of fundamental errors in a prior period are to be reported in the interim period statements by restating prior interim periods only when annual data for prior years is also restated. This follows from the concern about comparability: Unless prior year data is being presented and is being restated, making retroactive adjustments to earlier interim statements would not accomplish, and would actually hinder, comparability. If the allowed alternative treatment under IAS 8, prospective adjustment, is followed, then this approach should be utilized in the interim financial statements as well.

SEGMENT REPORTING

PERSPECTIVE AND ISSUES

Segment reporting, the disclosure of information about an enterprise's operations in different industries, its foreign operations and export sales, and its major customers, is a relatively recent development in financial reporting.

During the late 1960s, a large number of business combinations resulted in highly diversified corporations. Some of these companies voluntarily disclosed segment financial information in their annual reports, but the extent and nature of the disclosure varied widely. A non-binding official pronouncement in the US, issued in 1967, recommended further voluntary disclosure. In addition, organizations representing preparers of financial statements sponsored research studies that generally supported the desirability and feasibility of segment reporting.

The US securities regulator, the Securities and Exchange Commission, began requiring "line-of-business" information in registrants' annual reports in 1970, but many diversified companies still failed to include segment information in their annual reports issued to stockholders. By 1974, the SEC required registrants to include some of the line-of-business information in their annual reports to stockholders. SFAS 14, issued in December 1976, established specific guidelines for the required disclosure of segment information on financial reports issued to stockholders. These requirements were later dropped for interim reports, and shortly thereafter were deleted for non-publicly-held companies.

The first (and still governing) international standard, IAS 14, was issued in 1981 and largely followed the lead of the earlier US standard. However, the IASC has more recently proposed (in E51, issued in late 1995) changing the method of determining reportable segments to conform more closely to how the business enterprise is internally managed. Subsequent to the exposure draft of the revised international standard, the standard setters in the US and elsewhere essentially conformed their standards to this new reporting philosophy as well. The IASC has very recently approved the revised version of IAS 14, and it will be promulgated soon. Accordingly, the new requirements will be emphasized in the following discussion.

Sources of IAS
IAS 14, *IAS* 14 *(Revised)*

DEFINITIONS OF TERMS

Accounting policies. Specific principles, bases, conventions, rules and practices adopted by an entity in preparing and presenting its financial statements.

Business segment. A distinguishable component of an enterprise that is engaged in providing a product or service or group of related products or services, and that is subject to risks and returns that are different from those of other business segments.

Cash flows. Inflows and outflows of cash and cash equivalents.

Common costs. Operating expenses incurred by the enterprise for the benefit of more than one industry segment.

Consolidated financial information. Aggregate (financial) information relating to an enterprise as a whole whether or not the enterprise has consolidated subsidiaries.

Corporate assets. Assets maintained for general corporate purposes and not used in the operations of any industry segment.

Discontinued operation. Resulting from the sale or abandonment of an operation that represents a separate, major line of business of an enterprise; the assets, net profit or loss, and activities can be distinguished physically, operationally, and for financial reporting purposes.

Extraordinary items. Income or expenses that arise from events or transactions that are clearly distinct from the ordinary activities of the enterprise and, therefore, are not expected to recur frequently or regularly.

General corporate expenses. Expenses incurred for the benefit of the corporation as a whole, which cannot be reasonably allocated to any segment.

Geographical segment. Distinguishable component of an enterprise engaged in operations in individual countries or groups of countries within particular geographic areas, as may be determined to be appropriate in the circumstances to reflect the nature of the enterprise's operations.

Identifiable assets. Those tangible and intangible assets used by an industry segment, including those the segment uses exclusively, and an allocated portion of assets used jointly by more than one segment.

Industry segment. A distinguishable component of an enterprise engaged in providing a different product or service or a different group of related products or services, primarily to unaffiliated customers. This term has been superseded by **business segment**.

Intersegment sales. Transfers of products or services, similar to those sold to unaffiliated customers, between industry segments or geographic areas of the enterprise.

Intrasegment sales. Transfers within an industry segment or geographic area.

Minority interest. That part of the net results of operations and of net assets of a subsidiary attributable to interests which are not owned, directly or indirectly through subsidiaries, by the parent.

Operating activities. The principal revenue producing activities of an enterprise and other activities that are not investing or financing activities.

Operating profit or loss. An industry segment's revenue minus all operating expenses, including an allocated portion of common costs.

Ordinary activities. Any activities which are undertaken by an enterprise as part of its business and such related activities in which the enterprise engages in furtherance of, incidental to or arising from, these activities.

Revenue. The gross inflow of economic benefits during a period arising in the ordinary course of business activities from sales to unaffiliated customers and from intersegment sales or transfers, excluding inflows from equity participants.

Reportable segment. A business or geographical segment for which segment information is required to be disclosed.

Segment revenue. Revenue that is directly attributable to a segment, or the relevant portion of revenue that can be allocated on a reasonable basis to a segment, and that is derived from transactions with parties outside the enterprise and from other segments of the same enterprise.

Segment expense. Expense that is directly attributable to a segment, or the relevant portion of expense that can be allocated on a reasonable basis to a segment.

Transfer pricing. The pricing of products or services between industry segments or geographic areas.

CONCEPTS, RULES, AND EXAMPLES

Conceptual Basis for Segmental Reporting

As business organizations have become more complex over the years, and the conglomerate form of organization has become ever more popular, it has become necessary to concede that financial statements which present the full scope of an enterprise's operations have declined markedly in utility. While it is certainly possible to assess the overall financial health of the entity using such financial reports, it is much more difficult to evaluate management's operating and financial strategies, particularly with regard to its emphasis on specific lines of business. For example, the extent to which operating results for a period are the result of the development of new products with greater potential for future growth, vs. mature product lines which nonetheless still account for a majority of the entity's total sales, would be largely masked in financial statements which did not present results by business segment.

The need for the inclusion of some type of disaggregated information in general purpose financial reports became critical by the late 1960s, and national accounting rule-making bodies accordingly began to address this topic around that time. In the US, for example, the need for segment information was one of the first agenda items identified upon the FASB's formation in 1973. The present US requirement, SFAS 14, was promulgated in 1976; and a revised standard, embracing essentially the same approach that is anticipated for a revised international standard, was recently adopted as SFAS 131, to become effective in 1998. In the UK, the Companies Act of 1967 first mandated the disclosure of limited segment data; this requirement was expanded by later revisions of the Act, and disaggregated information was formally made part of the notes to the financial statements in 1981. A related professional accounting standard (SSAP 25) was adopted in 1990, with segments again defined either by "class of business" (similar to product or service areas) or by geographic location, with company management charged with the responsibility of determining which type of categorization would be most meaningful to financial statement users. As in the US, a threshold value of 10% is established for making a determination that a segment is material, and the criteria are virtually identical to those in the US under SFAS 14. Information to be disclosed is also modeled on the US requirement -- sales, operating results, and identifiable assets (called net assets under the UK standard, but not actually defined there). It is not clear whether the UK standard will be subject to the same sort of revisions as are likely in the US, Canada, and under IAS.

On the international standard setting scene, the relevant rules, which comprise original IAS 14, have been effective since 1983. The standard was reformatted, but not substantively altered, in 1995. The IASC has recently approved a successor to this standard, revised IAS 14, which will be used as the basis for the following discussion.

Applicability of IAS 14

In contrast to the new US standard on segment reporting (SFAS 131), which affects the financial reports (including interim ones) of only publicly held companies, the original international standard was intended to be applicable to both publicly held and "other economically significant entities." While this expression went undefined by that standard, presumably this meant that all business organizations, other than those which are small, locally-based, and nondiversified, were expected to apply the requirements of IAS 14.

Revised IAS 14, on the other hand, stipulates that the new standard will be applicable to those entities which have publicly traded equity or debt securities. This will essentially conform the international rules with those of the national standard-setting bodies, and limit this standard to publicly held entities. While the logic for presenting disaggregated information in the context of nonpublic enterprises is still strong, the counterarguments that owners and managers already have this information, and that general disclosure could place the entity in jeopardy from a competitive perspective, have been voiced so loudly for such a long time, that it has become politically nonfeasible to impose the requirement on privately owned entities at this juncture.

In determining which segments of a given entity should be separately presented, there was a contrast between the US approach and that of the original international accounting standard. Original IAS 14 asked that segment information be presented for industry segments or geographic segments whose level of revenues, profits, assets, or employment are significant in the countries in which their major operations are conducted. However, the term "significant" remained undefined, and in fact

IAS 14 declined to quantify this threshold, while duly noting that other standard setters had chosen to establish such guidelines, thereby implying that those could be used to fill the vacuum. In the US, the FASB mandated a 10% boundary for recognition, but level of employment was not stipulated as one of the criteria (only assets, revenues, and profits were so identified).

Thus, the intent under original IAS 14 was that the segment data prescribed by that standard was to be presented by any entity having substantial activities in more than one industry group or geographic region. It remained a matter of some judgement, however, as to where that threshold was to be placed.

Revised IAS 14 takes a very different approach to defining segments and to defining the threshold at which they become reportable segments. Under the new standard, the goal is to disaggregate business and geographical segments which have different risk and return profiles. The new standard sets forth a number of factors which can be used to determine whether the risks and returns are in fact at variance as between two or more segments. Furthermore, it is explicitly intended that the reporting entity's internal organization and financial reporting system should be used to help in making this determination. For example, the way in which the enterprise is organizationally structured should reveal whether geographical segments are defined in terms of location of productive operations or location of customers.

Not only is it necessary under revised IAS 14 to define which of the business and geographical segments are to be deemed reportable, it is also required that a determination be made about whether the business segments or the geographical segments will be the primary mode of segment reporting, with the alternative becoming the secondary mode. This depends, under the terms of the revised standard, upon whether the dominant source and nature of risk and return derives from the products and services it produces, or from operating in different countries or selling into different markets. The amount of information to be disclosed for the primary segments is much greater than for the secondary segments. (This will be covered in greater detail in a later section of this chapter.) The lack of quantitative thresholds, (under original IAS 14) provided under the US standard is consistent with the decision to use the enterprise's internal organization and operation as the driver of the segment reporting model. In other words, a definable portion of the business will be a segment if management behaves as if it is.

Defining Industry and Geographic Segments

Understanding what is meant by industry segments has proven to be a difficult task for many preparers and users of financial statement information, and furthermore, some preparers have been inclined to define a segment in an overly broad fashion, to reduce the amount of disaggregated information which they present. However, there are very legitimate questions which can, and have, been raised on this matter. For one hypothetical example, consider a large manufacturer of a range of automobiles which can convincingly argue that this represents a single segment, while other similar enterprises might hold that a number of segments exist, such as small cars, luxury cars, etc. Under the original IAS 14, the requirements for segment information appeared to tolerate using a liberal interpretation, so that in the foregoing example all automobile manufacturing could have been deemed to have been a single segment.

In revised IAS 14, the IASC has defined segments in terms more consistent with internal managerial decision making. Using the example above, if management makes distinct decisions about production and marketing of small cars vs. luxury cars, then those would be separate segments for disclosure purposes, regardless of brand names or other artificial distinctions among the product lines. According to the new standard, "an enterprise should look to its system of internal reporting to the board of directors and the chief executive officer for the purpose of identifying its business segments or geographical segments, for both its primary and secondary reporting formats, ..."

Characteristics of business and geographical segments. In the event that internally reported segments fail to satisfy the definitions of business and geographical segments, then the criteria in the standard are to be applied to ascertain the identities of the segments.

The standard stipulates the following factors to be considered in determining how to group products and services into business segments:

1. The nature of the products or services
2. The nature and technology of the production processes
3. The types of markets in which the products or services are sold
4. Major classes of customers
5. The distribution channels and methods for the products
6. A unique legislative or regulatory environment relating to part of the business, as might define banks, insurance companies, and utilities

The following factors can be used to group geographical areas into geographical segments:

1. Proximity of operations
2. Similarity of economic and political conditions
3. Relationships between operations in different geographical areas
4. Special risks associated with operations in a particular country
5. Underlying currency risks

In the absence of internal organizational indicators which suffice to define business and geographical segments, the foregoing criteria should be applied in an attempt to identify primary and secondary segment formats. In that situation, the disclosure of segment data should include a statement to the effect that the externally reported segment data does not conform to that used internally, and the following three supplemental disclosures must be made for each segment which has revenue from sales to external customers amounting to 10% or more of total enterprise revenue from external customers:

1. Segment revenue from external customers
2. The total carrying amount of segment assets
3 Capital expenditures

Internal indications of segments are to be used whenever possible, however. The informational items to be disclosed for the segments, however they are defined, are discussed below.

Defining Reportable Segments

Reportable segments are business or geographical segments, whether identified either by internal organizational or financial reporting factors, or by application of the criteria set forth above, which meet the threshold test for becoming reportable. A segment will be reportable if a majority of its revenue is earned from sales to external customers, and furthermore

1. Its revenue from sales to external customers and from transactions with internal customers (other segments) is 10% or more of total revenue of all segments, **or**
2. Its segment result, whether profit or loss, is 10% or more of the combined result of all segments recording a profit or of all segments recording a loss, whichever is the greater in absolute monetary terms, **or**
3. Its assets are 10% or more of the total assets of all segments.

Thus, the revised IAS 14 essentially has embraced the quantitative criteria of the former US GAAP standard, SFAS 14, regarding the threshold criteria for reportability of individual segments. Note that the segment will be deemed reportable if any one of the three foregoing criteria are satisfied: The test is disjunctive, not conjunctive. However, since only those segments which earn a majority of revenues from external customers are subjected to this testing, those which are essentially vertically integrated will typically not be required to report as separate segments.

Comparative financial statements. Revised IAS 14 also provides that if a segment were deemed to be reportable in the immediate preceding period (because one or more of the aforenoted 10% thresholds had been exceeded), then even failing each of these tests in the current year would not eliminate the need to present comparable segment data currently. However, this requirement is only applicable if management believes that the segment has continuing significance; absent this, such disclosure could be eliminated. The fact that continuing disclosure is dependent upon management attitudes introduces a subjective element. This may eventually be seen as permitting nondisclosure of important information, and more objective criteria may have to be imposed at some point in time.

Furthermore, if a segment is deemed to be reportable in the current reporting period because it satisfies a relevant threshold test for the first time, the comparative prior period disclosures should be restructured to include that segment as a reportable one; notwithstanding that it did not surpass the 10% thresholds in the prior year. In establishing these two requirements, comparability was obviously given a very substantial weighting.

Reporting Segment Information Under Original IAS 14

Original IAS 14 required descriptions of activities for each defined industry segment and the composition of the area for each geographic segment. Furthermore, for each defined segment, the following financial information was to be provided:

1. Sales or other operating revenues, with an indication of how much is derived from outside customers and how much is from sales to other segments of the same reporting entity
2. Operating results
3. Segment assets employed
4. The basis for intersegment pricing

Sales. Revenue by segment is generally easily determined, even in those instances when the definition of industry segments does not completely parallel the formal structure of the organization. With modern data processing capabilities, identification by product, by customer type, or by location is readily accomplished, and information can be appropriately aggregated for segment reporting purposes. Intersegment sales are to be reported separately from those to outside customers, so that users can better appreciate how substantial the operation could be in the possible absence of "captive" sales opportunities.

Segment operating results. A true measure of operating performance, on an "as if independent" basis, is typically very difficult to determine, since many costs, particularly administrative and other overhead items, are allocated from a common pool and the bases upon which these allocations are made will often be somewhat arbitrary. For this reason, IAS 14 provides that this is to be measured by the difference between segment revenue and segment expense, generally at the "income from operations" level, not at the "net income" level, and that common items such as executive office expenses are not expected to be allocated. On the other hand, where there are reasonable bases for allocations, such as utilities costs which could be allocated among segments sharing a common facility by reference to the relative space occupied, etc., it is expected that these allocations will be made.

Items which are not part of operations, particularly at the segment level, such as interest income and interest expense, should not be allocated, since any such allocations would be arbitrary and the resulting measure of performance would be weakened as a consequence. Since, absent a complete allocation of all revenue and expense items, the sum of all segments' operating results will not equal that of the enterprise as a whole, IAS 14 further requires that there be a reconciliation presented. An example of such a reconciliation is included in the comprehensive illustration later in this chapter.

Segment assets employed. Disclosure of assets in use by each segment gives yet another indication of the scope of the segment operations. This is more important in the case of manufacturing enterprises, and for service businesses this often will be of trivial interest, but unless immaterial, this information should be presented. The requirement applies to all assets in use, both tangible and intangible, if they can indeed be identified with a particular segment or if a reasonable basis for allocation exists. Some assets, such as those employed by corporate headquarters, should not be allocated, since the result would be arbitrary and would diminish the utility of the disclosures. There would, however, need to be a reconciliation between total assets per the entity's balance sheet and the sum of the assets shown for the identified segments.

Basis for intersegment pricing. A wide range of methods are used by enterprises in pricing goods and services which are sold internally. Such so-called transfer pricing may be set to approximate arm's-length prices, but very often intersegment sales will instead be consummated at negotiated prices, marginal production costs, variable costs, discounted market prices, long-run average costs, or completely arbitrary amounts. Since the users of the financial statements will be making judgements about the relative importance of intersegment activities vs. transactions with outside parties, any disparity between the measurement approaches will be potentially misleading.

For this reason, IAS 14 required that the method of determining intersegment revenues be disclosed when a material component of segment operations. This disclosure can be fairly general, however. Terms such as "approximating fair market prices" and "average direct costs of production" would be acceptable as descriptions under this standard.

Applying the rules under current IAS 14. For purposes of conforming with IAS 14, as it presently exists, segments should be defined in terms of groups of related products or services, or alternatively by types of customers to whom these are provided. It must remain a matter of judgement as to how this guideline is applied, and similar enterprises might reach different conclusions on this. For example, the previously referenced manufacturer of electronic and mechanical components used in the automobile industry might market these to original equipment manufacturers (OEM) of automobiles and of heavy construction equipment, and also to aftermarket suppliers, in a number of different geographic markets (e.g., Western Europe, the former Eastern Bloc nations of Europe, and the Middle East). In presenting segment data, the entity might reach four different conclusions on how to define the segments, as follows:

1. It might argue that the entire business represents a single segment.

2. It could find that electronics and mechanical components are essentially different product lines and, thus, that there are two segments of the business.
3. It might conclude that the OEM market is generically different from the after market, thus defining two different segments in another way.
4. It could reason that automobile OEM, construction equipment OEM, and after-market suppliers are each distinct, thus defining three segments of the business for which information is to be disclosed.

Thus, it is clear that management judgement will continue to play a large role in financial reporting of industry segments. In reaching its decisions, however, managements should weigh the similarities and differences among the products or services, the risk characteristics of the markets, the growth potential and the likely future importance of the segment to the entity as a whole. If some parts of the business are subject to particular or unusual regulatory oversight (such as banking typically is), this is a factor which suggests that it might constitute a separate segment for reporting purposes. The fact that a product or service line is produced in an organizationally separate unit, such as a division, may or may not be determinative; thus, internal accounting data might be usable for segment reporting, but might also need to be reclassified for that purpose.

The determination of geographic segments is likewise subject to the application of substantial amounts of judgement. Typically, however, it will be fairly obvious in any given circumstance how the breakdown among regions should be accomplished. The only real question, in most cases, will be how much detail to present. For example, if an enterprise has operations in western Europe and also in former Soviet Bloc nations such as Poland, some might conclude that these are separate segments since their economic systems were so different for so long, and the emerging nations of Eastern Europe represent materially different risks and growth opportunities. Others might conclude that Europe is a single region, based on transportation requirements and other criteria, especially when compared to North American, Latin American and Asian segments of the same business.

Comprehensive example of segment reporting under IAS 14

To illustrate the foregoing ideas, a comprehensive disclosure under the existing standard, original IAS 14, is presented herewith. The following is the set of disclosures made by the aforenoted producer of electronic and mechanical components sold to OEM and after-market suppliers in Western and Eastern Europe and the Middle East.

Note 9: Segment Information

	(All amounts in $ millions)	
	Electronic components	*Mechanical components*
Net sales		
1996	345.0	228.6
1997	378.5	219.8
Operating profit		
1996	29.6	13.2
1997	36.0	8.5
Capital expenditures		
1996	12.1	3.5
1997	21.4	2.5
Identifiable assets		
1996	122.9	128.4
1997	140.2	118.5
Depreciation and amortization		
1996	13.7	15.9
1997	17.5	13.6

Unallocated (corporate) assets totaled $7.6 million in 1996 and $8.1 million in 1997. Unallocated corporate expenses equaled $3.4 million in 1996 and $4.5 million in 1997. Intersegment sales, which are made at cost, are not material in amount. Operating profit by segment is defined as third party sales less operating expenses; corporate overhead and financing costs are excluded from segment expenses.

Revenue by geographic area is summarized below.

	(All amounts in $ millions)		
	Western Europe	*Eastern Europe*	*Middle East*
Net sales			
1996	348.8	113.4	111.7
1997	366.3	133.4	98.6
Operating profit			
1996	22.7	8.6	11.5
1997	20.6	13.9	10.0
Identifiable assets			
1996	178.4	63.2	9.7
1997	183.3	69.5	5.9

Western Europe includes primarily Germany and France, with a relatively small amount of activity in Belgium and the Netherlands. Eastern Europe includes Hungary, Poland, Slovakia and the Czech Republic. The Middle East is principally Lebanon and Syria, with a small level of activity in Egypt and Saudi Arabia. Sales in the Middle East are made almost entirely to after-market suppliers, whereas revenues derived from European markets are predominately from original equipment manufacturers of automobiles and construction equipment. Approximately 12% and 14% of sales in Western Europe, for 1996 and 1997, respectively, were made to after-market suppliers; for Eastern European sales, the corresponding percentages were 19% and 23% for 1996 and 1997, respectively.

Disclosure Requirements Under Revised IAS 14

The draft which preceded the issuance of revised IAS 14 offered an expansive listing of mandatory disclosures to be made in both the primary and the secondary segment reporting formats. The comments received to the exposure draft, not surprisingly, indicated that many preparers of financial statements believed that these requirements would be excessive. While the final standard has eliminated a handful of the proposed disclosures, what remains is a wide-ranging set of data to be presented in the notes to the financial statements of any enterprise which operates in more than a single segment, and which is subject to the requirements.

All reporting entities will need to define whether business segments are to be the primary reporting format, in which case geographical segments will become the secondary reporting format, or whether the opposite is to be the case. This determination is made, as noted before, based on the dominant source of risk and return to the organization. Thus, if strategic decisions are made primarily in terms of geographical location of either operations (e.g., siting of manufacturing plants, sourcing materials, etc.) or customers, then geographical segments will be the primary reporting format. If decisions revolve around product or service offerings, then business segments will be the primary format. In either case, the format not chosen as primary will be used as secondary, which implies a substantial amount of informative disclosure, although somewhat less than in the primary format.

Primary reporting format disclosures. The following informative disclosures are mandated for each reportable segment:

1. Segment revenue, with separate disclosure of revenue derived from external customers and revenue derived from internal customers (i.e., from other segments). Also, the nature of the segment's revenue should be described, in the manner set forth in IAS 18 (i.e., separately disclosing revenues arising from sales of goods, rendering of services, interest, royalties, dividends, and from the exchange [bartering] of goods and services in each category)
2. Segment result
3. Interest and dividend income and interest expense directly attributable to the segment or which can be reasonably allocated to the segment, separately--except that this need not be done for reportable segments the operations of which are primarily of a financial nature
4. Total assets at carrying value
5. Segment liabilities

6. The contingencies or commitments which can be directly attributed to a reportable segment or allocated on a reasonable basis to segments
7. Total expenditures to acquire segment assets during the reporting period (typically referred to as capital expenditures)
8. Total depreciation and amortization expense related to segment assets and included in segment results for the reporting period
9. The nature of any item of revenue or expense which due to size, nature or incidence needs to be disclosed to explain performance of the segment for the period
10. The nature and amount of extraordinary items which are directly attributable to a segment or reasonably allocable to it
11. Significant noncash expenses, other than depreciation and amortization, that were deducted in arriving at segment results
12. The segment's share of profit or loss of associates, joint ventures or other investments accounted for under the equity method, as well as the investment in that associate or joint venture
13. A reconciliation of the information presented for reportable segments (the 12 categories above) to the amounts presented in the consolidated or enterprise-wide financial statements. In reconciling revenue, segment revenue from outsiders should be reconciled to total revenue from outside customers; segment results should be reconciled to a comparable measure of enterprise performance as well as to enterprise net income or loss; and segment liabilities should be reconciled to enterprise liabilities.

Secondary reporting format. The nature of the data presented in the secondary reporting format depends upon which of the two possible criteria determined the primary format, business or geography. If the primary disclosures were based on business segments, then the secondary, geographical, format must contain, for each segment which has sales to external customers **or** segment assets totaling 10% or more of the comparable enterprise-wide amounts

1. Segment revenue from external customers, determined by the geographical location of customer or market
2. Total carrying amount of segment assets, determined by geographical location of the assets
3. The total amount of capital expenditure for the period being reported on, by location of assets

If the primary mode of reporting segment information is by geographical locations, on the other hand, then the secondary format information will be, for each business segment whose revenue from sales to external customers is 10% or more of total enterprise revenue from external customers, as follows:

1. Segment revenue from external customers
2. Total carrying amount of segment assets
3. The total amount of capital expenditures for the period

Finally, if the entity defines primary segment format in terms of geographical area, based on the location of the production or service facilities, and if the markets in which the goods or services significantly differ from the location of the assets, then revenue from sales to external customers must also be reported by location of markets. The geographical markets to be identified are those whose sales to external customers is 10% or more of the corresponding enterprise total.

Other Disclosures Which May Be Necessary

Disclosures are necessary when a business or geographical segment is not deemed to be reportable because it earns a majority of its revenue from intersegment sales, yet 10% or more of enterprise sales to external customers is comprised of sales to external customers by this segment. This fact should be disclosed, as well as the sales revenue from external and intersegment sales generated by the segment.

The basis for determining prices for intersegment sales should be stated. This should be the same basis that the enterprise actually uses to recognize such transactions for internal reporting purposes. If the method has changed from the previous period, that fact should be adequately disclosed as well.

Segment disclosures are to be prepared using the same accounting principles that the enterprise uses for general external reporting in accordance with international accounting standards. If there have been changes in accounting principles employed at the enterprise level which also impact on segment informative disclosures, these should be dealt with in accordance with IAS 8. Under that standard's benchmark treatment, prior period information is restated to conform with the new principles, unless impracticable to do so. Under the allowed alternative treatment, the cumulative effect of the change in accounting principle is reported as a charge or credit in determining current period net income. If the alternative treatment is utilized, the cumulative effect should be included in segment operating performance, if reasonable allocations can be made, with sufficient disclosure to explain the performance of the segments for the period.

If there have been changes in accounting principles employed in determining segment disclosures, which have a material impact on the data provided to users of the financial statements, such as the method of allocating revenue and expenses to segments, then again consistent with the benchmark treatment stipulated by IAS 8, the comparative prior period information should be restated to conform with the new methods utilized. This is important even though aggregate enterprise amounts will not have been affected by the change, since the users' understanding of segment performance may be distorted unless efforts are made to provide them with insights into these matters.

Unless it is clear from other disclosures or from the body of the financial statements themselves, the segment information should include descriptions of the activities of each reportable business segment and should also indicate the composition of each geographical segment, both for primary and secondary reporting formats. A fair amount of judgement is required in deciding on what information should be provided, but in theory, to take the geographical segment disclosure as an example, such matters as stability of currencies, political risks, and market growth expectations are all potentially useful to recipients of the data and possibly necessary to interpret the financial disclosures most meaningfully. While these are technically voluntary disclosures, in ultimately reaching a judgement as to whether the financial statements are fairly presented, the adequacy of disclosures will have to be weighed.

If an enterprise operates in a single business or geographical segment and therefore is not required to, and does not, report either primary or secondary segment data, that fact should be disclosed and the nature of its business segment or geographical operations should be stated. In some cases an entity will operate within a single segment, but derive revenues from a number of diverse products or services; in such instances, the new standard requires that these be described and the amounts of revenues derived from any such group of products or services which constitute 10% or more of enterprise revenue should be set forth. This clearly will require the exercise of judgement, since there will be a thin line between such disclosures and the admission that the entity, in fact, is operating in more than a single segment and thus should have made the full set of informative disclosures required by revised IAS 14.

Finally, if the aggregate revenue from external customers from all reportable segments totals less than 75% of the revenue reported by the entity as a whole, the standard requires that there be a general description of the nature of the remaining sources of revenue. This would normally occur when the balance of revenues are derived from a range of individually minor activities which do not constitute a single or group of segments. In practice, this situation will not occur very often, as the defined and reportable segments will typically add to more than the 75% threshold level.

Revisions to Definitions of Segments

Over time, an entity may determine that the definition of industry or of geographic segments needs to be revised. The effect of making such a change could be to make information presented in earlier years no longer comparable to that currently presented in the financial statements. Accordingly, at a minimum, the fact of having made this change must be disclosed, with a sufficient description so that users can appreciate the general impact that change might have had. The reasons why the change was made, such as to better reflect the way management is currently making decisions about the segments of the business, should also be stated. If reasonably determinable, the actual effect of the change should be disclosed.

As an example, the manufacturer of electronic and mechanical automobile parts used in the example below might at some point conclude that its former manner of presentation of segment data as a dichotomy between electronic and mechanical products is no longer meaningful given the growing pervasiveness of electronic components in what had previously been entirely mechanical items. Thus, the entity might determine that a more useful categorization would be by type of customer, say, original equipment manufacturers (OEM) vs. after-market, since the underlying economic forces differ substantially between these. In the year of the change in presentation, the fact of the change and the logic for it should be presented, and if possible the prior period's data, which had been presented earlier on the basis of product type, should be restated on the newly adopted basis of customer class. By doing this, the users of the financial statements would be able to understand the trends affecting the segments, as they are currently being defined.

Comprehensive example of segment reporting under revised IAS 14

To illustrate the expansion of reporting requirements under the new standard, revised IAS 14, a comprehensive illustration is given below. The same facts are assumed as in the preceding illustration of disclosures under original IAS 14, to better highlight the changes in the new standard. It is assumed that management has determined that the primary reporting format should be by business segment; the secondary reporting format, therefore, will by geographical segment.

Note 10: Segment Information

Management has determined that the primary determinant of its decision making is the major products offered by the company, with lesser attention being based on geographical location of its customers. Accordingly, the primary disclosures, below, are based on business segment, alternatively, electronic or mechanical components, with the following secondary disclosures based on geographic location of customers.

(All amounts in $ millions)

	Electronic components	*Mechanical components*
Net sales		
1996--In total	345.0	228.6
1996--To external customers	336.3	228.6
1996--Intersegment sales	8.7	0.0
1997--In total	378.5	219.8
1997--To external customers	371.0	219.5
1997--Intersegment sales	7.5	.3
Operating profit		
1996	29.6	13.2
1997	36.0	8.5

Interest and dividend income		
1996--Interest income	1.2	.2
1996--Dividend income	.1	0
1997--Interest income	1.1	.3
1997--Dividend income	0	0
Interest expense		
1996	1.5	1.1
1997	1.2	1.0
Identifiable assets, at net carrying amounts		
1996	122.9	128.4
1997	140.2	118.5
Segment liabilities		
1996	62.3	43.4
1997	59.6	40.1
Contingent liabilities related to contractual disputes		
1996	2.5	1.0
1997	4.4	1.2
Capital expenditures		
1996	12.1	3.5
1997	21.4	2.5
Depreciation and amortization		
1996	13.7	15.9
1997	17.5	13.6
Nonrecurring items		
1996--Revenue from government contract	6.7	0
1997--Gain from settlement of patent suit	2.3	0
Equity in income of investee		
1996	2.2	0
1997	.5	0
Investment in equity method investee		
1996	5.6	0
1997	6.9	0

Segment information is reconciled to corresponding enterprise totals in the following section:

Net sales	
1996--To external customers	
Electronic components	336.3
Mechanical components	228.6
Enterprise total sales	564.9

1997--to external customers	
Electronic components	371.0
Mechanical components	219.5
Enterprise total sales	590.5
Operating profit	
1996	
Electronic components	29.6
Mechanical components	13.2
Less: Unallocated corporate expenses	(3.4)
Enterprise total operating profit	39.4
1997	
Electronic components	36.0
Mechanical components	8.5
Less: Unallocated corporate expenses	(4.5)
Enterprise total operating profit	40.0
Identifiable assets, at net carrying amounts	
1996	
Electronic components	122.9
Mechanical components	128.4
Unallocated corporate assets	7.6
Enterprise total assets	258.9
1997	
Electronic components	140.2
Mechanical components	118.5
Unallocated corporate assets	8.1
Enterprise total assets	266.8
Segment liabilities	
1996	
Electronic components	62.3
Mechanical components	43.4
Enterprise total liabilities	105.7
1997	
Electronic components	59.6
Mechanical components	40.1
Enterprise total liabilities	99.7

Revenue by geographic area is summarized below (based on location of customers).

	(All amounts in $ millions)		
	Western Europe	*Eastern Europe*	*Middle East*
Net sales			
1996	348.8	113.4	111.7
1997	366.3	133.4	98.6
Identifiable assets			
1996	178.4	63.2	9.7
1997	183.3	69.5	5.9
Capital expenditures			
1996	8.2	4.4	3.0
1997	12.5	5.5	5.9

Western Europe includes primarily Germany and France, with a relatively small amount of activity in Belgium and the Netherlands. Eastern Europe includes Hungary, Poland, Slovakia and the Czech Republic. The Middle East is principally Lebanon and Syria, with a small level of activity in Egypt and Saudi Arabia. Sales in the Middle East are made almost entirely to after-market suppliers, whereas revenues derived from European markets are predominately from original equipment manufacturers of automobiles and construction equipment. Approximately 12% and 14% of sales in Western Europe, for 1996 and 1997, respectively, were made to after-market suppliers; for Eastern European sales, the corresponding percentages were 19% and 23% for 1996 and 1997, respectively.

19 ACCOUNTING CHANGES AND CORRECTION OF FUNDAMENTAL ERRORS

PERSPECTIVE AND ISSUES

Information contained in an enterprise's financial statements over a period of time must be comparable to be of value to users of those statements. Users of financial statements usually seek to identify trends in the enterprise's financial position, performance, and cash flows by studying and analyzing the information contained in those statements. Thus it is imperative that the same accounting policies be applied from year to year in the preparation of financial statements, and that any departures from this rule be clearly indicated.

Financial statements are the results of choices among different accounting principles and methodologies. Companies select those accounting principles and methods that they believe depict, in their financial statements, the economic reality of their financial position, results of operations, and changes in financial position. Changes take place because of changes in the assumptions and estimates underlying the application of these principles and methods, changes in the acceptable principles by a promulgating authority, such as an accounting standard-setting body or other types of changes.

Accounting for and reporting of these changes is a problem that has faced the accounting profession for years. Much financial analysis is based on the consistency and comparability of annual financial statements. Any type of accounting change creates an inconsistency; thus, a primary focus of management in making the decision to change should be to consider its effect on financial statement comparability.

IAS 8 (revised 1993), which became operative for financial statements covering periods beginning on or after January 1, 1995, deals with accounting changes (i.e., changes in accounting estimates and changes in accounting principles) and addresses the correction of fundamental errors. IAS 8 also prescribes the classification, disclosure, and accounting treatment of certain items in the income statement, such as "extraordinary items" and "discontinued operations," which are the subject matter of Chapter 3. The objectives of this standard in prescribing such accounting treatment and disclosures is to enhance comparability both with an enterprise's financial statements of previous years and with the financial statements of other enterprises. Even though the correction of a fundamental error in financial statements issued previously is not considered an accounting change, it is discussed in this standard and therefore is covered in this chapter.

In the preparation of financial statements there is an underlying presumption that an accounting principle, once adopted, should not be changed in accounting for events and transactions of a similar type. This consistent use of accounting principles enhances the utility of the financial statements. The presumption that an entity should not change an accounting principle may be overcome only if the enterprise justifies the use of an alternative acceptable accounting principle on the basis that it is preferable.

Sources of IAS
IAS 8 (revised)

DEFINITIONS OF TERMS

Accounting policies. Specific principles, bases, conventions, rules, and practices adopted by an enterprise in preparing and presenting financial statements.

Change in accounting estimate. A revision of an accounting measurement based on new information, more experience, or subsequent developments. The use of reasonable estimates is an essential part of the financial statement preparation process and does not undermine their reliability. Since uncertainties are inherent in day-to-day business activities, revisions to such accounting estimates are an acceptable practice in the accounting process.

Change in accounting principle. A switch from one generally accepted accounting principle to another generally accepted accounting principle, including the methods of applying these principles.

Comparability. The quality of information that enables users to identify similarities in and differences between two sets of economic phenomena.

Consistency. Consistency refers to conformity from period to period with unchanging policies and procedures. It enhances the utility of financial statements to users by facilitating analysis and understanding of comparative accounting data.

Cumulative effect. The difference between the beginning retained earnings balance of the year in which the change is reported and the beginning retained earnings balance that would have been reported if the new principle had been applied retrospectively for all prior periods that would have been affected.

Error. The effect on the financial statements that results from mathematical mistakes, mistakes in applying accounting principles, misinterpretations of facts, fraud, or oversights.

Fundamental error. An error that has such a significant effect on the financial statements of one or more prior periods that those financial statements can no longer be considered to have been reliable at the date of their issue.

Pro forma information. Financial information that is prepared on an "as if" basis. The disclosure of required numbers computed on the assumption that certain events have transpired. Where allowed alternative treatments are followed in lieu of the benchmark treatments established by IAS 8, additional pro forma information is to be presented.

Restatement of comparative financial information. The recasting of a prior period's balance sheet or income statement information where there has been a change in accounting policy or correction of a fundamental error and the benchmark treatment is followed.

CONCEPTS, RULES, AND EXAMPLES

Importance of Comparability and Consistency in Financial Reporting

Generally accepted accounting principles have long held that an important objective of financial reporting is to encourage comparability among financial statements produced by essentially similar enterprises. This is necessary to facilitate informed economic decision making by investors, creditors, prospective employees, joint venturers, and others. While complete comparability will not be achieved as long as alternative principles of accounting and reporting remain acceptable for like transactions and events, a driving force in developing new accounting standards is to enhance comparability. The IASC's efforts in the early 1990s (the "comparability project") did in fact narrow the range of acceptable alternative methods of accounting, and further narrowing will probably occur as the core set of standards undergoes development to comply with the historic agreement with IOSCO, as described in Chapter 1.

Comparability refers to the quality of information that enables users to identify similarities in and differences between two sets of economic phenomena. Normally, comparability is a quantitative assessment of a common characteristic.

An important implication of the qualitative characteristic of comparability is that users be informed of the accounting policies employed in the preparation of the financial statements, any changes in those policies, and the effects of such changes. Disclosure of accounting policies was discussed in Chapters 2, 3, and 4; this chapter addresses the appropriate communications of changes in accounting policies and related matters.

Compliance with IAS helps in achieving comparability since the adoption of IAS by enterprises facilitates relative evaluation of financial data using a common accounting language. The need for comparability, however, should not be confused with mere uniformity and should not be allowed to become a barrier or an impediment to the adoption of improved accounting methods.

As contrasted with comparability, consistency refers to a given reporting entity's conformity from period to period with unchanging policies and procedures. The quality of consistency enhances the utility of financial statements to users by facilitating analysis and understanding of comparative accounting data.

According to IAS 1 (revised), "the presentation and classification of items in the financial statements should be retained from one period to the next unless a significant change in the nature of the operations of the enterprise or a review of its financial statement presentation demonstrates that more relevant information is provided in a different way." It is, however, inappropriate for an enterprise to continue accounting for transactions in the same manner if the policies adopted lack qualitative characteristics of relevance and reliability. Thus, if more reliable and relevant alternatives exist, it is better for the enterprise to change its methods of accounting for defined classes of transactions.

Reporting Accounting Changes

IAS 8 describes three ways of reporting accounting changes and the type of change for which each should be used. These are

1. Retrospectively
2. Currently
3. Prospectively

Retrospective treatment requires an adjustment to all current and prior-period financial statements for the effect of the accounting change. Prior-period financial statements presented currently are to be restated on a basis consistent with the newly adopted principle.

Current treatment requires reporting the cumulative effect of the accounting change in the current year's income statement as a special item. Prior-period financial statements are not restated.

Prospective treatment of accounting changes requires **no** restatement of prior financial statements and **no** computing or reporting of the accounting change's cumulative effect in the current period's income statement. Only current and/or future periods' financial report data will reflect the accounting change.

Each type of accounting change and the proper treatment prescribed for them are discussed in detail in the following sections.

Change in Accounting Policy

A change in any accounting policy means that a reporting entity has switched from one generally accepted accounting principle to another. According to IAS 8, the term "accounting policy" includes the accounting principles, bases, conventions, rules and practices used. For example, a change in inventory costing from weighted-average to first-in, first-out would be a change in accounting policy, as would a change in accounting for borrowing costs from capitalization to immediate expensing.

An interpretation of a similar definition under US GAAP provides a meaningful framework by establishing that a change in the components used to cost a firm's inventory is a change in accounting principle. This FASB interpretation also clarified that the preferability assessment (relating to the selection of the appropriate accounting policy or principle in particular circumstances) must be made from the perspective of financial reporting basis and not from the income tax perspective.

Changes in accounting policy are permitted if

1. The change in accounting principle will result in a more appropriate presentation of events or transactions in the financial statements of the enterprise, or
2. The change in accounting principle is required by an accounting standard-setting body, or
3. The change in accounting principle is required by statute.

IAS 8 does not regard the following as changes in accounting policies:

1. The adoption of an accounting policy for events or transactions that differ in substance from previously occurring events or transactions; and
2. The adoption of a new accounting policy to account for events or transactions that did not occur previously or that were immaterial

The provisions of IAS 8 are not applicable to the initial adoption of a policy to carry assets at revalued amounts, although such adoption is a change in accounting policy. Rather, it is dealt with as a revaluation in accordance with IAS 16 or IAS 25, as appropriate under the circumstances.

Benchmark and Allowed Alternative Accounting Treatments

IAS 8 prescribes two methods of reporting a change in accounting policy, depending on whether the "benchmark treatment" or the "allowed alternative" method is used. If the benchmark treatment is used, a change in accounting policy is to be applied retrospectively (unless the amount of the resultant adjustment from the change relating to the prior-period is not reasonably determinable). With application of the retrospective effect to the change in accounting policy, the following adjustments will have to be made:

1. The comparative information presented for the prior periods will be restated to reflect the effect of the change in accounting policy; the effect will be computed under the assumption that the new accounting policy had always been in use.
2. The cumulative effect of the change (resulting from the retrospective application of the accounting policy to prior periods) net of income taxes, if any,

will be reported as an adjustment to the opening balance of the retained earnings.

3. Any other information with respect to prior periods, such as historical summaries of financial data, is also restated.

If the allowed alternative treatment is chosen by the enterprise instead of the benchmark treatment

1. The cumulative effect of the change (resulting from the retrospective application of the accounting policy) net of income taxes, if any, will have to be included in the determination of the current year's net profit or loss.
2. The comparative information for the prior period presented alongside the current year's figures need not be restated as in the case of the application of the benchmark treatment above. In other words, the comparative information will be presented as reported in the prior years' financial statements.
3. Additional pro forma comparative information (prepared based on the guidelines above for the application of the benchmark treatment) will also need to be presented.

The cumulative effect of a change in accounting principle is to appear as a single amount in the income statement between extraordinary items and net income if the allowed alternative treatment is used, and as a single amount shown as an adjustment to the opening retained earnings balance if the benchmark treatment is applied. This single amount should be the difference between

1. The amount of retained earnings at the beginning of the period, and
2. The amount of retained earnings that would have been reported at that date if the new accounting principle had been applied retroactively to all prior periods affected.

The cumulative effect is generally determined by first calculating income before taxes for both the new principle and the old principle for all prior periods affected. The difference between the two incomes for each prior period is then determined. Next, these differences are adjusted for tax effects. Finally, the net of tax differences for each prior period are totaled. This total represents the cumulative effect adjustment at the beginning of the current period. The cumulative effect will either be an addition to or a subtraction from current income, depending on how the change to the new principle affects income.

Generally, only the direct effects of the change and the related income tax effect should be included in the cumulative effect calculation (i.e., if the company changes its method of costing inventories, only the effects of the change in cost of goods sold, net of tax, are considered to be direct effects). Indirect effects, such as the effect on a profit sharing contribution or bonus payments that would have occurred as a result of the change in net income, are not included in the cumulative effect computation unless these are to be recorded by the firm (i.e., the expense is actually incurred).

The computation of income on a pro forma basis must be made for each period currently presented. The objective is to present income before extraordinary items and net income as if the new principle were being applied. This is achieved by adjusting each period's income before extraordinary items as reported previously (i.e., applying the old principle). The adjustment is made by adding or subtracting the difference in income net of tax for the period to income before extraordinary items as reported previously. The difference, net of tax, is the change in income that occurs when the new principle is applied instead of the old principle. This results in a figure for income before extraordinary items that reflects the application of the new principle. Net income is then calculated as normally done from the adjusted income before extraordinary items. The per share amounts required are based on the pro forma income before extraordinary items and net income amounts.

The pro forma calculation differs from that of the cumulative effect. It is to include both the direct effects of the change and the "nondiscretionary" adjustments of items based on income before taxes or net income. Examples of nondiscretionary items are profit sharing expense or certain royalties. Both of these expenses are in some way based on net income, generally as a specified percentage. The related tax effects should be recognized for **both** the direct and nondiscretionary adjustments.

The following example illustrates the computations and disclosures necessary when applying the cumulative effect method.

Example of benchmark and alternative treatments of changes in accounting policy under IAS 8

In 19X5, the Zircon Company adopted the percentage-of-completion method of accounting for long-term construction contracts. The company had used the completed-contract method for all prior years.

The following sections present extracts from the statements of earnings and retained earnings of Zircon Company before adjusting for the effects of the change in accounting policy. Net profit for 19X5 was determined under the percentage-of-completion method of accounting.

	19X5	*19X4*
Profit from ordinary activities before income taxes	$120,000	$130,000
Income taxes	(20,000)	(26,000)
Net profit	100,000	104,000
Retained earnings, beginning	134,000	30,000
Retained earnings, ending	$234,000	$134,000

The effects of the change in accounting policy are presented below.

	Difference in income under the percentage-of-completion method	*Effect of the change net of income taxes*
Prior to 19X4	$20,000	$14,000
For 19X4	15,000	10,500
Total as of the beginning of 19X5	35,000	24,500
For 19X5	$20,000	$14,000

The following pages provide an illustration of the accounting treatment and presentation of financial statements under the benchmark treatment and the allowed alternative treatment of the changes in accounting policies in accordance with IAS 8.

Changes in Accounting Policies: Benchmark Treatment

Zircon Company
Extracts from Income Statement

	19X5	*19X4 restated*
Profit from ordinary activities before income taxes	$120,000	$145,000
Income taxes	(20,000)	(30,500)
Net profit	$100,000	$114,500

Zircon Company
Statement of Retained Earnings

Retained earnings, beginning, as reported previously	$134,000	$ 30,000
Change in accounting policy, net of income taxes of $10,500 for 19X5 and $6,000 for 19X4 (see Note 1)	24,500	14,000
Retained earnings, beginning, as restated	158,500	44,000
Net profit	100,000	114,500
Retained earnings, ending	$258,500	$158,500

Zircon Company
Extracts from Notes to the Financial Statements

Note 1: During 19X5, Zircon Company changed the accounting policy for revenue and costs for a long-term construction contract from the completed-contract method to the percentage-of-completion method, to conform with the accounting treatment of contract revenue and contract costs under IAS 11, *Construction Contracts*. This change in accounting policy has been accounted for retrospectively. The comparative financial statements for 19X4 have been revised to conform to the changed policy. The effect of this change is to increase income from contracts by $20,000 in 19X5 and $15,000 in 19X4. Opening retained earnings for 19X4 has been increased by $14,000, which is the amount of the adjustment relating to periods prior to 19X4, net of income tax effect of $6,000.

Explanation. Under the benchmark treatment, a change in accounting policy should be applied retrospectively unless the amount of any resulting adjustment that relates to prior periods is not reasonably determinable. Any resulting adjustment should be reported as an adjustment to the opening balance of retained earnings. Comparative information should be restated unless impracticable to do so. The steps in preparing the revised financial statements and related disclosures are as follows:

1. The 19X5 income statement is not adjusted, since it already reflects application of the new policy.
2. The 19X4 income statement is restated as follows:

Profit from ordinary activities before income taxes, as previously reported	$130,000
Effect of the change in accounting policy	15,000
As restated	145,000
Income taxes as previous reported	26,000
Income tax effect of the change in accounting policy ($15,000 – $10,500)	4,500
As restated	30,500
Net income as restated	$114,500

3. As presented in the statement of retained earnings, the opening retained earnings for 19X4 was restated to reflect an increase of $14,000, which represents the amount of adjustment related to periods prior to 19X4, net of income tax effect of $6,000. The opening balance of 19X5 was adjusted by $24,500, which represented the effect of the change at the beginning of 19X5, net of income taxes.

Changes in Accounting Policy: Allowed Alternative Treatment

Under the allowed alternative treatment set forth in IAS 8, the amount computed from the retroactive application of the new accounting policy is included in income of the current period. Additional pro forma presentations are also required under this approach. Using the same facts as in the preceding discussion, the alternative treatment is illustrated as follows:

Zircon Company
Extracts from Income Statement

			Pro forma	
			(Restated)	*(Restated)*
	19X5	*19X4*	*19X5*	*19X4*
Profit from ordinary activities, before income taxes and effect of change in accounting policy	$120,000	$130,000	$120,000	$145,000
Cumulative effect of change in accounting policy	35,000	--	--	--
Profit from ordinary activities, before income taxes	155,000	130,000	120,000	145,000
Income taxes (including effect of a change in accounting policy)	30,500	26,000	20,000	30,500
Net profit	$124,500	$104,000	$100,000	$114,500

Zircon Company
Statement of Retained Earnings

			Pro forma	
			(Restated)	*(Restated)*
	19X5	*19X4*	*19X5*	*19X4*
Retained earnings, beginning, as previously reported	$134,000	$ 30,000	$134,000	$ 30,000
Change in accounting policy for construction contracts, net of income taxes of $10,500 for 19X5 and $6,000 for 19X4 (Note 1)	--	--	24,500	14,000
Retained earnings, beginning, as restated	134,000	30,000	158,500	44,000
Net profit	124,000	104,000	100,000	114,500
Retained earnings, ending	$258,500	$134,000	$258,500	$158,000

Zircon Company
Extracts from Notes to the Financial Statements

Note 1: An adjustment of $35,000 has been made in the income statement for 19X5, representing the effect of a change in the accounting policy with respect to revenue and costs for long-term construction contracts. The company now uses the percentage-of-completion method instead of the completed-contract method, to conform to the accounting treatment of contract revenue and costs prescribed by IAS 11, *Construction Contracts*. This change in accounting policy has been accounted for retrospectively. Restated pro forma information, which assumes that the new policy had always been in use, is presented. Beginning retained earnings in the pro forma information for 19X4 has been increased by $14,000, which is the amount of adjustment relating to periods prior to 19X4, net of income tax effect of $6,000.

Explanation. Under the allowed alternative, a retroactive computation is still required, but instead of including the cumulative effect of the change in the restated balance of opening retained earnings, it is included in income of the current period. Furthermore, if the alternative treatment is elected, additional pro forma information must be presented (effectively, this means that the benchmark treatment must also be presented if the allowed alternative is used) unless it is impracticable to do so.

Change in Amortization Method

Another special case in accounting for a change in principle takes place when a company chooses to change the systematic pattern of amortizing the costs of long-lived assets to expense. When a company adopts a new method of amortization for newly acquired identifiable long-lived assets and uses that method for all new assets of the same class without changing the method used previously for existing assets of the same class, there is a change in accounting principle. Obviously, there is no adjustment required to the financial statements or any cumulative type of adjustment. In these special cases, a description of the nature of the method changed and the effect on net income, income before extraordinary items, and related per share amounts should be disclosed in the period of the change.

If the new method is, instead, adopted for all assets, both old and new, the change would appear to be a change in accounting principle which should be accounted for as described above. However, under the provisions of IAS 16, *Property, Plant and Equipment*, this is not the case. That standard, discussed in greater detail in Chapter 8, establishes that a change in depreciation method should be made only if there has been a significant change in the expected pattern of economic benefits from the use of the assets; in such case, the change is to be accounted for as a change in accounting estimate, not a change in policy. (Change in accounting estimate is discussed in the following section.) It does not appear to be contemplated by international accounting standards that there could be a change in depreciation methods to a "better" method that would justify change in accounting policy treatment. Since such changes in depreciation method are fairly common under US GAAP, the international standard on this topic is certain to generate at least some controversy.

Change in Accounting Estimates

The preparation of financial statements requires frequent use of estimates for such items as asset service lives, salvage values, collectibility of accounts receivable, warranty costs, pension costs, and so on. These future conditions and events and their effects cannot be perceived with certainty; therefore, changes in estimates will be inevitable as new information and more experience is obtained. IAS 8 requires that changes in estimates be handled currently and prospectively. It states that "The effect of the change in accounting estimate should be accounted for in (a) the period of change if the change affects that period only or (b) the period of change and future periods if the change affects both." For example, on January 1, 1994, a machine purchased for $10,000 was originally estimated to have a 10-year life. On January 1, 1999 (6 years later), the asset is expected to last another 10 years. As a result, both the current period and the subsequent periods are affected by the change. The annual depreciation charge over the remaining life would be computed as follows:

$$\frac{\text{Book value of asset} - \text{Salvage value}}{\text{Remaining useful life}} = \frac{\$5{,}000 - 0}{10 \text{ years}} = \$500/\text{yr.}$$

A permanent impairment affecting the cost recovery of an asset should not be handled as a change in accounting estimate but should be treated as a loss of the period. (See the discussion in Chapter 8.)

In some situations it may be difficult to distinguish between changes in accounting policy and changes in accounting estimates. For example, a company may change from deferring and amortizing a cost to recording it as an expense when incurred because the future benefits of the cost have become doubtful. In this instance, the company is changing its accounting principle (from deferral to immediate recognition) because of its change in the estimate of the future value of a particular cost.

Although the international accounting standards do not address this matter per se, useful guidance is available by reference to the parallel standard under US GAAP, which is APB Opinion 20. In that standard, the board concluded that a change in accounting estimate that is in essence effected by a change in accounting principle should be reported as a change in accounting estimate, the rationale being that the effect of the change in accounting principle is inseparable from the effect of the change in estimate. In the example in the preceding paragraph, the company is changing its accounting principle (from deferral to immediate recognition) because of its change in the estimate of the future value of a particular cost. The amount of the cumulative effect would be the same as that attributable to the current or future periods.

Because the two changes are indistinguishable, changes of this type should logically be considered changes in estimates and accounted for in accordance with IAS 8. However, the change must be clearly indistinguishable to be combined. The ability to compute each element independently would preclude combining them as a single change. Also, for generally accepted auditing standards such a change is deemed a change in accounting principle for purposes of applying the consistency standard.

Correction of Fundamental Errors

Although good internal control and the exercise of due care will serve to minimize the number of errors made, these safeguards cannot be expected to completely eliminate errors in the financial statements. As a result, it was necessary for the accounting profession to promulgate standards that would ensure uniform treatment of accounting for error corrections.

IAS 8 is the promulgated international accounting standard dealing with the accounting for error corrections. It outlines the two methods of accounting for the correction of the fundamental errors, one of which is the preferred benchmark approach. IAS 8 indicates that fundamental errors are to be treated as prior-period adjustments if the benchmark treatment is followed (i.e., the amount of the correction, net of the tax effect, if any, should be reported as an adjustment to the opening balance of the retained earnings). Comparative information should also be restated unless it is impracticable to do so.

If the allowed alternative treatment is opted by an enterprise, the amount of the correction of the fundamental error should be included in the determination of net profit or loss for the current period. The comparative information need not be restated under this method; instead, the comparative figures should be presented as reported in the financial statements of the prior period. In such a case, additional pro forma information (prepared in accordance with the foregoing guidelines for the application of the benchmark treatment) should also be presented (unless it is impracticable to do so).

IAS 8 identifies examples of fundamental errors as resulting from mathematical mistakes, mistakes in the application of accounting principles, or the oversight or misinterpretation of facts known to the accountant at the time the financial statements were prepared. A change from an unacceptable (or incorrect) accounting principle to a correct principle is considered a correction of an error, not a change in accounting principle. This should not be confused with the preferability dilemma discussed earlier, which involves two or more acceptable principles.

Although errors occur that affect both current and future periods, we are concerned primarily with the reporting of the correction of an error occurring in financial statements issued previously. Errors affecting current and future periods require correction but do not require disclosure, as they are presumed to be discovered prior to the issuance of financial statements. The correction of an error in the financial statements of a prior period discovered subsequent to their issuance should be reported as a prior-period adjustment.

The essential distinction between a change in estimate and the correction of an error depends on the availability of information. An estimate requires correction because by its nature it is based on incomplete information. Later data will either confirm or contradict the estimate, and any contradiction will require correction. An error **misuses** existing information available at the time of the decision and is discovered at a later date. However, this discovery is not a result of additional information.

Under the benchmark treatment the required disclosures regarding the correction of a fundamental error include

1. The nature of the error
2. The amount of the correction for the current period and for each period presented
3. The amount of the correction relating to periods prior to those included in the comparative information
4. The fact that comparative information has been restated or that it is impracticable to do so

Under the allowed alternative treatment the disclosures differ since the accounting treatment differs. Under this method the clauses 2, 3, and 4 above will be replaced with

2. The amount of the correction recognized in the net profit or loss for the current period
3. The amount of the correction included in each period for which the pro forma information is presented and the amount of the correction relating to periods prior to those included in the pro forma information. If the pro forma information could not be presented due to impracticality, this fact should be disclosed, too.

The major criterion for determining whether or not to report the correction of the error is the materiality of the correction. There are many factors to be considered in determining the materiality of the error correction. Materiality should be considered for each correction individually as well as for all corrections in total. If the correction is determined to have a material effect on income before extraordinary items, net income, or the trend of earnings, it should be disclosed in accordance with the requirements set forth in the preceding paragraph.

Thus, under benchmark treatment, the prior-period adjustment should be presented in the financial statements as follows:

Retained earnings, 1/1/9X, as reported previously	xxx
Correction of error (description) in prior period(s) (net of $___ tax)	xxx
Adjusted balance of retained earnings at 1/1/9X	xxx
Net income	xxx
Retained earnings, 12/31/9X	xxx

In comparative statements, prior-period adjustments should also be shown as adjustments to the beginning balances in the retained earnings statements. The amount of the adjustment on the earliest statement shall be the cumulative effect of the error on periods prior to the earliest period presented. The later retained earnings statements presented should also show a prior-period adjustment for the cumulative amount as of the beginning of the period being reported on.

Example of accounting for fundamental errors under IAS 8

In 1996, the bookkeeper of Dhow Corp. discovered that in 1995 the company failed to record in the accounts depreciation expense in the amount of $20,000, relating to a newly constructed building. The following presents extracts from the statement of income and retained earnings for 1996 and 1995 before correction of the error:

	1996	*1995*
Gross profit	$200,000	$230,000
General and administrative expenses, including depreciation	(80,000)	(80,000)
Net income from ordinary activities, before income taxes	120,000	150,000
Income taxes	(20,000)	(30,000)
Net profit	100,000	120,000
Retained earnings, beginning	150,000	30,000
Retained earnings, ending	$250,000	$150,000

Dhow Corp.'s income tax rate was 20% for both years.

The following provides an illustration of the accounting treatment and presentation of financial statements under the benchmark treatment and the allowed alternative treatment, in accordance with IAS 8.

Correction of Fundamental Error: Benchmark Treatment

Dhow Corp.
Extracts From Income Statement

	1996	*1995 restated*
Gross profit	$200,000	$230,000
General and administrative expenses, including depreciation	(80,000)	(100,000)
Net income from ordinary activities, before income taxes	120,000	130,000
Income taxes	(20,000)	(26,000)
Net profit	$100,000	$104,000

Dhow Corp.
Statement of Retained Earnings

	1996	1995 restated
Retained earnings, beginning, as reported previously	$150,000	$ 30,000
Correction of fundamental error, net of income taxes of $4,000 (see Note 1)	(16,000)	--
Retained earnings, beginning, as restated	134,000	30,000
Net profit	100,000	104,000
Retained earnings, ending	$234,000	$134,000

Dhow Corp.
Extracts From Notes to the Financial Statements

Note 1: The company failed to record a depreciation charge in the amount of $20,000 in 1995. The financial statements for 1995 have been restated to correct this error.

Explanation. Under the benchmark treatment of fundamental errors, the amount of correction of a fundamental error that relates to prior periods should be reported by adjusting the opening balance of retained earnings. Comparative information should be restated unless it is impracticable to do so. The steps in preparing the revised financial statements and related disclosures are as follows:

1. As presented in the statement of retained earnings, the opening retained earnings was adjusted by $16,000, which represented the amount of error, $20,000, net of income tax effect of $4,000.
2. The comparative amounts in the income statement were restated as follows:

General and administrative expenses, including depreciation, before correction	$ 80,000
Amount of correction	20,000
As restated	$100,000
Income taxes before correction	$ 30,000
Amount of correction	4,000
As restated	$ 26,000

Correction of Fundamental Error: Allowed Alternative Treatment

Dhow Corp.
Extracts From Income Statement

			Pro forma	
			(Restated)	*(Restated)*
	1996	*1995*	*1996*	*1995*
Gross profit	$200,000	$230,000	$200,000	$230,000
General and administrative expenses, including depreciation (see Note 1)	(80,000)	(80,000)	(80,000)	(100,000)
Correction of error (Note 1)	(20,000)	--	--	--
Profit from ordinary activities, before income taxes	100,000	150,000	120,000	130,000
Income taxes (including effect of a correction of a fundamental error)	16,000	30,000	20,000	26,000
Net profit	$ 84,000	$120,000	$100,000	$104,000

Dhow Corp.
Statement of Retained Earnings

			Pro forma	
			(Restated)	*(Restated)*
	1996	*1995*	*1996*	*1995*
Retained earnings, beginning, as reported previously	$150,000	$ 30,000	$150,000	$ 30,000
Correction of fundamental error, net of income taxes of $4,000 (Note 1)	--	--	16,000	--
Retained earnings, beginning, as restated	150,000	30,000	134,000	30,000
Net profit	84,000	120,000	100,000	104,000
Retained earnings, ending	$234,000	$150,000	$234,000	$134,000

Dhow Corp.
Extracts From Notes to the Financial Statements

Note 1: The company failed to record a depreciation charge in the amount of $20,000 in 1995. An adjustment has been made in the income statement for 1995, representing the correction of the fundamental error. Restated pro forma information for 1996 and 1995 is presented as if the error had been corrected in 1995.

Explanation. Under the allowed alternative treatment of fundamental errors, the amount of correction of a fundamental error that relates to prior periods should be included in the determination of net profit or loss for the current period. Comparative information should be presented as reported in the financial statements of the prior period. Additional pro forma information (effectively, the benchmark treatment) should be presented, unless impracticable to do so.

APPENDIX A

ACCOUNTING FOR CORRECTION OF ERRORS AND CHANGES IN ACCOUNTING POLICY UNDER US GAAP

The accounting for corrections of errors and changes in accounting policies differs markedly under US GAAP from that under the international standards. Under US GAAP, there is only the prescribed treatment; there are no allowed alternatives to the mandatory (benchmark) procedures, in contrast to IAS 8's benchmarks and alternatives. Since the requirements differ in each of these very important areas, and since many users and preparers of financial statements have previously been exposed to US GAAP, this appendix will summarize the corresponding requirements under the US standards.

Accounting for the Correction of Errors

Under international accounting standards, the preferred approach to reporting the effect of errors (called "fundamental errors" in IAS 8) is to present the cumulative effect of the error on all years prior to the earliest period being reported on as an adjustment of opening retained earnings, with the financial statements for all years presented being restated. This is identical to the required treatment under US GAAP. While IAS contemplates an allowed alternative treatment (including the cumulative effect of the error in current period earnings), the corresponding US standard, SFAS 16, does not offer this alternative.

Example of accounting for corrections of errors

Consider the following facts: Assume that ABC Company had overstated its depreciation expense by $50,000 in 1990 and $40,000 in 1993, both due to a mathematical mistake. The errors that affected both the income statement and the tax return in 1992 and 1993 are found in 1994.

The following prior-period adjustment would be required in 1994 to correct the accounts (assuming a 40% tax rate):

Accumulated depreciation	90,000	
Income taxes payable		36,000
Retained earnings		54,000

Assuming that 2-year comparative statements are being presented, the resulting effects of the prior-period adjustment should be included in each statement presented. The comparative statement of retained earnings would appear as follows (all figures other than corrections are assumed):

	1994	*1993*
Retained earnings, beginning of year (as reported previously)	$305,000	$250,000
Adjustments (see Note 1)	54,000	30,000
Restated, beginning of year	$359,000	$280,000
Net income	90,000	104,000
	$449,000	$384,000
Dividends	45,000	25,000
Retained earnings, end of year	$404,000	$359,000

Note 1: Correction of accounting error.

The balance of retained earnings at the end of 1993 has been restated from amounts reported previously to reflect a retroactive credit of $54,000 ($90,000 net of $36,000 tax) for overstatement of depreciation in the previous periods. Of this amount, $24,000 ($40,000 net of $16,000 tax) is applicable to 1993 and has been reflected as an increase in income for that year, and the balance (applicable to years prior to 1993) has been credited to 1993 beginning retained earnings.

The retained earnings as reported in 1993 and as they would have appeared in 1994 if no adjustments were made are as follows:

	1994	*1993*
Retained earnings, beginning of year	$305,000	$250,000
Net income	90,000	80,000
	$395,000	$330,000
Dividends	45,000	25,000
Retained earnings, end of year	$350,000	$305,000

Accounting for Changes in Accounting Policies

Under US GAAP, the cumulative effect of most changes in accounting policies must be included in income in the period of the change. Certain defined categories of accounting changes, however, must be handled by means of retroactive restatement. Furthermore, unlike under international standards, all changes in accounting policies (referred to under US GAAP as "changes in accounting principles") are to be accounted for in the manner prescribed; under IAS, changes in depreciation methods, which in actuality are changes in accounting principle, are accounted for as changes in an estimate and handled prospectively.

Briefly, US GAAP requires all changes in accounting principle, except as specifically set forth (see the discussion below), to be accounted for by the "cumulative effect" method, whereby the net-of-tax effect of the change on beginning retained earnings is included as a separate item on the income statement of the year of change. The following example illustrates this approach.

Example of accounting for changes in accounting policies

ABC Co. decides in 19X8 to adopt the straight-line method of depreciation for plant equipment. The straight-line method will be used for all new acquisitions as well as for plant equipment previously acquired, for which depreciation had been provided on an accelerated method. The following assumptions are being made:

1. The direct effect of the change is limited to the change in accumulated depreciation.
2. The tax rate is a constant 40%.
3. The executive incentive bonus is the only nondiscretionary item affected by the change. It is 10% of the pretax accounting income.
4. There are 1,000,000 shares of common stock outstanding throughout the entire period affected by the change.
5. An additional 100,000 shares would be issued if all the outstanding bonds, which are not common stock equivalents, were converted. Annual interest on this bond obligation is $25,000 (net of tax).
6. For 19X7 and 19X8 the income before extraordinary items is given as $1,100,000 and $1,200,000 respectively. There is an extraordinary item in each year amounting to $100,000 for 19X7 and ($35,000) for 19X8. The extraordinary items are included to illustrate the proper positioning of the cumulative effect adjustment on the income statement.

Year	*Excess of accelerated depreciation over straight-line depreciation*	*Direct effects of change, net of tax*	*Nondiscretionary item, net of tax*	*Pro forma amounts*
Prior to 19X4	$ 20,000	$ 12,000	$ 1,200	$ 10,800
19X4	80,000	48,000	4,800	43,200
19X5*	70,000	42,000	4,200	37,800
19X6	50,000	30,000	3,000	27,000
19X7	30,000	18,000	1,800	16,200
Total at beginning of 19X8	$250,000	$150,000	$15,000	$135,000

The following narrative provides assistance in grasping the computational aspects of the information given above. The "excess of . . . depreciation" is given in this example. It is generally determined by recomputing the depreciation under the new method and obtaining the difference between the two methods. The "direct. . . tax" represents the effect of the actual change (i.e., depreciation) on income before extraordinary items adjusted for the tax effects. For example, in the years prior to 19X4, the change in depreciation methods (from accelerated to straight-line) resulted in a $20,000 reduction in depreciation expense (or an increase in income). The net of tax number is $12,000 because the $20,000 increase in income is reduced by an $8,000 (40% x $20,000) increase in income tax expense.

The "nondiscretionary item, net of tax" represents the income statement items affected indirectly as a result of the change. In this case it was given that the executive incentive bonus equal to 10% of pretax accounting income was the only nondiscretionary item affected. Thus, in years prior to 19X4, when pretax accounting income increased by $20,000, the bonus expense would have been $2,000 higher ($20,000 x 10%). It is generally agreed that this should also be computed net of tax, and because the expense would have increased by $2,000, the taxes would have decreased by $800 ($2,000 x 40%). The net of tax increase in expense is $1,200. The pro forma amounts are to include both the direct and indirect effects of the change. The computation for this example is as follows:

	Increase (decrease) in net income
Reduction in depreciation expense	$20,000
Increase in taxes (depreciation)	(8,000)
Increase in compensation expense	(2,000)
Reduction in taxes (compensation)	800
	$10,800

The pro forma amount is needed for disclosure purposes so that 19X7 income can be shown on a comparative basis with 19X8 net income (i.e., adding the 19X7 income before the change). The pro forma increase or decrease will result in an income figure that reflects the same accounting principles as the 19X8 income figure. Below are the necessary disclosures required by APB 20 for the aforementioned situation.

On the Face of the Income Statement

	19X8	*19X7*
Income before extraordinary item and cumulative effect of a change in accounting principle	$1,200,000	$1,100,000
Extraordinary item (description)	(35,000)	100,000
Cumulative effect on prior years (to December 31, 19X7) of changing to a different depreciation method	150,000	--
Net income	$1,315,000	$1,200,000
Per share amounts:		
Earnings per common share--assuming no dilution:		
Income before extraordinary item and cumulative effect of a change in accounting principle	$1.20	$1.10
Extraordinary item	(0.04)	0.10
Cumulative effect on prior years (to December 31, 19X7) of changing to a different depreciation method	0.15	--
Net income	$1.31	$1.20
Earnings per common share--assuming full dilution:		
Income before extraordinary item and cumulative effect of a change in accounting principle	$1.11	$1.02
Extraordinary item	(0.03)	0.09
Cumulative effect on prior years (to December 31, 19X7) of changing to a different depreciation method	0.14	--
Net income	$1.22	$1.11

Pro forma amounts assuming the new depreciation method is applied retroactively:		
Income before extraordinary item	$1,200,000	$1,116,200
Earnings per common share--assuming no dilution	$1.20	$1.12
Earnings per common share--assuming full dilution	$1.11	$1.01
Net income	$1,165,000	$1,216,200
Earnings per common share--assuming no dilution	$1.17	$1.22
Earnings per common share--assuming full dilution	$1.08	$1.11

In the Notes to the Financial Statements

Note A: Change in depreciation method for plant equipment.

During 19X8 the company decided to change its method of computing depreciation on plant equipment from sum-of-the-years' digits (SYD) to the straight-line method. The company made the change because the straight-line method better matches revenues and cost amortization and therefore is a preferable accounting principle. The new method has been applied retroactively to equipment acquisitions of prior years. The effect of the change in 19X8 was to increase income before extraordinary items by approximately $10,000 (or $0.01 per share). The adjustment of $150,000 (net of $100,000 in taxes) included in 19X8 income is the cumulative effect of applying the new method retroactively. The pro forma amounts shown on the income statement have been adjusted for the effect of the retroactive application of the new depreciation method, the change in the provisions for incentive compensation that would have been made had the new method been used, and the related income taxes for both.

If the company elected to disclose the pro forma amounts in notes to the financial statements and not on the face of the income statement, the following disclosure would have been included as part of Note A. The following pro forma amounts show the effect of the retroactive application of the change from the SYD to straight-line method of depreciation.

	Actual	*Pro forma*
19X8		
Income before extraordinary items	$1,200,000	$1,200,000
Primary earnings per share	$1.20	$1.20
Fully diluted earnings per share	$1.11	$1.11
Net income	$1,315,000	$1,165,000
Primary earnings per share	$1.31	$1.17
Fully diluted earnings per share	$1.22	$1.08
19X7		
Income before extraordinary items	$1,100,000	$1,116,200
Primary earnings per share	$1.10	$1.12
Fully diluted earnings per share	$1.02	$1.01
Net income	$1,200,000	$1,216,200
Primary earnings per share	$1.20	$1.22
Fully diluted earnings per share	$1.11	$1.11

In the example above, notice how the four steps provided in APB 20 are followed.

1. No restatement takes place on the face of the income statements. The 19X7 figures provided for comparative purposes are the same as those reported originally.
2. The cumulative effect of the change is included on the face of the income statement as a single amount. The $150,000 shown in 19X8 represents the total direct effect net of tax for all years prior to 19X8. The effect of the change in 19X8 is included in the computation of ordinary income for 19X8.
3. The required disclosure of the 19X8 effects of the change, in both total and per share amounts, is usually done in the notes to the financial statements. This is assumed to be $10,000 in the example above, or $0.01 per share.
4. The pro forma amounts are used to make the statements from the 2 years comparable. The 19X7 income before extraordinary items is increased by $16,200 to $1,116,200. This is the amount found in the original table across from 19X7. Notice also how the 19X8 net income figure no longer contains a cumulative effect adjustment. This is because 19X8 and 19X7 earnings, under the pro forma computations, are derived using the same accounting principles.

Under US GAAP there are five instances that require retroactive treatment. These are as follows:

1. Change from LIFO to another inventory method
2. A change in the method of accounting for long-term contracts
3. A change to or from the full cost method of accounting for exploration costs in the extractive industries
4. Any change made by a company first issuing financial statements for the purpose of obtaining additional equity capital, effecting a business combination, or registering securities
5. Any changes mandated by authoritative pronouncements (although this case is not specified by APB 20, the promulgating bodies have in most instances thus far required that the change be made retroactively). FASB Interpretation 20 has also indicated that AICPA SOP may mandate the treatment given the change.

The process of restating the financial statements in these situations was favored because it did not require that the cumulative effect of the change be included in net income. Rather, each of the years presented is adjusted to reflect the new accounting principle. The cumulative effect is calculated in the same manner as shown earlier for accounting changes receiving nonretroactive treatment. The cumulative effect of all periods prior to such period presented is treated as an adjustment to beginning retained earnings of the period. The net income of each period presented is recomputed applying the new principle. Thus, the adjustment to beginning retained earnings includes all income effects prior to each period presented, and the recomputed net income includes the effect of the new principle on income for each period presented. Together these two adjustments restate the retained earnings ending balance for the period presented to the amount it would have been had the new principle always been applied. This restatement process is followed consistently for all periods presented. According to APB 20, the nature of and justification for the change must be disclosed in the year the change is made. In addition, the effect of the change on income before extraordinary items, net income, and the related per share amounts should be disclosed for all periods presented. Again, subsequent financial statements do not need to repeat the disclosures.

The restatement need only reflect the direct effects of the change in accounting principle. The exception to this statement arises if the direct effect results in a change in a nondiscretionary item that will be recorded on the books. For example, assume that profit sharing expense is based on net income. The company changes its method of accounting for long-term construction contracts, which results in an increase in income in all prior years. This increase in income would have changed the amount of the profit sharing expense required during the applicable years. However, the expense would be changed for the purpose of the restatement only if it is to be paid. If the profit sharing agreement does not require an adjustment to the actual contribution, the increase in expense would not be recognized on the restated financial statements.

The following illustration (an adaption of Appendix B in APB 20) illustrates the proper restatement in a situation where the company changes its method of accounting for long-term construction contracts. As mentioned above, this is one of the five situations for which APB 20 requires retroactive treatment.

Example of retroactive treatment

During 19X8, XYZ Company decided to adopt the percentage-of-completion method in accounting for all of its long-term construction contracts. The company had used the completed-contract method in previous years and had maintained records that were adequate to apply the percentage-of-completion method retroactively.

The following assumptions are made for this example:

1. A constant tax rate of 40%.
2. There are 1,000,000 common shares outstanding in all periods affected by the change.
3. An additional 100,000 shares would be issued if all of the outstanding bonds, which are not common stock equivalents, were converted. The annual interest on this bond obligation is $15,000 (net of tax).

	Pretax accounting income		*Difference in income*	
Year	*Percentage-of-completion method*	*Completed-contract method*	*Direct*	*Net of tax effect*
Prior to 19X4	$1,800,000	$1,300,000	$500,000	$300,000
19X4	900,000	800,000	100,000	60,000
19X5	700,000	1,000,000	(300,000)	(180,000)
19X6	800,000	600,000	200,000	120,000
19X7	1,000,000	1,100,000	(100,000)	(60,000)

Total at beg. of 19X8	$5,200,000	$4,800,000	$400,000	$240,000
19X8	1,100,000	900,000	200,000	120,000
Total	$6,300,000	$5,700,000	$600,000	$360,000

Following is the proper method of disclosing this type of change as prescribed by APB 20.

On the Face of the Income Statement

	19X8	As adjusted (see Note A) 19X7
Income before extraordinary item	$660,000	$600,000
Extraordinary item (description)	--	(80,000)
Net income	$660,000	$520,000
Per share amounts:		
Earnings per common share--assuming no dilution:		
Income before extraordinary item	$0.66	$0.60
Extraordinary item	--	(.08)
Net income	$0.66	$0.52
Earnings per common share--assuming full dilution:		
Income before extraordinary item	$0.61	$0.56
Extraordinary item	--	(.07)
Net income	$0.61	$0.49

On the Statement of Retained Earnings

	19X8	As adjusted (see Note A) 19X7
Balance at beginning of year, as previously reported	$17,910,000	$17,330,000
Add adjustment for the cumulative effect on prior years of applying retroactively the new method of accounting for long-term contracts (Note A)	240,000	300,000*
Balance at beginning of year	$18,150,000	$17,630,000
Net income	660,000	520,000
Balance at end of year	$18,810,000	$18,150,000

**This is the resultant amount of the change less the tax effect through 19X6.*

In the Notes to the Financial Statements

Note A: Change in method of accounting for long-term construction contracts.

In 19X8 the company changed its method of accounting for long-term construction contracts from the completed-contract method to the percentage-of-completion method. The change was made because the company felt that the new method resulted in a more accurate recognition of revenue and a better matching of revenue and costs. The financial statements of prior periods have been restated to apply the new method retroactively. The company will continue to use the completed-contract method for income tax purposes. The effect of the accounting change in income of 19X8 and on income previously reported for 19X7 is

	Increase (decrease)	
	19X8	19X7
Effect on:		
Income before extraordinary item and net income	$120,000	$(60,000)
Earnings per common share--no dilution	0.12	(0.06)
Earnings per common share--full dilution	0.11	(0.05)

The balances of retained earnings for 19X7 and 19X8 have been adjusted for the effect (net of income taxes) of retroactively applying the new method of accounting.

Notice that the income statement does not highlight the change. This lack of disclosure has been the major argument surrounding the use of this method. Although both periods reflect the increase in income resulting from the change, it is assumed that the average user of the financial statements may not refer to the notes to understand the change.

The only change shown in the financial statements, per se, is the cumulative adjustment that is part of the statement of retained earnings. This amount is determined by totaling the effect of the change for all periods prior to the period presented in the financial statements. This amount is reflected as an adjustment to the beginning balance of retained earnings.

The notes to the financial statements must disclose the nature of and reason for the change. In addition, the effect of the change on income before extraordinary items and net income including the related per share amounts should be disclosed for all the years presented. In this case, the change for 19X8 and 19X7 is to increase (decrease) net income by $100,000 and ($50,000), respectively.

Cumulative effect not determinable. In promulgating APB Opinion 20, the APB realized that there would be certain circumstances in which the pro forma accounts or the cumulative effect amount would not be available. If the pro forma amounts cannot be determined or reasonably estimated for the individual prior periods, the cumulative effect should be shown on the income statement and the reason for not showing the pro forma amounts disclosed in the notes to the financial statements. In an instance where the cumulative effect cannot be determined, disclosure will be limited to showing the effect of the change on the results of operations for the period of the change (including per share data) and to explaining the reason for omitting accounting for the cumulative effect and disclosure of pro forma results. The board specified the change from the FIFO to LIFO method of inventory pricing as one circumstance under which it would be impossible to determine the cumulative effect.

Example of change from FIFO to LIFO

During 1994, Ramirez, Inc. decided to change the method used for pricing its inventories from FIFO to LIFO. The inventory values are as listed below for both FIFO and LIFO cost. Sales for the year amounted to $15,000,000 and the company's total purchases were $11,000,000. Other expenses amounted to $1,200,000 for the year. The company had 1,000,000 shares outstanding throughout the year.

Inventory values:

	FIFO	*LIFO*
12/31/93	2,000,000	N/A
12/31/94	4,000,000	1,800,000

The computations for net income would be as follows:

	FIFO	*LIFO*
Sales	$15,000,000	$15,000,000
Less: Cost of goods sold	9,000,000	11,200,000
Gross margin	$ 6,000,000	$ 3,800,000
Other expenses	1,200,000	1,200,000
Net income	$ 4,800,000	$ 2,600,000

The following footnote would be an example of the required disclosure in this circumstance:

Note A: Change in method of accounting for inventories.

During 1994, the company changed its method of accounting for all of its inventories from first-in, first-out (FIFO) to last-in, first-out (LIFO). The change was made because management believes that the LIFO method provides a better matching of costs and revenues. In addition, the adoption of LIFO conforms the company's inventory pricing policy to the one that is predominant in the industry. The change and its effect on net earnings ($000 omitted except for per share) and earnings per share for 1994 are as follows:

	Net earnings	*Earnings per share*
Net earnings before the change	$4,800	$4.80
Reduction of earnings by the change	2,200	2.20
Net earnings	$2,600	$2.60

There is no cumulative effect of the change on prior years because beginning inventory on January 1, 1994 at LIFO is the same as that which was reported on a FIFO basis at December 31, 1993. As a result of this change, the current period's financial statements are not comparable with those of any prior periods. The current cost of inventories valued at LIFO exceeds the carrying amount by $2,200,000 at December 31, 1994.

APPENDIX B

ACCOUNTING CHANGES IN INTERIM PERIODS

At the present time, there are no promulgated international accounting standards dealing with interim financial reporting, although the IASC has issued a draft statement of principles (DSOP) on this matter, which is expected to result in a far-reaching new set of requirements (see discussion in Chapter 18). A question that often arises when entities prepare interim financial reports is how to account for changes in accounting principles when decisions to make changes are taken during the year. To provide some guidance on this important subject, this appendix will set forth the approach mandated under US GAAP. Although this is not binding on entities that adhere to IAS, the logical approach adopted by US standards can be seen as a valid reference point in determining how to accomplish this.

APB 28 is the US GAAP standard concerned with interim reporting. APB 28 indicates that accounting changes are to be reported in interim periods in accordance with the provisions set forth in APB 20. The FASB then issued SFAS 3 to clarify the interim treatment of an accounting change and to provide examples. Of particular concern in SFAS 3 was the treatment to be accorded cumulative effect accounting changes (including a change to LIFO for which no cumulative effect can be determined) and accounting changes made in the fourth quarter by publicly traded companies.

The treatment of a cumulative effect change in an interim period depends on the quarter in which the change is made. If the cumulative effect accounting change is made in the first quarter, the cumulative effect on the beginning balance of retained earnings should be included in the net income of the first quarter. Again, the income for the first quarter of the current period is computed using the newly adopted method, and the cumulative effect of the change shall be shown on the income statement after extraordinary items and before net income. In accordance with APB 20, the comparative periods are not to be restated.

If the cumulative effect accounting change is made in a period other than the first quarter, no cumulative effect of the accounting change should be included in the net income of the period. Rather, the prechange interim periods of the year in which the change is made should be restated to reflect the newly adopted accounting principle. The cumulative effect on the beginning balance of retained earnings is then shown in the first interim period of the year in which the change is made. This includes any year-to-date or other financial statements that include the first interim period.

SFAS 3 requires that the following disclosures be made regarding a cumulative effect accounting change in an interim period in addition to the treatment described above for the actual amount of the cumulative effect:

1. In the financial statements for the period in which the change is made, the nature and justification of the change.

2. Disclosure of the effect of the change on income from continuing operations, net income, and related per share amounts for the interim period in which the change is made. If the change is made in other than the first interim period, they should also disclose the effect of the change on income from continuing operations, net income, and related per share amounts for each prechange interim period, and income from continuing operations, net income, and related per share amounts for each prechange interim period restated.
3. In the period in which the change is made, the pro forma amounts for income from continuing operations, net income, and the related per share amounts should be disclosed for:

   a. The interim period in which the change is made
   b. Any interim periods of prior years for which financial information is presented

   If no prior year fiscal information is presented, disclosure should be made, in the period of the change, of the actual and pro forma amounts of income from continuing operations, net income, and related per share amounts for the interim period of the immediately preceding fiscal year that corresponds to the interim period in which the change is made. The pro forma amounts are to be calculated in accordance with APB 20 (discussed earlier).
4. The same disclosures described in items 1 and 2 above should be made regarding any year-to-date or last-twelve-months financial statements that include the period of the change.
5. For a postchange interim period (same fiscal year), disclosure should be made of the effect of the change on income from continuing operations, net income, and the related per share amounts for the postchange period.

As mentioned earlier, a change to the LIFO method of pricing inventories generally results in a situation where the cumulative effect is not determinable. If such a change occurs in the first interim period, then the same disclosures described above for the cumulative effect accounting change should be made with the exception of the pro forma amounts. If the change is made in a period other than the first interim period, the disclosures should include those mentioned above **and** restatement of the financial information presented for prechange interim periods of that year reflecting the adoption of the new accounting principle.

The following examples illustrate the foregoing principles relative to a cumulative effect accounting change made both in the first interim period and in other than the first period. We use the same facts and assumptions for both examples.

Example of accounting change in first interim period

In 19X5, ABC Company decided to adopt the straight-line method of depreciation for plant equipment. The new method was to be used for both new acquisitions and previously acquired plant equipment. In prior periods, the company had used an accelerated method of computing depreciation on plant equipment. The following assumptions are made:

1. The effects of the change are limited to the direct effect on depreciation and the indirect effect on the incentive compensation, as well as the related tax effects.
2. The incentive compensation is 10% of pretax accounting income.
3. There is a constant tax rate of 50%.
4. There were 1,000,000 shares issued and outstanding throughout the periods covered, with no potential for dilution.
5. The company presents comparative interim statements.
6. Assume that the following information is given for years 19X4 and 19X5:

Period	*Net income on the basis of old accounting principle (accelerated depreciation)*	*Gross effect of change to straight-line depreciation*	*Gross effect less income taxes*	*Net effect after incentive compensation and related income taxes*
Prior to first qtr. 19X4		$ 20,000	$ 10,000	$ 9,000
First quarter 19X4	$1,000,000	30,000	15,000	13,500
Second quarter 19X4	1,200,000	70,000	35,000	31,500
Third quarter 19X4	1,100,000	50,000	25,000	22,500
Fourth quarter 19X4	1,100,000	80,000	40,000	36,000
Total at beg. of 19X5	$4,400,000	$250,000	$125,000	$112,500
First quarter 19X5	$1,059,500*	$ 90,000	$ 45,000	$ 40,500*
Second quarter 19X5	1,255,000	100,000	50,000	45,000
Third quarter 19X5	1,150,500	110,000	55,000	49,500
Fourth quarter 19X5	1,146,000	120,000	60,000	54,000
	$4,611,000	$420,000	$210,000	$189,000

**The net income for 19X5 has been broken down into income based on the old accounting principle and the effect of the change. These numbers are unrealistic in the sense that the 19X5 income figure would be computed based on the new principle (e.g., the first quarter net income is $1,100,000, which is $1,059,500 + $40,500).*

In the first example we apply the SFAS 3 criteria applicable to a change made in the first quarter. Notice that in interim reporting the same principles are followed as were set for annual financial reporting. The cumulative effect is considered to be a change in the beginning balance of retained earnings and, therefore, effective at the beginning of the year. To include the cumulative effect in any interim period other than the first, or year-to-date including the first, would be misleading. In this case we are dealing with the first period, and the $125,000, representing the direct effects net of tax, is presented on the face of the income statement. Also, as with the annual reporting, the pro forma amounts reflecting the direct and indirect effects of the change are also presented. In this case the 19X5 number already reflects the change, and from the information given we can see that the total effect on the first quarter of 19X4 was to increase net income by $13,500.

As required, the notes state the nature and justification of the change. Also included in the notes are the total cumulative effect, the effect on the earnings of the first quarter of the year in which the change is made (this disclosure makes allowable a comparison between statements), and the nature of the pro forma amounts. Essentially, if the change is made in the first quarter, the reporting and disclosure requirements are very similar to those in the annual financial statements.

The following quarterly financial statements and note illustrate the foregoing principles:

	Three months ended March 31,	
	19X5	*19X4*
Income before cumulative effect of a change in accounting principle	$1,100,000	$1,000,000
Cumulative effect on prior years (to December 31, 19X4) of changing to a different depreciation method (Note A)	125,000	--
Net income	$1,225,000	$1,000,000
Amounts per common share:		
Income before cumulative effect of a change in accounting principle	$1.10	$1.00
Cumulative effect on prior years (to December 31, 19X4) of changing to a different depreciation method (Note A)	0.13	--
Net income	$1.23	$1.00
Pro forma amounts assuming the new depreciation method is applied retroactively (Note A):		
Net income	$1,100,000	$1,013,500
Net income per common share	$1.10	$1.01

Note A: Change in depreciation method for plant equipment.

During the first quarter of 19X5, the company decided to change the method of computing depreciation on plant assets from the accelerated method used in previous periods to the straight-line method. The change was made to better match the amortized cost of the asset to the revenue produced by it. The retroactive application of the new method resulted in a cumulative effect of $125,000 (net of $125,000 in income taxes), which is included in the income for the first quarter of 19X5. The effect of the change on the first quarter of 19X5 was to increase income before cumulative effect of a change in accounting principle by $40,500 ($0.04 per share) and net income by $165,500 ($0.17 per share). The pro forma amounts reflect the effect of retroactive application on depreciation, the change in provisions for incentive compensation that would have been made in 19X4 had the new method been in effect, and the related income taxes.

Example of accounting change in other than first interim period

In this case we assume that the change is made in the third quarter of the year and that the company is presenting comparative financial information for both the current quarter and year-to-date. As mentioned above, the cumulative effect is not necessarily to be presented in the period of the change because it relates to the beginning of the year. Thus, in the illustration below, the 3 months ended September 30 do not include an amount for the cumulative effect; however, the 9-month statements do. The presentation of the 3-month statements reflects the effect of the accounting change for 19X5 and does not reflect this change for 19X4. The 19X4 statement is the same as it was presented in the prior year. The pro forma amounts and the disclosure in the notes provide the information necessary to make these two interim periods comparable.

The 9-month statement for 19X5 reflects the effect of the change for the entire 9-month period. Thus, the results of the 6-month period for 19X5 added to the 3-month results would not equal the amounts shown in the 9-month statement. This is because the prior statement for the 6-month period would not have reflected the new principle that the 3-month and 9-month figures do. Again, the 19X4 numbers are presented as they were in the preceding year. The remainder of the example is really no different from the disclosure required by another accounting change, with one exception. The exception is that the effect of the change on the preceding interim periods must also be disclosed. Note that the cumulative effect is included in the first period. The total of the three individual quarters will now equal the total income shown in the 9-month statement.

	3 months ended September 30,		*9 months ended September 30,*	
	19X5	*19X4*	*19X5*	*19X4*
Income before cumulative effect of a change in accounting principle	$1,200,000	$1,100,000	$3,600,000	$3,300,000
Cumulative effect on prior years (to December 31, 19X4) of changing to a different depreciation method (Note A)	--	--	125,000	--
Net income	$1,200,000	$1,100,000	$3,725,000	$3,300,000
Amounts per common share:				
Income before cumulative effect of a change in accounting principle	$1.20	$1.10	$3.60	$3.30
Cumulative effect on prior years (to December 31, 19X4) of changing to a different depreciation method (Note A)	--	--	0.13	--
Net income	$1.20	$1.10	$3.73	$3.30
Pro forma amounts assuming the new depreciation method is applied retroactively (Note A):				
Net income	$1,200,000	$1,122,500	$3,600,000	$3,367,500
Net income per common share	$1.20	$1.12	$3.60	$3.37

Note A: Change in depreciation method for plant equipment.

During the third quarter of 19X5, the company decided to change the method of computing depreciation on plant assets from the accelerated method used in previous periods to the straight-line method. The change was made to better match the amortized cost of the asset to the revenue produced by it. The retroactive application of the new method resulted in a cumulative effect of $125,000 (net of $125,000 in income taxes), which is included in the income for the 9 months ended September 30, 19X5. The effect of the change on the 3 months ended September 30, 19X5, was to increase net income by $49,500 ($0.05 per share); the effect of the change on the 9 months ended September 30, 19X5, was to increase income before cumulative effect of a change in accounting principle by $135,000 ($0.14 per share) and net income by $260,000 ($0.26 per share). The pro forma amounts reflect the effect of retroactive application on depreciation, the change in the provisions for incentive pay that would have been made in 19X4 had the new method been in effect, and the related income taxes.

The effect of the change on the first and second quarters of 19X5 is as follows:

	Three months ended	
	March 31, 19X5	*June 30, 19X5*
Net income as originally reported	$1,059,500	$1,255,000
Effect of change in depreciation method	40,500	45,000
Income before cumulative effect of a change in accounting principle	1,100,000	1,300,000
Cumulative effect on prior years (to December 31, 19X4) of changing to a different depreciation method	125,000	--
Net income as restated	$1,255,000	$1,300,000
Per share amounts:		
Net income as originally reported	$1.06	$1.26
Effect of change in depreciation method	0.04	0.04
Income before cumulative effect of a change in accounting principle	1.10	1.30
Cumulative effect on prior years (to December 31, 19X4) of changing to a different depreciation method	0.13	--
Net income as restated	$1.23	$1.30

20 FOREIGN CURRENCY

PERSPECTIVE AND ISSUES

At the turn of the century, globalization seems to have become the keyword. Most domestic corporations worldwide are reaching out beyond national boundaries and engaging in international trade. Global economic restructuring is rampant: signing of trade pacts such as GATT, NAFTA, and the recent setting up of the World Trade Organization (WTO) has lent further impetus to the process of internationalization. International activity by most domestic corporations has increased significantly, which means that transactions are consummated not only with independent foreign entities but also with foreign subsidiaries.

It is well known that foreign subsidiaries, associates, and branches handle their accounts and prepare financial statements in currencies of the countries in which they are located. Thus, it is more than likely that a multinational company (MNC) ends up receiving, at year end, financial statements from various foreign subsidiaries expressed in a number of foreign currencies, such as francs, pounds, lira, dinars, dirhams, riyals, and yen. However, for users of these financial statements to analyze the MNC's foreign involvement properly, these foreign currency financial statements must first be expressed in terms that the users can understand. This means that the foreign currency financial statements of the various subsidiaries will have to be translated into the currency of the country where the MNC is registered.

The international GAAP governing the translation of foreign currency financial statements and foreign currency transactions is found primarily in IAS 21 (revised 1993), *The Effects of Changes in Foreign Exchange Rates*. This standard supersedes International Accounting Standard IAS 21, *Accounting for the Effects of Changes in Foreign Exchange Rates*, approved in 1983. IAS 21 applies to

1. Accounting for foreign currency transactions (e.g., exports, imports, and loans) which are denominated in other than an enterprise's functional currency
2. Translation of foreign currency financial statements of branches, divisions, subsidiaries, and other investees that are incorporated in the financial statements of an enterprise by consolidation, proportionate consolidation, or by the equity method

As stated in IAS 21, this standard does not deal with hedge accounting for foreign currency items other than the classification of exchange differences arising on a foreign currency liability accounted for as a hedge of a net investment in a foreign entity. The IASC is currently working on the second phase of the financial instruments project, and the second standard on financial instruments (the first being IAS 32) will address other aspects of hedging, including criteria for the use of hedge accounting.

Sources of IAS
IAS 21

DEFINITIONS OF TERMS

Closing rate. This refers to the spot rate (defined below) at the balance sheet date.

Conversion. The exchange of one currency for another.

Exchange difference. The difference resulting from reporting the same number of units of a foreign currency in the reporting currency at different exchange rates.

Exchange rate. This refers to the ratio for exchange of two currencies.

Fair value. The amount for which an asset could be exchanged, or a liability could be settled, between knowledgeable, willing parties in an arm's-length transaction.

Foreign currency. A currency other than the reporting currency of the entity being referred to (e.g., the yen is a foreign currency for a US reporting entity). (Under the US GAAP composites of currencies, such as the Special Drawing Rights on the International Monetary Fund (SDR), used to set prices or denominate amounts of loans, and so on, have the characteristics of foreign currency for purposes of applying SFAS 52. No such clarification or interpretation is found in the IAS.)

Foreign currency financial statements. Financial statements that employ as the unit of measure a foreign currency that is not the reporting currency of the enterprise.

Foreign currency transactions. Transactions whose terms are denominated in a foreign currency or require settlement in a foreign currency. Foreign currency transactions arise when an enterprise (1) buys or sells on credit goods or services whose prices are denominated in foreign currency, (2) borrows or lends funds and the amounts payable or receivable are denominated in foreign currency, (3) is a party to an unperformed foreign exchange contract, or (4) for other reasons acquires or disposes of assets or incurs or settles liabilities denominated in foreign currency.

Foreign currency translation. The process of expressing in the reporting currency of the enterprise amounts that are denominated or measured in a different currency.

Foreign entity. When the activities of a foreign operation are not an integral part of those of the reporting entity, such a foreign operation is referred to as a foreign entity.

Foreign operation. A foreign subsidiary, associate, joint venture, or branch of the reporting enterprise whose activities are based or conducted in a country other than the country where the reporting enterprise is domiciled.

Functional currency. A term used under the US GAAP in relation to foreign currency translations wherein it is defined as the currency of the primary economic environment in which the entity operates; normally, that is the currency of the environment in which an entity primarily generates and expends cash.

Monetary items. Money held and assets and liabilities to be received or paid in fixed or determinable amounts of money. Stated differently, monetary items refer to cash, claims to receive a fixed amount of cash, and obligations to pay a fixed amount of cash.

Net investment in a foreign entity. This refers to the reporting enterprise's share in the net assets of that entity.

Nonmonetary items. All balance sheet items other than cash, claims to cash, and cash obligations.

Reporting currency. The currency in which an enterprise presents its financial statements.

Reporting enterprise. An entity or group whose financial statements are being referred to. Under this standard, those financial statements reflect (1) the financial statements of one or more foreign operations by consolidation, proportionate consolidation, or equity accounting; (2) foreign currency transactions; or (3) both of the foregoing.

Spot rate. The exchange rate for immediate delivery of currencies exchanged.

Transaction date. In the context of recognition of exchange differences from settlement of monetary items arising from foreign currency transactions, transaction date refers to the date at which a foreign currency transaction (e.g., a sale or purchase of merchandise or services the settlement for which will be in a foreign currency) occurs and is recorded in the accounting records.

CONCEPTS, RULES, AND EXAMPLES

Classification of Foreign Operations

Under IAS 21, the way in which the foreign operations are financed and operate (i.e., in relation to the reporting entity) determines the method that would be used to translate their financial statements. Stated differently, the classification accorded to a foreign operation will determine the methodology to be used in translating their financial statements. According to IAS 21, a foreign operation may be classified into either one of two categories: (1) a foreign operation that is integral to the operations of the reporting entity, or (2) a foreign operation that is not integral to the operations of the reporting entity (referred to as a foreign entity).

The following factors, if present, indicate that a foreign operation is a foreign entity (i.e., the foreign operation is not integral to the operations of the reporting entity):

1. Its activities are carried out with significant autonomy.
2. Transactions with the reporting entity are not a high proportion of the foreign enterprise's operations.
3. Its activities are financed principally from its own resources or through local borrowings in lieu of the reporting entity's funds.
4. Cost of labor, material, and other components of the foreign operation's products or services are paid or settled primarily in the local currency rather than the currency of the reporting entity.
5. Its sales are principally made in currencies other than the reporting currency.
6. Cash flows of the reporting enterprise are insulated from the day-to-day activities of the foreign operation rather than being affected directly by the activities of the foreign operation.

The classification of a foreign operation is to be based on the facts surrounding each case, and sometimes this could be quite subjective and unclear. Thus, a degree of caution is to be exercised in judgments relating to classification of borderline cases, since on such a classification will depend the method that will ultimately be used to translate the foreign operation's financial statements into the reporting currency.

Translation of Foreign Operations That Are Integral to the Operations of the Reporting Enterprise

The financial statements of foreign operations that are integral to the operations of the reporting enterprise should be translated based on the premise that these are, in substance, the transactions of the reporting enterprise itself. Thus, the rules contained within IAS 21, dealing with reporting of foreign currency items of an enterprise's own transactions, will generally apply to such a foreign operation with the exception of any rules that specifically override the foregoing provisions and stipulate otherwise. These requirements or rules for translating the financial statements of such a foreign operation are the following:

1. Foreign currency monetary items should be reported using the closing rate.
2. Foreign currency nonmonetary items when carried at historical costs should be reported using the exchange rate at the date of the transaction.

3. Foreign currency nonmonetary items when carried at fair values (e.g., revalued property, plant, and equipment under the allowed alternative treatment prescribed by IAS 16) should be reported using exchange rates that existed when the fair values were determined.
4. Generally, all income and expenses items should be translated using exchange rates at the dates of the transactions. In practice, a rate that approximates the actual rate at the date of the transaction is used. For instance, an average rate based on month-end exchange rates might be used for translation of the annual expense and income figures on the financial statement of the foreign operation into the reporting currency. However, as specifically provided by the standard, depreciation expense should be translated either using the exchange rate at the date of purchase of the asset, or if the asset is carried at fair value (i.e., revalued under the allowed alternative treatment prescribed by IAS 16), the rate that existed on the date of such valuation.
5. Generally, exchange differences arising from reporting an entity's monetary items at rates different from those in which they were initially reported in previous financial statements should be recognized as income or expense in the period in which they arise. Note, however, that an exception is made, in case of exchange differences relating to monetary items which are, in substance, part of the enterprise's net investment in a foreign entity. In such a case they should be classified as a separate component of equity in the reporting enterprise's financial statements until disposal of the net investment at which time they should be recognized as income or expense (of the same period the gain or loss on disposal is recognized). Similarly, exchange differences which arise from a foreign liability accounted as a hedge of an enterprise's net investment in a foreign entity should be classified as a separate component of equity on the balance sheet until the disposal of the net investment (at which time they should be recognized as income or expense in the same period as the gain or loss on disposal is recognized).

IAS 21 further elaborates the translation methodology for two items and stipulates as follows:

1. The translation of the cost and depreciation of property, plant, and equipment is to be done based on rates in effect at the date(s) of acquisition, and if revalued (i.e., carried at fair value), then at the exchange rate(s) at the date(s) of such revaluation.
2. Inventories should be translated at the rates in effect at the dates of acquisition; however, if carried at a lower realizable value (or recoverable amount), then the exchange rate prevailing on the date when such lower realizable value (or recoverable amount) was determined (the rate in which

case will be the closing rate, since determination of lower of cost or net realizable value is usually undertaken at the balance sheet date).

Sometimes an adjustment may be required to reduce the carrying amount of an asset in the financial statements of the reporting enterprise even though such an adjustment was not necessary in the financial statements of the foreign operation. This stipulation of IAS 21 can best be illustrated by the following case study.

Example

Inventory of merchandise owned by a foreign operation (which is integral to the operations of the reporting enterprise) is being carried by the foreign operation at 3,750,000 SR (Saudi riyals) on its balance sheet. Suppose that the exchange rate fluctuated from 3.75 SR = 1 US dollar at September 15, 19XX, when the merchandise was bought, to 4.25 SR = 1 US dollar at December 31, 19XX (i.e., the balance sheet date). The translation of this item (appearing on the balance sheet of the foreign operation) into the reporting currency will necessitate an adjustment to reduce the carrying amount of the inventory to its net realizable value if this value when translated into the reporting currency is lower than the carrying amount translated at the rate prevailing on the date of purchase of the merchandise.

Although the net realizable value, which in terms of Saudi riyals is 4,000,000 (SR), is higher than the carrying amount in Saudi riyals (i.e., 3,750,000 SR) when translated into the reporting currency (i.e., US dollars) at the balance sheet date, the net realizable value is lower than the carrying amount (translated into the reporting currency at the exchange rate prevailing on the date of acquisition of the merchandise). Thus, on the financial statements of the foreign operation the inventory would not have to be adjusted. However, when the net realizable value is translated at the closing rate (which is 4.25 SR = 1 US dollar) into the reporting currency, it will require the following adjustment:

1. Carrying amount translated at the exchange rate on September 15, 19XX (i.e., the date of acquisition) = SR 3,750,000 @ 3.75 SR to 1 US dollar = $1,000,000.
2. Net realizable value translated at the closing rate = SR 4,000,000 @ 4.25 SR to 1 US dollar = $941,176.
3. Adjustment needed = $1,000,000 – $941,176 = $58,824.

Conversely, IAS 21 further stipulates that an adjustment that already exists on the financial statements of the foreign operation may need to be reversed in the financial statements of the reporting enterprise. To illustrate this point let us consider the facts of the example above with some variation as below.

Example

All other factual details remaining the same as above, let's assume that the inventory above, which is carried on the books of the foreign operation at Saudi riyals (SR) 3,750,000, instead has a net realizable value of SR 3,250,000 on the closing date. Also assume that the exchange rate fluctuated from SR 3.75 = 1 US dollar at the date of acquisition of the merchandise to SR 3.00 = 1 US dollar on the balance sheet date.

Since in terms of Saudi riyals, the net realizable value on the balance sheet date was lower than the carrying value of the inventory, an adjustment must have been made on the balance sheet of the foreign operation (in Saudi riyals) to reduce the carrying amount to the lower of cost or net realizable value. In other words, a contra asset account (e.g., allowance for obsolete inventory) representing the difference between the carrying amount (SR 3,750,000) and the net realizable value (SR 3,250,000) must have been created on the books of the foreign operation.

On translating the financial statements of the foreign operation into the reporting currency, however, it is noted that due to the fluctuation of the exchange rates the net realizable value when converted to the reporting currency [SR 3,250,000 (@ 3.00 SR = 1 US dollar) = $1,083,333] is no longer lower than the translated carrying value which is to be converted at the exchange rate prevailing on the date of acquisition of the merchandise [SR 3,750,000 (@ SR 3.75 = 1 US dollar)= $1,000,000].

Thus, as required by IAS 21, para 28, a reversal of the adjustment (for obsolescence) is required on the financial statements of the reporting enterprise, on translation of the financial statements of the foreign operation.

Translation Methods Commonly Used in Translating Financial Statements of Foreign Operations

In practice, one encounters four methods that could be used to translate assets and liabilities of a company's foreign operations. The primary distinction among the methods is the classification of assets and liabilities that would be translated at either the current or historical rate. Although the IAS recognizes the current rate method to translate the financial statements of a foreign entity, all four methods have been explained briefly below since internationally these methods are used in certain countries.

The first method is known as the **temporal method**. This method translates cash, receivables, payables, and assets and liabilities carried at present or future values at the current rate, with the remaining assets and liabilities carried at historical costs translated at the applicable historical rates. In essence, the accounting principles used to measure the assets and liabilities in the foreign statements are retained. However, the foreign exchange gains or losses that arise from this method do so because of this method and not because the economic events that affect the foreign entity's operations are reflected.

It is worth noting that the temporal method was the mandated method in the United States under SFAS 8 until it was superseded by SFAS 52, which requires the current rate method to be used under US GAAP. In most cases the temporal method produces the same results as the second approach, the monetary/nonmonetary method.

The remeasurement technique, required by US GAAP (when the books and records are not maintained in the functional currency), is essentially the same as the **monetary/nonmonetary method**. This method translates nonmonetary assets and liabilities at the proper historical rates. Under this method, it is the characteristics of assets and liabilities that are used as the basis for classification rather than the method of accounting, as under the first approach. It is by mere coincidence that assets and liabilities are measured on bases that coincide approximately with the monetary/nonmonetary classification, which produces the aforementioned similar results. A problem with this method is that not all items may be classified as monetary or nonmonetary, and some arbitrary decisions must be made.

The third method is the **current/noncurrent method**, which, as implied, stresses balance sheet classification as the basis for translation. Current assets and liabilities are translated at the current rate and noncurrent assets and liabilities at the applicable historical rates. A major weakness under this approach is the treatment of inventory and long-term debt. Inventory, a current asset, would be translated at its current cost, a major departure from traditional GAAP. The translation of foreign-denominated long-term debt under this approach would be misleading to users, as it would be translated at its historical value.

For instance, from the perspective of a US reporting entity, if the dollar weakens internationally, it will take more dollars to repay this obligation, a fact that would not be apparent from the reporting entity's financial statements. Furthermore, some balance sheets are not classified and variations between current and noncurrent classifications of classified balance sheets may be based arbitrarily on management's intentions.

The last approach is known as the **current rate method** and is the approach mandated by IAS for translation of financial statements of a foreign entity. This is also the prescribed method under certain other accounting standards, for instance the US GAAP, when the functional currency is the foreign currency. A distinguishing feature of this method is that all assets and liabilities, both monetary and nonmonetary, are translated at the closing rate. The basis of this method is the "net investment concept," wherein the foreign entity is viewed as a separate entity that the parent invested into, rather than being considered as part of the parent's operations.

Standard setters in countries such as the United States have expressed a preference for this method. The reason for preferring this method over others was that users could benefit most when the information provided about the foreign entity retains the relationships and results created in the environment (economics, legal, and political) in which the entity operates. Under this approach, the reasoning follows that foreign-denominated debt is used to purchase assets that create foreign-denominated revenues. These assets act as a hedge against the debt from changes in the exchange rate. The excess (net) assets will, however, be affected by this foreign exchange risk, and this is the effect that is recognized by the parent.

Note that under the US GAAP, if the foreign entity's local currency is the functional currency, it requires the current rate method when translating the foreign entity's financial statements. On the other hand, if the US dollar is the functional currency, US GAAP requires the remeasurement method when translating the foreign entity's financial statements. (Both of these methods are illustrated through numerical case studies later in this chapter.)

Translation of Financial Statements of a Foreign Operation That Is Not Integral to the Operations of the Reporting Enterprise (i.e., Foreign Entity)

The following rules should be used in translating the financial statements of a foreign entity:

1. All assets and liabilities, whether monetary or nonmonetary, should be translated at the closing rate.
2. Income and expense items should be translated at the exchange rates at the dates of the transactions, except when the foreign entity reports in a currency of a hyperinflationary economy (as defined in IAS 29), in which case they should be translated at the closing rates.
3. All resulting exchange differences should be classified as a separate component of equity of the reporting enterprise until disposal of the net investment in a foreign entity.

Guidance Under IAS 21 in Special Situations

Minority interests. When a foreign entity is consolidated but is not wholly owned by the reporting enterprise, there will be minority interest reported in the consolidated balance sheet. IAS 21 requires that the accumulated exchange differences resulting from translation and attributable to the minority interest be allocated to and reported as minority interest instead of as a separate component of equity.

Goodwill arising on acquisition of a foreign entity. Any goodwill (which in the authors' opinion includes negative goodwill) arising on the acquisition of a foreign entity should be treated as either

1. An asset (or a liability in case of negative goodwill) of the foreign entity and translated at the closing rate, or
2. An asset (or a liability in case of negative goodwill) of the reporting entity which is either already expressed in the reporting currency or is converted to the reporting currency, such as nonmonetary items that are carried at historical costs and translated at the exchange rate on the date of the transaction in accordance with IAS 21.

Fair value adjustments to carrying amount of assets and liabilities arising on acquisition of a foreign entity. IAS 21 prescribes the same treatment for this as well as for goodwill arising on acquisition of a foreign entity (discussed above).

Exchange differences on elimination of intragroup balances. While incorporating the financial statements of a foreign entity into those of the reporting enterprise, normal consolidation procedures, such as elimination of intragroup balances and transactions, are undertaken as required by IAS 27 and IAS 31. However, IAS 21 requires that exchange differences arising from intragroup monetary items should not be eliminated against corresponding amounts arising on other intragroup balances. This is because monetary items represent commitments to convert one currency into another and expose the reporting enterprise to a gain or loss through currency fluctuations. Thus, on consolidation, such exchange differences would continue to be recognized either as income or expense, or if they arise from exceptional circumstances described in IAS 21, they should be classified as equity until the disposal of the net investment.

Different reporting dates. When reporting dates up to which the financial statements of a foreign entity and those of the reporting enterprise differ, the foreign entity normally switches and prepares financial statements with reporting dates coinciding with those of the reporting enterprise. However, sometimes this may not be practicable to do. In such circumstances IAS 27 allows the use of financial statements drawn up to different dates, provided that the difference is no more than 3 months. In such a case, the assets and liabilities of the foreign entity should be translated at the exchange rates prevailing on the balance sheet date of the foreign entity. Adjustments should be made for any significant movements in exchange rates between the balance sheet date of the foreign entity and that of the reporting entity in accordance with the provisions of IAS 27 and IAS 28 relating to this matter.

Disposal of a foreign entity. Any cumulative exchange differences are to be carried as a separate component of equity until the disposal of the foreign entity in terms of the specific stipulation in IAS 21. The standard prescribes the treatment of the cumulative exchange differences account, on the disposal of the foreign entity. This balance, which has in a way been deferred, should be recognized as income or expense in the same period in which the gain or loss on disposal is recognized.

Disposal has been defined to include a sale, liquidation, repayment of share capital, or abandonment of all or part of the entity. Normally, payment of dividend would not constitute a repayment of capital. However, in rare circumstances, it does; for instance, when an enterprise pays dividends out of capital instead of divisible profits, as defined in the companies' acts of certain countries where this expression is used, such as the United Kingdom, this would constitute repayment of capital. In such circumstances, obviously, dividends paid would constitute a disposal for the purposes of this standard.

IAS 21 further stipulates that in case of a partial disposal of an interest in a foreign entity, only a proportionate share of the related accumulated exchange differences is recognized as a gain or a loss. However, the standard clarifies that a write-down of the carrying amount of the foreign entity does not constitute a partial disposal, and thus the deferred exchange differences carried forward as part of equity would not be affected by such a write-down.

Change in classification of a foreign operation. Since the classification of a foreign operation either as a foreign entity or otherwise depends on the way the foreign operation operates in relation to the reporting enterprise or is financed, a subsequent change in these circumstances could sometimes lead to a change of the initial classification. In such circumstances the translation procedures applicable to the revised classification should be applied from the date of change in the classification.

Comprehensive example of the practical application of the current rate method

Assume that a US company has a 100%-owned subsidiary in Germany that began operations in 1996. The subsidiary's operations consist of leasing space in an office building. This building, which cost 500 deutsche marks (DM), was financed primarily by German banks. All revenues and cash expenses are received and paid in deutsche marks. The subsidiary also maintains its books and records in DM.

As a result, management of the US company has decided that the financial statements of the German subsidiary be translated for incorporation into its financials as if it were a foreign operation that was not integral to the operations of the reporting entity, in other words, as if it were a foreign entity. The subsidiary's balance sheet at December 31, 1996, and its combined statement of income and retained earnings for the year ended December 31, 1996, are presented below in DM.

German Company
Balance Sheet
At December 31, 1996

Assets		*Liabilities and stockholders' equity*	
Cash	DM 50	Accounts payable	DM 30
Note receivable	20	Unearned rent	10
Land	100	Mortgage payable	400
Building	500	Common stock	40
Accumulated depreciation	(10)	Additional paid-in capital	160
		Retained earnings	20
Total assets	DM 660	Total liabilities and stockholders' equity	DM 660

German Company
Combined Statement of Income and Retained Earnings
For the Year Ended December 31, 1996

Revenues	DM 200
Operating expenses (including depreciation expense of 10)	170
Net income	DM 30
Add retained earnings, January 1, 1996	--
Deduct dividends	(10)
Retained earnings, December 31, 1996	DM 20

Various exchange rates for 1996 are as follows:

1 DM = \$0.40 at the beginning of 1996 (when the common stock was issued and the land and building were financed through the mortgage)
1 DM = \$0.43 weighted-average for 1996
1 DM = \$0.42 at the date the dividends were declared and the unearned rent was received
1 DM = \$0.45 at the end of 1996

Since the German subsidiary is a foreign entity (as per IAS 21), the German company's financial statements must be translated into US dollars in terms of the provisions of IAS 21 (i.e., by the current rate method). This translation process is illustrated below.

German Company
Balance Sheet Translation
At December 31, 1996

Assets	*DM*	*Exchange rate*	*US dollars*
Cash	DM 50	0.45	\$ 22.50
Accounts receivable	20	0.45	9.00
Land	100	0.45	45.00
Building (net)	490	0.45	220.50
Total assets	DM 660		\$297.00
Liabilities and stockholders' equity			
Accounts payable	DM 30	0.45	\$ 13.50
Unearned rent	10	0.45	4.50
Mortgage payable	400	0.45	180.00
Common stock	40	0.40	16.00
Additional paid-in capital	160	0.40	64.00
Retained earnings	20	(see income statement)	8.70
Cumulative exchange difference (translation adjustments)	--	--	10.30
Total liabilities and stockholders equity	DM 660		\$297.00

German Company
Combined Income and Retained Earnings Statement Translation
For the Year Ended December 31, 1996

	DM	*Exchange rate*	*US dollars*
Revenues	DM 200	0.43	\$86.00
Expenses (including DM 10 depreciation expense)	170	0.43	73.10
Net income	DM 30		\$12.90
Add retained earnings, January 1	--	--	--
Deduct dividends	(10)	0.42	(4.20)
Retained earnings, December 31	DM 20		\$ 8.70

German Company
Statement of Cash Flows
For the Year Ended December 31, 1996

	DM	Exchange rate	US Dollars
Operating activities			
Net income	DM 30	0.43	$ 12.90
Adjustments to reconcile net income to net cash provided by operating activities:			
Depreciation	10	0.43	4.30
Increase in accounts receivable	(20)	0.43	(8.60)
Increase in accounts payable	30	0.43	12.90
Increase in unearned rent	10	0.42	4.20
Net cash provided by operating activities	60		$ 25.70
Investing activities			
Purchase of land	(100)	0.40	(40.00)
Purchase of building	(500)	0.40	(200.00)
Net cash used by investing activities	(600)		(240.00)
Financing activities			
Common stock issue	200	0.40	80.00
Mortgage payable	400	0.40	160.00
Dividends paid	(10)	0.42	(4.20)
Net cash provided by financing	590		235.80
Effect on exchange rate changes on cash	N/A		1.00
Increase in cash and equivalents	DM 50		$ 22.50
Cash at beginning of year	-0-		-0-
Cash at end of year	DM 50	0.45	$ 22.50

The following points should be noted concerning the current rate method:

1. All assets and liabilities are translated using the current exchange rate at the balance sheet date (1 DM = $0.45). All revenues and expenses should be translated at the rates in effect when these items are recognized during the period. Due to practical considerations, however, weighted-average rates can be used to translate revenues and expenses (1 DM = $0.43).
2. Stockholders' equity accounts are translated by using historical exchange rates. Common stock was issued at the beginning of 1996 when the exchange rate was 1 DM = $0.40. The translated balance of retained earnings is the result of the weighted-average rate applied to revenues and expenses and the specific rate in effect when the dividends were declared (1 DM = $0.42).
3. Cumulative exchange differences (translation adjustments) result from translating all assets and liabilities at the current rate, while stockholders' equity is translated by using historical and weighted-average rates. The adjustments have no direct effect on cash flows; however, changes in exchange rate will have an indirect effect

on sale or liquidation. Prior to this time, the effect is uncertain and remote. Also, the effect is due to the net investment rather than the subsidiary's operations. For these reasons the translation adjustments balance is reported as a separate component in the stockholders' equity section of the US company's consolidated balance sheet. This balance essentially equates the total debits of the subsidiary (now expressed in US dollars) with the total credits (also in dollars). It may also be determined directly, as shown next, to verify the translation process.

4. The cumulative exchange differences (translation adjustments) credit of $10.30 is calculated as follows:

Net assets at the beginning of 1996 (after common stock was issued and the land and building were acquired through mortgage financing)	200 DM (0.45 – 0.40)	=	$10.00 credit
Net income	30 DM (0.45 – 0.43)	=	.60 credit
Dividends	10 DM (0.45 – 0.42)	=	.30 debit
Exchange difference (translation adjustment)			$10.30 credit

5. Since the translation adjustments balance that appears as a separate component of stockholders' equity is cumulative in nature, the change in this balance during the year should be disclosed in the financial statements. In the illustration, this balance went from zero to $10.30 at the end of 1996. The analysis of this change was presented previously. In addition, assume that the following occurred during 1997:

German Company
Balance Sheet
December 31

	1997	1996	Increase/(decrease)
Assets			
Cash	DM 100	DM 50	DM 50
Accounts receivable	-0-	20	(20)
Land	150	100	50
Building (net)	480	490	(10)
	DM 730	DM 660	DM 70
Liabilities and stockholders' equity			
Accounts payable	DM 50	DM 30	DM 20
Unearned rent	-0-	10	(10)
Mortgage payable	450	400	50
Common stock	40	40	-0-
Additional paid-in capital	160	160	-0-
Retained earnings	30	20	10
Total liabilities and stockholders' equity	DM 730	DM 660	DM 70

German Company
Combined Statement of Income and Retained Earnings
For the Year Ended December 31, 1997

Revenues	DM	220
Operating expenses (including depreciation expense of DM 10)		170
Net income	DM	50
Add: Retained earnings, Jan. 1, 1997		20
Deduct dividends		(40)
Retained earnings, Dec. 31, 1997	DM	30

Exchange rates were:

1 DM = $0.45 at the beginning of 1997
1 DM = $0.48 weighted-average for 1997
1 DM = $0.50 at the end of 1997
1 DM = $0.49 when dividends were paid in 1997 and land bought by incurring mortgage

The translation process for 1997 is illustrated below.

German Company
Balance Sheet Translation
At December 31, 1997

	DM		*Exchange rate*	*US dollars*
Assets				
Cash	DM	100	0.50	$ 50.00
Land		150	0.50	75.00
Building		480	0.50	240.00
	DM	730		$365.00
Liabilities and stockholders' equity				
Accounts payable	DM	50	0.50	$ 25.00
Mortgage payable		450	0.50	225.00
Common stock		40	0.40	16.00
Addl. paid-in capital		160	0.40	64.00
Retained earnings		30	(see income statement)	13.10
Cumulative exchange difference (translation adjustments)		--		21.90
Total liabilities and stockholders' equity	DM	730		$365.00

German Company
Combined Income and Retained Earnings Statement Translation
For the Year Ended December 31, 1997

	DM		Exchange rate	US dollars
Revenues	DM	220	0.48	$105.60
Operating expenses (including depreciation of DM 10)		170	0.48	81.60
Net income	DM	50	0.48	$ 24.00
Add: Retained earnings 1/1/97		20	--	8.70
Less: Dividends		(40)	0.49	(19.60)
Retained earnings 12/31/97	DM	30		$ 13.10

German Company
Statement of Cash Flows
For the Year Ended December 31, 1997

	DM		Exchange rate	US dollars
Operating activities				
Net income	DM	50	.48	$24.00
Adjustments to reconcile net income to net cash provided by operating activities:				
Depreciation		10	.48	4.80
Decrease in accounts receivable		20	.48	9.60
Increase in accounts payable		20	.48	9.60
Decrease in unearned rent		(10)	.48	(4.80)
Net cash provided by operating activities	DM	90		$43.20
Investing activities				
Purchase of land		(50)	.49	(24.50)
Net cash used by investing activities		(50)		(24.50)
Financing activities				
Mortgage payable		50	.49	24.50
Dividends		(40)	.49	(19.60)
Net cash provided by financing activities		10		4.90
Effect of exchange rate changes on cash		NA		3.90
Increase in cash and equivalents	DM	50		$27.50
Cash at beginning of year		50		22.50
Cash at end of year	DM	100	.50	$50.00

Using the analysis that was presented before, the total exchange differences (translation adjustment) attributable to 1997 would be computed as follows:

Net assets at January 1, 1997	220 DM	(0.50 – 0.45)	=	$11.00 credit
Net income for 1997	50 DM	(0.50 – 0.48)	=	1.00 credit
Dividends for 1997	40 DM	(0.50 – 0.49)	=	0.40 debit
Total				$11.60 credit

The balance in the cumulative exchange differences (translation adjustment) account at the end of 1997 would be $21.90 ($10.30 from 1996 and $11.60 from 1997).

6. Use of the equity method by the US company in accounting for the subsidiary would result in the following journal entries based on the information presented above:

	1996		*1997*	
Original investment				
Investment in German subsidiary	80*		--	
Cash		80		--
**[$0.40 x common stock of 40 DM plus additional paid-in capital of 160 DM]*				
Earnings pickup				
Investment in German subsidiary	12.90		24**	
Equity in subsidiary income		12.90		24
***[$0.48 x net income of 50 DM]*				
Dividends received				
Cash	4.20		19.60	
Investment in German subsidiary		4.20		19.60
Exchange difference (translation adjustments)				
Investment in German subsidiary	10.30		11.60	
Translation adjustments		10.30		11.60

Note that the stockholders' equity of the US company should be the same whether or not the German subsidiary is consolidated (IAS 28). Since the subsidiary does not report the translation adjustments on its financial statements, care should be exercised so that it is not forgotten in application of the equity method.

7. If the US company disposes of its investment in the German subsidiary, the translation adjustments balance becomes part of the gain or loss that results from the transaction and must be eliminated. For example, assume that on January 2, 1998, the US company sells its entire investment for 300 DM. The exchange rate at this date is 1 DM = $0.50. The balance in the investment account at December 31, 1997, is $115 as a result of the entries made previously.

	Investment in German Subsidiary	
1/1/96	80.00	
	12.90	4.20
	10.30	
Total	103.20	4.20
1/1/97	99.00	
	24.00	
	11.60	19.60
Total	115.00	

The following entries would be made to reflect the sale of the investment:

	Debit	Credit
Cash (300 DM x $0.50)	150	
Investment in German subsidiary		115
Gain from sale of subsidiary		35
Translation adjustments	21.90	
Gain from sale of subsidiary		21.90

If the US company had sold a portion of its investment in the German subsidiary, only a proportionate share of the translation adjustments balance (cumulative amount of exchange differences) would have become part of the gain or loss from the transaction. To illustrate, if 80% of the German subsidiary was sold for 250 DM on January 2, 1998, the following journal entries would be made:

	Debit	Credit
Cash	125	
Investment in German subsidiary (0.8 x $115)		92
Gain from sale of subsidiary		33
Cumulative exchange difference (translation adjustments) (0.8 x $21.90)	17.52	
Gain from sale of subsidiary		17.52

For an illustration of the remeasurement method under US GAAP, refer to Appendix B of this chapter.

Translation of Foreign Currency Transactions

According to IAS 21, a foreign currency transaction is a transaction "denominated in or requires settlement in a foreign currency." Denominated means that the amount to be received or paid is fixed in terms of the number of units of a particular foreign currency, regardless of changes in the exchange rate.

From the viewpoint of a US company, for instance, a foreign currency transaction results when it imports or exports goods or services to a foreign entity or makes a loan involving a foreign entity and agrees to settle the transaction in currency other than the US dollar (the reporting currency of the US company). In these situations, the US company has "crossed currencies" and directly assumes the risk of fluctuating exchange rates of the foreign currency in which the transaction is denominated. This risk may lead to recognition of foreign exchange differences in the income statement of the US company. Note that exchange differences can result only when the foreign currency transactions are denominated in a foreign currency.

When a US company imports or exports goods or services and the transaction is to be settled in US dollars, the US company will incur neither gain nor loss because it bears no risk due to exchange rate fluctuations. The following example illustrates the terminology and procedures applicable to the translation of foreign currency transactions.

Assume that a US company, an exporter, sells merchandise to a customer in Germany on December 1, 1996, for 10,000 DM. Receipt is due on January 31, 1997, and the US company prepares financial statements on December 31, 1996. At the transaction date (December 1, 1996), the spot rate for immediate exchange of foreign currencies indicates that 1 DM is equivalent to $0.50.

To find the US dollar equivalent of this transaction, the foreign currency amount, 10,000 DM, is multiplied by $0.50 to get $5,000. At December 1, 1996, the foreign currency transaction should be recorded by the US company in the following manner: Accounts receivable--Germany 5,000; sales 5,000. The accounts receivable and sales are measured in US dollars at the transaction date using the spot rate at the time of the transaction. While the accounts receivable is measured and reported in US dollars, the receivable is denominated or fixed in DM.

This characteristic may result in foreign exchange differences if the spot rate for DM changes between the transaction date and the date of settlement (January 31, 1997). If financial statements are prepared between the transaction date and the settlement date, all receivables and liabilities that are denominated in a foreign currency (the US dollar) must be restated to reflect the spot rates in existence at the balance sheet date.

Assume that on December 31, 1996, the spot rate for DM is 1 DM = $0.52. This means that the 10,000 DM are now worth $5,200 and that the accounts receivable denominated in DM should be increased by $200. The following journal entry would be recorded as of December 31, 1996:

Accounts receivable--Germany	200	
Foreign currency exchange difference		200

Note that the sales account, which was credited on the transaction date for $5,000, is not affected by changes in the spot rate. This treatment exemplifies the two-transaction viewpoint (which is a US GAAP expression). In other words, making the sale is the result of an operating decision, while bearing the risk of fluctuating spot rates is the result of a financing decision. Therefore, the amount determined as sales revenue at the transaction date should not be altered because of a financing decision to wait until January 31, 1997, for payment of the account.

The risk of a foreign exchange transaction loss can be avoided either by demanding immediate payment on December 1 or by entering into a forward exchange contract to hedge the exposed asset (accounts receivable). The fact that the

US company in the example did not act in either of these two ways is reflected by requiring the recognition of foreign currency exchange differences (transaction gains or losses) in its income statement (reported as financial or nonoperating items) in the period during which the exchange rates changed.

This treatment has been criticized, however, because both the unrealized gain and/or loss are recognized in the financial statements, a practice that is at variance with traditional GAAP. Furthermore, earnings will fluctuate because of changes in exchange rates and not because of changes in the economic activities of the enterprise.

On the settlement date (January 31, 1997), assume that the spot rate is 1 DM = $0.51. The receipt of 10,000 DM and their conversion into US dollars would be journalized in the following manner:

Foreign currency	5,100	
Foreign currency transaction loss	100	
Accounts receivable--Germany		5,200
Cash	5,100	
Foreign currency		5,100

The net effect of this foreign currency transaction was to receive $5,100 from a sale that was measured originally at $5,000. This realized net foreign currency transaction gain of $100 is reported on two income statements: a $200 gain in 1996 and a $100 loss in 1997. The reporting of the gain in two income statements causes a temporary difference between pretax accounting and taxable income. This results because the transaction gain of $100 is not taxable until 1997, the year the transaction was completed or settled. Accordingly, interperiod tax allocation is required for foreign currency transaction gains or losses.

Benchmark vs. Allowed Alternative Treatment

The benchmark treatment for exchange difference requires that they be recognized as income or expenses in the period in which they arise. However, in case of exchange differences that arise from (1) a severe devaluation or depreciation of a currency against which there is no practical means of hedging and that affects liabilities which cannot be settled, and (2) the recent acquisition of an asset invoiced in a foreign currency, the standard permits (under an allowed alternative treatment) such exchange differences to be added to the carrying value of the related asset provided that such adjusted carrying value does not exceed the lower of the replacement cost and the amount recoverable.

Disclosure Requirements

A number of disclosure requirements have been prescribed by IAS 21. Primarily, disclosure is required of the amounts of exchange differences included in net income or loss for the period, exchange differences that are included in the carrying amount of an asset, and those that are classified as equity along with a reconciliation of the beginning and ending balance in cumulative exchange difference account carried as part of the equity.

When there is a change in classification of a foreign operation, disclosure is required as to the nature of the change, reason for the change, and the impact of the change on the current and each of the prior years presented. When the reporting currency is different from the currency of the country of domicile, the reason for this should be disclosed, and in case of any subsequent change in the reporting currency, the reason thereof should also be disclosed. An enterprise should also disclose the method selected to translate goodwill and fair value adjustments arising on the acquisition of a foreign entity. Disclosure is encouraged of an enterprise's foreign currency risk management policy.

APPENDIX A

HEDGING

As explained earlier, IAS 21 (revised 1993) does not address hedge accounting for foreign currency items other than classification of exchange differences arising on a foreign currency liability accounted for as a hedge of a net investment in a foreign entity. IAS 21 categorically states that other aspects of hedging will be dealt with in a forthcoming IAS on financial instruments. In the absence of comprehensive guidance presently available in the IAS, the treatment under US GAAP has been included herein as a source of guidance and reference only.

Relevant Provisions on Hedging Under US GAAP

Foreign currency transaction gains or losses on assets and liabilities which are denominated in a currency other than the functional currency can be hedged if the US company enters into a forward exchange contract. Hedges and other futures contracts that are not entered into with respect to a foreign currency transaction are accounted for in accordance with SFAS 80, *Accounting for Futures Contracts.*

In the previous example, which illustrated the accounting for foreign currency transactions, the US company could have entered into a forward exchange contract on December 1 to sell 10,000 DM for a negotiated amount to a foreign exchange broker for future delivery on January 31, 1997. This forward contract is a hedge against the exposed asset position created by having an account receivable denominated in DM. The negotiated rate referred to above is called a futures or forward rate.

In most cases, this futures rate is not identical to the spot rate at the date of the forward contract. The difference between the futures rate and the spot rate at the date of the forward contract is referred to as a discount or premium. Any discount or premium must be amortized over the term of the forward contract, generally on a straight-line basis. The amortization of discount or premium is reflected in a separate revenue or expense account, not as an addition or subtraction to the foreign currency transaction gain or loss amount. It is important to observe that under this treatment, no net foreign currency transaction gains or losses result if assets and liabilities denominated in foreign currency are completely hedged at the transaction date.

To illustrate a hedge of an exposed asset, consider the following additional information for the German transaction.

> On December 1, 1996, the US company entered into a forward exchange contract to sell 10,000 DM on January 31, 1997, at $0.505 per DM. The spot rate on December 1 is $0.50 per DM. The journal entries that reflect the sale of goods and the forward exchange contract appear as follows:

Sale transaction entries			*Forward exchange contract entries (futures rate 1 DM = $0.505)*		
12/1/96 (spot rate 1 DM = $0.50)			Due from exchange broker	5,050	
			Due to exchange broker		5,000
Accounts receivable--Germany	5,000		Premium on forward contract		50
Sales		5,000	Foreign currency transaction loss	200	
12/31/96 (spot rate 1 DM = $0.52)			Due to exchange broker		200
			Premium on forward contract	25	
Accounts receivable--Germany	200		Financial revenue ($25 = $50/2 months)		25
Foreign currency transaction gain		200	Due to exchange broker	5,200	
			Foreign currency		5,100
1/31/97 (spot rate 1 DM = $0.51)			Foreign currency transaction gain		100
Foreign currency	5,100		Cash	5,050	
			Due from exchange broker		5,050
Foreign currency transaction loss	100		Premium on forward contract	25	
			Financial revenue		25
Accounts receivable--Germany		5,200			

The following points should be noted from the entries above:

1. The net foreign currency transaction gain or loss is zero. The account "Due from exchange broker" is fixed in terms of US dollars, and this amount is not affected by changes in spot rates between the transaction and settlement dates. The account "Due to exchange broker" is fixed or denominated in DM. The US company owes the exchange broker 10,000 DM, and these must be delivered on January 31, 1997. Because this liability is denominated in DM, its amount is determined by spot rates. Since spot rates change, this liability changes in amount equal to the changes in accounts receivable because both of the amounts are based on the same spot rates. These changes are reflected as foreign currency transaction gains and losses which net out to zero.
2. The premium on forward contract is fixed in terms of US dollars. This amount is amortized to a financial revenue account over the life of the forward contract on a straight-line basis.
3. The net effect of this transaction is that $5,050 was received on January 31, 1997, for a sale originally recorded at $5,000. The $50 difference was taken into income via amortization. SFAS 52 does not require a forward exchange contract for a hedge to take place.

For example, it is possible for a foreign currency transaction to act as an economic hedge against a parent's net investment in a foreign entity if

1. The transaction is designated as a hedge.
2. It is effective as a hedge.

To illustrate, assume that a US parent has a wholly owned British subsidiary which has net assets of £2 million. The US parent can borrow £2 million to hedge its net investment in the British subsidiary. Assume further that the British pound is the functional currency and that the £2 million liability is denominated in pounds. Fluctuations in the exchange rate for pounds will have no net effect on the parent company's consolidated balance sheet because increases (decreases) in the translation adjustments balance due to the translation of the net investment will be offset by decreases (increases) in this balance due to the adjustment of the liability denominated in pounds.

APPENDIX B

ADDITIONAL GUIDANCE FROM US GAAP

Application of the Remeasurement Method

In the example presented in the earlier part of this chapter, the DM was the functional currency because the German subsidiary's cash flows were primarily in DM. Assume, however, that the financing of the land and building was in US dollars instead of DM and that the mortgage payable is denominated in US dollars (i.e., must be paid in US dollars). Although the rents collected and the majority of the cash flows for expenses are in DM, management has decided that, due to the manner of financing, the US dollar is the functional currency. The books and records, however, are maintained in DM. The translation of the German financial statements is accomplished by use of the remeasurement method (also known as the monetary/ nonmonetary method). This method is illustrated below using the same information that was presented before for the German subsidiary.

German Company
Balance Sheet Translation (Remeasurement Method)
(US dollar is the functional currency)

Assets	DM	Exchange rate	US dollars
Cash	DM 50	0.45	$ 22.50
Note receivable	20	0.45	9.00
Land	100	0.40	40.00
Building (net)	490	0.40	196.00
Total assets	DM 660		$267.50
Liabilities and stockholders' equity			
Accounts payable	DM 30	0.45	$ 13.50
Unearned rent	10	0.42	4.20
Mortgage payable	400	0.45	180.00
Common stock	40	0.40	16.00
Additional paid-in capital	160	0.40	64.00
Retained earnings	20	(see income statement)	(10.20)
Total liabilities and stockholders' equity	DM 660		$267.50

German Company
Combined Income and Retained Earnings Statement Translation
(Remeasurement Method)
(US dollar is the functional currency)
For the Year Ended December 31, 1996

	DM	Exchange rate	US dollars
Revenues	DM 200	0.43	$ 86.00
Expenses (excluding depreciation)	(160)	0.43	(68.80)
Depreciation expense	(10)	0.40	(4.00)
Translation loss	--	(see analysis below)	(19.20)
Net income (loss)	DM 30	--	$ (6.00)
Retained earnings, January 1	--	--	--
Dividends paid	(10)	0.42	(4.20)
Retained earnings, December 31	DM 20		$(10.20)

German Company
Translation (Remeasurement Method) Loss
For the Year Ended December 31, 1996

	DM			US dollars	
	Debit	Credit	Exchange rate	Debit	Credit
Cash	DM 50		0.45	$22.50	
Note receivable	20		0.45	9.00	
Land	100		0.40	40.00	
Building (net)	490		0.40	196.00	
Accounts payable		DM 30	0.45		$ 13.50
Unearned rent		10	0.42		4.20
Mortgage payable		400	0.45		180.00
Common stock		40	0.40		16.00
Additional paid-in capital		160	0.40		64.00
Retained earnings		--	--		--
Dividends declared	10		0.42	4.20	
Revenues		200	0.43		86.00
Operating expenses	160		0.43	68.80	
Depreciation expenses	10		0.40	4.00	
Totals	DM 840	DM 840		$344.50	$363.70
Loss from remeasurement				19.20	
Totals				$363.70	$363.70

The following observations should be noted about the remeasurement method:

1. Assets and liabilities that have historical cost balances (nonmonetary assets and liabilities) are translated by using historical exchange rates (i.e., the rates in effect when the transactions occurred). Monetary assets and monetary liabilities, on the other hand, are translated by using the current exchange rate at the balance sheet date.
2. Revenues and expenses that occur frequently during a period are translated, for practical purposes, by using the weighted-average exchange rate for the period. Revenues and expenses that represent allocations of historical bal-

ances (e.g., depreciation) are translated by using historical exchange rates. Note that this is a different treatment as compared to the current rate method. Note also that in 1997, the unearned rent from 1996 of 10 DM would be translated at the rate of 1 DM = $0.42. The unearned rent at the end of 1996 is not considered a monetary liability. Therefore, the $0.42 historical exchange rate should be used for all applicable future years.

3. If the functional currency is the US dollar rather than the local foreign currency, the amounts of specific line items presented in the reconciliation of net income to net cash flow from operating activities will be different for nonmonetary items (e.g., depreciation). Note, however, that the net cash flow from operating activities will be the same in the reporting currency regardless of the applicable functional currency.
4. In a purely mechanical sense, calculation of the translation gain (loss) is the amount needed to make the dollar debits equal to the dollar credits in the German company's trial balance.
5. The translation loss of $19.20 is reported on the US company's consolidated income statement because the US dollar is the functional currency. When the reporting currency is the functional currency, as it is in this example, it is assumed that all of the foreign entity's transactions occurred in US dollars. Accordingly, translation gains and losses are taken immediately to the income statement in the year in which they occur as they can be expected to have direct cash flow effects. They are not deferred in a translation adjustments account as they were when the functional currency was the DM (current rate method).
6. The use of the equity method of accounting for the subsidiary would result in the following entries by the US company during 1996:

	Debit	Credit
Original investment		
Investment in German subsidiary	80	
Cash		80
Earnings (loss) pickup		
Equity in subsidiary loss	6	
Investment in German subsidiary		6
Dividends received		
Cash	4.20	
Investment in German subsidiary		4.20

Note that translation gains and losses are included in the subsidiary's net income (net loss) as determined in US dollars before the equity pickup is made by the US company.

7. In highly inflationary economies, those in which cumulative inflation is greater than 100% over a 3-year period, the functional currency is the reporting currency (i.e., the US dollar; SFAS 52, para 11). The remeasure-

ment method must be used in this situation even though the factors indicate the local currency is the functional currency. The board made this decision to prevent the evaporation of the foreign entity's fixed assets, a result that would occur if the local currency were the functional currency.

Summary of Current Rate and Remeasurement Methods

1. Before foreign currency financial statements can be translated into US dollars, management of the US entity must select the functional currency for the foreign entity whose financial statements will be incorporated into theirs by consolidation, combination, or the equity method. As the example illustrated, this decision is crucial because it may have a material effect on the financial statements of the US company.
2. If the functional currency is the local currency of the foreign entity, the current rate method is used to translate foreign currency financial statements into US dollars. All assets and liabilities are translated by using the current exchange rate at the balance sheet date. This method ensures that all financial relationships remain the same in both local currency and US dollars. Owners' equity is translated by using historical rates, while revenues (gains) and expenses (losses) are translated at the rates in existence during the period when the transactions occurred. A weighted-average rate can be used for items occurring numerous times throughout the period. The translation adjustments (debit or credit) that result from the application of these rules are reported as a separate component in owners' equity of the US company's consolidated balance sheet (or parent-only balance sheet if consolidation was not deemed appropriate).
3. If the functional currency is the reporting currency (the US dollar), the foreign currency financial statements are remeasured into US dollars. All foreign currency balances are restated to US dollars using both historical and current exchange rates. Foreign currency balances that reflect prices from past transactions are translated by using historical rates, while foreign currency balances that reflect prices from current transactions are translated by using the current exchange rate. Translation gains/losses that result from the remeasurement process are reported on the US company's consolidated income statement.

A summary of the provisions of the US GAAP relating to foreign currency translation is presented below in tabular form.

Functional currency	*Functional currency determinants*	*Translation method*	*Reporting*
Local currency of foreign company*	a. Operations not integrated with parent's operations b. Buying and selling activities primarily in local currency c. Cash flows not immediately available for remittance to parent d. Financing denominated in local currency	Current rate (all assets/liabilities translated use current exchange rate; revenues/expenses use weighted-average rate; equity accounts use historical rates)	Translation adjustments are reported in equity section of the US company's consolidated balance sheet Analysis of changes in accumulated transaction adjustments disclosed via footnote or separate schedule
US dollar	a. Operations integrated with parent's operations b. Buying and selling activities primarily in the United States and/or US dollars c. Cash flows immediately available for remittance to parent d. Financing denominated in US dollars	Remeasurement (monetary assets/liabilities use current exchange rate; historical cost balances use historical rates; revenues/expenses use weighted-average rates and historical rates, the latter for allocations such as depreciation expense)	Translation gain/loss is reported on the US company's consolidated income statement

**The functional currency could be a foreign currency other than the local currency. If this is the case, the foreign currency statements are first remeasured in the functional currency before the current rate method is applied.*

21 PERSONAL FINANCIAL STATEMENTS

PERSPECTIVE AND ISSUES

Accounting practices have historically developed in the context of corporate financial reporting. Accordingly, there is little formal guidance for reporting on the financial position and results of operations of enterprises that are organized as partnerships, for example, or for nonbusiness enterprises and individuals. For noncorporate businesses the general rule has always been to analogize from corporate accounting guidelines, and in some jurisdictions national accounting standard setters have developed rules applicable to private sector not-for-profit organizations. International standards have not, however, been promulgated for this important category of enterprises.

Personal financial statements present an interesting set of accounting issues. Frequently, lenders and other interested parties will request or require that the financial statements of owners or other key personnel of a business enterprise be disclosed to them. In many cases, lenders will require that repayment of loans to business entities, particularly smaller or closely held enterprises, be personally guaranteed by the owners, and accordingly will demand that they be able to evaluate the guarantors' net worth. In other situations, individuals will simply wish to have a formal representation of their financial positions prepared for them. A set of relevant standards for the preparation of personal financial statements would thus be of great utility.

Unfortunately, the IASC has not addressed the question of accounting principles applicable to personal financial statements and, as of this date, the topic has not been placed on its work program (technical projects agenda). Given the importance of the topic, however, the authors have concluded that it would be worthwhile to provide suggested guidance to readers. This guidance necessarily will draw heavily from the existing guidance under US GAAP, with commentary on departures that might make the resulting financial statements more useful, as needed.

Personal financial statements are generally prepared to organize and plan an individual's financial affairs on a more formal basis. Specific purposes deal with the obtaining of credit, income tax planning, retirement planning, gift and estate planning, or public disclosure of financial affairs. The aforementioned purposes are such that the users of personal financial statements rely on them in determining whether to grant credit, in assessing the financial activities of individuals, in assessing the financial affairs of public officials and candidates for public office, and for similar purposes.

The most definitive standards on personal financial statements are from the United States. These are contained in AICPA statement of position (SOP) 82-1, *Personal Financial Statements,* which addresses the preparation and presentation of personal financial statements, or, more specifically, financial statements of individuals or groups of related individuals (i.e., family). The previous guidance provided by the 1968 AICPA Industry Audit Guide, *Audits of Personal Financial Statements*, had used historical cost as the primary basis of measurement for personal financial statements, while recommending the presentation of estimated current value amounts as additional information. The increasing use of personal financial statements created the need to reassess the conclusions found in the Industry Audit Guide due to the purposes for which personal financial statements are prepared, the users to whom they are directed, and the ways in which they are used. That reassessment resulted in SOP 82-1, which is drawn on in this chapter. Although this does not constitute generally accepted accounting principles under the international standards, it is probably the best guidance available and has the added virtue that it does not conflict with established international rules.

DEFINITIONS OF TERMS

Estimated current amount of liabilities. Payables and other liabilities should be presented at the discounted amounts of cash to be paid. The discount rate should be the rate implicit in the transaction in which the debt was incurred. If, however, the debtor is able to discharge the debt currently at a lower amount, the debt should be presented at the lower amount.

Estimated current value of an asset. The amount for which an item could be exchanged between a buyer and a seller, each of whom is well informed and willing and neither of whom is compelled to buy or sell.

CONCEPTS, RULES, AND EXAMPLES

Personal financial statements may be prepared for an individual, husband and wife, or family. The basic concept of financial statements are the same, whether for a business enterprise, a not-for-profit, a governmental unit, or an individual, and thus the goal is to present the entity's financial condition (or position) at a point in time and its results of operations for a period ending on that point in time. The first of these goals is accomplished by the balance sheet (or statement of financial position or financial condition), which is a "snapshot" of the financial health of the entity, as measured and defined by the applicable principles being employed. The other objective is achieved by the presentation of an income statement (or statement of operations or statement of changes in net worth), which summarizes activity over a period, such as a month or a year.

A basic issue in accounting for any type of entity is whether to measure assets and liabilities, and thus net worth, by reference to actual transaction prices (i.e., historical costs), or instead with regard to current values. As directed by international accounting standards, financial reporting for business enterprises is effectively based on a "mixed attribute" model, with some items measured by historical costs and others by some form of current value (such as realizable value, fair value, etc.). This largely reflects the events that have affected the historical development of accounting measures and may not be a coherent approach to economic measurement. However, there are a variety of theoretical arguments supporting each element in the model, and it is now fairly well accepted, if for no other reason than having been employed for many years in an essentially unchanged manner.

Personal financial statements, on the other hand, have been less widely employed than those for business entities, and accordingly there has been less resistance to taking a "fresh look" at which accounting principles should logically underlie their preparation. The recent consensus of the accounting profession in the United States has been that the nature of personal financial statements is such that the most meaningful measure of an individual's net worth would be provided if assets were stated at current (or fair) values rather than original historical cost, and if liabilities were presented at estimated current amounts rather than the original amounts owed. The balance sheet (usually denoted as the statement of financial condition in this context, however) will, under a current value approach, calculate net worth without distinguishing between realized and unrealized gains or losses; accordingly, the financial statement that is the surrogate for the income statement will include more than the results of the entity's current operations. For that reason, the primary "flow" statement used in the context of personal financial reporting is generally denoted as being a measure of changes in net worth, not results of operations.

Under existing US GAAP, personal financial statements consist of the following:

1. **Statement of financial condition**--Presents the estimated current values of assets, estimated current amounts of liabilities, estimated income taxes, and net worth at a specified date.
2. **Statement of changes in net worth**--Presents the main sources of increases (decreases) in net worth and includes both realized and unrealized changes in values.

Assets and liabilities, including changes therein, should be recognized using the accrual basis of accounting. In the statement of financial condition, assets and liabilities should be listed by order of liquidity and maturity, not on a current/noncurrent basis.

The logic underlying the use of current values for personal financial statements derives from the use to which such statements are commonly put. In reality, of course, the purposes are not that different from those to which the financial statements of business enterprises are put: to support decision making about the reporting entity's financial position at a point in time and its results of operations for a period ending on that date. However, users of personal financial statements are less concerned with the stewardship exercised by the managers of the entity than are users of businesses' statements. For that reason, the historical cost of assets employed is of less interest; it is the present and future, not the past, that is of exclusive concern in most instances. Thus, while a very sound argument can be made for current value accounting for all reporting entities (see the discussion of this in Chapter 23), it is easier to make this case for the financial statements of individuals or families.

In personal financial statements, assets should be presented at their estimated current value. This is an amount at which the item could be exchanged, assuming that both parties are well informed, neither party is compelled to buy or sell, and material disposal costs are deducted to arrive at current values. A specialist may have to be consulted in the determination of the current value of certain types of assets (e.g., works of art, jewelry, restricted securities, investments in closely held businesses, and real estate). Liabilities should be presented at the lesser of the discounted amount of cash to be paid or the current cash settlement amount. Reference to recent transactions involving similar types of assets and liabilities, conducted in similar circumstances, will generally constitute a satisfactory means of determining the estimated current value of an asset and the estimated current amount of a liability. If recent information cannot be obtained, other methods can be used as suggested in the chart that follows (e.g., capitalization of past or prospective earnings, the use of liquidation values, the adjustment of historical cost based on changes in a specific price index, the use of appraisals, and the use of the discounted amounts of projected cash receipts and payments). The methods used should be followed consistently from period to period unless the facts and circumstances dictate a change to different methods.

Income taxes payable should include unpaid income taxes for completed tax years and the estimated amount for the elapsed portion of the current tax year. Additionally, personal financial statements should include the estimated income tax on the difference between the current values of assets and amounts of liabilities and their respective tax bases as if they had been realized or liquidated. Failure to provide this deferred tax item could have the result of materially misstating the net worth of the individual, since unrealized gains and losses are not generally taxable or deductible for current tax purposes, in most jurisdictions, but will eventually be so when the items are ultimately realized.

Assets and liabilities	Discounted cash flow	Market price	Appraised value	Other
Receivables	x			
Marketable securities		x		If traded on valuation date, closing price; if not, average of bid and ask prices
Options on securities		x		Difference between exercise price and current value of asset; if material, discount the difference
Options on other assets				
Investment in life insurance				Cash value less any outstanding loans
Investment in closely held business	x		x	Liquidation value, multiple of earnings, reproduction value, adjustment of book value or historical cost
Real estate	x		x	Refer to sales of similar properties
Intangible assets	x			Net proceeds from current sale or discounted cash flows from asset
Future interests (nonforfeitable rights)	x			
Payables and other liabilities	x			Discharge amount if lower than discounted amount
Noncancelable commitments	x			
Income taxes payable				Unpaid income tax for completed years and estimated tax for elapsed portion of current year
Estimated income taxes on difference between current value of net assets and respective tax bases				Computed as if current value of net assets had been realized, under applicable tax laws in existence at date
Uncertain obligations				Follow guidance for contingencies

Source: Michael D. Kinsman and Bruce Samuelson, Personal Financial Statements, Journal of Accounting, September 1987, pp. 138-148.

Business interests often comprise a large portion of a person's total assets and should be shown separately from other investments since these are generically different (active involvement versus passive ownership, etc.). An investment in a separate entity that is marketable as a going concern (e.g., a closely held corporation) should be presented as a single amount. The individual assets and liabilities of that enterprise would not typically be presented in the individual's statement of financial condition, because the assets are not normally individually accessible and the liabilities will not be settled by the investor personally. On the other hand, if the investment is a limited business activity, not conducted in a separate business entity, separate asset and liability amounts should be shown (e.g., an investment in real estate and its related mortgage). Of course, only the person's beneficial interest in the investment is included in his or her personal financial statements.

Comprehensive example of personal financial statements

Marcus and Kelly Imrich
Statements of Financial Condition
December 31, 1997 and 1996

	1997	1996
Assets		
Cash	$ 381,437	$ 207,621
Securities		
Marketable (Note 2)	128,787	260,485
Tax-exempt bonds (Note 3)	1,890,222	986,278
Certificate of deposit	20,000	10,000
Loans receivable (Note 4)	262,877	362,877
Partnership and venture interests (Note 5)	935,000	938,000
Real estate interests (Note 6)	890,000	2,500,000
David Corporation (Note 7)	2,750,687	2,600,277
Cash surrender value of life insurance (Note 8)	388,000	265,000
Personal residences (Note 9)	2,387,229	2,380,229
Deferred losses from partnerships	68,570	60,830
Vested interest in David Corporation benefit plan	545,960	530,960
Personal jewelry and furnishings (Note 10)	513,000	6,700
Total assets	$11,161,769	$11,109,257
Liabilities		
Mortgage payable (Note 11)	$ 254,000	$ 267,000
Security deposits--rentals	--	5,700
Income taxes payable--current year balance	9,800	10,680
Total liabilities	263,800	283,380
Estimated income taxes on difference between estimated current values of assets and estimated current amounts of liabilities and their tax bases (Note 12)	555,400	731,000
Net worth	10,342,569	10,094,877
Total liabilities and net worth	$11,161,769	$11,109,257

Marcus and Kelly Imrich
Statement of Changes in Net Worth
For the Years Ended December 31, 1997 and 1996

	Year ended December 31, 1997	1996
Realized increases in net worth		
Salary and bonus	$ 200,000	$ 175,000
Dividends and interest income	184,260	85,000
Distribution from limited partnerships	280,000	260,000
Gain on sales of marketable securities	58,240	142,800
	722,500	662,800
Realized decreases in net worth		
Income taxes	180,000	140,000
Interest expense	25,000	26,000
Real estate taxes	21,000	18,000
Personal expenditures	242,536	400,000
	468,536	584,000
Net realized increase in net worth	253,964	78,800
Unrealized increases in net worth		
Marketable securities (net of realized gains on securities sold)	37,460	30,270
Benefit plan--David Corporation	15,000	14,000
Personal jewelry and furnishings	20,000	18,000
	72,460	62,270
Unrealized decrease in net worth		
Estimated income taxes on the difference between the estimated current values of assets and the estimated current amounts of liabilities and their tax bases	78,732	64,118
Net unrealized decrease in net worth	(6,272)	(1,848)
Net increase in net worth	247,692	76,952
Net worth at the beginning of year	10,094,877	10,017,925
Net worth at the end of year	$10,342,569	$10,094,877

Marcus and Kelly Imrich
Notes to Financial Statements

Note 1: The accompanying financial statements include the assets and liabilities of Marcus and Kelly Imrich. Assets are stated at their estimated current values, and liabilities at their estimated current amounts.

Note 2: The estimated current values of marketable securities are either (1) their quoted closing prices or (2) for securities not traded on the financial statement date, amounts that fall within the range of quoted bid and asked prices. Marketable securities consist of the following:

	December 31, 1997		*December 31, 1996*	
	Number of shares	*Estimated current values*	*Number of shares*	*Estimated current values*
Stock				
Susan Schultz, Inc.			1,000	$122,000
Ripley Robotics Corp.	500	$ 51,927	1,000	120,485
L.A.W. Corporation	300	20,700	100	5,000
Jay & Kelly Corp.	300	20,700	200	5,000
J.A.Z. Corporation	200	35,460	200	8,000
		$128,787		$260,485

Note 3: The interest income from state and municipal bonds is not subject to federal income taxes but is, except in certain cases, subject to state income tax.

Note 4: The loan receivable from Carol Parker, Inc. matures January, 2005, and bears interest at the prime rate.

Note 5: Partnership and venture interests consist of the following:

	% owned	*Cost*	*Estimated current value 12/31/97*	*Estimated current value 12/31/96*
East Third Partnership	50.0	$ 50,000	$100,000	$100,000
631 Lucinda Venture	20.0	10,000	35,000	38,000
27 Wright Partnership	22.5	10,000	40,000	50,000
Eannarino Partnership	10.0	40,000	60,000	50,000
Sweeney Venture	30.0	100,000	600,000	600,000
Kelly Parker Group	20.0	20,000	100,000	100,000
707 Lucinda Venture	50.0	(11,000)	--	--
			$935,000	$938,000

Note 6: Mr. and Mrs. Imrich own a one-half interest in an apartment building in DeKalb, Illinois. The estimated fair market value was determined by Mr. and Mrs. Imrich. Their basis in the apartment building was $1,000,000 for both 1997 and 1996.

Note 7: Kelly Imrich owns 75% of the common stock of the David Corporation. A condensed statement of assets, liabilities, and stockholders' equity (income tax basis) of David Corporation as of December 31, 1997 and 1996 is summarized below.

	1997	*1996*
Current assets	$2,975,000	$3,147,000
Investments	200,000	200,000
Property and equipment (net)	145,000	165,000
Loans receivable	110,000	120,000
Total assets	$3,430,000	$3,632,000
Current liabilities	$2,030,000	$2,157,000
Other liabilities	450,000	400,000
Total liabilities	2,480,000	2,557,000
Stockholders' equity	950,000	1,075,000
Total liabilities and stockholders' equity	$3,430,000	$3,632,000

Note 8: At December 31, 1997 and 1996, Marcus Imrich owned a $1,000,000 whole life insurance policy.

Note 9: The estimated current values of the personal residences are their purchase prices plus their cost of improvements. Both residences were purchased in 1995.

Note 10: The estimated current values of personal effects and jewelry are the appraised values of those assets, determined by an independent appraiser for insurance purposes.

Note 11: The mortgage (collateralized by the residence) is payable in monthly installments of $1,083 a month, including interest at 10% a year through 2010.

Note 12: The estimated current amounts of liabilities at December 31, 1997, and December 31, 1996, equaled their tax bases. Estimated income taxes have been provided on the excess of the estimated current values of assets over their tax bases as if the estimated current values of the assets had been realized on the statement date, using applicable tax laws and regulations. The provision will probably differ from the amounts of income taxes that eventually might be paid because those amounts are determined by the timing and the method of disposal or realization and the tax laws and regulations in effect at the time of disposal or realization.

The estimated current values of assets exceeded their tax bases by $1,850,000 at December 31, 1997, and by $1,770,300 at December 31, 1996. The excess of estimated current valucs of major assets over their tax bases are

	December 31,	
	1997	*1996*
Investment in David Corporation	$1,400,000	$1,350,000
Vested interest in benefit plan	350,000	300,000
Investment in marketable securities	100,000	120,300

22 SPECIALIZED INDUSTRY GAAP

BANKS AND SIMILAR FINANCIAL INSTITUTIONS

PERSPECTIVE AND ISSUES

Disclosure requirements relating to financial statements of banks and similar financial institutions are contained in IAS 30. A broad definition of the term "bank" has been given by IAS 30 and covers all those enterprises (whether the word bank is included in their name or not)

1. Which are financial institutions
2. One of whose principal activities is to accept deposits and borrow money with the intention of lending and investing
3. Which are within the scope of banking and similar legislations

Since banks' operations differ in many material respects from other commercial enterprises and liquidity and solvency is of paramount importance, their financial reporting inevitably will be somewhat specialized in nature. In recognition of their special needs, IAS 30 lays down a number of disclosure requirements. Some of these disclosures may seem unusual from the standpoint of other commercial enterprises and may be perceived by users of the banks' financial statements as excessive or superfluous; however, these disclosures have been made mandatory for banks, keeping in view the special characteristics of banks' operations and the role they play in maintaining public confidence in the monetary system of the country through their close relationship with regulatory authorities (such as the country's central bank) and the government. Further, a bank is exposed not only to liquidity risks but even risks arising from currency fluctuations, interest rate movements, changes in market prices, and counterparty failure. These risks are associated not only with assets and liabilities, which are recognized on a bank's balance sheet, but also with off-balance-sheet items. Thus, certain disclosure requirements as outlined by IAS 30 relate to off-balance-sheet items as well.

It is a well-known fact that, compared to the other international accounting standards, IAS 30 took an inordinate amount of time before issuance in its final form. Although the standard became operative for financial statements of banks covering periods beginning on or after January 1, 1991 after having finally been approved in 1990, it is worth noting that the due process was, in fact, initiated by the IASC through the publication of a discussion paper in 1980. This was followed by two exposure drafts: E29 and E34. It should be noted, however, that even though the promulgation of IAS 30 spanned a number of years, it encompassed numerous deliberations and consultations with regulatory authorities, and users of banks' financial statements. Also, representatives of bankers from around the world (including the United States and Europe) were consulted extensively. Thus, it is not surprising that this standard has such extensive disclosure requirements.

Although IAS 30 applies exclusively to financial statements of banks and similar financial institutions, it should be borne in mind that disclosure requirements according to other international accounting standards, such as IAS 24, *Related Party Disclosures*, IAS 16, *Property, Plant and Equipment*, and so on, also need to be considered while preparing a bank's financial statements. Further, IAS 7, *Cash Flow Statements*, stipulates special provisions that are applicable to financial institutions, and the appendix to IAS 7 illustrates the "direct method" for the preparation of cash flow statements by financial institutions.

Sources of IAS
IAS 1, 5, 7, 10, 13, 16, 18, 24, 25, 30

CONCEPTS, RULES, AND EXAMPLES

Accounting Policies

International Accounting Standard (IAS) 1, which applies to financial statements of all commercial, industrial, and business enterprises in general (which includes banks and similar financial institutions as well), requires that disclosure be made of all significant accounting policies that were adopted in the preparation and presentation of an entity's financial statements. To comply with the standard above and also since different banks use diverse methods for recognition and measurement of items on their financial statements, disclosure of accounting policies relating to certain important items has been prescribed by IAS 30. This will enable users of the bank's financial statements to better understand the basis of preparation of those financial statements. Specifically, disclosure of the following accounting policies is prescribed by the standard:

1. The accounting policy setting forth the recognition of the principal types of income. An example of this disclosure follows:

    a. "Interest income and loan commitment fees are recognized on a time proportion basis* taking into account the principal outstanding and the rate applicable. Other fee income is recognized when due."

b. "Accrual of interest ceases on loans placed in the non accrual status if in the opinion of the management the loans are unlikely to be repaid as per the terms of agreement or when the principal or interest is past due 90 days or more."**

* *IAS 18 specifically requires that interest income be recognized on a time proportion basis.*

** *In some countries this is referred to as "interest in suspense" or "reserved interest."*

2. Accounting policies relating to the valuation of investments and dealing securities. An illustration follows:

 Note 1: Valuation of Investments. Long-term investments are stated at cost with provision being made for any decline other than temporary in value. Trading investments are stated at the lower of cost or market, the carrying amount being determined on an aggregate portfolio basis.

3. Accounting policy explaining the distinction between transactions and events that result in the recognition of assets and liabilities on the balance sheet vs. those that give rise to contingencies and commitments, including off-balance-sheet items. An example follows:

 Note 1: Contingent Obligations. Loans and advances to customers result from and include facilities granted to customers and are utilized before year end; however, undrawn facilities, such as lines of credit, extended to customers that are irrevocable according to agreements with customers (and cannot be withdrawn at the discretion of the bank), are disclosed as commitments.

4. Accounting policy that outlines the basis for the determination of

 a. The provision for possible losses on loans and advances
 b. Write-off of uncollectable loans and advances

 Note 1: Provision for Loan Losses. Provision is made for possible losses in relation to loans and advances to customers that have been individually reviewed and specifically identified as doubtful and is referred to as specific provision. A general provision based on experience is also made based on the risks that are likely to be present in any portfolio of bank advances that have not yet been identified specifically. Loans and advances on which all legal and other possible courses of action for recovery have been exhausted are written off as bad debts.

5. Accounting policy explaining the basis for determining and setting aside amounts toward general banking risks and the accounting treatment accorded to this reserve.

 Regulatory bodies such as the central bank of the country in which the bank is incorporated or the local legislation may require or allow a bank to set aside amounts for general banking risks, including future losses or other unforeseeable risks or even reserves for contingencies over and above accruals required by IAS 10, *Contingencies and Events Occurring After the Balance Sheet Date.* It would not be proper to allow banks to charge these additional reserves to the income statement, as this would distort the true financial position of the bank. Thus, IAS 30 requires that the above mentioned reserves be appropriated out of the retained earnings and be separately disclosed as such. An example is

> **Note 1: Statutory Reserves.** In accordance with the bank's articles of association, 10% of the net income for the year is to be set aside as a contingency reserve each year. Such appropriations of net income are to continue until the balance in the contingency reserve equals 50% of the bank's issued capital.

Preparation and Presentation of Bank's Financial Statements

IAS 5, which contains provisions relating to the information to be disclosed in financial statements, requires that

1. All material information be disclosed in order to make the financial statements clear and understandable
2. Items in the financial statements be supplemented, if necessary, by additional information to make their meaning clear

IAS 5 also gives the layout and groupings of significant items appearing in the financial statements of commercial and industrial enterprises. However, the standard categorically states that the described layout and groupings of financial statement items might not be appropriate for enterprises such as financial and insurance companies. In the opinion of the authors, this could be interpreted to mean that although the general disclosure requirements of IAS 5 may very well be applicable to all kinds of enterprises, the given layout and groupings of financial statements items may not be applicable universally, especially to financial companies. For instance, IAS 5 makes it mandatory for financial statements to show corresponding figures for the preceding period (i.e., to present comparative financial statements). This and other requirements contained in the other international accounting standards are applicable to banks as well as nonfinancial enterprises.

Further, whether banks or other financial institutions which are usually organized as public share holding companies could be considered "financial companies" as contemplated by IAS 5 is also open to interpretation. Taking a cue from the language of IAS 30, which prescribes an unclassified balance sheet for banks, the authors are of the opinion that the layout and groupings of financial statement items as per IAS 5 are obviously not applicable to banks (since that standard categorizes assets and liabilities into current and noncurrent classes), and hence the exemption in paragraph 4 of IAS 5 is squarely applicable to banks. Thus, certain provisions of IAS 30, which set forth rules for the preparation and presentation of financial statements by banks, should be made the basis for the layout and groupings of financial statements by banks.

The following ground rules have been established by IAS 30 for the preparation and presentation of the financial statements of banks:

1. The income statement of a bank should be presented in a manner that groups income and expenses by nature and discloses the amounts of the principal types of income and expenses. This principle has been further elucidated by the standard as follows:

   a. Disclosures in the income statement or in the footnotes should include, but are not limited to, the following items:

      (1) Interest and similar income
      (2) Interest expense and similar charges
      (3) Dividend income
      (4) Fee and commission income
      (5) Fee and commission expense
      (6) Gains less losses arising from dealing securities
      (7) Gains less losses arising from investment securities
      (8) Gains less losses arising from dealing in foreign currencies
      (9) Other operating income
      (10) Losses on loans and advances
      (11) General and administrative expenses
      (12) Other operating expenses

      These disclosures, to be incorporated into the bank's income statement, are of course in addition to disclosure requirements of other international accounting standards.

   b. Separate disclosure of the principal types of income and expenses as above is essential in order that users of the bank's financial statements can assess the performance of the bank.

   c. To enhance financial statement transparency, IAS 30 prohibits the offsetting of income and expense items, except those relating to hedges and to assets or liabilities wherein the legal right of set-off exists and the offsetting represents the expectation as to the realization or settlement of the asset or liability. In case income and expense items were allowed to be offset, it would prevent users from assessing the return on particular classes of assets; this, in a way, would restrict users of financial statements in their assessment of the performance of the bank.

   d. The following income statement items are, however, allowed to be presented on a net basis:

      (1) Gains or losses from dealings in foreign currencies
      (2) Gains or losses from disposals of investment securities

(3) Gains or losses from disposals and changes in the carrying amount of dealing securities

Example of bank financial reporting

ABC Banking Corporation
Statement of Income
For the Years Ended December 31,19X2 and 19X1

	19X2	*19X1*
Income from banking activities:		
Interest income	$400,000	$380,000
Fees and commissions	50,000	40,000
Net gain from disposal of investment securities	20,000	13,000
Net income from dealing securities	2,000	2,000
Net gain from dealings in foreign currencies	14,000	10,000
Dividend income	1,000	2,000
Other operating income	7,000	6,000
	$494,000	$453,000
Expenses relating to banking activities:		
Interest expense	$205,000	$200,000
Provision for losses on loans and advances	70,000	50,000
Provision for diminution in value of investments	1,000	1,000
	$276,000	$251,000
Net income from banking activities	$218,000	$202,000
Other income	9,000	8,000
	$227,000	$210,000
General and administration expenses	$80,000	$75,000
Depreciation on fixed assets	11,000	10,000
Provision for taxation	6,000	6,000
Net income for the year	$130,000	$119,000

2. The balance sheet of a bank should group assets and liabilities by nature and list them in the order of their respective liquidity. This is explained further by the standard as follows:

   a. Disclosure of the grouping of assets and liabilities by their nature and listing them by their respective liquidity is illustrated by the standard. These are to be made either on the face of the balance sheet or in the footnotes. The following disclosures are prescribed with a proviso that disclosures should include but are not limited to:

Assets
Cash and balances with the central bank
Treasury bills and other bills eligible for rediscounting with the central bank
Government and other securities held for dealing purposes
Placements with, and loans and advances to, other banks
Other money market placements
Loans and advances to customers
Investment securities

Liabilities
Deposits from other banks
Other money market deposits
Amounts owed to other depositors
Certificates of deposits
Promissory notes and other liabilities evidenced by paper
Other borrowed funds

These disclosures, to be incorporated into the bank's income statement, are of course in addition to disclosure requirements of other international accounting standards.

b. Grouping the assets and liabilities by nature does not pose a problem and, in fact, is probably the most logical way of combining financial statement items for presentation on the bank's balance sheet. For instance, deposits with other banks and loans/advances to other banks are combined and presented as a separate line item on the asset side of a bank's balance sheet and referred to as placements with other banks. These items would, however, be presented differently on financial statements of other commercial enterprises since deposits with banks in those instances would be combined with other cash and bank balances, and loans to banks would probably be classified as investments. On the other hand, balances with other banks are not combined with balances with other parts of the money market, even though by nature they are placements with other financial institutions, sincc this gives a better understanding of the bank's relations with and dependency on other banks vs. other constituents of the money market.

c. Listing of assets by liquidity could be considered synonymous with listing of liabilities by maturity, since maturity is a measure of liquidity in case of liabilities. For instance, certificates of deposits are liabilities of banks and have contractual maturities of say, 1 month, 3 months, 6 months, and 1 year. Similarly, there are other bank liabilities, such as promissory notes that may not be due, say, for another 3 years from the balance sheet date. Thus, a relative maturity analysis would suggest that the certificates of deposit be listed on the bank's balance sheet before or above the promissory notes since they would mature earlier.

Similarly, assets of a bank could be analyzed based on their relative liquidity, and those assets that are more liquid than others (i.e., will convert into cash faster than others) should be listed on the balance sheet above the others. Thus, cash balances and balances with the central bank are usually listed above other assets on the balance sheets of all banks, being relatively more liquid than other assets.

d. Offsetting of assets against liabilities, or vice versa, is generally not allowed unless a legal right of set-off exists and the offsetting represents the expectation as to the realization or settlement of the asset or liability. This is true even in the case of other enterprises; IAS 13, which applies generally to all enterprises, contains similar provisions.

e. IAS 25 provides that enterprises that do not distinguish between current and long-term investments in their balance sheets nevertheless make a distinction for measurement purposes and determine the carrying amount for investments in accordance with the provisions of IAS 25 (which prescribes different treatments for the determination of the carrying values of short-term investments vis-à-vis long-term investments).

   IAS 30 specifically requires that a bank disclose the market value of investments in dealing securities and marketable investment securities if these values are different from the carrying amounts in the financial statements. It is important to note that investments in dealing securities are considered as short-term investments, since they are acquired and held with the intention of reselling. On the other hand, even though they are marketable, marketable investment securities are considered long-term investments since they are acquired and held for yield or capital growth purposes and are usually held to maturity (this is required not only by IAS 25 but even by IAS 30).

Example

ABC Banking Corporation
Balance Sheet
As at December 31, 19X2 and 19X1

	19X2	*19X1*
Assets		
Cash and balances with central bank	$ 480,000	$ 370,000
Trading investments	364,000	26,000
Funds under management	40,000	28,000
Deposits with banks	3,685,000	2,990,000
Loans and advances, net	8,286,000	6,786,000
Long-term investments	358,000	283,000
Property and equipment, net	90,000	89,000
Other assets	55,000	44,000
Total assets	$13,358,000	$10,616,000
Liabilities and Shareholders' Equity		
Liabilities:		
Due to banks	$ 2,187,000	$ 998,000
Customer deposits	8,040,000	6,536,000
Long-term loan from government	1,300,000	1,380,000
Other liabilities	108,000	96,000
Total liabilities	$11,635,000	$8,930,000
Shareholders' Equity:		
Share capital	$ 1,250,000	$ 1,250,000
Statutory reserve	73,000	60,000
Contingency reserve	29,000	12,000
General reserve	325,000	325,000
Retained earnings	46,000	39,000
Total shareholders' equity	$ 1,723,000	$ 1,686,000
Total liabilities and shareholders' equity	$13,358,000	$10,616,000
Commitments and contingent liabilities	$15,300,000	$12,100,000

Cash Flow Statement for a Financial Institution (Including a Bank)

Cash flow statements are an integral part of financial statements. Every enterprise is required to present a cash flow statement in accordance with the provisions of IAS 7 for financial statements covering periods beginning on or after January 1, 1994.

Although the general requirements of IAS 7 are common to all enterprises, the standard does contain special provisions that are applicable only to financial institutions. These specific provisions deal with reporting of certain cash flows on a "net basis." The following cash flows are to be reported on a net basis:

1. Cash receipts and payments on behalf of customers when the cash flows reflect the activities of the customer rather than those of the enterprise; the standard refers to "the accepting and repayment of demand deposits of a bank"
2. Cash receipts and payments for the acceptance and repayment of deposits with a fixed maturity date
3. The placement of deposits with and withdrawal of deposits from other financial institutions
4. Cash advances and loans made to customers and the repayment of those advances and loans

The appendix to IAS 7 (see the discussion below) illustrates the application of the standard to financial institutions preparing cash flow statements under the direct method (for a more detailed discussion of cash flow statements, see Chapter 4).

Example of cash flow statement for banks

Neighborhood Bank
Statement of Cash Flows
For the Year Ended December 31, 1996

Cash flows from operating activities:		
Interest and commission receipts	$28,447	
Interest payments	(23,463)	
Recoveries on loans previously written off	237	
Cash payments to employees and suppliers	(997)	
Operating profit before changes in operating assets	4,224	
(Increase) decrease in operating assets:		
Short-term funds	(650)	
Deposits held for regulatory or monetary control purposes	234	
Funds advanced to customers	(288)	
Net increase in credit card receivables	(360)	
Other short-term negotiable securities	(120)	
Increase (decrease) in operating liabilities:		
Deposits from customers	600	
Negotiable certificates of deposit	(200)	
Net cash from operating activities before income tax	3,440	
Income taxes paid	(100)	
Net cash from operating activities		$3,340

Cash flows from investing activities:		
Disposal of subsidiary Y	50	
Dividends received	200	
Interest received	300	
Proceeds from sales of nondealing securities	1,200	
Purchase of nondealing securities	(600)	
Purchase of property, plant, and equipment	(500)	
Net cash from investing activities		650
Cash flows from financing activities:		
Issue of loan capital	1,000	
Issue of preference shares by subsidiary undertaking	800	
Repayment of long-term borrowings	(200)	
Net decrease in other borrowings	(1,000)	
Dividends paid	(400)	
Net cash from financing activities		200
Effects of exchange rate changes on cash and cash equivalents		600
Net increase in cash and cash equivalents		4,790
Cash and cash equivalents at beginning of period		4,050
Cash and cash equivalents at end of period		$8,840

Disclosure Requirements for Banks and Similar Institutions

Contingencies and commitments including off-balance-sheet items. Contingencies represent conditions or situations, the ultimate outcome of which will be determined by future events which themselves may or may not occur. Accounting for and disclosure of contingencies has been addressed by IAS 10. Liabilities of life insurance companies arising from insurance policies issued by them and other entities, such as retirement benefit plans, have been specifically excluded from the scope of IAS 10. However, contingencies and events occurring after the balance sheet date relating to the banking industry are required to be disclosed in accordance with the provisions of this standard since it has not specifically been excluded from the purview of the standard. This is further reinforced by IAS 30, which makes it mandatory for banks to disclose certain contingencies and commitments dealt with by IAS 10. The disclosures required in this regard are the following:

1. The nature and amount of commitments to extend credit that are irrevocable because they cannot be withdrawn at the discretion of the bank without incurring significant penalty or expenses
2. The nature and amount of contingencies and commitments arising from off-balance-sheet items, including those relating to

a. Direct credit substitutes, which include general guarantees of indebtedness, bank acceptances, and standby letters of credit, which serve as financial backup for loans and securities
b. Transaction-related contingencies, which include performance bonds, bid bonds, warranties, and standby letters of credit related to particular transactions
c. Trade-related contingencies, which are self-liquidating and short-term trade-related contingencies arising from the movement of goods, such as documentary credit wherein the underlying goods are used as security for the bank credit; sometimes referred to as trust receipts, or simply as TR
d. Sales and repurchase agreements that are not reflected or recognized on the bank's balance sheet
e. Interest and foreign exchange rate related items, which include items such as options, futures, and swaps
f. Other commitments, including other off-balance-sheet items such as revolving underwriting facilities and note issuance facilities

It is important for the users of the bank's financial statements to be cognizant about the contingencies and irrevocable commitments because these may have an effect in the future on the liquidity and solvency of the bank. For instance, undrawn facilities, to which the bank is irrevocably committed, could serve as a good example of what could happen to a bank's liquidity position if a majority of the customers utilize them at the same time, say, when there is a sudden shortage of funds in the market, due to economic reasons or otherwise. Thus, disclosing such irrevocable commitments and contingencies, in the footnotes or elsewhere, is of paramount importance to the user of the bank's financial statements.

Also, off-balance-sheet items, such as letters of credit (LC), guarantees, acceptances, and so on, constitute an important part of the bank's business and thus should be disclosed in the financial statements, since without knowing about the magnitude of such items, a fair evaluation of the bank's financial position is not possible (mostly because it adds significantly to the level of business risk the bank is exposed to at any given point of time).

Certain items which are typically not included in the balance sheet are commonly referred to as memoranda accounts, and less frequently are called contra items. These are often interrelated items which are both contingent assets and contingent liabilities, such as bills held for collection for customers, which if and when collected will in turn be remitted to the customer and not retained by the bank. The logic is that since the asset and liability both have contingent aspects, and since the bank is effectively only acting as an agent on behalf of a customer, it is valid to exclude both elements from the statement of financial condition. The existence of such items, however, generally must be disclosed even if not formally recognized.

Example of disclosure of contingencies and commitments

	19X2	*19X1*
At December 31,19X2 and 19X1 the contingent liabilities and commitments were the following (in 000s of US dollars):		
Letters of credit	$10,000	$ 9,000
Guarantees	11,000	8,000
Acceptances	12,000	11,000
Forward foreign exchange commitments	13,000	12,000
Commitments under undrawn lines of credit	15,000	12,000
	$61,000	$52,000

Maturities of Assets and Liabilities

Information about maturities of assets and liabilities is the most important disclosures required of banks, since it gives users a concise picture of the bank's liquidity. Well managed banks typically exhibit closely aligned maturities of assets, such as loans and investments, and liabilities, such as time deposits. To the extent these are mismatched, it not only raises a liquidity (or even solvency) question, but also in periods of changing interest rates it places the bank at risk of having its normal "spread" (the difference between interest earned and interest paid) become diminished or turn negative. Since even an otherwise healthy institution, having positive net worth, can have mismatches in some of the maturities, potential problems are identified through the schedule of asset and liability maturities which would not otherwise be apparent from the financial statements.

Maturity groupings applied to assets and liabilities differ from bank to bank, and IAS 30 does not prescribe the periods but only gives examples of periods that are used in practice, as follows:

1. Up to 1 month
2. From 1 month to 3 months
3. From 3 months to 1 year
4. From 1 year to 5 years
5. From 5 years and above

It is imperative that the maturity periods adopted by a bank should be the same for assets and liabilities. This ensures that the maturities are matched and brings to light dependency, if any, on other sources of liquidity.

Maturities could be expressed in more than one way, for instance, by remaining period to the repayment date or by the original period to the repayment date. IAS 30 recommends that the maturity analysis of assets and liabilities be presented by the remaining period to the repayment date, as this provides the best basis to evaluate the liquidity of the bank.

In some countries time deposits could be withdrawn even on demand, and advances given by the bank may be repayable on demand, in which case, maturities according to the contractual dates should be used for the purposes of this analysis since it reflects the liquidity risks attaching to the bank's assets and liabilities.

Certain assets do not have a contractual maturity date. In all such cases the period in which these assets are assumed to mature is usually taken to be the expected date on which the assets will be realized. For instance, in case of fixed assets that have no maturity date as such, as in the case of a certificate of deposit, the authors are of the opinion that their remaining useful lives as of the balance sheet date could be used as a measure of the maturity profile of these assets.

Example of disclosure of maturities of assets and liabilities

The maturity profile of assets and liabilities at December 31, 19XX was as follows:

	($ in thousands)			
	Up to 3 months	*3 months to 1 year*	*1 year to 5 years*	*Over 5 years*
Assets				
Cash and short-term funds	$ 10,157	$ --	$ --	$ --
Deposits with banks	298,771	--	--	--
Marketable securities	101,013	--	--	--
Accounts receivable	113,109	76,173	--	--
Trading investments	121,243	148,456	14,582	--
Accrued interest and other assets	9,919	18,681	2,150	--
Investments	--	66,160	300,099	--
Fixed assets	--	--	--	57,997
Total assets	$654,212	$309,470	$316,831	$57,997
Liabilities				
Deposits from banks	$105,492	$18,400	$ --	$ --
Other deposits	36,062	1,033	130,127	--
Proposed dividend	15,000	--	--	--
Accrued interest and other payable	38,882	9,952	30,865	--
Medium-term facilities	--	250,000	330,000	--
Total liabilities	$195,436	$279,385	$490,992	$ --

Concentration of Assets, Liabilities and Off-Balance-Sheet Items

Banks are required to disclose any significant concentrations of its assets, liabilities, and off-balance-sheet items. Such disclosures are a means of identification of potential risks, if any, that are inherent in the realization of the assets and liabilities (the funds available) to the bank.

Concentration of assets, liabilities, and off-balance-sheet items could be disclosed in the following ways:

1. By geographical areas such as individual countries, group of countries, or regions within a country
2. By customer groups such as governments, public authorities, and commercial enterprises
3. By industry sectors such as real estate, manufacturing, retail, and financial

4. Other concentrations of risk that are appropriate in the circumstances of the bank

Example of disclosure of concentration of assets, liabilities, and off-balance-sheet items

	($ in thousands)					
	19X2			19X1		
	Assets	Liabilities	Off-balance-sheet	Assets	Liabilities	Off-balance-sheet
Geographical region						
North America	$ 679,829	$ 26,103	$ 57,479	$ 681,958	$ 86,267	$ 146,099
Europe	662,259	778,470	621,316	574,699	662,690	1,117,110
Middle East	93,003	184,485	114,984	71,328	216,486	98,236
Other	279	--	--	10,525	370	198,138
Total	$1,395,370	$989,058	$793,779	$1,338,510	$965,813	$1,559,583
Industry sector						
Banking and finance	$ 314,563	$866,483	$715,141	$ 482,874	$846,513	$1,484,248
Food processing	40,535	--	--	40,777	--	--
Luxury merchandise	336,966	3,797	11,811	224,829	--	1,649
Retail	356,879	--	--	315,554	--	--
Real estate	96,743	--	63,871	68,744	--	72,947
Manufacturing and services	153,151	--	--	124,366	--	--
Other	96,533	118,779	2,956	81,366	119,300	739
Total	$1,395,370	$989,058	$793,779	$1,338,510	$965,813	$1,559,583

Losses on Loans and Advances

Loans and advances to customers may sometimes become uncollectable, and in those circumstances the bank would have to suffer losses on loans, advances, and other credit facilities. The amount of losses that are specifically identified and the potential losses not specifically identified should both be recognized as expenses and deducted from the carrying amount of the loans and advances. The assessment of these losses is dependent on management judgment and it is essential that it should be applied consistently from one period to another. Any amounts set aside in excess of the foregoing provision for losses on loans and advances, say, if required by local circumstances or legislation, should be treated as an appropriation of retained earnings and is not to be included in the determination of net profit or loss for the period. Similarly, any credits resulting in the reduction of such amounts are to be credited to retained earnings.

A number of disclosure requirements are prescribed by IAS 30 in this regard, as summarized below.

1. The accounting policy describing the basis on which uncollectable loans and advances are recognized as an expense and written off.

2. Details of movements in the provision for losses on loans and advances during the period: These details should include the amount recognized as an expense in the period on account of losses on loans and advances, the amount charged in the period for loans and advances written off, and the amount credited in the period resulting from the recovery of the amounts previously written off.
3. The aggregate amount of the provision for losses on loans and advances at the balance sheet date.
4. The aggregate amount included in the balance sheet as loans and advances on which no interest has been accrued (referred to in some countries as "interest in suspense" or "reserved interest") and the basis used to determine the carrying amount of such loans and advances.

Example of disclosure of loans and advances

	19X2	*19X1*
Balance, beginning of the year	$500,000	$400,000
Provision during the year--against specific advances	50,000	50,000
Provision during the year--against potential losses	20,000	70,000
Written off during the year	(10,000)	(20,000)
Balance, end of the year	$560,000	$500,000

Example of disclosure of interest in suspense

	19X2	*19X1*
Loans and advances on which interest is not taken to income	$2,000,000	$1,500,000
Movements in interest in suspense:		
Balance, beginning of year	$ 500,000	$ 490,000
Reserved during the year	50,000	30,000
Released during the year	(10,000)	(20,000)
Balance, end of year	$ 540,000	$ 500,000

Related Party Transactions

Parties are considered to be related if one has the ability to control the other or exercise significant influence over the other in making financial and operating decisions. IAS 24 requires that related-party transactions be disclosed. When a bank has entered into transactions with related parties, the nature of the relationship (say, director, shareholder, etc.), the type of transaction (loans and advances or off-balance-sheet financing, etc.), and the elements of the transaction should be disclosed. The elements that are to be disclosed include the bank's lend-ing policy to related parties and, in respect of related party transactions, the amount included in or the proportion of

1. Each of loans and advances, deposits and acceptances, and promissory notes; disclosures may include the aggregate amounts outstanding at the beginning and end of the year as well as changes in these accounts during the year
2. Each of the principal types of income, interest expense, and commissions paid
3. The amount of the expense recognized in the period for the losses on loans and advances and the amount of the provision at the balance sheet date
4. Irrevocable commitments and contingencies and commitments from off-balance-sheet items

Example of related party disclosures

Note 5: Related Party Transactions. The bank has entered into transactions in the ordinary course of business with certain related parties, such as shareholders holding more than 20% equity interest in the bank and with certain directors of the bank.

At December 31, 19X2 and 19X1 the following balances were outstanding in the aggregate in relation to those related party transactions:

	19X2	*19X1*
Loans and advances	2,000,000	1,800,000
Customer deposits	750,000	600,000
Guarantees	3,000,000	1,500,000

For the years ended December 31, 19X2 and 19X1, the following income and expense items are included in the aggregate amounts arising from the above-related transactions:

	19X2	*19X1*
Interest income	300,000	270,000
Interest expense	40,000	35,000
Commissions	60,000	30,000

Disclosure of General Banking Risks

Based on local legislation or circumstances, a bank may need to set aside a certain amount each year for general banking risks, including future losses or other unforeseeable risks, in addition to the provision for losses on loans and advances explained earlier. The bank may also be required to earmark a certain amount each year as a contingency reserve, over and above the amounts accrued under IAS 10. All such amounts set aside should be treated as appropriations of retained earnings, and any credits resulting from the reduction of such amounts should be returned directly to retained earnings and not included in determination of net income or loss for the year.

Disclosure of Assets Pledged as Security

If the bank is required by law or national custom to pledge assets as security to support certain deposits or other liabilities, the bank should then disclose the aggregate amount of secured liabilities and the nature and carrying amount of the assets pledged as security.

Disclosure of Trust Activities

If a bank is holding in trust, or in any other fiduciary capacity, assets belonging to others, those assets should not be included on the bank's financial statements since they are being held on behalf of third parties such as trusts and retirement funds. If a bank is engaged in significant trust activities, this deserves disclosure of the fact and an indication of the extent of those trust activities. Such disclosure will take care of any potential liability in case the bank fails in its fiduciary capacity. The safe custody services that banks offer are not part of these trust activities.

Comprehensive example of bank financial statements*

ABC Banking Corporation
Balance Sheet
As at 31 December 19X2

		19X2	*19X1*
Assets	*Note*	*(US $000s)*	*(US $000s)*
Cash and balances with central banks		$ 106,792	$ 97,706
Treasury bills	3	487,424	954,030
Deposits and due from banks		749,049	615,790
Loans, advances and overdrafts	4	2,057,230	1,836,814
Investments	5	607,068	402,129
Investment in associated companies	6	96,320	93,219
Interest receivable and other assets	7	48,818	53,480
Government bonds		375,375	389,004
Premises and equipment		83,244	82,929
Total assets		$4,611,320	$4,525,101

		19X2	*19X1*
Liabilities and shareholders' equity			
Liabilities	*Note*	*(US $000s)*	*(US $000s)*
Deposits and due to banks and other financial instructions		$ 690,837	$ 595,616
Customers' current savings and other deposits		3,267,663	3,305,946
Interest payable and other liabilities	8	98,070	79,443
Proposed dividend		39,830	39,830
Total liabilities		$4,096,400	$4,020,835

* *In order to fully comply with all International Accounting Standards certain other disclosures may need to be added to these financial statements. This example is meant to illustrate certain common disclosures seen in published financial statements of banks. For full compliance with IAS, refer to earlier parts of this chapter and other chapters where applicable.*

Shareholders' equity			
Share capital	9	$ 398,342	$ 398,342
Statutory reserve	10	48,958	43,708
General reserve	10	42,070	36,820
Retained earnings		25,550	25,396
Total shareholders' equity		514,920	504,266
Total liabilities and shareholders' equity		$4,611,320	$4,525,101

Notes 1 to 19 form an integral part of these financial statements.

ABC Banking Corporation
Statement of Income and Retained Earnings
For the Year Ended 31 December 19X2

Operating income	Note	*19X2* (*US $000s*)	*19X1* (*US $000s*)
Interest income		$ 250,579	$ 238,350
Interest expense		182,266	163,940
Net interest income		$ 68,313	$ 74,410
Other operating income	12	38,003	43,316
Income from associated companies		7,000	6,510
Total operating income		$ 113,316	$ 124,236
Operating expenses			
Staff costs		$ 43,071	$ 39,830
Other operating expenses		33,369	32,970
Total operating expenses		$ 76,440	$ 72,800
		$ 36,876	$ 51,436
Profit before provisions and recoveries			
Net (provisions) and recoveries:			
Relating to loans, advances, and overdrafts		$ 25,200	$ 22,183
Relating to the value of investments	5	(1,232)	1,407
Relating to other contingencies		(2,723)	(175)
Profit before taxation		$ 58,121	$ 74,851
Taxation--foreign branch		(5,579)	(4,249)
Profit for the year		$ 52,542	$ 70,602
Retained earnings at beginning of the year		$ 25,396	$ 34,440
Translation adjustment	11	(553)	602
		$ 77,385	$ 105,644

Appropriations:			
Transfer to statutory reserve	10	(5,250)	(7,063)
Transfer to general reserve	10	(5,250)	(31,500)
Proposed dividend		(39,830)	(39,830)
Directors' remuneration		(455)	(455)
Donations		(1,050)	(1,400)
Retained earnings at end of the year		$ 25,550	$ 25,396

Notes 1 to 19 form an integral part of these financial statements.

ABC Banking Corporation
Statement of Cash Flows
For the Year Ended December 31, 19X2

Cash flows from operating activities	Note	*19X2 (US $000s)*	*19X1 (US $000s)*
Profit before taxation		$ 58,121	$ 74,851
Adjustment for:			
Dividend income		(6,608)	(5,684)
Net (provisions) recoveries:			
Relating to loans, advances, and overdrafts		(25,200)	(22,183)
Relating to the value of investments		1,232	(1,407)
Relating to other contingencies		2,723	175
Income from associated companies		(7,000)	(6,510)
Depreciation		10,010	9,905
Net gains on investments		(7,112)	(16,884)
(Increase) decrease in operating assets:			
Treasury bills		460,201	(56,021)
Deposits and due from banks		106,358	(167,979)
Loans, advances, and overdrafts		(192,668)	(282,086)
Government bonds		16,709	--
Interest receivable and other assets		4,662	14,210
Increase (decrease) in operating liabilities:			
Deposits and due to banks and other financial institutions		95,221	(8,806)
Customers' current savings and other deposits		(38,283)	470,512
Interest payable and other liabilities		8,771	(917)
Taxation of foreign branch		(5,579)	(4,249)
Net cash flow from operating activities		$ 481,558	$ (3,073)

Cash flows from investing activities	Note	19X2 (US $000s)	19X1 (US $000s)
Guarantee fund bonds redeemed		$ --	$ 262,857
Purchase of investments		(401,366)	(65,198)
Maturities and redemptions of investments		202,307	139,566
Purchase of shares in associated companies		(896)	(28,595)
Dividends from associated companies		4,795	3,374
Purchase of premises and equipment		(12,208)	(6,615)
Sale proceeds from disposal of premises and equipment		1,883	--
Dividend received		6,608	5,684
Net cash flow from investing activities		$ (198,877)	$ 311,073
Cash flows from financing activities			
Dividends paid		(39,830)	--
Effect of exchange rate changes		(553)	602
Net increase in cash and cash equivalents		242,298	308,602
Cash and cash equipments at beginning of the year	18	1,022,476	713,874
Cash and cash equivalents at end of the year	19	$1,264,774	$1,022,476

Notes 1 to 19 form an integral part of these financial statements.

ABC Banking Corporation
Notes to the Financial Statements
For the Year Ended December 31, 19X2

Note 1: Activities. The ABC Banking Corporation, a public share holding company, was incorporated in XXX by a government decree. The bank operates under a banking license issued by the Central Bank of XXX. The overseas branches operate under the laws of their respective countries.

Note 2: Summary of Significant Accounting Policies. The financial statements have been prepared in accordance with international accounting standards.* The significant accounting policies adopted are as follows:

a. **Accounting convention.** The financial statements are prepared under the historical cost convention.
b. **Foreign currencies**. Assets and liabilities in foreign currency at the date of the balance sheet are translated at market rates of exchange prevailing at the year end. Foreign exchange gains and losses arising from the translation of the net investment in foreign branches and the foreign associate of the bank are taken directly to shareholders' funds. Other translation gains or losses are credited to or charged against income. Gains and losses arising from the difference be-

* *In the authors' opinion, in order to fully comply with IAS certain other disclosures may need to be added to these financial statements. (Please refer to the authors' comments at the beginning of this example.)*

tween spot and forward rates on forward foreign exchange contracts which are entered into in connection with loans and deposits are credited to or charged against income over the periods of the related contracts. Other forward foreign exchange contracts are translated at rates of exchange prevailing at year end, and the resultant gains and losses are taken to income.

c. **Revenue recognition**. Interest receivable and payable are recognized on a time proportion basis taking account of the principal outstanding and the rate applicable. Loan interest that is 90 days or more overdue is excluded from income until received in cash. Fees receivable and payable are recognized when earned. Premiums and discounts on dated bonds, bills and other securities are amortized on a straight-line basis to the dates of maturity.
d. **Investments**. Investments acquired with the intention of being held for trading purposes are stated at market value. Unrealized gains and losses are taken to the statement of income. Investments held with the intention of being retained until maturity are stated at cost, adjusted for any premium or discount amortized from date of purchase to date of maturity on a straight-line basis. Long-term investments are stated at cost with reduction for any decline other than temporary in their value.
e. **Investment in associated companies**. Associated companies are companies in which the bank has a long-term investment comprising an interest of not less than 20% in the voting capital and over which it exerts significant influence. Investment in associated companies is accounted for using the equity method.
f. **Provision for loans, advances, and overdrafts**. Specific and general provisions for loans, advances, and overdrafts are made on the basis of a continuing appraisal of the lending portfolio have regard to the bank's previous experience and current economic conditions. The specific element relates to identified risk advances, whereas the general element relates to risks that are likely to be present in any portfolio of bank advances but which have not yet been specifically identified. Loans and advances are stated net of provisions.
g. **Government bonds**. Government bonds are stated at cost.
h. **Depreciation**. Freehold land is not depreciated. Leasehold premises are depreciated by equal annual installments over the remaining periods of the respective leases. All other fixed assets are depreciated over their estimated useful lives on a straight-line basis.
i. **Employees' end-of-service benefits**. Provision is made for amounts payable under the relevant labor laws applicable to employees' accumulated periods of service at the date of the statement of condition.
j. **Fiduciary assets**. Assets held in trust or in a fiduciary capacity are not included in these financial statements.

Note 3: Treasury bills. These are short-term treasury bills issued by the governments of XXX.

Note 4: Loans, Advances, and Overdrafts.

a. The composition of the loans, advances, and overdrafts portfolio, net of provisions, is as follows:

	19X2 *(US $000s)*	*19X1* *(US $000s)*
Banks and other financial institutions	$ 428,330	$ 345,345
Others	1,628,900	1,491,329
	$2,057,230	$1,836,674

b. Provisions against loans, advances, and overdrafts, calculated in accordance with the basis set out in Note 2f., are as follows:

	19X2 *(US $000s)*	*19X1* *(US $000s)*
Balance at beginning of the year	$ 566,552	$ 669,151
Recoveries credited to income	(44,345)	(61,089)
Charge against income	19,145	38,906
Amounts written off	(33,915)	(81,158)
Relating to debt relief scheme	30,695	--
Amount ceded to central bank	(6,573)	--
Other movements	3,927	742
Balance at end of year	$ 535,486	$ 566,552

Other movements include exchange adjustments relating to loans, advances, and overdrafts denominated in foreign currencies and transfers from interest suspense account.

c. Loans, advances, and overdrafts (net of provisions against principal and interest) on which interest is not being accrued amount to $16,384,000 (19X1: $16,700,000).

Note 5: Investments.

	19X2 *(US $000s)*	*19X1* *(US $000s)*
Quoted securities	$ 121,345	$ 116,403
Quoted bonds	178,073	127,043
Unquoted securities	56,966	77,518
Treasury bonds	154,042	--
Managed funds	108,738	92,029
Other investments	2,163	2,163
	$ 621,327	$ 415,156
Less: Provision for reduction in value	14,259	13,027
	$ 607,068	$ 402,129

The market value of quoted securities and bonds as of December 31, 19X2 amounted to $48,290,000 (19X1: $42,095,000).

Note 6: Investment in Associated Companies.

	19X2		*19X1*	
	% of interest held	*(US $000s)*	*% of interest held*	*(US $000s)*
XXX Inc.	49.00	$70,042	49.00	$67,956
National Commercial Facilities Co. PSC	20.25	25,382	20.25	25,263
Other		896		--
		$96,320		$93,219

Note 7: Interest Receivable and Other Assets.

	19X2 (US $000s)	*19X1 (US $000s)*
Interest receivable	$ 28,105	$ 28,889
Acquired assets pending sale	7,595	14,826
Other	13,118	9,765
	$ 48,818	$ 53,480

Note 8: Interest Payable and Other Liabilities.

	19X2 (US $000s)	*19X1 (US $000s)*
Interest payable	$ 26,446	$ 33,327
Accrued expenses	3,514	2,618
Other	68,110	43,498
	$ 98,070	$ 79,443

Note 9: Share Capital.

Authorized:		
700,000,000 shares of $1 each	700,000	700,000
Issued and fully paid:		
398,341,750 shares of $1 each	398,342	398,342

Note 10: Reserves.

	Note	*Statutory reserve (US $000s)*	*General reserve (US $000s)*
a. Balance at beginning of the year	10b.	$ 43,708	$ 36,820
Transfers for the year		5,250	5,250
Balance at end of the year		$ 48,958	$ 42,070

b. Transfers for the year

(1) **Statutory reserve.** As required by the Commercial Companies Law, 10% of the profit for the year has been transferred to statutory reserve. The bank may resolve to discontinue such annual transfers when the reserve is equal to 25% of the issued share capital. The reserve cannot be utilized for the purpose of distribution except in such circumstances as stipulated in the Commercial Companies Law.

(2) **General reserve**. The transfer to general reserve has been made in accordance with the provisions of the bank's articles of association and underlines the shareholders' commitment to enhance the strong equity base of the bank.

Note 11: Translation Adjustment. These arise from foreign exchange gains and losses relating to the investment in foreign branches and the foreign associate of the bank. Retained earnings are stated net of accumulated foreign currency translation losses of US $1,140,000 (19X1: US $1,061,000).

Note 12: Other Operating Income.

	19X2 (US $000s)	*19X1 (US $000s)*
Dividend income	$ 6,608	$ 5,684
Fees and commissions	16,604	11,431
(Losses) gains on managed funds	(1,876)	15,526
Net gains on trading investments	8,988	1,358
Profit on foreign exchange	3,647	6,013
Other income	4,032	3,304
	$38,003	$43,316

Note 13: Related Party Transactions. Certain related parties (principally associated companies and directors of the bank, their families, and companies of which they are principal owners) were customers of the bank in the ordinary course of business. Facilities in the personal names of the directors are fully collateralized. The transactions with these parties were made on substantially the same terms, including interest rates, as those prevailing at the same time for comparable transactions with unrelated parties and did not involve more than a normal amount of risk.

	19X2		*19X1*	
	Associated companies (US $000s)	*Other (US $000s)*	*Associated companies (US $000s)*	*Other (US $000s)*
Loan, advances, and overdrafts	23,982	48,468	21,350	49,182
Direct credit substitutes	48,811	8,183	18,305	10,535
Deposits	399	4,284	91	1,239

Note 14: Maturities of Assets and Liabilities. The maturity profile of the assets and liabilities as of December 31 was as follows:

	19X2		*19X1*	
	Assets (US $000s)	*Liabilities (US $000s)*	*Assets (US $000s)*	*Liabilities (US $000s)*
Call and maturing within 1 year	$2,590,434	$3,952,515	$2,772,644	$3,853,829
From 1 year to 3 years	738,199	86,954	488,285	150,185
Over 3 years	1,282,687	56,931	1,264,172	16,821
	$4,611,320	$4,096,400	$4,525,101	$4,020,835

Note 15: Concentration of Assets, Liabilities, and Off-balance-sheet Items.

19X2

	Assets (US $000s)	*Liabilities (US $000s)*	*Off-balance-sheet items (US $000s)*
Geographic region			
South America	$3,376,331	$3,868,487	$ 458,136
Asia	99,967	2,093	37,982
Africa	293,524	93,205	80,409
Australia	747,159	112,994	133,238
Others	94,339	19,621	26,040
	$4,611,320	$4,096,400	$ 735,805
Industry sector			
Trading and manufacturing	$ 539,224	$ 410,032	$ 180,936
Banks and financial institutions	1,550,787	506,905	313,152
Construction and real estate	128,380	22,967	117,649
Others	2,392,929	3,156,496	124,068
	$4,611,320	$4,096,400	$ 735,805

19X1

	Assets (US $000s)	*Liabilities (US $000s)*	*Off-balance-sheet items (US $000s)*
Geographic region			
South America	$3,482,913	$3,698,800	$ 380,716
Asia	124,873	31,423	91,378
Africa	221,732	66,983	95,242
Australia	597,016	222,516	35,938
Others	98,567	1,113	7,091
	$4,525,101	$4,020,835	$ 610,365
Industry sector			
Trading and manufacturing	$ 523,614	$ 121,926	$ 99,960
Banks and financial institutions	1,317,421	800,828	233,275
Construction and real estate	116,494	10,899	136,059
Others	2,567,572	3,087,182	141,071
	$4,525,101	$4,020,835	$ 610,365

Note 16: Segmental Information. The bank's operating results arise primarily from the activities of commercial and retail banking from its operations based in South America.

Note 17: Contingent Liabilities and Commitments. The bank has exposure in the normal course of business arising from transactions in interest rate swaps and forward rate agreements. In addition, the bank has the following contingent liabilities and commitments:

	19X2 (US \$000s)	*19X1 (US \$000s)*
Contingent liabilities		
Letters of credit	\$ 68,404	\$ 100,583
Guarantees	184,331	188,783
Acceptances	27,909	18,781
	\$ 280,644	\$ 308,147
Commitments		
Undrawn loan commitments	\$ 72,555	\$ 60,795
Forward foreign exchange contracts	382,431	241,087
Other commitments	175	336
	\$ 455,161	\$ 302,218
	\$ 735,805	\$ 610,365

The bank has irrevocably guaranteed to the holders of units in a guaranteed fund, on the maturity date, the return of either US \$1,000 per unit or the highest net asset value per unit as of the end of three annual dates.

A counter guarantee in favor of the bank has been issued by Bank International, South America.

Note 18: Cash Flow Reconciliation. Reconciliation of net increase in cash and cash equivalents.

	19X2 (US \$000s)	*19X1 (US \$000s)*	*Change (US \$000s)*
Cash and balance with central banks	\$ 106,792	\$ 97,706	\$ 9,086
Deposits and due from banks	687,428	447,811	239,617
Treasury bills	470,554	476,959	(6,405)
Cash and cash equivalents	\$1,264,774	\$1,022,476	\$ 242,298

Note 19: Components of Cash and Cash Equivalents. Cash and cash equivalents include cash on hand, amounts held by other banks and financial institutions, and treasury bills with maturities of 3 months or less.

AGRICULTURE

PERSPECTIVE AND ISSUES

The IASC has been primarily occupied with completion of the "core set of standards" which it agreed to finish by mid-1998, as part of its negotiated agreement which, hopefully, will culminate in IAS becoming acceptable for cross-border securities registrations before the end of the decade. At the same time, however, the IASC has recognized the need for the development of some specialized industry accounting and disclosure standards, as the existence of IAS 30 demonstrates. Given the importance of IAS to the nations of the developing world, the economies of which are often more dependent upon agriculture than are those of the major industrial nations, it is perhaps not surprising that the IASC produced a draft statement of principles on agriculture in late 1996. While this DSOP has garnered its share of criticism, the IASC has recently indicated its intention to move forward on this project, with only minor revisions. Accordingly, the following paragraphs will set forth the basic conclusions expressed in the agriculture DSOP.

Background

Traditionally, national and international accounting standard setters have ignored or deliberately excluded agriculture from the coverage of accounting pronouncements. It is generally acknowledged that the most highly developed sets of accounting standards are those of the US and the UK, arguably with certain other European nations perhaps having accounting standards which are almost as fully matured. Not coincidentally, then, these nations, the economies of which are far less dependent upon agriculture than are many less developed nations of the world, have had little interest in establishing accounting rules applicable to agriculture. This lack of interest has been abetted by the fact that much of agriculture is controlled by closely held or family held businesses, with few if any outside owners who might have demanded formal financial statements prepared in accordance with agreed-upon accounting principles. Furthermore, grantors of farm credit have historically looked to the character of the borrower, usually a long-time resident with deep roots in the community, rather than to financial statements. For these and other reasons, there has been little need and less inclination to develop financial reporting for agriculture enterprises.

In the realm of international accounting standards, most of the existing standards which logically could have addressed agricultural issues (IAS 2 on inventories, IAS 4 on depreciation, IAS 16 on plant, property, and equipment, and IAS 18 on revenue recognition) have deliberately excluded most or all agriculture-related applications. A review of published financial statements for agriculture related enterprises, however, shows the result of this neglect. A wide range of methods and principles are applied to such businesses as forest products, livestock and grain production. For example, some companies account for timberlands at original cost, charging depreciation only to the extent of net harvesting, with reforestation costs charged to expense as incurred; others capitalize reforestation costs and even carrying costs, and charge depletion on a units of production basis; and yet others value forest lands at net present value of expected future cash flows.

The exclusion of agriculture from most established accounting and financial reporting rules is understood in the context of the unique features of the industry: biological transformations (growth, procreation, production, degeneration) which alter the very substance of the biological assets; the wide variety of characteristics of the living assets which challenge traditional classification schemes; the nature of management functions in the industry; and the predominance of small, closely held ownership. On the other hand, in many nations agriculture is a major industry, ranging up to 50% of gross national product of some nations (as much as 58% in New Zealand, in fact), and logic would suggest that comprehensive systems of financial reporting for business enterprises cannot be deemed complete while excluding so large a segment of the economy.

Thus, the IASC has concluded that excluding agriculture from the scope of IAS is not appropriate, but also accepts the need for a relatively simple, uniform and coherent set of principles applicable to this industry grouping. It believes that extending certain modifications to the historical cost model, which have already been applied by existing IAS (e.g., to plant and equipment and to investments), offers the best solution to this problem. Finally, any new standard will apply only to biological assets, as those are the aspects of agriculture which have unique characteristics; the accounting for assets such as inventories and plant and equipment will be guided by existing standards such as IAS 2 and IAS 16.

Defining Agriculture

Agriculture will be defined as the management of the biological transformation of plants and animals to yield produce for consumption or further processing. This will encompass livestock, forestry, annual and perennial cropping, orchards, plantations, and aquiculture. However, pursuits such as fishing, where there is no attempt to manage regeneration of resources, would not be subject to the proposed rules. The DSOP distinguishes among **biological assets**, which are groups or plants or animals held for regenerative and self-generative abilities; **agricultural** produce, which is harvested and thus a non-living product of the biological assets; and **agriculture produce incorporated in further processing** in integrated agribusiness enterprises, that, involving activities which are not unique to agriculture, will be excluded from coverage under the standard.

The DSOP would apply to forests and similar regenerative resources excluded from IAS 16; producers' inventories of livestock, agriculture, and forest products, including those excluded from IAS 2, to the extent they are to be measured at net realizable value; and natural increases in herds and agricultural and forest products excluded from IAS 18. It would also address financial statement presentation and disclosure (the primary province of IAS 1 revised). Furthermore, it would establish that, unless explicit exclusions are provided, international accounting standards do apply to agriculture.

Basic Principles Set Forth in the DSOP

The statement of principles will (when it ultimately evolves into an international accounting standard) apply to all enterprises which undertake agricultural activities. Animals or plants will be recognized as assets when it is probable that the future economic benefits associated with the asset will flow to the entity, and the cost or value to the enterprise can be measured reliably. Most importantly, biological assets are to be measured at each balance sheet date at their fair values.

The departure from historical cost is the most important aspect of the IASC proposal, and one which has generated a good deal of debate already, even though the project has yet to reach the exposure draft stage. While differing income recognition methods would not alter the total income to be recognized over the lifetime of the asset in question, it would perhaps greatly alter the periodic recognition of income, and given the very long lifetimes associated with such assets as dairy herds or field of crops, this divergence could be extreme. For example, a forest may not yield a harvest for the first 30 years of existence, and the use of historical cost-based accounting might show no income (perhaps even a loss) during that entire period, while a fair value-based model would show income each period as the forest nears maturity.

Furthermore, each stage of the biological transformation process is considered to be significant, as each stage (growth, degeneration, procreation, and production) contributes to the amount of expected economic benefits to be derived from the biological assets. Unless a fair value model were used, there would be no explicit recognition (in effect, no matching) of the benefits associated with each of these discrete events. Furthermore, this recognition underlines the need to apply the same measurement concept to each stage in the life cycle of the biological assets; for example, with live weight change, fleece weight change, aging, deaths, lambs born, and wool shorn, in the case of a flock of sheep.

The obvious argument in favor of historical cost-based measures derives from the superior reliability of that mode of measurement. By contrast, superior relevance is the strongest argument for current value measurement schemes. The IASC evaluated various measures, including current cost and net realizable value as well as market value, as alternatives to historical cost, but ultimately identified fair value, which ironically is the one approach not addressed in the IASC's seminal document, the *Framework for the Preparation and Presentation of Financial Statements*, as having the best combination of attributes for the determination of agriculture related earnings. It was particularly influenced by the market context in which agriculture takes place and the transformative characteristics of biological assets, and concluded that fair value would offer the best balance of relevance, reliability, comparability, and understandability.

The IASC also concluded that annual determinations of fair value would be necessary to properly portray the combined impact of nature and financial transactions for any given reporting period. Less frequent measurements were rejected because of the continuous nature of biological transformations, the lack of direct correlation between financial transactions and the different outcomes arising from biological transformation (thus, the former could not serve as surrogate indicators of the latter during "off periods"), the volatilities which often characterize natural and market environments affecting agriculture, and the fact that market-based measures are in fact readily available. The idea of maintaining historical cost as an allowed alternative was similarly rejected, essentially because historical cost is not viewed as meaningful in this context, coupled with concerns about the extreme lack of comparability that would result from the acceptability of two so disparate methodologies.

Determining Fair Values

The primary determinant of fair value would be market value, just as it is for financial instruments having active markets, as set forth in IAS 32. The use of so-called "farm gate" market prices would reflect both the "as is" and "where is" attributes of the biological assets; where farm gate prices are not available, market values would have to be reduced by transaction costs, including transport, to arrive at net market values which would equate to fair values.

For products for which market values might not be readily available, other approaches to fair value determination would have to be employed. This is most likely to be an issue where market values exist but, due to market imperfections, are not deemed to be useful, for example when access to markets is restricted or unduly influenced by temporary monopoly or monopsony conditions, or when no market actually exists as of the balance sheet date. In such circumstances, it might be necessary to refer to such indicators as the most recent market prices for the class of asset at issue, market prices for similar assets (e.g., different varieties of the same crop), sector benchmarks (e.g., relating value of a dairy farm to the kilograms of milk solids or fat produced), net present value of expected future cash flows discounted at a risk-class rate, net realizable values for short-cycle products for which most growth has already occurred, and (last and probably least) historical cost (particularly suited to biological assets which have experienced little transformation thus far).

A practical problem arises when the indirect method of valuation implicitly values both the crop and the land itself. The DSOP indicates that such valuations should be allocated to the different assets to give a better indication of the future economic benefits each will confer. While this may involve added effort, the DSOP concludes that the usefulness of the resulting financial statements will be materially enhanced if this is done.

Recognition of Changes in Biological Assets

The DSOP proposed that the change in carrying amounts for a group of biological assets was to be allocated between changes due to differences in fair value and physical changes due to growth and other natural phenomena. The intent was to have the former, which corresponds to revaluations of plant and equipment assets under the alternative treatment permitted by IAS 16, reported directly in equity, while the latter would be included in current period operating results. However, even if this were conceptually sound, the practical difficulties of allocating such value changes has more recently been appreciated by the IASC, which reportedly will soon issue an exposure draft that calls for both of these value changes to be included in current operations. The DSOP also stipulates that the economic effects of extraordinary items should be separately presented in the income statement (as with other enterprises); distinguishing normal events which inevitably affect agriculture (storms, draught, etc.) from extraordinary ones (severe or extended storms and draughts, etc.) may present a unique challenge in practice, however.

Financial Statement Presentation

The DSOP states that biological assets should be classified as a distinct class of assets, being neither part of current nor noncurrent assets. Since biological assets are defined in the DSOP as those having unlimited life due to the regenerative properties which are not possessed by any other type of assets, it was concluded that aggregation with other traditional categories of assets would be meaningless.

Biological assets are to be further categorized according to class of animal or plant, nature of activities (e.g., being maintained for harvesting or as breeding stock), and the maturity or immaturity for the intended purpose. If the plant or animal is being maintained for consumption (to be harvested, etc.), maturity is gauged by attainment of harvestable specifications. If for bearing purposes, the maturity criterion will be the attainment of sufficient maturity to sustain economic harvests.

The DSOP encourages the use of natural classification of income and expenses in the income statement. Sufficient detail is to be included in the face of the income statement to support an analysis of operating performance.

Finally, a number of additional disclosures are mandated by the agriculture DSOP, including measurement bases used to derive fair values; whether an independent appraiser was utilized; further details about the changes in fair value from the prior period; any restrictions on title and any pledging of biological assets as security for liabilities; commitments for further development or acquisitions of biological assets; specifics about risk management strategies employed by the entity (the use of hedging is widespread; the futures market, now heavily employed to control financial risks, was developed originally for agricultural commodities); and activities which are unsustainable, along with estimated dates of cessation of those activities.

Agricultural Produce

When crops or animals are harvested, they become agricultural produce. The point of transition is the harvest, when the product is detached from the biological asset. Thereafter, the produce is either incapable of biological processes, or is in a state of dormancy (e.g., stored grain). When the goods enter trading activities or production processes within integrated agribusiness complexes, they are no longer produce, but become inventory the accounting for which is to be governed by the existing principles of IAS 2. As written, the DSOP prescribed fair value accounting for agricultural produce, with changes in those values included in current earnings. However, it has been reported that the IASC now is inclined to limit fair value accounting to only biological assets, and this would suggest that the principles of IAS 2 would be extended to agricultural produce as well. The cost basis upon making the transition to agricultural produce status would be the fair value of the biological asset at that point in time.

Agricultural Land

Agricultural land would not be considered a biological asset, and thus the principles espoused in the DSOP for such assets would not apply to land. The requirements of IAS 16, which are applicable to other categories of plant, property, and equipment, would equally apply to agricultural land. The DSOP encourages the use of the allowed alternative method (revaluation), particularly for land-based systems such as orchards, plantations, and forests, where the fair value of the biological asset was determined from net realizable values which included the underlying land. It is also suggested that land be further classified in the balance sheet according to specific uses; alternatively, this information can be conveyed in the notes to the financial statements.

23 ACCOUNTING FOR INFLATION AND HYPERINFLATION

PERSPECTIVE AND ISSUES

The historical cost-based accounting model, employed almost universally for at least the past 60 years, resulted largely from the profession's embracing of the concepts of conservatism (or prudence), realization, and the stable measuring unit following the crash of 1929. Despite the obvious attractiveness of historical cost, especially its susceptibility to "objective" measurement, periodically there have been movements to adopt an accounting model that would be more consistent with economic reality. These efforts usually have coincided with periods of price instability. The most recent one occurred in the mid-1970s through the early 1980s in many developed nations.

Popular interest in "inflation accounting" (as all the various methods are referred to collectively) has diminished markedly since price stability has been largely restored over the past decade, and most of the financial reporting standards adopted (including the US, UK, and international standards) have been dropped or have fallen into disuse during this time. However, the ultimate return of inflation is a likelihood borne out by historical experience, and it would be unfortunate if the development of reporting models would have to begin again with a "clean slate." Therefore, the financial reporting approaches to addressing both general and specific price changes are reviewed in this chapter.

The objectives of general price level (constant dollar or inflation) accounting, on the one hand, and specific price (current value, replacement cost, or current cost) accounting, on the other, are quite distinct, although often confused. The former attempts to address the measurement unit problem, which results from accounting's assumption that the unit of measurement of economic transactions (the US dollar, British pound, Swiss franc, etc.) remains immutable over time. For example, the results of transactions at different times, made with dollars of different purchasing power, are simply added together in the financial statements. As a consequence, statement users are given no insight into such matters as purchasing power gains or losses incurred by the entity.

Current cost accounting, in contrast, addresses the issue of valuation and the timing of earnings recognition. The realization principle generally precludes earnings recognition until all steps in the earnings process have been completed. (Losses, on the other hand, are often recognized earlier.) Many have argued, however, that when specific prices are rapidly rising, the failure to give these recognition until assets are sold causes significant economic events to be concealed from both outside parties (stockholders, employees, etc.) and from management, to the detriment of all concerned.

In the United States and the United Kingdom, general price level accounting or disclosures related thereto had been favored by professional standards setters. This was largely due to the greater ease with which these adjustments could be made, as well as to a conceptual opposition to breaching the realization principle. However, in both nations governmental agencies or commissions, as well as most academicians thinking about the issues, favored instead an accounting model that would address specific price changes, believing that such an approach would provide more useful information to decision makers. Once the momentum toward price level accounting was halted, standards were developed in the United States, the United Kingdom, and by the international standard setter, IASC, to require some disclosures on the current cost basis of accounting.

As noted, constant dollar and current value accounting are responses to different measurement issues and should not have been seen as true alternatives. However, the ability of statement users to comprehend a variety of different income measures presented to them simultaneously is limited. Accordingly, if historical costing is to remain as the primary measurement method for general purpose financial reporting, perhaps only one other measure will be required as a supplement. If so, some variant of current costing will undoubtedly be preferred. The current cost/constant dollar method first imposed by the US standard and later largely duplicated by the international standard (later made optional, however) is likely to be chosen for this mission.

IAS 29 addresses financial reporting in hyperinflationary economies. In general, this applies the same principles as general price level accounting, although the precise mechanism varies depending on whether the basic financial reporting model is one of historical costing or of current costing. Although IAS 15 has been made voluntary, IAS 29 remains mandatory where applicable.

Sources of IAS
IAS 15, 29

DEFINITIONS OF TERMS

Common dollar reporting. Synonymous with general price level or constant dollar financial reporting.

Constant dollar accounting. An accounting model that treats dollars of varying degrees of purchasing power essentially in the manner that foreign currencies are treated; dollars are translated into current purchasing power units and presented in restated financial statements. Constant dollar accounting converts all nonmonetary assets and equities from historical to current dollars by applying an index of general purchasing power. Specific value changes are ignored, and thus there are no holding gains or losses recognized. Monetary items are brought forward without adjustment, and these accounts (cash, claims to fixed amounts of cash, and obligations to pay fixed amounts of cash) therefore do give rise to purchasing power gains or losses. Constant dollar accounting does not attempt to address value changes.

Current cost accounting. An accounting model that attempts to measure economic values and changes therein, whether or not realized in the traditional accounting sense. In current cost accounting financial statements, nonmonetary items are reflected at current value amounts, measured variously by replacement cost, exit value, fair market value, net present value, or by other methodologies. Current cost-based statements of earnings will report as operating income the amount of resources that are available for distribution (to shareholders and others) without impairing the entity's ability to replace assets as they are sold or consumed in the operation of the business. Holding gains may or may not also be reportable as a component of income, although these are never deemed to be distributable unless the entity is liquidating itself. In a pure current cost accounting system, no purchasing power gains or losses are given recognition, but hybrid models have been proposed under US GAAP and IAS, which do recognize these as well as specific price changes.

Distributable (replicatable) earnings. The amount of resources that could be distributed (e.g., by dividends to shareholders) from the current period's earnings without impairing the entity's operating capacity vs. its level at the beginning of the period. This parallels the classic definition of economic income. It is generally conceded that current cost would provide the best measure of distributable earnings. Traditional historical cost-based financial reporting, on the other hand, does not attempt to measure economic income, but rather, seeks to match actual costs incurred against revenues generated; the result in many cases is that this measure of income will exceed real economic earnings.

Economic value. The ideal measure of current value/current cost; also known as deprival value. In practice, surrogate measures are often used instead.

Excess of specific price changes over general price level increase. A measure first introduced by the US GAAP standard on inflation accounting (SFAS 33) and usable under IAS 15 as well. This is the amount of increase in current cost of inventories and plant assets, in excess of the increase that would have occurred during the period had the change in values been at the rate of change of a broad-based "market basket" of goods and services.

Exit value. Also known as net realizable value, this is the measure of the resources that could be obtained by disposing of a specified asset, often for scrap or salvage value. Valuing assets at exit value is not generally valid as a measure of current cost, since "value in use" usually exceeds exit value, and most assets held by the enterprise will not be disposed of; however, for assets that are not to be replaced in the normal course of business, exit value may be a meaningful measure.

Fair value. Fair market value, or market value. For certain specialized properties, such as natural resources, this may be the most meaningful measure of current cost.

Fair value accounting. A now obsolete term which implies current cost or current value financial reporting.

Gains/losses on net monetary items. Synonymous with general purchasing power gains and losses.

Gearing adjustment. A term used in the proposed British inflation accounting standard, which reflects the conclusion that if an entity is financed externally (i.e., by debt), it may not need to retain resources in an amount equal to the replacement cost of goods sold and of depreciation in order to maintain existing productive capacity; sufficient borrowed funds must, however, continue to be available so that the existing degree of financial leverage ("gearing") can be maintained in the future. This adjustment is not addressed by IAS 15.

Holding gains/losses. In general, the increase or decrease in the current cost of nonmonetary assets (plant assets and inventories, for the most part) during a period. Notwithstanding the "gain/loss" terminology, such items are not generally recognized as part of income but rather as part of stockholders' equity, although practice varies. Holding gains are not distributable to shareholders without impairing operating capacity. In some models, only the excess of specific price changes over general price level changes are deemed to be holding gains/losses.

Hyperinflation. The condition in an economy in which there is such extreme inflation that historical cost financial statements become meaningless; characterized by a general aversion of the population to holding monetary assets, the conducting of business in ways that provide some protection against inflation, such as denominating transactions in a stable foreign currency or indexing to compensate for price changes, and a cumulative inflation rate over 3 years approaching 100%.

Inventory profits. The overstatement of income resulting from charging cost of sales at historical levels instead of at replacement costs; during periods of rapid inflation, historical cost based income will exceed real, economic earnings (distributable or replicatable earnings); this is partly the result of inventory profits. Not all entities are affected similarly. Those using LIFO costing will be less severely affected, and entities having faster inventory turnover will also have less inventory profits.

Monetary items. Claims to, or obligations to pay, fixed sums of cash or its equivalent. Examples are accounts receivable and accounts payable. If constant dollar accounting is employed, net monetary assets or liabilities will create purchasing power gains or losses in periods of changing general prices, since such fixed claims to cash or obligations to pay cash gain or lose value as the general purchasing power of the currency grows or shrinks.

Net present value. The future cash flows that will be generated by operation of an asset, discounted by a relevant factor such as the opportunity cost of capital, to an equivalent present value amount. This is a surrogate measure for economic value (deprival value) that is useful in certain circumstances (e.g., determining the future net cash flow of income producing real estate). For other assets, such as machinery, this is difficult to compute because future cash flows are difficult to forecast and because the assets are part of integrated processes generating cash flows that cannot be attributed to each component.

Net realizable value. Generally used in accounting to denote the amount that could be realized from an immediate disposition of an asset. Also known as exit value. Net realizable value is sometimes used for current costing purposes if the asset in question is not intended to be held beyond a brief period.

Nonmonetary items. Items that are not claims to, or obligations to pay fixed sums of cash or its equivalent. Examples are inventories and plant assets. When constant dollar accounting is employed, all nonmonetary items are adjusted to current dollar equivalents by application of a general measure of purchasing power changes. If current cost accounting is employed, nonmonetary items are recorded at current economic values (measured by replacement cost, deprival value, etc.); nonmonetary equity accounts may be explicitly adjusted or the necessary balancing amounts can be imputed. Holding gains and losses result from applying current cost measures to nonmonetary items.

Price level accounting. See constant dollar accounting.

Purchasing power accounting. See constant dollar accounting.

Purchasing power gains/losses. The economic benefit or detriment that results when an entity has claims to fixed amounts of cash (monetary assets) or has obligations to pay fixed sums (monetary liabilities) during periods when the general purchasing power of the monetary unit is changing. An excess of monetary assets over monetary liabilities coupled with rising prices results in a purchasing power loss; an excess of monetary liabilities results in a gain. These are reversed if prices are declining.

Realized holding gains/losses. Holding gains/losses can be realized or unrealized. If an appreciated item of inventory is sold, the holding gain is realized; if unsold at period end, it is unrealized. Historical cost based accounting does not recognize unrealized holding gains/losses (with some exceptions), and realized holding gains/losses are merged with other operating income and not given separate recognition. Use of the term "holding gain/loss" was prohibited by the inflation accounting standard under US GAAP and is not addressed by IAS 15.

Recoverable amount. The amount that could be obtained either from the continued use of an asset (the net present value of future cash flows) or from its disposal (exit or net realizable value).

Replacement cost. The lowest cost that would be incurred to replace the service potential of an asset in the normal course of the business.

Replicatable earnings. See distributable earnings.

Reproduction cost. The cost of acquiring an asset identical to the one presently in use. The distinction between reproduction cost and replacement cost is that operating efficiencies and technological changes may have occurred and the nominally identical asset would have a different productive capacity. Typically, replacement costs are lower than reproduction costs, and use of the latter would tend to overstate the effects of inflation.

Unrealized holding gains/losses. Holding gains or losses that have yet to be realized through an arm's-length transaction.

Value in use. Also known as value to the business, this is defined as the lesser of current cost or net recoverable amount.

INFLATION ADJUSTED FINANCIAL REPORTING

CONCEPTS, RULES, AND EXAMPLES

Historical Review of Inflation Accounting

Accounting practice today, on virtually a worldwide basis, relies heavily on the historical cost measurement strategy, whereby resources and obligations are given recognition as assets and liabilities, respectively, at the original (dollar, yen, etc.) amount of the transaction from which they arose. Once recorded, these amounts are not altered to reflect changes in value, except to the limited extent that GAAP requires recognition of impairments (e.g., lower of cost or fair value for inventories, etc.). Most long-lived assets such as buildings are amortized against earnings on a rational basis over their estimated useful lives, while short-lived assets are expensed as physically consumed. Liabilities are maintained at cost until paid off or otherwise discharged.

It is useful to recall that before the historical cost model of financial reporting achieved nearly universal adoption, various alternative recognition and measurement approaches were experimented with. "Fair value" accounting was in fact widely employed in the nineteenth and early twentieth centuries, and for some regulatory purposes (especially in setting utility service prices, where regulated by governmental agencies) remained in vogue until 25 years ago. The retreat from fair value accounting was in fact due less to any inherent attractiveness of the historical cost model than to negative reaction to abuses in fair value reporting. This came to a climax during the 1920s in much of the industrialized world, when prosperity and inflation encouraged overly optimistic reflections of values, much of which were reversed after the onset of the worldwide Great Depression.

Most of what are known as generally accepted accounting principles (GAAP) were developed after the crash of 1929. The more important of the basic postulates, which underlie most of the historical cost accounting principles, include the realization concept, the stable currency assumption, the matching concept, conservatism (or prudence), and historical costing. Realization means that earnings are not recognized until a definitive event, involving an arm's-length transaction in most instances, has occurred. Stable currency refers to the presumption that a $1,000 machine purchased today is about the same as a $1,000 machine purchased 20 years ago, in terms of real productive capacity. The matching concept has come to suggest a quasi-mechanical relationship between costs incurred in prior periods and the revenues generated currently as a result; the net of these is deemed to define earnings. Conservatism, among other things, implies that all losses be provided for but that gains not be anticipated, and is often used as an argument against fair value accounting. Finally, the historical costing convention was adopted as the most objectively verifiable means of reporting economic events.

The confluence of these underlying postulates has served to make historical cost based accounting, as it has been practiced for the past 60 years, widely supported. Even periods of rampant inflation, as the Western industrialized nations experienced during the 1970s, has not seriously diminished enthusiasm for this model, despite much academic research and the fairly sophisticated and complete alternative financial reporting approaches proposed in the United Kingdom and the United States and a later international accounting standard that built on those two recommendations. All of these failed to generate wide support and have largely been abandoned, being relegated to "suggested supplementary information" status, with which very few reporting enterprises comply.

What should accounting measure? Accounting was "invented" to measure economic activity in order to facilitate it. It is an information system, the product of which is used by one or more groups of decision makers: managers, lenders, investors, even current and prospective employees. In common with other types of decision-relevant data, financial statements can be evaluated along a number of dimensions, of which relevance and objectivity are frequently noted as being the most valuable. Information measured or reported by accounting systems should be, on the one hand, objective in the sense that independent observers will closely agree that the information is "correct," and on the other hand, the information should be computed and reported in such as way that its utility for decision makers is enhanced.

Objectivity has become what one critic called an occupational distortion of the accounting profession. While objectivity connotes a basic attitude of unprejudiced fairness that should be highly prized, it has also come to denote an excessive reliance on completed cash transactions as a basis for recording economic phenomena.

However, objectivity at the cost of diminished relevance may not be a valid goal. It has been noted that "relevance is the more basic of the virtues; while a relevant valuation may sometimes be wrong, an irrelevant one can never be of use, no matter how objectively it is reached." Both the FASB in the United States and the IASC in the international arena have published conceptual framework documents which support the notion that more relevant information, even if necessitating a departure from the historical costing tradition, could be more valuable to users of financial statements.

Why inflation undermines historical cost financial reporting. Actual and would-be investors and creditors, as well as entity managers and others, desire accounting information to support their decision-making needs. Financial statements that ignore the effects of general price level changes as well as changes in specific prices are inadequate for several reasons.

1. Reported profits often exceed the earnings that could be distributed to shareholders without impairing the entity's ability to maintain the present level of operations, because so-called inventory profits are included in earnings and because depreciation charges are not adequate to provide for asset replacements.
2. Balance sheets fail to reflect the economic value of the business, because plant assets and inventories, especially, are recorded at historical values which may be lower than current fair values or replacement costs.
3. Future earnings prospects are not easily projected from historical cost based earnings reports.
4. The impact of changes in the general price level on monetary assets and liabilities is not revealed, yet can be severe.
5. Because of the foregoing deficiencies, future capital needs are difficult to forecast, and in fact may contribute to the growing leveraging (borrowing) by many enterprises, which adds to their riskiness.
6. Distortions of real economic performance leads to social and political consequences ranging from suboptimal capital allocations to ill-conceived tax policies and public perceptions of corporate behavior.

Example

A business starts with one unit of inventory, which cost $2 and which at the end of the period is sold for $10 at a time when it would cost $7 to replace that very same unit on the display shelf. Traditional accounting would measure the earnings of the entity at $10 – $2 = $8, although clearly the business is only $3 "better off" at the end of the period than at the beginning, since real economic resources have only grown by $3 (after replacing the unit sold there is only that amount of extra resource available). The illusion that there was profit of $8 could readily destroy the entity if, for example, dividends of more than $3 were withdrawn or if fiscal policy led to taxes of more than $3 on the $8 "profit."

On the other hand, if the financial report showed only $3 profit for the period, there could be several salutary effects. Owners' expectations for dividends would be tempered, the entity's real capital would more likely be preserved, and projections of future performance would be more accurate, although projections must always be "fine tuned" since the past will never be replicated precisely.

The failure of the historical cost balance sheet to reflect values is yet another major deficiency of traditional financial reporting. True, accounting was never intended to report values per se, but the excess of assets over liabilities has always been denoted as "net worth," and to many that clearly connotes value. Similarly, the alternative titles for the balance sheet, "statement of financial position" and "statement of financial condition," strongly suggest value to the lay reader. The confusion largely stems from a failure to distinguish **realized** from **unrealized** value changes; if this distinction were carefully maintained, the balance sheet could be made more useful while remaining true to its traditions.

Evolving use of the financial statements. The traditional balance sheet was the primary, even the only, financial statement presented during much of accounting's history. However, beginning during the 1960s, the income statement achieved greater importance, partly because users came to realize that the balance sheet had become the repository for unmatched costs, deferred debits and credits, and other items that bore no relationship to real economic assets and obligations. In the aggressive and high-growth 1960s and early 1970s, the focus was largely on summary measures of enterprise performance, such as earnings per share, which derived from the income statement. During this era, the "matching concept" became the key underlying postulate that drove new accounting rules.

As a result of a series of unpleasant economic events, including numerous "credit crunches" and recessions in the 1970s and 1980s, the focus substantially shifted back to the balance sheet. Partly in response, the major accounting standard-setting bodies developed conceptual standards that urged the elimination of some of the items previously found on balance sheets that were not really either assets or liabilities. Some of these were the "leftovers" from double entry bookkeeping, which was oriented toward achieving income statement goals; an example is the interperiod tax allocations, that resulted in the reporting of ever-growing deferred tax liabilities that were never going to be paid. While the tension between achieving a meaningful balance sheet and an accurate income statement is inherent in the accounting model in use for almost 500 years, accountants are learning that improvements in both can be achieved. Inflation adjusted accounting can contribute to this effort, as will be demonstrated.

General vs. specific price changes. An important distinction to be understood is that between general and specific price changes, and how the effects of each can be meaningfully reported on in financial statements. Changes in specific prices, as with the inventory example above, should not be confused with changes in the general level of prices, which give rise to what are often referred to as purchasing power gains or losses, and result from holding net monetary assets or liabilities during periods of changing general prices. As most consumers are well aware, during periods of general price inflation, holding net monetary assets typically results in experiencing a loss in purchasing power, while a net liability position leads to a gain, as obligations are repaid with "cheaper" dollars. Among other effects, prolonged periods of general price inflation motivates entities to become more leveraged (more indebted to others), because of these purchasing power gains, although in reality creditors are aware of this and adjust interest rates to compensate.

Specific prices may change in ways that are notably different from the trend in overall prices, and they may even move in opposite directions. This is particularly true of basic commodities such as agricultural products and minerals, but may also be true of manufactured goods, especially if technological changes have great influence. For example, even during the years of rampant inflation during the 1970s some commodities, such as copper, were dropping in price, and certain goods, such as computer memory chips, were also declining even in nominal prices. For entities dealing in either of these items, holding inventories of these **nonmonetary** goods (usually a hedge against price inflation) would have produced large economic losses during this time. Thus, not only the changes in general prices, but also the changes in specific prices, and very important, the interactions between these can have major effects on an enterprise's real wealth. Measurement of these phenomena should be within the province of accounting.

Experiments and proposals for inflation accounting. Over the past 50 years there have been a number of proposals for pure price level accounting, financial reporting that would be sensitive to changes in specific prices, and combinations of these. There have been proposals (academic proposals) for comprehensive financial statements that would be adjusted for inflation, as well as for supplemental disclosures that would isolate the major inflation effects without abandoning primary historical cost based statements (generally, the professional proposals and regulatory requirements were of this type). To place the requirements of IAS 15 in context, a number of its more prominent predecessors will be reviewed in brief.

Price level accounting concepts and proposals. At its simplest, price level accounting views any given currency at different points in time as being analogous to different currencies at the same point in time. That is, 1955 US dollars have the same relationship to 1996 dollars as 1996 Swiss francs have to 1996 dollars. They are "apples and oranges" and cannot be added or subtracted without first being converted to a common measuring unit. Thus, "pure" price level accounting is held to be within the mainstream historical cost tradition and is merely a translation of one currency into another for comparative purposes. A broadly based measure of all prices in the economy should be used in accomplishing this (often, a consumer price index of some sort is employed).

Consider a simple example. Assume that the index of general prices was as follows:

January 1, 1970	65
January 1, 1983	100
January 1, 1992	182
December 31, 1992	188

Also assume the following items selected from the December 31, 1992 balance sheet:

	Historical cost	*Price level adjusted cost*
Cash	$ 50,000	$ 50,000
Inventories (purchased 1/1/92)	350,000	
x 188/182		361,538
Land (acquired 1/1/70)	500,000	
x 188/65		1,446,154
Machinery (purchased 1/1/83)	300,000	
x 188/100		564,000
Accumulated depreciation	(200,000)	
x 188/100		(376,000)
Book value of assets	$1,000,000	$2,045,692
Less monetary liabilities	(500,000)	(500,000)
Net assets	$ 500,000	$1,545,692

In the foregoing, all nonmonetary items were adjusted to "current dollars" using the same index of general prices. This is not based on the notion that items such as inventory and machinery actually experienced price changes of that magnitude, but on the idea that converting these to current dollars is a process akin to converting foreign currency denominated financial statements. The implication is that the historical cost balance sheet, showing net assets of $500,000, is equivalent to a balance sheet that reports some items in German marks, some in French francs, some in Italian lira, and so on. The price level adjusted balance sheet, by contrast, is deemed to be equivalent to a balance sheet in which all items have been translated into dollars.

This analogy is a weak one, however. Not only are such statements essentially meaningless, they can also be misleading from a policy viewpoint. For example, during a period of rising prices, an entity holding more monetary assets than monetary liabilities will report an economic loss due to the decline in the purchasing power of its net monetary assets. Nonmonetary assets, of course, are adjusted for price changes and thus appear to be "immune" from purchasing power gains or losses. The implication is that holding nonmonetary assets is somehow preferable to holding monetary assets.

In the foregoing example, the net monetary liabilities at year end are $500,000 – $50,000 = $450,000. Assuming the same net monetary liability position at the beginning of 1992, the gain experienced by the entity (due to owning monetary debt during a period of depreciating currency) would be given as

($450,000 x 188/182) – $450,000 = $14,835

This suggests that the entity has experienced a gain, at the obvious expense of its creditors, which have incurred a corresponding loss, in the amount of $14,835. This fails entirely to recognize that creditors may have demanded an "inflation adjusted rate of return" based on actual past and anticipated future inflationary behavior of the economy; if this were addressed in tandem with the computed purchasing power gain, a truer picture would be given of the real wisdom of the entity's financial strategy.

Furthermore, the actual price level "protection" afforded by holding investments in nonmonetary assets is a function of the changes in their specific values. If the replacement value of the inventory had declined, for example, during 1992, having held this inventory during the year would have been an economically unwise maneuver. Land that cost $500,000 might, due to its strategic location, now be worth $2.5 million, not the indicated $1.4 million, and the machinery might be obsolete due to technological changes, and not worth the approximately $190,000 suggested by the price level adjusted book value. In fairness, of course, the advocates of price level accounting do not claim that these adjusted amounts represent **values**, per se. However, the utility of these adjusted balance sheet captions for decision makers is difficult to fathom and the potential for misunderstanding is great.

US and UK proposals. A number of proposals have been offered over the years for either replacing traditional financial statements with price level adjusted statements, or for including supplementary price level statements in the annual report to shareholders. In the United States, the predecessor of the current accounting standard setter, the Accounting Principles Board, proposed supplementary reporting in 1969; no major publicly held corporation complied with this request, however. The FASB made a similar proposal in 1974 and might have succeeded in imposing this standard had not the US securities market watchdog, the SEC, suggested instead that a current value approach be developed. (Later the SEC did impose a replacement costing requirement on large companies, and the FASB followed with its own version a few years thereafter.)

In the United Kingdom a similar course of events occurred. After an early postwar recommendation (not implemented) that there be earnings set aside for asset replacements, a late 1960s proposal for supplementary price level adjusted reporting was made, followed a few years later by a more comprehensive constant dollar recommendation. As happened in the United States at about the same time, what appeared to be a private sector juggernaut favoring price level adjustments was derailed by governmental intervention. A Royal Commission, established in 1973, eventually produced the so-called Sandilands report, supporting current value accounting and not addressing the reporting of purchasing power gains or losses at all. This marked the end of British enthusiasm for general price level adjusted financial statements. Even a fairly complex later proposal (ED 18) made in 1977 did not incorporate any measure of purchasing power gains or losses, although it did add some novel embellishments to what basically was a current value model.

Other European nations have never been disposed favorably toward general price level accounting, with the exception of France. However, Latin American nations, having dealt with virtually runaway inflation for decades, have generally welcomed this type of financial reporting and in some cases have required it, even for some tax purposes. While price level adjustments are no more logical in Brazil, for example, than in the United States, since specific prices are changing, often at widely disparate rates, the role of accounting in those nations, serving as much more of an adjunct to the countries' respective tax collection and macroeconomic policy efforts than in European or other Western nations, has tended to encourage support for this approach to accounting for changing prices.

Current value models and proposals. By whatever name it is referred to, current value (replacement cost, current cost) accounting is really based on a wholly different concept than is price level (constant dollar) accounting. Current value financial reporting is far more closely tied to the original intent of the accounting model, which is to measure enterprise economic wealth and the changes therein from period to period. This suggests essentially a "balance sheet orientation" to income measurement, with the difference between net worth (as measured by current values) at year beginning and year end being, after adjustment for capital transactions, the measure of income or loss for the intervening period. How this is further analyzed and presented in the income statement (as realized and unrealized gains and losses) or even whether some of these changes even belong in the income statement (or instead, are reported in a separate statement of movements in equity, or are taken directly into equity) is a rather minor bookkeeping concern.

Although the proliferation of terminology of the many competing proposals can be confusing, four candidates as measures of current value can readily be identified: economic value, net present value, net realizable value (also known as exit value), and replacement cost (which is a measure of entry value). A brief explanation will facilitate the discussion of the IAS requirements later in this chapter.

Economic value is usually understood to mean the equilibrium fair market value of an asset. However, apart from items traded in auction markets, typically only securities and raw commodities, direct observation of economic value is not possible.

Net present value is often suggested as the ideal surrogate for economic value, since in a perfect market values are driven by the present value of future cash flows to be generated by the assets. Certain types of assets, such as rental properties, have predictable cash flows and in fact are often priced in this manner. On the other hand, for assets such as machinery, particularly those that are part of a complex integrated production process, determining cash flows is difficult.

Net realizable values (NRV) are more familiar to most accountants, since even under existing US, UK, and international accounting standards, there are numerous instances when references to NRV must be made to ascertain whether asset write-downs are to be required. NRV is a measure of "exit values" since these are the amounts that the organization would realize on asset disposition, net of all costs; from this perspective, this is a conservative measure (exit values are lower than entry values in almost all cases, since transactions are not costless), but also is subject to criticism since under the going concern assumption it is not anticipated that the enterprise will dispose of all its productive assets at current market prices, indeed, not at any prices, since these assets will be retained for use in the business.

The biggest failing of this measure, however, is that it does not assist in measuring economic income, since that metric is intended to reveal how much income an entity can distribute to its owners, and so on, while retaining the ability to replace its productive capacity as needed. In general, an income measure based on exit values would overstate earnings (since depreciation and cost of sales would be based on lower exit values for plant assets and inventory) when compared with an income measure based on entry values. Thus, while NRV is a familiar concept to many accountants, this is not the ideal candidate for a current value model.

Replacement cost is intended as a measure of entry value and hence of the earnings reinvestment needed to maintain real economic productive capacity. Actually, competing proposals have engaged in much hairsplitting over alternative concepts of entry value, and this deserves some attention here. The simplest concept of replacement value is the cost of replacing a specific machine, building, and so on, and in some industries it is indeed possible to determine these prices, at least in the short run, before technology changes occur. However, in many more instances (and in the long run, in all cases) exact physical replacements are not available, and even nominally identical replacements offer varying levels of productivity enhancements that make simplistic comparisons distortive.

As a very basic example, consider a machine with a cost of $40,000 that can produce 100 widgets per hour. The current price of the replacement machine is $50,000, that superficially suggests a specific price increase of 25% has occurred. However, on closer examination, it is determined that while nominally the same machine, some manufacturing enhancements have been made (e.g., the machine will require less maintenance, will require fewer labor inputs, runs at a higher speed, etc.) which have altered its effective capacity (considering reduced downtime, etc.) to 110 widgets per hour. Clearly, a naive adjustment for what is sometimes called "reproduction cost" would overstate the machine's value on the balance sheet and overstate periodic depreciation charges, thereby understating earnings. A truer measure of the replacement cost of the service potential of the asset, not the physical asset itself, would be given as

$$\$40,000 \times (50,000/40,000) \times 100/110 = \$45,454$$

That is, the service potential represented by the asset in use has a current replacement cost of $45,454, considering that a new machine costs 25% more but is 10% more productive.

Consider another example: An integrated production process uses machines A and B, which have reproduction costs today of $40,000 and $45,000, respectively. However, management plans to acquire a new type of machine, C, which at a cost of $78,000 will replace both machines A and B and will produce the same output as its predecessors. The combined reproduction cost of $85,000 clearly overstates the replacement cost of the service potential of the existing machines in this case, even if there had been no technological changes affecting machines A and B.

Some, but not all, proposals that have been made in academia over the past 60 years, and by standards setters and regulatory authorities over the past 20 years, have understood the foregoing distinctions. For example, the US SEC requirements of the mid-1970s called for measures of the replacement cost of productive capacity, which clearly implied that productivity changes had to be factored in. The subsequent private sector rules issued by FASB seemed to redefine what the SEC had mandated to highlight its own "current cost" requirement; in essence, the FASB's current costs were nothing other than the SEC's replacement costs. Other proposals have been more ambiguous, however. Furthermore, measuring the impact of technological change adds vastly to the complexity of applying replacement cost measures, since "raw" replacement costs (known as "reproduction costs") are often easily obtained (from catalog prices, etc.), but productivity adjustments must be ascertained by carefully evaluating advertising claims, engineering studies, and other sources of information, which can be a complex and costly process.

Limitations on replacement cost. While entry value is clearly the most logical of the alternative measures discussed thus far, under certain circumstances one of the other candidates would be preferable as a measure to use in "current cost" financial reporting. For example, consider a situation in which the "value in use" (economic value or net present value of future cash flows) is lower than replacement cost, due to changing market conditions affecting pricing of the entity's output. In such a circumstance, although the enterprise may continue to use the machines on hand and to sell the output profitably, it would not contemplate replacement of the asset, instead viewing it as a "cash cow." If current cost financial statements were to be developed that incorporated depreciation based on the replacement cost of the machine, earnings would be understated, since actual replacement is not to be provided for. A number of other hypothetical circumstances could also be presented; the end result is that a series of decision rules can be developed to guide the selection of the best measure of current cost. These are summarized in the following table, where NRC stands for net replacement cost, which is synonymous with current cost; NRV is net realizable value or exit value; and EV is the same as net present value.

Conditions	Value to the business
EV > NRC > NRV	NRC
NRC > EV > NRV	EV
NRC > NRV > EV	NRV
EV > NRV > NRC	NRC
NRV > EV > NRC	NRC
NRV > NRC > EV	NRC

Measuring Income Under the Replacement Cost Approach

There are two reasons to employ replacement cost accounting: (1) to compute a measure of earnings that can probably be replicated on an ongoing basis by the enterprise and approximates real economic wealth creation, and (2) to present a balance sheet that presents the economic condition of the entity at a point in time. Of these, the first is by far the more important objective, since decision makers' use of financial statements is largely oriented toward the future operations of the business, in which they are lenders, owners, managers, or employees.

Given the foregoing, the principal use of replacement cost information will be to assist in computing current period earnings on a true economic basis. The income statement items which on the historical cost basis are most distortive, in most cases, are depreciation and cost of sales. Historical cost depreciation can be based on asset prices that are 10 to 40 years old, during which time even modest price changes can compound to very sizable misrepresentations. Cost of sales will not typically suffer from compounding over such a long period, since turnover for most businesses will be in a matter of months (although this can be greatly distorted if low LIFO inventory costs are released into cost of sales), but since cost of sales will account for a much larger part of the entity's total costs than does depreciation, it can still have a major impact.

Thus, current cost/replacement cost/current value earnings are typically computed by adjusting historical cost income by an allowance for replacement cost depreciation and cost of sales. Typically, these two adjustments will effectively derive a modified earnings amount that closely approximates economic earnings. This modified amount can be paid out as dividends or otherwise disbursed, while leaving the enterprise with the ability to replace its productive capacity and continue to operate at the same level as it had been. (This does not, however, address the matter of purchasing power that may have been gained or lost by holding net monetary assets or liabilities during the period, which requires yet another computation.)

Determining current costs. In practice, replacement costs are developed by applying one or more of four principal techniques: indexation, direct pricing, unit pricing, and functional pricing. Each has advantages and disadvantages, and no single technique will be applicable to all fact situations and all types of assets. The following are useful in determining current costs of plant assets.

Indexation is accomplished by applying appropriate indices to the historical cost of the assets. Assuming that the assets in use were acquired in the usual manner (bargain purchases and other such means of acquisition will thwart this effort, since any index when applied to a nonstandard base will result in a meaningless adjusted number) and that an appropriate index can be obtained or developed (which incorporates productivity changes as well as price variations), this will be the most efficient approach to employ. For many categories of manufactured goods, such as machinery and equipment, this technique has been widely used with excellent results. One concern is that many published indices actually address only reproduction costs, and if not adjusted further, the likely outcome will be that costs are overstated and adjusted earnings will be artificially depressed.

Direct pricing, as the name suggests, relies on information provided by vendors and others having data about the selling prices of replacement assets. To the extent that these are "list" prices that do not reflect actual market transactions, these must be adjusted, and the same concern with productivity enhancements mentioned with reference to indexation must also be addressed. Since many enterprises are in constant, close contact with their vendors, obtaining such information is often straightforward, particularly with regard to machinery and other equipment.

Unit pricing is the least commonly employed method but can be useful when estimating the replacement cost of buildings. This is the "bricks and mortar" approach, which relies on statistical data about the "per unit" cost of constructing various types of buildings and other assets. For example, construction cost data may suggest that single story light industrial buildings in cold climates (say, Europe) with certain other defined attributes may have a current cost of $47 per square foot, or that a first class high-rise urban hotel in England has a construction cost of $125,000 per room. By expanding these per unit costs to the scale of the enterprise's facilities, a fairly accurate replacement cost can be derived. There are complications: for example, costs are not linearly related to size of facility due to the presence of fixed costs, but these are widely understood and readily dealt with. Unit pricing is typically not meaningful for machinery or equipment, however.

Functional pricing is the most difficult of the four principal techniques and is best reserved for highly integrated production processes, such as refineries and chemical plants, where attempts to price individual components would be exceptionally difficult. For example, a plant capable of producing 400,000 tons of polyethylene annually could be priced as a unit by having an engineering estimate made of the cost to construct similar capacity in the current environment. Clearly, this is not a merely mechanical effort, as indexation in particular is likely to be, but demands the services of a skilled estimator. Technological issues are neatly avoided since the focus is on creating a new plant with defined output capacity, using whatever mix of components would be most cost effective. This technique has been widely employed in actual practice.

Inventory costing problems. For a merchandising concern, direct pricing is likely to be an effective technique to assist in developing cost of sales on a current cost basis. Manufacturing firms, on the other hand, will need to build up replacement cost basis cost of goods manufactured and sold by separately analyzing the cost behavior of each major cost element (e.g., labor contracts, overhead expenses, and raw materials prices). It is unlikely that these will have experienced the same price movements, and therefore an averaging approach would not be sufficiently accurate. Also, as product mix changes over time the entity may be subject to varying influences from one period to the next. Finally, the inventory costing method used (e.g., LIFO vs. FIFO) will affect the extent of adjustment to be made, with (assuming that costs trend upward over time) relatively greater adjustments made to cost of sales determined on the FIFO basis, since relatively older costs are included in the GAAP income statement.

Whatever assortment of methods is used, the end product is a restated inventory of plant assets, depreciation on which must then be computed. For the current cost earnings data to be comparable with the historical cost financial statements, it is usually recommended that no other decisions be superimposed. For example, no changes in asset useful lives should be made, for to do so would exacerbate or ameliorate the impact of the replacement cost depreciation and make interpretation very difficult for anyone not intimately familiar with the company. Some ancillary costs may need to be adjusted in computing cost of sales and depreciation on the revised basis. For example, if the only replacement machines available will reduce the need for skilled labor, the (higher) replacement cost depreciation should be reduced by related cost savings, if accurately predictable. There are literally scores of similar issues to be addressed, and indeed entire volumes have been written providing detailed guidance on how to apply current cost measures.

Examples of current costing adjustments to depreciation and cost of sales

Example 1

Hapsburg Corp. is a wholesale distributor for a single product. For 1997, the company reports sales of $35,000,000, representing sales of 600,000 units of its single product. The traditional income statement reports cost of sales as follows:

	($000 omitted)
Beginning inventory	$ 8.8
Purchases, net	25.7
Ending inventory	(6.5)
Cost of goods sold	$28.0

Reference to purchase orders reveals the fact that product cost early in 1997 was $42 per unit and was $55 per unit late in December of that year. The company employs FIFO accounting.

Since there is no evidence presented to the effect that net realizable value of the product is below current replacement cost, current cost can be used without modification.

Beginning current cost	$42.0
Ending current cost	$55.0
Average	$48.5

Total cost of sales for the period, on a replacement cost basis, is therefore $48.5 x 600,000 units = $29,100,000.

Example 2

In the following example, "deprival value" is, for one product line, better measured by net realizable value than by replacement cost. The company, St. Ignatz Mfg. Co., manufactures and sells two products, A and B. Product A has been a declining item for several years, and management now believes that it must close this line due to the shrinking market share, which will not support higher costs. St. Ignatz will continue to produce Product B and may possibly expand into new products in the future.

Company records show the following results in 1996:

	($000,000 omitted)		
	Product A	*Product B*	*Total*
Sales	$19.5	$40.5	$60.0
Cost of sales			
Beginning inventory	12.5	6.8	
Purchases	8.7	20.0	
Ending inventory	(3.0)	(5.4)	
Cost of sales	18.2	21.4	39.6
Gross profit	$ 1.3	$19.1	20.4
All other expenses			(18.8)
Net income			$ 1.6

The company's manufacturing records show the following data:

Current costs, beginning of year	$52.0	$75.0
Current costs, ending of year	$63.0	$79.0
Current costs, average	$57.5	$77.0

Sales in 1996 comprised 390,000 units of Product A and 540,000 units of Product B. Management believes that the market for Product A cannot support further price increases, and thus the remaining inventory will probably be sold at a loss. Selling expenses are estimated at $6 per unit.

Product A has a recoverable value lower than current manufacturing costs. The net recoverable amount is given by the selling price per unit less selling expenses: $50 – $6 = $44 per unit. Current cost of sales is $44 x $390,000 = $17,160,000. Note that recoverable amount, not replacement cost, is used.

Product B has an average current cost of $77 per unit, so 1996 cost of sales on a current cost basis is $77 x $540,000 = $41,580,000.

Total cost of sales on the current cost basis is therefore $17,160,000 + $41,580,000 = $58,740,000.

Example 3

Jacquet Corp. reports depreciation of $16,510 for 1996 in its historical cost based financial statements prepared on the basis of GAAP. A summary of plant assets reveals the following:

Asset class	*Total depreciable cost**	*Useful life (yr.)*	*Depreciation rate (%)***
A	$24,000	8	12 1/2
B	50,000	10	10
C	45,000	12	8 1/3
D	60,000	15	6 2/3
E	19,000	25	4

* *Depreciable cost is historical cost less salvage value.*
** *Depreciation rate is 1/useful life.*

Management employs appraisals and other methods, including information from vendors and indices, to develop current cost data as shown below.

Asset	*Current costs*		
class	*1/1/96*	*12/31/96*	*Average*
A	$28,000	$31,000	$29,500
B	56,000	60,000	58,000
C	55,000	60,000	57,500
D	62,000	68,000	65,000
E	30,000	33,000	31,500

From this information, the current cost depreciation for the year 1996 can be computed as follows:

Asset class	*Depreciation rate (%)*	*Average current cost*	*Depreciation*
A	12 1/2	$29,500	$ 3,687.5
B	10	58,000	5,800.0
C	8 1/3	57,500	4,792.0
D	6 2/3	65,000	4,333.0
E	4	31,500	1,260.0
			$19,872.5

Note that the replacement cost basis depreciation for the year is $3,362.50 greater than was the historical cost depreciation.

Purchasing power gains or losses in the context of current cost accounting. Thus far, general price level (or purchasing power or constant dollar) accounting has been viewed as a reporting concept totally separate from current value (or current cost or replacement cost) accounting. As noted, advocates of price level adjustments have argued that these are not attempts to measure value, as current cost accounting is, but merely to "translate" old dollars into current dollars. For their part, advocates of current value accounting have generally been more focused on deriving a measure of the "replicatable" economic earnings of the enterprise, usually with no mention of the fact that changing specific prices of productive assets exist against a backdrop of changing general price levels.

In fact, the FASB requirements imposed in the late 1970s (and dropped in the 1980s for lack of interest) attempted to measure both general and specific price changes. That standard included a requirement for reporting purchasing power gains or losses, as well as for stating the amount of adjustment for current cost depreciation and cost of sales. The IASC has imposed a somewhat similar requirement in IAS 15 (compliance with which is now wholly voluntary), albeit with less specificity. The guidance in the now dormant FASB standard can be used by those attempting to report under IAS 15 without limitation, as there are no conflicts between these sets of rules.

Requirements Under IAS 15

The experience of the international accounting standard that was designed to reveal the effects of inflation is very similar to the experiences in the United States and the United Kingdom. That is, while there was a great clamor, primarily from the financial analyst community, in favor of this supplementary financial reporting model, once it was mandated there was a noticeable decline in interest. It would appear that analysts much prefer to develop their own estimates of the impact of inflation on the companies they follow and may have an inherent distrust of management-supplied data. As for management, it generally argued that such information was useless before the standard was imposed, which at the time, seemed to be self-serving posturing in the hope that an expensive new mandate could be averted.

As in the United States, after a few years of demanding the supplementary information (IAS 15 was imposed in 1981), the IASC announced in 1989 that due to lack of worldwide support for this noble experiment it would no longer be required to comply with the standard, although still encouraged. In the event that inflation again becomes a concern, which eventually it will as such cycles are almost inevitable, this standard can be reactivated.

Alternative approaches permitted. The standard was intended to require certain supplementary current value and constant dollar information. A great deal of latitude was given to entities, which could choose from among a range of supportable methods to accomplish this directive. As the standard notes, the two main methods are intended to (1) recognize income after the general purchasing power of shareholders' equity has been maintained (price level accounting), and (2) recognize income after the operating capacity of the enterprise is maintained (current value accounting, which may or may not also include adjustments related to the general price level).

General purchasing power approach. IAS 15 does not stipulate what index should be used to measure the change in the general level of prices but does identify depreciation and cost of sales as being subject to adjustment, as well as a need to measure the effect of changing prices on net monetary items held.

Current cost approach. IAS 15 acknowledges the existence of various methods, with replacement cost being identified as the principal measurement strategy, subject to the caveat that if replacement cost is higher than both net realizable value and present value, replacement value is not to be used. Instead, the higher of net realizable value and present value would denote current value, as explained earlier in this chapter. Replacement costs are said to be found in information about current acquisitions of new or used assets of similar productive capacities or service potentials. Specific price indices are also favorably noted as sources of current cost data. Net realizable value is generally a representation of net current selling price (i.e., exit value), while present value is the discounted amount of future receipts attributable to the asset.

The standard discusses at some length the need to determine an adjustment for the effects of changing prices on net monetary items, including long-term debt, but suggests that some current cost methods (which it does not name) may not need to address this separately. In particular, the discussion in IAS 15 alludes to the argument (made explicitly in the British proposal of the 1970s but not otherwise enacted in any standards) that since depreciable assets in particular are often acquired at least in part in exchange for monetary debt, the gross replacement cost adjustment exaggerates the negative effect on earnings and that this is moderated to the extent leveraging is used.

In fact, one can make this argument, but as noted earlier in the chapter, to do so assumes that added borrowing in periods of rising prices is "costless" in the sense that no premium is added by lenders to compensate for either (1) the borrowers' greater riskiness as they become more leveraged, or (2) for the loss to be incurred on repayment of the debt in devalued currency. It is not likely that in the long run lenders will go uncompensated for either of these, and therefore to offset the higher charges for depreciation and cost of sales by the fraction to be borne by the lenders may be imprudent.

Minimum disclosures required by IAS 15. The disclosures required (now made optional) include the following:

1. The amount of adjustment to, or the adjusted amount of, depreciation of property plant and equipment
2. The amount of adjustment to, or the adjusted amount of, cost of sales
3. The adjustments relating to monetary items, the effect of borrowing, or equity interests when such adjustments have been taken into account in determining income under the (inflation) accounting method adopted

4. The overall effect on results of the adjustments described above, as well as any other items reflecting the effects of changing prices.
5. If a current cost method is used, the current cost of property, plant and equipment and of inventories should be disclosed.
6. There should be a description of the methods used to compute the foregoing items.

Example of disclosure consistent with IAS 15

DeKalb Thermodynamics Inc.
Statements of Income From Continuing Operations
Year Ended December 31, 1996

	As reported in primary statements	*Adjusted for general inflation*	*Adjusted for changes in specific prices (current costs)*
Net sales and other revenue	$253,000	$253,000	$253,000
Cost of goods sold	$197,000	$204,384	$205,408
Depreciation and amortization	10,000	14,130	19,500
Other operating expense	20,835	20,835	20,835
Interest expense	7,165	7,165	7,165
Provision for income taxes	9,000	9,000	9,000
	$244,000	$255,514	$261,908
Income (loss) from continuing operations	$ 9,000	$ (2,514)	$ (8,908)
Gain from decline in purchasing power of net amounts owed		$ 7,729	$ 7,729
Increase in specific prices (current costs) of inventories and property, plant, and equipment held during the year			$ 24,608
Effect of general price level increase			18,959
Excess of increase in specific prices over increase in general price level			$ 5,649

Note: Current costs are determined by consulting current prices posted for plant assets, net of applicable discounts, and by reference to indexed or replacement costs adjusted for productivity increases. The gain on purchasing power change is determined by reference to the consumer price index for all urban consumers.

FINANCIAL REPORTING IN HYPERINFLATIONARY ECONOMIES

CONCEPTS, RULES, AND EXAMPLES

Hyperinflation and Financial Reporting

Hyperinflation is a condition that is difficult to define precisely, as there is not a clear demarcation between merely "rampant" inflation and true hyperinflation.

However, in any given economic system, when the general population has so lost faith in the stability of the local economy that business transactions are commonly either denominated in a stable, reference currency of another country, or are structured to incorporate an indexing feature intended to compensate for the distortive effects of inflation, this condition may be present. As a benchmark, when cumulative inflation over 3 years approaches or exceeds 100%, it must be conceded that the economy is suffering from hyperinflation.

Hyperinflation is obviously a major problem for any economy, as it creates severe distortions and, left unaddressed, results in uncontrolled acceleration of the rate of price changes, ending in inevitable collapse as was witnessed in post-World War I Germany. From a financial reporting perspective, there are also major problems, since even over a brief interval, such as a year or even a quarter, the income statement will contain transactions with such a variety of purchasing power units that aggregation becomes meaningless, as would adding dollars, francs, and marks. This is precisely the problem discussed earlier in this chapter, but raised to an exponential level.

In a truly hyperinflationary economy, users of financial statements are unable to make meaningful use of such statements unless they have been recast into currency units having purchasing power defined by prices at or near the date of the statements. Unless this "common denominator" is employed, the financial statements are too difficult to interpret for purposes of making management, investing, and credit decisions. Although some sophisticated users, particularly in those countries where hyperinflation has been endemic, such as some of the South American nations, including Brazil and Argentina, and for certain periods nations such as Israel, are able to apply "rules of thumb" to cope with this problem, in general modifications must be made to general purpose financial statements if they are to have any value.

Under international accounting standards, if hyperinflation is deemed to characterize the economy, a form of price level accounting must be applied to the financial statements to conform with generally accepted accounting principles. IAS 29 requires that all the financial statements be adjusted to reflect year-end general price levels, which entails applying a broad-based index to all nonmonetary items on the balance sheet and to all transactions reported in the income statement and the cash flow statement.

Restating Historical Cost Financial Statements Under Hyperinflation Conditions

The precise adjustments to be made depend on whether the financial reporting system is based on historical costs or on current costs, as described in IAS 15 and explained earlier in this chapter. Although in both cases the goal is to restate the financial statements into the measuring unit that exists at the balance sheet date, the mechanics will vary to some extent.

If the financial reporting system is based on historical costing, the process used to adjust the balance sheet can be summarized as follows:

1. Monetary assets and liabilities are already presented in units of year-end purchasing power and receive no further adjustment. (See the appendix for a categorization of different assets and liabilities as to their status as monetary or nonmonetary.)
2. Monetary assets and liabilities that are linked to price changes, such as indexed debt securities, are adjusted according to the terms of the contractual arrangement. This does not change the characterization of these items as monetary, but it does serve to reduce or even eliminate the purchasing power gain or loss that would have otherwise been experienced as a result of holding these items during periods of changing general prices.
3. Nonmonetary items are adjusted by applying a ratio of indices, the numerator of which is the general price level index at the balance sheet date and the denominator of which is the index as of the acquisition or inception date of the item in question. For some items, such as plant assets, this is a straightforward process, while for others, such as work in process inventories, this can be more complex.
4. Certain assets cannot be adjusted as described above, because even in nominally historical cost financial statements these items have been revised to some other basis, such as fair value or net realizable amounts. For example, under the allowed alternative method of IAS 16, plant, property, and equipment can be adjusted to fair value. In such a case, no further adjustment would be warranted, assuming that the adjustment to fair value was made as of the latest balance sheet date (although IAS 16 only demands that this be done at least every 3 years). If the latest revaluation was as of an earlier date, the carrying amounts should be further adjusted to compensate for changes in the general price level from that date to the balance sheet date, using the indexing technique noted above.
5. Consistent with the established principles of historical cost accounting, if the restated amounts of nonmonetary assets exceed the recoverable amounts, these must be reduced appropriately. This can easily occur, since (as discussed earlier in this chapter) specific prices of goods will vary by differing amounts, even in a hyperinflationary environment, and in fact some may decline in terms of current cost even in such cases, particularly when technological change occurs rapidly. Since the application of price level accounting, whether for "ordinary" inflation or for hyperinflation, does not imply an abandonment of historical costing, being a mere "translation" into more timely and relevant purchasing power units, the rules of that mode of financial reporting still apply. Generally accepted accounting principles require that assets not be stated at amounts in excess of

realizable amounts, and this constraint applies even when price level adjustments are reflected.

6. Equity accounts must also be restated to compensate for changing prices. Paid-in capital accounts are indexed by reference to the dates when the capital was contributed, which are usually a discrete number of identifiable transactions over the life of the enterprise. Revaluation accounts, if any, are eliminated entirely, as these will be subsumed in restated retained earnings. The retained earnings account itself is the most complex to analyze and in practice is often treated as a balancing figure after all other balance sheet accounts have been restated. However, it is possible to compute the adjustment to this account directly, and that is the recommended course of action, lest other errors go undetected. To adjust retained earnings, each year's earnings should be adjusted by a ratio of indices, the numerator being the general price level as of the balance sheet date, and the denominator being the price level as of the end of the year for which the earnings were reported. Reductions of retained earnings for dividends paid should be adjusted similarly.
7. IAS 29 addresses a few other special problem areas. For example, the standard notes that borrowing costs typically already reflect the impact of inflation (more accurately, interest rates reflect inflationary expectations), and thus it would represent a form of double counting to fully index capital asset costs for price level changes when part of the cost of the asset was capitalized interest, as defined in IAS 23 as an allowed alternative method. As a practical matter, interest costs are often not a material component of recorded asset amounts, and the inflation related component would only be a fraction of interest costs capitalized. However, the general rule is to delete that fraction of the capitalized borrowing costs which represents inflationary compensation, since the entire cost of the asset will be indexed to current purchasing units.

To restate the current period's income statement, a reasonably accurate result can be obtained if revenue and expense accounts are multiplied by the ratio of end-of-period prices to average prices for the period. Where price changes were not relatively constant throughout the period, or when transactions did not occur ratably, as when there was a distinct seasonal pattern to sales activity, a more precise measurement effort might be needed. This can be particularly important when a devaluation of the currency took place during the year.

While IAS 29 addresses the cash flow statement only perfunctorily (its issuance was prior to the revision of IAS 7), this financial statement must also be modified to report all items in terms of year-end purchasing power units. For example, changes in working capital accounts, used to convert net income into cash flow from operating activities, will be altered to reflect the "real" (i.e., inflation adjusted) changes. To illustrate, if beginning accounts receivable were $500,000 and ending receivables were $650,000, but prices rose by 40% during the year, the apparent $150,000 increase in receivables (which would be a use of cash) is really a $50,000 decrease [($500,000 x 1.4 = $700,000) – $650,000], which in cash flow terms is a source of cash. Other items must be handled similarly. Investing and financing activities should be adjusted on an item-by-item basis, since these are normally discrete events that do not occur ratably throughout the year.

In addition to the foregoing, the adjusted income statement will report a gain or loss on net monetary items held. As an approximation, this will be computed by applying the change in general prices for the year to the average net monetary assets (or liabilities) outstanding during the year. If net monetary items changed materially at one or more times during the year, a more detailed computation would be warranted. In the income statement, the gain or loss on net monetary items should be associated with the adjustment relating to items that are linked to price level changes (indexed debt, etc.) as well as with interest income and expense and foreign exchange adjustments, since theoretically at least, all these items contain a component that reflects inflationary behavior.

Restating Current Cost Financial Statements Under Hyperinflation Conditions

If the financial reporting system is based on current costing (as described earlier in the chapter), the process used to adjust the balance sheet can be summarized as follows:

1. Monetary assets and liabilities are already presented in units of year-end purchasing power and receive no further adjustment. (See the appendix for a categorization of different assets and liabilities as to their status as monetary or nonmonetary.)
2. Monetary assets and liabilities that are linked to price changes, such as indexed debt securities, are adjusted according to the terms of the contractual arrangement. This does not change the characterization of these items as monetary, but it does serve to reduce or even eliminate the purchasing power gain or loss that would have otherwise been experienced as a result of holding these items during periods of changing general prices.
3. Nonmonetary items are already stated at year-end current values or replacement costs and need no further adjustments. Issues related to recoverable amounts and other complications associated with price level adjusted historical costs should not normally arise.
4. Equity accounts must also be restated to compensate for changing prices. Paid-in capital accounts are indexed by reference to the dates when the capital was contributed, which are usually a discrete number of identifiable transactions over the life of the enterprise. Revaluation accounts are eliminated entirely, as these will be subsumed in restated retained earnings. The retained earnings account itself will typically be a "balancing account" un-

der this scenario, since detailed analysis would be very difficult, although certainly not impossible, to accomplish.

The current cost income statement, absent the price level component, will reflect transactions at current costs as of the transaction dates. For example, cost of sales will be comprised of the costs as of each transaction date (usually approximated on an average basis). To report these as of the balance sheet date, these costs will have to be further inflated to year-end purchasing power units, by means of the ratio of general price level indices, as suggested above.

In addition to the foregoing, the adjusted income statement will report a gain or loss on net monetary items held. This will be similar to that discussed under the historical cost reporting above. However, consistent with IAS 15, current cost income statements already will include the net gain or loss on monetary items held, which need not be computed again.

To the extent that restated earnings differ from earnings on which income taxes are computed, there will be a need to provide more or less tax accrual, which will be a deferred tax obligation or asset, depending on the circumstances.

Comparative Financial Statements

Consistent with the underlying concept of reporting in hyperinflationary economies, all prior-year financial statement amounts must be updated to purchasing power units as of the most recent balance sheet date. This will be a relatively simple process of applying a ratio of indices of the current year-end price level to the year earlier price level.

Other Disclosure Issues

IAS 29 requires that when the standard is applied, the fact that hyperinflation adjustments have been made be noted. Furthermore, the underlying basis of accounting--historical cost or current cost--should be stipulated, as should the price level index that was utilized in making the adjustments.

Economies Which Cease Being Hyperinflationary

When application of IAS 29 is discontinued, the amounts reported in the last balance sheet that had been adjusted become, effectively, the new cost basis. That is, previously applied adjustments are not reversed, since an end to a period of hyperinflation generally means only that prices have plateaued, not that they have deflated to earlier levels.

APPENDIX

MONETARY VS. NONMONETARY ITEMS

Item	Monetary	Nonmonetary	Requires analysis
Cash on hand, demand deposits, and time deposits	x		
Foreign currency and claims to foreign currency	x		
Securities			
Common stock (passive investment)		x	
Preferred stock (convertible or participating) and convertible bonds			x
Other preferred stock or bonds	x		
Accounts and notes receivable and allowance for doubtful accounts	x		
Mortgage loan receivables	x		
Inventories		x	
Loans made to employees	x		
Prepaid expenses			x
Long-term receivables	x		
Refundable deposits	x		
Advances to unconsolidated subsidiaries	x		
Equity in unconsolidated subsidiaries		x	
Pension and other funds			x
Property, plant, and equipment and accumulated depreciation		x	
Cash surrender value of life insurance	x		
Purchase commitments (portion paid on fixed-price contracts)		x	
Advances to suppliers (not on fixed-price contracts)	x		
Deferred income tax charges	x		
Patents, trademarks, goodwill, and other intangible assets		x	
Deferred life insurance policy acquisition costs	x		
Deferred property and casualty insurance policy acquisition costs		x	
Accounts payable and accrued expenses	x		

Item	Monetary	Nonmonetary	Requires analysis
Accrued vacation pay			x
Cash dividends payable	x		
Obligations payable in foreign currency	x		
Sales commitments (portion collected on fixed-price contracts)		x	
Advances from customers (not on fixed-price contracts)	x		
Accrued losses on purchase commitments	x		
Deferred revenue			x
Refundable deposits	x		
Bonds payable, other long-term debt, and related discount or premium	x		
Accrued pension obligations			x
Obligations under product warranties		x	
Deferred income tax obligations	x		
Deferred investment tax credits		x	
Life or property and casualty insurance policy reserves	x		
Unearned insurance premiums		x	
Deposit liabilities of financial institutions	x		

APPENDIX

DISCLOSURE CHECKLIST

This checklist provides a reference to the disclosures common to the financial statements of enterprises which are complying with International Accounting Standards (IAS). It covers IAS which are effective as of January 1, 1998. (Thus, revised IAS 1 and revised IAS 14, which become operative for financial statements covering periods beginning on or after July 1, 1998, have not been considered herein since they will mostly be applied starting 1999). Changes to IAS which have been proposed but which have not been promulgated, although discussed in earlier chapters, are not addressed in this appendix. Furthermore, this has been developed as a general-purpose disclosure checklist for use by commercial enterprises and does not deal with disclosures which might be needed for specialized industry financial statements, such as those outlined in IAS 30 for banks and similar financial institutions.

DISCLOSURE CHECKLIST INDEX

M. Employers' Accounting for Postretirement Benefits Other than Pensions
N. Leases--From the Standpoint of Lessees
O. Leases--From the Standpoint of Lessors
P. Stockholders' Equity

Income Statement

A. Basic Disclosures
B. Investments
C. Income Taxes
D. Extraordinary Items
E. Discontinued Operations
F. Segment Data
G. Construction Contracts
H. Research and Development
I. Foreign Currency Translation
J. Business Combinations and Consolidations
K. Earnings Per Share

Statement of Cash Flows

A. Basis of Presentation
B. Format

GENERAL

A. Basis of Reporting

1. Name of the enterprise whose financial statements are being presented;
2. Enterprise's country of incorporation;
3. Legal form of the enterprise;
4. Currency in terms of which financial statements are expressed;
5. Brief description of nature of activities of the enterprise;
6. Period covered by the financial statements.

(IAS 5, Para 7)

B. Accounting Policies

1. Description of all significant accounting policies adopted in the preparation and presentation of financial statements.

(IAS 1, Para 1)

2. Examples of areas in which such disclosure of accounting treatment may be required are as follows:

   a. General

(1) Basis of consolidation or combination;
(2) Translation of foreign currency transactions;
(3) Overall valuation policy (e.g., historical cost, general purchasing power, replacement value);
(4) Subsequent events;
(5) Leases, hire purchase, installment transactions and related interest;
(6) Construction contracts;
(7) Taxes on income;
(8) Franchises.

b. Assets

(1) Receivables;
(2) Inventories (including work in progress);
(3) Investments;
(4) Property, plant, and equipment and depreciation on depreciable assets;
(5) Research and development costs;
(6) Goodwill and the amortization policy;
(7) Intangibles assets and amortization thereon.

c. Liabilities, provisions and reserves

(1) Current and long-term liabilities;
(2) Deferred revenues;
(3) Commitments and contingencies;
(4) Warranties;
(5) Provision for pension costs and contributions to retirement plans;
(6) Provision for severance costs;
(7) Reserves (e.g., general reserve, statutory reserve).

d. Revenue and expenses

(1) Methods of revenue recognition;
(2) Gains and losses on disposal of property, plant and equipment.

(IAS 1, Para 14)

3. If fundamental assumptions such as going concern, consistency, and the use of accrual accounting are not adhered to in the preparation of the financial statements, this fact should be disclosed.

(IAS 1, Para 3)

C. Accounting Changes

1. Change in accounting policy (alternative disclosures rules apply based on election of benchmark or allowed alternative treatment).

a. If benchmark treatment is elected:

(1) Reason(s) for the change;
(2) Amount of adjustment on current period and for each period presented;
(3) Amount of adjustment relating to periods prior to those included in the comparative information; and
(4) (a) If comparative information has been restated, the fact that it has been restated, or
(b) If comparative is not restated because it is not practicable to do so, then disclosure of this fact.

(IAS 8, Para 53)

b. If allowed alternative treatment is elected:

(1) Reason(s) for the change;
(2) The amount of adjustment recognized in the net profit or loss for the current period;
(3) The amount of the adjustment included in each period for which "pro forma" information is presented and the amount of adjustment relating to periods prior to those included in the financial statements; and
(4) If it is not practicable to present "pro forma" information, this fact should be disclosed.

(IAS 8, Para 57)

2. Change in accounting estimate:

a. Nature and amount of change in an accounting estimate, if material.
b. If it is not practicable to quantify the amount, this fact should be disclosed.

(IAS 8, Para 30)

3. Correction of fundamental errors:

a. If benchmark treatment is elected:

(1) The nature of the fundamental error;
(2) The amount of the correction for the current period and for each period presented;
(3) The amount of the correction which relates to periods prior to those included in the comparative information; and
(4) (a) If comparative information has been restated, this fact should be made explicit, or

(b) If comparative information is not restated because it is not practicable to do so, then this fact must be disclosed.

(IAS 8, Para 37)

b. If allowed alternative treatment is elected:

(1) The nature of fundamental error;
(2) The amount of the correction of the fundamental error which is recognized in the net profit or loss for the current period;
(3) The amount of the correction of the fundamental error which is included in each period for which "pro forma" information is presented and the amount of correction relating to periods prior to those included in the "pro forma" information; and
(4) If it is not practicable to present "pro forma" information, this fact should be disclosed.

(IAS 8, Para 40)

D. Related Party Disclosures

1. Those related party relationships where "control" exists, should be disclosed--*whether or not there have been transactions between the related parties.*

(IAS 24, Para 20)

2. Where transactions have taken place between related parties, the following disclosures are required to be made by the reporting enterprise:

    a. The nature of the related party relationship;
    b. The types of related party transactions; and
    c. The elements of the transactions necessary for an understanding of the financial statements including:

        (1) An indication of the volume of the transactions either as an amount or as an appropriate proportion;
        (2) Amounts or appropriate proportions of outstanding items; and
        (3) Pricing policies.

(IAS 24, Para 22 & 23)

3. Aggregation of items of similar nature is permitted, unless separate disclosure is needed for an understanding of the effects of the related party transactions on the financial statements of the reporting enterprise.

(IAS 24, Para 24)

E. Contingencies and Commitments

1. When the amount of a contingent loss cannot be recognized as an expense and a liability because *probable loss* could **not** be *estimated,* the existence of a contingent loss should be disclosed in the financial statements, unless the possibility of a loss is *remote* .

(IAS 10, Para 9)

2. The existence of contingent gains should be disclosed if it is probable that the gain will be realized. It is important, however, that the disclosure should avoid giving misleading implications as to the likelihood of realization.

(IAS 10, Para 16)

3. When disclosure of contingencies is made as required (i.e., when conditions outlined above are met) the following information is to be disclosed:

   a. The nature of the contingency;
   b. The uncertain factors that have a bearing on the future outcome; and
   c. Either of the following:

      (1) An estimate of the financial effect of such contingency, or
      (2) Disclosure that such an estimate cannot be made.

(IAS 10, Para 22)

F. Events Occurring After Balance Sheet Date (Subsequent Events)

1. Subsequent events that provide additional evidence regarding conditions existing at balance sheet date require adjustment of financial statements.

(IAS 10, Para 25)

2. However, those subsequent events which do not affect the condition of assets or liabilities at the balance sheet date but are of such importance that omission to disclose them would affect the ability of the users of financial statement to make proper decision(s), should be disclosed.

(IAS 10, Para 28)

3. When subsequent events are disclosed, the following information should be provided:

   a. The nature of the subsequent event;
   b. Either of the following:

      (1) The estimate of the effect it has on the financial statements, or
      (2) Disclosure of the fact that such an estimate cannot be made.

(IAS 10, Para 33)

4. Dividends proposed or declared after the balance sheet date but before approval of the financial statements should either be adjusted for or disclosed.

(IAS 10, Para 31)

G. Comparative Financial Statements

Financial statements should show comparative figures for the preceding period.

(IAS 5, Para 9)

H. Other Disclosures

1. Restrictions on the title of assets.

   (IAS 5, Para 10)

2. Securities provided in respect of liabilities.

   (IAS 5, Para 10)

3. Methods of providing for pension and retirement plans.

   (IAS 5, Para 10)

4. Contingent assets and contingent liabilities, quantified if possible.

   (IAS 5, Para 10)

5. Commitments towards future capital expenditures.

   (IAS 5, Para 10)

6. The domicile and legal form of the entity, its country of incorporation and the address of the registered office (or principal place of business, if different).

   (IAS 1, Para 102)

7. A description of the nature of the enterprise's operations and its principal activities.

   (IAS 1, Para 102)

8. The name of the parent entity and the ultimate parent of the group.

   (IAS 1, Para 102)

9. The number of employees either at the end of the period or on average during the period being reported upon.

   (IAS 1, Para 102)

BALANCE SHEET

A. Cash

1. The amount of cash, which includes:

   a. Cash on hand, and
   b. Current and other accounts with banks.

2. Cash that is **not** available for use, such as balances frozen in foreign banks by exchange restrictions, should be disclosed.

   (IAS 5, Para 13 [a])

B. Receivables

Current receivables should be segregated into the following categories, as appropriate:

1. Trade accounts receivables and notes receivable;
2. Receivables from directors;
3. Intercompany* receivables;
4. Receivables from associates; and
5. Other receivables and prepaid expenses.

(IAS 5, Para 13[c])

C. Marketable Securities (other than long-term)

The market value of marketable securities to be disclosed if different from the carrying amount.

(IAS 5, Para 13[b])

D. Inventories

1. The accounting policies and the cost formula used in inventory valuation.

   (IAS 2, Para 34[a])

2. Total carrying amount and the breakdown of the carrying amount by appropriate subclassifications, such as merchandise, production supplies, work in progress and finished goods.

   (IAS 2, Paras 34(b) & 35)

3. Carrying amount of inventories carrying at net realizable value.

   (IAS 2, Para 34[c])

4. Carrying amount of inventories pledged as security for liabilities.

   (IAS 2, Para 34[f])

5. The amount of any reversal of write-down that is recognized as income, along with disclosure of circumstances or events that led to the reversal.

   (IAS 2, Paras 34 [d] & [e])

6. When the cost of inventories is determined using the last-in, first-out (LIFO) formula (under the "allowed alternative treatment"), disclose the difference between the amount of inventories as shown in the balance sheet and either:

---

* *IAS 5 clarifies, by way of a footnote, that the term "Intercompany" refers to balances or transactions between:*

1. *A parent and subsidiaries;*
2. *A subsidiary and its parent; or*
3. *A subsidiary and other subsidiaries in the group.*

a. The lower of amount arrived at using the "benchmark treatment" and the net realizable value; or
b. The lower of current cost at the balance sheet date and net realizable value.

(IAS 2, Para 36)

7. Disclose either of the following:

a. Cost of inventories reported in expense for the period; or
b. Operating costs, applicable to revenues, recognized as expenses for the period, classified by their nature (e.g., raw materials consumed).

(IAS 2, Para 37)

E. Property, Plant, and Equipment (PP&E)

1. Separate disclosure is required for the following items:

a. Land and buildings;
b. Plant and equipment;
c. Other categories of PP&E, suitably identified;
d. Accumulated depreciation;
e. Leaseholds; and
f. Assets being acquired on the installment purchase plan.

(IAS 5, Para 11)

2. In respect of each class (i.e., groupings of assets of a similar nature and use) of PP&E, the following disclosures are required:

a. Measurement basis (bases) used for the determination of the gross carrying amount; if more than one basis has been employed, then also the gross carrying amount determined in accordance with that basis in each category;
b. The depreciation method(s) used;
c. Either the useful lives or the depreciation rates used;
d. The gross carrying amount and the accumulated depreciation at the beginning and the end of the period;
e. A reconciliation of the carrying amount at the beginning and the end of the period disclosing:

(1) Additions;
(2) Disposals;
(3) Acquisitions by means of business combinations;
(4) Increases/decreases resulting from revaluations;
(5) Reductions in carrying value;
(6) Amounts written back to the asset accounts;

(7) Depreciation;
(8) Net exchange differences arising from translation of financial statements of a foreign entity (in accordance with IAS 21); and
(9) Other changes, if any.

(IAS 16, Para 66)

3. Additional disclosure to be made include the following:

    a. Whether, in arriving at the "recoverable amounts" of items of PP&E, expected future cash flows were discounted to their present values;
    b. The existence and amounts of restrictions on title, and PP&E pledged as security for liabilities;
    c. The accounting policy for restoration costs relating to items of PP&E;
    d. The amount of expenditures in respect of PP&E in the course of construction; and
    e. The amount of outstanding commitments for acquisition of PP&E.

(IAS 16, Para 67)

4. In case items of PP&E are stated at revalued amounts, disclose the following information:

    a. The basis used to revalue the items of PP&E;
    b. The effective date of revaluation;
    c. Whether an independent party prepared the valuation;
    d. The nature of the indices used to determine replacement costs;
    e. The carrying amount of each class of PP&E that would have been included in the financial statements had the assets been carried at cost less accumulated depreciation basis; and
    f. The revaluation surplus, including the movements for the period in that account and disclosure of any restrictions on the distribution of the balance in the revaluation surplus account to shareholders.

(IAS 16, Para 70)

5. Other recommended disclosures:

    a. The carrying amount of temporarily idle PP&E;
    b. The gross carrying amount of fully depreciated PP&E still in use;
    c. The carrying amount of PP&E retired from active use and held for sale; and
    d. In cases where items of PP&E are carried at cost less accumulated depreciation (in accordance with the "benchmark treatment") the fair value of PP&E if it is materially different from the carrying amount.

(IAS 16, Para 71)

F. Other Long-Term Assets

Disclose the following items separately, including, if applicable, the method and period of depreciation and any unusual write-offs during the period, per IAS 5, Para 12:

1. Long-term investments

   a. Disclosures about investments in subsidiaries include the following:

      (1) (a) When certain subsidiaries have not been consolidated (i.e., where control is intended to be temporary or where the subsidiary operates under severe long-term restrictions), and these instead have been accounted for as if they were passive investments, the reason(s) for not consolidating the subsidiary.

      (IAS 27, Para 32 [b(i)])

      (b) The names of any enterprises in which more than one-half of the voting power is owned, directly or indirectly through subsidiaries, but which, because of the absence of control, are not subsidiaries.

      (IAS 27, Para 32 [b(iii)])

      (2) A parent company, which is itself a wholly- (or virtually wholly-) owned subsidiary, and which is not presenting consolidated financial statements, should disclose the reasons why consolidated financial statements have not been presented, together with the bases on which subsidiaries are accounted for in its separate financial statements, as well as the name and registered office of **its** parent that publishes consolidated financial statements.

      (IAS 27, Para 8)

      (3) In separate financial statements of a parent company, investments in subsidiaries that would otherwise be included in the consolidated financial statements should be either:

      (a) Accounted for using the equity method; or
      (b) Carried at cost or revalued amounts under the parent's accounting policy for long-term investments

      A description of the method used to account for these subsidiaries should be disclosed.

      (IAS 27, Para 32 [c])

      (4) The following disclosures are required in consolidated financial statements (in addition to disclosures outlined above):

(a) A listing of significant subsidiaries, including the name, country of incorporation or residence, proportion of ownership interest and, if different, proportion of voting power held;

(IAS 27, Para 32 [a])

(b) The nature of relationship between the parent and a subsidiary of which the parent does not own, directly or indirectly through subsidiaries, more than one-half of the voting power, but which is being accounted for as a subsidiary due to the existence of effective control;

(IAS 27, Para 32[b(ii)])

(c) The effect of the acquisition and disposal of subsidiaries on the financial position at the reporting date, and the results for the period and the corresponding amounts for the preceding period; and

(IAS 27, Para 32[b(iv)])

(d) The fact that uniform accounting policies were not used for like transactions and other events affecting the parent and the subsidiaries, together with the proportion of the items in the consolidated financial statements to which the different accounting policies have been applied, if applicable.

(IAS 27, Para 21)

b. Investments in associates

(1) If an investment in an associate is carried at cost or revalued amounts, when the equity method would be the appropriate accounting method for the associate if the investor issued consolidated financial statements, the investor is required to disclose what would have been the effect had the equity method been applied.

(IAS 28, Para 14[b])

(2) Investments in associates accounted for using the equity method should be classified as long-term assets and separately set forth in the balance sheet. The investor's share of profits or losses of such investments should be disclosed as a separate item in the income statement and the investor's share of any extraordinary item or prior period items should be separately disclosed as well.

(IAS 28, Para 28)

(3) The following disclosures are also required:

(a) An appropriate listing and description of significant associates, including the proportion of ownership interest and, if different, the proportion of voting power; and
(b) The method(s) used to account for such investments.

(IAS 28, Para 27)

c. Other long-term investments

(1) *Mandated disclosures*

(a) The accounting policies for:

1] The determination of the carrying amounts of investments; and
2] The treatment of revaluation surplus upon the sale of a revalued investment.

(b) The market value of marketable securities, if they are not carried at market values;
(c) The fair values of investment properties, if they are accounted for as long-term investments and not carried at fair value;
(d) Significant restrictions on the realizability of investments or the remittance of income and the proceeds of disposal;
(e) In the case of long-term investments carried at revalued amounts:

1] The policy regarding the frequency of revaluations;
2] The date of the latest revaluation; and
3] The basis of revaluation and whether an external appraisal was obtained.

(f) The changes in the revaluation surplus for the period and the nature of such changes; and
(g) In the case of those entities whose principal business is the holding of investments, an analysis of the portfolio of investments.

(IAS 25, Para 49)

(2) *Recommended disclosures*

(a) An analysis of long-term investments by category;
(b) The directors' assessment of the fair value of investments that are not marketable;
(c) In case of investments that are not marketable, the method of assessing value used for comparison with cost, where applicable;

(d) Amount of any previous "revaluation surplus" which related to investments disposed of during the year and which had been previously distributed or converted into share capital; and
(e) Details of any single investment which represents a significant fraction of the reporting entity's assets.

(IAS 25, Para 50)

2. Long-term receivables should be categorized as follows:

   a. Trade accounts receivables and notes receivables;
   b. Receivables from directors;
   c. Intercompany* receivables;
   d. Receivables from associates; and
   e. Other

(IAS 5, Para 12[b])

3. Other long-term assets

   The following should be disclosed separately, including, if applicable, the method and period of depreciation and any unusual write-offs during the period:

   a. Goodwill;

(IAS 5, Para 12 [c])

   b. Patents, trademarks, and similar assets; and

(IAS 5, Para 12 [d])

   c. Deferred expenditures (carried forward, e.g., preliminary expenses, re-organization expenses, and deferred taxes).

(IAS 5, Para 12 [e])

G. Current Liabilities

The following should be disclosed separately:

1. Bank loans and overdrafts;
2. Current portions of long-term liabilities;
3. Payables, categorized as to:

---

* *IAS 5 clarifies, by way of a footnote, that the term "Intercompany" refers to balances or transactions between:*

1. *A parent and subsidiaries;*
2. *A subsidiary and its parent; or*
3. *A subsidiary and other subsidiaries in the group.*

a. Accounts payable and notes payable--trade;
b. Current portions of long-term liabilities;
c. Related parties (associates, directors, and intercompany);
d. Income taxes payable;
e. Dividends payable; and
f. Other payables and accrued expenses.

(IAS 5, Para 15)

H. Long-Term Liabilities

The following should be disclosed separately, net of the portion payable within 1 year (which should be included with current liabilities):

1. Secured loans;
2. Unsecured loans;
3. Intercompany loans; and
4. Loans from associates.

A summary of interest rates, repayment terms, covenants, conversion features and amounts of unamortized premiums or discounts should be disclosed.

(IAS 5, Para 14)

I. Financial Instruments

1. *Mandatory disclosures*

a. For each class of either financial asset, financial liability or equity instrument, whether recognized in the balance sheet or not, disclose the following:

(1) Information concerning the extent and nature of the instrument, including significant terms and conditions which may affect the amount, timing or certainty of future cash flows; and
(2) The accounting policies and methods used to account for the instruments, including relevant criteria for recognition and the basis of measurement employed.

(IAS 32, Para 47)

b. For each class of either financial asset or financial liability, whether recognized in the balance sheet or not, disclose the following information about exposure to interest rate risk:

(1) The dates of contractual repricing or maturity, whichever comes first; and
(2) The effective interest rates, if applicable.

(IAS 32, Para 56)

c. For each class of financial asset, whether recognized in the balance sheet or not, disclose the following information about exposure to credit risk:

   (1) The amount which represents the maximum credit risk exposure as of the balance sheet date, without regard to any collateral held, should the other party fail to perform under the terms of the instrument; and
   (2) Any significant concentrations of credit risk.

(IAS 32, Para 66)

d. For each class of financial asset or financial liability, whether or not recognized in the balance sheet, disclose fair value information, unless this cannot be developed on a timely basis with sufficient reliability, in which case that fact must be stated, together with relevant information about the principal characteristics which would be determinative of the fair values of the instruments.

(IAS 32, Para 77)

e. When financial assets are carried at amounts in excess of fair values, disclose the following:

   (1) The carrying amounts and fair values of individual assets or appropriately grouped assets; and
   (2) The reasons for not presenting the assets at fair values, including the nature of any evidence supporting management's belief that the carrying amounts will be recovered.

(IAS 32, Para 88)

f. For instruments accounted for as hedges of anticipated transactions, disclose the following information:

   (1) A description of the anticipated transactions, including the timing of expected occurrence;
   (2) A description of the hedging instruments used; and
   (3) The amount of any deferred (unrecognized) gains or losses, as well as the expected timing of recognition.

(IAS 32, Para 91)

2. *Recommended disclosures*

   a. The total amount of change in the fair values of financial assets and liabilities which has been recognized in income or expense for the year being reported on.

b. The total amount of deferred (unrecognized) gain or loss on hedging instruments, other than those associated with anticipated transactions.
c. The average aggregate carrying amount during the year of recognized financial assets and liabilities; the average aggregate principal, stated or notional amounts of unrecognized financial assets and liabilities; and the average aggregate fair value of all financial assets and liabilities, particularly when the amounts as of the balance sheet date may not be indicative of the level of activity during the year then ended.
d. Any other information which would enhance users' understanding of the financial instruments.

(IAS 32, Para 94)

J. Other Liabilities and Provisions

The significant items included in other liabilities and in provisions and accruals should be separately disclosed. Examples are provisions for pensions, deferred income taxes, etc.

K. Deferred Tax Liabilities and Assets

1. Tax assets and tax liabilities should be presented separately from other assets and liabilities; deferred tax assets and liabilities should be distinguished from those arising from current tax expense.

(Revised IAS 12, Para 69)

2. If a classified balance sheet is presented, deferred tax assets and liabilities should not be included in current assets and liabilities.

(Revised IAS 12, Para 70)

3. Current tax assets and tax liabilities should not be offset unless there is a legally enforceable right of offset and the enterprise intends to settle on a net basis, or to realize the asset and settle the liability simultaneously.

(Revised IAS 12, Para 71)

4. Deferred tax assets and tax liabilities relating to different jurisdictions should be presented separately.

(Revised IAS 12, Para 74)

5. Deferred tax assets and tax liabilities relating to different enterprises in a group which are taxed separately by the taxation authorities should not be offset unless there is a legally enforceable right of offset.

(Revised IAS 12, Para 74)

6. When utilization of deferred tax assets is dependent upon future profitability in excess of amounts from the reversals of taxable temporary differences, and the entity has incurred losses in either the current or preceding period, the amount of deferred tax asset should be disclosed together with the nature of any evidence of its realizability.

(Revised IAS 12, Para 82)

L. Retirement Benefits

1. For defined contribution plans, the following disclosures are required:

   a. A general description of the plans either individually or grouped, with an indication of the groups covered;
   b. The amount recognized as expense during the period;
   c. Any other significant matters that would affect comparability of the financial statements for the period with those of the prior period.

(IAS 19, Para 22)

2. For defined benefit plans, the following disclosures are required:

   a. A general description of the plans either individually or grouped, with an indication of the groups covered;
   b. The accounting policies adopted for retirement benefit costs, including the actuarial methods used;
   c. A statement about whether the plans are funded or not;
   d. The amount recognized as expense during the period;
   e. The actuarial present values of promised plan benefits as of the date of the most recent valuations;
   f. If the plans are funded, the fair value of plan assets, also as of the date of the most recent valuations;
   g. If the amounts funded since the inception of the plans differ from the amounts recognized as expense over the same period, the amount of any resulting assets or liabilities and the funding approaches adopted (any asset of one plan cannot be netted against any liability of another plan);
   h. A statement of the principal actuarial assumptions used in determining expense, and information about significant changes in those assumptions;
   i. The date of the most recent actuarial valuations and the frequency of such valuations; and
   j. Any other significant matters that would affect comparability of the financial statements for the period with those of the prior period, including matters about plan terminations, curtailments, or settlements.

(IAS 19, Para 51)

M. Employers' Accounting for Postretirement Benefits Other Than Pensions

NOTE: While the standards do not address these plans, the same types of disclosures as used for retirement benefit plans would be appropriate.

1. For defined contribution postretirement benefit plans, the following disclosures are suggested:

   a. A general description of the plans either individually or grouped, with an indication of the groups covered;
   b. The amount recognized as expense during the period;
   c. Any other significant matters that would affect comparability of the financial statements for the period with those of the prior period.

2. For defined benefit postretirement benefit plans, the following disclosures are suggested:

   a. A general description of the plans either individually or grouped, with an indication of the groups covered;
   b. The accounting policies adopted for postretirement benefit costs, including the actuarial methods used;
   c. A statement about whether the plans are funded or not;
   d. The amount recognized as expense during the period;
   e. The actuarial present values of promised plan benefits as of the date of the most recent valuations;
   f. If the plans are funded, the fair value of plan assets, also as of the date of the most recent valuations;
   g. If the amounts funded since the inception of the plans differ from the amounts recognized as expense over the same period, the amount of any resulting assets or liabilities and the funding approaches adopted (any asset of one plan cannot be netted against any liability of another plan);
   h. A statement of the principal actuarial assumptions used in determining expense, and information about significant changes in those assumptions;
   i. The date of the most recent actuarial valuations and the frequency of such valuations; and
   j. Any other significant matters that would affect comparability of the financial statements for the period with those of the prior period, including matters about plan terminations, curtailments, or settlements.

N. Leases--From the Standpoint of Lessees

1. For *finance leases*:

a. The amount of assets that are the subject of finance leases at each balance sheet date.

(IAS 17, Para 21)

b. Liabilities relating to the assets that are the subject of finance leases should be presented separately from other liabilities differentiating between current and noncurrent portions.

(IAS 17, Para 21)

c. Commitments for minimum lease payments in the summary form, giving the amounts and the periods in which they become due.

(IAS 17, Para 24)

2. For *finance and operating leases*:

   a. Significant financing restrictions imposed by leasing arrangement, such as limitations on additional borrowing or further leasing;
   b. The nature of renewal options, purchase options or escalation clauses in the leasing arrangement;
   c. The nature of any contingent rentals based on usage or sales; and
   d. The nature of any other contingent liabilities arising from the leasing arrangement (e.g., costs expected at the end of the lease term).

(IAS 17, Paras 26 & 27)

O. Leases--From the Standpoint of Lessors

Disclosure is required of the following at each balance sheet date:

1. Gross investment in finance leases.

(IAS 17, Para 51)

2. Related unearned finance income.

(IAS 17, Para 51)

3. Unguaranteed residual values of leased assets.

(IAS 17, Para 51)

4. If significant portion of business comprised of operating leases, the amount of each major class of asset and related accumulated depreciation.

(IAS 17, Para 54)

5. Disclosure of the basis used for allocating income so as to produce a constant periodic rate of return, indicating whether the return relates to the net

investment outstanding or the net cash investment outstanding in the lease. If more than one basis used, the bases should be disclosed.

(IAS 17, Para 53)

P. Stockholders' Equity

1. For each class of share capital disclose:

    a. Par or legal value;
    b. Number of shares authorized, issued, and outstanding;
    c. Number of shares held in treasury;
    d. Movements in share capital accounts during the period;
    e. The amount of cumulative preference dividends in arrears;
    f. Reacquired shares; and
    g. Shares reserved for future issuance under options and sales arrangements, including terms and amounts.

2. For other equity accounts, disclose separately the following:

    a. Capital paid-in in excess of par value;
    b. Revaluation surplus;
    c. Reserves; and
    d. Retained earnings

(IAS 5, Para 17)

INCOME STATEMENT

A. Basic Disclosures

1. Sales or other operating income;
2. Depreciation;
3. Interest income;
4. Income from investments;
5. Interest expense;
6. Taxes on income;
7. Extraordinary charges;
8. Extraordinary credits;
9. Significant intercompany transactions; and
10. Net profit or loss for the period

(IAS 5, Para 18)

B. Investments

1. Disclosure is required of the following significant amounts included in income:

   a. Interest, royalties, dividends and rentals on long-term and current investments;
   b. Profits and losses on disposal of current investments; and
   c. Changes in value of such investments.

(IAS 25, Para 49[b])

2. The following should be included in income:

   a. Investment income from:

      (1) Interest, royalties, dividends and rentals on long-term and current investments;
      (2) Profits and losses on disposal of current investments;
      (3) Unrealized gains and losses on current investments carried at market value, where such a policy has been adopted under IAS 25, Para 31; and
      (4) Reductions in market value and reversals of such reductions needed to carry current investments at the lower of cost and market.

   b. In relation to long-term investments, reductions of the carrying amount for other than a temporary decline in value and reversals of such reductions; and
   c. Profits and losses on disposals of long-term investments, computed in accordance with the provisions of IAS 25, Para 33.

(IAS 25, Para 41)

C. Income Taxes

1. Tax expense related to profit or loss from ordinary activities should be presented on the face of the income statement.

(Revised IAS 12, Para 77)

2. The major components of tax expense should be presented separately. These commonly would include the following:

   a. Current tax expense;
   b. Any adjustments recognized in the period for current tax of prior periods;
   c. The amount of deferred tax expense relating to the origination and the reversal of timing differences;

d. The amount of deferred tax expense relating to changes in tax rates or the imposition of new taxes;
e. The amount of deferred tax expense or benefit relating to changes in tax rates or the imposition of new taxes;
f. The amount of the benefit arising from a previously unrecognized tax loss, tax credit, or temporary difference of a prior period that is used to reduce current taxes;
g. The amount of a benefit from a previously unrecognized tax loss, tax credit, or temporary difference of a prior period that is used to reduce deferred taxes;
h. Deferred tax expense related to a write-down of a deferred tax asset or the reversal of a write-down; and
i. The amount of tax expense relating to changes in accounting policies and correction of fundamental errors, accounted for consistent with the allowed alternative method under IAS 8.

(Revised IAS 12, Paras 79 & 80)

3. The following items also require separate disclosure:

a. Tax expense relating to items which are charged or credited to equity;
b. Tax expense relating to extraordinary items;
c. An explanation of the relationship between tax expense or benefit and accounting profit or loss either (or both) as:

(1) A numerical reconciliation between tax expense or benefit and the product of accounting profit or loss times the applicable tax rate(s), with disclosure of how the rate(s) was determined; or
(2) A numerical reconciliation between the average effective tax rate and the applicable rate, also with disclosure of how the applicable rate was determined.

d. An explanation of changes in thc applicable tax rates vs. the prior period;
e. The amount and expiration date of deductible temporary differences, and unused tax losses and tax credits for which no deferred tax asset has been recognized;
f. Aggregate temporary differences associated with investments in subsidiaries, branches and associates and interests in joint venture, for which deferred tax liabilities have not been recognized;
g. For each type of temporary difference, and for each type of unused tax loss or unused credit, the amount of deferred tax asset and liability recognized in the balance sheet and the amount of deferred tax expense or benefit recognized in the income statement, unless otherwise apparent from changes in the balance sheet accounts; and

h. With regard to discontinued operations, the tax expense relating to the gain or loss on discontinuance and the tax expense on the profit or loss from ordinary activities of the discontinued operation.

(Revised IAS 12, Para 81)

D. Extraordinary Items

1. The net profit or loss for the period should be comprised of:

   a. Profit or loss from ordinary activities; and
   b. Extraordinary items.

2. Each of the above components should be disclosed on the on the *face of the income statement.*

(IAS 8, Para 10)

3. The nature and the amount of each extraordinary item should be separately disclosed.

(IAS 8, Para 11)

E. Discontinued Operations

The following disclosures are required to be made for each discontinued operation:

1. The nature of the discontinued operation;
2. The industry and geographical segments in which it is reported in accordance with IAS 14;
3. The effective date of discontinuance for accounting purposes;
4. The manner of discontinuance (i.e., by sale or abandonment);
5. Gain or loss on discontinuance and the accounting policy used in measuring that gain or loss; and
6. The revenue and the profit and loss from the ordinary activities of the operation for the current period along with the corresponding figures for each period presented.

(IAS 8, Para 20)

F. Segment Data

1. A description of each reported industry segment and the composition of each reported geographical segment should be set forth.

(IAS 14, Para 9)

2. For each reported industry segment and geographical segment, disclose the following information:

a. Sales or operating revenues, distinguishing revenues from outside customers from intersegment sales;
b. Segment results;
c. Segment assets employed, either in terms of monetary amounts or as percentages of consolidated totals; and
d. The basis used to price intersegment transfers.

(IAS 14, Para 16)

3. A reconciliation should be provided between the total of the individual segment data and the corresponding aggregated information in the financial statements.

(IAS 14, Para 21)

4. If the composition of the segments changes, or the accounting for segments has materially changed, this should be disclosed. The nature of the change, an explanation of the reasons therefore, and the effect of the change (if reasonably determinable) should be provided.

(IAS 14, Para 24)

G. Construction Contracts

1. An enterprise which accounts for construction contracts in accordance with IAS 11 should disclose the following in its financial statements:

   a. The amount of contract revenue recognized as revenue in the period;
   b. The methods used to determine the contract revenue recognized in the period; and
   c. The methods used to determine the stage of completion for contracts in progress.

(IAS 11, Para 39)

2. Each of the following should be disclosed for the contracts in progress:

   a. The aggregate amount of costs incurred and recognized profits (net of any recognized losses) to date;
   b. The amount of advances received; and
   c. The amount of retentions.

H. Research and Development (R&D)

1. Research costs should be recognized as an expense in the period in which they are incurred and should not be recognized as an asset in the subsequent period.

(IAS 9, Para 15)

2. If criteria laid down in IAS 9 are met, then development costs should be recognized as an asset.

(IAS 9, Para 17)

3. In relation to the R&D costs, IAS 9 prescribes the following disclosures:

   a. Accounting policies adopted for R&D costs;
   b. Amount of R&D costs recognized as an expense in the period;
   c. The amortization method(s) used;
   d. The useful lives or amortization rates used; and
   e. A reconciliation of the balance of unamortized development costs at the beginning and the end of the period showing:

      (1) Development costs recognized as an asset;
      (2) Development costs recognized as an expense;
      (3) Development costs allocated to other assets; and
      (4) Development costs written back.

(IAS 9, Para 30)

I. Foreign Currency Translation

1. Disclosure is required of the following:

   a. The amount of exchange differences included in net profit or loss for the period;
   b. Net exchange differences classified as a separate component of equity, and a reconciliation of the amount of such exchange differences at the beginning and the end of the period; and
   c. Amount of exchange differences that arose during the period and which is included in the carrying value of an asset in accordance with IAS 21, Para 21 under the "allowed alternative treatment."

(IAS 21, Para 42)

2. If the reporting currency is different from the currency of the country in which the enterprise is domiciled, disclosure is required of the following:

   a. The reason for using a different currency; and
   b. The reason for any change in the reporting currency.

(IAS 21, Para 43)

3. When there is a change in classification of a significant foreign operation, the following disclosures are required:

   a. The nature of the change;
   b. The reason for the change;

c. The impact of the change in classification on the shareholders' equity; and
d. The impact on the net profit or loss for each period presented as if the change had occurred at the beginning of the period presented.

(IAS 21, Para 44)

4. Disclosure is required of the method selected to translate:

   a. Goodwill arising on the acquisition of a foreign entity; and
   b. Fair value adjustments to the carrying amounts of assets and liabilities arising on the acquisition of that foreign entity.

(IAS 21, Para 45)

5. A change in exchange rates occurring after the balance sheet date which is of such an importance that nondisclosure would affect the ability of users of the financial statements to make proper evaluations and decisions should be disclosed.

(IAS 21, Para 46)

6. Recommended additional disclosure: An enterprise is encouraged to disclose its foreign currency risk management policy.

(IAS 21, Para 47)

J. Business Combinations and Consolidations

1. For all business combinations, the following disclosures are required in the period in which a business combination takes place:

   a. The names and descriptions of the combining enterprises;
   b. The method of accounting for the combination;
   c. The effective date of the combination for accounting purposes; and
   d. A description of any operations of the combining entities which are to be disposed of.

(IAS 22, Para 70)

2. For business combinations accounted for as acquisitions, the following disclosures are also required:

   a. The percentage of voting shares acquired;
   b. The cost of the acquisition and the nature of the consideration paid or payable; and
   c. The nature and amount of any restructuring, plant closure or similar costs provided for in connection with the acquisition and recognized at that time.

(IAS 22, Para 71)

3. The following disclosures are required in the financial statements:

   a. The treatment being used to account for goodwill or negative goodwill, including the amortization period;
   b. Justification of an estimated life for goodwill longer than 5 years, if applicable;
   c. Justification for an amortization method other than straight-line, if applicable, including identification of the method used; and
   d. A reconciliation of goodwill and negative goodwill at the beginning and end of the reporting period, showing:

      (1) The gross amount and the accumulated amortization at the beginning of the period;
      (2) Any additional goodwill or negative goodwill recorded during the period;
      (3) Amortization charged during the period;
      (4) Any other write-offs during the period; and
      (5) The gross amount and the accumulated amortization at the end of the period.

(IAS 22, Para 72)

4. If in an acquisition the fair values of assets and liabilities obtained or of consideration paid can only be provisionally determined at the end of the period in which it occurred, this must be stated and explained. Subsequent adjustments to the provisional fair values should be disclosed and explained in the financial statements of the period in which they occur.

(IAS 22, Para 73)

5. For unitings of interests, the following disclosures are also required:

   a. A description and amount of shares issued, together with the percentage of each entity's voting shares exchanged to effect the uniting;
   b. The amounts of assets and liabilities contributed by each entity; and
   c. Sales revenue, other operating revenues, extraordinary items and net profit or loss of each enterprise prior to the date of the combination that are included in the net profit or loss of the combined entity as reported in the financial statements.

(IAS 22, Para 74)

6. If a business combination occurs after the date of the financial statements, the disclosures set forth above should nonetheless be made, unless impractical to do so, in which case that fact should be stated.

(IAS 22, Para 76)

K. Earnings Per Share

1. Enterprises should present both **basic** EPS and **diluted** EPS on the face of the income statement for each class of ordinary shares that has a different right to share in the net profit for the period. Equal prominence should be given to both the basic EPS and diluted EPS figures for all periods presented.

(IAS 33, Para 47)

2. Enterprises should present basic EPS and diluted EPS even if the amounts disclosed are negative. In other words, the standard mandates disclosure of not just *earnings per share* but even *loss per share* figures.

(IAS 33, Para 48)

3. Enterprises should disclose amounts used as the **numerator** in calculating basic EPS and diluted EPS along with a reconciliation of those amounts to the net profit or loss for the period. Disclosure is also required of the weighted-average number of ordinary shares used as the **denominator** in calculating basic EPS and diluted EPS along with a reconciliation of these denominators to each other.

(IAS 33, Para 49)

4. a. In addition to the disclosure of the figures for basic EPS and diluted EPS, as required above, if an enterprise *chooses to disclose* **per share** amounts **using a reported component of net profit**, other than net profit or loss for the period attributable to ordinary shareholders, such amounts should be calculated using weighted-average number of ordinary shares determined in accordance with the requirements of IAS 33; this will ensure comparability of the per amounts disclosed;
   b. In cases where an enterprise chooses to disclose the above "per share" amounts using a component of net profit not reported as a line item in the income statement, a reconciliation is mandated by the standard, which should reconcile the difference between the component of net income used with a line item reported in the income statement; and
   c. When additional disclosure is made by an enterprise of the above per share amounts, basic and diluted per share amounts should be disclosed with equal prominence (just as basic EPS and diluted EPS figures are given equal prominence).

(IAS 33, Para 51)

5. Enterprises are encouraged to disclose the terms and conditions of financial instruments or contracts generating potential ordinary shares since such terms and conditions may determine whether or not any potential ordinary shares are dilutive and, if so, the effect on the weighted-average number of shares outstanding and any consequent adjustments to the net profit attributable to the ordinary shareholders.

(IAS 33, Para 50)

6. If changes (resulting from bonus issue or share split etc.) in the number of ordinary or potential ordinary shares occur, after the balance sheet date but before issuance of the financial statements, and the per share calculations reflect such changes in the number of shares, such a fact should be disclosed.

(IAS 33, Para 43)

7. Enterprises are also encouraged to disclose a description of ordinary share transactions or potential ordinary share transactions, *other than capitalization issues* and *share splits,* occurring after the balance sheet date and which are of such an importance that nondisclosure would affect the ability of the users of the financial statements to make proper evaluations and decisions.

(IAS 33, Para 45)

CASH FLOW STATEMENT

A. Basis of Presentation

1. A cash flow statement (CFS) should be prepared in accordance with IAS 7 and presented as an integral part of an enterprise's financial statements for each period for which the financial statements are presented.

(IAS 7, Para 1)

2. The CFS should report cash flows during the period classified by:

    a. Operating activities;
    b. Investing activities; and
    c. Financing activities.

(IAS 7, Para 10)

B. Format

1. Cash flows from operating activities should be reported using **either**:

   a. The direct method, under which major classes of gross cash receipts and gross cash payments are disclosed*; or*
   b. The indirect method, wherein net profit or loss for the period is adjusted for the following:

      (1) The effects of noncash transactions;
      (2) Any deferrals or accruals of past or future operating cash receipts or payments; and
      (3) Items of income or expense related to investing or financing cash flows.

(IAS 7, Para 18)

2. An enterprise should generally report (separately) major gross cash receipts and payments from investing and financing activities.

(IAS 7, Para 21)

3. Under the following circumstances, however, an enterprise's* cash flows arising from operating, investing, or financing activities may be reported on a net basis:

   a. Cash receipts and payments on behalf of customers when the cash flows reflect the activities of the customer rather than those of the enterprise; and
   b. Cash receipts and payments for items in which the turnover is quick, the amounts are large, and maturities are short.

(IAS 7, Para 22)

4. Cash flows arising from extraordinary items should be classified as either:

   a. Operating activities;
   b. Investing activities; or
   c. Financing activities.

   Each of these items should be disclosed separately.

(IAS 7, Para 29)

---

* *Cash flows of financial institutions may be reported on a net basis under the following cases:*

1. *Cash flows from the acceptance and repayment of deposits with fixed maturity dates;*
2. *Placement of deposits with and withdrawal of deposits from other financial institutions; and*
3. *Cash advances and loans made to customers and the repayment of those advances and loans.*

(IAS 7, Para 24)

5. Cash flows from interest received and dividends received and dividends paid should be classified consistently (from period to period) as either:

   a. Operating activities;
   b. Investing activities; or
   c. Financing activities.

   Each of these items should be disclosed separately.

   (IAS 7, Para 31)

6. In relation to cash and cash equivalents, a cash flow statement should:

   a. Disclose the policy which it adopts in determining the components;
   b. Disclose the components; and
   c. Present a reconciliation of the amounts in its CFS with similar items reported in the balance sheet.

   (IAS 7, Paras 45 & 46)

7. The effect of exchange rate changes on cash and cash equivalents held or due in foreign currency should be presented separately from cash flows from operating, investing and financing activities.

   (IAS 7, Para 28)

8. Noncash transactions arising from investing and financing activities should be excluded from the CFS. Such transactions do not require the use of cash and cash equivalents and thus should be disclosed elsewhere in the financial statements by way of a note that provides all the relevant information about these activities.

   (IAS 7, Para 43)

9. Cash payments and receipts relating to taxes on income should be separately disclosed and classified as cash flows from operating activities unless they could specifically be identified with financing and/or investing activities.

   (IAS 7, Para 35)

10. In relation to acquisitions or disposals of subsidiaries or other business units which should be presented separately and classified as investing activities, an enterprise should disclose the following:

    a. The total purchase or sale price;
    b. Portion of the consideration discharged by cash and cash equivalents;
    c. Amount of cash and cash equivalents acquired or disposed; and

d. Amount of assets and liabilities (other than cash or cash equivalents) summarized by major category.

(IAS 7, Para 40)

11. Significant cash and cash equivalent balances held by the enterprise which are not available for use by the group should be disclosed by the enterprise along with a commentary by management.

(IAS 7, Para 48)

C. Additional Recommended Disclosures

Additional disclosures which may be relevant to financial statement users in understanding an enterprise's financial position and liquidity have been encouraged by IAS 7 and include the following:

1. The amount of undrawn borrowing facilities including disclosure of restrictions, if any, as to their use;
2. The aggregate amount of cash flows related to interests in joint ventures reported using the proportionate consolidation;
3. The aggregate amount of cash flows that represent increases in operating capacity separately from those cash flows that are required to maintain the operating capacity; and
4. Disclosure of segmental cash flow information in order to provide financial statement users better information about the relationship of cash flows of the business as a whole vis-à-vis cash flows from its segments.

(IAS 7, Para 50)

A

B

D

E

J

Feedback to Authors

We invite your suggestions, corrections, typographical errors, etc. Please send these to Barry J. Epstein and Abbas Ali Mirza, c/o John Wiley & Sons, Inc., 155 N. 3rd Street, Suite 502, DeKalb, Illinois 60115 before June 1, 1998, for inclusion in the 1999 Edition.

1.

2.

3.

4.

5.

6.

7.

8.

9.

10.

11.

12.

13.

WILEY

IAS 98 for WINDOWS®

USER'S GUIDE

Interpretation and Application of
INTERNATIONAL ACCOUNTING STANDARDS
1998

Barry J. Epstein
Abbas Ali Mirza

JOHN WILEY & SONS, INC.
New York • Chichester • Weinheim • Brisbane • Singapore • Toronto

PERMISSIONS

This text is printed on acid-free paper.

Part #055-11651-4 (User's Guide)
ISBN 0471-19537-5 (Disks)
ISBN 0471-19358-5 (CD-Rom)

Printed in the United States of America.

10 9 8 7 6 5 4 3 2 1

TO THE READER

The diskettes in this package are not electronically or mechanically copyprotected. As a purchaser of the package, you are entitled to make a backup copy of the diskettes to protect your investment should the originals become damaged.

As a publisher and representative of the author, we are also entitled to a fair return on our investment. The diskettes are copyrighted, and we assume a personal commitment on your part to abide by the copyright laws, which expressly prohibit unauthorized copying of diskettes or documentation. Offering the diskettes without copy protection allows us to distribute them at reasonable prices. We hope for your cooperation--your assurance that you will not violate the law by making unauthorized copies, either to give away or to sell, so that John Wiley & Sons, Inc. can continue to produce the highest quality electronic products at the lowest possible prices.

Before breaking the security seal on the package, please examine the demo disk and the user's guide provided for your convenience. By breaking the security seal on the main diskettes, you make this product nonrefundable.

CONTENTS

CHAPTER 1
GETTING TO KNOW *IAS 98*

GETTING STARTED

Welcome to *IAS 98*!

This chapter will introduce you to *Interpretation and Application of IAS for Windows 1998 Edition*. You will learn how to install, run, and navigate throughout the program. The following chapters will teach you how to customize certain features, construct a search, and maneuver within this program.

Searches can be performed using key words or phrases. Bookmarks and annotations can be placed in the margins and selected text can be printed.

Most questions can be answered either in this manual or via Help. Help can be accessed at any time either by pressing F1 or using a Pull-Down Menu.

SYSTEM REQUIREMENTS

- IBM compatible PC with a 386 or higher microprocessor
- Windows® 3.1 or higher (Windows® 95 and Windows® NT)
- 4 MB of RAM (8MB of RAM recommended)
- 8 MB of hard disk space
- 3.5" high-density drive or CD-ROM drive, depending on media

INSTALLING *IAS 98*

The *Interpretation and Application of IAS for Windows 1998 Edition* (*IAS 98*) installation process has been designed to be as simple as possible. It consists of a series of prompts and instructions to copy the programs to your computer and set up some initial tailoring for your specific environment. You may wish to backup the disks before installation.

SINGLE USER INSTALLATION INSTRUCTIONS

Floppy Disk Installation

Windows 3.1x and NT 3.51

1. Place Disk 1 in the floppy drive of your computer.
2. From Windows 3.1x Program Manager, choose File, Run.
3. In the Command Line edit box, type A:\SETUP (where A is the letter of your floppy disk drive). Press Enter.

The installation process will begin.

Windows 95 and NT 4.0

1. Place Disk 1 in the floppy drive of your computer.
2. From the Start Menu, choose Run.
3. In the Command Line edit box, type A:\SETUP (where A is the letter of your floppy disk drive). Press Enter.

The installation process will begin.

CD-ROM Installation

Windows 3.1x and NT 3.51

1. Place the CD-ROM in the CD-ROM drive of your computer.
2. From Windows 3.1x Program Manager, choose File, Run.
3. In the Command Line edit box, type D:\SETUP (where D is the letter of your CD-ROM drive). Press Enter.

The installation process will begin.

Windows 95 and NT 4.0

1. Place the CD-ROM in the CD-ROM drive of your computer.
2. From the Start Menu, choose Run.
3. In the Command Line edit box, type D:\SETUP (where D is the letter of your CD-ROM drive). Press Enter.

The installation process will begin.

The procedure consists of a series of questions and answers. If you wish to cancel the operation at any time, click on the appropriate icon.

The installation process is completely menu driven, with occasional prompts for the names of directories and disk changes. Simply follow the prompts on the screen. The SETUP program will search your hard drive for existing versions of *IAS 98*. If this is the first time you have installed *IAS 98* on your machine, a full installation will be initiated. If the program finds an existing version, you will be prompted to overwrite (if an update) or you will be given the option of selecting a new directory in which to install this program. Otherwise, it will prompt you with a default directory, which you can change if you wish.

The installation process will now copy *IAS 98* programs and other files from the diskettes to the directory designated.

Setup will inform you when *IAS 98* is successfully installed on your hard drive.

NETWORK INSTALLATION INSTRUCTIONS

Upgrading From Single User Version to Network Version

Before beginning installation of the Network Version of *IAS 98*, make sure that

1. The Single User Version of *IAS 98* is installed on a network drive. You must know the drive and directory where the Single User Version of *IAS 98* is installed. *NOTE: You must have appropriate rights on your network for the installation to work properly.*
2. The Single User Version of *IAS 98* is not currently in use. If the Single User Version is in use, the Network Version will not be installed.

This installation will upgrade the Single User Version of *IAS 98* to the Network Version. The upgrade does *not* need to be installed to each individual work station. No local files are needed to run the Network Version. To access the Network Version from an individual workstation, please create Program icons or Start Menu shortcuts that map to WIAS98.EXE on the network drive. (See instructions below.)

Network Upgrade Installation

Please note that the Single User Version **must** be installed prior to installing the upgrade.

Windows 3.1x and NT 3.51

1. Place the network installation disk in the floppy drive of your computer.
2. From Windows 3.1x Program Manager, choose File, Run.
3. In the Command Line edit box, type A:\SETUP. Press Enter.
4. Follow the instructions on the screen. A dialog box will appear telling you to enter the drive and directory where the Single User Version is installed. Type in the directory path or choose the path from the Browse button. Press OK to complete installation.

Windows 95 and NT 4.0

1. Place the network installation disk in the floppy drive of your computer.
2. From the Start Menu, choose Run.
3. In the Command Line edit box, type A:\SETUP. Press Enter.
4. Follow the instructions on the screen. A dialog box will appear telling you to enter the drive and directory where the Single User Version is installed. Type in the directory path or choose the path from the Browse button. Press OK to complete installation.

Setting Up Individual Workstations

Program icons (Windows 3.1x and NT 3.51) or Start Menu shortcuts (Windows 95 and NT 4.0) should be created at each workstation that will access the Network Version of *IAS 98*.

Windows 3.1x and NT 3.51

1. From the Program Manager, choose File, New.
2. Choose New Program Group and press OK.
3. Type **John Wiley & Sons** in the Description field. Press OK. A new Program Group called John Wiley & Sons will be created.
4. To create a Program Icon, choose File, New.
5. Choose New Program Item and press OK.

    a. In the Description field, type **Wiley IAS 1998**.
    b. In the Command Line field, type the path to the WIAS98.EXE file. (For example, if the Network Version is installed to the F:\ drive in the Program directory, you need to type F:\PROGRAM\WIAS98\ WIAS98.EXE.) If you do not know where the *IAS 98* program file is located, you can use the Browse feature or contact your network administrator.
    c. In the Working Directory field type in the path to the directory where the program is installed (e.g., F:\PROGRAM\WIAS98).

6. Press OK and a Wiley IAS icon will appear in the John Wiley & Sons Group. Double click on the icon to launch *IAS 98*.

Windows 95 and NT 4.0

1. Place the mouse pointer on the gray bar that runs along the bottom of the screen.
2. Click the right mouse button to open a pop-up menu.
3. Select Properties.
4. Choose the Start Menu Programs tab and press Add.
5. In the Command Line field, type the path to the WIAS98.EXE file. (For example, if the Network Version is installed to the F:\ drive in the Program directory, you need to type F:\PROGRAM\WIAS98\WIAS98.EXE.) Press Next. If you do not know where the Wiley IAS program file is located, you can use the Browse feature or contact your network administrator.

6. Select a folder to place the shortcut (e.g., Programs). Press Next.
7. Select a name for the shortcut (e.g., Wiley IAS).
8. Press Finish. Press OK. Go to the Start Menu, choose the Wiley IAS shortcut to launch *IAS 98*.

RUNNING *IAS 98*

Once *IAS 98* has been installed through Windows, a Group Icon will appear in your Program Manager. To open *IAS 98*, click on the group icon and then click on the icon for the application. The opening screen of *IAS 98* will now appear.

EXITING *IAS 98*

To exit from the application, click Exit from the File menu, select Close from the Control Menu Box, double-click on the Control Menu Box in the topmost left corner of your window, or click on the Close button on the tool bar.

WILEY IAS 98 UNINSTALL UTILITY (REMOVE.EXE)

The Uninstall utility will automatically be installed when you complete the *Wiley IAS 98* installation. If you have installed *Wiley IAS 98* into a directory on your hard drive called **C:\WIAS98**, then the Uninstall utility will be located there.

Steps for Running the Uninstall Utility

1. Locate the directory in which *Wiley IAS 98* was installed. Go to this directory in *File Manager* (Windows 3.x and NT 3.51) or *Windows Explorer* (Windows 95 and NT 4.0), and double-click on the **REMOVE.EXE** file located there. This executable file is located in the same directory as *WIAS98.EXE*.
2. The Uninstall will display a *Welcome*...message, asking you if you want to continue or not. Click *Yes* to continue, or *No* to cancel the Uninstall.

3. If the Uninstall cannot find the key *Wiley IAS 98* files (such as the WIAS98.EXE), it will display a message telling you that it could not do so, and ask you if you want to continue or not. You may get this message if you started an Uninstall previously, and it did not complete successfully. Click *Yes* to continue, or *No* to cancel the Uninstall.
4. When you click *Yes*, the Uninstall will automatically begin deleting files from the Wiley directory. It will delete all of the standard program files (*.EXE, *.DLL, etc.) without prompting for confirmation.
5. If the Uninstall comes across user-created files (such as the *Bookmark**.MRK files), it will prompt you whether or not to delete them. Whenever it prompts you to delete a file, it will give you five different options.

Yes	Deletes this file and only this file.
Yes to All	Deletes this file, and all (remaining) files with this same extension.
No	Does not delete this file.
No to All	Does not delete this file, nor any other (remaining) files with this extension.
Cancel	Cancels (aborts) the Uninstall.

6. After you have been prompted to delete the user-created files, the Uninstall will attempt to remove remaining subdirectories, as well as Windows program groups and icons referring to *Wiley IAS 98*.
7. Based on whether or not Setup was able to remove all of the files pertaining to *Wiley IAS 98*, it will display one of two messages.

   1) *Wiley IAS 98* has been successfully removed from your hard drive.

2) *Wiley IAS 98*'s Uninstall Utility successfully removed all program files but left some files behind as instructed.

8. **Note:** In Windows 95 and NT 4.0, the Uninstall can delete itself from the *Wiley IAS 98* directory. However, in Windows 3.x and NT 3.51, the Uninstall *cannot* remove itself; you will therefore receive the following message before the *Success* message indicated in Step 7:

   The current operating system will not allow Uninstall to remove itself. You will have to manually delete "REMOVE.EXE" and the Wiley IAS 98 program directory after this application terminates.

OVERVIEW

Once you have started *IAS 98* you will be presented with the opening screen containing the Browse Screen.

The Browse Screen is where you activate all of your document searches. On the top line of the screen you will see the product name: *Interpretation and Application of IAS 1998.* This is the title bar. Along the top, under the title bar, is the menu line. These pull-down menus enable you to use a wide selection of search and setup options which will be described throughout this reference material as well as in the on-line help. The Tool-Bar buttons located below the Pull-Down Menus represent major functions of *IAS 98.* To select a function, click on the appropriate button. A brief description of each feature appears on the applicable button.

Once you are using the program, you will become familiar with other display features of *IAS 98.* These will be introduced here and discussed further in later chapters.

The Browse Window

Documents and other types of data are presented in the Browse Window. You may use your mouse to make selections or use the arrow and other text-navigation keys to move around the document.

Dialog Boxes

Many of the options in *IAS 98* require you to make selections or enter data in a dialog box. When you are entering data, the usual editing keys, such as Delete, Backspace, Home, and End, function as they do in DOS.

Begin entering your data at the flashing cursor. When you have finished your data entry, click on OK or press Enter. Dialog boxes that require you to make selections use the Arrow and Tab keys for navigation and the Enter key for completing selections. When using a mouse, simply click on the selection and choose OK.

Screen Functions

Upon entering certain screens, specific function buttons may be highlighted by default. To switch from one highlighted function to another portion of the screen, use the Tab key.

CHAPTER 2
THE MAIN MENU AND TOOL BUTTONS

The Browse Screen contains the Pull-Down Menu Bar. The following is a brief description of the features available. For a more detailed explanation of these features, please refer to the individual sections.

FILE MENU

Activate Word Processor

This File Menu item activates the specified word processor. A word processor can either be specified during the installation of the product or from the Preferences Screen, which can be accessed through the Edit Pull-Down Menu.

Print

This option is only available if a printer has been installed. This menu item controls how a document is printed. This option can also be performed by pressing the Control and P keys simultaneously.

Print Setup

This option is only available if a printer has been installed. This menu item changes the printer setup. Select either the default printer or specify another one. In addition, there are paper orientation, size, and source options. If you currently have a printer setup through another Windows application, you will probably not need to run the Print Setup here.

Exit

This option closes *IAS 98* and returns you to Windows.

EDIT MENU

Copy Selected Text

This option is only available if text has been selected. This menu item will copy selected text to the Windows Clipboard. The selected text can then be pasted into other Windows applications. Once text has been selected using the mouse, you may also perform this option by pressing the Control and C keys simultaneously. Graphics cannot be copied or printed.

Search on Selected Text

This option is only available if text has been selected. This feature searches the book for highlighted words or phrases and can also be accessed by pressing the Control and S keys simultaneously.

Preferences

This option accesses the Preferences Screen. The Preferences Screen controls the highlight color for a search match, how many lines of text will surround the search match in the List Screen, how root words and variations will be searched, what will appear on the screen at startup, and the addition or modification of word processor and browser information.

PREFERENCES SCREEN

The Expanded Hit section controls the amount of text surrounding the hit when it appears in the List Screen. Also, the color used to highlight the text can be changed by selecting a color from the Hit Color selection box.

The Searches section controls whether a search will look for root word and variations. Select the box by either clicking on the box with the mouse or by tabbing to the section and pressing the spacebar. The root words and variations for the text entered in the Find Screen will be found in the text and displayed as matches in the List Screen. If the box is not selected, only text exactly matching the find phrase entered in the Find Screen will be found and displayed in the List Screen.

The Startup section controls whether the Introductory Splash Screen will appear each time upon entry into *IAS 98*. Select the box by either clicking on the box with the mouse or by tabbing to the section and pressing the spacebar. The Introductory Splash Screen will automatically appear each time upon entry into *IAS 98*. If the box is not selected, the Splash Screen will not appear. Another control option available determines whether the Table of Contents Screen will automatically appear upon entry into the Browse Screen. If the box is selected, the Table of Contents Screen will automatically appear upon entry into the Browse Screen. If the box is not selected, the Table of Contents is still available by pressing the Contents button or by using the Pull-Down Menu, but will not automatically appear upon entry in the Browse Screen.

The addition, deletion, or modification of Word Processor setup information in the Word Processor section can also be accomplished in this section. The default word processor can be changed by scrolling through the available word processors and selecting a different one. Either use the mouse to select a word processor or use the vertical arrow keys to highlight the applicable word processor and press Enter. The Edit List button provides for the addition, deletion, or modification of word processor information. The maximum number of word processors on the list that can be saved is 10. An additional word processor cannot be entered if the maximum number has been reached until the user deletes a word processor from the list.

EDIT WORD PROCESSOR LIST

The Edit Word Processor List Screen allows for the addition, deletion, or modification of word processor information. In addition, the user can select a default word processor. To access the Edit Word Processor List, choose Edit List from the Preferences Screen.

To add a word processor, either click on the Add button with your mouse or tab to the Add button and press Enter. Then the path for the new word processor must be entered. If that path is unknown, press the Browse button to access the File Manager and select the word processor .exe file. Once a path has been selected, the name to be associated with the word processor must be entered. This is the name that will appear on the list. Once this information has been added select the OK button to save and return to the Edit Word Processor List Screen or select Cancel to return to the Edit Word Processor List Screen without saving the new word processor information.

If editing a word processor, move the highlight in the List of Word Processors section using the vertical arrow keys to the applicable word processor or click on the applicable word processor with your mouse. Once a word processor has been selected, click on the Edit button with your mouse or tab to the Edit button and press Enter. This will access the Add Word Processor Screen. Modify either the path or name information by moving to the applicable field, deleting the information in the field, then entering new information. Once the information has been modified, select the OK button to save and return to the Edit Word Processor List Screen.

To delete a word processor from the list, move the highlight in the List of Word Processors section using the vertical arrow keys to the applicable word processor. Then either click on the Delete button with your mouse or tab to the Delete button and press Enter. The selected word processor will be deleted from the list.

Selecting a new Default Word Processor can be achieved by moving the highlight in the List of Word Processors section using the vertical arrow keys to the applicable word processor. Then either click on the Default button with your mouse or tab to the Default button and press Enter.

ADD WORD PROCESSOR

To add a word processor, either click on the Add button with your mouse or tab to the Add button and press Enter. Then the path for the new word processor must be entered. If that path is unknown, press the Browse button to access the File Manager and select the word processor .exe file. Once a path has been selected, then the name to be associated with the word processor must be entered. This is the name that will appear on the list. Once this information has been added select the OK button to save and return to the Edit

Word Processor List Screen or select Cancel to return to the Edit Word Processor List Screen without saving the new word processor information.

Edit Internet Browser

The addition, deletion, or modification of an Internet Browser can also be accomplished in this section. The default browser can be changed by scrolling through the available browsers and selecting a different one. Either use the Mouse to select a browser or use the vertical arrow keys to highlight the applicable browser and press Enter. The Edit List button provides for the addition, deletion, or modification of browser information. The maximum number of Internet Browsers on the list that can be saved is 10. A browser cannot be entered if the maximum number has been reached until the user deletes a browser from the list.

Edit Saved Searches

This item accesses the Edit Saved Searches Screen. The Edit Saved Searches Screen allows for the addition, modification, and deletion of a saved search. The Edit option is disabled until a search is selected from your directory of searches.

Add Search to Saved Search List

This option is only available if a search has been performed. This item will add the current search to the Saved Search List. The saved search must be named in the Search Name box. The Search Text displays the keyword phrase to be saved. Either click on the OK button with the mouse or tab to the OK button and press Enter. To cancel the save, select the Cancel button with the mouse or tab to the Cancel button and press Enter. The maximum number of saved searches is 100. If the maximum number is exceeded, the oldest saved search will automatically be deleted.

VIEW MENU

Title Page

This menu item returns the user to the Title Page from anywhere in the text.

Context of Hits

This menu item accesses the List Screen. The List Screen provides places in the book that contain text that matches a search. These matches are called hits. The user may view the context in which the search word or phrase was used in the matching portion of the text by expanding the hit.

Next Chapter

This option moves to the next chapter in the book.

Previous Chapter

This option moves back to the last chapter viewed.

Next Chapter That Contains a Hit

This option is only available if a successful search has been performed. This item moves to the next chapter in the book that contains a hit.

Previous Chapter That Contains a Hit

This option is only available if a successful search has been performed. This item moves to the previous chapter in the book that contains a hit.

Next Hit

This option is only available if a successful search has been performed. This item moves to the next hit within the chapter.

Previous Hit

This option is only available if a successful search has been performed. This item moves back to a previous hit within the chapter.

Back

This button is only available in the Browse Screen. Upon entry into the Browse Screen each search that is performed (find, hyperlink jump, browse search, browse chapter, random, or table of contents search) is stored in memory (up to 15 searches). This option then moves backwards through each browse screen that was reached as a result of one of the searches performed. This option can also be performed by pressing the Control and B keys simultaneously. These searches are only remembered during the current session.

SEARCH MENU

Find

The Find option can be accessed by pressing the Control and F keys simultaneously or by clicking the Find button. The Find Screen performs a simple text search. This is accomplished by entering a key word in the Find Box and selecting the OK button. A more complex search can be performed by selecting the Options button on the Find Screen.

Once the Options button is selected the Find Screen drops down to reveal a number of options that can be used to place text in the Find Box. The Find Phrase button will locate an exact string of words. After selecting this option quotation marks will appear on the screen. Enter phrase between the quotation marks and click OK. The Word Builder option will build a word letter by letter (select "text search") or search for a word phonetically (select "phonetic search"). The Saved Searches option will display previous searches that were saved. The Copy from Clipboard option extracts information that was copied to the Windows Clipboard and pastes it into the Find Screen.

The Word Connector options appear in the middle of the screen. To select a word connector, either tab to the word connector field and use your arrow keys to move to the applicable word connector then press Enter or move your mouse to the applicable word connector and double-click.

See *Formulating a Search in the Find Screen* in Chapter 3 for an explanation of each Word Connector.

Table of Contents

This option displays the Table of Contents and can also be accessed by pressing the Control and T keys simultaneously. See *Searching with the Table of Contents* in Chapter 3 for more information.

Key Concepts

Key Concepts are topics that have been located in the text for you. To access Key Concepts, click on the Key Concepts button, choose Key Concepts from the Search Menu or type CTRL+K.

Double click on the appropriate topic to go to that section. In some instances, the topic will be found in more than one location in the book. If you have chosen one of those topics, you will see a **List Screen**. Double click on the chapter you wish to go to, or highlight the chapter and click on "Go to Hit."

Index

This option accesses the Index Screen and can also be accessed by pressing the Control and I keys simultaneously. See *Searching with an Index* in Chapter 3 for detailed information.

Clear Search Terms

Use Clear Search Terms to remove the highlights from the previous search. Either choose Clear Search Terms from the Search Menu or press CTRL+X.

HELP MENU

IAS 98 has context-sensitive Help. From most windows within *IAS 98*, you can press F1 to obtain information about the current feature being used. If you are unsure of how to proceed or if you need additional information on a particular function, press F1 for assistance.

About *IAS 98 Edition*

Provides copyright and version information pertaining to *IAS 98* software.

Wiley Web Links

Provides online information on all Wiley accounting products.

Contents

Additional help on various topics can be obtained by selecting Contents from the Help Menu and clicking on the topic of your choice.

BOOKMARKS MENU

First Marked Chapter

This option is only available if a mark has been placed in the text. This item moves to the first chapter containing a mark.

Previous Marked Chapter

This option is only available if more than one mark has been placed in the text and in multiple chapters. This item moves to the previous chapter containing a mark.

Next Marked Chapter

This option is only available if more than one mark has been placed in the text and in multiple chapters. This item moves to the next chapter containing a mark.

Last Marked Chapter

This option is only available if more than one mark has been placed in the text and in multiple chapters. This item moves to the last chapter containing a mark.

First Mark

This option is only available if a mark has been placed within the chapter. This item moves to the first mark within the chapter.

Previous Mark

This option is only available if more than one mark has been placed within the chapter. This item moves to the previous mark within the chapter.

Next Mark

This option is only available if more than one mark has been placed within the chapter. This item moves to the next mark within the chapter.

Last Mark

This option is only available if more than one mark has been placed within the chapter. This item moves to the last mark within the chapter.

New Mark

This option accesses the New Mark Screen. The New Mark Screen adds marks in the margins of the text. Optional bookmarks, text annotations, existing files, or objects can be placed in the margin.

The color of the mark can be selected in the Highlight Color section of the screen.

When a mark is added, it is always added to the top of the applicable section. The cursor location does not indicate marked text. To edit or delete a mark, the user must scroll to the top of the applicable section then use the Edit or Delete Mark buttons.

Edit Mark

This option accesses the Edit Mark Screen. The Edit Mark Screen is used to modify marks made in the margins of the text.

Delete Mark

This option is only available in a section with an existing mark. This item will delete one mark at a time from within the section. To delete an existing mark, you must scroll to the top of the applicable section containing the mark.

Show Mark

This option is only available if a mark has been placed in the text. This item will display the mark.

View Bookmark List

Use the View Bookmark List option to show a list of all of your bookmarks. Highlight an entry and click on VIEW or double click on an entry to go to that bookmarked location in the text.

THE TOOL BUTTONS

For your convenience, the Tool Bar buttons across the top of the Browse Window provide you with immediate access to various functions found on the Pull-Down Menus. To access Tool buttons, click on the button. A brief description of each feature appears on the applicable button.

The following is a brief description of the functions available:

Contents

This button will access the Table of Contents Screen from any part of the text. The left arrow around the Contents button takes you to the previous hit. The right arrow around the Contents button takes you back to the current hit.

Find

This button allows you to display the Find Screen. The Find Screen performs a simple text search. For additional information on performing a search, see *Formulating a Search in the Find Screen* in Chapter 3.

Results

This option is only available if a search has been successfully completed. The vertical arrows move from hit to hit within a chapter. The horizontal arrows move through to the first hit of every chapter that contains a hit. The Results button accesses the List Screen. The List Screen provides places in the book that contain text that matches a search. These matches are called "hits."

The List Screen contains four buttons that either go to the hit that is highlighted in the List Hits box, close the screen, expand the hit (view the context in which the search word or phrase was used in the matching portion of the text), or offer help.

The amount of text above and below a hit is controlled in the Expanded Hit section of the Preferences Screen.

Back

Upon entry into the Browse Screen each search that is performed (find, hyperlink jump, browse search, browse chapter, table of contents, or index search) is stored in memory (up to 15 searches). This option then moves backward through each Browse Screen that was reached as a result of one of the searches performed. This option can also be performed by pressing the Control and B keys simultaneously. These searches are only remembered during the current session.

History

This button allows you to display a list of the last 20 chapters visited. To go directly to one of the chapters, single click on that entry and you will be taken to the top of that chapter.

Key Concepts

This button allows you to display the Key Concepts screen. The Key Concepts screen provides topics that have been located in the text for you.

Index

This button allows you to display the Index.

Copy

This button allows you to place selected text onto the Windows Clipboard. Graphics cannot be copied or printed.

Bookmark

This button activates the Bookmark function as if you had selected New Mark from the View Menu.

Word Processor

This button activates your word processor if one has been added in the Preferences section of the Edit Menu.

Print

This button allows you to print to your Windows printer.

Close

The Close button will exit you from the *IAS 98* product.

Help

This button allows you to access the *IAS 98* help system.

CHAPTER 3
SEARCH FORMULATION

OVERVIEW

There are many different ways to locate the information you want in *IAS 98*. This chapter will discuss the various search techniques available.

FIND SCREEN

The Find Screen can be accessed by pressing the Control and F keys simultaneously or by clicking the Find button.

The Find Screen performs a simple text search. This is accomplished by entering a key word in the Find Box and selecting the OK button. A more complex search can be performed by selecting the Options button on the Find Screen.

FIND OPTIONS

Once the Options button is selected, the Find Screen drops down to reveal a number of options that can be used to place text in the Find Box.

Find Phrase

The Find Phrase button will locate an exact string of words. After selecting this option, quotation marks will appear on the screen. Enter phrase between the quotation marks and click OK.

Word Builder

The Word Builder option will build a word letter by letter (select text search) or search for a word phonetically (select phonetic search). The words from the text that match the search appear in the scroll region. These words may be used as key words in the Find Box. This is accomplished by using the mouse to select a word from the scroll region, a single-click on the Use button and then a single-click on the OK button, or by using the vertical arrows to highlight the applicable word and then pressing Enter twice.

Saved Searches

The Saved Searches option will display previous searches that were saved.

Copy From Clipboard

The Copy from Clipboard option extracts information that was copied to the Windows Clipboard and pastes it into the Find Screen.

Word Connectors

The Word Connector options appear in the middle of the screen. To select a word connector, either tab to the word connector field, use your arrow keys to move to the applicable word connector, and then press Enter, or simply move your mouse to the applicable word connector and double-click.

An explanation of each Word Connector option is provided below.

And: represented by the symbol "&." This word connector is used to locate chapters that contain both of the specified terms. For example

stocks And bonds

Or: represented by a blank space. This word connector is used to locate hits within a chapter that contain either of the specified terms. For example

stocks Or bonds

Not: represented by the symbol "%." This word connector is used to locate hits within chapters that contain the first term but not the second. For example

stocks Not bonds

Followed by: is represented by "...". This connector is used to locate hits that are followed by another term later in the same chapter. For example

stocks Followed by bonds

In the same paragraph as: represented by the symbol "//." This word connector is used to locate hits in which both terms appear within one paragraph. For example

stocks In the same paragraph as bonds

Within 10 words of: is represented by the symbol "/10." This word connector is used to locate hits in which both terms appear within the same paragraph within 10 words of each other. For example

stocks Within 10 words of bonds

The Search Results area of the Find Screen selects the specific area where the search will be conducted. The New Search option searches the complete text of the selected book; the Search Current Results option searches within the results currently displayed; and the Search Previous Results option searches within the results of the previous search.

? is a single-letter *universal character*. For example, typing kn?w will find both **know** and **knew**. ***** or **!** are *root expanders*. For example, typing **legislat!** will find words like **legislate**, **legislator**, **legislative**, and **legislature**. Anything used as an operand or wildcard cannot be searched upon. This includes the following symbols: **&**, %, !, *, ?.

SEARCHING WITH THE TABLE OF CONTENTS

The Table of Contents Screen allows chapters or sections of the book to be viewed by simply selecting them from the Table of Contents.

There are many ways to select a chapter or section from the Table of Contents. Double-clicking on a page will bring up that section of the book while double-clicking on a book will expand the Table of Contents to the next level. Searches can be performed from this screen by highlighting an item from the Table of Contents with the mouse, then clicking on the Flashlight icon on the Toolbar. This will search for all occurrences of the item highlighted.

There are many ways to expand and collapse the Table of Contents. The Tree Pull-Down Menu has menu options to expand all, collapse all, expand one level or collapse one level of items in the Table of Contents. The highlighted entry in the Table of Contents is the only level affected when the expand or collapse one level options are used. The mouse can be used to expand and collapse the Table of Contents by selecting the Tree Pull-Down Menu and clicking on the appropriate action or by clicking on the 1, 2, 3, 4, or 5 buttons on the Toolbar. (This is only available if the Toolbar has been selected from the Options Menu.) These buttons expand and collapse to the selected level simply by clicking on the appropriate button.

Once a section is found, either move the highlight to the applicable entry using the arrow keys and press Enter or use the mouse to move the pointer arrow to the applicable entry and double-click on it.

Expand All

This option is only available if the Table of Contents has not been fully expanded. This item will fully expand all levels of the Table of Contents.

Collapse All

This option is only available if the Table of Contents has been expanded. This item will collapse all levels back to first level.

Expand One Level

This option is only available if there is another level available. This item will expand the Table of Contents one level.

Collapse One Level

This option is only available if the Table of Contents has been expanded one or more levels. This item will collapse the Table of Contents by one level.

Expand Current Branch

This option is only available if the current branch has another level below it. This item will expand the current branch of the Table of Contents by one level.

Collapse Current Branch

This option is only available if the current branch has been expanded. This item will collapse the current branch of the Table of Contents.

Expand to Level 1

This option is only available if the Table of Contents contains a Level 1. This item will expand the Table of Contents to Level 1.

Expand to Level 2

This option is only available if the Table of Contents contains a Level 2. This item will expand the Table of Contents to Level 2.

Expand to Level 3

This option is only available if the Table of Contents contains a Level 3. This item will expand the Table of Contents to Level 3.

Expand to Level 4

This option is only available if the Table of Contents contains a Level 4. This item will expand the Table of Contents to Level 4.

Expand to Level 5

This option is only available if the Table of Contents contains a Level 5. This item will expand the Table of Contents to Level 5.

SEARCHING WITH THE INDEX

The Index Screen allows chapters or sections of the book to be viewed by simply selecting them from the Index.

There are many ways to select a chapter or section from the Index. Double-clicking on a page will bring up that section of the book, while double-clicking on a book will expand the Index to the next level. Searches can be performed from this screen by highlighting an item from the Index with the mouse, then clicking on the Flashlight icon on the Toolbar. This will search for all occurrences of the item highlighted. All highlighted items in the Index are accentuated in red-colored text throughout the program.

There are many ways to expand and collapse the Index. The Tree Pull-Down Menu has menu options to expand all, collapse all, expand one level, or collapse one level of items in the Index. The highlighted entry in the Table of Contents is the only level affected when the expand or collapse one level options are used. The mouse can be used to expand and collapse the Table of Contents by selecting the Tree Pull-Down Menu and clicking on the appropriate action or by clicking on the 1, 2, 3, 4, or 5 buttons on the Toolbar. (This is only available if the Toolbar has been selected from the Options Menu.) These buttons expand and collapse to the selected level simply by clicking on the appropriate button.

Once a section is found, either move the highlight to the applicable entry using the arrow keys and press Enter or use the mouse to move the pointer arrow to the applicable entry and double-click on it.

Expand All

This option is only available if the Index has not been fully expanded. This item will fully expand all levels of the Index.

Collapse All

This option is only available if the Index has been expanded. This item will collapse all levels back to first level.

Expand One Level

This option is only available if there is another level available. This item will expand the Index one level.

Collapse One Level

This option is only available if the Index has been expanded one or more levels. This item will collapse the Index by one level.

Expand Current Branch

This option is only available if the current branch has another level below it. This item will expand the current branch of the Index by one level.

Collapse Current Branch

This option is only available if the current branch has been expanded. This item will collapse the current branch of the Index.

Expand to Level 1

This option is only available if the Index contains a Level 1. This item will expand the Index to Level 1.

Expand to Level 2

This option is only available if the Index contains a Level 2. This item will expand the Index to Level 2.

Expand to Level 3

This option is only available if the Index contains a Level 3. This item will expand the Index to Level 3.

Expand to Level 4

This option is only available if the Index contains a Level 4. This item will expand the Index to Level 4.

Expand to Level 5

This option is only available if the Index contains a Level 5. This item will expand the Index to Level 5.

CUSTOMER SUPPORT

For customer service inquiries or information about other accounting books, call **800-272-2100**.

TECHNICAL SUPPORT

For technical support about this product, call **(212) 850-6753,** or fax **(212) 850-6800**. (Please send fax to the attention of Wiley Technical Support), or e-mail: **techhelp@wiley.com**.

JOHN WILEY & SONS, INC.
NETWORK LICENSE AGREEMENT

IMPORTANT-READ CAREFULLY BEFORE USING OR LOADING THE SOFTWARE

This is a legal agreement between you, defined as the Licensee (which definition includes the end-users where applicable) and John Wiley & Sons, Inc. ("Wiley"). The enclosed Wiley software program, including the User's Guide (collectively, the "SOFTWARE") is licensed by Wiley for use only on the terms set forth herein. Using or loading the SOFTWARE indicates that you accept these terms. If you do not agree to these terms, return the full product with proof of purchase within 15 days for a full refund.

---

1. GRANT OF LICENSE.

You have purchased a network license which permits use of the SOFTWARE on a local area network maintained by the entity identified by the "bill to" address (the "Site"), and which permits use by the maximum number of end-users that you identified to Wiley when you ordered the SOFTWARE (the "Designated Number"). This Network License Agreement allows you to support up to the Designated Number of end-users on the terms set forth below. Wiley grants to you the right to use one copy of the SOFTWARE on a server located at the Site which is capable of supporting up to the Designated Number of end-users. You agree to use the SOFTWARE only for your internal purposes. If you wish to change the Designated Number of end-users or the Site, you must contact Wiley at the address set forth in Paragraph 7 below. You hereby agree to take all measures to ensure (i) that all end-users shall use the SOFTWARE solely for the purposes set forth herein and (ii) that all end-users shall be advised of such purpose, restrictions and all provisions of use set forth herein.

---

2. WARRANTIES, INDEMNITIES, AND LIMITATION OF LIABILITY.

Wiley warrants that the disk(s) is free of defects in materials and workmanship under normal use for a period of 30 days from the date of purchase as evidenced by a copy of your receipt. If during the 30 day period a defect occurs, you may return the disk(s) for a replacement. Your sole and exclusive remedy in the event of a defect is expressly limited to the replacement of the defective disk(s) at no additional charge. If Wiley is unable to provide a disk that is free from such defects, you may terminate this License by returning the disk(s) and the User's Guide to Wiley for a full refund. In addition, if you are not satisfied with this product for any other reason, you may return the entire product with proof of purchase and your receipt within 15 days for a full refund.

EXCEPT AS SET FORTH ABOVE, THE SOFTWARE IS PROVIDED "AS IS", WITHOUT WARRANTY OF ANY KIND, EXPRESS OR IMPLIED, INCLUDING BUT NOT LIMITED TO THE IMPLIED WARRANTIES OF MERCHANTABILITY OR FITNESS FOR A PARTICULAR PURPOSE. WILEY NEITHER GIVES NOR MAKES ANY OTHER WARRANTIES OR REPRESENTATIONS UNDER OR PURSUANT TO THIS LICENSE. Wiley does not warrant, guarantee or make any representations that the functions contained in the SOFTWARE will meet your particular requirements or that the operation of the SOFTWARE will be uninterrupted or error free. The entire risk as to the results and performance of the SOFTWARE is assumed by you.

Wiley has made efforts to ensure the accuracy and efficacy of the SOFTWARE. HOWEVER, IN NO EVENT SHALL WILEY OR ANYONE ELSE WHO HAS BEEN INVOLVED IN THE CREATION, PRODUCTION OR DELIVERY OF THE SOFTWARE OR USER'S GUIDE BE LIABLE OR RESPONSIBLE FOR ANY LOSS OR INACCURACY OF DATA OF ANY KIND NOR FOR ANY LOST PROFITS, LOST SAVINGS, OR ANY OTHER DIRECT OR INDIRECT, SPECIAL, INCIDENTAL OR CONSEQUENTIAL OR EXEMPLARY DAMAGES ARISING OUT OF OR RELATED IN ANY WAY TO THE USE OR INABILITY TO USE THE SOFTWARE, EVEN IF WILEY OR ITS SUPPLIERS HAVE BEEN ADVISED OF THE POSSIBILITY OF SUCH DAMAGES. THIS LIMITATION OF LIABILITY SHALL APPLY TO ANY CLAIM OR CAUSE WHATSOEVER WHETHER SUCH CLAIM OR CAUSE IS IN CONTRACT, TORT, OR OTHERWISE.

The limited warranty set forth above is in lieu of all other express warranties, whether oral or written. The agents, employees and distributors of Wiley are not authorized to modify this warranty, nor to make additional warranties binding on Wiley. Accordingly, additional statements such as distributor representations, whether written or oral, do not constitute warranties of Wiley and should not be relied upon as a warranty of Wiley. Wiley's pricing of the SOFTWARE reflects this allocation of the risk and limitations of liability contained in this clause; in no case shall

(continued on back)

Network License Agreement Continued . . .

Wiley's liability exceed the amount paid for use of the SOFTWARE. You agree to indemnify and hold Wiley and all of its officers, directors, employees, and agents, as well as all those individuals or organizations providing information for inclusion in the SOFTWARE incorporated into the SOFTWARE, harmless from any and all claims of third parties resulting from or incidental to your use or operation of the SOFTWARE, or arising from any breach by you or end-users of any provisions of this License. Wiley may, at its option, institute or defend any action arising out of the aforesaid clauses with counsel of its own choice. No action, regardless of form, arising out of this License may be brought by you more than one year after the cause of action has accrued.

(Some states do not allow exclusions or limitations of implied warranties or liability in certain cases, so the above exclusions and limitations may not apply to you.)

3. COPYRIGHT.

All intellectual property rights, trade secrets, and confidential information in the SOFTWARE and User's Guide are owned by Wiley or its suppliers and are protected by the United States copyright laws, other applicable copyright laws, and international treaty provisions.

You may not: (a) copy or distribute the SOFTWARE, except to load the SOFTWARE into computers to support the Designated Number of end-users; (b) modify, adapt, translate, publish (except as set forth in the preceding paragraph), transmit, reverse engineer, decompile, disassemble, or create derivative works based on the SOFTWARE or User's Guide except as set forth in this License; (c) transfer (except with Wiley's prior written permission), resell, rent, lease, sublicense, or grant any other rights of any kind to any individual copy of the SOFTWARE, including the User's Guide, to any other person; and (d) remove any proprietary notices, labels or marks on the SOFTWARE or User's Guide.

You shall take reasonable measures to maintain the security of the SOFTWARE and shall not allow any other parties, including your employees or students, to have access to or to use the SOFTWARE except as set forth herein, and you shall be responsible for any such use or access.

4. TERM.

This License is effective from the date you first use or load the SOFTWARE until it is terminated. If you should fail to perform in the manner required in this License, this License shall terminate and Wiley may exercise any other rights it may have. Upon termination, you agree to destroy all copies of the SOFTWARE (including all component parts) and the User's Guide. All provisions of this License with regard to the protection of the proprietary rights of Wiley shall continue in force after such termination.

5. GOVERNMENT RESTRICTED RIGHTS.

The SOFTWARE and User's Guide are provided with restricted and limited rights. Use, duplication, or disclosure by the Government is subject to restrictions as set forth in FAR 52.227-14 (June 1987) Alternate III (g)(3) (June 1987), FAR 52.227-19 (June 1987), or DFARS 52.227-701 (c)(1)(ii) (June 1988), as applicable.

6. CANADIAN PURCHASE.

If you purchased this product in Canada, you agree to the following: The parties hereto confirm that it is their wish that this License, as well as all other documents relating hereto, including Notices, have been and shall be drawn up in the English language only.

7. GENERAL.

This License will be governed by the laws of the State of New York, except for that body of law dealing with conflicts of law. Should you have any questions concerning this License or if you desire to contact Wiley for any reason, please write: Manager, Electronic Sales, John Wiley & Sons, Inc., Customer Sales and Service, 605 Third Avenue, New York, NY 10158 or call (212) 850-6553. This License may not be modified except in a writing signed by Wiley.

WILEY
Publishers Since 1807